RESEARCH
DESIGN
IN
COUNSELING

RESEARCH DESIGN IN COUNSELING

P. Paul Heppner
University of Missouri, Columbia

Dennis M. Kivlighan, Jr.
University of Missouri, Columbia

Bruce E. Wampold
University of Oregon, Eugene

BROOKS/COLE PUBLISHING COMPANY
PACIFIC GROVE, CALIFORNIA

I⟨T⟩P ™ The trademark ITP is used under license.

Brooks/Cole Publishing Company
A Division of Wadsworth, Inc.

© 1992 by Wadsworth, Inc., Belmont, California 94002.

Printed in the United States of America
10   9   8   7   6   5   4   3

Library of Congress Cataloging in Publication Data

Heppner, P. Paul. [date]
    Research design in counseling / P. Paul Heppner, Dennis M.
  Kivlighan, Jr., Bruce E. Wampold.
       p.   cm.
    Includes bibliographical references and index.
    ISBN 0-534-16284-3
      1. Counseling—Research—Methodology.   I. Kivlighan, Dennis M.
  II. Wampold, Bruce E., [date].   III. Title.
  BF637.C6H42   1991
  158'.3'0724—dc20   91-13832
                                                                CIP

Sponsoring Editor: CLAIRE VERDUIN
Editorial Assistant: GAY C. BOND
Production Editor: LINDA LOBA
Manuscript Editor: LORRAINE ANDERSON
Permissions Editor: MARIE DUBOIS
Interior Design: VERNON T. BOES
Cover Design: LISA BERMAN
Art Coordinator: LISA TORRI
Interior Illustration: LISA TORRI
Typesetting: EXECUSTAFF, INC.
Cover Printing: PHOENIX COLOR CORPORATION
Printing and Binding: ARCATA GRAPHICS/FAIRFIELD

We dedicate this book to:

Mary, my best friend and partner in life.
$$P.P.H.$$

Mary Suzanne, Mary Clayton, and Martin for their support and encouragement.
$$D.M.K.$$

My family and friends whose love and support mean even more than a statistically significant F.
$$B.E.W.$$

PREFACE

This book has been written for those learning the fundamentals of conducting empirical research in counseling. The book can also serve as a text for master's and doctoral level students in counseling psychology and counselor education programs who are enrolled in research methodology courses. In particular, the book is aimed at first and second year graduate students in the early phases of beginning work on research projects. Although there are numerous research design books in experimental psychology, there is a notable absence of research design texts that address the unique needs and concerns for graduate students in the specialty area of counseling. Such a book is long overdue.

There are several problems in teaching research methods to graduate students in counseling. Often students are quite anxious about conducting research, and view research activities (and particularly their thesis and dissertation) with more than a little apprehension. Another problem is students' lack of interest in research, in part because they do not adequately understand the philosophy of science, the history of counseling research, and the current research literature. Consequently, when they read a journal article they are confused by the methodology and procedures, and cannot place the study in a broader context of research within counseling. Many times students become too focused on the limitations of research, losing sight of the benefits. Moreover, many students learn about research methods in general research methods courses (that is, research methods in education), that enroll students from higher and adult education, counseling, educational psychology, and school psychology. Counseling students often become bored with research methods taught abstractly (or content-free), or methods taught with what seems like irrelevant examples from other areas (for instance, school psychology).

A primary purpose of the book is to provide an introduction to the basics of research design, with particular reference to issues relevant to counseling. However, the book does not provide recipes for how to do research. Rather, the text is directed toward a conceptual understanding of research design, and an emphasis on acknowledging the strengths and weaknesses of all designs. Thus, the book does not favor one design over another per se, but rather emphasizes the need to consider the inherent strengths and weaknesses of a particular design in the context of prior research (knowledge bases), and the particular type of information that is needed at the time.

The book is divided into four sections. The first section focuses on philosophical, ethical, and training issues. Basic philosophical and paradigmatic issues are introduced as well as ethical responsibilities of the researcher. In essence, the first section establishes the basic foundation for conducting empirical research.

The second section of the book discusses structural aspects of major research designs: between-group and within-subject designs, quasi-experimental and time-series designs, single-subject designs, and descriptive designs. In these chapters, we introduce the strengths and weaknesses of basic research designs, and provide research examples from the counseling literature to illustrate the various designs.

In the third section, we discuss some basic methodological issues in research design: designing and evaluating the independent variable, designing and choosing the dependent variable, population issues, experimenter and subject bias, analogue research, and methodological considerations in process research.

The final section focuses on writing and publishing the research report. Many students (and professionals) have trouble approaching that last hurdle—writing. Hopefully this section will provide a framework that will help organize the research report.

A unique feature of the book is the attention given to methodological issues pertaining to analogue research as well as process research. This focus provides information relevant to students in counseling, that is not addressed in previous research design texts. It is important to note that we make reference to appropriate statistical issues that are tied to design and methodological issues to avoid an artificial separation of these two areas. However, no particular statistical training is needed to understand the concepts presented.

Beyond introducing students to basic design issues, a second purpose of the book is to introduce counseling students to the counseling literature. Thus, the book discusses and provides examples of studies not only to illustrate design issues, but also to provide a background of previous research in counseling. Although the book is not comprehensive of all the research in counseling, the book provides the beginning graduate student with an overview of some of the research literature, as well as some of the researchers within the profession.

The final purpose of the book is to demystify the research process, as well as to attend to the typical affective reactions of beginning-level graduate students in counseling. Thus, early in the book we focus on issues relating to research training, in part to stimulate discussion among students and faculty about the issues that can arise in various research training methods. Moreover, we focus on and normalize common fears about science in general and about identifying research topics in particular. We have attempted to communicate that research is a challenging and stimulating endeavor. Research can be fun!

Many people have been very helpful in the preparation of this book. A number of graduate students in the counseling psychology programs at the

University of Missouri, Columbia and the University of Oregon over the last ten years have contributed ideas and observations, and have been a constant source of inspiration, support, and challenge that ultimately contributed to the development of this book. In addition, a number of faculty and students at the University of Missouri and the University of Oregon have provided particularly helpful feedback on various chapter drafts; we gratefully acknowledge the helpful comments of N. Francis J. Asama, Stephen Cook, Wayne Dixon, Denise Colombini, Patricia Frazier, Linda McBride, Melissa Grace, Mary Heppner, Mike Hinz, Carol Jacquet, W. Cal Johnson, Jr., Donna Koechig, Marie Knowles, Brent Mallinckrodt, Karla McClure, Philip Mothershead, Kelly Morrow, Judy Ogle, Toti Perez, Keith Ray, Patrick Schmitz, Mark Sharpe, and Debbie Wright. In addition, we are grateful to the following reviewers who provided insightful suggestions: Dr. Brent Mallinckrodt, University of Oregon, Eugene; Dr. Nancy Murdock, University of Missouri, Kansas City; Dr. Don Polkinghorne, University of Southern California; and Dr. Norman Stewart, Michigan State University, Lansing. And our thanks to the students who used typescript copies as their course text.

A special acknowledgment goes to Marty Heesacker, a valued colleague from the University of Florida, and seven graduate students in counseling: Kathryn Fraser, Diane Freeman, Michael Gillaspie, Linda Kay Hellmich, Martha Allison Kemp, John Francis Leso, and Jane Marie Parr. They not only piloted the chapters in 1990, but each student provided a detailed critique of each chapter. Marty in turn provided each student with feedback on each of their chapter critiques. In short, the feedback from Marty and his students was outstanding and very instrumental in many minor and several major revisions.

Karen Kitchener from the University of Denver also kindly provided extremely helpful observations and suggestions on the ethics chapter (Chapter 4); her comments stimulated a major revision of our thinking about ethics and our writing in that chapter.

David Knipp, Judy Letourneau, and Brenda Backer diligently and efficiently typed innumerable drafts of the chapters, and were instrumental in managing all of our writing on the computer. They deserve our sincerest gratitude for deciphering our writing.

In Chapter 15 (The Research Report), we neglected to advise writers to seek help from skillful editors. Linda Loba and her staff helped immensely in correcting our grammar and clarifying our writing.

And finally, our thanks to Claire Verduin of Brooks/Cole, for her enthusiasm and patience in helping us to develop this book.

P. Paul Heppner
Dennis M. Kivlighan, Jr.
Bruce E. Wampold

C O N T E N T S

RESEARCH DESIGN IN COUNSELING

PART ONE

PHILOSOPHICAL, ETHICAL, AND TRAINING ISSUES

CHAPTER 1

SCIENCE AND TRAINING IN COUNSELING

Counselors help people with a wide variety of personal, educational, and career-related problems. People come to counselors because they have problems they are unable to solve (Dixon & Glover, 1984; Fretz, 1982; Heppner, 1978a; Horan, 1979).

We as professionals assume responsibility for not only promoting the welfare of the people who seek our services, but also protecting clients from harm. Thus, as professionals we need to continually update and extend our knowledge about human nature and the field of counseling as well as evaluate our services, especially because the applied nature of our work affects the daily existence of thousands of people.

Consider the real-life example of a husband and wife who sought career planning assistance. After a thorough intake, they were assigned to a computerized career planning program. They both completed the program and were amazed to learn that they received exactly the same results.

> Careful checking of the program revealed that the program was reporting scores accurately for the first individual who used the program each day. The second and all subsequent users that day, however, were getting an identical printout of the first user's results. The first user's results continued to appear until the machine was turned off. In essence, every user, except the initial user each day, was receiving invalid results. For us, this resulted in many hours of calling clients to inform them that they had received invalid results. After expressing our shock to the manufacturer, we were told simply: "Oh, yes, we found that out a month ago and it has been fixed on new disks. We'll send you a new set." One wonders how many other career centers never found this error and continued to use a program that gave users blatantly invalid results (Johnston, Buescher, & Heppner, 1988, p. 40).

This example involves a computer programming error that was not caught through careful evaluation. Many other examples could be listed in which clients receive less than desirable treatments because of outdated information, ineffective or inappropriate counselor interventions, or erroneous knowledge about human behavior and the change process.

3

Medical professionals also aid people, although they obviously focus primarily on medical problems. The medical profession has advanced over the centuries, and has become increasingly more sophisticated. It is clear that important lessons can be learned from the trials and tribulations of the medical profession. Consider the historical lesson from the so-called thalidomide babies. In the early 1960s a drug called thalidomide was prescribed in England, Canada, the United States, and several other countries for pregnant women experiencing morning sickness. The drug was administered before adequate empirical tests had been completed on it. Some medical scientists in England argued that the effects of the drug should have been tested scientifically, especially in comparison with groups of women who did not receive the drug. Others, however, argued more convincingly that it was unethical to withhold (from the comparison group) a drug that was "known" to greatly ease women's problems with pregnancy. For some time after the drug was introduced, a number of medical professionals observed an increase in the number of deformed babies who had arms and legs resembling buds that precede limb development in the human embryo. Years later, after appropriate empirical tests had been completed, it was discovered that thalidomide administered to women during the critical embryonic period caused these major deformities in the babies. Although the drug was quickly taken off the market, for thousands of infants the damage had already been done.

How do we know whether we are promoting the welfare of or actually harming those people seeking our services in the counseling profession? None of us in the profession would intentionally want to harm clients. Counseling, however, can have detrimental effects on people (see Lambert, Bergin, & Collins, 1977). How do we know our interventions are effective? What is sufficient proof that we as a profession can afford to accept? If someone proclaims that a certain intervention is effective, should we believe it? If your supervisor maintains that a certain technique is effective, is that sufficient evidence? What kind of *knowledge* must a profession be based on to succeed? The answer to these questions rests in the manner in which the profession has developed its knowledge base.

The purpose of this chapter is to examine how the counseling profession has developed its knowledge base. This chapter is divided into two major sections. The first half of the chapter focuses on the role of science in the counseling profession. In the second half of the chapter we introduce you to training issues related to the scientific enterprise in counseling.

THE ROLE OF SCIENCE IN COUNSELING

Science plays an essential role in developing the knowledge upon which the counseling profession is based. In this section, we take a close look at science as it relates to counseling. We first discuss different ways of knowing, and particularly the scientific way of knowing. Second, we discuss the scientific method as applied to human behavior and introduce you to some of the issues being debated in the philosophy of science. Finally, we discuss some issues pertaining to a philosophy of science for the counseling profession. These philosophical issues are complex and intricate; our purpose is to introduce you to the basic issues, and thus we only provide a brief overview. Nonetheless, these issues form the foundation for future research and training in the profession.

Science as a Way of Knowing

Charles Peirce, a nineteenth-century American mathematician, philosopher, and logician, stated that there are at least four ways of knowing, or of "fixing belief" (Buchler, 1955). The first method is the method of tenacity. That is, whatever belief one firmly adheres to is truth. These "truths" are known to be true because we have always known them to be true; Kerlinger (1986) noted that frequent repetition of these "truths" seems to enhance their validity! A second method of knowing is the method of authority. If noted authorities, such as the president of the United States, a state governor, a well-known psychologist, or a clinical supervisor says it is so, then this is the truth. A third method of knowing is the a priori method, or method of intuition (see Cohen & Nagel, 1934). This method is based on the notion that what agrees with reason, what makes sense, is true. The fourth method of knowing is the scientific method, which involves empirical tests to establish objective, verifiable facts. We would add a fifth way of knowing, and that is what is learned through one's own direct experiences in the world. Through countless experiences, each individual construes a "reality" of the world; some of his or her perceptions may match those of others with similar experiences, while other perceptions and conclusions about the world may not match those of others. Dangers exist if this method is used alone, because biases can develop or information can be distorted. Moreover, the events we experience can represent a biased sample, which in turn can lead to inaccurate conclusions.

Given the overwhelming complexity of life, and the vast amounts of knowledge needed even in daily living, people most likely acquire "truths" through all five of these ways of knowing. Obviously, there can be error involved in any of these ways of knowing. Such error, if it affects the knowledge on which counseling is based, can be dangerous for the counseling profession and our clients.

To be credible, reliable, and effective, a profession must be built on dependable facts or truths, rather than on tenacity, decrees from authority figures, or subjective opinions. Knowledge on which to base a profession that aims to facilitate growth and positive change in clients must be based as much as possible in a reality outside of the professionals' personal beliefs and biases. The scientific method has been developed to create such knowledge. Basically, the scientific method is a set of assumptions and rules about collecting and evaluating data. The explicitly stated assumptions and rules enable a standard, systematic method of investigation that is designed to reduce bias as much as possible. Central to the scientific method is the collection of data, which allows investigators to put their ideas to an empirical test, outside of or apart from their personal biases. In essence, "the proof of the science is in the experiment" (Ruch & Zimbardo, 1970, p. 40). "Stripped of all its glamour, scientific inquiry is nothing more than a way of limiting false conclusions about natural events" (Ruch & Zimbardo, 1970, p. 31).

There are obvious costs to acquiring knowledge by using the scientific method. Conducting empirical investigations is costly in terms of time, energy, and resources. Putting complex and internal cognitive and affective processes to empirical test is a difficult and elusive task. Sometimes as we try to identify specific processes or variables, we become mechanistic and lose the Gestalt or whole picture. Sometimes, the lack of sophistication of our research methods results in conclusions that tell us little about real-life processes.

But the risks of building a profession on nonscientific evidence are far greater. The thalidomide babies are one clear example of the risks associated with not empirically testing one's opinions. Conducting therapy based only on personal hunches and opinions is risky and might well result in harming clients (see Lambert, Bergin, & Collins, 1977, for data regarding client deterioration as evidenced by increased social maladjustment, more negative views about oneself, and decreases in overall problem-solving skills). It is important that the knowledge on which the profession is built be based on objective or verifiable information that can be put to empirical or quantifiable tests. In this way, the methods used to establish our "truths" have a built-in self-correction process; each empirical test is independent of previous findings, and can either verify or disconfirm the previous knowledge. In contrast, subjective ways of knowing that do not involve empirical tests run the risk of creating myths. These myths hinder the progress of a profession.

This does not mean that the professionals' beliefs, hunches, and even biases are not useful in exploring ideas and perhaps extending the field's knowledge. Undoubtedly, we can learn a great deal about human behavior from the more subjective ways of knowing; it is clear that many ideas and breakthroughs regarding therapeutic orientations and techniques have initially sprung from practitioners' direct experience with people. However, it is important to note that these ideas must be empirically tested. In fact, no major orientation has been maintained in the profession without substantial empirical support. Parenthetically, even though the scientific method tends to provide data that is prone to less bias or distortion, Howard (1982) cogently recommended that we "periodically obtain evidence demonstrating the adequacy" of the various assumptions or procedures involved in the scientific method (p. 324).

In short, the knowledge on which the credibility of a profession is based must be objective and verifiable rather than subjective and untestable. While the scientific method has costs and is not problem-free, building a helping profession without it is too risky. Credibility is important for the counseling profession as a whole, as well as for each person in the profession.

Science as Applied to Human Behavior

In the mid-1800s there was much confusion and speculation about the nature of human behavior. John Stuart Mill suggested that "the backward state of the moral (human) sciences can be remedied by applying to them the methods of physical science, duly extended and generalized" (Mill, 1843/1953). Mill's suggestion was not only adopted by the newly emerging social and behavioral sciences, but has dominated research in these areas ever since (see Polkinghorne, 1983, 1984) as well. The basic philosophy of science that has been generalized from the physical sciences has been referred to as the received view (Putman, 1962) or the standard view of science (Manicas & Secord, 1983). This view has drawn heavily on the logical positivism of the 1930s (Hanfling, 1981), and contains the following elements:

1. Knowledge, as opposed to mere opinion, is contained only in state-ments based on or linked to direct observation. The only kind of statements free from personal bias (and thus distortion) are those grounded in observation.
2. The accumulation of facts or knowledge will result in general laws of human behavior. Human nature is lawful; the goal of science is to identify the causal relationships among variables. The overall goal of science is to develop theories of human behavior, which consist of a network of knowledge statements that are grounded in observation and tied together by deductive logic.

The idea of a rigorous link between observations, hypotheses, and theory was appealing; after all, "the hard-nosed scientist," like the proverbial Missourian, wants to be "shown" the evidence (Manicas & Secord, 1983). In addition, the notion of discovering laws of human behavior based on the accumulation of objective data promised credibility as well as utility for a young profession.

In the last two or three decades, psychology has become more sophis-ticated in its methodologies and procedures, but the basic elements of the received view of science still predominate within science (Manicas & Secord, 1983; Polkinghorne, 1984). The received view, however, has come under attack from philosophers of science (for example, Bhaskar, 1975; Harré, 1970, 1972; Kuhn, 1970; Lakatos, 1970; Suppe, 1977; Toulmin, 1972). As a result, an alternative paradigm referred to as the realist's view of science has emerged (see Manicas & Secord, 1983, for a brief overview). Basically, this view proposes that (1) knowledge is a social and historical product and cannot be obtained only by studying the individual in isolation; (2) the experiences of an individual, whether observable or not, are appropriate topics of study; and (3) the focus of research should not be on events and finding relationships among events, but rather on examining the underlying "causal properties of structures that exist and operate in the world" (Manicas & Secord, 1983, p. 402).

The received view also has been criticized by counseling psychologists (such as Howard, 1984; Patton, 1984; Polkinghorne, 1984). Critics have maintained that observations are not absolute but rather are filtered through the subjective, phenomenological world of the observer (see Patton, 1984; Polkinghorne, 1984). Moreover, some have contended that people's subjective internal activities, such as their plans, intentions, feelings, and thoughts, are essential domains of counseling (for example, Howard, 1984) and thus merit scientific examination. Finally, it also has been argued that our view of human nature is becoming increasingly more sophisticated (Polkinghorne, 1984), which makes it more difficult to delineate single "laws" of human behavior, and subsequently makes prediction of human behavior more complex.

The debate over the philosophy of science is exceedingly complex and intertwined with our view of human nature, the adequacy of our research methods, the content of our research investigations, and the perceived utility of our research findings. The interested reader might explore these issues further by examining some of the following: Bhaskar (1975), Caple (1985), Dar (1987), Harré (1974, 1980), Lakatos (1970), Manicas and Secord (1983), Meehl (1978, 1987), Polkinghorne (1983), Schutz (1964), Serlin (1987), Serlin and Lapsley (1985), Toulmin (1972), as well as the special issue of the *Journal of Counseling Psychology* focusing on the topic of philosophy of science and counseling research (Borgen, 1984b; Dawis, 1984; Ford, 1984; Howard, 1984; Patton, 1984; Polkinghorne, 1984; Strong, 1984; Tyler, 1984).

A Philosophy of Science for the Counseling Profession

With regard to a philosophy of science for the counseling profession, we will discuss four issues: (1) the goals of science in counseling, (2) the importance of methodological diversity, (3) the need to examine and expand our assumptions regarding human nature, and (4) our responsibility for applying research tools. All of these issues affect the quality and type of research conducted within counseling.

Goals of Science in Counseling

Science is a mode of controlled inquiry to develop an objective, effective, and credible "way of knowing." Historically, the basic functions of the scientific approach were typically discussed as twofold (see, for example, Kerlinger, 1986). The first function was to advance knowledge, to make discoveries, and to learn facts in order to improve some aspect of the world. The second function was to establish relations among events, develop theories, and thus help professionals to make predictions of future events. We will now discuss philosophical issues related to each of these functions, specifically within the field of counseling.

In our view, the goal of the scientific method in counseling is indeed to advance knowledge, to make discoveries, and to acquire facts about counseling. However, in the realm of counseling, phenomena of interest include both observable events and subjective, self-report experiences. Indeed, researchers have examined a wide range of phenomenological or self-report variables in counseling for some time (for example, client satisfaction with counseling, perceived counselor expertise, client self-efficacy, supervisee self-efficacy, client reactions to counselor statements). The expansion of our knowledge is often guided, in part, by pressing questions or problems that professionals in the field have about their work. For example, one pressing question has been whether client expectations about the counselor or the counseling process affect later outcomes in counseling, such as problem resolution or premature termination (see Hardin, Subich, & Holvey, 1988; Tinsley, Bowman, & Ray, 1988). Or the pressing question may result from a practitioner's dissatisfaction with her or his inability to help certain clients make effective decisions about their career plans (see Rubinton, 1980, for a study that explored the utility of different career interventions for clients with different decision-making styles). Thus, scientific research is designed, in part, to provide answers to pressing questions or problems. In this way, research in counseling can be very practical; in fact, one view is that the adequacy of our research can be evaluated by how relevant the findings are for practitioners (Krumboltz & Mitchell, 1979). Scientific research in counseling can thus increase our understanding by providing data that describe and explain counseling phenomena. In short, there is a great deal of value in the ordinary description of behavior and the human experience.

It is also important to develop knowledge bases and research perspectives that emphasize the social and historical context of the individual. People do not think, feel, or behave in isolation, but rather in the context of a rich personal and social history. Research that increases an understanding of how individuals interact within a broader social and personal environmental context is critical to the development of knowledge about counseling. For example, the role of counseling centers on university and college campuses has received considerable attention since the early 1950s. A critical issue within this line of research has involved the types of problems that are viewed by various groups (such as students, faculty, counseling center staff) as appropriate to bring to a counseling center. (This line of research is sometimes referred to as problem appropriateness research.) In reviewing the research accumulated during a thirty-year span, Heppner and Neal (1983) observed that some of the findings seemed inconsistent. However, upon examining the research more closely, especially in conjunction with broader social events, they observed that historical events (like the Vietnam War) seemed to explain some discrepancies in the research. Thus, the goal of science is not only to expand our knowledge about individuals, but also about the interactions between individual actions and a larger personal, social, and historical context.

Research, however, is guided by more than practical problems. To achieve scientific understanding, the researcher often needs to organize observations and facts into a logical framework that explains some aspect of behavior. Thus, research is often guided by theoretical issues within a line of work, and seeks to establish general relations and conditional statements among events that help professionals to understand phenomena. The accumulation of facts or knowledge will probably not result in general laws or broad-scale theories of human behavior as was earlier conceived. Human behavior is multidetermined; that is, a single action can be determined by any one of several preceding events. Moreover, human actions consist of complex chains in which preceding events increase or decrease the probability that some action will occur, but it is not a uniform process across individuals or even within individuals over time. Meehl (1978) likewise concluded that for a variety of reasons (such as individual differences, polygenic heredity, random events, nuisance variables, cultural factors), human psychology is hard to scientize and that "it may be that the nature of the subject matter in most of personology and social psychology is inherently incapable of permitting theories with sufficient conceptual power" (p. 829). Thus, the range of human variability and complexity does not lend itself to description by general principles or broad theories, and much less to prediction.

In short, we are suggesting that it is exceedingly difficult (if not futile) to develop broad-scale theories aimed at predicting human behavior in general. However, skilled therapists are able to make better predictions about individual people when they combine research knowledge about specific relations among variables with a host of qualifying information, namely the biographical and social history of the individual. In this way, therapists use "the discoveries of science, but in order to bring about changes in the everyday world, also employ a great deal of knowledge that extends beyond science" (Manicas & Secord, 1983, p. 412). Thus, it is useful for those in the counseling profession to continue to organize facts and knowledge into theoretical frameworks that can be used as ingredients within more complex conditional models of behavior. Theoretical frameworks that consist of sets of conditional statements that can be qualified by specific information about an individual may allow the needed specificity as well as complexity in explaining and predicting individuals' behavior. In sum, we believe that the second function of science is to help explain and predict human action, but in a much more complex and idiographic manner than acknowledged in the received view.

The Importance of Methodological Diversity

Inherent in the traditional view of science was the assumption that the "best" knowledge (and thus best research methodology) could be obtained from tightly controlled, experimental research that used randomization and control groups. There was an implicit hierarchy, with the experimental studies at the top and correlational and descriptive studies at the bottom, seemingly based on an assumption that the experimental investigations resulted in superior information. We disagree with such assumptions and maintain rather that the selection of the research method must fit the phenomenon under investigation and the type of information that is being sought (also see Ford, 1984; Howard, 1982, 1984; Patton, 1984; Polkinghorne, 1984). For example, we believe that far too often we attempt to do experimental, between-groups studies before we have an adequate description of some phenomenon; thus, in some cases,

descriptive studies might very well yield more useful and important information than a controlled experimental investigation.

There does seem to be a growing consensus for methodological diversity
within counseling. Authors such as Borgen, 1984a, 1984b; Ford, 1984; Gelso,
1979, 1982; Goldman, 1982; Harmon, 1982; Hill, 1982; Hill & Gronsky, 1984;
Howard, 1982, 1983, 1984; Neimeyer & Resnikoff, 1982; Patton, 1984; and
Polkinghorne, 1984 have cogently argued for greater creativity and flexibility
in using existing research methods to examine important questions within
counseling. Howard (1982) provided a parable that underscores the notion
that different methods present advantages and limitations:

> In practice, one never demonstrates that one methodological approach is
> always superior to another. An elaboration and extension of a parable by
> the astronomer Eddington might draw this point into sharp relief. Eddington
> tells of a scientist who wished to catalogue the fish in the sea (the research
> question). He took a net of two-inch mesh (a research method) and cast
> it into the sea repeatedly. After carefully cataloguing his findings he con-
> cluded that there were no fish in the sea smaller than two inches. In this
> apocryphal example, the scientist's trust in the adequacy of his method was
> somewhat misplaced and led the researcher to draw an inaccurate conclu-
> sion. However, if someone had doubted the adequacy of the netting pro-
> cedure and performed an investigation specifically to test its adequacy
> relative to some specific alternative procedure, the misinterpretation might
> have been recognized. For example, our researcher might have considered
> an alternative research method: namely damming a small inlet of the sea,
> draining the water, and examining the bodies of the fish left behind. In
> finding fish smaller than two inches, the limitations of the netting procedure
> would become apparent. One would not be surprised, however, to find
> that the largest fish obtained via the damming approach was substantially
> smaller than was obtained with the netting approach: another potential
> problem. Therefore, research testing the adequacy of research methods does
> not prove which technique is better but provides evidence for the poten-
> tial strengths and limitations of each. From this information, researchers
> can determine when one of two approaches, or both, should be the method
> of choice. (p. 319)

Methodological diversity is essential for important advances to be made in the
field of counseling and development.

The Need to Examine and Expand Our View of Human Nature

The assumptions one makes regarding the basic qualities of human nature (that
is, cognitive, affective, behavioral, and physiological processes) affect how one
conceptualizes human behavior. Moreover, our view of human nature affects
the research problems we examine in counseling. Our views of human nature
have changed dramatically in the last one hundred years and are still evolving. Consistent with the beliefs of some of the previously mentioned writers
(such as Borgen, 1984a; Howard, 1984; Patton, 1984; Polkinghorne, 1984;
Strong, 1984), we believe there is a need to expand our view of how human

beings operate, particularly within counseling. One major change of view concerning human nature that is gaining support pertains to human rationality. For example, Gelatt (1989) has recently noted that his view of human decision making, especially within a counseling context, has changed dramatically in the last 25 years. In 1962 he stressed rational processes in decision making, while in 1989 he stressed intuitive processes and positive uncertainty (that is, accepting uncertainty and inconsistencies). Gelatt's 1989 perspective is consistent with those of a host of other writers at this time who have emphasized nonrational and unsystematic processes within human decision making (for example, Heppner, 1989; Meehl, 1978; Strohmer & Blustein, 1990; Tversky & Kahneman, 1981). Related to unsystematic processing are chance events or luck. Meehl has cogently argued that our view of human nature should also include chance events; "luck is one of the most important contributors to individual differences in human suffering, satisfaction, illness, achievement, and so forth, an embarrassingly 'obvious' point that social scientists readily forget" (Meehl, 1978, p. 811).

A number of suggestions have been made for how we might expand our view of human beings, such as human agency (Howard, 1984), phenomenological perspectives within language (for example, Patton, 1984; Pepinsky, 1984), cognitive mediational processes (for example, Martin, 1984), and information processing (for example, Heppner & Krauskopf, 1987), particularly in nonlinear causal chains (for example, Ford, 1984; Maruyama, 1963). It is striking to note that all of these suggestions are process-oriented, thus suggesting that it may be fruitful to examine more dynamic and microscopic processes at this point within counseling research. The major point of this discussion is that our view of human nature affects the research problems we examine in counseling. Thus, researchers must examine their assumptions about human nature, and be creative in investigating human processes within counseling. In this regard, other areas of psychology (like social psychology, developmental psychology, cognitive psychology) provide rich sources of information for investigating basic human processes in a counseling context.

The Responsibility for Applying Research Tools

Much of the responsibility for adequately applying the scientific method to counseling phenomena rests with researchers. Strong (1984) aptly depicted this issue.

> Scientific development in counseling psychology has not been as helpful to the pragmatic enterprise of counseling and therapy as we would like. It would be wrong to conclude that it has not been helpful, as many practices of counseling today have grown out of scientific efforts, such as behavior therapy, relationship skills, and psychological tests. There is a frustration that scientific efforts have had less pragmatic import than desired. I believe that this state of affairs is not the result of inherent limitations of the scientific enterprise, but of inadequacies in our conceptions of the objects of inquiry—human beings and the phenomenon of behavior change through interpersonal interaction. (pp. 472–473)

The methods of science are only tools, tools that we use to obtain knowledge about phenomena. A flashlight is a good analogy. A flashlight is a useful tool but it will only shine light where we point it. If we cannot see the object we are looking for with a flashlight, it does not necessarily follow that we should throw the flashlight away, but rather change the direction of the light. Similarly, our research methods will only provide us with information about the content that we examine. If we are dissatisfied with the results, it does not necessarily follow that we should eliminate the research methods, but rather that we should try new angles with our research methods. It is possible, however, that one may need a bigger flashlight, or a flashlight that could reflect light around a corner. Thus, sometimes new research methodologies may be needed to help us acquire new or different types of knowledge. Developing new methodologies or alternative ways of collecting data obviously challenges the problem-solving and creative abilities of researchers. Presently, there are many ideas that we cannot examine adequately because we do not have the appropriate methodologies or measurement instruments. Researchers must be creative and diverse not only in the methodologies they use but also in the type of data they collect in order to examine the phenomena that are central to counseling and human development.

The Importance of a Scientific Approach

Consider this true story of a group of faculty who were ardent believers in Freud's conception of psychoanalysis. These faculty members were relatively isolated from other professionals and had a habit of hiring only their own graduates. (They noted that since they rarely had a faculty opening, and since the job market was so restricted, they would feel like traitors to hire someone else's student rather than one of their own.) These people believed that clients' paranoid fantasies could be major obstacles to uncovering unconscious psychological conflicts. Consequently, they would not allow any live recording (audio or visual) or direct observation of therapy sessions. Nor would they allow any kind of written self-report data to be collected from clients. Their primary method of knowing seemed to be the method of authority (Freud), with little opportunity to objectively confirm or disconfirm Freud's ideas. Moreover, they so firmly believed in their truths that they scoffed at the utility of other therapeutic techniques such as systematic desensitization, the Gestalt empty chair, and reflection. Consequently, this group of psychologists, in the absence of any objective data, discovered very little beyond Freud's early formulations of the therapeutic process. The bottom line is that this group did not advance the knowledge of their field; by today's standards (as well as students' evaluations), their therapy practices were archaic, and their training philosophies and methods totally inadequate.

This story illustrates how the lack of a scientific approach can hinder growth within a discipline, even to the point of stagnation. The counseling profession will best be advanced by methodological diversity, a broader view of human processes, and tolerance toward a broad range of inquiry systems. Polkinghorne (1984) aptly summarizes this perspective:

> When a discipline gives priority to understanding its object of inquiry over its commitment to a particular research form, and when it recognizes that all research methods—including those developed within the received view—abstract from the object of investigation only certain information, there is a strong indication that this discipline will also open itself to multiple strategies of investigation. It will train its members in the scholarly and rigorous use of the various logics of understanding, and it will support, through its publications and conventions, the sharing of knowledge gained through multiple forms of research. Finally, the discipline will participate in the further development and refinement of all of the research methods that offer understanding and information for practice in the field. (p. 428)

TRAINING IN COUNSELING

Although training within counselor education programs varies considerably, most counselor education programs incorporate science and scientific activities. In this section we discuss the dominant training model, the scientist-practitioner model of training. It is important to note, however, that even within this model there is considerable latitude for various interpretations and training activities. Thus, various training programs that espouse the scientist-practitioner model each have their unique interpretations and variations. We first provide a brief overview of the scientist-practitioner model, followed by a summary of some concerns about this model. Then we focus specifically on the scientific domain of training, and discuss ideas within two areas to broaden our concept of scientific training: basic scientific thinking skills and basic research application skills. Finally, we discuss students' typical reactions to scientific activities and delineate training strategies.

The Scientist-Practitioner Model

Most graduate training programs in counseling espouse the scientist-practitioner model of training. The scientist-practitioner model has been referred to as a "living tradition"; it is "one of our oldest ideas; it remains the foundation of most training programs" (Claiborn, 1984). Basically this model consists of training in both scientific and practitioner activities. The scientific activities include courses such as statistics, research design, evaluation, counseling research literature, and philosophy of science, while the practice side includes courses such as counseling methods, counseling theories, personality, assessment, and practica.

When students enter a graduate training program in counseling, they typically have a wide range of interests along the scientist-practitioner continuum. Most students are primarily interested in being practitioners, a few are interested in being researchers, and others are interested in both research and practice. (It is critical to note that these interests often change over time, not only during graduate training but throughout one's career as well; thus, we will discuss later in this section the need for students to prepare themselves broadly to allow for career changes over time.)

The scientist-practitioner model goes back at least 40 years. In 1949 and 1950, the first national conferences for the training of clinical and counseling psychologists were held in Boulder, Colorado, and Ann Arbor, Michigan, respectively. One major purpose of the Boulder conference was to develop a broad model of training. After two weeks of meeting daily, the clinical psychologists developed what they called the scientist-practitioner model of training, which is also referred to as the Boulder model (Raimy, 1950). The creators of that model stressed the philosophy that students need to be trained to do research as well as to learn the skills of the practitioner. The counseling psychologists affirmed this model in Ann Arbor. In addition, the field of counseling psychology has repeatedly reiterated its commitment to the scientist-practitioner model, most notably in 1951 at the Northwestern conference (Whiteley, 1984), in 1964 at the Greystone conference (Thompson & Super, 1964), and again in 1987 at the Atlanta conference (Meara et al., 1988). The scientist-practitioner model also has been incorporated into the *Standards for the Preparation of Counselors and Other Personnel Service Specialists* (1977) established by the American Association for Counseling and Development (AACD).

Meara et al. (1988) succinctly amplified on the scientist-practitioner model:

> Those at the Georgia [Atlanta] conference agreed that because psychology is a science, both the generation and application of psychological knowledge are based on scientific views of the world. Psychologists, whatever their work, are professionals and their attitude toward their work is scientific.
>
> The scientist-professional model is an integrated approach to knowledge that recognizes the interdependence of theory, research, and practice. The model emphasizes systematic and thoughtful analyses of human experiences and judicious application of the knowledge and attitudes gained from such analyses. An attitude of scholarly inquiry is critical to all the activities of those educated in the scientist-professional model.
>
> The model encompasses a variety of research methods, assessment techniques, and intervention strategies. The counseling psychologist is engaged in the pursuit and application of psychological knowledge to promote optimal development for individuals, groups, and systems (including families), and to provide remedies for the psychological difficulties that encumber them. To implement these goals, the scientist-professional psychologist adopts a scientific approach based on observation of psychological phenomena. This approach generates theoretical constructs and propositions, which are in turn tested as hypotheses (Claiborn, 1987; Pepinsky & Pepinsky, 1954). (p. 368)

Concerns with the Model

An increasing number of writers from both counseling and clinical psychology, however, have questioned the utility of the scientist-practitioner model (for example, Albee, 1970; Gelso, 1979). In addition, several writers have questioned the value of psychological research for practitioners (for example, Goldman, 1976; Howard, 1984; Levine, 1974; Polkinghorne, 1983; Raush, 1974). They have contended that most practitioners do not use research findings in their practice, and that, in fact, research findings are often meaningless. This contention has led some writers to the conclusion that research training is not necessary for practitioners (for example, Frank, 1984; Hughes, 1952; Meehl, 1971). Others have suggested that students are not receiving adequate training in how to think scientifically, whether it be about clients or about research (for example, Anderson & Heppner, 1986; Claiborn, 1984; Goodyear & Benton, 1986). In assessing professional training issues pertaining to counseling research, Gelso (1979) noted that the "modal counseling psychologist publishes no research following the attainment of the doctoral degree" (p. 25). Carkhuff (1968) suggested a more extreme estimate: The last research project of 95% to 99% of graduates is the doctoral dissertation. These data are in contrast to the widely espoused scientist-practitioner training model as well as the research training goals established by the AACD in their *Standards for the Preparation of Counselors* (1977).

The debate regarding the utility of the scientist-practitioner model is a complex one that intertwines multiple factors. For instance, the model itself could be unrealistic and impossible to fulfill in reality (for example, Albee, 1970; Gelso, 1979). Conversely, maybe the training students receive in scientific activities is inadequate or even inappropriate (for example, Anderson & Heppner, 1986; Claiborn, 1984, 1987; Gelso, 1979; Goodyear & Benton, 1986; Heppner, Gelso, & Dolliver, 1987; Magoon & Holland, 1984; Royalty, Gelso, Mallinckrodt, & Garrett, 1986; Wampold, 1986). Moreover, it could also be that graduate training in practitioner activities does not adequately incorporate scientific activities (for example, Anderson & Heppner, 1986; Claiborn, 1984, 1987; Goodyear & Benton, 1986; Heppner & Anderson, 1985). It does seem questionable whether graduate students are taught to think about applied problems and to process information as scientists (for example, Betz, 1986; Claiborn, 1987). Perhaps the type of research being conducted is too distant from the reality of the practitioner (for example, Howard, 1984; Polkinghorne, 1984), or our research methods reduce counseling phenomena to senseless numbers (for example, Goldman, 1976). Or maybe our professional journals are structured in ways that make it cumbersome for practitioners to find and assimilate the information they need (for example, Anderson & Heppner, 1986; Gelso et al., 1988). Yet another factor could be that students admitted to graduate programs have predominantly social or interpersonal interests (for example, Holland, 1986; Magoon & Holland, 1984).

There is no doubt that research has enhanced the practice of counseling. Although a practitioner may not be able to cite a specific reference, his or her graduate school training was likely based on a tremendous amount of research data, all the way from personality theory to intervention strategies. The accumulation may be slow, but the data eventually advance our working knowledge of the field (Heppner & Anderson, 1985). The fact that research continues to be criticized for not being relevant, however, is noteworthy and should be cause for concern for educators (that is, the people responsible for training). Perhaps the truth occupies a middle ground: the scientific method and research have advanced the field, but they have not been as helpful as we would like them to be.

A central issue in the debate over the scientist-practitioner model is the role of scientific training in the development of a competent and professional counselor. Hans Strupp, a noted clinical psychologist with a great deal of experience in practice, research, training, and professional affairs, concluded in 1981 that inadequate training in the scientific process has been a major problem in the development of the mental health profession in general:

> Despite notable exceptions, the mental health professions have not done an impressive job of training truly first-rate clinicians and practicing therapists. These deficiencies are now coming back to haunt us in the form of demands by the government, insurance companies, and society at large for more stringent controls. I cannot do justice to these important issues in a few words, but the declining status of organized psychoanalysis may teach some lessons of what not to do, to wit, total commitment to a single theoretical and technical model; enshrinement of theoretical formulations as dogma; imperviousness to research progress in neighboring fields; rigid indoctrination of trainees; failure to inspire students to become critical and independent thinkers, failure to teach students abiding respect for empirical data and rival hypotheses; insufficient attention to clinical realities—patient selection, formulation of treatment goals, bold experimentation with alternative technical approaches, systematic exploration of the limits of existing approaches, and the like. How many of our own training programs and clinical supervisors take these matters seriously? How many students are given thorough training in diverse theoretical and technical approaches? How many supervisors are intimately familiar with the frontiers of current research? The influence of research, as noted previously, must make itself felt largely through the kinds of attitudes instilled in student therapists toward clinical work. Harry Stack Sullivan once expressed amazement at how difficult it is for most people to think seriously of even one alternative hypothesis to explain clinical observations. In short, clinical training must not only be comprehensive and thorough, but it must educate students to become thinking clinicians who can effectively apply quality control in their daily practice. Unless we succeed in selecting and training clinicians who can exercise this kind of self-surveillance, who practice responsibly and effectively while being mindful of their human and professional limitations, it is predictable that governmental controls and bureaucratic rules will make a charade of professional work in this area. It may already be later than we realize. (pp. 217–218)

The scientist-practitioner model in its ideal form (that is, implicitly 50% practitioner and 50% scientist/researcher) may be just that: an ideal that is rarely found in reality. Gelso (1979) proposed that it may be more realistic to train students in both domains (in varying degrees depending on their interests) with the expectation that students will find a suitable place for themselves on the scientist-practitioner continuum. Thus, one student might prefer a 20%-80% split, while another might choose a 75%-25% split. Such training goals may be more realistic and, as Gelso speculated, entail less discouragement for both faculty and students. Gelso's idea is promising. Moreover, it is important for the profession to value both ends of the continuum equally, as well as various points along that continuum. It also seems that even if a person were trained within a scientist-practitioner model, he or she might choose not to engage in any research per se; we suggest that such a choice would not negate the model necessarily, because *other training outcomes* are associated with the scientific domain of the model. For example, a psychologist can be a scientist-practitioner and not engage in any research activity. What we are suggesting is that the product of a scientist-practitioner program is not necessarily a researcher but rather a counselor who thinks scientifically. In fact, equating science with only research activities may be the major problem with previous operationalizations of the scientist-practitioner model.

A counseling center staff member might be engaged primarily in direct client service and, let's say, one research project; this might be a 5%-95% science-practice split of *professional activities.* A faculty member (three-quarters time) with a quarter-time direct service appointment in the counseling center might have a 75%-25% split of *professional activities.* Regardless of the type of professional activities a counselor selects along the scientist-practitioner continuum, we nonetheless still maintain that all graduate students in counseling should receive basic training in both the scientific and practice domains.

The Need to Broaden Scientific Training

Most counselor education programs provide comprehensive training in the practice domain (for example, courses in counseling methods, counseling theory, multiple practica, and a year-long internship). The basic training most provide in the scientific domain, however, is deficient in at least two areas: basic scientific thinking skills and basic research application skills. We will discuss these two topics in some detail.

Training in Basic Scientific Thinking Skills

All counselors, regardless of where their professional activities fall on the scientist-practitioner continuum, need basic scientific thinking skills. Scientific thinking refers to a controlled method of inquiry and reasoning, typically to collect data of some kind for the purpose of testing a hypothesis. Clearly, it is essential to have research scientists within the counseling profession to continually expand our knowledge bases; these people obviously need training not only in basic scientific thinking skills, but also in research methods, statistics, philosophy of science, writing, and logic, and they need a multitude of opportunities to apply and extend their research skills. Moreover, a critical characteristic of a professional counselor is the integration of "scientific thinking" into the daily activities of professional practice (see Anderson &

Heppner, 1986; Berdie, 1972; Claiborn, 1984, 1987; Goodyear & Benton, 1986; Pepinsky & Pepinsky, 1954). Scientific thinking can be instrumental in how counselors process information about a specific client during counseling as well as how counselors evaluate the counseling process. (We will elaborate further on these two activities.)

How a person thinks is an exceedingly complex process (for example, see Anderson, 1983; Neisser, 1976). It is becoming increasingly clear over time that human beings often think or process information in both rational and irrational ways, in systematic and unsystematic ways, and in linear and nonlinear ways (for example, see Fiske & Taylor, 1984; Heppner, 1989; Kanfer & Busemeyer, 1982; Nisbett & Ross, 1980; Strohmer & Blustein, 1990; Tversky & Kahneman, 1974). Moreover, there is reason to believe that one's cognitive processes (that is, how one thinks) interact with both one's affective processes and behaviors, thus creating a complex triadic process (Heppner & Krauskopf, 1987). At this point the research clearly indicates that people do not think as "objective computers," but rather are selective or biased in the type of information to which they attend (Nisbett & Ross, 1980; Turk & Salovey, 1988). In particular, people often attend to information that confirms their existing beliefs, or discount information that is contrary to their existing beliefs (see Lichtenberg, 1984; Slusher & Anderson, 1989). Such biases can lead to problems for professional counselors as they process information about clients and evaluate the effectiveness of their work. (For references that discuss thinking processes and biases in counseling, see: Abramson, 1988; Heppner & Frazier, in press; Ingram, 1986; Turk & Salovey, 1988.)

Carl Rogers was very aware of this danger of counselor bias; in 1955 he observed that he could "deceive himself in regard to my creatively formed subjective hunches" about a client (p. 275). He believed that the scientific method, as a way of thinking, led him to check "the subjective feelings or hunch or hypothesis of a person with the objective fact" (Rogers, 1955, p. 275). Rogers would often check his hunches very directly by asking the client, "Do you mean this?" or "Could it be this?" Rogers would sometimes go a step farther and develop a written transcript of an interview to analyze the relationships between counselor and client statements. Years later his face would still light up with excitement about what he would learn about a particular client, or the counseling process, by stepping back from the immediacy of an interview to analyze those transcripts (Rogers, personal communication with P. P. Heppner and L. A. Lee, January 1984).

Pepinsky and Pepinsky (1954) initially articulated a prescriptive model of counselor thinking based on the scientific method. Strohmer and Newman (1983) succinctly summarized their model:

> The counselor observes the client, makes inferences about his or her current status and the causal inferences, and then, based on these inferences, makes a tentative judgment about the client. The counselor then proceeds in an experimental fashion to state the judgment as a hypothesis and to test it against independent observations of the client. Through a series of such tentative judgments and tests based on these judgments, the counselor constructs a hypothetical model of the client. This model then serves as the basis for making predictions (e.g., which treatment approach is most appropriate) about the client. (p. 557)

In essence, Pepinsky and Pepinsky (1954) were suggesting that the counselor incorporate a scientific thinking model by (1) generating hypotheses based on (2) the data that the client presents, followed by (3) empirical testing of the hypotheses, to develop (4) a model that can be used (5) to make predictions about the client. The essence of this approach is that it is *data-based* or *empirical,* which lessens the chance of personal biases or subjectivity. Scientific thinking in this way involves a continual generation and evaluation of hypotheses based on data.

Training in scientific thinking may be particularly important in evaluating counseling outcomes. Goodyear and Benton (1986) have referred to a particular counselor bias in assessing counseling outcomes, one which they call a "walk-through empiricism" mentality:

> That is, as the counselor has successes, he or she will form impressions of what techniques are proving useful. Although this walk-through empiricism can be valuable, it is also subjective and therefore unreliable if it is used as the sole source of data.
>
> An analogy might be drawn from medicine where not so long ago a frequent remedy was to treat people by bleeding them of "bad blood." Physicians believed a cause-effect relationship—that the bleeding caused a cure—and continued to offer this as a common treatment for many years. Yet, the treatment was no doubt responsible for many patient deaths that might have been avoided if the procedure had been tested empirically. (p. 291)

Thus, training in scientific thinking and methodologies can help the counselor to evaluate the effectiveness of counseling interventions more objectively and with less personal or subjective bias.

The empirical approach is a critical feature that distinguishes the counselor from a nonprofessional layperson, in large part because of its self-corrective characteristics:

> Both layman and scientist tend to construct "possible worlds," but whereas the layman's attitude predisposes him to fit what he sees and hears into a preconceived set of ideas about his world, the scientist tends to look upon his assumptions as tentative and problematic and subject to change as his observations fail to confirm his theoretical expectations. (Pepinsky & Pepinsky, 1954, p. 198)

Thus, Claiborn (1987) concluded that the difference between the counselor-as-scientist and the scientist is more a matter of goals than of procedure. We believe that it would be worthwhile to pursue more thorough training in basic scientific thinking skills to reflect training outcomes associated with a more integrated scientist-practitioner model.

It seems important to address one final point concerning the debate over the utility of the scientist-practitioner model. This model is in fact a hypothesis: it hypothesizes that scientific thinking enhances practice skills, and that practice training positively influences scientific endeavors. It is surprising that this hypothesis has not been put to an empirical test. Research is long overdue on this fundamental hypothesis.

Training in Basic Research Application Skills

The counseling research literature contains a great deal of information about client populations, counseling processes and outcomes, assessment, interventions, crisis intervention, professional issues, and a variety of special topics (see reviews by Borgen, 1984a; Gelso & Fassinger, 1990). A great deal of the counseling research literature appears in professional journals such as the *Journal of College Student Development,* the *Journal of Counseling and Development,* the *Journal of Counseling Psychology, The Counseling Psychologist,* the *Journal of Vocational Behavior,* and *Counselor Education and Supervision.* In addition, a number of other journals in other areas of psychology and education, such as the *Psychological Bulletin,* the *Journal of Personality and Social Psychology,* the *Journal of Aging,* the *Journal of Consulting and Clinical Psychology, Behavior Therapy, Cognitive Therapy and Research,* the *Journal of Educational Psychology, Educational and Psychological Measurement, Developmental Psychology, American Psychologist,* and the *Journal of Clinical and Social Psychology* contain a broad range of articles relevant for those in the counseling profession. Finally, more concentrated or condensed information is also available in several handbooks, such as *Effective Psychotherapy: A Handbook of Research* (Gurman & Razin, 1977), *Handbook of Counseling Psychology* (Brown & Lent, 1984), and *Handbook of Psychotherapy and Behavior Change* (Bergin & Garfield, 1971; Garfield & Bergin, 1978, 1986). There are also many specialized books on various counseling topics that are useful resources; for example, two books that are useful in developing research projects on career planning in the school system are *Designing Careers: Counseling to Enhance the Quality of Education, Work, and Leisure* (Gysbers & Associates, 1984) and *Developing and Managing Your School Guidance Program* (Gysbers & Henderson, 1988).

In short, the counseling research literature as well as literature from other areas in psychology and education contains a wealth of information about counseling and human behavior. This information is obviously essential for any person engaging in counseling research. Moreover, this information also can be an extremely useful data base or tool for a practitioner to help solve particular client problems. Anderson and Heppner (1986) observed that counselors' knowledge bases can quickly become out of date. While preparing a book of readings on recent innovations in counseling, Anderson was impressed with the number of articles being published on topics that counselors in training were not being taught about ten years ago (such as bulimia, sleep disorders, spouse abuse). Thus, counselors in the field need to train themselves continually to work effectively with new client problems.

Gelso (1985) has also observed that reading the research literature affects his thinking about the counseling process:

> I would offer that it is important to think about research as that which helps us use our heads more clearly and less prejudicially. It helps us think about what we do and organize our ever-changing personal theory of the processes in which we are involved, be they counseling, psychotherapy, consultation,

> supervision, and so on. We should not expect empirical research to capture
> the felt essence of those processes. Only the practice of them will do that.
> Most of the research findings that I read are relevant to my clinical practice
> in the following way: they help me think in a less biased way, they help
> me further refine my usually private theory of my practice, and they allow
> me to add small pieces of new information to my conceptual system. (p. 553)

The professional research literature is a resource that can provide a wealth
of useful information about specific client problems as well as topics for additional research. Moreover, reading the literature may affect the counselor's
thinking and refine his or her conceptualizations of the counseling process.
Thus, a basic skill for all graduate students in counseling is to become active
consumers of research (see Goodyear & Benton, 1986).

The research literature has at times been criticized for not having much
value for the practitioner for a wide variety of reasons (for example, Gadlin
& Ingle, 1975; Goldman, 1976, 1977, 1982; Howard, 1985; Levine, 1974;
Raush, 1974; Ross, 1981). Learning how to use the research literature (for
example, becoming familiar with the types of articles in different journals,
learning how to access information most efficiently) and making the literature
a part of one's problem-solving repertoire does not simply happen, but rather
typically involves specific training. A number of suggestions have appeared
in the literature to facilitate students' perusal and application of the research
literature, such as (1) identifying key articles for students rather than allowing
students to select what they read almost at random, (2) specific training in using
the literature as a problem-solving tool to help solve client problems, (3) specific
training in applying research methods to provide answers to client or agency
problems, and (4) increasing the efficiency of the information communicated
in the professional journals (for more detail regarding specific training
strategies, see Anderson & Heppner, 1986; Claiborn, 1984; Heppner &
Anderson, 1985; Wampold, 1986). In short, we suggest that the profession
examine methods to train students to apply the results of scientific research
to practice.

Students' Typical Reactions to Scientific Training

Typically, beginning graduate students have a number of fears associated with
the training they are about to receive, although it is not uncommon that these
fears remain unexpressed. Some students have doubts whether they can be
effective counselors (Will I be able to really listen and understand my clients?
Will I be able to help my clients change? What if my clients don't like me as
a person? What if my clients don't return for counseling?). Other students question whether they can succeed academically (Will I get through the required
courses? Dr. Groucho Knails has a reputation for being very demanding in class;
can I make it through his required courses?). Many students question whether
they can adequately learn the skills associated with research and science (How
can I, a mere graduate student, come up with a good research idea? Can I do
a thesis? A dissertation? Will I get bogged down in my research and never finish

my degree? Statistics scare me—I don't like math.). These and other fears are common and even developmentally normal. For the rest of this section, we will focus primarily on students' typical reactions to science and the scientific enterprise and possible training strategies. We believe it is essential to discuss the affective components associated with scientific activities to facilitate development in this area.

Most incoming graduate students have had some experience (or even a lot) with helping other people, and consequently the benefits of counseling and other practitioner activities are abundantly clear. Moreover, for most of us, helping people is a personally rewarding experience, and students have an understanding of those rewards. Conversely, most incoming students have had considerably less experience with science (Gelso, 1979). Typically, students do not imagine themselves making contributions to the profession by publishing in our professional journals. Moreover, students do not have a long history in the profession and are unable to identify how previous research has contributed to the profession. Similarly, students do not have a clear understanding about the utility of the scientific method as a way of thinking, either about research or clients. Finally, the student typically has not had the experience of *learning,* of discovering new insights, of expanding one's understanding about clients and applied problems by engaging in research activities, reading the professional literature, contemplating one's empirical findings, and hours of concentrated thinking. From our experience teaching research methods, we have been struck by *many* students' surprise and actual delight as they get past their initial fears and begin to apply their new knowledge about research design. We often have heard comments like "I am actually *enjoying* this research course"; "I never thought I would be a researcher; now, I am beginning to re-consider my career goals"; "This research stuff is contagious; I am starting to think about research studies a lot and I want to collect data now!" In sum, the major point is that often beginning graduate students have considerably less information about research and science than about practitioner activities. Moreover, there is evidence that as students obtain more experience with scientific activities (especially if it is early in their training), their research interests increase and they place a higher value on the role of research (Gelso, Raphael, Black, Rardin, & Skalkos, 1983; Royalty et al., 1986).

From our experience working with students, a major issue is students' affective reactions to science, and especially to research. In particular, students' performance anxiety is a central and critical affective issue. Other educators have come to similar conclusions (for example, Claiborn, 1984; Gelso, 1979). Common student disclosures include: "I don't know enough to conduct any meaningful research on my own. How can I do a thesis? How can I criticize previous research?" "Any data that I could uncover using 'science' would be so basic and bland as to make it worthless." "I feel completely inadequate in even conceiving a study that comes at counseling from a unique perspective." "Although I made it through the statistics and research design courses, once I start to do some research I will be 'found out'; it will become clear that I am incompetent and really don't know how to do research." "What if I make a mistake and report inaccurate findings?" "I have had trouble writing before, and I am scared that I will run into debilitating writing blocks again in my research." "I fear that my results will be statistically nonsignificant, and all of my research efforts and time will just be one big waste." "I have seen other students in the throes of a dissertation. The whole process seems overwhelming: tedious, long, anxiety-producing, confusing, and complicated." All of these feelings, and many others, are usually developmentally normal. That is, since students have had little, if any, research experience, they have reason to question and doubt their skills and abilities. It is important to remember, however, that the reason for attending graduate school is to acquire new skills—skills the student currently does not have. If the student had enough previous experience to ease all of these doubts, he or she probably would not need to be in a training program.

In fact, some of these performance-anxiety fears are common developmentally many years post-Ph.D. This suggests to us that acquiring the necessary research and thinking skills occurs over a long period of time; it does not happen all at once. Just as it is unreasonable to expect to become an Olympic downhill skier in four years, it is also unreasonable to expect to become an expert researcher in four years (Nancy Downing, personal communication, June 28, 1990).

Clara Hill, a creative and innovative researcher from the University of Maryland, was invited to write a personal account of her evolution as a researcher (Hill, 1984). Her account illustrates how she made decisions, how complex the process of research can be, and most importantly, how she coped with the ups and downs along the way. For example, consider her comments regarding her "crisis of faith in research":

> After this series of studies I underwent a crisis in terms of research. I had achieved tenure, had my first baby, and turned 30. I started questioning everything. Because I could see so many imperfections in my research, I was not very proud of my work. It had taken an incredible amount of time for little "hard information." I could not even remember the results of many of my studies. Further, I seemed woefully far from even describing what happens in the counseling process let alone understanding what counselor behaviors were useful in effecting change. I despaired that counseling was far too complex to be studied. I had previously had lots of doubts about my research, but it was mostly related to self-confidence in my research abilities. This crisis seemed to have more to do with whether I felt that research was a viable means to answer questions about the counseling process. (p. 105)

Hill's behind-the-scenes disclosures are illuminating as well as relieving. The article should be required reading for all graduate students in counseling, perhaps during their first course on research methods. We have found that students resonate strongly with Hill's frustrations, jubilations, feelings of inadequacy, and doubts about the role of research. (In fact, informal data collected from a beginning-level research methods course taught by the first author suggests that some students rated Hill's article as one of the most important readings in the course.) The evolution of her confidence in studying her own ideas in her own way not only sends a useful message, but also presents some data about the developmental processes of a researcher.

Another major issue pertains to beginning students' understanding of science and its role in our profession for both research and practice. Most beginning students do not have much of an understanding of the role of science in our profession. One unfortunate outcome is that students sometimes fill this void with misinformation, like "science = statistics." Or "the scientific method is too intellectual, too cognitive, and unrelated to the experiences of real people." Or "the scientific method is so mechanical and reductionistic that it cannot be used adequately to study the complexities of real human behavior." Or students say to themselves, "I just want to be a therapist, not a scientist"; very simply stated, they "just want to help people."

In our view, all of these statements reflect a lack of understanding of science, of the scientific method, and of the counseling process as well. A noted counselor-educator from the University of Minnesota, Ralph Berdie, discussed the role of science in training professional counselors almost two decades ago (Berdie, 1972). At this point, Berdie was discouraged with the outcomes of the typical counselor-education training:

> Counselors repeatedly ask for training that will be of more practical assistance. They want their periodicals and literature to provide them with examples of how to solve problems—recipes or cookbooks that will aid them. A survey of counselors in 1971 reported that "a majority seemed to think they would like the content of counseling journals changed to something more practical, more realistic, and less theoretical" (Bradley & Smith, 1971).
>
> The present counselor's difficulty is not that he [sic] has too much theory, but rather too little. He [sic] does not have enough ideas and concepts to understand the problems that face him or to develop approaches and solutions to these problems. He [sic] asks to be told what to do and how to do it, because he does not know enough to figure this out for himself. His professional preparation has failed to provide him with knowledge, theory, and concepts, and these are what he needs. (pp. 452–453)

Counseling has been characterized frequently as *either* an art *or* a science, but as Goodyear and Benton (1986) note, this is a rather narrow view:

> This dichotomy, however, oversimplifies the situation and perhaps exists because of a misunderstanding of the scientist role. Scientists are too often confused with technicians, the people who apply the findings of science but without theoretical understanding. . . . The best scientists overlap with the best artists in their capacity for alternative ways of perceiving, in their creativity, and in their openness to new experiences. (p. 290)

There is no doubt that counseling is a very complex process, one that defies a simple description. But this complexity does not mitigate against a scientific way of thinking about that complex process. The scientific method is simply a set of tools to establish a controlled mode of inquiry about our professional activities. Those of us in the profession are in control of how we use those tools, or we can develop new ones. If we cannot "make the tools work," the fault could lie with the tools, or it could lie with the users; however, to simply throw up our hands and throw our tools away is dangerous. Similarly, after much deliberation Carl Rogers concluded that "science will never depersonalize, or manipulate, or control individuals, only people could do that" (Rogers, 1955, p. 277).

The final issue we'll discuss is the idea that students' research training is often less than rewarding. Gelso (1979) offered the following proposition: "Training programs tend not to take the [students'] ambivalence toward research into account and, to a remarkable degree, lack deliberateness in their attempts to capitalize on and strengthen the positive side of the ambivalence" (p. 27). In general, the research training most graduate students receive is less sophisticated and thorough than their practitioner training.

Consider this not-too-hypothetical example, offered by Gelso (1979):

> Harold/Hannah Helpful, our typical student, enters graduate school with much ambivalence and anxiety about the scholarly requirements of that situation, as well as the role of science in his/her career. He/she knows he/she has done quite well in school all along, but the scholarly demands of a doctoral program are a different ballgame for him/her. Yet he/she is indeed ambivalent, not negative. At the same time, he/she probably endows the faculty with some degree of omniscience. What the student runs into during the first year is a bewildering array of requirements, including courses (unfortunately, sometimes even in his/her specialty) that are demanding but unexciting. Usually this includes one or two statistics courses that teach little if anything about counseling research, but seem wedded to the scientific enterprise. These courses often deepen the student's anxiety and deaden motivation. The task is to get through them.
>
> Toward the end of the first year our hypothetical student must start thinking thesis. More anxiety. Up to that point he/she has done no research, acquired no confidence, and at best has gotten through statistics unscathed. The student does not know how to generate ideas that later may be translated into scientifically answerable questions. The process goes on, through the preliminary meeting with the advisor, the thesis proposal meeting, and the thesis orals. All steps along the way are all too often filled with more threat and anxiety than pleasure of discovery. The fortunate student gets by without massive revisions of the thesis and can take a deep breath until the next major scientific hurdle, the dissertation. When assessed against the criterion of, "Is it positively reinforcing?" this unfortunately not very exaggerated description of the scientific regimen of graduate school hurdles is a dreadful failure. (p. 28)

Unfortunately, when students have little experience with research and science, one bad experience can create tremendous attitudinal and motivational damage and move a student a long way from future scientific activities. Although empirical evidence is scant on graduate-level research training, it does appear that some training programs actually decrease students' interest in research (Royalty et al., 1986). Moreover, some students report feeling "disenchanted with research" when they perceive unethical and unprofessional approaches to conducting research in their training environment (more on this in Chapter 4).

A number of ideas have been published in approximately the last two decades aimed at increasing the effectiveness of graduate-level training in science and research (for example, Anderson & Heppner, 1986; Claiborn, 1984; Gelso, 1979; Gelso et al., 1988; Goodyear & Benton, 1986; Heppner, Gelso, & Dolliver, 1987; Magoon & Holland, 1984; Royalty & Magoon, 1985; Seeman, 1973; Wallerstein, 1971; Wampold, 1986). The ideas range from broader programmatic philosophies to more specific events, such as seminars and workshops, and focus on faculty, students, curricula, and environmental variables. Some of these ideas include the following:

- Encourage faculty to provide more complete self-disclosure and modeling of positive and negative aspects associated with research
- Provide more positive reinforcement to students, such as publicly acknowledging research publications
- Organize early and minimally threatening involvements in research training during students' training
- Separate the artificial connection between research and statistics
- Teach students to integrate their own experiences with the findings from the research literature to facilitate involvement and thinking
- Develop more social activities within the research enterprise, such as research teams
- Provide more explicit training on how science and counseling practice can be wedded
- Emphasize the suitability of multiple research methodologies, depending on different research questions
- Train students in how to conduct research in an agency
- Promote workshops aimed at increasing graduate students' awareness of and interest in professional writing
- Develop a sequence of training events to create conducive academic environments for learning
- Specifically focus training on emotional fears of students about research
- Emphasize the role of scientific thinking in graduate training
- Increase the amount of feedback to and supervision of students regarding the development of specific scientific thinking and research skills
- More systematically introduce students to the research literature and emphasize its applications to practice
- Teach students how to apply research findings as a problem-solving tool
- Teach students how to apply research methods to solve real-life problems or answer real-life questions (for example, within an agency)
- Have graduate students keep a log of their own research ideas, starting at the beginning of their graduate study
- Develop a graduated series of experiential and didactic research training courses analogous to counseling practice, including prepractica, practica, advanced practica, and internship
- Open students' proposal and defense committee meetings to other students

- Link dissertations to journal publications
- Reorient research advisors to assume more of a detective, consultative role
- Train students to make their work environments more conducive to research activities
- Train students to seek researcher support in their work environments
- Cultivate research environments that are consistent or congruent with the personalities of the researchers
- Focus graduate training on three interrelated factors in students: their sense of efficacy as scientists, their interest in doing research, and the value they place on research during their forthcoming careers
- Create postdoctoral research opportunities for counseling psychologists
- Develop theory and conduct research on all aspects of research training
- Develop more specific accreditation standards for research training

Despite all of these ideas, training students in research and scientific thinking is an "area of inquiry in its infancy" (Gelso et al., 1988, p. 402). More attention should be given to the sequence of training activities as well as students' affective reactions to research training. In addition, it seems important to attend much more to individual differences among students. For example, one study found support for the notion that psychologists with different personalities (using Holland code high points) preferred different research environments (Royalty & Magoon, 1985). Thus, it may be helpful for students to understand their personality style more clearly and the implications for finding research endeavors more or less rewarding. "For example, investigative researchers may be more willing to conduct theoretical research, whereas social researchers may be more willing to conduct practical, applied research and may be more interested in team research. Artistic researchers may be more creative with less traditional and less restrictive methods of research (e.g., case studies)" (Royalty & Magoon, 1985, p. 461). Perhaps consideration of students' affective reactions, values, and individual differences will enhance our training endeavors.

SUMMARY AND CONCLUSIONS

The counseling profession helps people with a wide variety of personal, educational, and career-related problems. Most of all, we must be very cognizant that we are working with real people, many of whom are experiencing psychological pain of some sort and are in need of professional assistance. To be credible, reliable, and effective, the profession must be built on a dependable knowledge base, rather than on tenacity, decrees from authority figures, or subjective opinions.

Science represents a way of knowing, a way of establishing truths about the profession. There is much debate over how we might best proceed in our scientific endeavors as well as how students should be educated. The careers professional counselors choose will most likely demand professional activities that will continue to fall at various points along the scientist-practitioner continuum. It is important to note, however, that one's professional interests and desires often change throughout one's career. Thus, we strongly encourage students to prepare themselves broadly throughout graduate school to acquire skills within both the scientific and practice domains. From our experience, it is sad to witness students who have not acquired necessary skills within either the science or practice domains and then do not have career options available to them later in life.

We strongly believe that there can be a much greater integration between the science and practice domains, not only within counselor training but also within the professional activities of all counselors. Carl Rogers's hope for the future was that "each researcher would be a practitioner in some field and each practitioner would be doing some research (Heppner, Rogers, & Lee, 1984, p. 19). This is one type of integration; we have also suggested that scientific research training be broadened (and integrated) to include basic scientific thinking and basic research application skills. In our personal experience, our research has clearly been facilitated by observations made during many hours of counseling practice. Moreover, our experience has been that our thinking and counseling skills have been sharpened, extended, and clearly enhanced by subjecting our thinking to empirical tests as well as contemplating new ideas from the research literature. Integration might also happen on another level: between those who are primarily research-oriented and those who are practice-oriented. In some ways, the people who have the most well-developed set of observations of the counseling process are those people who are heavily engaged in counseling practice; it behooves the typical researcher to develop collaborative relationships with such practitioners. In short, we suspect that scientific and practice-oriented professional activities could both be enhanced by a more complete integration of the two domains.

We have suggested in this opening chapter that a critical ingredient of counseling is the counselor's attitudes toward science and research. We have discussed some common fears that students have about scientific activities that may present obstacles and negatively affect students' attitudes. It is sad to see students not only have bad experiences with research, but also feel so angry and hurt that their attitudes about science are adversely affected. Educators must attend to students' affective experiences during training in the scientific domain, and develop more effective didactic and experiential components in the training curriculum. Moreover, students must help by "educating" faculty about their experiences; we strongly encourage students to take the necessary risks to disclose and encourage faculty to try to listen.

We have also maintained that a basic issue in scientific training is scientific thinking. Those at the Atlanta conference in 1987 concluded that "an attitude of scholarly inquiry is critical to all the activities of those educated in the scientist-professional model" (Meara et al., 1988, p. 368). Such an outcome requires not only scientific skills but also scientific values. The latter are also important goals and need specific attention in training (perhaps by way of discussions about the philosophy of science, research methods, the slow but steady accumulation of knowledge, and students' own research experiences).

An attitude of scholarly inquiry goes beyond scientific thinking and involves curiosity, inquisitiveness, healthy skepticism, exploration, and a desire to learn. In a way, all counseling professionals are pioneers in extending the boundaries of their own knowledge throughout their careers, and possibly extending the knowledge bases of the profession as well. In this way, scholarly inquiry involves discovery, excitement, and even a sense of adventure. Not surprisingly, pioneers in the field of counseling and development report they were motivated to achieve, in part, by the joys of intellectual discovery, "the thirst to know something" (Pepinsky, cited in Claiborn, 1985, p. 7).

Maintaining a pioneering attitude in one's professional scholarly inquiry can also be a way of life. Following is a quote from Enos Mills (1924) that aptly depicts qualities of a pioneer's life. Mills was an early pioneer in the mountains of Colorado in the area that is now Rocky Mountain National Park. Although Mills was referring to pioneering in the early American West, the qualities of life he describes apply to the pioneering attitude we are referring to with regard to discovering professional knowledge through scholarly inquiry.

> Those who live pioneer lives are usually the most fortunate of people. They suffer from no dull existence. Each hour is full of progressive thought, and occasions which call for action accompanied by the charm of exploration— action that makes their lives strong, sincere, and sweet. Their days are full of eagerness and repose, they work with happy hands. The lives of pioneers are rich with hope and their future has all the promise of spring. . . . (p. 9)

CHAPTER 2

IDENTIFYING AND OPERATIONALIZING RESEARCH TOPICS

The purpose of this chapter is to provide an overview of selecting a research topic and developing the research idea into a testable investigation. The chapter describes the five main components of this process: identifying research topics, specifying research questions and hypotheses, formulating operational definitions, identifying research variables, and collecting and analyzing data. For pedagogical reasons, we present these activities in separate sections. However, in reality these activities are often intertwined, and the researcher often intersperses thinking and planning across all of these activities as she or he progresses from identifying the topic to developing specific research hypotheses.

IDENTIFYING RESEARCH TOPICS

A wide range of experiences can play a role in helping the researcher develop research ideas. At times, developing a research idea can involve a great deal of creativity, as the researcher integrates information from diverse sources and in novel ways. It is often exciting to develop innovative ideas that may lead to important contributions of new knowledge, and to think that no one has thought of this idea before (at least for a short period of time!). Various pioneers in the field of counseling have commented on the joys of discovery and learning they have experienced by engaging in research. (The interested might read some of the interviews with early counseling pioneers that have appeared in the "Pioneers in Guidance" and "Lifelines" series in the *Journal of Counseling and Development.* For example, Anne Roe, in reflecting on her career, stated simply that "nothing is as much fun as research. . . . I miss that [in retirement]" [Wrenn, 1985, p. 275].) At other times, developing a research idea can involve very little creative thought as the researcher takes a previous research idea one logical step farther. But even here there is the fun of learning and discovery.

At first, developing research ideas often seems difficult for inexperienced researchers; they cringe at the thought of developing an original research idea that *no one* has *ever* had before! Typically, the experienced researcher has little difficulty in developing research ideas. In fact, often the veteran researcher has too many research ideas and a more difficult problem is deciding which ideas to pursue. Several ingredients differentiate the experienced researcher from the inexperienced. The experienced researcher usually has a very large knowledge base, not only about one topic but about several other topics as well. The researcher can most likely process information about these topics in sophisticated ways, identifying the most important findings, combining research findings, dovetailing an idea from one topic with another, and elaborating on or extending ideas in novel ways. In addition, the experienced counseling researcher often has a considerable wealth of information from his or her applied counseling experiences that can be the source of many ideas and hypotheses. The veteran researcher also typically has a great deal of knowledge about the skills needed to conduct research, such as research design, methodology, assessment, statistics, data collection, data analysis, and professional writing. All of these knowledge bases are important in facilitating the processing of large amounts of information about specific research projects in sophisticated and often novel ways. Perhaps equally as important, the experienced researcher typically has confidence that he or she can effectively conduct research, and thus has the needed level of self-efficacy.

In contrast, the inexperienced researcher has far less knowledge about specific research topics, and often has trouble identifying the most important or relevant information. The trainee often has less applied experience in counseling, and most likely has less-developed conceptualizations of the counseling process. The inexperienced researcher has perhaps only a vague sense of the various research activities (such as recruitment of subjects, data collection), and harbors doubts about his or her ability to do research as well as his or her interests in conducting research. In fact, in many counseling programs, well-articulated guidelines for conducting research are not available to students, leaving the impression that the research process is rather mystical. Drew (1980) noted that a logical place to turn to for information is a college or departmental catalog, which describes the thesis or dissertation project. Typically such documents say something to the effect that the thesis "must be an original contribution to the field." When viewed literally, such phrases can be very threatening. The word "original" can engender considerable anxiety as the trainee tries to develop a completely novel research idea. In addition, the idea must represent "a contribution to the field," which makes the task even more formidable. It is the rare trainee who believes at the outset that he or she can make a "real contribution" to the field; after all, we are talking about *Science!* Most often the inexperienced researcher interprets the "original contribution" phrase much too broadly and tries to develop a new topic area by creating a new assessment instrument to measure new constructs, a new research methodology to collect data previously not collected, and new statistical procedures to handle old problems. In reality, most experienced researchers would feel quite a sense of accomplishment if they did all of these things during an entire career. In short, the inexperienced researcher often assumes too much in trying to develop an "original contribution." Not surprisingly, our experience has been that graduate students in beginning research design courses ask questions about how to identify "good" research topics and "good" research ideas. Also not surprisingly, they often ask whether a particular idea is "enough" for a thesis.

We will make some suggestions here to help beginning researchers in identifying a research topic. Essentially, the task is to identify some general topic that may (1) contribute to the profession's bases in meaningful ways, and (2) simultaneously stimulate and motivate you to explore and learn more about this topic. Most inexperienced researchers in counseling need to acquire more knowledge about what research has been done as well as the directions of current research efforts. Thus, for such students we do not simply recommend sitting and thinking hard about research topics and hoping that the ideal research question will present itself, but rather a more active, information-collecting approach. A good first step in identifying possible research topics is to start collecting information about previous research, both within and outside of counseling. Thus, read widely in the professional journals, such as those listed in Chapter 1. Reading widely will not only provide you with information about what is being published, but also may help you to clarify what topics are of most interest to you. Sometimes it is useful to start with a general review of the counseling literature (see Borgen, 1984a; Gelso & Fassinger, 1990); another strategy is to begin by looking for more focused literature reviews on specific topics (the *Psychological Bulletin* is a journal devoted to evaluative and integrative reviews; see Dolliver, 1969, for an excellent example of an influential evaluative review of measured versus expressed vocational interest). There is no substitute for this time-consuming process, although at first you might peruse the literature and read abstracts to develop a broad overview. A good beginning is to spend at least five hours a week reading and exploring the journals for six weeks or more.

In addition to regularly reading the journals, capitalize on the faculty and student resources on your campus. While this sounds simplistic, it often provides useful information. Talk with these people about their past and present research projects. What are they most excited about now? What was the most stimulating idea at a recent national, regional, or state convention they attended? What do they consider as hot or promising topics? Follow your discussion with these people with readings they might suggest to you.

In addition to faculty in general, your advisor or research supervisor is often an invaluable resource. Typically, your advisor's role is to facilitate your work on the thesis. Thus, another strategy is to begin research training by working closely within the advisor's research interests, which resembles an apprenticeship model. An advantage of this strategy is that the advisor can more easily facilitate the identification of workable research ideas, methods, and procedures. Some faculty believe that master's-level students should be assigned research topics, because students are typically overwhelmed with their first research project. Assigning research topics may be directive, but sometimes appropriate for students who have trouble getting started.

Although we said earlier that we do not recommend simply sitting and thinking hard, we do recommend thinking and reflecting *after* you have collected a wide variety of information. What do you like and dislike about a particular line of research? Pay attention to what bothers you about a study. Was something omitted? How could you improve the study? Also try to bring your own observations and beliefs into your research topics. Many experienced counselors use their own observations about a topic (for example, the counselor supervision process, counselor self-disclosure) as a source of ideas for research topics. This is more risky, however, for the inexperienced counselor and researcher, because a lack of experience may provide less-reliable observations. To facilitate reflecting and brainstorming, sometimes it is helpful to record ideas, observations, and questions in a journal or log.

While reading and thinking about previous research in counseling, it is important to keep in mind at least four issues: your particular interests, building on previous research, the role of theory, and the utility of research in answering real-life applied questions.

It is essential to continually assess which topics intrigue you most within the broad field of counseling. What are you most curious about? Are there certain topics that you are motivated to pursue, or perhaps feel a special commitment to investigating because of your beliefs or values? Are there any topics that you believe previous researchers have overlooked? In short, pursuing research topics that you are curious about and are motivated to pursue will likely provide the intellectual stimulation needed to sustain you through various research tasks.

It is important to realize that a great deal of research in counseling is extending the results from previous research. Typically, our research proceeds by adding one or two new pieces of information per study. Thus, a researcher might extend a previous study by adding one or two new constructs or developing a new assessment instrument to operationalize a construct. Often a researcher uses a method of data collection similar to that used in previous research, or instruments used in three or four previous studies. In short, it is essential to focus on investigation of just a few constructs, and not to try to do too much in developing an "original contribution." Most often our knowledge bases in counseling increase in small steps by building only slightly on previous research.

A considerable amount of research within counseling applies or tests theories about personality, human behavior, and the persuasion process as they apply to topics in counseling. For example, Stanley Strong (1968) initially conceptualized counseling as a social influence process and used research and theory on persuasion from social psychology to develop a two-phase model of influence within counseling. Subsequently, a great deal of research has examined the persuasion or social influence process within counseling (see reviews by Corrigan, Dell, Lewis, & Schmidt, 1980; Heppner & Claiborn, 1989; Heppner & Dixon, 1981). Likewise, another theoretical perspective that is influencing counseling research is that of developmental models in counselor training (see Holloway, 1987). Thus, another strategy in identifying research topics is to note the theories that are being examined in the counseling literature as well as to consider theories outside of the counseling literature that might be helpful to the work of counselors.

A considerable amount of research within counseling stems from questions about applied problems. Thus, another way to identify research topics is to contemplate what is unknown or unclear about the counseling process, various treatment programs (such as social skills training, marriage enrichment workshops, men's support groups), or outreach programs (for example, rape prevention programs, alcohol awareness programs). Most important, are there some real-life questions that an agency director, or some other personnel, would like some information about? For example, perhaps the counseling center director would like to know how clients would react to a detailed, computer-assisted intake like CASPER (see McCullough & Farrell, 1983; McCullough, Farrell, & Longabaugh, 1986). Many times unresolved problems or questions about applied aspects of counseling are a rich source of research topics.

In summary, ideas for research projects can come from a wide range of sources. It is often useful for students to use several of the strategies mentioned as they enter the world of research.

SPECIFYING RESEARCH QUESTIONS AND HYPOTHESES

Typically, the purpose of research is to answer questions, solve problems, or develop theories of interest to counseling, and ultimately add to the existing knowledge in the field. It is one thing to identify a *topic* you want to research (such as client thoughts-not-said in group therapy or the effects of art therapy). It is a significant step to move beyond the research topic to an unresolved problem or specific research question or hypothesis that can guide your research. In fact, developing testable research questions is often quite troublesome for inexperienced researchers as they develop research ideas and proposals.

After identifying a possible research topic (for example, counselor supervision), it is important that you become knowledgeable about the previous research on that topic, perhaps even resulting in writing a formal review paper. There is again no substitute for becoming thoroughly knowledgeable about a topic to identify current research findings, previous research obstacles, and previous researchers' suggestions for future research. As we indicated earlier, many times developing a specific research idea means extending a line of research one logical step farther. Thus, regarding key studies or incisive reviews is essential. Pay particular attention to the discussion section in those studies. Often there is explicit discussion of future research needs or the next logical step. The authors often identify these needs by phrases such as "future research should . . . " or "additional research might examine . . . " These suggestions could be the basis of your research idea.

Conversely, sometimes previous research is based on certain assumptions, procedures, and manners of thinking that have blinded previous researchers in identifying the obvious or critical constructs on a particular topic. Thus, a researcher can be at an advantage by coming at a research topic with a new or fresh perspective, untainted by the assumptions of previous researchers.

At this point, begin to attend more closely to the constructs that have been used in the previous research. What psychological processes are interesting and important to researchers in the field? Perhaps stated most simply, research explores or examines relationships among constructs. *Research questions* are questions about the relations among or between constructs. For example, "Does the level of dysfunction of the client affect the working alliance formed in counseling?" is a research question. A *research hypothesis* is more specific in that it states the expected relationship between the constructs—for example, "More dysfunctional clients will form poorer alliances in counseling than will less dysfunctional clients." Often, distinctions are not made between questions and hypotheses. However, it should be kept in mind that hypotheses specifically state the expected relationship.

From our experience, students have difficulty developing research questions and hypotheses for several reasons. Perhaps most frequently, students often lack a theoretical structure for their investigation and thus cannot conceptualize relevant research hypotheses that will empirically test or extend previous research. Research hypotheses are often deduced from theory (Wampold, Davis, & Good, 1990). At other times students select constructs they do not have ways of measuring or testing. For example, one doctoral student was stymied because he could not clearly assess what he meant by counselor personal power and autonomy. Sometimes students have not thought in depth beyond the research topic, and have not asked themselves what specific constructs they are most interested in examining. Thus, they are unable to be more specific than being interested in "something about computerized career information services." At other times, students are reluctant to decide on specific constructs, choosing rather to delay or procrastinate for an array of conscious and unconscious avoidant reasons. All of these difficulties in developing research questions and hypotheses are not atypical for inexperienced researchers. Most important, such difficulties suggest that additional reading and thinking are necessary. Researchers can make serious errors by proceeding to select subjects and assessment instruments without ever being clear about their research questions or hypotheses and exactly what they are looking for in their research.

Drew (1980) has identified three general categories of research questions (or hypotheses), which we find useful: descriptive, difference, and relationship. *Descriptive questions* essentially ask what some phenomena or events are like. In these studies, experimental manipulations typically are not used, but rather information is collected on inventories, surveys, or interviews. Sometimes we have questions about events or phenomena pertaining to counseling that are best answered by collecting information to describe events, like types of events that trigger counselor anger (Fremont & Anderson, 1986). At other times we use statistical procedures such as factor analysis (see Tinsley & Tinsley, 1987) or cluster analysis (see Borgen & Barnett, 1987) to describe how people or events might be categorized. For example, one group of researchers recently used cluster analysis to describe different types of career indecision in students (Larson, Heppner, Ham, & Dugan, 1989). Descriptive research is discussed more fully in Chapter 8.

Difference questions ask if there are differences between groups of people or even within the same subjects. The key feature in this type of question is a comparison of some sort. Such research questions tend to focus on groups of individuals; the groups may differ on some dimension or may receive different treatments. For example, a study by Mallinckrodt and Helms (1986) examined a difference question as they determined whether physically disabled counselors enjoy certain therapeutic advantages relative to able-bodied counselors due to their disability. Likewise, Tracey, Leong, and Glidden (1986) compared help seeking and problem perception of Asian-American clients and white clients. Difference questions are often examined in between-group and within-group designs (see Chapter 5).

Relationship questions explore the degree to which two or more constructs are related, or vary together. Such questions tend to use correlational statistics, or more complex regression analyses. For example, a study by Marx and Gelso (1987) examined a relationship question by studying the relationship between client satisfaction with termination and five client variables suggesting loss in the termination process. Relationship research questions are also discussed more fully in Chapter 8.

What constitutes a testable research question? Kerlinger (1986) specified three criteria: a research question (1) asks a question about (2) the relationships between two or more constructs that can be (3) measured in some way. First, the question should be stated clearly and unambiguously in question form. Second, the research question should inquire into a relationship between two or more constructs, asking if Construct A is related to Construct B. (If a particular relationship is stated, the research question becomes a hypothesis.) This second criterion pertains mostly to difference and relationship questions, while descriptive questions often seek to collect or categorize information. Finally, not only is a relationship stated between constructs, but somehow this relationship also must be measurable.

For example, consider a research question like, Is supervision effective? One might immediately ask, "Effective at what?" Is the researcher interested in the effectiveness of supervision at lowering the trainee's stress level, ability to conceptualize clients, or ability to intervene with clients? In short, such a question lacks specificity. Conversely, consider the research questions developed by Wiley and Ray (1986). These researchers were interested in the topic of the changing nature of supervision over the course of training. In particular, they were interested in testing Stoltenberg's 1981 counselor complexity model about developmental levels of counselor trainees. (Stoltenberg proposed that counselor trainees develop in a predictable way over the course of graduate training, and that counseling supervision environments should be adapted in ways that match the needs of the trainee.) Wiley and Ray developed three specific research questions. Each one inquired about relationships between two or more constructs, and were amenable to being measured or tested in some way. For example, one of their questions was: To what extent do supervision dyads with a more congruent person-environment match on developmental level report higher satisfaction and learning than those with a less congruent match? The construct of the congruent person-environment match was concretely operationalized via the use of an assessment instrument called the Supervision Level Scale. Likewise, satisfaction and learning were operationalized in terms of a brief outcome instrument. Parenthetically, while Wiley and Ray obtained results that provided some support for conceptualizing supervisees and supervision environments developmentally, mean satisfaction and learning ratings did not differ by person-environment congruency.

Thus, the function of a testable research question or hypothesis is to provide direction for experimental inquiry. The testable research question or hypothesis not only identifies the topic but also identifies specific constructs of interest within that topic. After a researcher has developed a specific research question or hypothesis, he or she can then proceed to determine how data can be collected, what subjects to use, what instruments to use, and so on. Many of these methodological decisions are directly dependent on the investigator's specific question or hypothesis.

Although the research question provides direction for designing a study, it is important to note that in the formative stages as an investigator continues to develop the design and methodology of a particular study, it is not uncommon to revise or change the original research question. The investigator may encounter measurement or subject availability problems, which may dictate a slightly different research question. Or the researcher may find new information or data that suggests additional complexity in the topic, and thus the need to revise the research question. In short, any of a number of events may lead the researcher to process more information and subsequently to revise or sharpen his or her research questions in the formative stages of designing a study.

Sometimes graduate students get discouraged about their false starts, and begin to feel a sense of inadequacy because they "couldn't get it right the first time." There often is an assumption that the "real researcher" proceeds through a logical series of ordered steps, starting first of all with a brilliant, incisive research question. Our experience has been that effective researchers generally intersperse thinking about a wide range of design issues when developing a research question, such as thinking about instruments, subjects, and external validity issues; rereading studies; and so forth. In short, revision of research questions is typical during the formative design stages, and often is desirable. Of course, after data collection has begun, revision of the research question is no longer functional or appropriate.

FORMULATING OPERATIONAL DEFINITIONS

After the initial development of the research question or hypothesis, it is critical that all terms or constructs in the question be defined concretely so that the research idea can be empirically tested. More specifically, each construct must be operationally defined, which means specifying the activities or operations necessary to measure it in this particular experiment. Kerlinger (1986) referred to operational definitions as "a sort of manual of instructions" that spells out what the investigator must do to measure or manipulate the variables during the procedures of the study.

For example, considerable interest has been shown in developmental models of supervision, which in essence postulate that trainees' skills and supervisory needs change over time as trainees attain different developmental levels (see Holloway, 1987). A critical issue is how one operationally defines developmental level. Some of the initial investigations operationally defined developmental level by the training level of the student, such as beginning practicum student, advanced practicum student, and doctoral-level intern (for example, Heppner & Roehlke, 1984; Reising & Daniels, 1983; Worthington, 1984). Thus, developmental level was concretely or operationally defined in terms of training level.

The primary function of an operational definition is to define the constructs involved in a particular study. In a way, the operational definition provides a working definition of the phenomenon (Kazdin, 1980). Thus, the operational definition allows the researcher to move from general ideas and constructs to more specific and measurable events.

A problem arises when researchers investigate the same construct, but develop different operational definitions. Consider again the example of developmental levels of counseling trainees. Whereas developmental level was initially defined as trainee level (for example, Reising & Daniels, 1983), Wiley and Ray (1986) defined developmental level in terms of supervisors' ratings on an instrument (the Supervision Level Scale) that assesses the trainee developmental level along five dimensions. Wiley and Ray's definition is more specific, and based on Stoltenberg's (1981) theoretical model. Interestingly, Wiley and Ray (1986) found that these two definitions of developmental level result in quite different categorizations of trainees.

This example aptly depicts the problem of different operational definitions for the same construct. As research information accrues over several investigations, it is difficult to summarize information on supervisees' developmental level because of the different operational definitions. More important, different operational definitions sometimes lead to very different results. This is a critical point for the inexperienced researcher to comprehend, because it implies that the results from a particular study must be qualified or restricted according to the operational definitions used in the study. It is also important to note that, as research within a topic progresses and becomes more complex, often operational definitions undergo revision as knowledge accumulates and researchers become more sophisticated, as in the supervision literature.

IDENTIFYING RESEARCH VARIABLES

Up to this point we have referred to variables rather generally. Often there is confusion and debate about the terms used to describe or designate the variables in a research study. We hope to alleviate some of this confusion by using specific terms throughout this book to describe the various types or classes of variables found in research designs. Specifically, the terms *independent variable* and *dependent variable* have been used in both experimental and descriptive research to define different types of variables.

In classical or "true" experiments, the researcher attempts to examine causality by systematically varying or altering one variable or set of variables and examining the resultant changes in or consequences for another variable or set of variables. In this classical or "true" experiment, the variable that is varied or altered is called the independent variable. More specifically, the independent variable is the variable that is manipulated or controlled in a study. Usually in an experiment there are two or more levels of the independent variable (for example, high and low), sometimes referred to as conditions. For example, in a study that compares cognitive versus interpersonal treatments for depression, the type of treatment (cognitive vs. interpersonal) would be the independent variable.

To examine the effects of the manipulation of the independent variable, concomitant changes in another variable, the dependent variable, are observed. In an experimental study, changes in the dependent variable are supposed to depend on or be influenced by changes or variations in the independent variable. In the previous example, the comparison is made by measuring some dependent variable. One possible example of a dependent variable would be the depression scores on a standardized test (for example, the MMPI-D scale). In classical or "true" experiments we infer that a change (if one exists) in the dependent variable was caused by the manipulation of the independent variable. Thus, the terms *independent variable* and *dependent variable* have causal implications.

Unfortunately, the terms *independent variable* and *dependent variable* are sometimes used to describe the variables in nonexperimental studies. For instance, the predictor variables in a regression equation are sometimes referred to as independent variables and the criterion variable is sometimes referred to as a dependent variable. This can be confusing because of the notions of causality implied in the terms *independent variable* and *dependent variable*. To alleviate this type of confusion, we will primarily utilize the terms *independent variable* and *dependent variable* to describe variables in experimental studies, although some exceptions will have to be made. Independent and dependent variables are discussed further in Chapters 9 and 10.

COLLECTING AND ANALYZING DATA

Once the constructs referenced in the research question or hypothesis have been operationally defined and the design of the study determined, the researcher collects data. The actual process of data collection depends, of course, on the design of the experiment.

The design of the study must be determined—and that is the primary focus of the remaining chapters of this book. The final step of collecting and analyzing data, which is most appropriately discussed in various statistical books, will be briefly addressed in several statistical issues presented throughout the book.

Once the data are collected, sense must be made of this data. Data usually consist of numbers that index characteristics of the subjects. The data are summarized and analyzed with the express purpose of testing the research question or hypothesis. Specifically, the data are examined to determine whether or not the hypothesized relationship was indeed present.

When you are imbedded in the intricacies of data collection and analysis, it is often difficult to remember that the goal is to answer a question or test a hypothesis. Inevitably, decisions need to be made during the course of a study. At these times, always think about how various alternative methods will affect your ability to shed light on the original problem. Will a course of action obscure or clarify the original research question?

SUMMARY AND CONCLUSIONS

The purpose of this chapter was to provide an overview of selecting a research topic and developing the research idea into a testable investigation. A number of activities are involved in narrowing a general topic to a series of specific, testable research hypotheses, such as developing research questions or hypotheses, identifying specific variables, and operationalizing variables. Typically, researchers intersperse thinking and planning across all of these activities as they proceed in reading relevant research literature and developing a particular topic. The outcome should be a specific, well-defined, clearly articulated research hypothesis.

We want to emphasize that it is normal, and even expected, for inexperienced researchers to make false starts and to modify aspects of their research project as they hone the final research question and hypothesis. Sometimes students get the impression that once they have had courses in research methods, statistics, and counseling theory, they ought to produce research questions that have all the bugs worked out. They fear that if they do not perform flawlessly, their competence as a researcher will not only be questioned but it will be clear that they do not have the right stuff to complete the program or have a research career. Regardless of how many courses a student has taken, there is no reason why a graduate student should be an expert researcher. Rather, it may be useful for students to regard their initial research attempts as training projects.

It is also important to note, especially for beginning researchers, that all research studies have limitations of one kind or another (such as lack of experimental control, concerns regarding generalizability). Gelso (1979) referred to this phenomenon as the Bubble Hypothesis and suggested that all research studies have some type of flaw or weakness. Sometimes inexperienced researchers create problems for themselves by trying to develop the perfect study or dissertation. In truth, these entities do not exist. Thus, it is essential for the inexperienced researcher to keep in mind the necessity of developing a study that provides the profession with another piece of information, not the definitive study. Most often our knowledge bases in counseling are increased by adding one or two more pieces of information per study, with each study building on the previous research in some relatively small way. Over time, these small pieces accumulate and our knowledge about a particular topic is substantially increased.

CHAPTER 3

CHOOSING RESEARCH DESIGNS

In the past, researchers have examined questions like: Does counseling/therapy work? What is the best type of counseling? Which clients benefit the most from therapy? The common thread among these three questions, and many like them, is their assumption of what Kiesler (1966) labels a uniformity myth. Simply stated, we have oversimplified counseling to assume that psychotherapeutic treatments are a standard (uniform) set of techniques, applied in a consistent (uniform) manner, by a standard (uniform) therapist, to a homogeneous (uniform) group of clients. Kiesler believed that these myths have greatly hampered progress in psychotherapy research; subsequently, he advocated research that addresses the question of what the best types of treatments are for particular types of clients across different settings.

No doubt, the uniformity myth has hampered and still does hamper research within counseling. We believe that counseling researchers often operate under an equally pervasive, often subtle, and definitely hindering uniformity myth about research design. This myth is embodied in the question What is the best research design? Many times, students and, unfortunately, experienced researchers believe that there is one right or best type of research design. We believe that just like there is not one best therapy, there is also not one best type of research design. In this chapter, we will maintain that the more helpful question is What is the best research design for this particular problem at this point in time?

Kiesler (1966) suggested that client characteristics should determine the choice of therapeutic interventions. But what characteristics should then determine the choice of an experimental design? This chapter will address the question of choosing a research design to examine a particular research question. First, we will define research design and discuss its role in the scientific method. In this section we introduce three major concepts: experimental control, generalizability, and the idea of drawing inferences. Next, we expand this notion of inferences into a more detailed discussion of four major types of validity in terms of which we can evaluate specific research studies. Most important, we delineate a broad range of threats to each of the four types of validity. The third topic is a classification of the types of research designs in relationship to various types of validity. In particular, internal and external validity will be used to describe four types of research designs. Finally, we refocus on the topic of choosing a research design by integrating and extending the previous discussion. A common theme throughout all of these sections is the balance between experimental control and generalizability of the research.

WHAT IS A RESEARCH DESIGN?

In the first chapter we identified the roles of science as extending the profession's knowledge bases and theoretical understandings. Moreover, we maintained that the best way to establish credible knowledge bases (ways of knowing) was through a systematic and controlled method of inquiry, known as the scientific method. In this chapter we will focus more on what we mean by *systematic* and *controlled*.

The basic task of the experimenter is to design research in such a way as to identify relationships between constructs and simultaneously rule out as many plausible rival hypotheses or explanations as possible. Basically, research designs help the researcher to examine specific research questions in a valid, systematic, and objective manner by reducing as many rival hypotheses or explanations as possible and yet isolating the variables of interest to the research question. Perhaps an analogy might help. Ever since human beings began harvesting grains, there has been a need to separate the grain itself (the wheat) from its protective shield (the chaff). The chaff is a dry, coarse material that is not edible. In a way, the chaff gets in the way of digesting the wheat. In a similar way, the researcher wants to isolate the constructs of interest to his or her research question (the wheat) and remove as much as possible the other constructs (the chaff) that might contaminate, confound, bias, or distort the constructs of interest. Although the analogy with separating the wheat from the chaff is an oversimplification, it does highlight the essential feature of the scientific method, which is *isolating the constructs of interest and trying to draw conclusions about the relationships among those constructs.* Any particular experiment never removes all of the possible explanations; it is always a matter of degree as well as the type of explanations left untested. This is actually a very critical point to understand about research design; we will elaborate on this point throughout the chapter.

How does the researcher separate the "wheat" from the "chaff"? The basic tool of the researcher is what we call research design. Research design involves developing a plan or structure for an investigation, and a way of conducting or executing the study that reduces bias and distortion. Thus, research design helps us to provide answers to our research question while minimizing bias. Sometimes the latter is referred to as error, error variance, or noise.

A central issue in research design is experimental control. The experimenter uses the research design to exercise as much experimental control as possible to insure an accurate investigation of his or her research question.

Kerlinger (1986) described this process as the "MAXMINCON" principle. He observed that the researcher first of all tries to *max*imize the variance of the variable or variables pertaining to his or her research questions. Second, the researcher tries to *min*imize the error variance or random variables, particularly due to errors of measurement or individual differences of subjects. Third, the experimenter tries to *con*trol the variance of extraneous or unwanted variables that might affect or bias the variables in the research question. Whereas the "MAXMINCON" principle applies most directly to traditional experimental research (between-group or within-group designs), the essence of Kerlinger's principle applies to all research designs: control the experiment so as to obtain the most accurate investigation of one's research question. In essence, experimental control increases the certainty of the conclusions or inferences that one can draw from an investigation. *Thus, a research design is a set of plans and procedures that reduce error and simultaneously help the researcher obtain empirical evidence (data) about isolated variables of interest.* From the evidence, or data, the researcher then draws inferences about the constructs in his or her research question. We say "inferences" because the researcher can never rule out all of the rival hypotheses.

It is important to note that in an applied field such as counseling, experimental control is often difficult and sometimes unethical. For example, it is often difficult to minimize error variance due to individual differences across clients. Or there may be ethical dilemmas associated with particular treatment interventions or experimental manipulations. In short, within an applied context that involves the lives of real people who are struggling and needing psychological assistance, experimental control often presents obstacles for the researcher. Moreover, the more steps a researcher takes to maximize control, the more simplified (or even artificial) the research context can become.

Counseling is first and foremost an applied specialty. It is therefore important to ascertain that the phenomenon one wishes to examine has some relevance to counseling. Whereas we have maintained that experimental control is a central ingredient of research design, a second key issue is generalizability of the results to applied settings. Our research knowledge must be grounded in and responsive to our application of counseling. Herein lies a major research design issue for the counseling researcher: the balance and trade-offs between experimental control and generalizability. We will elaborate on this control-generalizability issue throughout the chapter. To examine this issue we will first discuss the types of inferences important to counseling researchers, which greatly affect the validity of research conclusions.

FOUR TYPES OF VALIDITY AND THE THREATS TO THEM

Chapter 2 presented an overview of the research process. Based on theory, clinical practice, or observation, the researcher states a research hypothesis or a set of research hypotheses. Recall that a research hypothesis is a conjecture about the relationship between or among constructs. The next step is to operationalize the constructs so that they can be measured. In a true experimental design, the independent variable is manipulated by the researcher to assess the effect of the manipulation on a dependent variable. Statistical methods are often (although certainly not always) used to help the researcher decide whether or not the manipulation had the intended effect.

As an illustration, consider the following example. Suppose that a researcher theorizes that cognitive treatments of social anxiety have found limited success because the interventions do not generalize to behavioral situations. The researcher hypothesizes that in vivo behavioral exercises added to cognitive therapy will improve the efficacy of the therapy. In vivo behavioral exercises are operationalized carefully by designing homework that involves a progressive set of situations in which clients first smile at a stranger, later engage strangers in a short conversation, and finally arrange a social encounter. Social anxiety is operationalized by having the subjects report on the (fictitious) ABC Anxiety Test the anxiety that they experienced after talking with a stranger that the researcher arranged for them to meet (called a confederate). The independent variable is manipulated by randomly assigning the subjects to one of two conditions: cognitive therapy alone or cognitive therapy plus behavioral exercises. Further suppose that 40 subjects are randomly chosen from people who (1) answered an advertisement for a program to treat social anxiety, and (2) were assessed in a clinical interview to be socially anxious by the researcher. After the ten-week program, anxiety is assessed using the confederate and the ABC Test; a statistical test indicates that there is a reliable difference between the groups in the expected direction. That is, the mean level of anxiety, as indicated on the ABC Test, is lower for the group that received the exercises, and this difference has a low probability of occurring by chance.

Pleased with these results, the researcher concludes that (1) a true relation exists between the independent variable and the dependent variable (that is, subjects who receive exercises in addition to cognitive therapy have lower scores on the ABC Test than subjects who receive just cognitive therapy), (2) the manipulation of the independent variable was indeed the cause of the difference in scores (that is, the exercises were the cause of the lower anxiety scores), (3) behavioral exercises increase the effectiveness of the cognitive treatment of social anxiety, and (4) the results are applicable to socially anxious subjects generally (and not just to the subjects in this particular study). The conclusions, or more specifically inferences, made by the researcher in this case seem reasonable; however, there are always flaws in any research and it is appropriate to keep in mind that one of these inferences may be incorrect.

The degree to which inferences reflect the actual state of affairs is referred to as validity. If in vivo exercises really do reduce anxiety, then the inferences made by the researcher in our example are valid. The purpose of this section is to discuss the principles of validity so that researchers and consumers of counseling research can evaluate the probable validity of the inferences made in a particular study. Although there are many ways to look at the validity of research, the framework presented by Cook and Campbell (1979) is a generally accepted and particularly useful model. Cook and Campbell have created a taxonomy that classifies validity into four types: statistical conclusion validity, internal validity, construct validity of putative causes and effects, and external validity. This typology was derived from Campbell and Stanley's (1963) original conception of internal and external validity. Other discussions of validity are presented by Bracht and Glass (1968) and by Wampold, Davis, and Good (1990).

In this section we present an overview of the four types of validity identified by Cook and Campbell, and examine threats to each of these types of validity. Many of the subsequent chapters in this book focus on these types of validity in more detail.

Overview of Four Types of Validity

We will approach Cook and Campbell's four categories by examining the four major inferences made by the researcher in the anxiety example. The first question was whether or not there was a relationship between the in vivo exercises used in this study and scores on the ABC Test. In our example, there was a statistically significant relationship between the independent variable and the dependent variable. One of the major inferences made in interpreting research is whether or not there is a relationship between (or among) the variables in the study. The researcher may conclude that there is a relationship or that there is no relationship. *Statistical conclusion validity* refers to the degree to which the researcher has come to the correct conclusion about this relationship.

The second major inference to be made in interpreting research is in answer to the following: Given that there is a relationship between the variables, is it a causal relationship? In our anxiety example, the researcher concluded that the statistically significant differences between the anxiety levels for the two groups was due to (or caused by) the addition of the exercises. *Internal validity* refers to the degree to which such statements can be made about whether there is a causal relationship between variables.

The third major type of inference relates to the cause and effect of the constructs that are represented by the measured variables, and is referred to generally as *construct validity of putative causes and effects.* Construct validity concerns how well the variables chosen to represent a hypothetical construct actually capture the essence of the hypothetical construct. One of the major issues with construct validity is confounding, or the possibility that what one researcher interprets as a causal relationship between constructs A and B, another researcher might interpret as a causal relationship between A and C, or D and B. In our example, it was presumed that the ABC Anxiety Test used in a contrived situation with a confederate was a suitable measure of the social anxiety of the subject and that the particular exercises used in this study were truly in vivo exercises appropriate for social interactions. If the operationalizations of the constructs of this study were adequate, then the causality attributed to the independent and dependent variables justifies statements about the causality of the constructs used in the research hypotheses. Thus, construct validity of putative causes and effects refers to the degree to which the measured variables used in the study represent the hypothesized constructs. In our example, in vivo exercises (in conjunction with cognitive therapy) were the putative cause and anxiety was the putative effect.

To be of any value to researchers and practitioners, the causal relationship between the hypothesized constructs must be generalizable to persons other than those in the particular study. Thus, in our fictitious example, to what extent can we generalize the use of in vivo behavioral exercises to other socially anxious people? *External validity* refers to the degree to which the causal relationship is generalizable across persons, settings, and times.

The question arises of how these types of validity can be assessed. This is a difficult process since one can never be totally certain of what is true, but the basic procedure is to establish estimates of validity by ruling out as many threats to validity, sometimes called sources of invalidity or rival explanations, as possible. For each of the four types of validity, we will discuss here several threats or sources of invalidity. Each threat represents a possible explanation that would invalidate the inference made in the study.

Researchers strive to conduct research that rules out as many threats to validity as possible. It is crucial to understand that no study will adequately eliminate all threats to validity. Moreover, different research designs place different emphases on the importance of these four types of inference (validity). Ideally, a researcher should be able to choose a design that will let him or her be fairly certain about all four types of inference. Unfortunately, these types of inferences are not independent. Designs that increase the certainty of causal inferences (internal validity) and statistical conclusion validity often do so at the expense of decreasing the certainty of inferences from samples to populations (external validity) or the meaning of the operations (construct validity). Likewise, designs that increase the certainty of inferences from samples to populations or about constructs do so at the expense of decreasing the certainty of inferences about the extent of relationships or causality. The point is that there are trade-offs with different types of research designs, not only with regard to these four types of inferences, but other factors as well.

A study that has reasonable levels of validity will be useful scientifically because the conclusions reached can be tentatively accepted. Additional studies should be designed that will rule out threats that were plausible in the original study. Through the accumulation of studies, threats to a research hypothesis can be ruled out and a strong conclusion can be reached. For example, no single study of smoking and health has unequivocally established a causal relationship between smoking and disease; however, the accumulation of many studies (and there have been thousands) rules out, with almost absolute certainty, any threats to this conclusion. (The Tobacco Institute's statement that no *one* study has ever established scientifically an unequivocal causal relationship between smoking and health is true, as far as it goes.)

We will now discuss specific threats to the four major types of validity. Cook and Campbell (1979) indicate, and we concur, that the boundaries between threats are not rigid. Rather than debate whether one aspect of a study represents one threat or another, we think it is more important for you to come to understand the major concepts so that you can make a reasonable assessment of the validity of studies you review or design.

Threats to Statistical Conclusion Validity

In this section, we will define statistical conclusion validity and delineate seven threats to this type of validity. First, however, we need to examine the role of statistics in counseling research. Although most students will study statistics independently from design, it is necessary to realize that statistical analysis is just one of many parts of the research process. Typically, a statistical test is used to examine whether there is indeed a relation between the variables in a study. In the anxiety example, most likely a two-independent-group *t* test would be conducted.

Traditional statistical tests are employed to test two competing hypotheses: the null hypothesis and the alternative hypothesis. The null hypothesis predicts that there is not a true relationship between the variables in the study. The alternative hypothesis is that there is some true relationship between the variables (and hopefully the relationship that the authors have predicted!). In the anxiety example, the null hypothesis would be that the mean scores on the ABC Anxiety Test for those who received in vivo exercises would be equal to the mean scores for those who did not receive the exercises; that is, the manipulation of the independent variable (in vivo exercises) does not generally affect (or is not related to) anxiety scores. The alternative hypothesis would be that the mean anxiety scores for those who received the in vivo exercises would be lower than for those who did not receive this treatment. Rejection of the null hypothesis and acceptance of the alternative hypothesis lends credence to the hypothesis that in vivo experiences add to the efficacy of cognitive therapy.

Now for a crucial point. Statistical hypotheses are stated in terms of what is true in a population. When we speak of a true relationship between variables, we mean that generally the relationship exists across all persons in a population, although certainly there will be variability among persons. The behavioral exercises might be generally helpful, even though perhaps slightly less helpful for some persons than for others or maybe even a hindrance for a few. Thus, when we conduct a study on a sample drawn from a population, it may be possible that the results of the analysis for the sample are not indicative of the true relationship between the variables. For our example, it is possible that the subjects selected to be in the study were unusual in some way and the results obtained are not indicative of the true relationship.

Statistical tests are used to indicate whether one should reject the null hypothesis of no relationship and accept the alternative that there is a relationship. A statistically significant *t* test in the anxiety example (say at $p < .05$) would indicate that one could comfortably believe that a true relationship exists between the independent and dependent variables. However, it is possible that this conclusion is in error. That is, the null hypothesis of no relationship may be true, while a statistically significant result was obtained due to sampling error. The significance level of .05 indicates, however, that the chances of incorrectly concluding that a true relationship exists is less than 5 in 100. Incorrectly concluding that a true relationship exists is called a Type I error. Type I errors are pernicious because claims are made that something is going on when it is not; for example, a Type I error in the anxiety study would perpetuate the belief that in vivo exercises were helpful when they were not.

Another type of error can be made: one can incorrectly conclude that there is no relationship. Suppose that the *t* test in the anxiety example was not statistically significant; in this case, the researcher could not conclude that the independent variable was related to the dependent variable. Nevertheless, there might have been a true relationship between these two variables but for a variety of reasons the researcher did not find it. This type of error is called a Type II error. One of the major reasons for Type II errors is that variability in the subjects' responses tends to obscure true relationships. This variability, often called error variance, can be thought of as static on a radio receiver that obscures the true signal. Even if the true signal is strong, an electrical storm can generate sufficient static that one cannot hear a favorite program. Conditions that create error variance lead to threats to statistical conclusion validity (more on this later).

It is important to realize that one is never totally certain that a statistically significant result indicates that a true relationship exists. Similarly, a nonsignificant result does not absolutely indicate that no relationship exists. Nevertheless, various factors or threats can decrease the confidence with which we conclude that either there is or there is not a true relationship between variables. These threats are discussed next. Although some of these topics are more appropriately discussed in statistics or measurement courses, discussion of them here will, we hope, facilitate an understanding of statistical conclusion validity.

Low Statistical Power

Power refers to the probability of correctly deciding that there is a true relationship, if indeed a true relationship exists. Clearly, if there is a true relationship, we want to design a study that is able to detect this relationship. Studies with low power often result in the conclusion that no relationship exists when in fact a true relationship exists. Insufficient power most often results from using too few subjects. For example, in a study with less than ten subjects, the probability of obtaining a statistically significant result (that is, concluding that there is a relationship) will likely be very small even when the relationship between the variables is strong. Power will be discussed in more detail in Chapter 11; here we need only note that inadequate statistical power is a threat to statistical conclusion validity.

Violated Assumptions of Statistical Tests

All statistical tests rely on various assumptions (for example, traditional parametric tests typically rely on the assumption that scores are normally distributed). When the assumptions are violated, the researcher and consumer may be misled about the probabilities of making Type I and Type II errors. For example, if the p level of a statistical test is set at .05 and the test is statistically significant (that is, $p < .05$), one commonly believes that the chance of incorrectly concluding that there is a true relationship is less than 5 in 100. However, if the assumptions of the test are violated, this probability may be much higher. Thus the statistical conclusion validity is reduced because there is more chance for making Type I and II errors. The pernicious aspect of violated assumptions is that it is difficult to determine whether or not there are violations, and the degree to which the violation affects the results. We advise you to be aware of the importance of assumptions when using statistical tests; the details of violated assumptions are left to statistics texts and courses.

Fishing and Error-Rate Problems

As previously discussed, when the researcher employs any one statistical analysis there is a chance of incorrectly concluding that a relationship does exist. The probability of making this error is given by the significance level for the test (for example, $p < .05$ or 5 chances in 100). However, the probability of this error escalates dramatically when more than one test is conducted. For example, if ten statistical tests are conducted, the probability of making at least one Type I error (incorrectly concluding that a relationship exists) is at least .40 (see Hays, 1988, for a discussion and calculations of experiment-wise error rates). The point is this: when a researcher conducts many statistical tests, some are likely to be statistically significant by chance and thus lead to false interpretations, sources of statistical conclusion invalidity. Sometimes researchers engage in "fishing," which is simply conducting many statistical tests on a data set without specific hypotheses. This procedure capitalizes on chance events. Matching the statistical test to the research hypothesis is preferable (Wampold, Davis, & Good, 1990).

Unreliability of Measures

Unreliable measures introduce error variance and obscure the true state of affairs, and thus cannot be expected to be related to other measures. For example, think of a scale that yields a dramatically different weight each time you get on it (that is, the readings are random). It is unlikely that scores obtained from this scale will be related to any other scores (such as caloric intake) in a systematic manner. Thus, the unreliability of measures provides another threat to statistical conclusion validity. Reliability is discussed further in Chapter 10.

Unreliability of Treatment Implementation

Although a researcher might have carefully developed a particular treatment intervention, it is still possible for treatments to be delivered or implemented in a variety of ways. For example, the in vivo homework exercises in our fictitious study may have been assigned in a variety of ways. One of the group therapists may have given the exercises to the clients in written form at the end of the session with no explanations, while another therapist may have explained them and their rationale in detail. These variations tend to lead to uncontrolled variability that obscures the true relationship between the independent and dependent variables. Thus, unreliability of treatment implementation is another threat to statistical conclusion validity. Standardization of treatments is desirable and is discussed in more detail in Chapter 9.

Random Irrelevancies in the Experimental Setting

Any aspect of the experimental setting that leads to variability in responding will increase the error variance and obscure a true relationship. In the fictitious anxiety study, the situations in which the exercises were practiced were not controlled. Some subjects may have completed their exercises in a singles bar, others at work, and still others in the grocery store. The differences in these situations would likely have led to variability in responding, which again increases the error variance and threatens statistical conclusion validity.

Random Heterogeneity of Respondents

Differences in subjects can often lead to variability in responding. For example, in our anxiety study, personally attractive subjects may have had more success in the exercises than less attractive subjects. Thus differences in attractiveness would have led to variability in responding, adding to the error variance (and again obscuring any true relationship). From this point of view, homogeneous samples (for example, all subjects being equally attractive) are preferable to heterogeneous samples (subjects having varied levels of attractiveness). However, the results from homogeneous samples can be appropriately generalized only to populations with similar characteristics (see Chapter 11). Statistical procedures, such as the analysis of covariance, can be used to remove variance due to some nuisance factor, such as personal attractiveness in heterogeneous populations (see Porter & Raudenbush, 1987; Wampold & Drew, 1990). The essential point is that random heterogeneity of respondents increases variability of responses, and is a threat to statistical conclusion validity.

Threats to Internal Validity

Internal validity refers to the confidence that one can place in inferring a causal relationship among variables while simultaneously eliminating rival hypotheses. Internal validity is concerned with the most basic aspect of research, the relationships among the variables of interest (typically the independent and dependent variables). Thus, internal validity in an experimental study focuses on whether or not the manipulation of the independent variable was responsible for the differences found in the dependent variable. In our example, was it the in vivo behavioral exercises that caused the lower anxiety scores in the treatment group, or is there another explanation for the results? Since one can never know the true state of affairs, internal validity is assessed by the extent that alternative explanations for the results can be ruled out. The more alternative explanations that can be ruled out, the higher the internal validity. As will become evident, internal validity is directly related to experimental control, such as through the random selection of subjects, random assignment to groups or treatments, manipulation of the independent variable, and determination of measurement times.

Our discussion of internal validity will begin by examining three very basic research designs. We will then discuss in considerable detail 13 specific threats to internal validity.

To illustrate internal validity, consider the three designs diagrammed in Figure 3-1. We will discuss each of these designs briefly and then in more detail as each of the threats to internal validity is discussed. In Figure 3-1, the "O" stands for an observation (or collection of data vis-à-vis the dependent variable), the "X" for a treatment (or some manipulation of an independent variable), and "R" for random assignment. The subscripts on the observations (for example, O_1) are used to differentiate the order of different observations.

The first design, which is called a one-shot pretest/posttest design (Campbell & Stanley, 1963), involves observing a sample of subjects (O_1), administering some treatment (X), and then observing the subjects afterward (O_2). Consider a study designed to test the efficacy of a psychoeducational intervention to teach second graders about sexual abuse. Suppose that the pretest is a 30-item knowledge test related to sexual abuse (for example, "What should you do if a stranger asks to touch you under your bathing suit?"). The psychoeducational intervention consists of puppet shows, plays, discussions,

Design 1: One-shot pretest/posttest design O_1 X O_2

Design 2: Non-equivalent group posttest-only design   X O_1

O_2

Design 3: Randomized posttest-only design   R   X O_1

O_2

FIGURE 3-1
Three possible research designs, where O = observation, X = treatment, and R = random assignment.

and workbooks, which last throughout the school year. At the end of the school year, the knowledge test is readministered. It would be expected that the post-test scores would be higher than the pretest scores (that is, $O_2 > O_1$). Suppose that this relationship is observed: generally the subjects score higher after the psychoeducational program than before. The question is this: Was the psycho-educational program the cause of the increase in scores on the knowledge test? (Take a few minutes and think of alternative explanations for this increase.) There are actually many alternative explanations. Perhaps over the course of the school year the subjects learned about sexual abuse from their parents, friends, or televi-sion. Or perhaps they scored better at the second administration of the test because they had taken the test before and were more comfortable with the format of the questions. Or their reading had improved during the year and they scored better because they understood the questions better. Clearly, there are a number of problems with attributing causality in this example.

One of the problems with the first design is that the performance of the subjects who receive the treatment is not compared to the performance of subjects who do not receive the treatment. In Design 2 (Figure 3-1), there are two groups of subjects; one group receives the treatment and one does not. After the treatment, observations are made. Let's say the psychoeducational program is implemented in Chris Jones's class whereas it is not in Sammy Wong's class. If the psychoeducational program increased knowledge, then we would expect the scores in Jones's class to be higher than those in Wong's class (that is, $O_1 > O_2$). Again, assume that this is the case; was the psycho-educational program the cause of this difference? Possibly, but again there are strong possibilities of alternative explanations for the difference. The most problematic is that it is possible that Jones's class already knew more about sexual abuse before the intervention began. The students may have been placed in Jones's class because it was the accelerated track or the students may have been placed in Wong's class because they had behavioral/emotional problems. Basically, the problem here is that there is no way of knowing or inferring that the students in the classrooms were comparable before the intervention. (There are other problems as well—for example, Jones may have discussed sexual abuse with his students.)

The best way to make groups comparable is to randomly assign subjects to the groups. Although random assignment will be discussed in more detail in later chapters, the principle is that each subject has the same likelihood of being assigned to one group as to the other group. Or, said another way, subjects are not assigned in a systematic way that may bias the composition of the groups. (Keep in mind that random assignment most likely will result in some small initial differences between groups. This is sampling error and is accounted for in statistical tests.) Design 3 (Figure 3-1) involves two groups containing subjects who were randomly assigned. For example, students are randomly assigned to a treatment group (they receive the psychoeducational program) or to a group that does not receive treatment (called a no-treatment control group; in our example study, suppose that they have a study period during the time the other group receives the psychoeducational program).

Suppose that the expected pattern of scores is obtained ($O_1 > O_2$). Now it is more difficult to find alternative explanations to the conclusion that the psychoeducational program was responsible for the higher scores. However, there are still some alternative explanations. Perhaps a student in the treatment group had been abused and this led to a very emotional discussion during the treatment; it may well have been this event and the discussion rather than the content of the psychoeducational program that caused the higher scores for the treatment group.

The anxiety study described at the start of this section is an example of Design 3, which is called a randomized posttest-only design. In this context, one group receives cognitive therapy plus the in vivo behavioral exercises whereas the other receives only the cognitive therapy. In this way, statistically significant differences can be causally attributed to the addition of the exercises (although there are still some threats to this attribution).

We will now discuss 13 threats to internal validity (also see Cook & Campbell, 1979). Keep in mind that each of these threats is basically an alternative explanation for causal attributions.

History

History refers to an event that transpires during the time when the treatment is administered that may affect the observations. Thus, history refers to any events in the subjects' school, work, or home life (for instance, a television program, a newspaper article, a term paper, the death of a family member). In our example, history is a threat in Design 1 because a television special on sexual abuse may have been aired during the time that the intervention was being administered. There is no way to determine whether or not the television special or the psychoeducational program resulted in the increase in knowledge.

The primary way to control history is to use two groups (as in Designs 2 and 3 in Figure 3-1) so that the event affects both groups equally (or nearly equally). In our example, the subjects in the treatment and control groups would have equal access to the television special, equalizing this threat. (Actually, in Design 2 students in one class may stay up later, possibly due to increased homework or some other reason unique to one group, making late night specials more accessible.) Still, try as the researcher might, it is possible that an event would occur that would affect only one of the groups. The threat that occurs from an event that affects only one of the groups is called local history. The sexual abuse of a student in the treatment group is an example of local history.

Threats due to history can be reduced in a number of other ways. First, observations on the groups should be made at the same time. For example, in Design 3, O_1 and O_2 should occur at the same time. Delaying observations for one group leaves open the possibility that some important event may occur after one group is tested and before the other is tested, creating a threat due to local history. Second, the shorter the treatment, the less opportunity there is that an event will occur. Third, the subjects can be isolated during the treatment, thereby reducing the likelihood that an extraneous event will affect them. This is similar to sequestering a jury; however, this is extremely difficult to accomplish with human subjects in naturalistic settings.

Maturation

Maturation refers to normal developmental changes in subjects between the pretest and posttest that might affect the results. Obviously, studies of physical and mental abilities will be affected by maturation. Design 1 (Figure 3-1) is an example of a study that is particularly vulnerable to the threat of maturation, especially if the time span between O_1 and O_2 is long. For example, if the treatment in a study is a one-year program to increase the physical strength of third graders, gains in strength (that is, $O_2 > O_1$) could be due to maturation rather than to treatment.

Design 3 controls for maturation provided O_1 and O_2 take place at the same time. Because the subjects in this study were randomly assigned to groups (and therefore were comparable before the study began), it would be expected that subjects in each group would mature at the same rate.

Testing

Testing refers to changes in scores on a test due to taking the test more than once. Subjects' scores often improve due to familiarization with the test, recall of items and previous responses, and so forth. For example, subjects might be asked to perform anagram tasks both before and after a problem-solving intervention. However, the practice on the first anagram task might account for improved performance on the posttest, apart from the effect due to treatment. Testing is a threat in Design 1 because improvement in scores from the pretest to posttest could be due to taking the test a second time. Effects of testing should always be considered when pretests are given. Testing is not a threat in Designs 2 and 3 because the subjects are tested only once in these designs.

Instrumentation

Instrumentation refers to changes in the measuring device or procedure over the course of a study. One might think that a test is a test, so its properties cannot change from, say, pretest to posttest. Realize that scores are often obtained from assessments not involving tests; for example, observations, interviews, electronic and/or mechanical devices, and so forth. Observations by "objective" coders are known to change or "drift" systematically during the course of a study (Kazdin, 1982). Often raters may change or refine definitions as a result of increased experience with the rating process, and thus change their rating behavior over time. Electronic devices are subject to changes in weather. Even paper-and-pencil tests are subject to the threat of instrumentation. Scoring of the tests may differ systematically from pretest to posttest, especially if the tests are subjectively scored.

Statistical Regression

Statistical regression refers to changes in scores due to the fact that generally subjects who score low on the pretest will score higher on the posttest and subjects who score high on the pretest will score lower on the posttest. (For this reason, statistical regression often is referred to as regression toward the mean.) An example is the batting champion of professional baseball. Obviously, he obtained this title because he is a good hitter. Still, his batting average for a given year is due in part to serendipity as well: perhaps there was a warm spell in his home city in the spring, the player next in the lineup had a good year (and so the opposing team couldn't pitch around the champion), he was injury-free, he had more than his share of luck as several balls just eluded the outstretched hands of defensive players, his personal life was stable, and so on. It is unlikely that all these factors will be favorable the next year, and so it is logical to predict that although he will have a good year, he will not be the batting champion again. (Indeed, batting champions rarely repeat.)

Similarly, someone who scores low initially likely will score higher the next time around. Take the example of a state bar examination. The examinee who obtains the lowest score during an administration is obviously deficient in his or her knowledge. However, because the examination does not perfectly measure knowledge of the law, this score is also due to other factors: the examinee may have been late to the examination (and therefore more anxious), may have misunderstood some questions, may have missed all questions on which he or she guessed, and so forth. On reexamination, all of these factors are unlikely to be in operation and he or she will do better, although still below average. (Interestingly, the examinee might attribute the gain to better study habits!)

Statistical regression is a problem especially when an experimenter chooses subjects for research based on their extreme standing on some variables (such as high levels of depression). If subjects are selected based on their extremely low scores, then, as a group, they can be expected to score higher on the post-test, *regardless of whether or not they have received any treatment*. Again, consider Design 1 in Figure 3-1. Suppose that subjects were selected for a study because they fell above a certain cutoff score on a paper-and-pencil test of depression (higher scores indicate greater depression). Upon subsequent testing (that is, at posttest), these subjects generally will score lower (less depressed) than they did previously. Therefore, a statistically significant difference from pretest to post-test (that is, $O_1 > O_2$) may be due entirely to statistical regression.

Design 3 in Figure 3-1 controls for regression because the subjects are randomly assigned (that is, comparable with regard to the extremeness of their scores) and thus the regression toward the mean for both groups will be about the same.

Selection

Selection refers to differences between groups that exist prior to implementation of the treatment. Selection is often a threat when subjects are initially chosen for a study based on some group membership; that is, subjects are assigned to a particular treatment or control group because they are part of an existing group. Design 2 is a design that is subject to the threat of selection. Recall that in our example, the students in Jones's class may be very different from the students in Wong's class, and therefore observed differences (for example, $O_2 > O_1$) could well be due to these initial differences rather than to the treatment. In the absence of random assignment of subjects to groups, selection is always a potentially serious threat to the internal validity of a study.

Attrition (or Mortality)

Attrition or mortality refers to the effect of subjects dropping out of a study. (Cook & Campbell, 1979, use the term *mortality;* we prefer *attrition* because it is free of epidemiological connotations.) Attrition can be a particularly pernicious threat because it can affect all designs and because its severity is difficult to assess. When subjects drop out of a study, the scores that remain at posttest may not be representative. For example, consider Design 1 with subjects who are depressed. If the most depressed subjects drop out, then the observations at posttest will tend to display less depression because the most extreme scores are no longer considered. Therefore, the fact that $O_1 > O_2$ could very well be due to the fact that the scores that remain at posttest are unrepresentative. (In this instance, the pretest scores for those who drop out would not be analyzed either, but it illustrates the problems of attrition that follow.)

When more than one group is involved and the attrition across the groups is not comparable, *differential attrition* is said to exist. Design 3, which has been immune to most of the threats to internal validity so far discussed, is subject to differential attrition. We will consider a few applications of Design 3 to indicate how differential attrition may work. First, consider the psychoeducational example where the subjects were randomly assigned to a treatment group or a control group. It may be that five of the subjects in the treatment group moved from the district whereas none of the control subjects dropped out of the study. If the five subjects were representative of the other subjects, then dropping these five would have no effect on the outcome (other than to reduce power and possibly make the tests more sensitive to violations of assumptions).

Now consider Design 3 for our fictitious anxiety study. Recall that one group received cognitive therapy plus in vivo exercises whereas the second group received only cognitive therapy. Because the exercises are anxiety-provoking in their own right, it may well be that the most anxious subjects will drop out of the cognitive therapy plus exercises group rather than complete the exercises (a not uncommon avoidance reaction). Because the subjects who drop out of the first group are the most anxious, this will tend to decrease the anxiety scores in this group (that is, decrease O_1) and could be responsible for a significant difference between the groups (that is, $O_1 < O_2$), in favor of the treatment group (cognitive therapy plus exercises).

The third application of Design 3 will demonstrate how differential attrition can act against determining that a treatment is effective. Consider a treatment for depression that is effective and provides an immediate palliative effect.

Again suppose that the subjects are randomly assigned to the treatment condition and to a waiting-list control group (the subjects in this group will receive the treatment after the study ends, if it is found to be effective). Because depression is a particularly distressing disorder, the most depressed subjects in the control group might be most inclined to drop out of the study and seek treatment elsewhere. Let's say this does occur. The control group scores will reflect a drop in depression because the lowest scores have been removed. If this drop due to differential attrition is about the same as the effect of the treatment, then the posttest scores will be about equal (that is, $O_1 = O_2$), even though the treatment was effective!

In short, attrition can serve as a threat to internal validity. To some extent, the effects of differential attrition often can be assessed by administering a pretest. This topic will be discussed in Chapter 5.

Interactions with Selection

Many of the threats to internal validity so far discussed can work in concert with selection to affect the results of a study. Consider the psychoeducational example in Design 2. Suppose that even though the subjects were not randomly assigned to Jones's and Wong's classes, they were roughly equivalent on all relevant characteristics (intelligence, previous knowledge, motivation, socioeconomic status, and so forth). Suppose as well that a local television station ran a series on the late-night news about sexual abuse. It would appear that selection is not a threat because of the comparability of the groups and that history is not a threat because the television series aired during the period when both groups of subjects could watch it (assuming that O_1 and O_2 occurred at the same time). However, selection and history could interact because it may be that Wong assigned a great deal of homework, children stayed up late to complete the homework, and therefore they were awake at the time when this series aired. In this example, the scores in the control group could be improved by the interaction of selection and history, obviating treatment effects. It could also work in the opposite direction: if for some reason Jones's students were the students who stayed up late and watched the series, then it would be difficult to know whether an observed effect for the treatment group was due to the psychoeducational treatment or to the television series.

When designing or reading research, keep in mind that selection can exacerbate problems with the other threats. While we illustrated a selection-history interaction, it is important to remember that all of the aforementioned threats can interact with selection.

Ambiguity about the Direction of the Causal Influence

In the examples given in this chapter, the independent variable is manipulated to determine its effect on the dependent variable. Although there are threats to the internal validity of the studies, if these threats can be ruled out, it would appear that the manipulation of the independent variable caused the concomitant change in the dependent variable, rather than vice versa. However, the direction is not as clear in designs where the independent variable is not manipulated. Consider studies in counseling that examine the role of counselor empathy and therapeutic gains in clients; several studies have found a positive relation between these two variables (Mitchell, Bozarth, & Kraft, 1977). Does the empathy of the counselor cause client progress or does client progress cause the counselor to be more empathic? Unless the temporal order is known, the directionality of causality in correlational or passive designs is difficult to determine.

Diffusion or Imitation of Treatments

Occasionally, the treatment delivered to one group unknowingly is allowed to spread to other groups. This is particularly true when the treatment is primarily informational and of much interest. Suppose a study is being conducted on sexual abuse. Because of the relevance of this topic, students in the treatment group may discuss it with students in the control group, thereby effectively delivering the treatment to both groups. Diffusion of treatments makes it difficult to find differences among or between groups even when the treatment is effective.

Compensatory Equalization of Treatments

There is a natural reluctance by most counselors to withhold programs from subjects in control groups. When personnel directly or indirectly involved in a study provide some type of service to subjects in a control group to compensate for their assignment to a group that does not receive treatment, compensatory equalization of treatments is said to exist and might be a threat to internal validity. In counseling, subjects in the control group will often seek services elsewhere (clergy, other counseling services, and so forth). In school settings, administrators, feeling bad for the control group, may provide extraordinary experiences, such as field trips, movies, and so forth. These experiences may well affect the scores for these subjects, especially if the dependent variable is nonspecific (for example, self-concept).

Compensatory Rivalry by Subjects Receiving Less-Desirable Treatments

Compensatory rivalry refers to efforts by the subjects in the control group to outperform the subjects in the treatment group to prove that they are "just as good, if not better." This threat occurs most often when the performance of subjects will be publicized and there are consequences of not performing well. To illustrate this threat, suppose that counselors in a mental health center are randomly assigned to a treatment group and a control group. The treatment consists of refresher courses on assessment, diagnosis, and service delivery. Because the counselors find such courses remedial and demeaning, they are determined to demonstrate that they do not need the courses. Therefore, the subjects in the control group work extra hard to demonstrate that they are competent in these areas.

Resentful Demoralization of Subjects Receiving Less-Desirable Treatments

Resentful demoralization is, in some ways, the opposite of compensatory rivalry. Rather than working extra hard to perform, subjects in the less-desirable treatment (or a control group) will often become demoralized, which tends to decrease performance. For example, subjects in a study of depression, although informed that they might be assigned to a control group, might feel more depressed than usual when actually assigned to the control group. Their sense of having little control over the reinforcers in their world is reiterated. The demoralization of the subjects in the control group adds to the level of depression of these subjects and therefore differences between scores on the posttest (that is, $O_1 < O_2$) may be due to the demoralization of the control subjects rather than the effectiveness of the treatment.

Threats to Construct Validity of Putative Causes and Effects

Construct validity refers to how well the independent and dependent variables represent the constructs they were intended to measure. When there is ambiguity about the constructs, a confound is said to exist. More technically, a confound is an alternate construct that cannot be logically or statistically differentiated from a hypothesized construct. Suppose that a researcher hypothesizes that male clients with personal problems prefer female counselors. Male clients are randomly assigned to one of two groups. One group reads a description of a counselor who has a female name and views a photograph of a female counselor; the other group reads the same description, but with a male name and a male photograph. Each subject, after receiving the materials, indicates his willingness to see the counselor for a personal problem. Suppose that the results indicate that the clients prefer, as predicted, the female counselor (and further suppose that the statistical conclusion validity and the internal validity are adequate). A logical conclusion is that male clients prefer female counselors for personal problems. However, there is an alternative explanation: it may well be that the female in the photograph is more physically attractive than the male counselor. Therefore, the willingness to see the female counselor may be due to personal attractiveness rather than to gender. In this example, the two constructs (physical attractiveness and gender) have been confounded.

Construct validity is relevant to both the independent variable and the dependent variable. With regard to the independent variable, the groups should vary along the dimension of interest but should not systematically vary on some other dimension. If the independent variable is meant to operationalize gender (as in our previous example), the groups should differ on this dimension (which was the case), but should not differ on any other dimensions (such as physical attractiveness). Likewise, the dependent variable or variables should measure what they are intended to measure and should not measure irrelevant factors. Issues related to independent and dependent variables are discussed in more detail in Chapters 9 and 10, respectively.

Cook and Campbell (1979) identified ten threats to construct validity. We briefly review these threats, following their nomenclature. Keep in mind that these threats are discussed in more detail in later chapters. These threats were seen to cluster into two main groups: construct underrepresentation and surplus construct irrelevancies. Construct underrepresentation involves operations that fail to incorporate all of the important aspects of the construct. On the other hand, surplus construct irrelevancies involve operations that include irrelevant or capricious aspects as part of the construct. An analogy may help to explicate the differences between the two types of threats to construct validity. If we use a fishing net with holes that are too big, some of the fish that we want to catch will get away (construct underrepresentation). If we use a net with holes that are too small, we will catch a lot of smaller fish that we do not want (surplus construct irrelevancies). In many ways, the search for construct validity is like trying to find a net with the right size holes to use to catch our target fish.

Inadequate Preoperational Explication of Constructs

To make a construct operational, one must first have a careful rational analysis of the important or essential components that make up a construct. A threat to construct validity from inadequate preoperational explication of constructs occurs when this careful rational analysis has not taken place. To adequately operationalize a construct, it should be defined clearly. When a construct is referenced by a name but not discussed in detail, it is often difficult to ascertain exactly what is intended. *Spouse abuse* may refer to physical acts with the intent to harm, any physical acts, physical and verbal attacks, and so forth. Decisions about the nature of a construct should not be arbitrary; proper definitions are needed so that the research hypotheses follow from theories and so that they can be properly operationalized.

Mono-Operation Bias

Mono-operation refers to single exemplars of the levels of the independent variable or single measures of the dependent variable. Mono-operations are problematic because frequently the essence of a construct cannot be captured by a single exemplar or a single measure. Most likely, mono-operations underrepresent the construct and contain irrelevancies.

Mono-operations of the independent variable result when only one exemplar of each treatment is used. For example, in the gender study mentioned earlier, all of the subjects in the female-counselor group read the same description and name of the counselor as well as viewed the same photograph. That is, a single exemplar of a female counselor was used; similarly, a single exemplar of a male counselor was used. Clearly, this operationalization of gender is narrow and the results are restricted to this particular operationalization, thereby creating a threat to the larger construct of gender. It would have been preferable to have several descriptions, male and female names, and photographs. Including variations of exemplars raises the issue of whether the variations have an effect on the dependent variable; if this is of concern, the experiment can be designed to test the effect of the variations (see Chapter 5).

With regard to the dependent variable, a single measure often will not reflect the construct adequately. The ABC Anxiety Test may reflect social anxiety to some extent, but will fail to do so perfectly. By adding other measures of social anxiety, the construct is operationalized more completely. The technical bases for the use of multiple dependent measures to operationalize a construct are found in statistics and measurement; these bases are discussed conceptually in Chapter 10. The essential point to note at this time is that mono-operation bias presents a threat to construct validity, typically by underrepresenting a construct.

Mono-Method Bias

As mentioned previously, multiple measures are important to capture the essence of a construct. However, if all the dependent measures use the same method, there may well be a bias introduced by the method. For example, self-report measures often share a common bias by the respondents. If a subject responds in a socially desirable way to all self-report instruments, then consistent bias is introduced by this method. If two constructs are measured in the same way (for instance, self-report), the correlation between variables may be due to method variance rather than a true correlation between constructs. Another example of mono-method bias pertains to the measurement of depression. Rather than using only self-report measures, a more valid method of operationalizing the construct of depression would be to use a client self-report measure coupled with a therapist and observer measure of depression.

Mono-method bias can also apply to independent variables. Presenting written descriptions, names, and photographs (even multiple exemplars of each) operationalizes gender using one method. The question remains: Would the results be similar if gender were operationalized using a different method (such as videotapes of the counselor)? In short, mono-method bias introduces threats to construct validity.

Hypothesis Guessing within Experimental Conditions

Hypothesis guessing occurs when the experimental subjects try to figure out what the researcher wants (that is, his or her hypothesis) and then attempt to either comply or rebel against these presumed expectations. One of the most problematic things about hypothesis guessing is that it is very difficult to determine when it occurs, how often it occurs, and the direction and magnitude of its effect. For example, in the gender study, if the subjects guess that the hypothesis is actually related to their willingness to see the counselor of a specific gender, then they may respond in a certain way to please the researcher, to show that they are open-minded, nonsexist, and so forth. Ethical principles dictate that the purpose of research be explained to subjects prior to their consent to participate; however, frequently it is desirable to make the specific research hypothesis difficult to guess (see Chapter 4 for a discussion of these ethical issues). In short, hypothesis guessing can obscure or diminish true treatment effects and is thus a threat to construct validity.

Evaluation Apprehension

Subjects often are apprehensive about being evaluated, especially by experts, and will respond in ways that make them appear better adjusted or more healthy than is actually the case. (This is related to mono-method bias because self-report measures most easily reflect the effects of evaluation apprehension.) When apprehension about being evaluated affects the responses of subjects, the dependent measure is confounded with this bias, and thus it is a threat to construct validity.

Experimenter Expectancies

Although experimenters are portrayed as objective scientists, there is evidence that this is not the case. They are often eager to find particular results and this bias is often communicated to subjects in subtle (and sometimes not-so-subtle) ways. For example, if the experimenter is also the counselor in a treatment study, he or she may be overly eager to help the clients to show the effectiveness of his or her valued treatment. Thus, when this happens, it is unclear whether the causal element is the treatment or the expectations, which again threatens the construct validity of the study. Experimenter expectancies are discussed in detail in Chapter 12.

Confounding Constructs and Levels of Constructs

Frequently constructs that are continuous are operationalized with discrete exemplars. For example, the experience level of the counselor is often an independent variable in treatment studies. Experience is a continuous variable with a wide range. If the experience levels are chosen at the low end of the continuum (for example, a study with novice counselors, those with one practicum course, and those with a master's degree) or at the high end of the continuum (doctoral-level counselors with 10, 15, and 20 years of experience), then it might be concluded that experience does not affect counseling outcomes. A very different result might be obtained with experience levels that span the continuum. When restricted levels of the construct are chosen, the construct is confounded with levels of the construct.

Interaction of Different Treatments

When subjects receive more than one treatment, it is difficult to determine whether an effect is due to a single treatment or to the latest treatment in the context of the previous treatments. Suppose that it was found that the psychoeducational program for sexual abuse was not effective; afterward a computer-assisted instruction program was tested with the same subjects and found to be effective. Would the computer-assisted instruction program have been effective had it not followed the psychoeducational program? In the present example, this question is unanswerable. Thus, the interaction of different treatments provides a confound and is a threat to construct validity of the treatment. This problem is inherent in within-subjects designs (see Chapter 5).

Interaction of Testing and Treatment

Occasionally the pretest can sensitize subjects to the treatment so that their performance on the posttest is due in part to the effects of the treatment in conjunction with the pretest. That is, the treatment would not have been effective (or as effective) had the pretest not been given. Ways to control this threat are discussed in Chapter 5.

Restricted Generalizability across Constructs

Any treatment can have an effect on multiple constructs. For example, a treatment may have a positive effect on some outcome variables, a negative effect on others, and no effect on still other possible outcome variables. Restricted generalizability across constructs occurs when an overly narrow range of outcome variables is examined. Establishing the relationship between two constructs restricts conclusions to those variables. Often other important constructs are not investigated and the research can be criticized because these other constructs might be the most interesting piece of the psychological puzzle. There have been numerous investigations of minority group preference for types of counselors (Atkinson, 1983); however, missing from most of this research are constructs related to counseling outcomes. Does the fact that an Asian-American client prefers a directive counselor imply that a directive counselor would produce the most desirable outcome in this context? Thus, restriction of the constructs used in a study is a threat to the construct validity of a study.

Threats to External Validity

External validity refers to the generalizability of the results of a study. To what group of persons, settings, and times do the results of the study apply? Traditionally, external validity has been approached by examining samples from populations. First, a population is defined; second, a random sample is drawn from that population. Based on the results of the research with the sample, conclusions are made about the population. Unfortunately, true or even approximate random sampling is possible only infrequently. Consider the study with socially anxious subjects. It is impossible to randomly sample from the population of all socially anxious subjects in the United States. The concepts of sampling and the inferences that can be drawn in the absence of random sampling are discussed in Chapter 11.

Cook and Campbell (1979) broadened the concept of external validity to include generalization *to* the population and generalization *across* populations. Random sampling from a well-defined population refers to the generalizability *to* the population; however, since true random sampling is infrequently conducted, generalization to the population is difficult. Of greater practical importance is the generalizability of results *across* different populations. Consider the social anxiety example and suppose that the study finds that cognitive therapy plus exercises is significantly more effective than cognitive therapy alone in reducing social anxiety (assume that the statistical conclusion validity, internal validity, and construct validity are adequate to draw valid inferences). Across which populations are these results generalizable? Do they apply equally to all socially anxious subjects? Males and females? Adolescents and adults? Various minority groups? As well, do the results apply to subjects in various settings (social gatherings, public places, with people of different ages than the subjects, and so forth)?

Generalizability across populations is of particular interest to counseling researchers. Paul (1967) admonished researchers to determine which treatments work with which types of clients in which settings. The intricacies of testing for generalizability across persons, settings, and times are discussed in detail in Chapter 11. As indicated there, generalizability across populations is determined by examining possible interactions between the treatment and various population characteristics. For example, if a statistical interaction occurs between a treatment variable and gender, then the treatment is not equally effective with males and females.

Generalization across various kinds of persons, settings, and times is tested by examining statistical interactions between the treatment (or the independent variable) and persons, settings, or times. We will briefly discuss three threats to external validity that serve to limit the generalizability of research results.

Interaction of Selection and Treatment

Interaction of selection and treatment refers to generalizability across persons (that is, how the persons are selected). Person variables relevant to counseling research include gender, racial or ethnic background, experience level, degree of dysfunction, intelligence, cognitive style, personality, level of acculturation, and sex role orientation, among others. Clearly, there are many choices for populations to be studied; in Chapter 11, some considerations in choosing populations are discussed. In short, the external validity of a study is strengthened when the research examines the relationship between the independent and dependent variables across different categories of persons.

Interaction of Setting and Treatment

Interaction of setting and treatment refers to generalizability across settings. How generalizable are results obtained in a university counseling center to a community mental health setting, hospital setting, or private practice? There are obvious differences between these settings and there is little reason to believe that results necessarily generalize across these settings. Much research is conducted at counseling centers, we conjecture, because the staff are motivated, interested, and proactive; however, there are factors that may differentiate this setting from others. Thus, the external validity of a study is strengthened when the relationship between the independent and dependent variables is examined across different settings.

Interaction of History and Treatment

Interaction of history and treatment refers to generalizability across times. Counseling approaches valued in the 1960s may no longer be valued in the 1980s and 1990s. Epidemiological studies of anxiety in Cuba during the Cuban Missile Crisis may not apply to anxiety levels during *glasnost* in the Soviet Union. To be of much use, results of research should be applicable to the future, but obviously one cannot sample from future populations. Generalizability across times is often achieved through replications across time or by analyzing prior research across time periods (for an example of the latter, see Heppner & Neal, 1983). In short, establishing external validity across time periods is more difficult and often requires retrospective analyses or replications after the passage of time.

Assessing Validity

Our discussion of validity provides a framework for assessing the types of inferences made in research and the subsequent validity of a study. The fact that many threats were presented indicates that many things can weaken or strengthen any particular study. Keep in mind that no research can be designed that is not subject to threats to validity to some degree. The objective is to design and conduct research in such a way as to minimize the threats and maintain the possibility of obtaining interpretable findings. In this respect, programmatic research is needed because studies can build on each other and a threat to one study can be ruled out in a future study.

The question is raised: How does one assess the severity of a threat? In some instances, statistical tests can be used to determine whether or not a threat is problematic. For example, if pretests are administered, differences between subjects who drop out of a study can be compared statistically to those remaining subjects. Or external validity can be assessed by examining the statistical interaction between the independent variable and some person, setting, or time variable.

A second way to assess validity is to logically examine the chances that a threat is or is not likely to occur. In some instances, it is very unlikely that a particular threat is problematic even though there will be no direct evidence. For example, although maturation may be a threat in some designs, if the treatment lasts only one hour, it is very unlikely that subjects will mature much during that time. Or if the pretest is a commonly used test and the treatment is lengthy, interaction of testing and treatment probably will have little impact on the results. Diffusion of treatments will be impossible if subjects are strangers and do not have the opportunity to meet.

It is also possible to reduce threats to validity by building in some aspects of the study to control for the threat. Consider the example of the gender study in which photographs of counselors of different genders were presented to the subjects. Recall that personal attractiveness was a potential confound in that study. To control for the confound, the researchers could have judges rate the personal attractiveness of various photographs and then match them so that the personal attractiveness of the photographs was constant across the groups.

A CLASSIFICATION OF RESEARCH DESIGNS BASED ON VALIDITY

Now that we have delineated in detail the concept of validity, we can use this concept, particularly internal and external validity, to delineate the different types of research designs. Historically, several broad categorizations of different research designs have been described. Campbell and Stanley (1963) discussed design in terms of preexperimental designs, experimental designs, and quasi-experimental designs. Kazdin (1980) referred to experimental designs, quasi-experimental designs, and correlational designs. It is important to note that the different types of research designs may present particular strengths or weaknesses with regard to internal and external validity. In short, we are talking about different trade-offs.

Gelso (1979) used the concepts of external and internal validity to create a typology of research designs that we find helpful. Basically, Gelso proposed that we can organize counseling research along two dimensions; he argued that research can be either high or low in control (internal validity) and carried out in a field or a laboratory setting (external validity). Gelso acknowledged that these categories were inevitably simplifications, but nonetheless useful in understanding the strengths and limitations of types of research designs. Studies that are high in control typically use random selection of subjects, random assignment of treatments, and manipulation of an independent variable or variables. These studies usually permit the researcher to make inferences about causality. Studies that are low in control lack either or both random assignment to treatments (quasi-experimental studies) or manipulation of an independent variable (descriptive studies and ex post facto designs). In low-control studies, researchers can make inferences about relationships but not about causality.

The second dimension reflects the setting in which the research is conducted. Field studies use subjects from the population of interest in a naturally occurring form. This may involve real clients seeing experienced therapists or students who are truly undecided about a major or career choice. Laboratory studies use subjects who resemble the subjects from the population of interest;

these subjects may be recruited clients in the case of counseling process research or students with low scores on a career maturity scale to study career choice antecedents.

We believe that the internal and external dimensions are not independent of each other. A study that exerts a high amount of experimental control will most likely depart from a naturalist setting, and a study that examines variables in a highly naturalistic setting can only have limited experimental control. In general, the field study will have less internal validity than the laboratory study. Likewise, the laboratory study will typically not have the level of external validity of the field study.

Figure 3-2 is a representation of the different types of research using Gelso's (1979) two (high, low) internal validity by two (high, low) external validity matrix. We have made changes in two aspects of Gelso's classification system to reflect a broader set of operations. Specifically, we have modified the shape of the matrix, and changed some of his labels. The most significant change involves the changed shape of the matrix. In our figure, the box that represents high internal and high external validity is smaller than the other three boxes. This change represents the nonindependence of the internal and external validity dimensions. Since internal and external validity are not independent, it is difficult to have an experimental field study with internal validity as high as that of an experimental laboratory study, or with external validity as high as that of a descriptive field study. A second change involves using the label *descriptive* rather than Gelso's label *correlational* to describe studies low in internal validity. This change was made because the term *correlational* seemed to unnecessarily limit our thinking about the nature of studies low in internal validity. The *descriptive* label was chosen because it does not imply limiting the use of these designs to one statistical operation (correlation).

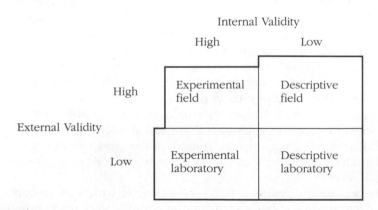

FIGURE 3-2
Types of research designs classified by levels of external and internal validity.

Descriptive Laboratory Studies

Descriptive laboratory studies have low external and internal validity. These studies are characterized by investigations that do not exercise experimental controls (such as randomization or manipulation of independent variables) and that are conducted in a laboratory setting of some kind. A descriptive laboratory study is low in external validity because it uses a setting that in some ways simulates a real-life setting. For instance, undergraduate students recruited to be clients and beginning counselor trainees can be used to study some aspect of the counseling process. This "counseling" may or may not be like that which takes place between real clients and experienced counselors. In other words, there would certainly be questions about the extent of generalizability of findings from this type of study.

A descriptive laboratory study is low in internal validity because there is a lack of experimental control in the sense of manipulation of an independent variable or randomization of subjects. Rather, the descriptive laboratory study involves describing in detail some aspect of counseling, by identifying, labeling, or categorizing data, as well as obtaining basic descriptive statistics such as means, standard deviations, and correlations among variables. Returning to the counseling example, a researcher may want to determine the likelihood of client self-exploration given certain counselor responses. Rather than manipulating counselor responses, the researcher may want to study their natural occurrence. In this way, the study is descriptive, not experimental.

You may wonder why, if internal and external validity are so important, a researcher would conduct a study that is low along both dimensions. There are two main reasons for conducting these types of studies. First, a laboratory setting allows the researcher some control over extraneous variables, even though the experimenter chooses not to manipulate some variables. Data can be more easily collected, the researcher does not have to worry as much about experimental variables adversely affecting the therapeutic assistance a client receives, and the researcher can expect and encourage more involvement from the subjects. A second reason for employing descriptive laboratory studies is that it is impossible to study some phenomena in a field or real-life setting. The data collection procedures may be so extensive and/or intensive that the very presence of these procedures alters the process under examination to the point where it is no longer natural or real.

Elliott's (1985) study of helpful and nonhelpful events in counseling interviews is a good example of a descriptive laboratory study. He had counselor trainees conduct an interview with a recruited client. After the interview, the client reviewed the tape and rated each counselor statement on a nine-point helpfulness scale. Most and least helpful counselor statements from each counseling dyad were then given to judges who sorted the statements into categories. Cluster analysis was then used to put the statements into categories. In this manner, Elliott was able to develop a taxonomy of helpful and nonhelpful events in early counseling interviews.

This study is low in internal validity because no manipulation of counselor statements occurred. Rather, statements were classified as helpful or nonhelpful on the basis of an a posteriori (after the fact) rating of helpfulness. The study is low in external validity because counselor trainees and recruited clients served as the subjects, and because the video-recall procedure probably altered aspects of the counseling. This study does, however, provide important information about the counseling process that certainly advances our understanding of an important concept, perceived helpfulness to clients of counselor statements.

For the researcher considering a descriptive laboratory study, Chapter 13 contains information about the conduct of analogue research, with special emphasis on the issue of generalizability of laboratory studies. In addition, Chapter 8, on descriptive research, contains information on different types of descriptive designs.

Descriptive Field Studies

Descriptive field studies have high external and low internal validity. These studies are characterized by investigations that do not exercise experimental controls (randomization, manipulation of variables) and are conducted in a real-life setting. A descriptive field study is often high in external validity because a sample of subjects can be taken directly from a population of interest. In counseling research, for example, this would mean the study of real clients seeing actual therapists. The descriptive field study is low in internal validity because variables are studied as they occur naturally rather than being manipulated.

For a study to be truly high in external validity, the data-gathering procedures must not have a large enough impact on the subjects to disrupt them from their normal set of actions. The two most common examples of this type of study are retrospective studies that use data that is routinely collected as part of an agency policy, and single-subject studies of individual counseling. A classic study representing descriptive field research is the Menninger project (Wallenstein, 1989). This project was a very large study conducted over a 35-year period that examined the effectiveness of counseling (thus, an outcome study) with patients who received more than 1000 hours of analysis. Client-therapist pairs were selected for this study only after counseling had formally ended. As Wallenstein (1989) states, clients and therapists were totally unaware during treatment of which cases would be analyzed. In addition, the study used only data that was routinely collected during treatment. Because of the lack of experimental control in this study, there are certainly a number of problems regarding internal validity, such as threats from history, selection, and so forth. The real-life nature of this study does make it intriguing because it has high external validity and applicability, even though the findings are only suggestive at best.

A study by Anderson, Hogg, and Magoon (1987) demonstrates some of the advantages and disadvantages of descriptive field studies. These authors were interested in examining the impact of an administrative procedure, time on the waiting list, on client premature termination. Time on the waiting list and premature termination were determined from existing client records. Time on the waiting list was operationally defined as the elapsed time between an intake interview and client assignment to a counselor. Premature termination was operationally defined as counselor-judged nonmutual termination. These data were routinely collected by the counseling center where the study was conducted (at the University of Maryland). This study was high in external validity because real clients in a real agency were studied. In addition, clients and counselors could not react to the data collection procedures because they were unaware that their data was going to be used.

This study was low in internal validity because time on the waiting list was not manipulated. The results suggested that time on the waiting list was not related to premature termination. From a methodological viewpoint, the lack of manipulation of the time variable was not critical in interpreting the results in this study. The lack of a correlation can rule out the possibility of causality, but the presence of a correlation cannot prove causality. If, for instance, Anderson et al. (1987) had found a relationship between time on the waiting list and premature termination, they could not, with the descriptive field study design, say that time on the waiting list caused premature termination. It is possible that more-disturbed clients were assigned to counselors sooner. If a relationship had been found between time on the waiting list and premature termination, it would be impossible to know if this relationship was caused by the wait, difference in client disturbances, or some unknown third variable. Only by randomly assigning clients to specified waiting periods could a researcher conclude that delays in therapeutic assistance caused premature termination. Most agencies, however, probably would not agree to put their disturbed clients in this type of jeopardy, and even if they did, the study would lose external validity because normal administrative procedures would no longer be involved in the study.

For the researcher interested in conducting descriptive field studies, Chapter 7 on single-subject designs and Chapter 14 on process research provide guidance for the conduct of this type of research, with an emphasis on therapeutic counseling. Chapter 8, on descriptive designs, provides an overview of some common descriptive designs, while Chapter 6 covers ex post facto designs.

Experimental Laboratory Studies

Experimental laboratory studies have low external and high internal validity. These studies are characterized by investigations that manipulate independent variables and are conducted in a laboratory setting. An experimental laboratory study is low in external validity because rather than using a sample of subjects directly from a population of interest, the experimenter sets up a situation to resemble one that naturally occurs. This research is often high in internal validity because the experimenter can randomly assign subjects to treatment and manipulate one or more independent variables. Because these studies are high in internal validity, the researcher can and does make inferences about causality. The extent to which these inferences about causality can be generalized to the populations and settings of interest is the critical question raised by the experimental laboratory study.

A number of studies applying social psychological processes to the counseling relationship exemplify the experimental laboratory study. Many of these studies can be traced to Strong's (1968) classic formulation of counseling as a social influence process.

Strong reasoned that since expertness, attractiveness, and trustworthiness seemed to be important source characteristics in the persuasion literature, then perhaps counselors who were perceived as expert, attractive, and trustworthy would have more persuasive power or more influence on clients. One line of research that followed from this formulation was to vary the amount of expertness the counselor displayed and examine the amount of influence he or she had on a subject (for reviews, see Corrigan, Dell, Lewis, & Schmidt, 1980; Heppner & Claiborn, 1989; Heppner & Dixon, 1981). More recently, Strong and his colleagues have examined the influence of paradoxical versus nonparadoxical symptom prescription on client depression (Feldman, Strong, & Danser, 1982). To increase the external validity of this research, Feldman et al. (1982) used recruited clients who met certain criteria for depression. The independent variable (paradoxical vs. nonparadoxical intervention) was controlled by using scripted interviews in which the exact same interventions were given to subjects, depending on which condition they were in. In this study, Feldman et al. found that paradoxical interventions were more helpful in relieving depression. The authors could, because of the experimental controls used, conclude with a high degree of certainty that the paradoxical interventions did cause the decrease in depression symptomology. Because of the recruitment of clients and the scripted nature of the interviews, however, there is certainly doubt about the generalizability of these results to real counseling interviews.

For readers interested in using an experimental laboratory design, Chapter 13 details issues in the conduct of analogue research. Chapter 5 describes between-groups and within-subjects designs. These designs are what many authors refer to as "true" experiments.

Experimental Field Studies

Experimental field studies have moderate external and internal validity. These studies are characterized by investigations that manipulate independent variables and are conducted in a real-life setting. An experimental field study attempts to examine causality by the introduction of random assignment of treatments and control of independent variables. Such experimental control moves the study away from the examination of naturally occurring counseling. At best, the researcher has a study moderately high in external validity. An experimental field study does, however, attempt to examine causality in a naturally occurring setting. Still, the researcher can never exercise the same control in the field as in the laboratory. Hence, the experimental field study can be at best moderately high in internal validity. The experimental field study does allow for the best inferences about cause and generalizability within one study. Typically, though, the experimental field study does not obtain the same level of certainty about causality as is possible in the experimental laboratory study nor the same level of certainty about generalizability as in the descriptive field study.

Hogg and Deffenbacher (1988) offer an example of an experimental field study. These authors were interested in comparing an interpersonal and a cognitive approach in the group treatment of depression. They also included a no-treatment control condition in the design. External validity was emphasized by using clients seeking help at a university counseling center and experienced group therapists. There were, however, threats to external validity because of pretesting and possible reactions to experimental procedures (tape recordings). Internal validity was emphasized by random assignment of clients to interpersonal and cognitive groups and by standardized treatment for the two conditions. Internal validity was threatened by the nonrandom assignment of clients to the control condition (clients who came to treatment late in the semester were used to form the control group). This study is a good example of the sacrifices that researchers must often make in external and internal validity considerations in order to conduct an experimental field study. Researchers wanting to do experimental field studies should read Chapter 5 describing between-groups and within-subjects designs, and Chapter 6 on quasi-experimental designs.

ON CHOOSING A RESEARCH DESIGN

We now return to the question of choosing the best research design. If, as we have argued, there is no a priori best design, then one could conclude that the choice of a design does not matter; all designs are equally good and bad. This, of course, would be true only if research were conducted in a vacuum. It might be that there is not a best design for research within the counseling profession as a whole, *but at any particular time in the history of a topic area there may be more or less useful ways to approach a specific research question.* We propose that the usefulness of a particular research design to examine a specific research question is a function of (1) the existing knowledge bases pertaining to the specific research question, (2) the types of research designs used and inferences made to develop the existing knowledge bases, (3) the resources available to the researcher, (4) the specific threats to the validity of the particular design being considered, and (5) the match or fit between previous research knowledge (factors 1 and 2), the design being considered (factor 4), and one's resources (factor 3). Moreover, we believe that it is essential to be aware of Gelso's (1979) Bubble Hypothesis (the idea that all experiments will be flawed somehow), and thus maintain that both paradigmatic diversity and programmatic research are also basic considerations in selecting a design.

Typically, research on a particular question is conducted within an existing body of knowledge. Thus, it is imperative for the researcher to determine what the previous research suggests about a particular topic area, as well as what kinds of questions remain unanswered. As the particular research question of the researcher is formed, it is important to ask what kind of knowledge will now add to the existing literature. Simultaneously, the researcher must evaluate what type of research design will provide the kind of knowledge that is needed. Perhaps a descriptive study would add the most useful knowledge or basic normative information about a topic. Or perhaps an experimental study that isolates the interactive effects of two independent variables would help explain previous contradictory findings. Thus, the utility of a research design needs to be evaluated in the context of the existing research knowledge in a particular area.

Equally important is the type of research design used and the inferences drawn to develop the existing knowledge bases. The types of research designs used affect the types of inferences made in developing a knowledge base. Thus, if a particular topic has been predominantly researched in laboratory settings, then perhaps research focused on field settings will now add the most useful knowledge in that area. Or if a topic has been investigated through tightly controlled experimental studies, then perhaps descriptive studies might now add some useful information. Any type of design can be overused in a particular area, a condition that can produce an unbalanced and subsequently weak knowledge base. (In Chapter 13 we present a brief overview of the social influence literature in counseling, and we provide details of an example of this problem of overusing one particular design.)

Many times inexperienced researchers do not read the methods sections of research studies. One of this book's authors admits (sheepishly) to committing this sin for much of his early time in graduate school. Instead, students usually read the introduction and the discussion. While this might suffice for obtaining content knowledge in an area, it misses the important aspect of learning about how the studies were conducted. We suggest a simple technique that inexperienced researchers can use in examining a body of literature. Make a copy of Figure 3-2. As you read the method sections of various studies within a topic area, record the study into the appropriate cell. It should quickly become apparent which designs have been used and perhaps overused.

It is also important to note that different designs require different resources and have different costs. For instance, a researcher might decide that a descriptive field study was needed to examine the relationship between counselor techniques and a client's perception of the working alliance. But should she do a correlational study or use an intensive single-subject design? The answer to this question should be obtained, in part, by examining the resources available. To do the correlational study, the researcher would probably need to find 30 to 50 client-counselor dyads. It may take a great deal of work to find these dyads, but the data analyses may be fairly easy and painless. On the other hand, for an intensive single-subject study the researcher may easily be able to find one dyad to participate. However, there will probably be a rather involved, intensive process of analyzing the data from this study. This example illustrates that a researcher must not only examine resources available but also must look at costs in choosing a particular design.

In choosing a research design, it is also of utmost importance to understand and keep in awareness that each experiment has strengths and weaknesses, and moreover that each experiment is typically flawed in some way. Gelso (1979) understood this idea as he offered the Bubble Hypothesis. The Bubble Hypothesis suggests that doing research is similar to trying to place a sticker on a car windshield. When an air bubble forms between the sticker and the windshield, the owner presses the bubble in an attempt to eliminate it. No matter how hard he tries, however, the bubble reappears somewhere else. The only way to get rid of the bubble is to throw the sticker away, but then the owner is left without a sticker. In a similar manner, every piece of research and every research design is flawed (that is, it has a bubble). The different research designs have different limitations and strengths (the different designs may change the location of the bubble). No design can entirely eliminate the bubble. The researcher can either stop doing research (throw the sticker away), or can be cognizant of the size and location of the bubble in the design that he or she chooses.

Using the Bubble Hypothesis, it is easy to see that if only one type of research design is advocated by a discipline, then the "bubble" will always be in the same place on the sticker. If only one type of design is seen as appropriate for counseling research, then all the research will contain the same flaws or blind spots. On the other hand, if multiple research designs are advocated, with different "bubble" locations, the cumulative effect will be a clearer, more accurate picture of the research problem. Viewed in this manner, the usefulness of a particular design at a particular time will be determined by where the "bubbles" are in the studies that have previously addressed this question. This type of reasoning led Gelso (1979) to suggest that all types of research designs are useful and that knowledge can only be advanced when the same problem is examined using multiple design strategies. He thus argued for paradigmatic diversity. In fact, there is a growing consensus within (and outside) the field of counseling that the discipline is strengthened when alternative designs are used (for example, Gelso, 1979; Harmon, 1982; Kazdin, 1978; Polkinghorne, 1984).

The Bubble Hypothesis and the need for paradigmatic diversity underscores the importance of programmatic research on a particular topic. That is, a series of investigations, conducted by the same or different researchers, that successively extend our knowledge bases along a particular line of research on a particular topic is highly desirable for the profession. A series of related investigations that build on each other tends to accumulate more useful knowledge bases that does a series of isolated investigations. Consider the following examples and notice how the researchers used different research methods for different purposes.

Hill and her colleagues (Hill, Helms, Spiegel, & Tichenor, 1988) used a descriptive laboratory study as the first step in developing a client reactions system. Recruited clients seen by counselors-in-training used a preliminary version of the reactions system to record their reactions to interviews. Based on client feedback and item analysis, a revised reactions list was formulated that was then used in a descriptive field setting. Thus, Hill et al. (1988) initially used a descriptive laboratory strategy to develop a measure, followed by a descriptive field design to evaluate the utility of the measure as well as the implications of the findings. In short, once appropriate measures have been found or developed, it is then important to examine how these variables operate in real-life settings.

A study by Marx and Gelso (1987) also illustrates programmatic research. Since little research had been done on the termination of individual counseling, these authors sought to describe the termination process using a descriptive field study. They did this in two ways: first, by content analyzing termination sessions, and second, by examining variables that correlated with client satisfaction with termination. One variable that related to satisfaction with termination was the amount of time spent talking about termination. This finding could serve as a springboard for the next step in a program of research, perhaps through an experimental laboratory study. One might wonder if there is a causal relationship between the amount of time the counselor spends talking about termination and client satisfaction with terminating. Recruited clients and volunteer counselors could be used to examine this question. For instance, dyads could be assigned to a high- or a low-termination-discussion condition. Subsequently, more refined questions could be asked, like how soon (first session, middle session, next-to-last session) the counselor should begin to address termination.

SUMMARY AND CONCLUSIONS

In this chapter we have extended our discussion of science and the scientific method to basic research design considerations. We have maintained that the basic task of the experimenter is to design research in such a way as to identify relationships between constructs and simultaneously eliminate as many rival hypotheses as possible. Kerlinger (1986) has labeled this the "MAXMINCON" principle. Research design involves developing a plan or structure for an investigation, and a way of executing the study that reduces threats to the validity of the research.

We have further maintained that two central issues in research design are experimental control and generalizability. Our discussion of internal and external validity identified specific threats with regard to both control and generalizability. We have maintained that different types of research designs represent different trade-offs between these two central issues. While it can be debated which of these issues is of most importance, or which issue a researcher should attend to first in beginning a line of research (for example, Campbell & Stanley, 1963; Gelso, 1979; Stone, 1984), we believe that in an applied specialty such as counseling, both issues are essential. While internal validity may be the sine qua non (Campbell & Stanley, 1963), the applied nature of our work in counseling cannot be ignored, but must be emphasized. Although we have maintained that internal and external validity are not independent, they also are not incompatible, especially across multiple investigations. Thus, we need programmatic research that is designed to maximize the benefits of both internal and external validity across investigations. Moreover, within such an investigative blend, we also suggest that there is a useful place for laboratory research extension of theoretical issues. As Stone (1984) has argued, "a pre-occupation with immediate application can lead us to dismiss important research" (p. 108) that extends our theoretical understanding. In essence, we are underscoring the need for balance in our research; we suggest that investigative styles that prohibit certain types of research (such as naturalistic research) are dangerous because they reduce the possibility of gaining certain types of knowledge.

We have also suggested that the goodness of a particular design rests not only on the threats to validity it allows, but also on the context provided by previous research and existing knowledge bases. Thus, in addition to evaluating the threats to validity, the researcher needs to consider (1) the existing research content, (2) the type of research designs used, and (3) the resources available to him or her. The researcher must choose a research design with strengths and weaknesses that match the needs of the research question, a design that will provide the type of knowledge needed at this particular time in history. In this way, a series of research studies, each with different strengths and weaknesses, may add the greatest breadth to our knowledge bases. Thus, we strongly encourage programmatic research that also emphasizes paradigmatic diversity to build broad knowledge bases for the counseling profession.

CHAPTER 4

ETHICAL ISSUES
IN COUNSELING RESEARCH

Ethics are not simply proper etiquette, but rather "they are expressions of our values and a guide for achieving them" (Diener & Crandall, 1978, p. 14). Ethical principles help researchers not only achieve their goals, but also avoid strategies that compromise their values, and help them make decisions when their values are in conflict (Diener & Crandall, 1978). We believe that ethics are nothing less than central to the conduct of research. Just as morality is a way of living, ethics is a way of living that permeates the research enterprise. Because of the centrality of ethics in research, this chapter is placed toward the beginning of the book so that ethical reasoning can be integrated into basic design considerations, not as an afterthought but as intrinsic to the research endeavor. To assume that being a counseling researcher only involves technical research design skills is a very incomplete picture. We will maintain that it is essential for researchers to be aware of their ethical responsibilities to the people who participate in the research, co-workers, the profession, and society as a whole.

In this chapter we will focus on the investigator's responsibility in two general categories: ethical issues related to scholarly work and ethical issues related to subjects. In today's complex world, these topics take on a complexity not even imagined several decades ago. It is important to underscore at the outset that ethical issues in research are often not cut-and-dried, and sometimes one ethical principle will conflict with another to create a tangled and muddy dilemma. Our main goals in this chapter are to (1) introduce and sensitize you to the ethical issues involved in counseling research, (2) underscore the complexity of real-life ethical dilemmas, which sometimes do not have clear answers, and (3) discuss common strategies and the reasoning process for designing research with ethical rigor.

The first section of this chapter discusses fundamental ethical principles that form the core of our professional values. Specifically, we will discuss nonmaleficence, beneficence, autonomy, justice, and fidelity. In addition, we will introduce ethical guidelines that have been suggested by the American Psychological Association and the American Association for Counseling and Development. The central ethical principles as well as both sets of ethical guidelines will be used throughout the rest of the chapter. In the second section of the chapter, we discuss ethical issues related to scholarly work, specifically with regard to (1) execution of the research study, (2) reporting the results, (3) publication credit, and (4) plagiarism. In the final section, we discuss ethical issues pertaining to subjects, such as (1) risks and benefits, (2) informed consent, (3) deception and debriefing, (4) confidentiality and privacy, and (5) special considerations for treatment issues.

FUNDAMENTAL ETHICAL PRINCIPLES

To facilitate professionals' decision making with regard to ethics, both the American Psychological Association (APA) and the American Association for Counseling and Development (AACD) have developed a set of ethical principles or guidelines: *Ethical Principles for Psychologists,* referred to hereafter as *EPP* (APA, in press) and *Ethical Standards,* referred to hereafter as *ES* (AACD, 1988). These principles are presented in Appendixes A and B, and will be referred to in the discussion of ethical issues throughout the chapter. Implicit in these professional codes of ethics are more general and fundamental ethical principles. "Because ethical codes may be too broad in some cases and too narrow in others, [the more fundamental] ethical principles both provide a more consistent framework within which cases may be considered and constitute a rationale for the choice of items in the code itself" (Kitchener, 1984, p. 46). In this chapter we will focus on five fundamental ethical principles: nonmaleficence, beneficence, autonomy, justice, and fidelity. In essence, these fundamental ethical principles are central but implied building blocks for the professional codes of AACD and APA. We briefly discuss these general principles in this chapter to clarify the essence of ethical issues as well as to facilitate an understanding of the professional ethical codes. Readers interested in a fuller discussion of such fundamental ethical principles could read the following: Beauchamp and Childress, 1979; Diener and Crandall, 1978; Drane, 1982; Kitchener, 1984; Lindsey, 1984.

Nonmaleficence

Diener and Crandall, in their book *Ethics in Social and Behavioral Research* (1978), succinctly concluded that "the most basic guideline for social scientists is that subjects not be harmed by participating in research" (p. 17). This central principle has been referred to as the principle of nonmaleficence (above all do no harm: Beauchamp & Childress, 1979). This includes not inflicting intentional harm nor risking harming others. Thus, it is the responsibility of the investigator to plan and act thoughtfully and carefully in designing and executing research projects, because harm can occur intentionally or unintentionally. Kitchener (1984) noted that a number of ethicists and psychologists have argued that nonmaleficence should be the most critical ethical principle in applied psychology (Beauchamp & Childress, 1979; Brown, 1982; Frankena, 1963; Rosenbaum, 1982; Ross, 1930). Thus, these professionals have argued that if we must choose between harming someone and perhaps helping another person, the strongest obligation would be to avoid harm. Diener and Crandall (1978) have argued that nonmaleficence can only be superseded if volunteers knowingly participate and the benefits are of great import.

Beneficence

Beauchamp and Childress (1979) concluded that acting ethically not only involves preventing harm, but also contributing to health and welfare of others. Doing good for others is beneficence. This central ethical principle is the essence of the goal of counseling, to help people resolve problems that they have been unable to resolve on their own. Moreover, beneficence constitutes the core of the ethical principles advocated by APA and AACD. In the Preamble to *Ethical Principles for Psychologists* (APA), the first sentence indicates that "psychologists promote the welfare . . . of the individual." Likewise, in the Preamble to *Ethical Standards* (AACD, 1988), the first sentence proclaims that "members are dedicated to the enhancement . . . of each individual and thus to the service of society."

Inherent in beneficence is competence. If our value is to help others, particularly those in need who come to rely on our services, then we have an obligation to help others in as competent a manner as possible. Such reasoning raises a number of implications for service delivery, professional training, and research. With regard to the latter, Lindsey (1984) noted that the beneficence principle mandates the profession to do effective and significant research to maximally promote the welfare of our constituents. Likewise, White and White (1981) argued that it is our responsibility as a profession to provide all the knowledge and skill we can marshall to benefit our clients.

Autonomy

The principle of autonomy centers around the liberty to choose one's own course of action. This includes freedom of action and freedom of choice (Kitchener, 1984). The principle of autonomy is woven into American political institutions, law, and culture. Not surprisingly, Rokeach (1973) found that Americans ranked individual freedom as one of their most esteemed values. In many ways, autonomy is the cornerstone of subjects' rights to voluntarily participate in psychological research, or conversely to decline to participate. Since the Nuremberg trials after World War II, the principle of autonomy has received increased attention in research. At the center of this attention is the notion of informed consent, or informing potential subjects about a particular research project so that they can make informed decisions about participation.

Justice

The principle of justice implies fairness (Benn, 1967). Because the quantity of services and goods in any society is limited, there are conflicts between people. Thus, in the United States, a vast array of laws have developed as part of our judicial system for deciding what is fair. In essence, the principle of justice is based on the assumption that people are equals. Thus, as initially suggested by Aristotle, equals should be treated as equals, and unequals should be treated unequally only in proportion to their relevant differences (Beauchamp & Childress, 1979; Benn, 1967). For example, gender or race are not relevant characteristics for deciding access to mental health services, but this is not to suggest that gender and race might be relevant for consideration for different treatments. The concept of justice also implies just rewards for one's labor, and ownership of the fruits of one's labor.

Fidelity

The principle of fidelity implies faithfulness, keeping promises or agreements, and loyalty (Ramsey, 1970). This principle applies directly to voluntary interpersonal relationships, such as counselor-client, student-teacher, researcher-subject. Not fulfilling a contract (by, for example, engaging in deception, breaching confidentiality) is a violation that infringes upon the other individual's choice to enter into an agreed-upon relationship. Issues of fidelity and trustworthiness are central to the helping professions such as counseling. The principle of fidelity is important for the reputation of the profession as well as for individual professionals in their work as counselors, supervisors, consultants, educators, and researchers.

ETHICAL ISSUES RELATED TO SCHOLARLY WORK

The study of human behavior is constantly evolving and progressing. This evolution and progress reflects a commitment "to increasing knowledge of human behavior" (*EPP,* General Preamble). One of the basic purposes of scientific endeavors in counseling is to increase our knowledge about topics of value to the counseling profession. This broad and vital goal reflects the fundamental ethical principle of beneficence. In a very simple way, the counseling researcher has a responsibility to provide accurate information about counseling-related phenomena for the "promotion of human welfare" (*EPP,* General Preamble) and the "enhancement of the worth, dignity, potential, and uniqueness of each individual and thus to the service of society" (*ES,* Preamble). It can be argued that accurate information promotes the profession's knowledge bases, and inaccurate and misleading information may distort or even falsify the profession's knowledge bases. In short, given the role of science within the profession, there is a very important responsibility for scientists "to under-take their efforts in a totally honest fashion" (Drew, 1980, pp. 58–59). Although any of a number of factors may tax the typical researcher (for instance, publication pressure, boredom), it is imperative that the researcher keep in focus the ultimate aim of the scientist, to extend our knowledge bases with accurate, reliable, and thus usable information. If the researcher loses sight of this essential goal, in our opinion she or he has no business conducting research and may only hinder rather than aid the profession and the people we try to help.

It is important to note that the goal of providing "accurate information" and extending the profession's "knowledge bases" can sometimes be at odds with promoting the welfare of others and society. It can be argued that research that led to the atomic bomb extended existing knowledge bases and was instrumental for the Allied troops in winning World War II. However, strong arguments can be made that this research did not promote the welfare of many people, as it actually resulted in the deaths of thousands of people. Seeman (1969) aptly concluded: "The existence of Hiroshima in man's history demonstrates that knowledge alone is not enough, and that the question 'knowledge for what?' must still be asked. If knowledge in psychology is won at the cost of some essential humanness in one person's relationship to another, perhaps the cost is too high" (p. 1028). Likewise, Jensen (1969, 1985) published research (and there is considerable controversy about whether the data were biased) that has been interpreted as showing that Blacks are intellectually inferior. A strong argument can be made that Jensen's writing did not promote the welfare of Blacks. In short, the essential point is that more information does not necessarily always result in promoting human welfare. At a minimum, expanding our knowledge bases raises multicultural issues and deeper moral issues about right and wrong (K. S. Kitchener, personal communication, January 2, 1990). Thus, it is imperative to note the complexity and sometimes contradictions in these seemingly straightforward goals of extending knowledge bases and promoting human welfare.

At this point, we will discuss the implications of the researcher's responsibility to provide accurate information in four areas: execution of the research study, reporting the results, publication credit, and plagiarism.

Execution of the Research Study

A study must be properly executed to establish valid knowledge bases and protect the fundamental ethical principle of beneficence. The researcher has a responsibility for accurately and reliably planning and conducting the research investigation (*EPP*, II.C.1, V.D.1, V.D.2; *ES*, D.3, D.8). The researcher also has the responsibility of planning the study to evaluate its ethical acceptability, weighing scientific values and rights of participants, and then conducting all aspects of the study in a careful, deliberate manner "that minimizes the possibility that results will be misleading" (*ES*, D.8). Conducting research typically involves a lot of tasks, and many of these tasks are menial and boring.

For example, typical procedural tasks include contacting subjects, arranging experimental conditions, randomly assigning subjects to conditions, locating and assembling assessment instruments, administering instruments, coding data, entering the data into the computer, and analyzing the data. Within these major tasks are a myriad of steps and processes, such as collating questionnaires, checking the accuracy of the coded data with the original data set, and checking for keypunching errors. In short, many, many tasks confront the researcher in a typical research project, and the researcher is responsible for the accuracy and reliability of carrying out all of them.

Problems can occur if the investigator becomes lax during any phase of executing a study. For example, differential subject biases may be created if subjects are solicited in slightly different ways for an experiment because the experimenter is not careful to maintain a standardized recruitment procedure (see Chapter 12 for a detailed discussion of such biases). Or distortion can occur if the researcher does not impress upon the assistant the need for accuracy in matching subjects carefully to all of their questionnaire data. Research assistants can be invaluable resources, but they typically need close supervision. Moreover, sometimes it is difficult for research assistants to maintain high levels of performance with extremely difficult or very boring tasks, and especially when they do not understand the purpose of the task (or study), or the need for exact precision. Drew (1980) noted incidents where research assistants actually recorded fictitious data rather than conscientiously performing the needed task, such as counting specified subject behaviors. Investigators are responsible for the competence of assistants working with them (*EPP,* V.D.2) as well as for the ethical treatment of research assistants themselves. In short, the researcher needs to maintain constant vigilance over all phases of executing a study to ensure the planning and collection of accurate and reliable data.

Reporting the Results

Reporting the results of a study, although seemingly a straightforward task, entails responsibilities and often complexities. The fundamental ethical principles include beneficence and nonmaleficence. The investigator has a responsibility to accurately report and prevent misuse of research results (*EPP,* III.B.2, III.B.3, III.B.4; *ES,* D.7, D.8). This implies that the researcher must honestly report findings and present them in a way that is clear and understandable to readers. The investigator's task is to present the facts of what happened in the study. Sometimes researchers believe that their data will have more value if they confirm their hypotheses or support a well-known researcher's theory. It is probably true that published research consists mostly of statistically significant findings. However, it is imperative to note that the researcher is not responsible for whether the data support or do not support a particular theory. Perhaps the theory is incorrect. As Carl Rogers once said, "The facts are always friendly," implying that one should not feel bad about data not supporting a hypothesis (personal communication to P. P. Heppner & L. A. Lee, January 1983). Thus, the job of the investigator is to honestly report the results, regardless of preconceived predictions, theories, or personal desires.

Investigators have a responsibility to provide a discussion of the limitations of their data, and qualify their conclusions accordingly (*EPP*, III.B.2). Discussion of limitations is especially important where the research can be "construed to the detriment of persons in groups of specific age, disability, ethnicity, gender, national origin, race, religion, sexual orientation, social class, or other vulnerable groups" (*EPP*, III.B.2). Moreover, it is important to explicitly mention "all variables and conditions known to the investigator" that might have affected the results of the study (*ES,* D.7). Sometimes researchers believe that the results will be weakened if limitations are discussed and perhaps even prohibit publication in a professional journal. It is important to remember that the goal of the researcher is to provide the most accurate information possible about the phenomenon of interest. Specifying the limitations is helpful to the profession and often to future researchers as well. In our view, if the limitations are such that they do substantially weaken the probability of publishing the results, then the long-term consequences for the profession are probably best if the results are not published. It is antithetical to the long-term goals of the scientist to publish information that is misleading, or to suppress disconfirming data.

The investigator also has a responsibility, after research results are in the public domain, to make available original data to other qualified researchers who may want to inspect the data or run additional analyses (*EPP*, III.B.5; *ES,* D.9). This necessitates storage of raw data for some time after a study is published. Although no specific amount of time is indicated in *EPP* or *ES,* some investigators routinely store data for three to five years after a study is published.

Perhaps one of the most serious problems is the conscious fabrication of data. It is clearly unethical to produce fraudulent data (*EPP*, III.B.3). There are at least three basic varieties of concocting fraudulent data: (1) inventing findings without any actual data collection, (2) tampering with or doctoring actual findings to more closely resemble the desired outcome, and (3) trimming actual findings to delete unwanted or discrepant information (Keith-Spiegel & Koocher, 1985). Such fabrication obviously provides misinformation to the profession and serves only to add confusion and misunderstanding in place of knowledge. Unfortunately, numerous instances of fraudulent research have been reported in the scientific community in the last decade (see Keith-Spiegel & Koocher, 1985, pp. 363–364) and have even received attention in the general media as well as evoked congressional investigations (Broad & Wade, 1982).

Perhaps the most publicized report of fabricating data involves Sir Cyril Burt, a noted British psychologist whose research on identical twins was read and cited internationally. Posthumously, Burt has been exposed for publishing implausible and fictitious data that supported his own theory of inherited intelligence. Not only did such fabrication present misinformation and mislead the psychological profession for many years, but it is also a major source of embarrassment to the profession. Burt was a well-known scientist who was knighted in 1946 in recognition of the importance of his work (Drew, 1980).

Clearly, the fabricating of data represents a loss of "scientific responsibility" (Keith-Spiegel & Koocher, 1985, p. 364) and does little to promote human welfare. The goals of science have been lost in the pursuit of personal rewards and short-term consequences. Although a quest for personal recognition and fame and the pressure to publish (the academic publish-or-perish dilemma) may distort a researcher's motivations, probably the most significant factor pertains to securing grant funds. The researchers who make startling discoveries often are awarded grant funds; grant renewals are contingent upon continued research performance and breaking new ground. But sometimes in this pursuit is lost the basic aim of science, extending the knowledge bases of a profession. Fabrication of data results in especially negative consequences for the counseling profession because most of our research is not only aimed at enhancing our knowledge bases, but also at enhancing knowledge bases that are used to improve psychological services to people in need. Thus, fabrication of data creates confusion and misleading knowledge, and can also weaken the effectiveness of the counseling profession, which affects the lives of real people. The federal government has promulgated rules that define fabrication, falsification, or plagiarism as *misconduct*. Furthermore, the rules indicate that institutions must have procedures for investigating and sanctioning misconduct of scientists that it employs (see the Department of Health and Human Services, 1989).

Publication Credit

Researchers have a responsibility to accurately and adequately assign credit for contributions to the project (*EPP*, IV.C.1, IV.C.2; *ES*, D.12). The issues involved with publication credit revolve primarily around the fundamental ethical principle of justice. On the one hand, assigning publication credit seems like a straightforward and simple process. Those people who made minor contributions are acknowledged in a footnote, while those making major contributions are given authorship and listed in order of how much they contributed. In reality, these decisions can be complicated and emotional primarily because of ambiguity surrounding the term *contribution*. What constitutes minor and major contributions? Sometimes it is reasoned that the person who contributed the most time to a project deserves to be first author, while others argue that expertise, or even seniority, should determine author order. At other times, it is reasoned that the one who conceived the idea for the study should be the principal or first author. Determining the author order often becomes difficult when the authors were primarily engaged in different activities, such as writing the manuscript, analyzing the results, collecting the data, designing the study, and supervising the implementation of the study. Assigning publication credit becomes complicated as researchers debate whether all of these contributions are equally important, or whether some contributions should be assigned greater weight than others.

Accurately assigning publication credit is important for several reasons. First and foremost, it is important to publicly acknowledge the contributions of all the people involved in the study, to give credit where credit is due (*EPP*, IV.C.2; *ES*, D.12). In addition, publication credit is often important in one's professional career, helping one gain entrance into graduate school, obtain professional employment, and earn professional promotion. Moreover, public acknowledgment of one's professional contributions can serve as a "psychic reward" to compensate for the low monetary rewards associated with writing for scholarly outlets (Keith-Spiegel & Koocher, 1985). Sometimes the order of authorship on a publication is important, as the first author is accorded more credit (and responsibility) for the scholarly work than are the other authors; thus, determining the order of authorship is relevant to career-related issues.

Ethical Principles for Psychologists and *Ethical Standards* are ambiguous in determining most of these issues. For example, *EPP* ambiguously suggests that "minor contributions to publications" be credited in footnotes, but does not define those activities. Typically, minor professional contributions that receive acknowledgment in a footnote include such activities as giving editorial feedback, consulting on design or statistical questions, serving as raters or judges, administering an intervention, providing extensive clerical services, and generating conceptual ideas relevant to the study (for example, directions for future research). Thus, a common introductory footnote (which is usually found at the bottom of the first page of a journal article) reads something like: "The authors would like to thank Josephine Computer for statistical assistance and Helen Grammar and Chris Critical for helpful editorial comments." Usually, these contributors went out of their way to help the authors in minor but significant ways. Thus, it is important to publicly recognize these minor contributions. However, the author should receive permission from contributors before thanking them in a footnote. Another type of footnote is a public acknowledgment of a funding source that sponsored the research (*EPP*, IV, B.2). A footnote might acknowledge, "This research was supported by a grant received by the first author from the National Institute of Mental Health" (complete with reference to the grant number).

How to distinguish between a minor contributor and a major contributor (an author) and how to determine the order of multiple authors are not clearly specified in *EPP* and *ES*. *EPP* does state that "publication credit accurately reflects the relative contributions of the individuals involved, regardless of professional status" (IV.C.2). Spiegel and Keith-Spiegel (1970) surveyed over 700 professionals to empirically examine their opinions about determining authorship. They found modal trends, but not a firm consensus, for the following criteria, in their respective order: (1) generation of hypotheses and design, (2) writing the manuscript, (3) establishing the procedure and collecting the data, and (4) analyzing the data. Contributions tend to be valued according to their scholarly importance as opposed to the amount of time they required. Moreover, respondents in two studies did not rate professional status as a determining variable (Bridgewater, Bornstein, & Walkenbach, 1981; Spiegel & Keith-Spiegel, 1970), which suggests that merit rather than degrees or status is typically a stronger determinant of professional contribution. In short, the list of authors should include those individuals who made a major scholarly contribution to the study in the ways just listed.

The order of authorship (in the case of multiple authorship) should reflect differential amounts of scholarly contributions. That is, the person who made the greatest scholarly contribution should be the principal or first author, with the others listed in order of their relative contributions.

The process of determining authors and order of authorship is very important, and probably as important as the outcome (who the authors are and the respective author order). Because a great deal of ambiguity enters into deciding authorship, authors may have different opinions about author order. The potential for authors to feel slighted or cheated is greater when author order is autocratically decided by one person, such as the first author. Thus, from our experience, a mutual decision-making process is most desirable, and preferably a consensus model where all those involved discuss these issues.

Sometimes the order of authorship is decided at the conclusion of a study (a post hoc strategy) and just prior to submitting a manuscript for editorial review to a journal or a professional convention. The advantage of assigning authorship at this time is that it is possible to assess how much each person actually contributed. The disadvantage is after-the-fact disappointments: a person might have wanted to be or expected to be first author, but was unaware of how the order was to be decided or of other members' contributions. Or a worse scenario: a person might have thought that his contribution was sufficient to qualify him as an author, but then learned after the study that his scholarly contribution was minor and he would be acknowledged only in a footnote. Another strategy (the a priori strategy) is to assign authorship prior to implementing a study. The advantage here is that as a result of the opportunity to discuss and clarify the relevant issues beforehand, informed decisions and agreements can be made by all participants. One disadvantage to this strategy is that a person might contribute either considerably more or less than he or she initially agreed to. Or an inexperienced researcher might want to be first or second author but not clearly understand the implications of such an assignment in terms of the tasks and skills needed.

A third strategy is to combine both the post hoc and a priori strategies, discussing author-related issues before the study is conducted, perhaps developing a tentative author order, and then evaluating the accuracy of that initial order after all the tasks have been completed. This strategy offers the benefits of both of the other strategies and minimizes the disadvantages and disappointments.

A final strategy is to assign the order of authorship by chance (for example, by drawing straws). This strategy is sometimes used when it truly seems that each author contributed equally, and it is literally impossible to differentiate among the contributors. It may also seem that any author order would misrepresent the contributions of both the first or last author. In these situations, authors may use some arbitrary method of assigning the order of authorship.

If this strategy is used, an introductory footnote should acknowledge that the author order was determined by chance. Parenthetically, assigning author order by alphabetizing names is not a random process (ask people with names like Zimmer or Zytowski). If chance is to be used as the method of assignment, then drawing straws, pulling numbers from a hat, drawing cards from a deck, or some other random means of assigning order is more desirable.

One final note. A very complicated issue pertaining to publication credit involves graduate students' theses and dissertations. Often graduate students believe and feel that because they have contributed a great deal of time, effort, and sometimes money, they have contributed the most to this scholarly project. Faculty advisor input might range from providing encouragement and technical assistance to designing the study, developing major interpretative contributions, and writing major parts of the manuscript. However, it is unclear how much of the faculty advisor's contribution is a part of her or his teaching and training role within the university. There is a real potential for exploiting graduate students if the faculty member has them conduct most if not all of the research tasks and then claims publication credit, particularly first authorship. *EPP* indicates that "a student is generally listed as the principal author of any multiple authored article based primarily on the student's thesis or dissertation" (IV.C.2). Keith-Spiegel and Koocher (1985) noted that the number of ethical complaints about this issue has resulted in a policy statement issued by the APA Ethics Committee (1983), which provides detailed guidelines. Whereas the Ethics Committee wrote specifically about dissertations, their guidelines pertain equally well to theses. The guidelines are as follows:

1. Only second authorship is acceptable for the dissertation supervisor.
2. Second authorship may be considered *obligatory* if the supervisor designates the primary variables or makes major interpretative contributions or provides the data base.
3. Second authorship is a courtesy if the supervisor designates the general area of concern or is substantially involved in the development of the design and measurement procedures or substantially contributes to the write-up of the published report.
4. Second authorship is *not* acceptable if the supervisor provides only encouragement, physical facilities, financial support, critiques, or editorial contributions.
5. In all instances, agreements should be reviewed before the writing for publication is undertaken and at the time of submission. If disagreements arise, they should be resolved by a third party using these guidelines.

Winston (1985) has developed a system for analyzing contributions to data-based articles that can facilitate decisions about author order. The system delineates eleven activities common to a research project: (1) conceptualizing and refining research ideas, (2) literature search, (3) developing a research design, (4) instrument selection, (5) instrument construction/questionnaire design, (6) selection of statistical analyses, (7) collection and preparation of data, (8) performing statistical analyses, (9) interpreting statistical analyses, (10) drafting manuscripts (first draft, second draft, and so on), and (11) editing the manuscript. Winston suggested that the people involved in the project, as a group and through consensus, assign points for each task. Because some tasks require more or less skill and time than others, and vary in importance, the assigned points should vary for the different activities; the interested reader might compare his or her assignment of points to those initially specified by Winston. The next step is to, again through group consensus, assign points to each person for each of the eleven activities. Points are then totaled, and the order of authorship is decided based on the point distribution. This system appears promising not only because it provides more specific criteria for determining author order but also because it could facilitate communication and make explicit the decision-making process within the research group.

Plagiarism

Researchers have a responsibility to acknowledge the original contributions of other writers and clearly distinguish their own original scholarly insights from the work of others (*EPP,* IV.C.3; *ES,* D.11). Again, these issues revolve primarily around the fundamental ethical principle of justice. Plagiarism can occur in the direct, verbatim copying of another's work or less explicitly in duplicating ideas from others' work without proper citation. In both cases, the original author does not receive proper acknowledgment or credit for his or her work. Keith-Spiegel and Koocher (1985) nicely depicted this issue:

> Copying the original work of others without proper permission or citation attribution is often experienced as "psychic robbery" by the victims, producing the same kind of rage expressed by those who arrive home to find the TV set and stereo missing. When plagiarizers reap financial rewards or recognition from passing someone else's words off as their own, the insult is still greater. Readers are also misled and, in a sense, defrauded. Plagiarism and unfair use of previously published material are among the more serious ethical infractions a psychologist can commit. (p. 356)

Plagiarism can occur on several levels. A researcher might omit necessary citations through inattention, perhaps by not being as careful or conscientious as might be desired. The plagiarism in such cases is unintentional and more due to inattention. Another level involves the difficulty sometimes encountered in determining what is original in a researcher's ideas. For example, after a researcher has read and written in an area for twenty years, ideas from a variety of sources often blend together in a complex knowledge base. The researcher may one day conceive of what seems like a new insight to him or her, and publish it. However, in reality the "insight" was published two years ago; the researcher simply did not remember the original source. Or, as researchers work together and not only share ideas with each other but also build upon each other's ideas, the ownership of ideas becomes unclear. Or researchers working in slightly different areas may duplicate each other's ideas without being aware of their common work. Thus, in such cases plagiarism may be the result of memory loss or the convoluted nature of developing original ideas. These types of plagiarism are difficult to control; one needs to be as conscientious as possible but acknowledge that there are memory lapses that create less-than-ideal conditions.

Another level of plagiarism involves the conscious or intentional exclusion of another person's writing because of petty jealousies or interpersonal competition. Thus, a writer might intentionally not cite the relevant work of a particular researcher in part because the writer does not want to publicly acknowledge the researcher's work, but also because the writer would like to have sole credit for an idea or contribution. A final level of plagiarism involves the verbatim copying of another's writing or duplicating of ideas, with the motive being to present oneself as the original contributor while knowing full well this is not the case. In these situations, the plagiarist does have control and is able to make some deliberate choices.

Removing all of the complications, acknowledging the contributions of others is basically a matter of fairness and integrity; in essence, giving credit where credit is due. Not citing the original author may seem like a rather small issue, but really it is quite important. Imagine that you have worked very hard for two to three years, creating and building a new conceptual model. Naturally, you are very proud of this accomplishment. Then someone "steals" it and takes credit for it. Being cited is often meaningful to authors and serves as an important psychic reward. In addition to fairness and integrity, there is also an issue of saluting (in a small way) previous researchers for their accomplishments. From a historical perspective, it is important not only to recognize those authors' work that preceded one's own, but also to recognize where one's work fits within the bigger picture. It is a sad comment on the profession when petty jealousies prevent mutual recognition or even collaboration that might result in important contributions. Keep in mind as well that plagiarism is considered misconduct in science by the federal government and that employing institutions are required to investigate all cases of suspected plagiarism and provide sanctions where appropriate.

ETHICAL ISSUES RELATED TO SUBJECTS

A central issue in all psychological and educational research is the dignity and welfare of the people who participate in the study. The goal of the ethical researcher is to develop a fair, clear, and explicit agreement with the subject so that the subject's decision to participate in an experiment is made voluntarily, knowingly, and intelligently (Keith-Spiegel & Koocher, 1985). In this manner, the subject is not coerced and makes an informed decision about the benefits and risks associated with participating in a particular experiment. The most fundamental ethical principles implied in the treatment of subjects involve nonmaleficence, autonomy, and fidelity.

Historically, the dignity and welfare of those participating in research have not always been of foremost concern. Probably the most notorious example of abuse of subjects occurred in the experiments conducted in World War II Nazi prison camps, where many prisoners died from lethal doses of chemical trials and varying levels of physical abuse. Physicians conducted research on such topics as effective ways of treating severe frostbite (which involved subjecting individuals to freezing temperatures) and treatment of infected wounds and deadly diseases such as malaria and typhus (which involved subjecting individuals to infectious germs) (Stricker, 1982). Fortunately, the Nuremberg trials at the end of World War II, which tried 23 physicians for these research atrocities, served as an initial impetus for ethical treatment of research subjects. In fact, the Nuremberg Code has been the basis for later ethical principles regarding human subject participation in research (Keith-Spiegel & Koocher, 1985). Unfortunately, it was other research tragedies that stimulated additional concern and additional regulation. In 1962, the thalidomide scandal (as discussed in Chapter 1) came to public attention along with the innumerable gross neonatal deformities. Consequently, the Food and Drug Administration introduced much stricter regulations for tightly controlled experimentation on drugs and other products (Stricker, 1982). Not long afterward, public attention became focused on a program conducted by a hospital in Brooklyn where 22 chronically ill patients were injected with cancer cells as part of a study to examine the body's capacity to reject foreign cells. The patients were not informed of their participation. Subsequently the issue of informed consent crystallized and obligations to research subjects were made clearer (Stricker, 1982).

Diener and Crandall (1978) discuss a number of research studies that have raised concern about ethical issues in research (for example, inducing extreme levels of fear in subjects, suppressing disconfirming data, jeopardizing continued employment of subjects). As awareness of and sensitivity to the rights of both human and animal subjects in psychological and educational research have increased, there have been major changes in the regulation of research.

One of the major changes has been development of the Code of Federal Regulations (rev. March 3, 1983), which implemented Public Law 93-348 (July 12, 1974) establishing institutional review boards (IRBs) and an ethics guidance program to protect human subjects in biomedical and behavioral research.

All research projects with human subjects are subject to federal regulations governing research. Initially, IRBs were established as five-person panels to preview research proposals and weigh potential risks and benefits for all research that sought funding from the Department of Health, Education, and Welfare (now the Department of Health and Human Services, hereafter referred to as DHHS). Although IRBs still serve this function, most institutions now routinely have all research proposals reviewed by an IRB committee of peers at their institution. In essence, the typical IRB certifies that projects comply with the regulations and policies set forth by the DHHS regarding the health, welfare, safety, rights, and privileges of human subjects. The general procedure is for the investigator to complete and submit a form to the IRB that summarizes basic information about the research (see Exhibit A at the end of this chapter for an example of one such form). Key issues in evaluating the ethicality of any research project are the risks involved to the subjects and whether subjects have been fully informed about the study so they can make an informed decision to voluntarily participate in the research (informed consent). Given the increased sensitivity to informed consent, documentation of the subject's consent is now required unless specifically waived. General requirements have been developed for documenting informed consent (see *Federal Register,* Volume 46, Number 16, January 26, 1981).

In this section of the chapter, we will discuss a number of complexities and complications related to using human subjects that often arise for the psychological researcher in general, and the counseling researcher in particular. Assessing potential harm or risk is a difficult process and sometimes inaccurate. Because there is some level of risk (even if it is minuscule) in every experiment, how much risk or harm is too much? In some research, deception is needed to adequately investigate a particular construct, and if the full truth were known to a subject, the validity of the experiment might be significantly reduced. Thus, without deception, knowledge of some aspect of human behavior may be inaccessible. But deception conflicts with informed consent and the fundamental principles of autonomy and fidelity. This section will focus on these issues in greater detail as we discuss the issues involved in protecting the dignity and welfare of the people who participate in research investigations. Specifically, we will discuss issues pertaining to risks and benefits, consent, deception and debriefing, confidentiality and privacy, and treatment issues.

Risks and Benefits

The ethical researcher's goal is to conduct an investigation that creates new knowledge (the beneficence principle) while preserving the dignity and welfare of the participants or subjects (the nonmaleficence and autonomy principles). It almost goes without saying that one would not want to harm subjects in any way. Particularly for the counseling researcher, the goal is usually to alleviate human suffering; thus harm is antithetical to the immediate and long-term goals of the professional counselor. But harm can be manifested in many ways. The most obvious way involves physical harm, or even death, as in the Nazi "research" during World War II. However, harm can also consist of embarrassment, irritation, anger, physical and emotional stress, loss of self-esteem, exacerbation of stress, delay of treatment, sleep deprivation, loss of respect from others, negative labeling, invasion of privacy, damage to personal dignity, loss of employment, and civil or criminal liabilities. Part of the difficulty in predicting harm is that different people may react to the same experimental condition in very different ways. For example, most clients may feel very comfortable rating their expectations for the counseling they are about to receive; some clients might even enjoy this reflection. However, a few clients might experience stress or embarrassment or even guilt by participating in this exercise. Sometimes cross-cultural differences contribute to unintended reactions, which underscores the complexity of this issue. Researchers need to not only assess harm in a general sense, but also with regard to the intended subjects' perceptual world and cultural background.

It is the researcher's responsibility to identify potential sources of risk and eliminate or minimize them to protect the potential subjects (*EPP*, II.C.3, II.C.4, II.C.5; *ES*, D.4). The professional codes of ethics specifically indicate that the researcher should carefully assess the potential of risk for subject participation (*EPP*, II.C.3), and take precautions to protect the participant from physical and mental discomfort, harm, and danger that might occur in a study (*EPP*, II.C.5; *ES*, D.4). Implied in these statements is that it is the responsibility of the investigator to reduce risk and prevent harm by detecting and removing any negative consequences associated with a study.

One of the problems inherent in assessing risk potential is that the task is often subjective, ambiguous, and involves an estimation of probabilities. Typically one does not have beforehand empirical, objective data about whether the experimental condition is stressful (and to collect such data would require administering the experiment to subjects). Moreover, the type and level of stress that would be harmful is ambiguous and most likely varies across cultures and individuals. That is, what is perceived as harmful in one culture may not be perceived as such in another culture. Thus, assessing harm may also involve cross-cultural sensitivity. In short, assessing risk is difficult, if not impossible, to quantify.

Acknowledging the difficulty, ambiguity, and imperfectness of the task, there are at least two main strategies for evaluating potential risk. The first strategy involves making a best estimate of the cost/benefit ratio of the study. That is, a comparison should be made of the potential benefits that might accrue from the study in comparison with the potential risks to subjects. For example, a study might be considered ethically acceptable if the potential benefits greatly outweighed the potential risks, or failure to use the experimental procedures might expose the participant to greater harm (*EPP*, II.C.5). Assessing the benefits derived from a particular study, however, is also a difficult and ambiguous task. This assessment is complicated by the question of "benefit for whom?" That is, should the subject be the one to receive the benefit directly, or could it be to a larger group, such as increasing a profession's knowledge base. Some may argue that benefits from any single study may be minimal, but over time programmatic research does increase the profession's knowledge base. Yet balancing individual costs against societal benefits is a difficult task. Moreover, it can be argued that the investigator is at a disadvantage to accurately judge the cost/benefit ratio because he or she may be overly biased regarding the benefit of the study (Diener & Crandall, 1978). In short, in principle the cost/benefit ratio is appealing, but in reality it is difficult to weigh the issues precisely. Nonetheless, the cost/benefit ratio is one useful strategy to employ in assessing the ethical issues associated with a particular study.

The second strategy involves several procedures to minimize risk or reduce the probability of harm. Whenever the potential for substantial risk is present, the investigator should engage in a search for other possible designs or procedures. The researcher needs to exhaust other possibilities to obtain the same or similar knowledge by using a slightly different design. A common practice is to consult with colleagues not only to obtain ideas regarding alternative designs or procedures, but also to obtain alternative perspectives in assessing risks and benefits. Consultation with colleagues is particularly important in planning socially sensitive research or research in which cross-cultural issues and investigator bias may be a factor. Counselors "have a duty to consult with those knowledgeable about the individuals or groups most likely to be affected, in order to preserve the integrity of the research methodology and to prevent harm" (EPP, II.C.4). Often the researcher's problem solving with regard to ethical issues can be greatly stimulated and facilitated by successively conferring with a wide variety of colleagues. The process of consulting with colleagues has now been formalized at many institutions and agencies, as we indicated earlier, into institutional review boards (IRBs) or human subject review committees. From our experience, the IRBs serve the extremely valuable function of providing additional perspectives in assessing risk and suggesting possible alternative designs that are often not immediately apparent to the researcher. Even if not technically required to do so, researchers are encouraged to solicit feedback from such committees.

The researcher can also engage in other strategies to minimize risk. One of the problems we indicated earlier in assessing risks and benefits is the lack of empirical data on which to make informed decisions. Thus, another strategy is to collect some data through safer channels, such as using pilot subjects and role playing, to facilitate a more accurate assessment of risks and benefits. For example, the researcher and his or her assistants might role-play the experimental procedures in question (which is often a good idea in general), and perhaps explore alternative procedures. Perhaps a colleague or two could also be asked to serve as a subject to pilot the procedures and provide feedback on potential risks. Colleagues often can provide very useful feedback because they can discuss their experience as a subject while at the same time being familiar with ethical and design issues. Depending on the outcome of such role plays (that is, if the risks do not appear to be substantial), the researcher might take another step by conducting a very small-scale pilot study with two to five subjects. In such a pilot, the researcher should not only monitor the experimental procedures very carefully, but also take the opportunity to interview subjects at length either during or after the experiment about their experience, as well as solicit suggestions for alternative procedures. Pilot subjects' feedback can be extremely valuable, and its utility should not be underplayed. In short, role plays and pilots provide the researcher with at least some data from which to assess risks and benefits. Additional data can also be obtained by careful monitoring of the actual experiment, and even interviewing randomly selected subjects immediately after the experiment as well as several days later throughout the study. The researcher should not stop evaluating the potential risks of a study after the study is approved by an IRB committee, but rather needs to be vigilant and constantly evaluating the risks and benefits as more data about the subjects' experiences becomes available.

Another strategy to minimize risk is to screen subjects for a particular study, and select only those subjects who have certain characteristics that make them more resistant to the risks involved in a study (or deselect subjects that might be particularly at risk in the study) (Diener & Crandall, 1978). For example, depressed subjects with very low self-esteem might have an increased risk if they participated in a protracted study that involved a great deal of interpersonal feedback from other students. In this regard, special populations (such as children, patients from a psychiatric hospital, prisoners in solitary confinement) merit careful consideration as a subject group.

In summary, the ethical researcher's goal is to conduct an investigation that creates new knowledge while preserving the dignity and welfare of the participants. A central issue in preserving the subjects' dignity and welfare is preventing harm. Thus, a major task for the researcher is to carefully assess potential risks and make every attempt to eliminate or minimize such risks. Two strategies were discussed for evaluating potential risks: (1) attempting to assess and weigh the cost/benefit ratio of the study and (2) engaging in a variety of procedures to eliminate, minimize, and more accurately evaluate potential risks. Both strategies should be used in any study involving more than minimal risk. It is important to note, however, that a great deal of ambiguity often enters into assessing costs and risks, particularly in cross-cultural situations; the researcher may often experience conflict and struggle with the imperfectness of this important task. Consultation is strongly encouraged.

Consent

A critical issue in conducting studies that involve risk pertains to informed consent. After a researcher has carefully evaluated potential harm and developed the best design to answer his or her question while preserving the subject's dignity and welfare, the researcher is then ready to approach the subject and develop a fair, clear, and explicit agreement about the experiment in question (informed consent). The issue of informed consent revolves around the fundamental ethical principles of autonomy and fidelity. Consent refers to the process of giving subjects the opportunity to decide whether or not to participate in a particular research study. This might seem like a rather simple process: simply ask the subject if he or she would like to participate. Actually, a number of factors make obtaining consent a rather complicated process, and a considerable amount of attention has been given to this topic in the last 15 years (see Keith-Spiegel & Koocher, 1985; Schmidt & Meara, 1984).

The professional codes of ethics clearly indicate that the investigator has a responsibility to obtain informed consent from subjects (*EPP,* I.C.1, I.C.2, I.C.3, I.C.4, I.C.6, I.C.8, I.C.9, I.C.10, I.C.11, IIC.5; *ES,* D.5, D.6). The investigator seeks to develop a specific type of relationship with the potential subject, and thus ethically is bound to establish a clear and fair agreement with potential research participants that clarifies obligations, risks, and responsibilities prior to the study.

Turnbull (1977) discussed consent in this special relationship in terms of three key elements: capacity, information, and voluntariness. Capacity refers to the ability to process information and involves two issues: a legal age qualification and an ability issue. Minors, under the age of 18, are not considered to be legally able to make some decisions and thus do not have the needed capacity in these instances. The principle of autonomy creates difficult issues when applied to using children in research (*EPP,* I.C.2). Ramsey (1970) has argued that since children have a reduced or limited capacity, it is impossible to obtain a fully rational consent from them. Moreover, the parent or legal guardian of the child cannot know whether the child, if he or she were fully rational, would choose to participate or not. He argued that children should not be used in any research except research from which they would benefit directly. Ramsey's position has been regarded as too extreme (see Cooke, 1982; Powell, 1984), and parents or legal guardians are allowed to give consent. However, federal regulations indicate that a child's assent (defined as an affirmative agreement to participate) is required whenever in the judgment of an IRB the child is capable of providing assent, taking into account age, maturity, and psychological state. We encourage counseling researchers to explain to children (in addition to their parents or guardians) in language that they can understand, what they will be asked to do in the course of the research and to secure their agreement to participate if possible.

Ability typically refers to mental competence and thereby protects individuals who may be at risk because of diminished mental capacities. Autonomy is again an issue. If a researcher uses institutionalized adults, consent must be obtained from parents or legal guardians. We also suggest obtaining assent from adults with diminished capacity if at all possible. In short, a critical element of consent involves the capacity to process information about the merits of participating in a particular study.

The second key element of informed consent pertains to the type of information that potential subjects are given about a study (*EPP,* I.C.1, I.C.11, II.C.5; *ES,* D.5). Subjects must be given all of the relevant information about a study so that they can make an informed decision about the merits of participating. Turnbull (1977) noted that two issues are important: the kind of information provided as well as the process of providing it. Thus, the information given must be complete and presented in an understandable manner. Drew (1980) referred to these issues as fullness and effectiveness. To satisfy the requirement of fullness, the information presented should contain a description of what the investigation is about and what the subject will be asked to do (for example, complete two questionnaires about study habits). This should include a discussion of any type of electronic recording or filming (and subject approval: *EPP,* I.C.4). Moreover, the explanation should include a discussion of possible risks or potential harm involved in the study as well as a discussion of potential benefits that might accrue from participation. Failure to make full disclosures, as in the case of deception, requires additional safeguards that we will discuss later.

The third element of consent is voluntariness: it must be given without some element of explicit or implicit coercion, pressure, or undue enticement (*EPP*, I.C.3, I.C.6; *ES*, D.6). Examples of coercion include requiring students to participate in a study because they are enrolled in a class, in an institution, in a therapy group, or seeking individual therapy; publicly humiliating subjects if they choose not to participate; paying excessive amounts of money or other financial rewards as an inducement to participate; repeatedly contacting clients and soliciting participation; and creating undue social pressure by indicating that all of the other clients have agreed to participate. University courses (such as large introductory psychology classes) sometimes offer bonus credits for or require participation in research studies; in such situations it is essential to offer students viable alternatives in addition to research studies in order to protect their autonomy. In a counseling context, voluntariness can also be a complex issue. For example, situations in which therapists ask their clients to participate may contain elements of undue influence (for example, the therapist is very likable, or the client is vulnerable and wants to be a "good client"). In short, a critical aspect of consent is that subjects can voluntarily decide on participating free from blatant or subtle extraneous factors that may compel them to participate.

The notion of voluntariness does not end when a potential subject decides to participate in a study, but actually continues through the completion of a study (*EPP*, I.C.8, I.C.9). Thus, subjects are typically informed prior to the commencement of a study that they have the right to withdraw from the experiment at any time, and that their initial agreement to participate is not binding. Keith-Spiegel and Koocher (1985) astutely observed that the wise investigator will be alert to signs of discomfort or anxiousness that might influence subjects to withdraw, and rather than coerce continued involvement, be concerned about the usefulness and validity of data collected under stressful conditions. Moreover, it is useful to contact subjects "within a reasonable time period following participation should stress, harm, or related questions or concerns arise" (*EPP*, I.C.12).

In short, an important ethical consideration in recruiting subjects to participate in counseling research involves the informed consent of the participants. It is important that potential subjects have the capacity to process information about the study, have received complete and effective information about the content and procedures of the study, and can decide on the merits of participating voluntarily without extraneous compelling factors.

As we indicated earlier, documentation of the subject's consent is now common practice. There are a few exceptions; several categories of research are typically considered exempt from these requirements, such as observation of public behavior, the study of anonymous archival data, and certain types of survey and interview procedures. Subjects are asked to sign a formal consent form indicating their informed agreement to participate if there is more than what is referred to as a minimal risk (that is, more risk to the subject than he or she would encounter in daily life). Even in studies involving minimal risk to subjects, obtaining a signed consent form is advisable to avoid misunderstandings as well as for the researcher's own protection. It is important to note that cross-cultural issues can also create confusion or misunderstandings that may be relevant during the process of obtaining informed consent, which again reinforces the need for sensitivity to these matters while obtaining consent.

Specifically, the following elements are to be incorporated into a written consent form:

- Name, phone number, and address of the person(s) conducting the study, and whom to contact for additional information or questions; name, phone number, and address of faculty member if investigator is a student; whom to contact in the event of a research-related injury to the subject
- A statement that the study involves research, along with the title, purpose, and general description of the study
- A description of the procedures, including amount of time involved and any plans for contacting subjects at a later time
- A description of any reasonably foreseeable risks or discomforts to the subject
- A description of the benefits to the subject, or to others, that can reasonably be expected
- In cases involving treatment or therapy, a statement of appropriate alternative procedures or courses of treatment, if any, that might be advantageous to the subject
- A statement describing the extent to which confidentiality will be maintained
- A statement that the results of the study may be published or reported to government or funding agencies
- A statement indicating that participation is voluntary, and that the subject may discontinue participation at any time without any penalty
- For research involving more than minimal risk, an explanation of whether compensation or medical treatments are available if injury occurs

A sample of a typical consent form for adults is provided as Exhibit B, and a sample of a typical consent form for children (note the appropriate language level) is provided as Exhibit C.

Deception and Debriefing

Deception is a topic that has received considerable attention and been the subject of much debate (*EPP,* II.C.6., II.C.8; *ES,* D.5). Deception in psychological research refers to misinforming or withholding information from potential subjects about the nature of the experiment or the procedures involved in the study. Thus, deception refers to misrepresenting the facts pertaining to a study, either through acts of omission or commission. That is, an investigator might omit or withhold some information about a study and thus disguise the true nature of the study in some way; or the researcher might purposefully provide false or misleading information, an act of commission, to deceive the subject in some way. Either way, the thorny issues of deception revolve around the fundamental ethical principles of autonomy, fidelity, and to some extent nonmaleficence.

It is important to note that there are many types or levels of deception. Perhaps at the simplest and most benign level, the experimenter may accurately describe the study but not disclose all the facts about it, largely because of the tremendous level of detail involved. Or the experimenter might accurately disclose the nature of the experiment but not reveal the hypotheses so as to not bias the subjects. These acts of omission usually do not bother subjects. It is typically recognized that an experimenter cannot be completely disclosing about all aspects of a study (including the researcher's hypothesis plus complete descriptions of all experimental conditions); in fact, revealing such information can bias or confound the results of a study (see Chapter 12). Other types of deception, however, mislead the subjects in major ways and often lead them to feel "duped" or "had." For example, subjects might be told that they failed a problem-solving test (their score was in the fifth percentile) in order to examine their behavior following failure. In reality, subjects probably did not perform that poorly on the test, but merely were given bogus feedback. For the most part, the major controversy surrounding deception pertains to these situations where subjects are entirely misled. It is these instances of deception that we will focus on here.

Obviously, the use of deception is antithetical to fully informing potential subjects about the essence of a particular study. The use of deception in psychological research is quite a controversial topic. Schmidt and Meara (1984) reported that in revising the APA Ethical Principles in 1981, a large minority of psychologists agreed to forbid the use of any deception. The majority, however, thought that although deception should generally be avoided, important research would be impossible to conduct and would never be done if deception were unethical. For example, sometimes deception is necessary in psychological research to adequately examine certain phenomena, like the process of persuasion. Specifically, in a study of the social influence process in counseling, some subjects might very well be biased to not change a particular belief or attitude if they were told beforehand that the study was investigating variables related to changing the subject's beliefs. In this case, not using deception would result in a study that did not have much generalizability or resemblance to the attitude change process in counseling.

Schmidt and Meara (1984) noted, however, that deception may have especially troublesome consequences for counseling researchers. A core ingredient of the counseling relationship is perceived counselor trustworthiness; deception would most likely destroy client perceptions of trustworthiness and the working alliance. Thus, researchers examining real-life counseling processes must address additional considerations and consequences in using deception because of therapeutic considerations as well.

Our view is that researchers should avoid deception whenever possible. In particular, subjects should not be deceived about "aspects that subjects might find negative, such as physical risk, discomfort, or unpleasant emotional experiences" (*EPP,* II.C.6). But we believe there are exceptions in which deception may be allowed. Specifically, when there is little or minimum risk, and the benefits from the research are socially significant or directly benefit the subject, deception may be allowed. However, we agree with Lindsey (1984) that "if the risk is significant and subjects are deceived, it is a fundamental violation of the principle of autonomy" (p. 85). In addition, before conducting a study using deception it is the responsibility of the investigator to (1) "determine whether the use of deceptive techniques is justified by the study's prospective scientific, educational, or applied value;" and (2) "determine whether alternative procedures are available that do not use concealment or deception" (*EPP,* II.C.6). Kazdin (1980) noted two other considerations. First, the aversiveness of the deception itself is an important factor to consider, as there are many types of deception with varying consequences. Some deception does not result in any harm to a subject, while other types of deception might result in considerable harm. Second, the researcher must weigh the potential for and magnitude of the harmful effects caused by the deception. Thus, the extent or magnitude of the harm is important to consider. In short, if an investigator decides to use deception, additional responsibilities and safeguards are required to protect the welfare and dignity of the research subjects, and the researcher must carefully assess the potential consequences and risks to the subject. Finally, given the nature of the counseling relationship, deception in real-life counseling with actual clients would seem to be rarely justifiable.

If deception is justified, the investigator is responsible for informing subjects about the nature of the study and removing any misconceptions as soon as possible within the experiment (*EPP,* II.C.6, II.C.8; *ES,* D.5). Providing a sufficient explanation is commonly referred to as debriefing. Moreover, in educational settings, if students are serving as subjects to earn research credits and learn about psychological research, then debriefing also should emphasize educational issues. Exhibit D provides examples of both oral and written debriefings for an analogue study that examined variables affecting laypersons' perceptions of grief reactions. Since this study was conducted with undergraduates who earned extra credit, the debriefing nicely emphasizes educational components. Moreover, the example explains the need for the minimal level of deception employed in the analogue study.

It is important to note that the effectiveness of debriefing is unclear and probably varies with each study or experimenter. Moreover, in some cases, debriefing can itself create stress or harm. For example, if the researcher preselected two groups of subjects who had very high or very low self-concepts, communicating this information may not be well received by some subjects. In this regard, Baumrind (1976) identified debriefing as "inflicted insight." In other situations, subjects may feel angry because they were misled or "duped." Thus, sometimes debriefing adds additional complications and results in delicate situations that the investigator must examine.

Confidentiality and Privacy

Investigators ask subjects for a wide array of information, and often it is of a very personal nature and could be harmful if publicly released. Often experimenters promise confidentiality to increase honest responses from subjects. If a subject agrees to participate confidentially in an experiment, the principles of fidelity, autonomy, and to some extent nonmaleficence suggest that any information that the subject discloses should be treated confidentially to protect the welfare of the client. The professional codes of ethics clearly indicate that care should be taken to protect the privacy of subjects (*EPP*, I.C.5, I.C.14; *ES*, D.10). Maintaining the anonymity or confidentiality of subjects is now standard in counseling research. Anonymity exists when there are no identifiers whatsoever on project materials that can link data with individual subjects; often researchers will assign subjects code numbers to place on their respective questionnaires in lieu of their names. Thus, the subjects' responses are anonymous, and even the investigator cannot identify the participants. At other times, investigators will collect data and ask for subjects' names. Researchers have an obligation to maintain the confidentiality of information obtained in the research. Thus, confidentiality involves a right of privacy and nonrelease of disclosed personal information. If names are used, typically code numbers will be assigned to subjects when the data are transferred to coding sheets, and the original questionnaires along with subject names will be destroyed. If someone other than the experimenter will have access to the subjects' data (for example, a research assistant), this should be explained to the subjects (and usually is stated in the consent form) along with plans for maintaining confidentiality. In field settings, researchers also should be sensitive to minimizing the invasiveness of data collection so as to protect the subjects' privacy within a social milieu (*EPP*, II.C.7).

Schmidt and Meara (1984) indicated that because confidentiality is central to the counseling relationship, counseling researchers often need to be especially sensitive to maintaining confidentiality, particularly with regard to research conducted in an agency such as a university counseling center. For example, researchers must be sensitive to releasing demographic information that might identify particular clients, such as participants in a small therapy group (for example, an eating disorder group, a consciousness raising group for men over 30); on small college campuses, demographic information about the group composition can easily identify clients. Likewise, research using an intensive single-subject design or an intra-subject design that uses only a few subjects also demands sensitivity to identifying characteristics; typically, it is advisable to provide fictitious descriptive information similar to the truth if it is necessary to describe a particular client in detail, and to explicitly indicate this in whatever written or oral report is made. Sometimes investigators also communicate to subjects how the data will be used (*EPP*, I.C.14) as well as obtain feedback and written approval from clients on written descriptions of the results of the study, to further reduce any breaches of confidentiality.

Another confidentiality issue arises if researchers want to investigate some aspect of a particular treatment procedure, but *after* clients have already begun treatment at an agency. For example, suppose there is an active relaxation training program at a university counseling center, in which students, staff, and faculty are encouraged to participate. Clients enter this program with the usual assurance of confidentiality. Let's say a researcher from the psychology department (outside the agency) is interested in evaluating some aspect of the treatment program and examining the effect of certain individual difference variables (such as coping style) on the relaxation training. Given that the clients have been assured of confidentiality at the outset, it would be a breach of confidentiality to reveal client names at this point to a researcher outside the agency. Some clients might also feel their privacy has been invaded if they are identified to a researcher *in the agency,* as they did not consent to having that person know of their seeking such services. Likewise, an investigator might conduct a study with a counseling center sample that gave their consent to participate in a study with certain specified procedures; the investigator is limited to accessing only the information or data that the clients consented to disclosing or providing, as opposed to any information in the clients' agency files (see Keith-Spiegel & Koocher, 1985). In short, counseling researchers sometimes have dual responsibilities; they need to be sensitive to confidentiality issues pertaining to research endeavors as well as to confidentiality issues inherent in therapeutic relationships in general.

Confidentiality and privacy issues can also intersect in research settings with a psychologist's duty to protect the welfare of the subject and other individuals, and can thus create an ethical dilemma for the researcher. The most notable examples involve subjects with homicidal and suicidal intentions that become evident during the course of a research investigation. For example, counseling researchers routinely assess the psychological adjustment of subjects in various ways, such as by using the Beck Depression Inventory (BDI) (Beck, Ward, Mendelson, Mock, & Erbaugh, 1961). The difficult question revolves around what to do when the investigator finds that a subject scored very high on the BDI. Or let's say the researcher is investigating suicidal intentions and in administering the Scale for Suicide Ideators (SSI) (Schotte & Clum, 1982) learns that one or more subjects scored very high on the SSI. Another ethical dilemma can arise if a subject reveals some information such that the subject or others will be liable for a violation of the law. In short, sometimes the counseling researcher obtains information about subjects that creates considerable concern for the general well-being of a particular subject or another individual, or that brings up criminal or civil liabilities.

Concern for the well-being of a particular subject must also be considered in relationship to the individual's right to privacy. In approaching one subject who had a very high BDI score after a particular investigation, the investigator was curtly informed that the subject "consented to participate in a psychological experiment, not psychotherapy." Some subjects may feel embarrassed if attention is called to them within a group setting; obviously, care must be taken to avoid breaching confidentiality to other subjects and to be sensitive to the effects of isolating particular individuals.

Concern for the well-being of a particular subject must also be considered in reference to how much information an investigator has about a subject. That is, one researcher might only have a BDI score that is causing some concern; another researcher might have a much broader array of information (for example, questionnaire data, interview data, information about environmental stressors, knowledge about past suicide attempts) that more strongly suggests there is considerable reason for concern.

Clearly, the counseling researcher has ethical obligations beyond the research ethical issues. Moreover, each situation presents a slightly different context and calls for slightly different interventions. The researcher faces a complex decision as he or she weighs the strength of the evidence, the individual's right to privacy, the consequences of approaching a subject with the topic, and the obligation to promote human welfare. Some IRBs now require investigators to include a statement in the consent form that indicates that if the subject reveals information that signals danger to the subject or another person, confidentiality may need to be broken. Another strategy is for researchers who collect data of a sensitive psychological nature to routinely attach a statement to the research questionnaire communicating that it asks questions of a personal nature, and that if subjects want to discuss their feelings reflected in the questionnaire, they are strongly encouraged to do so. Resources should then be listed, such as the address and phone number of the university counseling center or local mental health center. In addition, verbal announcements can also be made before administering the questionnaire.

Following is an example of a statement designed to facilitate such an exchange. This paragraph was developed as part of an introduction to the Scale of Suicide Ideators.

> The following questionnaire inquires about a variety of thoughts, feelings, attitudes, and behaviors that are sometimes related to suicide. We are interested in how frequently college students think about suicide. We realize that this is not a rare occurrence. In fact, by some estimates, up to 70% of the population at one time or another contemplate suicide. However, we want you to be aware that counseling services are available to you should your thoughts about suicide cause you some distress. To inquire about counseling, you can contact the Counseling Center [address and phone], or the Psychological Clinic [address and phone]. In the event that your score on this inventory indicates that you are seriously contemplating suicide we will contact you to express our concern and urge you to seek counseling. (Dixon, 1989, p. 42)

Treatment Issues

In the past a common strategy among researchers was to use a between-groups design to compare two or more groups of subjects, with one group receiving a particular treatment and often one of the other groups not receiving treatment, by receiving a placebo instead or having treatment delayed. Although such designs offer methodological rigor, they can present ethical problems in withholding treatment from people in need. Clients in a waiting-list or placebo group could be at risk as they continue to struggle under duress. Thus, researchers who are interested in examining questions about comparative treatments often must examine additional ethical issues.

One of the essential issues pertains to the necessity of withholding treatment. Does the researcher need to compare a particular treatment against a no-treatment group? The researcher might also consider alternatives, like comparing a particular treatment against a well-known treatment. Or the researcher might examine treatment comparisons in an alternative design, like a within-subjects design. In short, as with the standards for using deception, researchers need to assess potential risk and consider alternative designs to answer treatment questions.

Another consideration is the type of subjects who are being asked to participate in the experiment. Kazdin (1980) suggested that volunteer clients solicited from a community setting may be more appropriate for a waiting-list group than clients from a crisis intervention center. Assessing the risk potential not only involves an assessment of the setting that subjects are drawn from but also consideration of the type and severity of the subject's presenting problem (for instance, depression versus assertiveness).

Kazdin (1980) also suggested that assigning subjects to delayed-treatment groups might be more ethically appropriate if the subjects initially came from a waiting list, which is in essence delayed treatment. For example, many agencies have waiting lists because service demands are heavier than can be met by the staff. Thus, a treatment study might be conducted by randomly assigning clients from the waiting list to the experimental conditions (treatment and delayed treatment). In such a case, some clients would actually receive treatment earlier than if they had stayed on the agency's waiting list.

Other ethical considerations that merit attention in delayed-treatment conditions include informed consent and ultimately arranging for treatment to occur. Ethically, subjects should be informed prior to an investigation if there is a possibility that they may be placed in a delayed-treatment group; they then may or may not decide to participate in the study. Moreover, subjects who are in a delayed-treatment group ethically deserve to receive treatment after the experiment has been conducted; and these subjects deserve the same quality of treatment as the experimental group.

In short, counseling researchers who contemplate using placebo or delayed-treatment conditions must carefully examine additional ethical issues. As with the standards for the use of deception, we suggest that researchers need to assess the potential risk and consider alternative designs, or ways of minimizing risks.

SUMMARY AND CONCLUSIONS

We have suggested that ethics are central to the conduct of research and, in fact, permeate the entire research enterprise. Broadly speaking, ethics are a "set of guidelines that provide directions for conduct" (Keith-Spiegel & Koocher, 1985, p. xiii). For counselors, research ethics provide directions for how we are to interact with the larger profession, other professionals, and those people who participate in our research. Moreover, how we design and conduct our research reflects our basic values, such as autonomy, fairness, promoting the welfare of others, fidelity, and above all, avoiding harm to others. Sometimes it seems that the business of life overshadows our basic values, as corners are cut to save time. It is essential to keep in mind, however, that the health and longevity of our counseling profession rests on such basic values as honesty and fairness. These values need to be stressed throughout graduate training in a wide range of situations, and particularly with regard to research. Our values may communicate more about who we are and what we do in our research than any other aspect of our behavior. In essence, "ethical rigor needs to find as central a place of prominence in research as does methodological rigor" (Lindsey, 1984, p. 85).

It is important to note that every researcher most likely cannot be entirely ethical all of the time. In fact, almost all researchers will unknowingly engage in some aspect of research that might infringe upon one of the ethical principles at some time or another. This is not to condone infringements, but rather to acknowledge that oversights and mistakes happen. Most often, infringements occur due to a lack of sensitivity, knowledge, or experience. We can all help each other by consistently educating each other in our endeavor to conduct our research ethically and uphold our professional responsibilities. Thus, it is important to talk with each other about ethical issues and dilemmas, and particularly about events that we witness that make us uncomfortable. From our experience, most often inexperienced professionals become paralyzed when they witness what appears to be an ethical infraction and withdraw from the situation. Informed peer monitoring of ethical issues is a powerful mechanism to not only monitor the appropriateness of our behavior, but also to increase our sensitivity and knowledge about ethical issues. For more serious ethical violations, sanctions may be sought from local, state, or national ethics committees (such as state licensing boards or professional organizations such as AACD or APA) as well as the judicial system. The interested reader should consult Keith-Spiegel and Koocher (1985), who provide excellent guidelines for a range of options (and sanctions) in responding to ethical situations.

• • • • • • • • • • • • • • • • • •

EXHIBIT A

Protocol Review Number _____

University of Oregon
HUMAN SUBJECTS ACTIVITY REVIEW FORM [1]

I. PROJECT INFORMATION:

Investigator name:_____ Date_____

Unit (see appendix in Manual for list of units)_____ ext._____

Project title:_____

_____

II. PROJECT SUPPORT:

Funded _____   If funded, indicate source: unit _____

Unfunded _____   UO biomed grant _____

                                                  other UO source _____ specify: _____

If grant proposal: pending _____ approved _____   non-UO source _____ specify: _____

III. INVESTIGATOR STATUS: (check one)

Student _____   Faculty _____   Administrator _____   Other _____
(to IV.)   (to V.)   (to V.)   (to V.)

IV. FACULTY SUPERVISOR REVIEW: My signature verifies that 1) I will supervise this student's research project and 2) it complies with federal and University policies regarding protection of human subjects.

Approval _____
Date _____ (to V.)

V. UNIT REVIEW: Signature verifies that the project 1) has been reviewed by the unit and 2) complies with federal and University regulations for research with human subjects.

Approval _____
Date _____ (to VI.)

VI. OFFICE OF RESEARCH & SPONSORED PROGRAMS/REVIEW CATEGORIES:

EXEMPT

Category no._____
Approval _____
Date _____
(to VIII.)

EXPEDITED REVIEW
Dates:
Assigned _____/_____
Cond. approval _____/_____
Approval _____/_____
Refer to IRB _____/_____
(to VIII. if approved; to VII. if not approved)

FULL REVIEW
Dates:
Assigned _____/_____
Cond. approval _____/_____
Approval _____/_____
Disapproval _____/_____
(to VII.)

VII. INSTITUTIONAL REVIEW BOARD (IRB)

Meeting date _____
Conditional approval _____
Approval _____
Disapproval _____ (to VIII.)

VIII .
Signature of IRB Chair _____ Date _____

Submit Human Subjects Activity Review form, sample informed consent form(s), and other pertinent information such as sample of survey instrument or questionnaire, grant proposal, etc., in triplicate to Office of Research and Sponsored Programs, 120 Chapman Hall (ext. 5131) following unit review and approval. Consult the Investigator's Manual on Research with Human Subjects for additional detail.

Please provide answers to all of the following questions (attach additional pages as needed). Forward in triplicate, along with the signed cover page and accompanying informed consent form(s), and proposal if available, to Office of Research and Sponsored Programs (ORSP), 120 Chapman Hall, for review and approval by the Committee for the Protection of Human Subjects/Institutional Review Board (CPHS/IRB). References are found in the Investigator's Manual on Research with Human Subjects, available from ORSP.

I.   **PURPOSE AND OBJECTIVES OF THE RESEARCH**

II.   **DESCRIPTION OF SUBJECT POPULATION(S)**

     1.   Who are the subject groups and how are they being recruited?

     2.   Approximate number of subjects in each group to be used: _____

     3.   If advertising for subjects, include a copy of the proposed advertisement. (Refer to section V in the Manual)

     4.   What are the criteria for selection and/or exclusion of subjects? (Refer to sections V and VIII in the Manual)

     5.   If special populations are being used, please justify. (Refer to section X in the Manual)

III.   **ACTIVITIES INVOLVING HUMAN SUBJECTS**

    1.   Describe the activities involving each subject group described in #II.1. Include the expected amount of time subjects will be involved in each activity and where the activities will be conducted.

    2.   How will the data be collected (check):
        ___ questionnaires? (submit a copy)
        ___ interviews? (submit sample of questions)
        ___ observations? (briefly describe)
        ___ standardized tests? (If yes, list names)
        ___ other (describe)

IV.   **DATA**

    1.   How will the data be recorded (notes, tapes, computer files, completed questionnaires or tests, etc.)?

    2.   Who will have access to the gathered data and how will confidentiality be maintained during the study, after the study, and in reporting of results?

    3.   What are the plans for the data after completion of this study and how and when will data be maintained or destroyed? (Refer to section VIII in the manual)

V.   BENEFITS, RISKS, COSTS

1.   What are the potential benefits to humanity?

2.   What are the potential benefits to the subjects?

3.   What compensation, if any, will be offered to the subjects and how will payment be scheduled throughout the study? (Refer to sections V and VIII in the Manual)

4.a.   What risks to the subjects are most likely to be encountered, and at what level? (Refer to section VIII in the Manual) (check):

	None	Minimal	More than Minimal	Not sure
physical	—	—	—	—
psychological (emotional, behavioral, etc.)	—	—	—	—
sociological (employability, financial, reputation, etc.)	—	—	—	—
loss of confidentiality	—	—	—	—
criminal or civil liability	—	—	—	—
deception	—	—	—	—
other (explain)	—	—	—	—

4.b.   Describe any risks identified above in 4.a.

5.   What safeguards will you use to eliminate or minimize these risks? If subjects experience adverse reactions, how will they be managed?

6.   What are the costs, if any, to the subjects (monetary, time, etc.)?

VI.   OTHER COMPLIANCE ISSUES

1.   If this project may be subject to other regulations, such as state or local laws protecting special populations or the use of a new drug or device, please identify and discuss.

2.   If this project involves any of the following activities, requiring consideration by another review committee, please check.
        ___ animal use and care
        ___ radiation safety (including use of x-rays, microwaves)
        ___ biological safety (including recombinant DNA, biohazards)
        ___ chemical safety (including hazardous waste materials, chemical carcinogens, flammables, lab safety)

VII.   INFORMED CONSENT

1.   How will the study be explained to the subjects and by whom?

2.   Attach informed consent form(s) you will use in the study (Refer to section IX in the Manual).

3.   Indicate rationale for any special conditions relating to informed consent (e.g. request for approval to obtain oral consent or waiver of documentation). (Refer to section IX in the Manual).

CERTIFICATION:

In submitting this proposed project and signing below, I certify that: I have read and understand the Investigator's Manual on Research with Human Subjects; I will conduct the research involving human subjects as presented in the protocol and approved by the unit, faculty supervisor (if a student project), and IRB; I will meet all responsibilities of the research investigator as outlined in the Manual, including obtaining and documenting informed consent and providing a copy of the consent form to each subject; I will present any proposed modifications in the research to the IRB for review prior to implementation; and I will report to the IRB any problems or injuries to subjects.

Signed: _____   Date: _____

8/89

• • • • • • • • • • • • • • • •

EXHIBIT B
Consent to Serve as a Subject in Research[2]

I consent to participate in the research project entitled "Gender Role Conflict," conducted by Mark Sharpe under the sponsorship of P. Paul Heppner, Ph.D., and the Psychology Department at the University of Missouri-Columbia.

I understand that the only requirement of the study will be to complete four questionnaires in this one session which will take approximately forty-five minutes.

I understand that results of this research will be coded in such a manner that my identity will not be attached physically to the data I contribute. The key listing my identity and subject code number will be kept separate from the data in a locked file accessible only to the project director. This key listing subjects' identities will be physically destroyed at the conclusion of the project in approximately one year. In addition, I realize the purpose of this project is to examine the performance of groups of individuals, not to evaluate the performance of a particular individual.

This research project is expected to provide further information on gender role conflict, which increases our understanding of the psychological effects of traditional gender roles.

I understand that the results of this research may be published or otherwise reported to scientific bodies, but that I will not be identified in any such publication or report.

I understand that my participation is voluntary, that there is no penalty for refusal to participate, and that I am free to withdraw my consent and discontinue participation at any time.

I understand that this project is not expected to involve any risks of harm any greater than those ordinarily encountered in daily life. I also understand that it is not possible to identify all potential risks in such research, but that all reasonable safeguards will be taken to minimize the potential risks.

If at any time I have questions about any procedure in this project, I understand that I may contact the investigator at 882-4351.

Signature _____

Date _____

• • • • • • • • • • • • • • • •

• • • • • • • • • • • • • • • •

EXHIBIT C
Sample Informed Consent (Children)[3]

Child's name: _____

We are interested in what attention is, so that one day we can try to help people who find it hard to concentrate on things, and we'd like you to help us. We'd like you to play a kind of game on a computer. All you'll have to do is press a button when some lights come on. It will take about an hour, but you can rest as much as you'd like, and you can stop the game whenever you want.

If you want to rest, or stop completely, just tell us—you won't get into any trouble! In fact, if you don't want to play the game at all, you don't have to. Just say so. Also, if you have any questions about what you'll be doing, or if you can't decide whether to do it or not, just ask us if there is anything you'd like us to explain.

If you do want to try it, please sign your name on the line below. Your parent(s) have already told us that it is alright with them if you want to play the game. Remember, you don't have to, and once you start you can rest or stop whenever you like.

Signed: _____   Date: _____

• • • • • • • • • • • • • • • • •

• • • • • • • • • • • • • • • •

EXHIBIT D
Oral Debriefing[4]

That concludes your participation in the study. Thanks so much for your help. Now that you have finished giving your opinion, I can explain more to you about the whole purpose of the study. I could not do so before now without biasing your responses. First, the study is concerned with more than "interviewing styles." We are more interested in impressions of college students about bereaved and depressed persons. Specifically, we wanted to find out both about your personal reactions to someone who is bereaved and also your attitudes about what is normal or pathological grief. We didn't want people to know exactly what we were looking for in advance, because it could have influenced who signed up for the experiment or the answers they gave. We regret that we could not more fully inform you before you participated. We strongly hope you will respect the need to withhold this information and not discuss this experiment with your fellow classmates.

Some of you received instructions that you were listening to a tape of a middle-aged widow; some were told that she had become widowed three weeks ago and some were told she became widowed two years ago. If you received these instructions, you were in one of the experimental groups. Others received instructions that you were listening to a tape of someone who had lost a job. You were in a control group. In addition, some subjects hear a depressed woman on tape and others hear a nondepressed woman. We will be looking for differences in the answers of these various conditions depending on whether the subjects are male or female.

I want to tell you now that none of you will come back to participate in a further part of the experiment. When you leave today, your participation will end. It was important that you think you might come back, so we could get your reaction about whether you were willing to meet the woman you heard on the tape.

Next, let me explain that this is an analogue experiment. That means that the people you heard on tape were playing parts that were written for them in advance. The purpose of this is so each time a new group hears a particular conversation, it is done exactly the same as the last time a group heard that conversation. This allows for better control of the experiment and helps to eliminate unknown influences on the answers you gave.

I want to thank you for your participation today. Again, it is very important that you do not talk about this experiment with anyone once you leave this room. If people who participate later in the study are aware of its purpose or procedures, their answers may be biased. This would cause us to report misleading results. As we hope our research may some day assist actual bereaved persons, this is a serious problem. Please give others the chance to fairly contribute as you have today.

Does anyone have any questions? [Pause for questions.] I will sign your research cards and you are free to leave. I will stay for a moment in case you have other questions.

If you're having any difficulty dealing with either bereavement or depression, I have the telephone numbers of our University Psychology Clinic and of the Counseling Service, and I will be glad to give them to you when you have finished.

Written Debriefing[5]

This sheet will further explain the purpose of this research project beyond the oral explanation you have already heard. It will outline the independent and dependent variables and research hypotheses. It is crucial that you do not discuss the information on this sheet with any of your friends (who might inadvertently communicate with future subjects) or with the experimenter who is present today. She must remain blind (uninformed) concerning the hypotheses in order to avoid influencing the experiment. You may direct any questions to Carol Atwood at 484–7276 (leave message if no answer). Please sign this sheet as soon as you finish reading it, place it back in the envelope provided, and seal the gummed flap. Thank you very much for your help.

1. Nature of the project: This project would best relate to the major research area of social psychology—attitudes and social perception.

   Findings of related studies: There is little prior research concerning the layperson's views of what is a healthy versus an unhealthy grief reaction, and whether or not laypersons reject or avoid the bereaved. Vernon (1970) asked subjects how they would respond to a recently bereaved person that they knew. Only one-fourth of subjects indicated they would spontaneously mention the death; another one-fourth preferred that neither side mention the death at all. Other researchers, such as Lopata (1973) and Glick, Weiss, and Parkes (1974) have indirectly addressed the question by interviewing widows themselves, who frequently reported experiencing strained relationships or the break-up of friendships after the death of their husbands.

2. Independent variables: These are the variables in the experiment that the investigator manipulates or controls. There are three independent variables in this project. The first is gender of the participants. We will look for differences in the responses of male and female subjects. Second is depression condition (whether the woman heard on the tape is depressed or nondepressed). Third is the "bereavement (or widowhood) status"; that is, the woman on the tape is either recently widowed, long-term widowed, or not widowed (loss of a job is mentioned), depending on which written instructions you recieved.

3. Dependent variables: Used to measure the effects of manipulation of the independent variables. In this project, the dependent variables consisted of the written questionnaire you completed. We want to find out how much you would reject the woman heard on the tape, what your social perceptions were of her, and how pathological you found her to be.

4. Hypotheses: The research questions to be examined in the project. Please do not share this information with today's experimenter.

   A. How do college students' judgments of emotional disturbance compare, based on whether the woman on the tape is recently bereaved, long-term bereaved, or nonbereaved? How do ratings of disturbance differ, depending on whether the woman on tape sounded depressed or not depressed?

B. Do college students reject a bereaved person or a nonbereaved person more, and is this rejection affected by whether the woman sounds depressed or not depressed?

C. How does the gender of the subject (male or female) affect subjects' responses?

5. Control procedures: Procedures to reduce error or unwanted variance. In this study, random assignment of subjects to experimental conditions was used, except that it was not possible to randomly assign subjects based on subject gender. Other control procedures used include keeping the experimenter blind to the study hypotheses, not informing subjects before the experiment about the true purpose, use of an analogue procedure in which actors were used on the tapes, and use of a control group of subjects who listen to the tape of a woman who is neither a widow nor depressed.

I have read the above information concerning the nature of the study, Reactions to Stressful Life Experiences. I agree not to disclose this information either to potential future participants or to the experimenter present today.

Name (Print) _____

Signature _____

Date _____

•   •   •   •   •   •   •   •   •   •   •   •   •   •   •   •

NOTES

1. This form was developed by the Committee for the Protection of Human Subjects/Institutional Review Board at the University of Oregon.
2. This consent form was written by Mark Sharpe. At the time this chapter was written, Mark was a doctoral student in counseling psychology at the University of Missouri-Columbia.
3. This form was developed by the Committee for the Protection of Human Subjects/Institutional Review Board at the University of Oregon.
4. This oral debriefing was written by Carol Atwood. At the time this chapter was written, Carol was a doctoral student in clinical psychology at the University of Missouri-Columbia.
5. This written debriefing was written by Carol Atwood. At the time this chapter was written, Carol was a doctoral student in clinical psychology at the University of Missouri-Columbia.

PART TWO
MAJOR RESEARCH
DESIGNS

CHAPTER 5

BETWEEN-GROUPS AND WITHIN-SUBJECTS DESIGNS

In Chapters 2 and 3 we identified the goal of research as being to isolate relationships among constructs of interest, operationalizing constructs into the independent and dependent variables, while simultaneously eliminating sources of bias, contamination, and error. Perhaps the essence of research is expressed by Kerlinger's "MAXMINCON" principle, which has researchers try to maximize the systematic variance of the variables under study, minimize error variance, and control extraneous variables. The latter two, extraneous variables and error variance, can mask or obscure the effects of the independent variable on the dependent variable.

In this chapter we will discuss two designs that often adhere to the "maxmincon" principle, and are often referred to as true experimental designs because of their emphasis on experimental control and internal validity. Sometimes students anticipate that they will feel intimidated or confused about true experimental designs because of the heavy, ominous meaning that the words sometimes convey. Actually, the designs are quite straightforward; the label is more ominous than the actual design. The two true experimental designs are commonly labeled between-groups design and within-subjects design. We will first discuss between-groups design, and then later in the chapter we will discuss within-subjects design.

The between-groups design often adheres to the "MAXMINCON" principle. Differences between treatments can be maximized by making the treatment (independent variable) stronger or even exaggerated. Thus, researchers will often examine the effects of extreme treatments, such as five counselor disclosures in ten minutes, or three counselor influence attempts in three minutes. Moreover, the between-groups design can be arranged to control extraneous variables and minimize error variance through randomization and experimental control.

The essential feature of between-groups design is the comparison of variables across two or more groups under tightly controlled experimental conditions. In early counseling research, a common comparison group was some type of control group, which was a group that did not receive one of the active treatments in the study. More recently, differences between experimental treatments have been compared. To adequately make comparisons across groups necessitates that the groups do not differ in important ways before the experiment. Thus, initial differences between groups in terms of individual difference variables, demographics, and situational variables must be minimized prior to experimental manipulations to reduce threats to internal validity. Because of the emphasis on comparison and equivalent groups, assignment of subjects to groups is a critical consideration in between-groups design. In fact, one of the major identifying features of between-groups design is the random assignment of subjects. This design is used to compare the effect of an independent variable across groups that were comparable at the beginning of the study. This design is a powerful investigative tool, and often the most strongly favored design (Campbell & Stanley, 1963; Cook & Campbell, 1979; Kerlinger, 1986).

The hallmark of the within-subjects design is that it attempts to minimize error variance due to individual variation by having each subject serve as his or her own control. Thus, the identifying feature of within-subjects design is that each subject serves as his or her own control as all subjects are exposed to all of the treatment conditions. This design, like the between-groups design, is often called a true experimental design because of the random assignment of treatments and manipulation of the independent variable. The random assignment that occurs in the within-subjects design is assignment to a time period in which the treatments are delivered. For example, let's say an experimenter wants to make a comparison between two treatments, X_1 and X_2. One group of subjects could get treatment X_1 before X_2, while the other group would receive the opposite sequence, X_2 before X_1. In within-subjects design, each subject is assigned to either sequence through random assignment, as a matter of chance. Hence, the comparison in a within-subjects design is between different time periods in which separate treatment conditions are in effect.

BETWEEN-GROUPS DESIGNS

In this section we will initially discuss some of the historical events affecting the emergence and development of the between-groups design. We will follow with a discussion of the strengths and weaknesses of three specific between-groups designs. Because our discussion of these designs will focus on simple between-groups designs that contain one independent variable and control groups, the next section will explicitly discuss issues pertaining to control groups. Subsequently we will discuss more complex designs that contain two or more independent variables, which are called factorial designs. Finally, we will examine a central issue of between-groups design, randomization and subject assignment. The strength of the between-groups design is based on group equivalence before the experimental manipulation, which underscores the importance of subject assignment. After our discussion of subject assignment and group equivalence, we will discuss related issues of matching and dependent samples designs.

Historical Perspective

The origins of the group-comparison approach have been related to the discovery and measurement of individual differences, and the development of inferential statistics (Barlow & Hersen, 1984). Adolphe Quetelet, a Belgian astronomer, initially discovered in the nineteenth century that human traits (for example, chest expansion of Scottish soldiers) followed a normal curve (Gleitman, 1986). Rather than interpreting his findings as indicating that some traits are normally distributed in nature, Quetelet inferred that nature was actually striving to create the "average" person, the ideal. But nature obviously failed, which resulted in errors, or variances in traits, that grouped around the mean in orderly ways. Quetelet found that the traits of the "average" person could be estimated by applying statistical techniques to the errors or differences from the mean. The study of individual differences mushroomed in the early to mid-1900s, notably through the work of F. Galton, E. S. Pearson, A. Binet, and R. B. Cattell.

As traits were being identified and measured, the next logical step was to compare one group of people to another. Various descriptive statistics facilitated such comparisons, although Fisher's work on inferential statistics in the 1930s was one of the most influential statistical advances. Fisher's work not only provided statistical techniques, but also made an important contribution in the realm of making inferences from samples, or generalizing the results. Being an agronomist, Fisher was interested in learning about the results from a particular plot of land and generalizing the results to many plots of land. Thus, Fisher developed statistical techniques that made it possible to estimate the relevance of data from one small group, or plot, with certain characteristics to the universe with these characteristics. Such developments in sampling theory (that is, making inferences from a sample to a larger population) greatly facilitated the group-comparisons approach within basic psychological research. By the 1950s, the zeitgeist in psychological research was group comparison and statistical estimation (Hersen & Barlow, 1976). Not surprisingly, as research was conducted in counseling in the 1950s and 1960s, the between-groups design began to appear. For example, the between-groups design was used to examine differences in adjustment changes between students receiving counseling versus a control group (Williams, 1962), and in the effects of time limits (limited or unlimited) on adjustment changes (Shlien, Mosak, & Dreikurs, 1962). The group-comparison approach has also been and still is extremely popular in counseling.

Three Common Experimental Between-Groups Designs

We will initially discuss the three most commonly identified experimental between-groups designs. To do so, we will again use the symbolic representation used by Campbell and Stanley (1963) to depict each of the designs. R indicates random assignment of subjects to each of the groups; O indicates an "observation" or point where data is collected as a dependent variable;

X indicates the exposure of a group to an experimental variable, often a treatment intervention of some kind. The purpose of O, in essence, is to measure the effects of X. The subscripts following O and X indicate the sequence of occurrence: O_1 is the first observation, O_2 is the second, and so on.

After describing each of these three designs, we will then discuss advantages and disadvantages of each, referring particularly to validity issues. It is important to note that these three designs are initially most easily conceptualized as using one independent variable. For example, the independent variable may represent treatments and contain two levels—treatment and no treatment (that is, control group). After our initial discussion of the three commonly used between-groups designs, we will discuss the use of two or more independent variables in what is known as factorial designs.

Posttest-only Control Group Design

Notationally, the posttest-only control group design is conceptualized as

$$R \quad X \quad O_1$$
$$R \qquad O_2$$

Basically, this design involves subjects being randomly assigned to two (or more) groups, with one of the groups receiving exposure to a treatment while one of the groups serves as a control group and thus receives no treatment. Both groups receive a posttest, but neither group receives a pretest. The basic purpose of the design is to test the effect of X, the independent variable, on the dependent variable vis-à-vis O_1.

STRENGTHS. The posttest-only control group design controls for most of the threats to internal validity and thus is a powerful experimental design. For example, history would have affected each group equally because O_1 and O_2 occurred at the same time. Likewise, maturation, instrumentation, testing effects, and regression are controlled in that they are expected to be equally manifested in both the experimental and control groups. For example, if extreme scores were used, the control group would be expected to regress as much as the experimental group. Both selection and selection-maturation effects are controlled for in that randomization would most likely make the groups comparable on these dimensions prior to the study. Mortality rates can be examined to determine if differential losses may have occurred across groups, although again randomization would decrease the probability of differential mortality due to preexisting differences in subjects.

In many ways, the posttest-only control group design is the prototypical experimental design and most closely reflects the characteristics necessary to attribute a causal relationship from the independent variable to the dependent variable (Cook & Campbell, 1979). The difference between O_1 and O_2 reflects the degree to which treated subjects are different from untreated subjects at the end of the treatment period. Of course, the observed difference would need to be statistically significant (have statistical conclusion validity) to claim that the treatment indeed is effective.

In spite of the veridicality of the posttest-only design, many are reluctant to embrace this design. The primary concern is that because the dependent variable is examined only at the end of treatment, statements about actual change cannot be made. That is, there is no evidence to show whether the treatment group improved vis-à-vis their level of functioning prior to treatment. However, the central question is the comparison of the level of functioning of treated individuals (at O_1) with their level of functioning had they not been treated (O_2), not the change from pre- to posttreatment. The logic of experimentation does not require that pretreatment levels of functioning be assessed; thus, a pretest is not used.

One of the strengths of the posttest-only control group design, therefore, is that a pretest is unnecessary. Practically speaking, sometimes the repeated testing of subjects is bothersome to the subjects and expensive to the researcher in terms of time and effort. Furthermore, the absence of pretests obviates the need to collate the pretest and posttest scores and hence it may be possible to have subjects respond anonymously, thereby protecting the confidentiality of responses. Another advantage of the posttest-only control group design is that it eliminates pretest sensitization (which will be discussed more fully as a disadvantage to the pretest-posttest control group design).

WEAKNESSES. The absence of a pretest in this design can present some problems, some of which cannot be known before the research is conducted. The arguments for pretests are discussed along with the following design, the pretest-posttest control group design.

Although the posttest-only control group design is generally an internally valid experimental design, there are issues pertaining to external validity, namely the interaction of selection and the treatment (Campbell & Stanley, 1963). From an internal validity perspective, selection of subjects is not a threat because subjects are randomly assigned across groups. However, from an external validity perspective, it is often unknown whether the results of the study would generalize to another population. For example, it is possible that a treatment is effective (for example, a career-planning workshop) but only for the particular sample (for example, returning adults who have a broader set of work experiences). It may very well be that the career planning workshop is not at all effective for the typical 18-year-old freshman student. Or it may be that different samples of returning adults (for instance, in a community college versus a four-year university) might also respond very differently to the career-planning workshop. In short, the interaction between selection of a particular sample and the treatment is an issue that needs to be tested empirically, and again needs to be considered and acknowledged by the researcher.

Closely related is another threat to external validity, reactivity to the experimental situation. That is, subjects may react differently, perhaps in biased or socially desirable ways, because they are in an experiment, and thus again threaten the generalizability of the findings. The issues of reactivity and generalizability across populations are also threats to external validity of the pretest-posttest control group design, as well as many other designs. Because counseling is an applied field, we are especially concerned with external validity, and these and other threats to external validity merit serious consideration.

Finally, a practical issue pertaining to this design is that of timing. To adequately control for history effects, the investigator needs to conduct the experimental and control sessions simultaneously. Sometimes this requirement places excessive time and energy constraints on the experimenter. Nonetheless, history effects may not be controlled for if the experimenter conducts the two groups, let's say, one month apart. The greater the time differential between the group administrations, the greater the likelihood of confounding history effects.

AN EXAMPLE. A study examining stress management with math anxiety depicts the unique advantages of the posttest-only design. Sime, Ansorge, Olson, Parker, and Lukin (1987) were interested in examining whether combining cognitive and relaxation techniques would be an effective intervention for math anxiety, and ultimately to improve academic performance on an introductory statistics examination. The authors chose to conduct their research with students in a real-life testing situation; thus, participants were 56 students enrolled in an undergraduate statistics course. The authors randomly assigned the students to one of two groups, the treatment and the control group. Dependent measures included anxiety measured both before and after the exam, and actual performance on the statistics examination. Training for the experimental group consisted of three 15-minute training sessions, and focused on both relaxation and cognitive interventions. The control group did not receive any intervention and thus served as a no-treatment control group. The results suggested that the treatment intervention did lower subjects' ratings of anxiety both before and after the exam, but that it did not affect students' actual performance on the examination.

In this study, pretesting the subjects on the anxiety measures and an actual classroom examination would have demanded considerably more time of both subjects and researchers, but probably would not have added relevant information. Thus, the advantages of not administering a pretest allowed the researchers to add other features to their design, such as reversing the treatment conditions before the next examination. In addition, the study avoided the pretest sensitization threat to external validity.

Pretest-Posttest Control Group Design

Notationally, the pretest-posttest control group design is conceptualized as

$$R \ O_1 \ X \ O_2$$
$$R \ O_3 \quad O_4$$

This design involves the random assignment of subjects to two (or more) groups, with one group receiving treatment while the other group receives no treatment and thus serves as a control group. Both groups receive a pretest and a posttest. The purpose of the design is to test the effect of the independent variable, the X, which is reflected in the differences between O_2 and O_4.

STRENGTHS. This design controls for most of the threats to internal validity discussed by Campbell and Stanley (1963) and in that way is similar to the posttest-only control group design. The unique strength of this design pertains to the use of the pretest, which allows the researcher to perform various analyses that may be helpful in making valid inferences.

One of the most important reasons for giving a pretest is that pretest scores can be used to reduce variability in the dependent variable, thereby creating a more powerful statistical test. In essence, such a strategy attempts to minimize error variance, in line with the "MAXMINCON" principle. Much of the variance in any dependent variable is due to individual differences among the subjects. Knowledge of the pretest level of functioning allows the researcher to use statistical methods, such as the analysis of covariance, that remove the variance found in the pretest from the variance in the posttests. Such procedures can reduce drastically the number of subjects needed to achieve a desired level of statistical power (Porter & Raudenbush, 1987). Of course, the pretest in this case does not need to be the same measure as the posttest; however, it must be linearly related to the posttest to use an ordinary analysis of covariance. For example, in a study of covert desensitization, a measure of the degree to which subjects can produce imagery could be measured before treatment and be used as a covariate.

Another important reason to give a pretest is that it can be used to help eliminate post hoc threats to internal validity. In this regard, one strategic use of pretests is to compare subjects who drop out to those who remain. If more subjects drop out of the treatment group than from the control group, differential attrition is a particularly troublesome threat; however, if it is found based on pretest scores that those subjects who dropped out did not differ significantly from those who remained, concern about differential attrition is attenuated.

Pretests often are used to select or deselect subjects. For example, in a study on depression, the researchers may wish to select only those subjects who are in the moderately depressed range. Although selection is a primary reason to use a pretest in this example, determination should be made whether or not using the depression pretest as a covariate would be advisable.

Pretest scores can also be used to describe the subjects used in a study. For example, it would be important to describe the level of anxiety of undergraduate subjects in a study of test anxiety to determine whether or not the subjects were representative of those disabled by test anxiety.

Finally, the pretest-posttest scores allow the researcher to examine the individual performance of specific subjects. Kazdin (1980) suggests that in this way, researchers might examine those subjects who benefited the most versus the least from the treatment intervention. Identifying subjects in such a fashion, combined with anecdotal information the researcher has, may suggest hypotheses for future research. In short, the pretest provides additional information for researchers, and perhaps some clues for future research directions.

There are two often-stated advantages of pretests that are controversial. The first pertains to comparing posttest to pretest scores to determine the degree to which the treatment was beneficial. There are problems with making inferences from pretest measures to posttest measures, as will be illustrated with the three possible patterns of results portrayed in the graphs in Figure 5-1. The graphs depict three scenarios where the treatment group is statistically different at posttest from the control group. In Graph 1, the treated subjects scored higher than the control subjects on the posttest and treated subjects appear to have improved from the pretest whereas the controls have remained the same. In Graph 2, the treatment group was also superior on the posttest, but it appears that the treated subjects did not improve vis-à-vis the pretest. Finally, consider the third pattern of results (Graph 3), where the treatment group was superior to the control group at posttest and both groups' scores were higher at posttest than at pretest. It would appear that Graph 1 represents the clearest outcome, but this may be illusory due to several threats to internal validity that interfere with comparing pretest scores with posttest scores. The apparent improvement in Graph 1 for the treated subjects may be due to regression toward the mean, whereas the apparent lack of change of the control subjects actually may be a deterioration that was masked by regression toward the mean. In Graph 2, it appears that the treatment did result in improvement, but actually there was no change from pretest to posttest. If the subjects were deteriorating, as would be the case with a progressive dysfunction such as some anxiety disorders, then the control group shows the natural progression whereas the treatment successfully maintained the treated subjects' current level of functioning. However, this interpretation of Graph 2 cannot be made unambiguously because the pattern may also be due to a historical event, such as the announcement of mobilization for war, which would exacerbate anxiety disorders. The results for Graph 3 could be due to regression toward the mean, maturation, or spontaneous remission.

The point is that there are too many rival hypotheses to infer the degree to which treatment was effective by comparing pretest to posttest scores. For this reason, "gain scores" (differences from pretest to posttest) are typically not recommended for statistical analyses. Rather it is better for researchers to restrict themselves to making inferences only about differences at the posttest, because fewer threats are involved. Parenthetically, statisticians typically recommend using the pretest as a covariate in analyzing the posttest scores (see Huck & McLean, 1975). These techniques adjust or reduce error variance across individuals.

Another use of pretest scores is controversial. Recall that random assignment was a means to make the groups comparable. Clearly, the groups will not be exactly the same in all aspects; random error typically characterizes

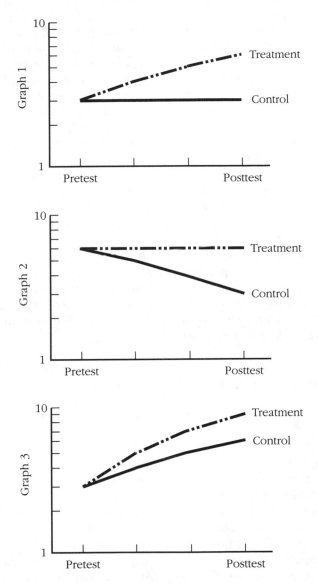

FIGURE 5-1
Three possible patterns of results for pretest-posttest control group design.

the process so that there are some differences between groups. Often there is a tendency to check whether or not random assignment succeeded; that is, to see whether or not the groups were indeed comparable. Accordingly, one often finds preliminary analyses of pretest scores to ascertain whether or not there are significant differences between the groups before treatment. However appealing this process is, there are some problems associated with it (Wampold & Drew, 1990). First, how big a difference is necessary to decide

whether random assignment failed? For small sample sizes, statistically significant differences between pretest scores are unlikely to be obtained; however,
this is exactly the instance where sampling error is most pernicious. Second,
pretest scores only represent possible differences on the particular characteristics measured; what about differences in age, gender, intelligence, education,
and a host of other factors? Third, if a large number of factors are compared
before treatment, by chance some differences will be found and it will be
unlikely that the researcher will ever conclude that random assignment succeeded. Finally, it should be remembered that statistical tests indicate the degree
to which the results may have occurred by chance (the significance level), and,
therefore, checking on sampling error is unnecessary. In short, it is important
to note that however appealing it is to check whether or not random assignment succeeded, there are some problems and controversial issues associated
with this procedure.

Parenthetically, if one wants to insure that a nuisance factor is evenly
distributed across the groups, another alternative is to use a matching procedure. For instance, to equate groups based on intelligence, subjects in the
treatment group and the control group should be matched on intelligence. This
process, and its advantages and disadvantages, are discussed in a following
section on dependent samples designs.

WEAKNESSES. It is perhaps ironic that the unique strength of the pretest-posttest
control group design, namely the pretest, is also the main weakness. It is often
assumed that pretesting will not sensitize subjects to a particular treatment.
In the two-group pretest-posttest control group design, the effect of repeatedly
administering a test to the treatment group (O_1 to O_2) is the same for the
control group (O_3 to O_4). Therefore, the effect of repeated testing is not a
threat to internal validity.

However, the pretest may have a potential sensitizing effect pertaining
to external validity, or generalizing the results from the study to other samples.
It is unclear if any changes found at posttest might be due to the groups' being
sensitized by the pretest. That is, it is unclear if the same effect of X on O_2
would be found again without the sensitizing effect of O_1. For example, a
pretest questionnaire on attitudes about rape might cue subjects not only to
reflect on this topic, but also to process information differently in the ensuing
treatment, an awareness-enhancing workshop about date rape. Although the
treatment may or may not have an impact by itself, the interactive effects of
the pretest may result in substantially greater changes at posttest. A real problem
could result if practitioners implemented the workshop, but without the
pretest, and thus had a much weaker treatment effect than they thought they
would have. When researchers use the pretest-posttest control group design,
they need to be cautious in generalizing the results of the study, and they need
to explicitly discuss this sensitization issue.

AN EXAMPLE. A study by Nezu (1986) nicely depicts the pretest-posttest control
group design. In the mid 1980s, research was consistently finding relationships

between problem solving and depression, as well as psychological health in general. However, very little outcome research had been conducted to systematically evaluate the efficacy of a problem-solving approach for the treatment of depression (for more background see D'Zurilla, 1986; Nezu, Nezu, & Perri, 1989). In Nezu's study, 26 individuals who were diagnosed as experiencing nonpsychotic, unipolar depression were randomly assigned to one of three conditions: problem-solving therapy (PST), problem-focused therapy (PFT), and a waiting list control group (WLC). The design can be depicted as follows:

$$R \; O_1 \; X_{pst} \; O_2 \; O_3$$
$$R \; O_4 \; X_{pft} \; O_5 \; O_6$$
$$R \; O_7 \; X_{wlc} \; O_8 \; O_9$$

Note that Nezu used two treatment groups in addition to the control group; such a variation of the pretest-posttest control group design allowed Nezu to not only compare the treatment groups to the control group, but also to compare the treatment groups to each other. Also note that Nezu used a follow-up procedure to assess the impact of the training over time (O_3, O_6, O_9). Follow-up data can be extremely valuable, but often can be difficult to obtain because it can be difficult to locate subjects, or the subjects may not be motivated to respond to the assessments. The PST treatment was based on a systematic model of social problem solving emphasizing five components: problem orientation, problem definition and formulation, generation of alternatives, decision making, and solution implementation and verification. The PFT treatment was conceptualized as a traditional group therapy approach. Subjects were administered the Beck Depression Inventory (BDI: Beck, Ward, Mendelson, Mock, & Erbaugh, 1961), the Problem Solving Inventory (PSI: Heppner & Petersen, 1982), the Depression scale of the Minnesota Multiphasic Personality Inventory (MMPI-D: Hathaway & McKinley, 1967), and the Internal-External Locus of Control Scale (I-E, Rotter, 1966); these instruments were administered at both pretest and posttest. Since questions have been raised about the long-term effects of problem-solving training, Nezu extended the design by also including a six-month follow-up where he administered the same instruments again. Treatment was conducted over eight weeks, with hour-and-a-half weekly sessions. Nezu did check on whether random assignment succeeded by doing preliminary analyses on the pretest scores (O_1 versus O_4 versus O_7). In these preliminary analyses, Nezu found that the groups did not differ on any of the dependent variables at the pretest. Thus, at least with regard to these variables, random assignment was successful. The results indicated that PST subjects had significantly lower posttreatment depression scores than either the PFT or WLC groups (O_2 versus O_5 versus O_8). This improvement was found to have been maintained at the six-month follow-up. Parenthetically, Nezu also found that decreases in depression covaried with concurrent increases in perceived problem-solving effectiveness and the adoption of an internal-locus-of-control orientation.

The results of this study provided very useful information about problem-solving training. The pretest-posttest control group design was useful to check the adequacy of the random assignment of clients (but only with regard to the dependent variables) as well as changes in the dependent variables. Nezu varied the basic design by adding another treatment group, which then allowed him to compare the efficacy of the treatment groups as well. Comparisons with existing treatments (such as traditional group therapy) provide a kind of benchmark that often helps to evaluate the usefulness of a new treatment program. The six-month follow-up added an extremely useful piece of information about more long-term benefits of training; such follow-up data is typically difficult to obtain but often does provide very useful data.

Solomon Four-Group Design

When there is a desire to use a pretest but there is a concern about the effect that the pretest may have on the subjects (such as test-by-treatment interaction), the Solomon four-group design is appropriate. Notationally, this design is conceptualized as follows:

$$
\begin{array}{llll}
R & O_1 & X & O_2 \\
R & O_3 &   & O_4 \\
R &   & X & O_5 \\
R &   &   & O_6 \\
\end{array}
$$

This design is a combination of the pretest-posttest control group design (first two groups in the diagram) and the posttest-only control group design (last two groups). The main purpose of this design is to examine potential effects of the pretest, which is one of the main weaknesses or unknowns of the pretest-posttest control group design.

STRENGTHS. In terms of internal validity, this design controls for most threats to internal validity. The Solomon four-group design contains the strengths of both the pretest-posttest control group and the posttest-only control group designs. The unique strength of the Solomon four-group design is that it explicitly examines the potential sensitizing effect of the pretest as it might interact with the treatment, X. The researcher can easily test for pretest sensitization by comparing O_2 to O_5, the only difference between these observations being the pretest prior to the treatment for O_2. Thus, this design is useful if the investigator not only wants to test the effect of some treatment, X, but also wants to examine whether the pretest sensitizes subjects to the treatment.

Another strength of this design is that it inherently includes a replication test of the treatment intervention. That is, if there is a significant treatment effect found when comparing O_2 to O_4, this design allows the researcher to examine whether this treatment effect will be replicated by comparing O_5 versus O_6. If the researcher finds a treatment effect in both cases, the results of the study will be considerably stronger because the treatment has been found to be effective across two trials. In this way, the replication results will enhance the generalizability of the treatment, and thus the external validity of the study.

WEAKNESSES. The major drawback to using this design is that it costs the investigator a great deal in terms of time, energy, and resources. In essence, the Solomon four-group design contains the two prior designs (pretest-posttest control group and posttest-only control group), which means that the experimenter is almost conducting two investigations. The Solomon four-group design is especially costly if the treatment, X, is long and a rather complex intervention. Such treatments often require considerable effort, such as training therapists (perhaps prior to each treatment session), preparing training materials, and obtaining financial compensation for therapists. Many times ethical considerations are involved in the intervention, particularly with regard to the control group, such as withholding treatment from this group during part or all of the research study. A common option is to offer treatment to control subjects after the experiment is over; it is important to plan on this additional cost (that is, additional service delivery for two more groups of subjects).

AN EXAMPLE. Our examination of the professional journals revealed that the Solomon four-group design is used infrequently in counseling research. A study by Dixon, Heppner, Petersen, and Ronning (1979) depicts most of the major elements of the Solomon four-group design. In the mid-1970s the utility of training clients in some sort of problem-solving method was unclear, and there were many unanswered research questions. The investigators wanted to assess the effects of problem-solving training in general, but also wanted to test the effects of pretesting. Because of costs involved, the Solomon design was modified and subjects were assigned to one of three groups: a pretest-posttest treatment group, a pretest-posttest control group, and a posttest-only control group. Treatment consisted of didactic presentations, group discussions, and directed practice in five hour-and-a-half sessions that were designed for systematic training in five stages of problem solving (problem definition, goal selection, strategy selection, strategy implementation, and evaluation). The investigators used dependent variables such as the generation of alternatives, decision-making skill, and subjects' perceptions of their problem-solving skills. The results indicated that training did influence the quality of responses but did not necessarily increase the number of alternatives. However, it was also found that the treatment group only differed from the posttest-only control group, and did not differ from the pretest-posttest control group. These results suggested a practice effect; simply taking the dependent measure twice resulted in the same outcome as the treatment. Subjects participating in the workshop also described themselves as using fewer impulsive behaviors during the problem-solving process than the control subjects.

The value of the Solomon design in this particular study is rather compelling. By using two control groups, the authors were able to isolate the effects of training as well as the practice effects. Erroneous conclusions might well have been drawn if only a posttest-only control group design or a pretest-posttest control group design had been used.

Use of Control Groups

To this point, the designs discussed have included a control group. The expressed purpose of this arrangement is to compare treated subjects with non-treated subjects. In this way, the effect of the treatment vis-à-vis no treatment can be determined. However, the use of control groups is oftentimes precluded. For instance, it is unethical to withhold treatment from subjects who are in need of treatment and who have a condition for which a treatment is known to work. For example, it would be unethical to have a control group of suicidal clients in a study of a new crisis-intervention technique. Furthermore, the research question may not refer to the absence of a treatment. For example, a study by Malkiewich and Merluzzi (1980) examined within conceptual-level theory the relative effectiveness of matching client conceptual level with treatments (desensitization, and rational restructuring) differing in structure. To examine this matching question, a control group is not needed; inclusion of a control group, however, would answer the additional question of whether either of these two treatments is more effective than no treatment.

Although some research questions do not call for control groups, the logic of much research dictates the use of a control group. *Control group* refers generically to a class of groups that do not receive one of the active treatments in the study. The *no-treatment control group* receives no treatment. It should be realized that this implies that the researchers do not provide any treatment, although we know that subjects in such groups often seek treatment elsewhere (for example, Frank, 1961; Gurin, Veroff, & Feld, 1960).

Often it is practically and ethically difficult to have a group that does not receive any treatment. However, a viable control condition can be obtained by using a *waiting-list control group*. Typically, subjects are randomly assigned to the treatment condition and to the waiting-list control group; at the end of the treatment phase and the posttests, the treatment is made available to the subjects in the waiting-list control group. (If more than two treatments were studied, the subjects might be given the choice of the available treatments, or the one that proved most effective.) In either the pretest-posttest control group design or the posttest-only control group design, the treatment given to the waiting-list subjects is not part of the design, but may be analyzed anyway to strengthen the results (Kazdin, 1980) or to rule out threats to validity of quasi-experimental designs (Cook & Campbell, 1979). One disadvantage of the waiting-list control group is that long-term follow-up of the control subjects is precluded (because they have by then received treatment). Another disadvantage is that although ultimately the subjects in the waiting-list control group receive treatment, the treatment is withheld for some time.

Another type of control group is the *placebo control group*. Subjects in a placebo control group are led to believe that they are receiving a viable treatment, although the services rendered them are nonspecific and supposedly ineffective. For example, in a group counseling outcome study, subjects in the placebo condition may be in a discussion group with no active group counseling. The rationale for including a placebo control is that it enables separating out the specific effects of a treatment from effects due to client expectations, attention, and other nonspecific aspects. There are those who think that the major effects of counseling process are due to nonspecific factors (for example, Frank, 1961); inclusion of a placebo control group allows determination of whether the effects of a treatment are greater than those obtained under conditions that appear to clients to be viable but do not contain the major aspects of the active treatments. One commonly used placebo is the subconscious reconditioning placebo (SRP). Subjects are told that the SRP reconditions the subconscious by using subliminal messages, when actually nonsense syllables are presented. Subjects believe they are receiving a viable treatment; in fact, SRP has been found to be as effective as other treatments in the areas of smoking cessation (Sipich, Russell, & Tobias, 1974), test anxiety (Russell & Lent, 1982), and speech anxiety (Lent, Russell, & Zamostny, 1981). Of course, inclusion of a no-treatment or a waiting-list control group with a placebo control group strengthens the design considerably because differences between the placebo and no-treatment control groups gives an estimate of the strength of the effect of nonspecific factors.

A final type of control group is the *matched control group.* Subjects in the matched control group are paired in some way with subjects in the treatment group. Although the primary purpose of this type of design is to reduce variance due to a matching factor (and will be discussed later in this chapter under dependent group designs), one application of this design is worth mentioning here. Length of counseling is often a troublesome variable in outcome studies. If the length of treatment is constrained to a given length of time, the treatment may not adequately represent the real way in which the treatment is delivered, reducing the construct validity of the independent variable. However, if the treatment is allowed to vary from one client to another as determined on a case-by-case basis, the timing of the posttest for the control subjects is problematic. That is, if the treatment lasts from 7 to 20 weeks and the posttest is administered immediately following termination, when should the posttest be administered to the control subjects? The matched control group design solves this problem by administering the posttest to a control subject at the same time the posttest is administered to his or her paired subject in the treatment group, thereby holding time of treatment constant over the treatment and the control groups.

Factorial Designs

Factorial designs are used when two or more independent variables are employed simultaneously to study their independent and interactive effects on a dependent variable. It is cumbersome initially to relate factorial designs to the three between-group designs previously discussed; basically, factorial designs are extensions of these earlier designs, namely by the addition of independent variables. Whereas previously we used the notation of Campbell and Stanley, with factorial designs it is more useful to visualize the design by diagramming the levels of the independent variables into cells. For example, if a study were examining three levels of an independent variable, there would be three cells, diagrammed like this:

The scores on the dependent variables are conceptualized as being placed in each of the cells. If there were 30 subjects (10 subjects per cell), there would be 10 scores for each dependent variable in each cell.

In the Nezu (1986) study previously discussed, the design was a pretest-posttest control group design with three levels of the independent variable, problem-solving treatment. This design could also be diagrammed as follows:

Let's suppose that Nezu was curious about how gender of the participants might affect their reactions to the treatments. Perhaps he had observed some female subjects reacting more favorably, or had had some other experiences that led him to hypothesize that females might respond more favorably to the treatments than males. Therefore, we have a situation where there are now two independent variables of interest, the problem-solving treatments and the gender of the participants. The dependent variables could be the same as before: BDI, MMPI-D, PSI, and I-E. Subjects could be randomly assigned to the treatment conditions (a manipulated variable) but obviously not to the gender conditions (an attribute variable). Subject assignment therefore must be altered slightly, perhaps by first assigning females at random to the treatment/control cells, and then randomly assigning males to the treatment/control cells. The cells for these two independent variables would be diagrammed like this:

	Treatments		
	PST	PFT	Control
Males			
Females			

Gender

This design is verbally described as a 2 (gender: males versus females) × 3 (treatment: PST, PFT, and control group) design, which results in six cells. (Conversely, if there were two independent variables that each had three levels, the design would be a 3 × 3 design and have 9 cells.) It is important to note that this 2 × 3 hypothetical study is essentially a pretest-posttest control group design, but now we have two independent variables.

STRENGTHS. The unique strength or advantage of the factorial design is that it does test the effects of two or more independent variables, and their interaction with each other, on the dependent variable. The factorial design provides more information than the single-independent-variable designs because it simultaneously tests two or more variables. In our hypothetical study, the researcher could examine whether the levels of problem-solving training have an effect on the dependent variables, as well as whether the subject gender has an effect on the dependent variables. (The effect of an independent variable on a dependent variable is often referred to as a main effect.) Because of the efficiency of such simultaneous tests in factorial designs, it is not uncommon for researchers to test two, three, or even four independent variables in one study. Usually these added independent variables are person (personality) variables. For example, Kivlighan, Hageseth, Tipton, and McGovern (1981) examined how Holland type (Holland, 1985, 1987) interacted with treatments that varied in terms of the amount of interpersonal involvement. More important, factorial designs allow the investigator to examine the interaction of the independent variables. An interaction means that the effect of one of the independent variables depends on the level of one of the other independent variables. In our hypothetical example, the investigator could examine whether the effects of gender interact with the effects of treatment. For example, the researcher might find that one of the treatments does not have the same effect on all participants, but that it results in more favorable responses with females than male subjects. Thus, factorial designs not only result in more information because they examine the effects of more than one independent variable, factorial designs also result in more complex information about the combined effects of the independent variables.

Another advantage of factorial designs is that if the independent variable added to the design is related to the dependent variable as expected, then the unexplained variance in the dependent variable is reduced. Reducing unexplained variance is again related to Kerlinger's "MAXMINCON," which in essence increases the power of the statistical test for analyzing factorial design (for example, in the analysis of variance, the denominator of the F ratio is reduced).

In a way, our fictitious example indicates how the factorial design can provide important qualifications about relationships between variables. The factorial design provides some answers about the conditions in which a treatment may operate, such as the gender of participants, the type of therapist, the age of clients, or the problem-solving style of clients. Whereas the single-variable study most often investigates whether a variable (most notably some treatment) has any effect, the factorial design examines more complex questions that approximate the complexity of real life.

WEAKNESSES.   While at first one might think the more information, the better, it is important to realize the costs involved as more variables are added to designs. With the addition of variables, the results of the study become more complex. In a 2 × 2 design, the researcher would typically examine the main effects of variable A, the main effects of variable B, and the interaction of A with B. In a 2 (A) × 2 (B) × 3 (C) design, the investigator would typically examine the main effects of variables A, B, C; the two-way interactions of A with B and B with C; and the three-way interaction of A, B, and C. Complex interactions between three, four, or more independent variables typically are difficult to interpret and the results of the study may be unclear. Researchers should not add independent variables just to have more than one independent variable, but rather independent variables should be carefully selected on theoretical and empirical grounds after thought is given to the research questions of interest.

   Another disadvantage of the factorial design is the flip side of an advantage. If additional independent variables are added to the design and these variables turn out to be unrelated to the dependent variable, then the power of the statistical test may be reduced rather than increased.

AN EXAMPLE.   A study by Stein and Stone (1978) is a frequently cited investigation that used a factorial design. These researchers were interested in assessing the utility of a conceptual-level (CL) matching model in the initial phase of counseling. Conceptual level has been described in terms of personality development, and related to both cognitive complexity and interpersonal maturity (Harvey, Hunt, & Schroder, 1961). In general, the CL matching model generally predicts an inverse relation between CL and degree of structure preferred. Thus, low CL people profit more from a highly structured environment while high CL people benefit more from a less structured environment. In essence, Stein and Stone sought to determine if these relationships between CL and structure would occur in counseling. They used a 2 (client conceptual level: high versus low) × 2 (counselor-offered structure: high versus low) × 2 (interviewers: A versus B) design to compare the effects of matching in a 40-minute counseling interview. They predicted that matched persons (low CL, high structure; high CL, low structure) would respond better than mismatched persons (low CL, low structure; high CL, high structure). No differences were expected across interviewers, and none were found; still, the authors tested the effects of this variable to determine if there might be any systematic bias due to the interviewers themselves. Dependent measures included client participation, client self-disclosure, client satisfaction, and perceived counselor helpfulness and understanding. Although the results did not totally support their hypotheses, their results clearly suggested that CL did interact with counselor-offered structure to produce some of the predictable effects of client verbal behavior, perceptions of the counselor, and satisfaction with counseling. The authors interpreted their results as suggesting that it may be important for the counselor to alter his or her interviewing style to capitalize on the apparent strengths or preferences of each client. In sum, this study nicely depicts one advantage of a factorial design—namely, testing the interaction between two variables. In this study, the interaction between CL and counselor-offered structure was predicted and, in general, supported.

Subject Assignment

Because the basic purpose of the between-groups design is to make comparisons between subjects from different groups, it is critical that the people in the groups do not differ in important ways before the experiment or measurement begins. Subject assignment is also predicated on subject selection, which pertains to external validity. That is, a researcher might satisfactorily assign undergraduate students to one of four group conditions (subject assignment), but the results might not be generalizable to counseling center clients (a subject selection issue).

The intended outcome of assigning people to groups is to eliminate systematic differences across groups before the experiment so that if any changes are detected in one or more of the groups after the experiment, the change can be attributed to the independent variable. Subjects therefore need to be assigned to groups in an unbiased fashion and free from extraneous variables.

The most effective way of insuring comparable groups is to assign subjects to groups so that each subject has the same probability of being assigned to each group. Such assignment tends to equalize both known and unknown sources of subject variation across groups so that extraneous variables will not bias the study.

A number of procedures exist for randomly assigning subjects to groups; the most common method is to use a table of random numbers to determine the order of assigning subjects to groups. For example, if a researcher had four groups, subjects could be randomly assigned by the order that the numbers 1, 2, 3, and 4 appear consecutively in the list of numbers (for example, 4, 1, 4, 2, 2, 3, 1, and so on). Numbers other than 1 through 4 would be ignored. Thus, the first subject would be assigned to group 4, the next to group 1, the third to group 4, and so on. In short, such a procedure would reduce the probability of systematic biases or variations in subjects between groups.

Note that random assignment would most likely result in unequal numbers of subjects in each of the four groups. Statistically speaking it is better to have equal numbers across groups. To deal with this issue, Kazdin (1980) suggested assigning subjects in blocks, or in the preceding example, in blocks of four subjects. Within each block of four subjects, the experimenter would simply randomly assign one subject to each of the four groups. This procedure is particularly useful when subjects begin the experiment periodically, or at different times.

In counseling research, a researcher will often have a total sample identified and available at the beginning of an investigation. For example, a researcher might have available 20 people who have expressed an interest in some kind of treatment group, such as assertiveness training or group therapy. In this situation, the investigator knows the total number of subjects, their names, and general characteristics such as age and gender. Underwood (1966) has labeled this type of subject pool as captive. In this situation, random assignment is easily accomplished at one time via a random table or even by drawing names from a hat. Quite often in counseling research, however, we do not have the entire sample at the outset, but rather must engage in sequential assignment (Underwood, 1966). For example, imagine that a researcher is investigating the effect of two types of precounseling information on client expectations of therapy. Most counseling centers have only a few clients beginning therapy each day, which would necessitate randomly assigning clients to the two types of precounseling information each day. In this case, clients can be assigned to either treatment as they enter counseling via some sort of randomization process.

Does randomization *always* result in equivalent groups? No. Random assignment refers to a method of assigning subjects in a bias-free manner; the method should be considered distinctly different from the outcome or results. Randomization distributes subjects, and thus extraneous variables, by chance across the researcher's groups. Because randomization distributes by chance, it is possible that by chance some extraneous variable will not be distributed equally across groups.

Consider a study conducted on ways to enhance the problem-solving effectiveness of college students (Heppner, Baumgardner, Larson, & Petty, 1988). Subjects were randomly assigned to two groups, a treatment group and a delayed-treatment group. Four instruments were used as pretest-posttest measures: the Problem Solving Inventory (PSI: Heppner & Petersen, 1982), the Level of Problem Solving Skills Estimate Form (LPSSEF: Heppner, 1979), the Ways of Coping Scale (WCS: Folkman & Lazarus, 1980), and the Mooney Problem Checklist (MPC: Mooney & Gordon, 1950). Given the random assignment of subjects, one would typically expect the two groups to be equivalent on the four pretest measures. Statistical analyses of the pretest measures revealed no significant differences on the PSI, LPSSEF, and WCS; however, the delayed-treatment group had significantly lower scores on the MPC. In this case randomization did not result in totally equivalent groups. Thus, sampling error can exist even when one uses randomization. Randomization simply *decreases the probability* of creating differences in groups due to sampling errors.

Dependent Samples Designs

One of the concerns raised in this chapter was with regard to whether or not random assignment equated groups adequately on some factor, such as intelligence or pretest level of psychological functioning. Implicit in this concern is the assumption that the factors identified are important factors in the study— that is, intelligence or level of psychological functioning are important variables in the study. Importance in this context can be defined in two ways.

First, the factor may be theoretically important to understanding the phenomenon under investigation. In this case, the factor should be examined for its own sake. For example, if intelligence is thought to be an important variable theoretically, then it should be included as an independent variable in a factorial design. In this way, the effects of intelligence as well as the effects of the interaction of intelligence with the treatments (or other independent variables) can be determined.

If the factor is not interesting for its own sake, it is labeled a nuisance factor. Although a nuisance factor is not examined explicitly (that is, by inclusion as an independent variable in a factorial design), it remains an important consideration in the design of an experiment. For example, pretest level of functioning may not be interesting to the researcher in the sense that the effectiveness of treatment for clients at different levels of psychological functioning is not a burning research question. Nevertheless, it is desirable to have the treatment and control groups comparable on psychological functioning. A particularly useful way to accomplish this goal is to match subjects on the basis of their pretest scores and then to randomly assign one of the matched subjects to the treatment group and the remaining subject to the control group, as illustrated in Table 5-1. Thus the two samples are dependent. In this way, the researcher can be relatively certain that levels of psychological functioning are comparable across the two groups. More important, if the nuisance factor is related to the dependent variable as expected, then the variance in the dependent variable can be removed from the variance in the outcome variable, resulting in a more powerful statistical test (Wampold & Drew, 1990). The typical statistical test for this type of design is the dependent samples t test (sometimes called the paired t test or correlated t test).

Essentially, the dependent samples t test accomplishes the same purpose as the analysis of covariance—that is, to reduce unexplained variance and yield a more powerful test. The analysis of covariance does not require that subjects be matched, and the reduction in unexplained variance is accomplished statistically. In the dependent samples t test, the reduction is accomplished by the design of the experiment. The dependent samples design reduces uncertainty

T A B L E 5-1
Assignment of Subjects to Treatment and Control Groups in a Dependent Samples Design

Pairs of Subjects	Treatment		Control
1	S_{11}	is matched with	S_{12}
2	S_{21}	is matched with	S_{22}
3	S_{31}	is matched with	S_{32}
–	–		–
–	–		–
–	–		–
N	S_{n1}	is matched with	S_{n2}

Note: Paired subjects have comparable scores on pretest.

by matching comparable subjects. Two subjects who have high pretest scores are also likely to have high posttest scores; difference in posttest scores for these two matched subjects is due presumably to the treatment (and other uncontrolled factors).

Dependent samples can be accomplished in other ways as well. Often natural pairs, such as monozygotic twins, are used. Because monozygotic twins have identical genetic materials, using such pairs holds all hereditary factors constant. Other natural pairs include litter mates (not often applicable to counseling researchers), marital partners, siblings, and so forth.

Another means to create dependent samples is to measure the subject in more than one condition. Although this is difficult to accomplish in the treatment and control conditions, consider two treatments, say for increasing the degree to which subjects use a computerized career exploration software. Each subject would be exposed to one of the treatments (for example, token reinforcement for use of the system) and use of the system assessed; then the subject would receive the other treatment (for example, social reinforcement for use of the system) and use of the system assessed. Of course, the order of the treatments would need to be randomized. In this way, all nuisance factors are controlled because the subject serves as his or her own control. Such a design is called a repeated measures design and contains many of the aspects of the within-subjects design discussed in the next section.

The idea of two dependent samples can be expanded to include more than two groups (for example, two treatment groups and a control group). Typically, the dependency is created by matching or by repeated measures (it is a bit difficult to find enough monozygotic triplets for such a study!). For example, Haupt (1990) was interested in counseling students on religious issues; he had reason to believe that the type of counselor responses to a client's religious statements would affect how the client perceived the counselor's expertness, attractiveness, and trustworthiness. Haupt believed that subjects' beliefs about Christianity would most likely affect how subjects would react to the counselor responses. In considering assigning subjects to one of three group conditions, Haupt decided to force group equivalency on this attitudinal variable. Consequently, as he assigned subjects to one of the three groups, he first identified three subjects who had identical scores on a scale measuring beliefs about Christianity, and then randomly assigned each of these subjects to a different group. As a result, subjects had identical scores on their beliefs about Christianity across each of the three groups. When more than two subjects are matched and assigned to conditions, the design is called a randomized block design. Each group of matched subjects is called a block and the subjects within blocks are randomly assigned to conditions. The randomized block design is typically analyzed with a mixed model analysis of variance (see Wampold & Drew, 1990).

In sum, matching is a method to control for a nuisance factor that is believed or known to have an effect on the dependent variable. Dependent samples designs are powerful tools for increasing the power of statistical tests. Properly used, these designs can enable the researcher to accomplish the same purpose with far fewer subjects. Unfortunately, dependent sample designs are underused in counseling research.

One final note. Many times in counseling research, randomly assigning subjects to groups is not possible. For example, ethical problems would arise if a researcher tried to randomly assign clients to therapists with different levels of counseling experience, such as beginning practicum, advanced practicum, doctoral-level interns, and senior staff psychologists. It is quite likely that a client with complex psychological problems would be assigned to an inexperienced therapist who was ill-equipped to work therapeutically with such a client. In such applied situations, randomization may well introduce more practical problems than it solves experimentally. Sometimes researchers will attempt to show that clients are equivalent (matched) on several dimensions such as age, gender, presenting problem, and personality variables. Matching in this type of post hoc fashion can rule out some dimensions in comparing clients, but it is important to realize that many variables, known or unknown, are simply left uncontrolled. Thus, a weakness of such field designs is that unknown variables may confound the relationships among the variables being investigated.

WITHIN-SUBJECTS DESIGNS

The remainder of this chapter examines within-subjects designs. Remember that the hallmark of the within-subjects design is that it attempts to minimize error variance due to individual variation by having each subject serve as his or her own control. Similar to the between-groups design, subjects are randomly assigned to groups or treatments and independent variables are manipulated. The unique feature of the within-subjects design is that all subjects are exposed to all of the treatment conditions; random assignment involves assigning people to different sequences of treatment. In this section we first provide an overview of two types of within-subjects designs: crossovers and Latin Square designs. We then discuss the strengths and limitations of the traditional within-subjects design.

Crossover Designs

Suppose a researcher wanted to compare the effects of two treatments—test interpretation of the Strong Campbell Interest Inventory (SCII) and work genograms—on a dependent variable, vocational clients' career maturity. The researcher could use the following within-subjects design:

$$O_1 \quad X_1 \quad O_2 \quad X_2 \quad O_3$$

O_1, O_2, and O_3 represent different observations—in this case, administration of a career maturity inventory (let's say the Career Maturity Inventory: Crites,

1978). X_1 represents the test interpretation treatment and X_2 represents the genogram treatment. This is called a crossover design; all subjects are switched (that is, crossed over) to another experimental condition usually halfway through the study. Let's say that the researcher conducted this study with 20 vocationally undecided adults as diagrammed. Suppose the researcher found significantly more change in career maturity between O_2 and O_3 than between O_1 and O_2 ($p < .01$); could he or she conclude that genograms are better at promoting career maturity than test interpretation? This conclusion would be quite tenuous because of the threats to internal validity embedded in this design, such as history (events may have happened to the subjects between the administrations), maturation (normal development may have occurred), order effects (that is, maybe genogram treatments are more effective if they are presented as a second treatment), or sequence effects (that is, maybe the genogram treatment is effective only if it follows and perhaps adds to a SCII test interpretation). In point of fact, a major difficulty in the within-subjects design is the possibility of confounding order or sequence effects.

How might the researcher control these threats to internal validity? One of the primary mechanisms used to control such threats is counterbalancing. Counterbalancing involves "balancing" the order of the conditions. The following is a diagram of a counterbalanced crossover design:

$$R \quad O_1 \quad X_1 \quad O_2 \quad X_2 \quad O_3$$
$$R \quad O_4 \quad X_2 \quad O_5 \quad X_1 \quad O_6$$

The R's in the design indicate that subjects are randomly assigned to two groups. The X_1 and X_2 in the diagram represent the two treatments again and the O's represent the different observation periods. O_1 and O_4 designate a pretesting assessment, O_2 and O_5 represent an assessment at the crossover point, while O_3 and O_6 indicate testing at the end of the experiment. Thus, the groups only differ in the order in which they receive the treatments. In this case, counterbalancing also controls for sequence effects: X_1 precedes X_2 once, as X_2 precedes X_1 once.

It is important to be aware of two issues with regard to counterbalancing. First, the researcher can now use some simple statistical procedures to determine if the order of the treatment conditions made any difference vis-à-vis the dependent variables. For example, a simple t test can be conducted on O_2 versus O_6 to determine if the treatment X_1 resulted in differential effects depending on whether the treatment was administered first or second. A similar t test can be conducted on O_3 versus O_5 for treatment X_2. These analyses are important for the researcher to conduct not only for the present research but also for future researchers to know about order or sequence effects. A second issue is that even if there is an order effect, it can be argued that these effects are "balanced" or equal for both treatments (given the preceding example), and thus order effects are controlled.

Stiles, Shapiro, and Firth-Cozens (1988) used a counterbalanced crossover design to examine differences in session evaluation and client postsession mood for an interpersonal-psychodynamic treatment and a cognitive-behavioral treatment. Of the 40 clients studied, 19 were randomly assigned to receive eight sessions of interpersonal-psychodynamic treatment followed by eight sessions of cognitive-behavioral treatment. The remaining 21 clients first received eight sessions of cognitive-behavioral treatment followed by eight sessions of interpersonal-psychodynamic treatment. Session evaluation and postsession mood (both client and counselor ratings) were assessed by having the client, counselor, and external raters fill out a Session Evaluation Questionnaire (Stiles, 1980) for each session. Results showed that counselors and external raters saw interpersonal-psychodynamic sessions as significantly more powerful (that is, deep) and uncomfortable (that is, rough) than cognitive-behavioral sessions. Likewise, clients rated the interpersonal-psychodynamic sessions as significantly more uncomfortable (that is, rough), and their post-session mood was significantly more positive following cognitive-behavioral sessions. Finally, external raters saw counselors' moods as more positive following cognitive-behavioral sessions. It is also important to note that Stiles et al. (1988) found no evidence for carryover effects (that is, one treatment affecting the rating of another treatment).

Latin Square Designs

A second type of within-subjects design is the "Latin Square" design. As the number of treatments being compared increases, the counterbalancing of treatment order and sequence becomes increasingly complex. The critical issue is insuring that all treatments are "balanced" or presented in the same ordinal position (that is, first, second, third) with the same frequency (for example, three times). How should the researcher decide on the order of treatments? Let's say a researcher wanted to compare three treatments (X_1, X_2, and X_3), using a within-subjects design. He or she could randomly assign the order of treatments for each subject. The problem with random assignment is that with a large number of subjects, the treatment order normally balances out—that is, an equal number of subjects receive the X_1 treatment first, second, and third (likewise for X_2 and X_3). But with a small number of subjects, there can be large discrepancies in the distribution of treatments. For example, with 12 subjects, let's say 8 of these subjects are randomly assigned to receive treatment X_1 at the first point in the sequence, and 4 receive X_2 first, but no one receives X_3 first. Thus, X_2 and X_3 would not be presented first with the same frequency as X_1. This is critical because a number of studies have shown that treatments given first are more effective (Morrison & Shapiro, 1987).

   The researcher can guard against such an imbalance by predetermining a set sequence of treatments that is balanced for order and then randomly assigning clients to a particular order of treatments. A Latin Square is a way of predetermining the order of treatments. The major characteristic of a Latin Square is that each treatment appears in each ordinal position. The following is an example of a Latin Square design for three treatments, X_1, X_2, and X_3.

Group	Order of Treatment		
	1st	*2nd*	*3rd*
1	X_1	X_2	X_3
2	X_3	X_1	X_2
3	X_2	X_3	X_1

The one problem with the Latin Square design is that the particular sequence of treatments cannot be controlled (or assessed statistically). In the preceding design, for instance, treatment X_1 never directly follows treatment X_2. Because all possible sequences are not represented in the Latin Square, it is not possible to entirely rule out this type of sequence effect as a rival hypothesis. This problem is usually considered minor, however, compared to order effects.

Hermansson, Webster, and McFarland (1988) used a Latin Square design to examine the effects of counselor deliberate postural lean on levels of communicated empathy, respect, and intensity. They manipulated three levels of the independent variable, postural lean (forward, backward, and counselor's choice). Each counselor conducted three consecutive sessions with a different client. For the first 9 minutes of an 18-minute session, the counselor was seated upright, then for the next 9 minutes each counselor leaned forward, backward, or counselor's choice. The particular order of forward, backward, or choice was determined by the Latin Square. Each counselor was randomly assigned to a particular sequence. The results of this study suggested a compensatory process between deliberate counselor lean and verbal communication. Specifically, a required forward lean was associated with decreased levels of intensity and empathy while a required backward lean showed a significant increase in the levels of intensity and empathy. There were no significant effects for the choice condition.

Strengths and Limitations

At least six factors specific to the design itself can affect the appropriateness of a within-subjects design for a particular research question. These six factors are (1) experimental control, (2) statistical power, (3) time, (4) order and sequence effects, (5) measurement issues, and (6) restriction of certain independent variables.

Experimental Control

The traditional within-subjects design is potentially a powerful design because of its reliance on random assignment of treatments and manipulation of independent variables. The experimenter can often obtain a great deal of experimental control with this design, and the threats to internal validity tend to be low with a counterbalance crossover design. Moreover, the within-subjects design tends to minimize error variance due to normal individual variability by using each subject as his or her own control. The reduction of individual error variance is a noteworthy advantage of the within-subjects design, and merits consideration when the researcher is especially concerned about such error.

Statistical Power

Because each subject receives all levels of the independent variable, there are also some advantages from a statistical perspective. In general, a researcher can use half the number of subjects in a counterbalanced crossover design and still retain the same statistical power as in the between-subjects design (see Kerlinger, 1986, for a more complete statistical discussion of this matter).

Time

Although a within-subjects design can use fewer subjects to obtain statistical power similar to a between-groups design, the trade-off is that the within-subjects design involves more time to conduct the study. Consider the researcher who wants to compare interpersonal and cognitive-behavioral approaches to the treatment of depression. Let's say he or she recruits 24 depressed clients. If the experimenter chooses to use a between-subjects design, he or she can randomly assign 12 subjects to 12 sessions of interpersonal treatment and the remaining subjects to 12 sessions of cognitive-behavioral treatment. In this design, at the end of 12 weeks the researcher has conducted the study and has collected the data. If the researcher alternately uses a within-subjects design with only 12 clients, randomly assigning 6 clients to receive 12 sessions of interpersonal therapy followed by 12 sessions of cognitive therapy and the remaining six subjects to receive treatment in the reverse order, the researcher would need 12 more weeks than in the between-subjects design to collect data. Thus, an important consideration is the trade-off between subjects and time. Because of dissertation deadlines or pressure to maintain publication records, it may seem that time is often a more valuable resource than subjects. We would encourage researchers, however, not to be too quick to overlook within-subjects designs only because of a time factor.

Order and Sequence Effects

As we indicated earlier, a special problem of within-subjects design is the effect of order and sequence. *Order effects* refers to the possibility that the order (that is, the ordinal position, such as first or third) in which treatments were delivered rather than the treatment per se might account for any changes in the dependent variable. As such, order effects can be seen as threats to internal validity. Even when order effects are controlled as in the counterbalance crossover and Latin Square designs, it is still important to check whether the order of the treatments affected the dependent variable. It can be argued that because counterbalancing equalizes any effects due to order, the researcher can ignore such order effects. This strategy, however, does not provide any information about the basic question: Were there any order effects in a particular study? Such information can be useful to future researchers as they design their investigations on a similar topic. Likewise, practitioners may be interested in knowing if the order of treatments makes any difference as they plan to maximize their interventions.

Sequence effects can also create threats to internal validity. *Sequence effects* refers to the interaction of the treatments (or experimental conditions) due to their sequential order—that is, treatment X_1 may have a different effect when it follows treatment X_2 than when it precedes treatment X_2. In a counterbalanced crossover design this sequence, or carryover effect, can be statistically examined because all possible sequences are represented in the study. Remember that in the Stiles et al. study (1988) the researchers examined for and found no sequence effects. However, in the Latin Square design all possible sequences are not represented. Thus, the Latin Square design typically has less internal validity because sequence effects are more difficult to eliminate.

Measurement Considerations

There are two measurement issues that merit attention when one is considering a within-subjects design: (1) ceiling and floor effects, and (2) equivalency of scale points. *Ceiling and floor effects* refers to problems associated with the upper or lower limits of dependent measures. In essence, the upper or lower limit of a dependent variable may limit the amount of change that can be demonstrated on that variable. Although this can be a problem for any research design, it can be a particular problem for within-subjects designs because they rely on multiple testing, which examines continued increases or decreases in the dependent variable. Consider the Stiles et al. (1988) study again, which is diagrammed as follows:

$$R \quad O_1 \quad X_1 \quad O_2 \quad X_2 \quad O_3$$
$$R \quad O_4 \quad X_2 \quad O_5 \quad X_1 \quad O_6$$

Suppose that in that study the effect of the two treatments, interpersonal-psychodynamic and cognitive-behavioral, on client depression was also assessed. Further suppose that at pretest (O_1 and O_4) all clients had a pretest score > 15 on the Beck Depression Inventory (BDI). Say that after the first treatment for both groups of subjects, the crossover testing (O_2 and O_5) reveals that all clients had a BDI mean score of 2. Since the BDI score cannot be lower than 0, there is little or no room for the second treatment to show improvement.

There is a related measurement problem in within-subjects designs that involves the equivalency of scale points. For example, is a change in the mean BDI score from 15 to 10 equivalent to a change from 10 to 5? Again, this problem is not atypical of between-subjects designs, but these problems are exacerbated by the within-subjects design. For example, variables involving instructions or subject expectancies may be difficult to reverse at the cross-over point.

Restriction of Variables

A final consideration in the use of within-subjects designs involves the restriction of certain independent and dependent variables. It may not be possible to use certain independent variables in a within-subjects design. It is impossible, for example, to induce both the expectation that a given treatment will be effective and then later the expectation that it will not be effective. Or two treatments may be too incompatible with each other. Kazdin (1980) offered the conflicting approaches of systematic desensitization and flooding. It is important for the researcher considering using a within-subjects design to closely examine the impact that multiple treatments may have on one another. Given that each subject receives all treatments, the experimenter must assess whether the combination of multiple treatments can be administered realistically and fairly. Finally, variables that involve some personality, demographic, and physical characteristics may not vary within the same subject in a given experiment (Kazdin, 1980). For example, a subject cannot be both a male and female subject, or be a subject from both a rural and an urban community.

One final note. It also seems important not to limit research by concluding too quickly that particular treatments are incompatible. Kazdin (1980) suggested that "behavioral and psychodynamic therapy could not easily be compared within a particular set of subjects." However, Stiles et al. (1988) did use, quite successfully, a within-subjects design comparing eight sessions each of exploratory (interpersonal-psychodynamic) and prescriptive (cognitive-behavior) therapy. Although worries about treatment contamination may be present or even pervasive among counseling researchers, this study challenges us to fairly evaluate the crossover effect, and to be creative in our thinking about within-subjects designs.

SUMMARY AND CONCLUSIONS

There are two types of true experiments: between-groups and within-subjects designs. These are true experiments because in both cases there is random assignment of treatments and manipulation of an independent variable. In between-groups designs the random assignment that occurs is an assignment of subjects to treatment conditions to create experimental control groups. In contrast, in within-subjects designs, all subjects are exposed to all treatment conditions. Thus, the overall goal of the within-subjects design is to compare the effects of different treatments on each subject. Both designs lend themselves to Kerlinger's "MAXMINCON" principle.

In terms of between-groups designs, we discuss the posttest-only control group design, the pretest-posttest control group design, and the Solomon four-group design. These experimental designs are clearly powerful designs as they can rule out many rival hypotheses. Each design controls for all of the common threats to internal validity. A key feature of these designs is the random assignment of subjects; randomly assigning subjects to groups is a major source of control with regard to internal validity. Kerlinger (1986) concluded that between-groups designs "are the best all-around designs, perhaps the first to be considered when planning the design of a research study" (p. 327). Likewise, Campbell and Stanley (1963) indicate that these designs are "most strongly recommended" (p. 13). Since control groups are commonly used in these designs, we discussed issues pertaining to different types of control groups, such as no-treatment groups, waiting-list control groups, placebo groups, and matched control groups. Since randomization of subjects is a defining characteristic of between-groups design, we also discussed subject assignment, group equivalence, and dependent samples designs.

We also described two traditional within-subjects designs, the crossover and Latin Square designs. Both of these designs make comparisons between two or more groups of subjects, but in a different way from the between-groups design. In the crossover design, all subjects are switched to another experimental condition, usually halfway through the study. Counterbalancing was introduced within this design as a way of reducing bias due to order effects. The Latin Square design was introduced as a design suitable for research questions that examine more than two levels of the independent variable. We suggested that at least six factors specific to the traditional within-subjects design can affect its utility for examining a particular research question, namely (1) experimental control (particularly with regard to individual subject variation), (2) statistical power, (3) time, (4) order and sequence effects, (5) measurement issues, and (6) restriction of certain independent variables. In particular, we encouraged researchers to be creative in the application of traditional within-subjects designs. In short, within-subjects designs offer a powerful means of identifying causal relationships. The advantage of these designs has to do with the ability to reduce error variance by using each subject as his or her own control and the ability to reduce the number of subjects needed in a particular study.

Within-subjects designs have been underused in counseling research. In developing this chapter, we scanned several counseling journals in search of research examples that used a within-subjects design; we were struck by the relatively less frequent use of this design than between-groups design. For example, in the 1988 volume of the *Journal of Counseling Psychology* were reports of 17 time-experimental designs (within subjects and between groups). Of these, 14 (82%) were between-groups designs and 3 (18%) were within-subjects designs. These percentages would probably be similar if other years or other counseling-related journals were examined. In addition, within-subjects designs have not been used to examine a particular content area or particular population in counseling research. While these numbers may suggest that the between-groups design may be better suited for research questions in counseling, we suspect this is not the case. The within-subjects design has a number of strengths, most notably the reduction of subject variability, that ideally suit it for research in counseling.

Clearly, the between-groups and within-subjects designs are useful designs to examine research questions of interest to those in the counseling profession. These designs are flexible and can be made applicable to a wide variety of research problems; in fact, the factorial design is widely used in counseling research. However, it is important for the researcher in counseling to evaluate the strengths and limitations of these designs in relationship to the type of research question being asked and type of subjects needed. Given the applied nature of many of our research questions in counseling, the researcher needs to carefully consider a broad range of issues pertaining to external validity to evaluate the utility of the true experimental designs in providing the most needed information. In addition, many times the random assignment of subjects to groups cannot be done because of ethical constraints, such as in a study of the effects of different levels of sexual harassment. We think it is erroneous for students to be taught that the between-groups design is simply ''the best''; rather, students should be encouraged to consider the strengths and weaknesses of various designs in relation to different research questions. In other words, the utility of the design needs to be evaluated in the context of the research question, the existing knowledge bases, and internal and external validity issues.

CHAPTER 6

QUASI-EXPERIMENTAL
AND TIME-SERIES DESIGNS

As discussed in Chapter 5, one of the hallmarks of a true experimental design is random assignment of subjects to treatments. Random assignment allows the researcher to control many of the threats to internal validity described by Cook and Campbell (1979). A true experimental design always includes random assignment of subjects to conditions, manipulation of the independent variable(s), and comparisons between or among groups. The researcher, however, may not always be in a position to use a true experimental design.

According to Cook and Campbell (1979), the most compelling reason to deviate from a true experimental design is the cost. Usually, carrying out a true experiment is quite expensive in terms of both time and resources. It is a lot less expensive to evaluate naturally occurring differences in treatment settings. In addition, true experiments usually involve the comparison of two, or more rarely three, treatments. It is critical in these situations that the treatments compared be ones that are very likely to be successful and conceptually important. To conduct a true experiment with treatments that are not well conceived and have little prior empirical support is a waste of time and resources, and raises ethical issues. Quasi-experimental and time-series designs can be especially useful in providing preliminary empirical evidence for verifying potentially effective treatments.

The researcher may not be in a position to randomly assign subjects to conditions. For example, in many clinical settings, clients may have to be assigned to a treatment based on their available times or some other situational variable; or it may be unethical to withhold treatment. When the researcher encounters a situation where it is not practical or feasible to randomly assign subjects to conditions, he or she can use a quasi-experimental design. Like the true experiment, the quasi experiment involves the manipulation of one or more independent variables, but there is no random assignment of subjects to conditions. Thus, a major identifying characteristic of a quasi-experimental design is the lack of random assignment of subjects to conditions.

In other circumstances, a researcher may want to investigate the effects of an intervention or treatment when there is no appropriate control or comparison group available. In this situation, the researcher can infer whether the intervention or treatment had an impact by comparing observations made prior to and subsequent to the onset of the intervention. This design is referred to as a time-series design. Hence, a time-series design requires multiple observations over time and the introduction of a treatment at a specified point in time. In other words, in a time-series design, the researcher can and does manipulate one or more independent variables, but there is no random assignment to groups or between-group comparisons.

Because the researcher has less control in quasi-experimental and time-series designs than in an experimental design, there is less certainty about the meaning and interpretation of the results of these studies. In terms of the "MAXMINCON" principle, the researcher using a quasi-experimental design can maximize differences in the independent variable(s) as well as minimize error variance due to measurement issues just as with true experimental designs. However, because there is no random assignment of subjects to treatments, he or she cannot control all of the various threats to internal validity. Many research design texts cover quasi-experimental and time-series designs in a superficial manner. These texts emphasize the increased certainty that accrues when interpreting the results of a true experiment. The emphasis on true experiments may be appropriate for the more laboratory-oriented specialties within psychology, but for many counseling researchers the controls of the laboratory are not available or may even be undesirable (because of reduced external validity) in the applied setting. Given the applied nature of counseling research, this chapter will focus on delineating quasi-experimental and time-series designs that can be useful for the counseling researcher.

The first half of the chapter focuses on quasi-experimental designs. There are two major classes of quasi-experimental designs: nonequivalent-groups designs and cohort designs. In nonequivalent-groups designs, comparisons are made between or among subjects in groups that have been nonrandomly formed. We initially discuss three types of uninterpretable as well as four types of interpretable nonequivalent-groups designs. We then discuss cohort designs. Cohort designs are a special case of nonequivalent-groups designs. Cohorts are groups of subjects that are assumed to be similar to each other because they temporarily follow each other through a formal or informal institution. The second half of the chapter focuses on time-series designs. The defining characteristic of a time-series design is multiple observations over time (Cook & Campbell, 1979). These observations can involve the same object, for instance, the client's level of perceptual processing for each statement during a counseling session, or different but similar subjects, for example, monthly totals of clients requesting service at a counseling center.

QUASI-EXPERIMENTAL DESIGNS

In many clinical situations, the experimenter cannot randomly assign subjects to treatments because of institutional, practical, or ethical constraints. In such cases the experimenter may have to work with preestablished groupings. For instance, an investigator may want to examine the impact of a group session summary (a therapist's written summary of the group session that is mailed to each group member prior to the next session) on session quality and group member involvement (Yalom, 1985). Group leaders may not agree to randomly assigning clients to groups, because many leaders believe that selecting members to form a compatible mixture is one of the most important decisions a leader makes. The investigator may consequently be restricted to already formed groups. In this case he or she could use summaries in two already formed groups and not use summaries in two other already formed groups. The researcher could then compare ratings of session quality and member involvement in the groups that did and did not receive the summaries. This design would be a quasi-experimental design because there would be a manipulation of an independent variable (summary versus no summary) and a between-conditions comparison, but no random assignment of subjects to conditions.

This example also nicely illustrates some of the drawbacks and the major problem with quasi-experimental designs. In this case, the members were selected and the groups composed for a reason (perceived compatibility). If the investigator does find a difference between the groups that did and did not receive the group summaries, one possible explanation for this finding is the effect of the independent variable (group summaries). Another equally plausible explanation for these results, however, could be selection differences. Perhaps the group leaders who led the groups that received the summaries were more effective at composing counseling groups. Thus, the differences between the two conditions may reflect differences in clients and not in the experimental manipulation. In short, whenever an investigator uses previously established groupings (classes in schools, wards in a hospital, therapy groups) he or she must always be aware that these groups were probably established for some reason. Differences found between groups may have more to do with the selection process than with the experimental manipulation.

Selection may also have a more indirect effect, as it interacts with other variables (Kazdin, 1980). A selection-by-threat interaction effect occurs when the threats to internal validity operate differently across the conditions. For example, in our group summary example, the group leaders may have used very different selection criteria in establishing their groups. The group leaders in the treatment (receiving summaries) condition may have selected only passive-dependent clients for the group (believing that these clients get the most from a group treatment) while the leaders in the control condition may have selected clients with varying interpersonal styles (believing that heterogeneity of group composition leads to a better outcome). If passive-dependent clients mature at a faster rate than clients with other interpersonal styles, there may be a selection-maturation interaction that could account for any observed differences across conditions. Likewise, history, testing, regression, mortality, or other factors may interact with selection to produce differences across conditions (see Chapter 3).

The preceding examples illustrate that selection is a critical variable in examining the adequacy and usefulness of a quasi-experimental design. We will suggest in this chapter that the usefulness of quasi-experimental designs in advancing our knowledge is directly related to how thoroughly the investigator examines and controls for the selection criteria used in forming the initial groupings.

Historical Perspective

One of the most important and confusing questions that psychotherapy and counseling researchers have grappled with concerns the effects of counseling: Does counseling work? In order to answer this question we need to compare a group of clients who have received counseling to a group of clients who have not received counseling. The most rigorous (in terms of internal validity) test of the effects of counseling would involve the random assignment of clients to a treatment (receiving counseling) versus no-treatment condition. The random assignment of clients to a no-treatment condition would in effect constitute the withholding of service. Withholding services can of course raise ethical issues for the counseling researcher. To avoid this type of ethical dilemma, early counseling researchers attempted to find other groups of subjects with which to compare the effects of counseling.

Many of the classic outcome studies in counseling used quasi-experimental designs. For example, Klingelhofer (1954) was interested in examining the effects of academic advisement on the scholastic performance (grade point average) of students placed on academic probation. He compared three groups of students in this study, all of whom were on academic probation. One group received four one-hour counseling sessions, a second group received one one-hour counseling session, and the third group received no counseling interviews. The students who received one or four hours of counseling were randomly assigned to groups. The students in the uncounseled group were drawn from students who had been on academic probation during the preceding year. In essence, Klingelhofer's study had elements of both an experimental and a quasi-experimental design.

The comparison between the students receiving one or four hours of counseling was a true experiment because there were random assignment of subjects to treatments, manipulation of the treatment variable, and a between-groups comparison. The comparison between the students who did and did not receive counseling was a quasi-experimental design because the students were not randomly assigned to conditions. This particular type of quasi-experimental design is called a cohort design. Cohorts are groups of subjects that follow each other through an institution. The students who had been on probation the year prior to the study formed one cohort, and the students on probation during the experimental year formed a second cohort. Klingelhofer assumed that the students in the two cohorts were similar because the same rules were used to place students on academic probation both years.

The results of this study did not reveal any differences in subsequent grade point average for the students counseled for either one or four sessions. There was, however, a significant difference in grade point average between students who had and had not received counseling. Nonetheless, this result must be interpreted with some caution because pretreatment differences between the students in the two cohorts may have existed due to some unknown selection factor or to different historical events during their year on probation. Despite these possible limitations, Klingelhofer's study was a test of the effectiveness of one widely used counseling intervention. It represents a typical quasi-experimental study of counseling in the 1950s and 1960s.

Types of Quasi-Experimental Designs

There are two major classes of quasi-experimental designs: nonequivalent-groups designs and cohort designs. In nonequivalent-groups designs, comparisons are made between or among subjects in groups that have been nonrandomly formed. For example, a researcher may want to examine the effects of a video tape that provides precounseling information on subsequent counseling dropout rates. He or she may be able to find a counseling agency that uses such a tape and compare the dropout rate for this agency with the dropout rate for an agency that does not use this type of tape. Obviously, the clients at the two agencies may or may not be different on a number of variables that relate to dropout rate (for example, ethnicity). The clients in the two agencies represent non-equivalent groups. As we will discuss subsequently, the usefulness of a nonequiv-alent-groups design is related to how much the researcher knows about possible pretreatment differences among subjects in the nonequivalent groups.

Cohort designs are a special case of nonequivalent-groups designs. Cohorts are groups of subjects that are assumed to be similar to each other because they temporarily follow each other through a formal or informal institution. For example, subsequent classes of graduate counseling students are cohorts. According to Cook and Campbell (1979), cohort designs are "particularly useful for drawing causal inferences [because] a 'quasi-compatibility' can often be assumed between [adjacent] cohorts that do and do not receive a treatment." However, the compatibility in a cohort design will never be as high as in an experiment with random assignment. Nonetheless, cohort designs do share a relative advantage over other types of nonequivalent-groups designs.

In the following examples, we will visually depict the quasi-experimental designs. The symbol Non R represents the nonrandom assignment of subjects to groups. As in the previous chapters, X indicates the independent variable or treatment, and O indicates observations of the dependent variable.

Uninterpretable Nonequivalent-Groups Designs

We will begin our discussion of nonequivalent-groups designs with three designs that are virtually uninterpretable because of multiple threats to internal validity. We describe these three designs so that you can be aware of their shortcomings and as a basis for comparison with the more interpretable nonequivalent-groups designs.

The one-group posttest-only design can be diagrammed as follows:

X_1 O_1

In this design, observations are made of the dependent variable only after subjects have undergone some type of treatment. This design is impossible to interpret because there is no way to infer that any type of change has taken place. In addition, the lack of a control group makes it impossible to investigate the presence of maturational or historical processes.

A nonequivalent-control-group posttest-only design can be diagrammed as follows:

Non R   X O_1
Non R O_2

In this design, the two groups are formed in a nonrandom manner. The subjects in the first group receive the experimental treatment (X) while the subjects in the second group do not receive any treatment. Change is measured by comparing the posttests (O_1 and O_2).

The posttest-only nonequivalent design does not have to compare a treatment with a control group. Two or more active treatments can be compared using this type of design. The following is a diagram of a nonequivalent posttest-only design comparing three active treatments:

Non R X_1 O_1
Non R X_2 O_2
Non R X_3 O_3

Once again, the groups are formed on a nonrandom basis. Treatments (X_1, X_2, and X_3) are administered to the subjects in the three groups and then posttests (O_1, O_2, O_3) are used to assess changes.

The posttest-only quasi-experimental designs are especially weak, because of the difficulty in attributing results to the intervention. The lack of random assignment of subjects to groups allows the possibility that the groups may differ in some important manner prior to treatment. Typically, students are assigned to classes, patients to wards, clients to groups, and residents to living groups based on some reason or rationale. This suggests that the natural groupings that we encounter will differ prior to treatment on a few, or in some cases many, dimensions. Thus, one of the problems with the posttest-only nonequivalent-groups design is that it does not allow for an assessment of any of the possible differences that exist prior to treatment.

Consider the following example. Let's say an investigator wants to examine the usefulness of an in-class program in alleviating depression in children. He or she might select two classes of sixth graders in a school and then provide one class with the intervention. After the month is over he or she assesses the students' level of depression. Let's say that after treatment, the students who received the intervention show less depression. This result may indicate an effect of the treatment, or it may reflect differences between the two classes in their levels of depression prior to the intervention. Perhaps the principal decided to assign students to classes on the basis of their social skills level. Much research has documented the relationship between social skills and depression (for example, Lewinsohn, Mischel, Chapel, & Barton, 1980). Since there was no pretest, the possible differences in the initial levels of depression could not be assessed.

The third type of uninterpretable design is the one-group pretest-posttest design. This design is diagrammed as follows:

$$O_1 \quad X \quad O_2$$

In this design, pretest observations (O_1) are recorded, then a treatment is administered, and finally posttest observations are made. This design is better than the one-group posttest-only design because by examining the pretest-posttest difference we can determine if a change occurred. However, the possible cause of this change is still quite ambiguous. For example, the treatment might be responsible for any observed change, or history (the occurrence of other events between pretest and posttest) might account for the change. Alternately, if the intervention or treatment was initiated because of a particular problem (for example, academic probation, as in the Klingelhofer study), the posttest scores might improve because of statistical regression toward the mean. Another possible explanation for changes in the posttest score involves maturation. The change may have nothing to do with the treatment; rather, it may reflect simple growth and development. Without a comparison group, it is impossible to rule out these and other threats to internal validity.

Interpretable Nonequivalent-Groups Designs

A more useful nonequivalent-groups design is the pretest-posttest design. The following diagram depicts this design:

$$
\begin{array}{llll}
\text{Non R} & O_1 & X & O_2 \\
\text{Non R} & O_3 & & O_4
\end{array}
$$

In this design, subjects are nonrandomly assigned to groups and then pretested on the dependent variable. One group then receives the experimental treatment while the other does not. It is important to note that this design does not have to involve a treatment-control group comparison; it may involve the comparison of two or more active treatments.

The pretest-posttest nonequivalent-groups design is a stronger, and therefore more interpretable, design than the posttest-only nonequivalent design because it allows for an examination of some of the inevitable pretreatment differences. The investigator using a pretest-posttest nonequivalent-groups design can assess similarity of subjects on the dependent variable(s) of interest and on other variables that may be related to the dependent variable. It is important for the researcher to remember, however, that pretest equivalence on the dependent variable(s) and on other assessed variables does not mean that the groups are comparable on all dimensions that are important to behavior change. A demonstration of pretest equivalence, however, does increase one's confidence in attributing any observed posttest differences between groups to the experimental manipulation rather than to some selection difference.

In the pretest-posttest nonequivalent design it is unlikely that observed differences between groups can be attributed to factors such as history, maturation, or testing. However, there can be a selection-by-threat interaction that can pose a threat to internal validity. In other words, an event might affect subjects in only one group or might affect them differently from subjects in the other group(s). For example, the subjects in one group, because of some selection bias, may mature faster (selection × maturation) or be more likely to encounter some historical event (selection × history) than those in the other group.

Like its experimental equivalent, the pretest-posttest nonequivalent-groups design may have problems with external validity related to pretest sensitization. Subjects in the different groups might react to the intervention(s) based on a sensitizing effect of the pretest. Also, subjects in one group may react differently to the pretest than subjects in the other group(s). Still, Kazdin (1980) argued, and we agree, that the possible problem of pretest sensitization is minor compared to the problems of trying to interpret the results of a nonequivalent-groups design when there has been no check on pretreatment equivalence.

Sometimes the researcher may not want or be able to pretest the subjects in the groups in a nonequivalent-groups design. This may happen when he or she is worried about the possible effects of pretest sensitization or when he or she is working with archival data and no pretest was given. In this case, the researcher may choose to use a nonequivalent-groups design with a proxy pretest measure (a proxy pretest involves a similar but not identical variable). This design is diagrammed as follows:

Non R O_{A1} X O_{B2}
Non R O_{A1} O_{B2}

In this design, groups are formed nonrandomly and a proxy pretest (O_{A1}) is administered to both groups. Later, one group gets the experimental treatment (X). Then, both groups are retested with a different posttest (O_{B2}). The viability of this design depends on the ability of the researcher to find a pretest measure (O_{A1}) that relates conceptually and empirically to the posttest (O_{B2}).

For example, a researcher may want to examine a new method of counselor training. He or she finds two training programs willing to participate and institutes the new method in one program. At the end of the first year the researcher administers a paper-and-pencil counseling skills test to all students in the two programs and finds that the students in the treatment program scored higher on this test. However, the researcher is worried about possible pretreatment differences in counseling skill level. Suppose the researcher finds that Graduate Record Exam (GRE) scores are correlated $r = .80$ with scores on the paper-and-pencil counseling skills test. In this case, the researcher can use the pretreatment GRE score (O_{A1}) to examine possible pretreatment differences between students in the two programs.

The pretest-posttest nonequivalent-groups design can be strengthened by the use of an additional pretest. This design is illustrated below:

$$\text{Non R} \quad O_1 \quad O_2 \quad X \quad O_3$$
$$\text{Non R} \quad O_1 \quad O_2 \quad X \quad O_3$$

This design is similar to the nonequivalent-groups pretest-posttest design except for the addition of a second pretesting to enhance the interpretability of the design. One of the main threats to the internal validity of a pretest-posttest nonequivalent-groups design involves a selection-by-maturation interaction. In other words, the subjects in the two groups may be maturing at different rates because of some selection characteristic. The addition of a second pretest allows the researcher to examine this possibility. The difference between O_1 and O_2 for the treatment and control groups can be examined to see if the groups are maturing at different rates.

The addition of a second pretest significantly enhances the interpretability of the nonequivalent-groups design. A review of the counseling literature, however, suggests that two pretests are rarely, if ever, used. We strongly recommend that researchers contemplating the use of a nonequivalent-groups design consider the addition of a second pretest.

Although the reversed-treatment pretest-posttest nonequivalent-groups design is also rarely used in counseling research, we include a discussion of this design because it is one of the stronger nonequivalent-groups designs. We hope that an understanding of the strengths of this design will encourage its use in counseling research. The design is diagrammed as follows:

$$\text{Non R} \quad O_1 \quad X + \quad O_2$$
$$\text{Non R} \quad O_1 \quad X - \quad O_2$$

In this design, the $X +$ represents a treatment that is expected to influence the posttest (O_2) in one direction and the $X -$ represents a treatment that is expected to influence the posttest in the opposite direction.

For example, a researcher may want to test the hypothesis that structure is related to productive group development. Certain schools of therapy contend that ambiguity enhances therapy because lack of structure increases anxiety, and anxiety is necessary for productive work to occur. Other schools contend that anxiety interferes with group work and that structure should be used to lessen the amount of anxiety that group members experience. To test this hypothesis, the researcher could obtain pretest and posttest measures of the quality of group interactions from two groups of clients. One group of these clients could be given explicit information about group procedures and the other group could be given more ambiguous information. Posttest scores could be examined to see if the levels of quality of group interactions moved in opposite directions.

This design renders a selection × maturation threat to internal validity improbable. It is hard to imagine that two groups of subjects would spontaneously mature in different directions. The usual pattern of differences in maturation between two groups is in rates, not directions of maturation.

The reversed-treatment design is also stronger in terms of construct validity. As Cook and Campbell (1979) point out, the "theoretically causal" variable has to be rigorously specified if a test is made that depends on one version of the cause affecting one group one way and another group the other way. The main problem with a reversed-treatment design is an ethical one. For example, it is usually unethical to administer a treatment that would cause subjects to become more depressed. The researcher wanting to use the reversed-treatment design must, therefore, display a good deal of thought and creativity.

Cook and Campbell (1979) discuss several other nonequivalent-groups designs (for example, repeated treatments). Because these designs are so rarely used in counseling research, we believe that a discussion of them is not warranted here. The interested reader is referred to Cook and Campbell (1979) for a discussion of the less common designs. In addition, Cook and Campbell provide an excellent summary of the statistical analysis of nonequivalent-groups designs.

An Example of a Nonequivalent-Groups Design from Counseling Research

Taussig (1987) used a nonequivalent-groups design with a proxy pretest to examine the effects of client-counselor ethnicity matching and the time of goal setting on the number of kept, canceled, and broken appointments. In addition, she analyzed possible interactions between these variables and client ethnic status and gender. In this study, client-counselor-ethnicity match and the time of goal setting were used to form nonequivalent groups. In other words, clients were not randomly assigned to counselors nor was the time of goal setting specified on a random basis.

Taussig hypothesized that client-counselor pairs mismatched on ethnic status would share fewer cultural expectations about counseling and thus would have fewer kept and more canceled and broken appointments than client-counselor pairs matched on ethnic status. She also hypothesized that early goal setting with Mexican-American clients would lead to fewer kept and more canceled and broken appointments than early goal setting with Anglo-American clients. Taussig reasoned that relationship building was expected to take longer with Mexican-American clients, and the early goal setting was predicted to disrupt this relationship building process.

The data for this study were obtained from the archival client records of 70 Mexican-American and 72 Anglo-American clients seen at a community mental health center. The independent variables in this study were client ethnicity (Anglo-American, Mexican-American), counselor ethnicity (Anglo-American, Mexican-American, other Spanish speaking), and goal-setting duration (setting goals within 14, 21, or 28 days or not at all). Client-counselor match was examined by noting the ethnicity of clients across types of counselor ethnicity.

Four pretest proxy variables were used in the design. These variables were annual income of the client, client age, client employment status, and goal resetting (number of times goals were set for the client). Each of the variables was related to one or more of the dependent variables: kept, canceled, and broken appointments. Specifically, these pretest variables were used as covariates in an analysis-of-variance design. In this manner, the author hoped to control several pretreatment differences that could have affected the analysis of counselor-client match and/or duration of goal setting. The results of the analysis of covariance showed that none of the dependent variables were related to duration of goal setting. However, in terms of the counselor-client ethnic match, when Mexican-American clients were matched with other Spanish speaking counselors, there were more kept appointments. Counselor-client ethnic match was not related to appointments kept for the Anglo-American clients.

The Taussig study is a good example of the use of a nonequivalent-groups design. It was certainly less expensive (in time and money) for Taussig to access client records than to go into an agency and set up a system whereby clients would be randomly assigned to counselors and duration of goal setting within a particular client-counselor dyad also would be determined by random assignment. Her finding that ethnic matching was related to kept appointments but probably not to goal-setting duration provides preliminary information for future research and avoided wasting time and effort in a more costly true experimental design. Another strength of the study was the use of proxy pretest variables to examine for possible selection differences. The major weakness of the Taussig study is a question of possible selection effects. We do not know, for instance, why clients were assigned to particular therapists or why goals were set with some clients within 14 days and never set with other clients. In other words, the conditions examined in the study (client-counselor ethnicity match and duration of goal setting) were formed on some basis that was unknown to the researcher. The reason(s) for the client-counselor matches or the duration of goal setting could have affected the results of the study.

Cohort Designs

Cohort designs are typically stronger than nonequivalent-groups designs because cohorts are more likely to be similar to each other since their environment is the same except for the treatment variable. For example, the sixth grade class at a particular school one year is likely to be similar to the sixth grade class the following year. This would not be the case, however, if school district lines were redrawn between the two years. It is therefore important for the researcher to have as much knowledge as possible about conditions that could affect the cohorts. Cohort designs are strengthened when the researcher can argue conceptually and empirically that the two cohorts did share similar environments, except of course for the treatment. Three types of cohort designs have been used in counseling research. We will use the notations suggested by Cook and Campbell (1979) to diagram these designs. The first design is diagrammed as follows:

$$\frac{O_1 \text{-----}}{X \quad O_2}$$

In this design, the broken line indicates that the two groups are successive cohorts and not nonequivalent groups. The O_1 represents a posttest administered to one cohort, while the O_2 represents the same posttest administered to the second cohort. It is important to note that these testings occur at different points in time because the cohorts follow each other through the system; however, the posttesting does occur at a similar point in each cohort's progression through the institution.

Slate and Jones (1989) used a posttest-only cohort design to test the effect of a new training method for teaching students to score the Wechsler Intelligence Scale for Children-Revised (WISC-R). One cohort of students took the intelligence testing course during the fall semester and the other cohort took the course during the spring semester. The fall cohort group received a standard scoring training procedure and the spring cohort group received the new training method. The students in the spring cohort group made fewer scoring errors on the WISC-R than did the students in the fall cohort group. Slate and Jones (1989) concluded that the new training method was effective. These authors assumed that the students in the fall and spring cohorts were similar prior to training. They buttressed this assumption by examining several possible sources of pretreatment differences. For example, they found that the gender composition was similar across the two cohort groups and that the students in the two cohort groups had similar GRE scores and grade point averages.

Posttest-only cohort designs can be strengthened by partitioning the treatment. Partitioning treatments involves giving different amounts of the treatment to different groups of subjects within a cohort group. A posttest-only cohort design with partitioned treatments is diagrammed as follows:

$$\frac{O_1 \text{\_\_\_\_\_}}{\begin{array}{cc} X_1 & O_2 \\ X_2 & O_2 \end{array}}$$

The O_1 is the posttest given to the first cohort group. X_1 represents one level of treatment and X_2 represents the second level of treatment. O_2 is a posttest measure given to all the members of the second cohort group regardless of level of treatment administered.

In the Slate and Jones (1989) study, suppose that some of the students in the second cohort practiced the new scoring procedure for two hours and that the other students in the cohort practiced it for four hours. Slate and Jones could have analyzed the results separately for these two groups of students. If the students who had practiced for four hours committed significantly fewer scoring errors than the students who practiced for two hours, and if the treatment cohort committed fewer errors than the no-treatment cohort, then the assertion that the treatment was effective would be strengthened, particularly with regard to the amount of training needed.

In short, the posttest-only cohort design can be useful, particularly relative to the posttest-only nonequivalent-groups design. Since clients experience various aspects of counseling treatments in different amounts, we urge researchers to use partitioning as a way of strengthening the internal validity of the posttest-only cohort design in counseling research.

The final cohort design that we will discuss is the pretreatment-posttreatment cohort design. This design is diagrammed as follows:

$$\frac{O_1 \quad O_2}{O_3 \quad X \quad O_4}$$

As in the previous design, the broken line represents the use of cohorts. The first cohort group is pretested (O_1) and posttested (O_2), and then the second cohort group is pretested (O_3), treated (X), and posttested (O_4).

This design is illustrated in the following paragraphs. The main advantage of the pretest-posttest cohort design over the posttest-only cohort design is the increased assurance that the pretest provides for asserting that the two cohorts were similar prior to the treatment. In addition, the use of the pretest as a covariate in an analysis of covariance provides a stronger statistical test. The main disadvantage of this design is in terms of the pretest operating as a threat to construct validity. We believe in most cases that the advantages of having the pretest to examine pretreatment compatibility across groups outweighs the disadvantage involved with the pretest as a threat to construct validity.

An Example of a Cohort Design from Counseling Research

Hogg and Deffenbacher (1988) used both an experimental design and a quasi-cohort design in their comparison of cognitive and interpersonal-process group therapies for treating depression. Depressed students seeking treatment at a university counseling center were screened in an intake interview, for (1) presence of nonpsychotic, unipolar depression; (2) absence of major psychopathology; and (3) absence of high suicide lethality. Additionally, prospective subjects had to receive a score of 14 or greater on the Beck Depression Inventory (BDI; Beck, Rush, Shaw, & Emery, 1979). Clients meeting these criteria were randomly assigned to cognitive or interpersonal group treatments. A cohort control group was formed by selecting clients who met the same screening criteria but who came to the counseling center too late in the fall semester to be assigned to any type of treatment. Hogg and Deffenbacher assumed that students who came to the counseling center early versus late were similar. The subjects in the control group received no formal treatment during the semester break. The comparison of the treatment subjects and the control subjects constituted the cohort part of the design.

Subjects in the treatment and control groups were administered the BDI, the Minnesota Multiphasic Personality Inventory-Depression scale (MMPI-D; Hathaway & McKinley, 1942), the Automatic Thoughts Questionnaire (ATQ; Hollon & Kendall, 1980), and the Self-Esteem Inventory-Adult Form (SEI; Coopersmith, 1981). Treatment subjects were assessed at pretreatment, mid-treatment (4 weeks), posttreatment (8 weeks), and follow-up (12–14 weeks). Control subjects were assessed before the semester break and 8 weeks later, which was equivalent to the pretest-posttest assessment period for the treatment group. The comparison of the treatment and control groups constituted a pretest-posttest cohort design.

Hogg and Deffenbacher performed initial analyses to assess equivalence across groups prior to treatment. They found no pretreatment differences across groups on the BDI, MMPI-D, ATQ, or SEI scales. A repeated measures (pretesting, posttesting) MANOVA (BDI, MMPI-D, ATQ, and SEI) was used to compare treatment and control groups. The treatment versus control comparison and the treatment-control by time (pretest-posttest) interaction were not significant. However, a significant change was found for both groups from pretest to posttest; such differences over time are sometimes referred to as time effects. The findings indicated that subjects in both the treatment and control groups significantly decreased depression and distorted cognitions, and increased self-esteem.

Hogg and Deffenbacher highlighted one of the problems inherent in the use of cohort designs in their discussion of the lack of difference between the experimental and control groups. No significant differences were found between those who received active treatments and members of the waiting-list control group. However, using Christmas vacation as a naturalistic waiting-list period may have produced a significant temporal confound. Students who are depressed at the end of a semester may differ significantly from those seeking counseling services at the beginning of the semester. Additionally, interview data indicated that many waiting-list students felt considerable relief of depression over the holiday. These changes were evidenced in dramatic differences in posttest scores. The evidence of symptom transiency and wide client variability is in sharp contrast to other studies (for example, Fuchs & Rehm, 1977; Shaw, 1977) that have reported little improvement for depressed subjects in waiting-list groups, although those studies did not coincide with a holiday break. The potential temporal and subject-selection confounds made the validity of the finding of apparent equivalence between the waiting-list and treatment cohorts highly questionable. For future research, the use of vacation periods as a naturalistic waiting-list condition is not recommended as a solution to the "rigorous methodology versus professional ethics" dilemma inherent in depression research (Hogg & Deffenbacher, 1988, p. 309).

In sum, the Hogg and Deffenbacher (1988) study was well conceived and executed. The authors used time of semester break to form a cohort group to use as a comparison in addition to the comparison of the two active treatments. They also comprehensively addressed the issue of pretreatment equivalence by comparing treatment and control groups across multiple measures. Interestingly, Hogg and Deffenbacher used the limitations (selection, temporal confound) inherent in the cohort design to argue against accepting the null hypothesis. One could possibly argue that, in fact, the treatments actually had no additional effect greater than the passage of time. Alternatively, Hogg and Deffenbacher could have used an additional control group. For instance, they could have recruited nonclients (through a subject pool) who had BDI scores greater than 14 and who met the criteria for nonpsychotic unipolar depression. These subjects could have been tested during the same time frame as the treatment subjects. This type of control could rule out the temporal (Christmas holiday) confound in examining the results.

TIME-SERIES DESIGNS

The defining characteristic of a time-series design is multiple observations over time (Cook & Campbell, 1979). These observations can involve the same subject (for instance, the client's level of perceptual process for each statement during a counseling session) or different but similar subjects (for example, monthly totals of clients requesting services at a counseling center). In an interrupted time-series design, a treatment is administered at some point in the series of observations. (The point at which the treatment takes place is called the interruption.) In order for the researcher to use an interrupted time-series design, he or she must know the specific point in the series of observations when the treatment occurred. The logic of the interrupted time-series design involves a comparison of the observations before and after the treatment or interruption. If the treatment has an effect, there should be a difference in the observations prior to and following the interruption.

While the logic of comparing pre- and postinterruption observations for signs of difference is simple and straightforward, the statistical analysis can be complex. The reader who is interested in their statistical analysis is referred to Cook and Campbell (1979). In this section we will concentrate on the logical analysis of interrupted time-series designs. (Chapter 7 discusses time series as applied in single-subject designs.)

Although we could not find an example of a time-series design published in the counseling journals, we do believe that these designs can be profitably used in counseling research. In this section we will describe three time-series designs with the hope of stimulating counseling researchers to think about using these designs in planning their research.

Types of Time-Series Designs

The most basic time-series design is the simple interrupted time series. This design is diagrammed as follows:

$$O_1 \quad O_2 \quad O_3 \quad O_4 \quad O_5 \quad O_6 \quad X \quad O_7 \quad O_8 \quad O_9 \quad O_{10} \quad O_{11} \quad O_{12}$$

As shown in the diagram, there are multiple observations both before (O_1–O_6) and after (O_7–O_{12}) the treatment (X) is initiated. The diagram shows an equal number of observations before and after the treatment, but this is not a requirement for the design.

The interrupted time-series design has two advantages over the quasi-experimental designs previously described. First, the time-series design allows the researcher to detect maturational changes that may be occurring prior to treatment initiation. The researcher does this by looking for changes in the pretreatment observations. If found, these maturational changes can be controlled for in a statistical analysis, allowing a more powerful test of the effect of the treatment. The second advantage of the time-series design is that it also allows for the analysis of seasonal trends. Many data examined by counseling researchers vary systematically over time. For example, more clients seek counseling around holiday periods. It is obviously important to account for this type of systematic variation if a researcher is interested in testing an intervention that affects clients' use of counseling services. The statistical analysis of time-series designs can also control for these types of systematic variations.

An example of a simple interrupted time-series design could involve a researcher wanting to assess the effects of a counseling center's adopting a time-limited model of counseling. The center could initiate the time-limited model in September of one year. The researcher could examine the number of clients on the waiting list each month for the preceding three years and the number of clients on the waiting list during the current year. The analysis of this design would require a comparison of the number of clients on the waiting list prior and subsequent to the initiation of the time-limited model.

One of the main threats to the internal validity of a simple interrupted time-series design is history. In other words, something other than treatment could affect the observations that the researcher makes. One way to reduce such a threat is to add a second dependent variable. This design, with a second dependent variable, is called an interrupted time-series design with non-equivalent dependent variables. This design is diagrammed as follows:

$$O_{A1} \quad O_{A2} \quad O_{A3} \quad O_{A4} \quad X \quad O_{A5} \quad O_{A6} \quad O_{A7} \quad O_{A8}$$
$$O_{B1} \quad O_{B2} \quad O_{B3} \quad O_{B4} \quad X \quad O_{B5} \quad O_{B6} \quad O_{B7} \quad O_{B8}$$

In this design O_A represents one dependent variable and O_B represents a second. Otherwise, the design is exactly the same as the simple interrupted time-series design. If the O_A series shows an interruption at the time of treatment and the O_B series does not, then the internal validity of the treatment effect is enhanced. In other words, it is unlikely (although possible) that history would have an effect on one conceptually related dependent variable but not the other.

In the simple interrupted time-series design described earlier, the researcher could add a second set of observations—for example, the number of clients requesting services each month. If the number of clients on the waiting list (O_A) shows an interruption at the time that the time-limited model was introduced and the number of clients requesting services (O_B) does not show a similar interruption, the researcher can conclude that the initiation of the time-limited model caused a reduction in the waiting list. It is unlikely that history could cause this effect because history would likely also affect the number of clients requesting services.

At times, counseling researchers are interested not in examining the effect of a treatment in a time series, but whether changes in one variable in the time series cause subsequent changes in another variable in a time series. For instance, do changes in the counselor's level of self-disclosure affect the client's level of self-disclosure? This type of analysis is referred to as an analysis of concomitances in time series. The design is diagrammed as follows:

$$O_{A1} \quad O_{A2} \quad O_{A3} \quad O_{A4} \quad O_{A5} \quad O_{A6} \quad O_{A7} \quad O_{A8}$$
$$O_{B1} \quad O_{B2} \quad O_{B3} \quad O_{B4} \quad O_{B5} \quad O_{B6} \quad O_{B7} \quad O_{B8}$$

In essence, the researcher observes two dependent variables over time. In the example just given, the researcher checks in the analysis if the counselor's level of self-disclosure adds predictability to the client's level of self-disclosure over and above the predictability obtained from patterns in the client's level of self-disclosure. An introduction to the statistical analysis of concomitances in time series can be found in Cook and Campbell (1979).

An Example of a Time-Series Design in Counseling Research

As stated earlier, time-series designs have not been used often in counseling research. When used in other disciplines, time-series designs have been used to study large macro-level systems and interventions. An example of this type of analysis would be an examination of the effect of changing the speed limit on the number of traffic fatalities. This level of analysis can also be used in counseling research to study, for instance, the impact of prevention programs or environmental interventions. We believe that time-series analyses can also be used to study more micro-level systems and treatments. The following study illustrates this type of use.

Kivlighan (1990) used an interrupted time-series with nonequivalent dependent variables design to study the effects of live supervision in counselor training. Beginning counselor trainees saw a recruited client for four 50-minute counseling interviews. Advanced counseling doctoral students provided live supervision for the counselor trainees. This supervision involved viewing the counseling interview from behind a one-way mirror and at approximately the session midpoint entering the session and commenting on the counseling process and providing direction for the counselor. The observations in this study consisted of ratings of each of the counselor statements. Observers rated each counselor statement on a cognitive-affective dimension and an immediacy dimension (outside statement versus statements about the client-counselor relationship). Based on the training model used, Kivlighan predicted that after the interruption (the supervisor entering the room), the counselor's statements would be less cognitive and more immediate.

Figure 6-1 shows statements taken from one counselor-client-supervisor triad, made during the interview. The supervisor intervened between the 60th and 61st counselor statements. A visual inspection of these graphs suggests that the counselor's statements became more immediate and less cognitive after the supervisor's intervention. A statistical analysis of this time series was performed with the SPSS-X Box-Jenkins procedure. Kivlighan concluded that the live supervision interventions influenced the novice counselor to use more affective and immediate statements with clients.

This study illustrates the usefulness of interrupted time-series analysis in studying counseling process. By using two dependent variables, Kivlighan strengthened his confidence in the assertion that the observed changes were not due to a history compound. The study could have been further strengthened by replicating this analysis with other counselor-client-supervisor triads. This type of replication could enhance the generalizability of the results.

SUMMARY AND CONCLUSIONS

We believe that quasi-experimental and time-series designs do have a place in contemporary counseling research. They are especially useful when we are

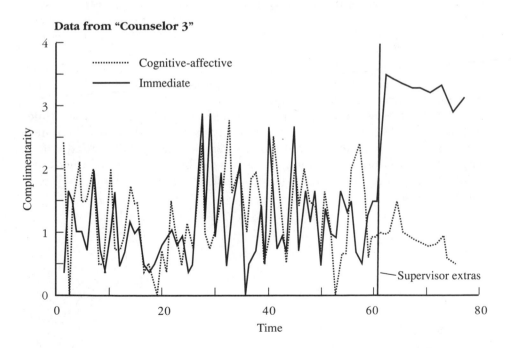

FIGURE 6-1

trying to examine relationships in applied settings. It is critically important that counseling psychologists and counselors conduct their research with real clients, workers, and students. Often, experimental designs are not possible in these settings for a variety of logistical, methodological, and ethical reasons. Especially with findings from studies that do not use real clinical populations or settings, it is important to have replications in a more applied, real-life setting. Studies using quasi-experimental or time-series designs in real settings could be the final point in a series of investigations.

Because there are inherent problems with the interpretation of the results of quasi-experimental and time-series designs, however, researchers must exercise caution when employing these designs. We strongly recommend against the use of posttest-only nonequivalent-groups designs in counseling research. As discussed earlier, having no way to assess pretreatment equivalence makes the results from a posttest-only nonequivalent-groups design virtually uninterpretable. In addition, when using a pretest-posttest nonequivalent design, we recommend that the researcher attend carefully to how the naturally occurring groups were formed. In applied settings, there is usually some basis on which groupings are made. The more the researcher can understand the basis on which the naturally occurring groupings were formed, the better he or she can examine or control for preexisting differences. This can be accomplished by using the selection variable as a covariate in the analysis.

When using the pretest-posttest nonequivalent-groups or cohort designs, we recommend that researchers consider using multiple pretest measures or multiple times of pretesting to examine pretreatment equivalence. Using multiple measures or measurement periods strengthens the assertion of equivalence of conditions prior to intervention. Also, when using a cohort design, the researcher needs to be vigilant in looking for obvious or not-so-obvious differences (other than the experimental manipulation) in what is occurring for subjects during the different time periods.

Finally, we believe that counseling researchers have underused time-series designs. These designs can be especially useful in the evaluation of new and innovative programs. Because time-series designs are often used with a single example from a population, questions can be raised as to their external validity. Therefore, researchers should consider replication when they plan their research.

C H A P T E R   7

SINGLE-SUBJECT DESIGNS

The focus of counseling is on helping people to cope more effectively with their environment; thus, most often those in the counseling profession are concerned with the welfare of individuals. However, methodological issues have plagued the development of a scientific analysis of individuals, to the point where single-subject research designs have sometimes been regarded as unscientific. Error variance, extraneous variables, and numerous sources of bias—major threats to Kerlinger's "MAXMINCON" principle—have beset researchers using single subjects. The purpose of this chapter is to discuss issues pertaining to experimental designs that use a single subject, counselor-client dyad, group, or organization. The central thesis of this chapter is that single-subject designs, like other experimental designs, can play an important role in the pursuit of knowledge within the counseling profession. However, certain methodological considerations must be addressed within Kerlinger's "MAXMINCON" principle. Thus, this chapter will present a variety of approaches that can be considered single-subject designs. However, important distinctions must be made about different types of studies that use a single subject and about the varying amounts of experimental control that are used. Moreover, the researcher must be aware of the strengths and weaknesses of this particular design and qualify his or her conclusions accordingly (which is also the case with the other designs as well).

This chapter considers two major types of single-subject designs: (1) the traditional nonbehavioral designs, the single case study and intensive single-subject design, and (2) the traditional behaviorally oriented designs. You will find many similarities between the behaviorally oriented and nonbehaviorally oriented designs, although the former are usually distinguished by comparisons between baselines and different treatment phases. Actually, the theoretical orientation (behavioral or nonbehavioral) need not be restricted to the type of single-subject design, but for now those traditional labels help to identify the two basic types of designs.

As a preface to both of these types of designs, the first section of this chapter will provide a brief historical picture of designs using a single subject, in psychology as well as in counseling. Then we will discuss the traditional nonbehavioral designs, which sometimes have been referred to as associational designs (Tracey, 1983, 1985). We will draw a distinction between the traditional uncontrolled case study and the more intensive single-subject design. We will then focus on the traditional behaviorally oriented designs, which are sometimes referred to as behavioral intrasubject designs (Kazdin, 1980) or as time-series designs (Drew, 1980). We will discuss several defining features of these behaviorally oriented time-series designs, and then describe and illustrate two different types of designs: AB time series and multiple baseline. In the next section we will discuss limitations and advantages of single-subject designs.

A HISTORICAL PERSPECTIVE ON SINGLE-SUBJECT DESIGNS

The study of individual subjects not only has a long history in psychology, but also has played a prominent role in the development of the applied professions. Perhaps the most extensive chronology of the historical sequence of events affecting the development of the single-subject design is to be found in Barlow and Hersen (1984); the interested reader may want to pursue that source for a more detailed account. When psychology was initially developing into a science, the first experiments were performed on individual subjects. For example, during an autopsy of a man who had been unable to speak intelligibly, Broca discovered a lesion in the third frontal convolution of the cerebral cortex. The discovery that this area was the speech center of the brain led to the systematic examination of various destroyed brain parts and their relationship to behavior (Barlow & Hersen, 1984). Likewise, Wundt made pioneering advances in perception and sensation by examining the introspective experience of light and sound of specific individuals. Ebbinghaus, using a series of repeated measurements, made important advances in learning and memory by examining retention in specific individuals. Both Pavlov's and Skinner's conclusions were gleaned from experiments on single organisms, which were repeatedly replicated with other organisms. In short, important findings and advances in psychology with wide generalizability have been made from systematic observations of individuals.

At the beginning of the twentieth century, a number of advances were made that facilitated the examination and comparison of groups of subjects. The invention of descriptive and inferential statistics not only facilitated group comparisons but also emphasized a philosophy of comparing the averages of groups rather than being preoccupied with individuals. Barlow and Hersen (1984) noted that the pioneering work and philosophy of Fisher on inferential statistics was most likely influenced by the fact that Fisher was an agronomist. He was concerned with the farm plots that yielded better crops on the average given certain fertilizers, growing conditions, and so forth. Individual plans per se were not the focus of agronomists. In short, as psychology developed in the middle of the twentieth century, the methods of inquiry were primarily influenced by statistical techniques such as the analysis of variance.

Meanwhile, at the beginning of the twentieth century within the applied fields of psychiatry, counseling, and clinical psychology, the primary, if not sole, methodology for investigating emotional and behavioral problems was the individual case study. Thus, cases such as Breuer's treatment of Anna O. and Freud's Frau Emmy formed the basis of "scientific" observations, which gradually grew into theories of personality and psychotherapy. These studies of therapeutically successful and unsuccessful cases were not tightly controlled investigations from a methodological viewpoint. In addition, the typical practitioner was not well trained in the scientific method of critical thinking, and such practitioners extrapolated from the early case studies in fundamentally erroneous ways. Consequently, outlandish therapeutic conclusions were reached; for example, Max (1935) concluded on the basis of uncontrolled case studies that electrical aversion therapy resulted in "95 percent relief" from the compulsions of homosexuality.

However, as the fields of counseling and clinical psychology developed in the 1940s and 1950s, more clinicians became aware of the inadequacies of the uncontrolled case study (Barlow & Hersen, 1984). Greater methodological sophistication led the applied psychologists to operationalize variables and to adopt the model of between-groups comparisons as well as Fisher's methods of statistical analysis. Armed with these new methodological tools, researchers attempted to document the effectiveness of a wide range of therapeutic techniques as well as the efficacy of therapy itself. These efforts were most likely fueled by the writing of Hans Eysenck, who repeatedly claimed that the profession did not have very compelling evidence for the effectiveness of therapy (Eysenck, 1952, 1961, 1965). In fact, Eysenck claimed that a client's chance of improving was about the same whether he or she entered therapy or was placed on a waiting list (Eysenck, 1952). Eysenck's charges about the lack of empirical support for therapy's effectiveness challenged the very existence of the therapeutic professions.

Although it has taken considerable time, researchers have begun to unravel the outcome question. Paul (1967) noted that a global measurement of therapeutic effectiveness was inappropriate because of the overwhelming complexity and number of confounding variables. Rather, he suggested that investigators examine the question "What treatment, by whom, is most effective for this individual with that specific problem, and under which set of circumstances?" (p. 111). Others noted that clients were erroneously conceptualized as being similar to each other (the uniformity myth; Kiesler, 1966) rather than as individuals with differences that clearly interact with counseling outcomes. Still other investigators noted that the group comparisons masked important variations across clients, specifically that some clients improved but others actually got worse (Truax & Carkhuff, 1967; Truax & Wargo, 1966). In short, although group comparison methods and inferential statistics substantially facilitated research on the effects of psychotherapy, researchers quickly encountered a number of confounding variables that underscored the complexity of the therapeutic experience.

In response to the confusion and complexity within the therapeutic process, other methodologies have been subsequently proposed and explored, such as naturalistic studies (Kiesler, 1971), process research (Hoch & Zubin, 1964), and a more intensive, experimental single-subject design (Bergin & Strupp, 1970). On the surface, it might seem that the applied professions have come full circle, returning to the study of the individual. This is true only in part, because currently there is considerably more methodological sophistication in scientifically studying an individual subject than there was during the early part of the twentieth century.

TRADITIONAL NONBEHAVIORAL DESIGNS

Perhaps the prototypical nonbehavioral single-subject design has been the uncontrolled case study. A case study here refers to a study that simply consists of observations of an individual client, dyad, or group made under unsystematic and uncontrolled conditions, and often made in retrospect. Observations may not be planned and sometimes consist of "recollections" or of intermittently recording statements or behaviors that seem to support a particular hypothesis. The lack of experimental control means that it is difficult to exclude many rival hypotheses that might be plausible in explaining the client's behavior, and thus this type of study provides ambiguous information that is difficult to interpret clearly.

A good example of the traditional case study is provided by Daniels (1976) in his investigation of the effects of thought stopping in treating obsessional thinking. He reported that he found the sequential use of several techniques to be beneficial with clients who wished to control depressing thoughts, obsessive thinking, constant negative rumination, or acute anxiety attacks. The sequential use of techniques consisted of thought stopping (Wolpe, 1969), counting from 10 to 1 (Campbell, 1973), cue-controlled relaxation (Russell & Sipich, 1973), and a modification of covert information. The training consisted of three one-hour sessions to teach the client the various techniques. Daniels reported that these procedures were successful, and that clients responded positively to the "sense of control and immediate success" (p. 131). Although this report may be a source of ideas on generating hypotheses for future research, the lack of experimental control makes it difficult to unambiguously interpret the results. It is possible that clients felt compelled in some way to report success, or maybe the successful effects were temporary and short-lived, or maybe techniques other than thought stopping were responsible for any client changes.

More recently, investigators have used a single subject in counseling research by examining variables much more intensively and rigorously. An intensive single-subject design is defined here as the systematic, repeated, and multiple observation of a client, dyad, or group to identify and compare relationships among variables. More specifically, observations regarding a clearly identifiable variable are made in a systematic manner, and typically are planned prior to the beginning of data collection. Many times these observations are made repeatedly over time to allow a comparison across time. Observations are often made from multiple sources allowing a multimodal assessment, including, for instance, (1) cognitive, behavioral, and affective variables, and (2) process and outcome data. The data or observations are collected in such a way as to provide information about the relationships among certain variables or comparisons of variables within the same subject (especially pre-to-post). When comparisons are made within the same subject, the subject serves as his or her own control. In short, the intensive single-subject design is quantitative and is characterized by multiple observations over time that closely scrutinize some variables of interest within a client. The single-subject design involves comparisons of some sort, which is essential for establishing scientific evidence (Campbell & Stanley, 1963). The comparisons can be on the same variable across time, or across different variables.

Hill, Carter, and O'Farrell (1983) provide an example of an intensive single-subject design. They observed one client and one therapist over 12 sessions of insight-oriented therapy; measurements consisted of both process and outcome data that were obtained through subjective and objective means. More specifically, process measures were used to assess verbal behavior, anxiety, and verbal activity level (rated by judges) for both the client and counselor. In addition, both the client and counselor gave subjective impressions of session effectiveness and significant events for each session. The client and her mother also made summary evaluative statements following treatment. Outcome measures, which consisted of the Hopkins Symptom Checklist, Tennessee Self-Concept Scale, Target Complaints, and satisfaction and improvement ratings, were collected immediately after the completion of counseling and at two-month and seven-month follow-ups. The first goal of the study was to describe the process and outcome of the therapeutic treatment. The second aim was to explore the mechanisms of change within the counseling process. With regard to the second goal, (1) comparisons were made between the best and worst sessions, (2) positive and negative events in each session for both the client and counselor were analyzed, and (3) the immediate effects of counselor verbal behavior on client verbal responses were analyzed statistically through sequential analysis.

Outcome measures indicated that treatment was generally positive and resulted in improvement after the 12 sessions. While this improvement was maintained at the two-month follow-up, the client seemed to have relapsed at the seven-month follow-up. The process measures suggested that interpretations, direct feedback, Gestalt exercises, and examination of the therapeutic relationship (all within the context of good rapport and support) seemed to be important mechanisms of change. More recently, Wampold and Kim (1989) conducted more sophisticated sequential analyses on the process data and found that the counselor's minimal encourager responses reinforced description responses (storytelling) by the client, and that confrontation did not lead to opening up or greater client experiencing.

The Hill et al. (1983) study nicely depicts an intensive examination of a single subject within a therapeutic context. A great deal of data were systematically collected in this situation from multiple sources (client, counselor, mother, judges) and across time. For example, over 11,000 responses were categorized in examining client and counselor response modes. In addition, the objective and subjective data collected from various perspectives allowed for comparisons to be made, and subsequently, for conclusions to be developed based on the convergence of a wide range of information rather than a single data point. It is important to note from a scientific perspective that the generalizability of the conclusions obtained from this single case is unclear and replications are needed. Later research by Hill and her colleagues has resulted in important replications as well as extensions (see Hill, Helms, Spiegel, & Tichenor, 1988; Hill, Helms, Tichenor, Spiegel, O'Grady, & Perry, 1988; Hill & O'Grady, 1985; O'Farrell, Hill, & Patton, 1986).

Martin, Goodyear, and Newton (1987) provide another good example of an intensive single-subject design with their study of a supervisory dyad during the course of an academic semester. This investigation used a strategy that merits attention. The authors employed an intensive single-subject design to compare the "best" and "worst" supervisory sessions as a means to increase scientific knowledge about the supervisory process. Similarly to the Hill et al. (1983) investigation, this study used multiple measures of process and outcome variables from multiple perspectives (trainee, supervisor, judges). Specifically, information from the supervisor and trainee perspective were obtained by assessing perceptions of themselves, each other, and the supervisory process. Thus, each person (1) evaluated the quality of each session in terms of depth, smoothness, positivity, and arousal; (2) reported expectations about supervision in terms of interpersonal attraction, interpersonal sensitivity, and task orientation; (3) identified and discussed the occurrence of critical incidents within supervision; and (4) maintained a personal log of their reactions within and to supervision on a weekly basis. Two other measures, activity level and the categorization of interactions, were employed to allow inferences about the supervisory process to be made by objective judges. All of these data were examined by comparing the "best" and "worst" sessions.

Conclusions from this study were made based on the convergence of data from the multiple sources, and also in reference to findings from previous counseling and supervision research. For example, multiple sources of data suggested that the "best" session focused around clarifying the supervisory relationship very early in the semester (second session), a finding that substantiated and extended an earlier conclusion reached by Rabinowitz, Heppner, and Roehlke (1986). Another conclusion was that substantial differences in activity levels differentiated the "best" from the "worst" session, which is consistent with a pattern noted in the Hill et al. (1983) study as well as by Friedlander, Thibodeau, and Ward (1985). Methodologically, the important point here is that conclusions and hypotheses that can direct future research were obtained by examining the convergence of information or data from multiple sources over time from an intensive single-subject design. Webb, Campbell, Schwartz, and Sechrest (1965) called this convergence from multiple sources and multiple observations "triangulation." They maintained that multiple internal measures can provide a form of cross-validation.

TRADITIONAL BEHAVIORAL DESIGNS

The traditional behavioral intrasubject designs also examine the relationship between two or more variables, typically within one or a few subjects. Clearly, the largest single influence in the development of this design has come from researchers operating within an operant conditioning paradigm, using specific target behaviors and clearly identifiable treatment phases, although most definitely the utility of the intrasubject design need not be restricted to that theoretical orientation. Moreover, these designs revolve around multiple or continuous measurements of a dependent variable. Comparisons are made on the dependent variable across specific treatment phases, which makes these intrasubject designs a special type of within-subjects designs (see Chapter 5). The multiple measurements are often referred to as time-series designs; time-series designs have been used in economics for almost half a century (Davis, 1941). A considerable amount of writing has been done on the traditional behavioral intrasubject design, most notably in the last twenty years. Readers interested in this topic might examine the following: Baer, Wolf, and Risley, 1968; Barlow and Hersen, 1984; Kazdin, 1978; Kratochwill, 1978.

In this section, we will first discuss several common features of intrasubject designs (Drew, 1980; Kazdin, 1980). Next we will describe and illustrate two different types of intrasubject designs: AB time series and multiple baseline.

Common Features of Intrasubject Designs

The first common characteristic of intrasubject designs involves the specification of treatment goals. Since intrasubject designs grew out of an operant conditioning paradigm, most studies have specified behavioral goals, often referred to as "targets" or "target behaviors." In essence, the target behaviors are the dependent variables of the investigation. The treatment goal can consist of cognitions, affective reactions, behaviors, physiological responses, or personality characteristics. If systems (groups, families, organizations) are used as the subject of the design, system characteristics (communication patterns, cohesion, involvement) can be designated as treatment goals.

The second defining feature of intrasubject designs is the repeated measurement of the dependent variables over time. The measurement might occur on a weekly basis, or daily, or even several times a day. Many times this assessment process starts before the initiation of treatment, in which case it is referred to as a baseline assessment. Because this assessment process is continuous, or nearly continuous, the researcher can examine the patterns in the dependent variable over time. The independent variable is typically a treatment intervention, often referred to as the intervention. The multiple measurement of the intrasubject design is in stark contrast to other research designs that might employ a single data point before and after an intervention.

The third characteristic of intrasubject designs is the inclusion of different treatment phases, each one representing a different experimental condition. One method of phase specification is to designate a baseline and a treatment phase. Baseline data is collected before treatment initiation and is used to describe the current state of functioning and make predictions about subsequent performance. The second method of defining time periods involves the random assignment of different treatments to different time periods (days, sessions). The basic purpose of changing from one phase to another is to demonstrate change due to the onset of the independent variable or intervention.

The stability of the baseline data is an important feature of most of the intrasubject designs. Change cannot be detected after the onset of an intervention if the baseline data are unstable, and are either increasing, decreasing, or lack consistency. Thus, before the researcher can demonstrate causality due to an intervention, he or she must obtain an accurate and stable assessment of the dependent variable prior to the introduction of the intervention. This is especially the case when a baseline-versus-treatment-intervention-phase comparison is used. This is not true, however, in designs that randomly assign treatments to phases, like the randomized AB design.

AB Time-Series Designs

There are many variations on the AB time-series design. Here we will discuss three specific designs: AB, ABAB, and randomized AB.

The AB Design

The AB design is basically a two-phase experiment; the A phase is a baseline period and the B phase is an intervention phase. Typically, multiple measurements or observations are taken during each phase. For example, each phase might be six weeks long, with two observations each week. These multiple observations enable the researcher to ascertain first of all if the baseline period is stable, and thus allow a suitable assessment of the subject before the intervention. If the baseline period is unstable (that is, measurements are accelerating or decelerating), it is often difficult to draw inferences about the effects of the intervention. Multiple observations after the intervention has begun enable a thorough assessment of the effects of the intervention over time. If one were to collect only one observation per phase, this would basically be a one-group pretest-posttest design (see Chapter 6), which typically has a number of threats to internal validity. The multiple measurements within an AB design, referred to as a time-series format, give more stability over time. The AB design, like the traditional within-subjects design discussed earlier, has the subject serve as his or her own control or comparison. Thus, the basic comparison is between the A phase (baseline) and the B phase (intervention) within the same subject. If a researcher only measured the B phase, he or she would have no basis for comparison and would find it impossible to infer any effects due to the intervention.

Wampold and Freund (in press) noted that the use of statistical methods to analyze the data generated by single-subject designs is controversial. Rather than employing statistical techniques, researchers plot the raw data and make inferences from the graph. This visual analysis, however, is imprecise and can be unreliable and systematically biased (for example, DeProspero & Cohen, 1979; Furlong & Wampold, 1982; Wampold & Furlong, 1981a). Consequently, a variety of statistical tests have been proposed for single-subject designs (see Kazdin, 1980; Wampold & Freund, in press). The interested reader might examine statistical procedures such as the two standard deviation rule (Gottman, McFall, & Barnett, 1969), the relative frequency procedure (Jayaratne & Levy, 1979), lag analysis (Gottman, 1973, 1979), Markov chain analysis (Lichtenberg & Hummel, 1976; Tracey, 1985), time-series analysis (for example, Glass, Willson, & Gottman, 1974), randomization tests (for example, Edgington, 1980, 1982, 1987; Wampold & Worsham, 1986), the split middle technique (White, 1974), and the binomial test (Kazdin, 1980).

In sum, the AB design is a two-phase experiment with a single subject (or group, family) that typically employs multiple observations over time. The basic comparison is between phase A and B; thus each subject serves as his or her own control or comparison.

Consider the following example. Yalom (1985) has suggested that an agenda-go-round (where the therapist asks each member at the beginning of the session to set an agenda for himself or herself for that session) can be used to improve group cohesion and member involvement. A researcher might examine this suggestion by using an AB design. This could be done by identifying a therapy group and for the first ten group sessions measuring the level of cohesion and member involvement in each session. This would be the A phase, or baseline. For the next ten sessions, the researcher could have the group leader use Yalom's agenda-go-round technique and once again measure cohesion and member involvement for each session. This would be the B phase, or intervention. The researcher could compare cohesion and member involvement during the A and B phases to see if the agenda-go-round intervention had an effect. A graph of this design is shown in Figure 7-1. In this figure it seems apparent that the agenda-go-round intervention did have an effect. This type of obvious difference is not always apparent in graphic analyses.

A problem with this simple AB design is that the researcher cannot rule out threats to internal validity from history and maturation as possible explanations for his or her results. (For instance, most groups increase in cohesion over time.) Thus, although the multiple measurements strengthen this study over the one-group pretest-posttest design, this particular time-series design contains some threats to internal validity. Expansions of the AB design such

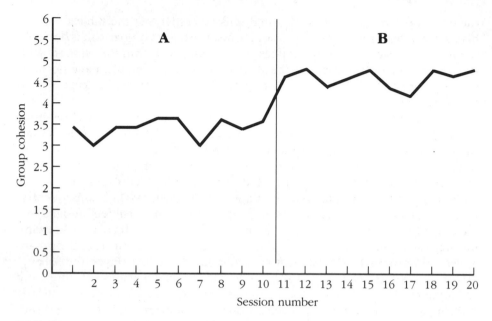

FIGURE 7-1

AB design examining group cohesion (measured on a five-point Likert, with 1 = low cohesion, 5 = high cohesion) by session number (the agenda-go-round exercise was instituted at session 11).

as the ABA, ABAB, and multiple-baseline designs were developed to circumvent some of these weaknesses.

The ABAB Design

Whereas the AB design is basically a two-phase experiment, the ABAB is a four-phase experiment, frequently referred to as a reversal design. In essence, the ABAB examines the effect of a treatment (or independent variable) by either presenting or withdrawing the variable during different phases in an attempt to provide unambiguous evidence of the causal effect of the independent variable. The ABAB design starts with a period of baseline data gathering (A_1) and then a treatment phase (B_1). In this design, however, there is a return to a baseline period (A_2) where the intervention is withdrawn and then a second treatment phase (B_2).

The assumption underlying this reversal is that if the independent variable caused the change in the dependent variable in the B_1 phase, then a removal of the independent variable ought to return the subject to a level similar to the baseline phase. Moreover, if the reversal does result in a return to the baseline, then readministering the independent variable at B_2 will serve as a replication and further strengthen the inferred causal relationship. If the behavior at A_2 does not revert back to the baseline levels, a causal relationship cannot be inferred between the independent and dependent variable, as other (unknown) variables may be accounting for the change. Thus, in the agenda-setting example given earlier, an ABAB design would be as follows: there would be ten group sessions where the researcher collected the baseline cohesion and member involvement data (A_1), ten sessions in which the group leader implemented the agenda-go-round intervention, with continued data collection (B_1), followed by another ten group sessions of just data collection (A_2), and then a final ten sessions with the agenda-go-round intervention reinstituted (B_2). Figure 7-2 presents a graph of data from this ABAB design. Because the group climate improved in both B phases, we can infer that the agenda-go-round exercise caused a change in group climate.

Patterson and Forgatch (1985) used an ABAB design to examine the relationship between therapist behavior and client resistance. (This study is also a good illustration of programmatic research that uses both descriptive and experimental designs to study a phenomenon.) First, using a descriptive research strategy, Patterson and Forgatch examined the likelihood of client resistance following various types of counselor behavior (that is, supportive or teaching responses). In essence, they found that client resistance following the therapist teaching responses was significantly higher than the clients' base rate of resistance. Since this first study was only descriptive, the authors could not infer that therapist teaching caused client resistance. To examine this causal hypothesis, the researchers used an ABAB design. Six counselors met with their clients for video-taped sessions. The counselors started with a baseline phase (A_1) in which they interacted with their clients without using teaching interventions; this was followed by a treatment phase (B_1) in which

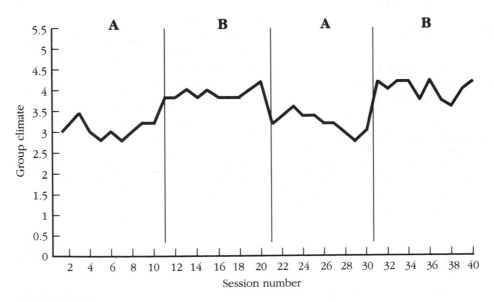

FIGURE 7-2
ABAB design examining group climate by session number (the agenda-go-round exercise was instituted at session 11, withdrawn at session 20, and reinstituted at session 31).

the counselors increased their use of teaching responses. Then a second baseline phase followed in which the counselors returned to interacting without the teaching responses (A_2); and then there was a final treatment phase (B_2) in which the counselors once again increased their use of teaching responses. The results of this ABAB study showed that the counselors did give significantly more teaching responses during the two treatment phases. This indicates that the experimental manipulation was successful (such a procedural check is referred to as a manipulation check). More important, the clients were more resistant during the treatment phases (B_1 and B_2). This data more strongly suggests that therapist teaching behavior caused client resistance.

There are three problems with the ABAB design. The first problem is a statistical one. Most authors and editors want to report some statistical test that describes the amount of difference between the two phases (A and B: see earlier references regarding statistical issues for these designs). When reported, this test is usually a t test or an F test. Both t and F tests, however, assume independent observations, and this is not the case in the ABAB design (Wampold & Freund, in press). A second problem with the ABAB design is the possible presence of carryover efects (that is, effects from the manipulation at phase B_1 that affect A_2 or B_2). It could be that the effects of the B_1 intervention are irreversible and cannot be withdrawn. For example, if the dependent variable involves learning or skill acquisition (for example, study skills such as test-wiseness), it is difficult to reverse these treatments and return the subject to the A_1 level. Obviously, there are many interventions where treatments are reversible and carryover effects are not present. However, in some ABAB designs, the interventions are not reversible and the carryover effects present problems in drawing inferences and in isolating causal relationships. Finally, there may be therapeutic situations in which it is undesirable or unethical to reverse the treatment phase. Both the client and counselor may be reluctant to withdraw an effective treatment. These concerns, in part, have led authors (such as Edgington, 1987) to call for the use of randomized single-subject experiments or randomized AB designs.

The Randomized AB Designs

There are many randomization tests for intrasubject designs (see Edgington, 1980, 1987; Wampold & Furlong, 1981b; Wampold & Worsham, 1986). These statistical tests are beyond the scope of this book. However, we wanted to present one example to introduce you to the design possibilities within randomized AB designs.

The randomized AB design involves two phases that are repeated in a randomized fashion. Thus, in a randomized AB design, the presence of an A or B phase at any point in time is dependent on random assignment. For example, the randomized AB design for examining the effects of an agenda-go-round exercise on group cohesion and member involvement might look like this:

```
         A  A B A B A B B B  A  B  A  A  B  B  A  B  A  B  A
Session  1  2 3 4 5 6 7 8 9 10 11 12 13 14 15 16 17 18 19 20
```

In this example, A represents sessions where the agenda-go-round is not used, and B represents sessions where this exercise is used. Because the occurrence of A and B phases is random, randomization tests or traditional parametric tests can be used (Edgington, 1980) to compare cohesion and involvement scores for the A and B sessions.

This design has a second advantage: it enables the researcher to analyze carryover effects. This can be done by setting up the following simple 2 × 2 factorial design.

Preceded by Phase	Phase A	Phase B
A	(1) Data from sessions 2, 13	(2) Data from sessions 4, 6, 10, 12, 16, 18, 20
B	(3) Data from sessions 3, 5, 7, 11, 14, 17, 19	(4) Data from sessions 8, 9, 15

Data are assigned to cells based on whether they come from phase A or B and based on which phase preceded the phase in question. For example, the first cell in the table contains the data from all phase-A sessions (all sessions without the agenda-go-round) that were preceded by a phase-A session (session without the agenda-go-round). In a like manner, the second cell of the table contains all data from phase-A sessions (without agenda-go-round) that were preceded by a phase-B session (with agenda-go-round). A factorial ANOVA using this setup would provide a main effect for phase A versus B, a main effect for preceding phase (preceding A versus preceding B), and an interaction effect for phase × preceding phase. The interaction analysis directly tests for carryover effects.

Jauquet (1987) actually used this randomized AB design to examine the effects of an agenda-go-round on group cohesion and member involvement. The leader of a training group for graduate students either did (B) or did not (A) begin group sessions with an agenda-go-round exercise, based on a random AB schedule. Since research by Kivlighan and Jauquet (1990) had shown that agenda quality was related to cohesion, cohesion at each meeting was measured by member ratings on the Engaged and Avoiding scales of the Group Climate Questionnaire (MacKenzie, 1983). Involvement was rated by objective observers who viewed video tapes of the session, unaware of the purpose of the study. A 2 (agenda-go-round, non–agenda-go-round) × 2 (preceded by an agenda-go-round, preceded by a non–agenda-go-round) ANOVA revealed no main or interaction effects for observer-rated involvement. There were also no main effects for phases or preceding phases on the Engaged and Avoiding scales.

There was, however, a significant interaction effect on the Engaged and Avoiding scales. An examination of the means showed that non–agenda-go-round sessions that followed agenda-go-round sessions were rated by the group members as more engaged and less avoidant than any of the other combinations. This finding suggests that a periodic use of the agenda-go-round intervention may enhance members' perception of cohesion in groups.

Not only is Jauquet's study important in demonstrating the usefulness of a randomized AB design from a statistical analysis standpoint, it also demonstrates the usefulness of examining for carryover effects. A simple *t* test comparing the results during the A and B phases would have suggested that the agenda-go-round intervention did not have an effect on the dependent variable. The factorial analysis suggested that the simple question of whether or not to use an agenda-go-round is misleading. Rather Jauquet's study suggested that the more appropriate question is when and how much to use the agenda-go-round. In a nonrandomized ABAB design the researcher would never have been alerted to this possible interaction effect.

Some final comments about the AB time-series designs seems warranted. First, although we have discussed and illustrated AB designs as having only two (A and B) phases, this does not have to be the case. A design could contain three (A, B, and C) or more phases. A three-phase design could compare a baseline phase to two different treatments or it could compare three different levels of an independent variable. The basic logic of the AB design remains the same no matter how many phases are involved; the researcher is attempting to isolate the effects of the independent variable by examining different levels (or trends) across different phases.

Many times AB designs are not considered because of possible ethical concerns. For instance, is it appropriate to withdraw a treatment that is having a positive effect on a client? This is a valid concern if the researcher is faced with a question of treatment or no treatment for a client. However, the time-series AB designs can be modified to compare treatments, as in an ABC design, which probably more accurately reflects the reality of the practitioner. For example, rarely is it the case that the clinician decides between one intervention or no treatment at all; rather, he or she has to decide among alternative interventions. Modified AB time-series designs that still allow basic comparisons between phases can be particularly helpful in this situation.

Another concern with AB designs is related to carryover effects of an intervention. For example, Gelso (1979) reasoned that one cannot reverse a client's insight (the theoretical effect of an appropriate interpretation), and thus the AB designs would not be well suited for such content. We believe that the AB designs can be successfully applied to a wider range of topics than is typically acknowledged, although the researcher may need to be creative in adapting the AB designs. For example, we believe that the interpretation-insight link is not a one-time event, but rather that multiple interpretations lead to increasing client insight. One current debate in analytic psychotherapy is over the relative importance of here-and-now versus there-and-then interpretations. This could be studied in a randomized AB design by randomly altering the focus of a counselor's interpretations across sessions. In the then-and-there condition, the counselor's interpretations might focus on how the relationship the client is talking about is similar to past relationships. Conversely, in the here-and-now condition, the interpretations might focus on how those events (or feelings or thoughts) apply to the counseling relationship. Our point is to illustrate that AB designs are not only appropriate for behavioral researchers, but can be fruitfully employed within other theoretical orientations as well.

Multiple-Baseline Designs

The second type of intrasubject design is the multiple-baseline design. The essential feature of this design is that data are recorded on more than one dependent variable, or target behavior, simultaneously. Like the AB designs there is continual collection of data, but in the case of the multiple-baseline design there are two or more data collection baselines on different dependent measures. The intervention being examined is applied to the different dependent measures at different points in time. If the intervention is truly the causal agent, there should be change on the dependent variable that was targeted by the intervention but not on the nontargeted dependent variables. Thus, whereas the ABAB design attempts to identify causal relationships by withdrawing the intervention and reversing the change, the multiple-baseline design attempts to identify causality by changes in some but not all of the multiple dependent measures. In short, the basic assumption is that with several dependent measures, one or more of these variables can serve as controls while the intervention is simultaneously applied to one of the dependent measures. One of the problems with the multiple-baseline approach is the possible nonindependence of the dependent variables; thus, when the intervention is targeted at one of the dependent variables but all of the dependent variables change, this raises confusion as to what caused the change (more on this later).

There are three different versions of the multiple-baseline design. The first variation is to collect data on two or more dependent variables in the same individual. For example, a researcher may want to examine the effects of therapeutic homework assignments on the amount of family communication. To use a multiple-baseline design, he or she would have to identify at least two behaviors to measure family communication. These two behaviors might be (1) the amount of time after dinner the husband and wife spend talking and (2) the amount of time after dinner the parents spend talking with the children. Like the AB designs, the multiple-baseline design starts with a period of baseline assessment. Thus, in our example, this would involve daily recordings of interaction time between (1) spouses and (2) parents and children. Next the intervention is targeted at one of these dependent variables; a homework assignment is initiated that is designed to increase interspousal communication. The basic assumption in this example is that the second behavior (amount of communication between parents and children) serves as a control for the first behavior (amount of communication between spouses). If the intervention is causally related to interspousal communication, there should be a change in the amount of time the husband and wife spend communicating but not in the amount of time the parents spend communicating with the children. Similarly to the AB designs, data are collected on these two behaviors for a specified period of time, let's say one week. Finally, a homework assignment can be designed to increase parent-child communication. A change in the amount of time spent in parent-child communication would be expected to occur only after the introduction of this intervention. Sometimes three to five different behaviors are identified and these behaviors are targeted over successive time periods to assess the effects of a particular intervention. Continuation of stable baselines in the behaviors not targeted for intervention (that is, the controls) indicates the absence of coincidental influences other than the experimental intervention.

The second variation of the multiple-baseline design is to identify the same response across different subjects. Returning to our earlier example about agenda setting, a researcher may want to test Yalom's (1985) hypothesis concerning the relationship between the quality of group member agendas and their subsequent involvement in the group. Specifically, Yalom stated that group members will initiate more high-level interactions when the agendas for the group are realistic, interpersonal, and here-and-now oriented. The researcher could begin by making a baseline assessment of each group member's interactions over the first five group sessions. He or she could then begin to train individual group members to set relative, interpersonal, and here-and-now agendas. Only one group member would be trained at a time and the initiation of the training with the individual group members would be staggered; let's say the researcher might train a different member every fifth group session. A change in any individual's quality of group participation would be expected to occur contingent on his or her receiving the agenda training, while no change would be expected in those not trained. The basic assumption in this example is that individuals can serve as controls when they have not been intervened with. Data collection is continuous, and only those individuals who have received the intervention are expected to change on the dependent measure. A possible source of contamination in this example is that subjects who have not received training might learn how to set effective agendas by observing their peers who have received training.

The third variation of the multiple-baseline design is to identify the same response for one subject but across different situations. As in all illustrations of the multiple-baseline design, a subject can refer to an individual subject, group, classroom, or larger unit. As an example, a researcher may want to examine the effects of token reinforcement (the independent variables) on a child interacting with peers (the dependent variable). The amount of interaction with peers could be observed both before and after school on the playground, during a baseline period. The researcher could then start token reinforcement of prosocial interactions only during the morning before school.

The researcher would expect to then find a change in the amount of inter-action with peers in the morning but not in the afternoon. Later the token reinforcement could be done in the afternoon also, and a consequent change in this baseline would then be expected.

Because the logic of the multiple-baseline design requires that the researcher show changes in one assessed behavior while the other assessed behavior remains constant, one of the main concerns in using this type of design is the indepen-dence of the dependent variables. If there is a relationship between two or more of the behaviors, then a change in one behavior may well lead to a change in the other. If two behaviors show simultaneous change, and only one received the independent variable, then it is impossible to rule out threats to internal validity like history and maturation as causal agents. Such unintended changes in baselines seriously jeopardize the strength of the multiple-baseline design and typically produce a study with uninterpretable results.

One way to guard against this complication is to carefully assess the independence of the behaviors, perhaps by correlating the baseline behaviors (Christensen, 1980). Another possible solution to this problem is the use of several dependent variables. Kazdin and Kopel (1975) recommended using four or more variables. By increasing the number of baselines the researcher can guard against the possibility that two of the baselines are dependent on each other.

A final comment about multiple-baseline designs seems warranted. In reviewing articles from counseling journals for inclusion as examples in this section, the authors were not able to find any recent studies using multiple-baseline designs in the major counseling journals. This absence is in stark contrast to journals in clinical psychology, and especially the behaviorally oriented journals (for example, *Behavior Therapy, Behavioral Assessment, Journal of Applied Behavior Analysis*). This suggests that this design is being used infrequently in counseling research.

ADVANTAGES AND DISADVANTAGES OF SINGLE-SUBJECT DESIGNS

The single-subject design has a number of advantages and limitations. We will initially discuss these in a rather simple and absolute sense. We would like to highlight the fact that in weighing these advantages and limitations, it is imperative to distinguish between the uncontrolled case study on the one hand and the intensive single-subject design and traditional behavioral design on the other. In our view, much less can be learned from the uncontrolled case study because of the multitude of rival hypotheses. Conversely, the comparisons and control in the intensive single-subject design and traditional behavioral design provide stronger empirical support, and thus lend more utility to the research design. It is also important to note that the advantages and limitations need to be considered relative to two variables: the existing scientific knowledge pertaining to a specific question and the previous research methodologies employed in examining that particular research question.

Advantages

Single-subject designs are versatile. They can be used as a means of collecting information and ideas, and generating hypotheses about the therapeutic process; as a means of testing therapeutic techniques; as a means of testing new methodologies; as a means of studying individuals and rare phenomena; and as a means of providing exemplars and counterinstances.

A Means of Collecting Information and Ideas, and Generating Hypotheses about the Therapeutic Process

Although the traditional between-groups design has been useful in examining outcomes in psychotherapy, a prominent difficulty has been the obscuring of individual variations in group averages. The therapeutic process is complex and highly variable. Clients differ from each other in significant ways; they are not uniform (Kiesler, 1966). Rather, clients process information about themselves, their experiential worlds, and counseling in idiographic ways, and even differently from one time to the next. The same can be said of counselors; therapists not only differ in important ways from each other, they also are different from one time to another. The counselor-client relationship is equally complex and idiographic. Thus, in the context of the complex and detailed process of therapy, intensive single-subject methodologies in particular are ideally suited for microscopic analyses and expanding scientific knowledge. In fact, more than twenty years ago Bergin and Strupp (1970) maintained that the intensive single-subject design would be one of the primary strategies to clarify the mechanisms of change within the therapeutic process. More recently, intensive single-subject designs have also been recommended for obtaining an in-depth analysis of the therapeutic process (Bergin & Lambert, 1978; Gelso, 1979; Hill, Carter, & O'Farrell, 1983; Resnikoff, 1978).

Both the intensive single-subject design and the traditional behavioral design offer a unique opportunity to carefully scrutinize aspects of the therapeutic process in depth. Methodologies that employ very time-consuming procedures such as interpersonal process recall (Kagan, 1975) or assessing cognitive structures by using an associative network (Martin, 1985) are often impossible when large numbers of subjects are involved. However, these procedures are more feasible when only one or a few clients are involved. In a way, the single-subject design can allow for a more complete description of what happens in counseling and the mechanisms involved in change. The studies mentioned earlier by Hill et al. (1983) and Martin et al. (1987) provide good examples of microscopic analyses of variables involved in the change process. These studies provide important in-depth information that contributes to our scientific knowledge base about counseling and supervision. More specifically, Hill et al. (1983) noted that intensive single-subject designs (1) permit a more adequate description of what actually happens between a counselor and client, (2) facilitate more integration of process data with positive or negative outcomes, (3) allow a close examination of the change process in the therapeutic relationship, and (4) allow outcome measures to be tailored to an individual client's problems.

Tracey (1986) provides a good example of using a single-subject design to initially examine a relatively new counseling variable, topic determination, followed by a larger study using a between-groups design. Topic determination pertains to reaching agreement between the counselor and client on what is to be discussed and how it is to be discussed. In his first study, Tracey (1986) compared four continuing counseling dyads (two dyads were determined to be successful while two dyads were identified as unsuccessful), and two dyads that had terminated prematurely. All dyads involved nonpsychotic clients seen at a university counseling center using a time-limited therapy format. Consistent with his hypothesis, the premature termination dyads had lower levels of topic determination than the continuing dyads. Tracey then conducted a second study in which he examined 18 dyads (6 who terminated prematurely, and 12 who were continuing). The results from his between-groups analysis confirmed his first study in identifying a significant relationship between premature termination and topic determination.

The single-subject design also provides a rich source of data that can spark ideas or hypotheses. For example, a case study approach, even though it typically is uncontrolled, can offer suggestive data about some aspect of counseling. Let's say a therapist has developed a special interest in counseling clients who have an especially difficult time with grieving the loss of a significant other. As the therapist's skills are honed over time, she begins to detect certain patterns in the grief victims she works with in therapy, such as overdependence and problems with intimacy. The therapist then collects some objective test data with the next client to check her hunches, which are verified. Thus, the case study approach, first informally with individual clients and later with more objective test data, can be a rich source of ideas and hypotheses for more systematic research. It is important for the therapist to be cognizant, however, that such observations and ideas are subject to information processing biases and subjective inference processes (see Turk & Salovey, 1988). Although such observations obviously do not provide rigorous scientific data, nonetheless important information can be obtained from single-subject studies of some aspect of counseling, even from a relatively uncontrolled case study.

It is important to qualify our comments regarding the use of single-subject designs in generating ideas. Historically, individual cases not only have been the source of ideas, but also have been influential in the formulation of personality and psychotherapy theories. For example, Freud's psychoanalytic theory depended heavily on his observations of individual clients. Cases such as those of Ann O., Frau Emmy von N., and Fraulein Elizabeth von R. greatly affected the development of Freud's ideas regarding catharsis, repression, and free association (Monte, 1980). Thus, the core of Freud's psychoanalytic theory was based largely on observations from case studies. Still, the scientific merit of generalizing from uncontrolled case studies to the development of entire theoretical models is extremely suspect and generally ill-advised. The process of collecting suggestive information and generating hypotheses is only a small part of a broader process of developing theories.

A Means of Testing Therapeutic Techniques

Single-subject designs provide a useful means to test the effects of specific therapeutic techniques. The testing of techniques might happen at several levels: (1) the discovery of a new technique, (2) an intentional examination of a relatively new technique, (3) the application of an established technique to a new population or treatment situation, and (4) an in-depth examination of well-established technique.

Occasionally, therapists will discover new techniques through a trial-and-error process with individual clients. Breuer's work with Anna O. resulted in the discovery of a "talking cure" or catharsis. In essence, Breuer found through trial and error that some of Anna's symptoms were relieved or disappeared simply by talking about them (Breuer & Freud, 1893–1895/1955). George Kelley, in part out of boredom with the Freudian interpretations, began fabricating "insights" and "preposterous interpretations," and discovered that often clients could change their lives in important ways if they believed these "alternative constructions of the world" (Monte, 1980, p. 434). Likewise, Rogers abandoned the traditional directive and diagnostically oriented therapeutic style after a dismal therapeutic failure in which a client reentered and redirected therapy by initiating a discussion of her troubled marriage. Rogers discovered "it is the client who knows what hurts, what direction to go, what problems are crucial, and what experiences have been deeply buried" (Rogers, 1961, pp. 11–12). In short, therapists often will stumble onto or create new techniques through their therapeutic work with individual clients. The intentional and consistent examination of new techniques within the informal case study as well as the more formal single-subject design can yield useful information about the counseling process. Thus, new observations by the therapist might be informally or formally tested with additional clients to further determine the effectiveness and generalizability of the technique.

The single-subject design can also be used effectively to test the application of an established technique with a new problem or a new population. Kazdin (1980) noted that the extension of a given technique to a new problem is really quite common in the literature. For example, systematic desensitization has been found to be applicable to a wide range of phobias or fears, such as fear of heart attacks (Furst & Cooper, 1970) and fear of sharks (Krop & Krause, 1976).

Finally, the single-subject design also lends itself well to an in-depth examination of the effectiveness of a certain technique. For example, a great deal of information could be collected about how a client is processing or reacting to repeated use of a certain technique, such as the Gestalt empty-chair

technique, counselor touch, or counselor self-disclosure. Thus, in-depth information could be collected on the use of a specific technique over time.

A Means of Testing New Methodologies

The single-subject design is especially well suited to testing new research
methodologies. This design allows the investigator to "experiment" in a way
with a new methodology or procedure. The investigator can determine whether
a new methodology provides new or more useful information, or if some aspect
of counseling is better understood in some way.

Several investigations by Jack Martin provide excellent examples of testing
new methodologies by using single-subject designs. Martin has conceptualized
counseling through a cognitive mediational paradigm (Martin, 1984), in which
he maintained the necessity to examine the cognitive processes of clients.
Martin suggested that the information contained in a client's cognitive structures, and the organization of that information, would have considerable appeal
to researchers of counseling outcomes. Using an information-processing
perspective, Martin tested a methodology to assess a client's cognitive structures (Martin, 1985). At the end of each session with a client, fictitiously called
Carla, he would ask her to relax and then give the first associations to the
following words: *problem, Bill* (fictitious name for her husband), and *Carla*.
As the client mentioned specific word associations, Martin wrote each word
on a small square. After Carla had responded to the three memory probes, she
was asked to arrange the labels on a laminated board using distance and drawing lines to symbolically depict relationships among the words. Martin found
this procedure produced "an incredible amount of data" (p. 558). The pre-
to postcounseling diagrams revealed that Carla had acquired important
knowledge about battering (the presenting problem) and options of what she
should do about this particular problem (for example, take advantage of Women
Center's programming). Carla's outcomes also reflected important changes in
her affective processes, from passive, reactive emotions (such as guilt, shame)
to more active emotions (like hope, anger). Martin (1985) thus concluded that
this particular method of assessing a client's cognitive structures provided very
useful data that nicely captured some of the richness and subjective nature of
the change process in counseling. Thus, this particular single-subject study
provided important information about a new methodological procedure. Given
the idiosyncratic nature of the data from this new method, group data would
initially be quite overwhelming and not lend itself well to "averaging" across
clients. The important point is that the results of Martin's initial study provided
empirical support for additional examination of this new methodology.

A Means of Studying Individuals and Rare Phenomena

A major difficulty noted by many applied researchers and practitioners is the
obscuring of individual variations and outcomes when subjects are examined
in groups and their data is simply "averaged." In fact, trying to think about

the "average" or "typical" client is generally not very useful when developing interventions. Clients are seldom homogeneous or "uniform."

By contrast, the single-subject design is particularly well suited to describing the idiosyncracies of individual clients, because of its intensive and often microscopic analyses. Thus, the single-subject design can be considered a useful tool for examining change within a single individual. In fact, in the early 1970s Bergin and Strupp (1970) proposed that the single-subject design be used as the primary methodology to isolate specific mechanisms of change. The case study approach can provide some information as well, but most often it lacks experimental control, which confounds even tentative conclusions.

The single-subject design also lends itself to more qualitative approaches in studying individuals (see Neimeyer & Resnikoff, 1982; Polkinghorne, 1984). In this way, the single-subject design can be used to collect data about the "thinking frameworks" of individuals (Edgington, 1987; Neimeyer & Resnikoff, 1982) or higher mental processes (Wundt, 1900/1916). Polkinghorne (1984) aptly suggested that human action and decision making, which are central to the therapeutic and counseling process, appear to be related to a "means-end rationality" or mode of processing information. Heppner and Krauskopf (1987) noted similar thinking processes by using an information-processing model to describe client problem solving in a counseling context. The single-subject design may be particularly well suited for gathering information about (1) how clients process information, (2) the thinking steps or means involved in reaching some end or goal (logically or illogically), (3) an individual's plans and intentions (Heppner & Krauskopf, 1987; Howard, 1985), and (4) how such plans affect the processing of information and subsequent behavior. The complexity of such information processing may be examined more feasibly via a single-subject design, at least initially. In short, single-subject designs are useful to study individuals, particularly as counselors use some of the more qualitative approaches in examining higher mental processes.

Although the single-subject design is useful in studying specific individuals, it is particularly useful in studying rare phenomena, such as a multiple personality. Kazdin (1980) illustrates this particular advantage of single-subject designs by discussion of the well-publicized report of the "three faces of Eve" (Thigpen & Cleckley, 1954, 1957). Eve represented a rare personality and offered a unique opportunity to study this phenomenon.

In addition to rare phenomena, the single-subject design can also be used to study relatively low-frequency occurrences, such as male anorexics and foreign college students under situational stress (for example, Iranian students during the Iran Hostage Crisis of 1980, and aborted grief reactions; see Corazzini, 1980). Although a typical university counseling center usually has a very broad range of clients, it is often difficult to study infrequent occurrences in a group comparison format. It is not usually feasible, nor ethical, to withhold treatment until enough of these low-occurrence clients seek counseling to randomly assign clients to groups, and so forth. Thus, the single-subject design is useful to investigate various idiosyncracies or commonalities across clients with similar presenting problems, such as clients with aborted grief reactions.

A Means of Providing Exemplars and Counterinstances

The single-subject design can be used to provide exemplars to highlight findings, particularly if these findings run counter to existing beliefs or theories (in which case exemplars become counterinstances). Given that the intensive and behavioral designs generally provide stronger experimental control, these findings obviously lend themselves better to such highlighting.

More specifically, the findings from a single-subject design can be used to provide data in support of a particular point, argument, or theory. For example, Strupp (1980a, 1980b, 1980c) conducted a series of single-subject studies, comparing therapists each with a successful and unsuccessful case in brief psychodynamic therapy. A wide variety of process and outcome measures were used to examine events related to therapeutic effectiveness. Negative outcomes were related to client characterological problems (as compared to neurotic problems) or counseling countertransference issues. Positive outcomes were related to the client's ability to take advantage of the therapeutic relationship and to work within the therapist's framework. Strupp then used these results to propose that patient variables were more powerful events in assessing therapeutic outcomes, even to the point of overshadowing therapists' attitudes and technical skill.

Kazdin (1980) points to the early beliefs about symptom substitution, stemming primarily from psychoanalytic thinking. The general assumption was that treatment of overt, problematic behavior rather than the underlying cause may result in symptom substitution. However, research on specific problematic behaviors such as phobias or bed wetting did not result in the appearance of substitute symptoms (for example, Jones, 1956; Meyer, 1957; Yates, 1958). Thus, this early research using primarily uncontrolled case studies cast doubt on the unqualified notion of symptom substitution, suggesting that this phenomenon may be more complex than previously assumed.

Caution obviously must be used when employing findings from single-subject designs as exemplars or as counterinstances. As mentioned previously, in early research relatively uncontrolled case studies were not just overused as exemplars but were used as the primary data base in the construction of personality theories. Although the generalizability of the findings from single-subject designs must always be questioned, the results can highlight a particular point or cast doubt on previously held beliefs and suggest that, at a minimum, there are exceptions to the rule, or suggest that the rule is somehow incorrect. However, exemplars should not become the only or even primary data base relating to a particular phenomenon. Thus, it is imperative to consider both the need for additional empirical evidence as well as the advantages and limitations of single-subject designs in giving such findings persuasive value.

Disadvantages

As traditionally conceived and conducted, the individual case study represents an almost total lack of experimental control. Many of Cook and Campbell's

(1979) threats to internal validity are present, such as history, maturation, testing, selection, and mortality. In addition, many times "data" are collected in unsystematic and even retrospective ways. After a counselor has worked with a particular client for some time, the therapist reflects back (sometimes months later) to collect his or her "observations" about the case. Such retrospective analyses most likely involve multiple sources of bias and distortion (for example, memory loss, memory distortion, subjective impressions, selective attention) and blur any temporal succession pertaining to causal relationships. Sometimes the "data" also consist of self-reports collected verbally from the client by the counselor. Sometimes the client may believe he or she is doing the counselor a favor by completing a questionnaire. Data obtained in such a manner may very well be contaminated or biased, most likely by demand characteristics inherent in the situation. Likewise, data may be collected from the client with instruments of unknown reliability or validity, thereby calling into question the adequacy of the client data. In short, any of a number of biases of uncontrolled variables obscure the relationship between the variables under examination and thus obscure interpretation of the findings. While it *may* be true that variable x affected variable y in some way, it also may be the case that many other variables created the effect on variable y. The upshot of the uncontrolled case study is that there may be several plausible explanations for the observed effect on variable y, thus limiting the scientific value of the study. The uncontrolled case study is a weak source of "data" and at best is suggestive.

By contrast, the intensive single-subject design and the behavioral design typically involve more systematic observations and experimental control. For example, the study by Hill et al. (1983) involved combining subjective and objective data from multiple sources (client, counselor, judges, the client's mother). In addition, the study made comparisons within the data collected, specifically between the "best" and "worst" sessions. Such comparisons serve to identify relationships among variables within the same subject. When comparisons are made within the same individual (and thus the subject serves as his or her own control), some of the threats to internal validity are controlled for. These well-controlled investigations typically provide stronger empirical evidence, allowing fewer rival hypotheses and subsequently more definitive conclusions. A disadvantage of the intensive single-subject design is that experimenters may find what they expected to find and overlook information that is contrary to their expectations. For example, subsequent analyses of the Hill et al. (1983) data revealed several facets of the interaction between the counselor and client that were undetected by those researchers' analysis (Wampold & Kim, 1989).

A major issue in using single-subject designs is the generalizability of the findings to other individuals or situations. Even if one isolates specific relationships among variables, it is unclear whether the results would generalize to other clients with similar concerns or diagnosis (client generality) or whether a particular technique would work in a different setting (setting generality) (Barlow & Hersen, 1984). In short, the generalizability issue has been a major limitation of the single-subject design.

The generalizability issue is also a major concern for studies comparing groups. Neimeyer and Resnikoff (1982) persuasively argued that inferences derived from *any* sampling procedure must be tentatively ventured and carefully restricted. They note that quantitatively oriented studies deal with the representativeness issue primarily by using statistical sampling. Qualitatively oriented approaches rely more on theoretical sampling, generalizing only to people with characteristics similar to those of the individuals studied.

Tracey and Ray (1984) provide an example of replicating single-subject designs. They conducted a study that focused on the interactional stage differences between successful (n = 3) and unsuccessful (n = 3) time-limited counseling by examining six counseling dyads; data from each dyad were examined individually, which meant that Tracey conducted six single-subject studies. They hypothesized that the successful (but not unsuccessful) dyads would be characterized by three fairly distinct stages of high, low, and again high levels of complementarity. To examine complementarity, Tracey and Ray examined who determined the topic of discussion in the counseling session. Specifically, the sequence of topic-following/topic initiation was used as an index of complementarity and was analyzed using a Markov chain model to test for differences in the sequence of topic responses over time. Analyses of each dyad revealed support for their hypothesis for each successful and unsuccessful dyad. Specifically, topic determination was found to change significantly over time for successful dyads but remain constant for unsuccessful dyads. Thus, replicating the pattern of results across six dyads adds considerable strength to the external validity of this study. Parenthetically, Tracy and Ray (1984) also found that the differences between unsuccessful and successful dyads disappeared when the data were combined or aggregated across dyads, which underscores the potential loss of information when averaging across individuals.

SUMMARY AND CONCLUSIONS

The common goal of all counseling research methods is to facilitate an understanding of human behavior. Different methodologies provide different types of data and information about human behavior. Single-subject designs permit an examination of an individual person, dyad, or group. It can be argued that a practitioner counseling a specific client is less concerned with group averages than with the individual's behavior. It is not sufficient to rely on normative data that suggest a particular intervention strategy works with three out of four clients and thus simply to rely on probabilities. Single-subject designs, particularly those of an intensive, systematic, or time-series nature, can provide information about the uniqueness of client responses and counselor interventions. However, researchers must be particularly sensitive to various sources of bias and extraneous variables, and must make every attempt to control such variables when considering Kerlinger's "MAXMINCON" principle.

More specifically, we discussed two main types of single-subject design, the nonbehavioral single-subject design and the traditional behaviorally oriented intrasubject time-series design. Within the former, we discussed the uncontrolled case study as well as the more recent intensive single-subject design. A case study refers to a study that consists simply of observations of an individual, dyad, or group that are made under unsystematic and uncontrolled conditions. The intensive single-subject design typically involves more experimental control and consists of systematic, repeated, and multiple observations of an individual, dyad, or group under experimental conditions designed to identify and compare relationships among variables. In our view, the comparisons and control in the intensive single-subject design provide stronger empirical support and thus give it more utility than the case study as a research design.

The traditional behaviorally oriented intrasubject time-series designs also examine the relationship between two or more variables, typically within one or a few subjects, and involve considerable levels of experimental control. These designs are characterized by specific treatment goals, numerous and repeated measurements of the dependent variable, and the inclusion of different phases or periods of time (each one representing a different experimental condition such as a baseline phase or an intervention phase). The basic purpose of changing from one phase to another is to demonstrate change, presumably due to the onset of the independent variable or intervention. Two major types of intrasubject designs were discussed: AB time-series designs (AB, ABAB, randomized AB) and multiple-baseline designs. We maintained that the time-series designs are not only appropriate for behavioral researchers, but can be fruitfully employed within other theoretical orientations as well.

The uncontrolled case study appears infrequently, if at all, in the major counseling journals at this time. The intensive single-subject design has begun to appear in the counseling journals, particularly since the appearance of Hill et al. (1983). It is extremely rare for any counseling journal to contain a report of a study using an intrasubject design. For example, during all of 1988 the *Journal of Counseling Psychology* contained no reports of studies using an intrasubject design.

We strongly believe that the intensive single-subject design can be a powerful methodology to increase understanding of counseling and the counseling process. The single-subject design can be used for (1) collecting information and ideas, and generating hypotheses about the therapeutic process, (2) testing therapeutic techniques, (3) testing new methodologies, (4) studying individuals and rare phenomena, and (5) providing exemplars and counterinstances. However, limitations imposed by threats to both internal and external validity must be clearly examined and considered. Bergin and Strupp (1970) initially predicted that the single-subject design would be one of the primary strategies to clarify the process of counseling; this remains to be demonstrated. Nonetheless, we strongly believe in the potential of this methodology; thus our first recommendation is to use the single-subject design more frequently in counseling research. Intensive single-subject designs that use both quantitative and qualitative data can be especially rich in providing more holistic data of both a content and process nature. Moreover, we believe that it is erroneous to relegate the single-subject design to merely ''exploratory'' research, in which any "findings" must later be subject to the "real" methods of science (Neimeyer & Resnikoff, 1982).

A number of the examples used in this chapter were drawn from group counseling. This was quite deliberate. One of the main obstacles in group counseling research is the sample size of the study. Many times in group counseling research, the variable of interest is a group-level variable like cohesion. Often, however, researchers use individual scores, like each subject's attraction to the group, so they can increase the size of their groups in their between-groups design. Researchers could circumvent this sample size problem by using more intrasubject time-series designs.

Accordingly, our second recommendation is an increased use of intrasubject designs in group (and family) research. This recommendation could also help address a second problem in group research, that of most group counseling studies using analogue groups of very short duration. Time-series designs would allow the researcher to study the group as an entity and to use real client groups without having to line up a prohibitively large number of subjects.

Our third recommendation is the increased use of randomized designs in AB intrasubject research. Randomized designs offer additional complexity and flexibility, and enable the researcher to examine for the presence of carryover effects between treatments. In addition, randomized designs permit the use of powerful parametric statistical analyses. Editors are often reluctant to publish studies that do not have statistical comparisons, and readers rely on these statistical comparisons as a way of comparing studies for AB intrasubject designs; parametric statistical tests can only be performed appropriately when AB phases are randomly assigned.

We would like to mention one other methodological consideration in discussing the use of the single-subject methodology, namely the type of data or knowledge currently available on a particular research question. For example, a considerable number of studies have investigated the therapeutic technique of thought stopping. In 1978, Heppner reviewed the published investigations to determine the clinical efficacy of thought stopping. This body of literature consisted of 22 studies, 20 of which were case studies that lacked experimental control (Heppner, 1978b). Thus, this body of "knowledge" concerning the clinical efficacy of thought stopping was based largely on data collected from the same methodological perspective, indicative of what has been called paradigm fixation (Gelso, 1979). Our point is that it is insufficient to ascertain the advantages and limitations of the single-subject design in an absolute sense. Rather, it is also imperative to weigh the advantages and limitations with reference to the existing scientific knowledge base on a particular question and the type of designs that have been used in past research.

CHAPTER 8

DESCRIPTIVE DESIGNS

Descriptive designs are research strategies that enable the investigator to describe the occurrence of variables, the underlying dimensions in a set of variables, or the relationship between or among variables. Basically, descriptive designs help to define the existence and delineate characteristics of a particular phenomenon. For example, a descriptive study might present information that establishes the frequency of date rape, problems faced by college students, or vocational undecidedness in entering freshman students. Observation is at the core of the descriptive process; the utility of a descriptive study is directly dependent on the quality of observations, or more commonly in counseling, the quality of the instruments or assessments. Moreover, it is impossible to observe all instances of a phenomenon, so instead the researcher carefully studies the phenomenon in a sample drawn from the population of interest. Thus, the reliability and validity of the observations and the generalizability of the sample are two critical issues in descriptive research.

Unfortunately, many texts on research design devote little attention to descriptive designs. This lack of attention stems partially from what we call the "pure science myth," which holds up the experimental design paradigm a priori as the "correct" or "best" mode of scientific investigation.

Moreover, the received view of science tends to emphasize the testing and verification of theories, as well as comparisons among competing theories. Consequently, research in counseling has become largely a science of verification and less a science of description and discovery. Greenberg (1986) argued that counseling psychology should place more emphasis on discovery paradigms. He believes that the empiricist tradition with its emphasis on the controlled between-groups experiment has been overvalued by counseling researchers. We strongly agree. Consequently, a great deal of research in counseling is based on poorly described phenomena and most likely is poorly understood. Too often researchers attempt to manipulate and control variables before enough is known about those variables.

Physical scientists, by contrast, spend a great deal of time observing, describing, and classifying events. Tests of competing theories are relatively infrequent in the physical sciences. This order of things has seemingly been reversed in counseling research. Inadequately described phenomena are often subjected to rigid verification with disappointing results. Before one can test the adequacy of a theory in explaining a phenomenon, one needs a reliable and detailed description of the phenomenon. A central thesis of this chapter is that descriptive designs do have an important role in the scientific process, and that one should strongly consider using these designs to address certain research questions. Thus, we see considerable value in descriptive research in counseling.

At first glance, the "MAXMINCON" principle that we have stressed seems antithetical to descriptive research. For example, by exercising experimental control, it might seem like the experimenter would interfere with or change the natural phenomenon he or she was attempting to describe. On the one hand, many variables are left uncontrolled in descriptive research, and thus cause-and-effect statements are inappropriate. Conversely, the investigator can exercise considerable care in making observations so as to minimize measurement errors, which can create considerable error variance. Thus, the quality of the observations is the heart of descriptive design. Likewise, the researcher can exercise experimental control to reduce bias and extraneous variables by selecting his or her sample through random sampling. Accordingly, in this chapter we will emphasize measurement, observation, and sampling as we review the different types of descriptive designs.

There are two major classifications of descriptive research: qualitative and quantitative. This chapter devotes a major section to each. According to Patton (in press), quantitative and qualitative research can be distinguished along four dimensions. The first distinguishing characteristic involves ontological assumptions. Quantitative research, because it emanates from a post-positivistic tradition, asserts that the major constituents of the world are physical objects and processes. In contrast, qualitative approaches, which emanate from a phenomenological perspective, tend to emphasize internal mental events as the fundamental reality of existence. The second distinguishing characteristic involves epistemological assumptions. Quantitative designs assume that knowledge arises from observations of the physical world. For the qualitative researcher, however, knowledge is actively constructed, not passively observed, and thus arises from examination of people's internal constructions. A third distinction between quantitative and qualitative research involves methods of data collection. In quantitative research the investigator either directly or through coding schemes observes events and then makes inductive inferences based on these observations. The qualitative researcher, rather than rely on outside observational schemes, tries to retain the perspective of the people being studied. This usually involves an analysis of field or observational notes or a study of audio or video recordings. Finally, quantitative and qualitative researchers usually address different research questions. According to Patton, the goal of quantitative research is to describe cause-and-effect relationships in the physical world. Qualitative researchers, on the other hand, attempt to describe and understand the ways that people give meaning to their own and others' behavior (Patton, 1984).

QUALITATIVE DESIGNS

Qualitative designs include naturalistic-ethnographic and phenomenological designs. Naturalistic-ethnographic research attempts to holistically describe a phenomenon with particular attention to the participants' beliefs about the phenomenon. Phenomenological research is particularly interested in examining consciousness. In other words, phenomenological researchers attempt to understand how participants make meaning of and through their interactions.

Naturalistic-Ethnographic Research

Naturalistic-ethnographic research is characterized by an emphasis on inductive observation and description (Hoshmand, 1989). In this paradigm the researcher attempts to describe and understand the perceptions of the research participant, with a particular emphasis on the context in which the behaviors occur. The methodology, particularly the procedures, are often unique to the individual investigation. Nevertheless, there do seem to be some standard phases involved in the conduct of these studies. Smith (1981) described four: (1) entrée and access to the site, (2) data collection, (3) interpretation and analysis, and (4) writing.

Perhaps most important, the researcher attempts to make the research subject a collaborator in the research. Rather than standing apart from and looking at the subject, the naturalistic-ethnographic investigator becomes intimately involved with the research participants. Most writers talk about the researcher's stance as being that of a participant-observer (for example, Hoshmand, 1989). Since the researcher is more intimately involved with the subject in this type of research, the entrée into the system is critical. In essence, the quality of the data that the researcher collects is directly related to the quality of the relationship that she or he establishes with the subject(s). The entrée process in naturalistic-ethnographic research is very similar to the building of a working alliance with a counseling client. Thus, an important focus for the researcher is building a collaborative working relationship with the subject.

Only after this collaborative relationship has been established can the researcher begin the actual data collection process. In most naturalistic-ethnographic studies, multiple methods of data collection are used and data are obtained from multiple sources. The typically used data collection methods are archival research, ethnographic observation, oral history, qualitative interview, and critical incident reports (Hoshmand, 1989). Archival records or literature can provide background or history about the subjects. Ethnographic observation involves the researcher's entering the subjects' environment and either recording verbatim or through notes the interactions. A qualitative interview is an interactive open-ended dialogue between the researcher and the subject(s). Oral history is similar to the qualitative interview, but more in the form of a monologue. Critical incident reports are either written or verbal descriptions by the subjects of important or significant events. According to

Hoshmand (1989), the form of data collection should match the subjects' natural style of interacting.

Data analysis can range from systematized methods like Glaser and Strauss's (1987) constant comparative method to more intuitive approaches. The main method of analysis is a reading and rereading of the data with the goal of identifying core constructs or deep levels of meaning. The conclusions derived from this analysis can be strengthened by having independent judges engage in the same analytic process and/or by having the research participants confirm or disconfirm the derived conclusion. Regardless of how formalized, the analysis involves a process of categorization, resorting, and recording that eventuates in emergent categories of meaning.

The final step is writing the report. While writing is important in any form of research, it is critical in the naturalistic-ethnographic paradigm. This is because the final test of the quality of a naturalistic-ethnographic study is a sense of agreement. In other words, the reader should be convinced that the researcher reached an appropriate or reasonable conclusion; the reader needs to feel that she or he would reach the same conclusion if she or he had been intimately involved with the data. It is therefore incumbent on the writer to use precise language, descriptions, and clear presentation of ideas (Smith, 1981).

Smith (1981) describes eight characteristics to look for in determining the quality of a naturalistic-ethnographic design. We believe that these characteristics can also be used as a checklist to evaluate the quality of a proposed design. The eight characteristics modified from Smith are as follows:

1. *Duration.* Will the researcher be in contact with the research subject(s) long enough to sufficiently understand both the subject(s) and the context?
2. *Scope.* Will the researcher have a comprehensive view of the subject(s) (that is, from multiple perspectives)?
3. *Ethics.* Is there evidence that the researcher will maintain confidentiality and protection of the subject(s)?
4. *Logic.* Does the internal logic hang together? In other words, is there a consistency between the type of data and the proposed or actual method of data collection?
5. *Verification.* Will the researcher use triangulation? Triangulation refers to the process of using multiple sources of data and/or having independent observers examine the data.
6. *Stance of the Researcher.* Did or will the researcher maintain a nonideological stance toward the data? Is there evidence that the researcher either has no previous conceptions about the phenomenon or can be explicit about stating these preconceptions?
7. *Writing.* Is there evidence that the report will be written in a clear manner?
8. *Contribution to Knowledge.* Is there evidence that the research will provide new information?

Phenomenological Research

Phenomenological research is similar to naturalistic-ethnographic research except that it focuses specifically on describing human consciousness. In other words, a researcher interested in using this paradigm would be attempting to understand how, for instance, a client and counselor make sense of their counseling interactions. What sense does the interaction make to the participants? Methodologically, phenomenological research is similar to a counseling interview. The researcher engages in a collaborative interview with the research subject. In this manner the researcher tries to gain an empathic understanding of the subject's frame of reference. This process is usually referred to as a qualitative interview. The qualitative interview itself is unstructured, with the researcher acting as a participant-observer. The interviewer is not only interested in what is reported, but also in how it is reported. The goal of the qualitative interview is to describe the essential meaning of the experience (Hoshmand, 1989).

   Two major processes are used in the conduct of a qualitative interview: bracketing and horizontalization. Bracketing is a suspension of prejudices and biases so that the researcher can approach the interview in an open manner. Denton (1980) described three types of bracketing: cognitive, existential, and dramaturgical. Cognitive bracketing is the conscious and intentional act of setting aside one's usual ways of perceiving and interpreting phenomena. This is usually done by asking oneself a series of intellectual questions concerning alternate ways of viewing phenomena. Existential bracketing involves a disruption in the normal flow of events in the subject's life. This disruption (such as a death) allows the researcher to obtain new perspectives and interpretations because the subject's everyday world and usual process of meaning making have been interrupted. Dramaturgical bracketing involves the use of enacted dramas to set aside the everyday world or events. In other words, the researcher may ask the subject to enact certain scenes based on identified themes. Finally, the concept of horizontalization refers to treating all sources of data as equal. In other words, there is no a priori decision that an observer's (or interactant's) view will provide a more valid description. In short, the phenomenological researcher uses bracketing and horizontalization to obtain a broad and hopefully unbiased view of the subject's experiences.

An Example of Qualitative Research

One variant of the naturalistic-ethnographic tradition of qualitative research is called grounded theory (Glaser, 1967). The purpose of grounded theory is to systematically observe a phenomenon as a way of generating theory. This is opposed to theory verification, which is the goal of most quantitative research approaches. According to Rennie, Phillips, and Quartaro (1988), there are five steps in the conduct of a grounded theory investigation: (1) data collection, (2) categorization, (3) memoing, (4) movement toward parsimony, and (5) writing the theory.

The extent of and sources for data collection in a grounded theory investigation, unlike traditional data collection, are not determined before the study. Rather, the data collection is influenced by the outcomes of the analysis. Initially, subjects are chosen who are similar to each other and who are likely to represent "ideals" of the phenomenon under investigation. Next, the researcher attempts to enlarge or generalize the emerging theory by picking comparison groups or subjects. Rennie et al. call this type of sampling "theory-based data selection."

The next step in a grounded theory analysis is categorization. This process begins with the choice of a unit of analysis. While this choice is arbitrary, the researcher must be consistent once the unit is defined. Usually, with interview material, this unit is either the line or the thought unit. These units can be transcribed to index cards and then sorted into categories. Rennie et al. suggest that initial categories should be descriptive, using labels that come directly from the language used by the subjects. These authors also advocate a process of "open categorization," which involves assigning a unit to as many categories as possible. Descriptive categorization continues until saturation occurs—that is, until all new data can be subsumed into existing categories. Next, the researcher constructs categories from the descriptive categories. These constructed categories should explain the descriptive categorizing and their interrelationships. Rennie et al. suggest that independent categorization be used to verify these constructed categorizations. The third step in the process of grounded theory analysis, referred to as memoing, is the process of recording the ideas that occur to the researcher during the categorization process. These memos serve as a record of the process of theory building and also serve to get the researcher to think about themes and patterns in the data.

The fourth step is the movement toward parsimony. After the categories are saturated, the researcher focuses on the relationships among categories. The researcher begins to search for "central" categories. The researcher also tries to develop a hierarchical structure with more central categories subsuming lower-level categories. The ultimate goal of this process is the identification of a "core" category that can explain the phenomenon in question.

The final step involves writing the theory. According to Rennie et al., there are four criteria for judging the quality of the theory and the report. First, it should be believable to the reader. Second, it should be comprehensive, accounting for all important parts of the phenomenon. Third, the theory should be inductively tied to the data. Finally, the theory should be applicable and heuristic.

Rennie and Brewer (1987) used a grounded theory analysis to study the process of thesis blocking. They were interested in why some graduate students completed their theses in a timely and efficient manner, while others either bogged down in the process or never finished the process.

The data for this study consisted of transcribed interviews with 16 individuals. These interviews were semistructured, revolving around ten interviewer-generated, open-ended questions (for example, "What characteristics do you think a person needs to have in order to successfully complete a thesis in the required time?"). Of the 16 subjects interviewed, 10 had had difficulty in finishing his or her thesis and 6 had had little difficulty with this project.

Rennie and Brewer used a "complete thought" communicated by an interviewee as the unit of analysis. These thought units were transcribed onto index cards and then physically arranged in descriptive categories. This physical arrangement permitted a visual display of the emergent categorical structure.

According to Rennie and Brewer, their analysis consisted of three phases. First, they formed a number of descriptive categories that closely followed from the verbatim reports. Examples include support versus nonsupport and approach versus avoidance. Next they created hierarchical categories to subsume these descriptive categories. There were two major categories in their hierarchy: dependence-independence and structuring the task. Structuring the task was further divided into project meaningfulness, political expertise, and time management.

The dependence-independence category involved the quantity and quality of a student's dependence on others in completing the thesis. According to Rennie and Brewer, the students who did not have difficulty completing the thesis preferred to work alone but were able to turn to others for emotional or technical help when needed. On the other hand, the students who were blocked seemed to be unable to ask others for assistance or got stuck in feelings of dependency.

Project meaningfulness refers to how personally meaningful the students found either their particular subject matter and/or the process of doing research. The "blockers" tended to feel that their research was not meaningful because they saw that the research could not satisfy their ideals. The "nonblockers" tended to view the thesis as a stepping-stone on their career path; it was meaningful to the nonblockers because they could learn something about the process of doing research.

Political expertise refers to an awareness of the political nature of the thesis project. This usually revolved around issues of picking committees in regard to personality conflicts, technical expertise, and research interest. The students who struggled to finish their thesis usually had little recognition of the political nature of the process or became angry and resentful about the political nature of the project. The students who did not have difficulty with the project were aware of the political nature of the process and actively intervened in the process.

The final category, time management, involved the process that the students used to structure their thesis project. Students who did not have difficulty completing the thesis tended to set subgoals for completion of aspects of the project. The students who had difficulty completing the project tended to approach the project in a global manner and rarely attempted to break it down or to attach time deadlines to the components.

In the final stage of this research, Rennie and Brewer attempted to define a core category that would subsume their identified categories. In this example, they identified control as the core category. By this the authors meant how much mastery or ownership the student felt in relation to the thesis.

In addition, Rennie and Brewer appropriately discussed in the final section of their report aspects of the validity of the grounded theory approach in general and relative to their particular project. They particularly pointed to issues of alternate interpretation and to generalizability.

The Rennie and Brewer study is a good example of qualitative research. This study has several strengths. First and foremost, the validity of a qualitative study is in many ways related to the believability of the categories. In other words, the reader asks himself or herself if he or she would have come up with the same or a similar explanation or categories if he or she had examined the data. To make this type of decision, readers must be presented with enough examples so that they can have an understanding of the data. Rennie and Brewer did an excellent job of this in their report. Thus, readers were able to judge how believable the analysis was for them. Second, the authors effectively and clearly delineated their choice points (that is, unit of analysis) in the research process. Finally, the authors did use a contrast group (students with or without difficulty completing the thesis) as a means of extending the applicability of the developed model.

Limitations of the study include a fairly small sample size and the use of only one comparison group. In grounded theory, the notion of theoretical sampling is of critical importance. The researcher should pick contrast groups that will extend and expand the developing theory. In the Rennie and Brewer example, only one contrast group was used. The study could have been strengthened by the addition of an alternate group to test the limits of generalizability. For example, the researchers could have recruited students in the physical sciences (their subjects were mostly social science students) as an additional source of data.

Final Thoughts on Qualitative Designs

For several years, authors (Hoshmand, 1989; Patton, in press; Polkinghorne, 1984) have advocated the use of qualitative designs in counseling research. Studies using these designs have rarely if ever been published in the more mainline counseling journals. Unfortunately, the usefulness of these designs remains at a more theoretical or speculative level. We too believe that our understanding of counseling could be enhanced by the use of more qualitative designs.

We, however, want to caution the reader who thinks that qualitative research is an easier or less-involved research approach than quantitative research. This is not the case. The conduct of a qualitative study can be quite time-consuming and expensive. It is certainly not an "easy way out" in writing a thesis or dissertation. In addition, there are few concrete guidelines or rules for the day-to-day or mundane conduct of the qualitative study. The researcher may at times feel like he or she is operating in a vacuum, having to create his or her own rules and decision guidelines. Also, few research advisors have had the experience of conducting or supervising a qualitative study, so the student may feel particularly alone or without guidance in the process of conducting a qualitative study. Finally, few thesis committee members or editorial reviewers have had the experience of reading and reacting to a qualitative study. The student, therefore, has little basis for knowing what type of reactions to expect. In spite of these caveats, we do think that qualitative studies can profitably be conducted and that our knowledge of counseling can be enriched accordingly.

QUANTITATIVE DESIGNS

In this section we discuss three major types of quantitative descriptive research: (1) survey or epidemiological research, (2) classification or categorization research, and (3) passive research designs. More specifically, research strategies designed to examine the occurrence of behaviors are commonly known as epidemiological or survey designs. Classification research uses factor and cluster analysis as strategies for categorizing and reducing data, primarily by identifying underlying dimensions or groupings in a set of variables. Research strategies that examine the relationship among or between variables are referred to as passive or correlational designs. This type of design includes correlational, regression, and ex post facto designs.

Survey or Epidemiological Research

Hackett (1981) observed that survey research is one of the oldest and most widely employed research methods in the social sciences. The use of surveys have been traced back to ancient Egypt, and surveys were employed to assess social conditions in England in the eighteenth century (Glock, 1967). Today surveys are commonplace, particularly public opinion polls and political surveys.

The basic aim of survey research is to document the nature or frequency of a particular variable (for instance, the incidence of rape) within a certain population (for example, American college students). Thus, surveys typically identify facts, opinions, attitudes, behavioral self-reports, and relationships among psychological variables; data are often collected through questionnaires, mailed surveys, telephone interviews, or personal interviews. The functions of survey research are to describe, explain, or explore phenomena (Babbie, 1979). Descriptive research provides basic information about a variable or phenomenon (for example, the frequency of rape on college campuses). Explanatory research attempts to identify variables (such as beliefs about women, beliefs about the acceptability of physical aggression) that might explain the occurrence of a phenomenon (such as rape on college campuses). Exploratory research is often conducted when little is known about a phenomenon, and the researcher wants to learn more about it (for instance, how rapists rationalize rape).

Often it is useful for counselors to carefully observe or describe the occurrence of a variable; consequently, survey research has made important contributions to the counseling profession. For example, early researchers (such as Brotemarkle, 1927; Schneidler & Berdie, 1942) documented the frequency and types of problems that college students experienced. A large number of studies have been conducted to assess college students' problems and needs (thus, they were referred to as needs-assessment studies) from the 1940s through the present (for example, Blos, 1946; Carney & Barak, 1976; DeSena, 1966; Koile & Bird, 1956; McKinney, 1945; Rust & Davie, 1961). As college populations have changed over time, needs assessments have been used to document changes in students' needs (Heppner & Neal, 1983) as well as to identify needs within specific populations (for example, adult students; Warchal & Southen, 1986). This documentation has had both theoretical and practical significance. On a theoretical level, the description of the types of problems encountered by college students has facilitated the formulation and testing of student development theory (for example, Chickering, 1969). On a practical level, this information has aided the staffs of college counseling centers to design programs and deliver services appropriate to the needs of students. Parenthetically, this line of research has led to a number of studies that have examined not only the typical problems experienced by students, but also the appropriateness of services delivered by counseling centers (as viewed by students, faculty, and counseling center staff), and ultimately larger issues such as the role and functions of university counseling centers (see a review by Heppner & Neal, 1983). Other examples of survey research include studies examining the level of distress in psychologists (for example, Thoreson, Miller, & Krauskopf, 1989), alcoholism among psychologists (for example, Thoreson, Budd, & Krauskopf, 1986), job analysis of psychology internships in counseling center settings (Ross & Altmaier, 1990), and career development of college women (Harmon, 1981, 1989) and men (Super, 1957).

A common strategy using survey designs is to compare information across two or more groups. For instance, Koplik and DeVito (1986) compared the problems identified by members of the college classes of 1976 and 1986; this is known as a survey cross-sectional design. Other times a researcher might employ a survey longitudinal design and compare, let's say, students' responses when they were freshmen versus their responses when they were sophomores. A number of authors have also examined gender differences in, for example, students' perceptions and reporting of problems (for example, Koplik & DeVito, 1986; Nagelberg, Pillsbury, & Balzor, 1983) and in academic careers (Thoreson, Kardash, Leuthold, & Morrow, 1990). Comparisons have also been made based on race, year in school, educational level, time of year, type of academic program, and type of service requested. The accumulation of this type of research, particularly with a college population, enables counselors to describe with a high degree of confidence the types of problems encountered on college campuses and also their differential distribution across segments of the student population. In addition, the accumulation of these descriptive findings is instrumental in the process of theory building. For instance, one consistent finding in this body of research is the difference between males and females in the number and type of problems recorded. This finding has led to theoretical speculation about gender differences in problem perception.

Survey research is not limited to documenting the existence of problems within a population. In fact, a wide range of other types of behavior or variables can be described using this type of approach. For example, Hill and O'Grady (1985) were interested in counselor intentions, which they described as the "why" of a counseling intervention. They analyzed the responses of 42 experienced therapists and documented the relative frequency of use for 19 theoretically derived intentions. In addition, they examined the differential rate of using the different intentions as a function of the therapist's theoretical orientation. From these descriptive analyses, Hill and O'Grady were able to provide a profile of intention use for experienced counselors and identified intentions that characterized various theoretical positions.

In sum, the aim of epidemiological research is to describe, explain, or explore the occurrence of a variable. This design is most useful in describing a phenomenon about which we lack information, either in terms of frequency of occurrence or categorization of occurrence.

The Design of Epidemiological or Survey Research Procedures

At least four major activities are included in the conduct of survey research: (1) matching the survey design to the researcher's questions, (2) defining the sample, (3) selecting and developing a data collection method, and (4) analyzing the data. These activities are generic in that they apply to all forms of research rather than specifically to the conduct of survey research. We discussed matching the survey design to the researcher's question in Chapters 2 and 3, and will look at deriving the sample in Chapter 11, and selecting and developing the data collection method in Chapter 12. The actual design of a survey study is fairly straightforward. Unlike for true or quasi-experimental designs, the researcher does not form the actual groups a priori. Although groups may be formed for comparison's sake (for example, males versus females), the survey is given to the entire identified sample. Even in instances where the researcher knows ahead of time that he or she will compare, for example, males and females, he or she must find these subjects as they occur in the population. Also, in survey designs the researcher does not manipulate an independent variable, so the researcher is not concerned with manipulation checks.

Perhaps the most frequent way of collecting data in survey research is through self-report questionnaires, and particularly mailed questionnaires. The primary advantage of mailed surveys is the ease of data collection, particularly when the sample covers a geographical distance, in which case it would be difficult to collect on-site data. Perhaps one of the biggest potential disadvantages is the difficulty of getting subjects to return the questionnaires (assuming they were mailed). Often the return rate from the first mailing is only 30% of those mailed, which raises questions about the external validity of the results. Was there some reason why the majority of the subjects did not respond? Would their responses be different from those of the 30% who responded? It is doubtful that one could safely generalize from a 30% return rate (of a sample) to the target population. Because the return rate is such a critical issue in mail surveys, researchers usually try to make it easy to complete the questionnaire by keeping it short and including a stamped, addressed return envelope. Two sets of reminder letters or postcards are usually sent. Babbie (1979) suggested a follow-up letter be sent about two to three weeks after the initial mailing, and subsequently two to three weeks later as a final follow-up. Researchers commonly report obtaining around a 30–40% return rate from an initial mailing, and around 20% and 10% from two successive follow-ups. There is not a commonly agreed-upon "acceptable" return rate. Some survey research is published based on a less than 40% return rate. Some researchers recommend at least a 50% return rate as an "adequate" basis for findings (Baddie, 1979), while others recommend at least 80–90% (Kerlinger, 1986).

Whatever method the researcher uses to collect data, the final step entails data analysis. A critical starting point for data analysis is checking the adequacy of the sample. This involves checking how closely the sample resembles the general population along a number of important dimensions. For instance, is the proportion of male and female (or black and white, young and old) respondents in the sample similar to the proportion of males and females in the general population? Another type of check that is especially important when using mailed questionnaires is a comparison of respondents and nonrespondents. For example, when using a college population, do respondents and nonrespondents differ in sex, year in school, major, grade point average, and such? Only after this type of checking has been done should the data be analyzed and interpreted.

An Example of Survey Research

Muehlenhard and Linton (1987) were interested in documenting the incidence of and risk factors associated with date rape and sexual aggression in dating situations. Their specific research questions were: (1) How prevalent is sexual aggression in college dating? (2) What sexual activities are being done against a woman's will? and (3) What risk factors are involved in sexual aggression? The first two questions called for an examination of the occurrence or frequency of these events. To address the third research question, the authors choose six possible variables based on their review of the current literature. These included familiarity with partner, power differential between the two persons, miscommunication about sex, alcohol or drug use, particular dating activities or locations, and attitudes likely to be associated with sexual aggression (traditionality of attitude toward women and sex roles, acceptance of rape myths, acceptance of interpersonal violence, and adversarial sexual beliefs).

Apparently the authors wanted to generalize their results to the population of single college women. A convenience sample was chosen that consisted of 380 women and 368 men enrolled in introductory psychology classes at a large southwestern public university. The study population was limited to students who were single and interested in dating members of the opposite sex.

The researchers decided to use written questionnaires administered in group testing situations. The questionnaires were a combination of researcher-developed and previously developed instruments with known psychometric properties. The previously developed instruments were the Attitude Toward Women Scale (Spence & Helmneich, 1972), the Adversarial Sexual Beliefs Scale (Burt, 1980), the Acceptance of Interpersonal Violence Scale (Burt, 1980), and the Rape Myth Acceptance Scale (Burt, 1980). In addition, the authors asked the respondents to describe their most recent date, including how long the two persons had known each other; how many times they had dated; how old each person was; who initiated; who paid the dating expenses; how many people went on the date; what transportation was used; where they went; whether each person used alcohol or drugs; how suggestively each person dressed; how much each person wanted sexual contact and intercourse; and whether the man felt led on. Respondents were also given a list of 17 sexual activities and asked to check the activities (1) the woman did willingly and (2) the man tried against the woman's wishes. Finally, the respondents who had experienced unwanted sexual contact were asked to describe their worst experience and to respond to several other questions.

Unfortunately, Muehlenhard and Linton did not report any attempt to check the adequacy of their sample. Were the students in introductory psychology classes comparable to students throughout the university? How did students at this particular university compare to students on other campuses across the country? The authors did examine variations in reports of unwanted sex across college class, and found no differences for men or women across classes.

For the first research question—How prevalent is sexual aggression in college dating?—the authors' results revealed that sexual aggression was reported by 77.6% of the women and 57.3% of the men surveyed. In response to the second research question—What sexual activities are being done against a woman's will?—the researchers found that 14.7% of the women and 7.1% of the men reported being involved in sexual intercourse against the woman's will. To determine risk factors involved in sexual aggression, the authors compared the questionnaires filled out about recent dates and those filled out about a date in which the subject had experienced sexual aggression. Additionally, they compared attitudes of people who had been involved in sexual aggression with those of people who had not. These comparisons are in fact correlational or ex post facto analyses. The researchers examined whether group membership (involved versus noninvolved in sexual aggression) was related to or correlated with certain risk factors. Briefly, their results identified the following risk factors: the man's initiating the date, paying all the expenses, and driving; miscommunication about sex; heavy alcohol or drug use; "parking"; and men's acceptance of traditional sex roles, interpersonal violence, adversarial attitudes about relationships, and rape myths.

The study by Muehlenhard and Linton is exemplary in many ways. They carefully defined the research questions and used the previous research literature to select probable risk factors. The use of their tailor-made questionnaire in conjunction with previously constructed questionnaires with known psychometric characteristics strengthened the design. Finally, using multiple methods to assess risk factors was a form of replication within the sample. The relative weakness of the study involves the sampling procedure. Would we expect introductory psychology students to be representative of university students on the whole? Are there data that could strengthen this assumption? Are there data that could clarify how this particular college sample compares with a college population in general? Nonetheless, the data from this descriptive study are important because date rape is a phenomenon we know relatively little about. These findings have immediate implications for preventive programming and other psychological interventions.

Classification or Categorization Research

Often in counseling research it is necessary to reduce or simplify a data set that contains a number of variables to only a few variables by developing categories, subgroups, factors, or in general some sort of classification system. Frequently, a taxonomic system not only simplifies a data set, but also has important theoretical implications. In chemistry, for example, the periodic table provided a means of classifying elements and also described underlying dimensions of atomic structure (protons, electrons, and neutrons). The establishment of reliable and valid categorical and dimensional systems likewise can advance the counseling profession.

Greenberg (1986), in writing about psychotherapy research, contended that there is a "dearth of conceptually clarifying classification schemes" (p. 712). He believes that comprehensive classification schemes are a critical base for counseling research and that there is a need for more research with such a focus. In fact, all sciences start from commonly accepted bases of description and classification.

Two commonly used classification strategies are factor and cluster analysis. Both of these procedures describe data sets by reducing or categorizing the data into underlying or simpler structures or subgroups. We will define and discuss these two techniques, give an overview of the steps involved in using them, and provide illustrations from contemporary counseling research.

Factor Analysis

Factor analysis is a class of multivariate statistical methods whose primary purpose is data reduction and summarization (Hair, Anderson, & Tatham, 1987). Factor analysis analyzes the interrelationships among a large number of variables and condenses (summarizes) that information into a smaller set of common underlying dimensions or factors. Thus, the fundamental aim of factor analysis is to search for common dimensions that underlie the original variables (Hair et al., 1987). This statistical technique is often used in developing and validating assessment inventories. There are two major approaches to factor analysis: exploratory and confirmatory. In exploratory factor analysis, the most commonly used, the researcher examines a set of data to determine underlying dimensions, without any a priori specification in terms of the number or content of the dimensions. In confirmatory factor analysis, the researcher first identifies theoretically (or through previous research) the number of dimensions he or she expects to find and the items or scales in the data set that will load on or form each factor; this is called the model. Then the researcher examines how well the model fits the actual relationships observed in the data. The analysis can either confirm (hence the name) or disconfirm the researcher's model. Because the researcher can specify a model, confirmatory factor analysis allows him or her to test theoretical propositions.

As an example of exploratory factor analysis, let's say a researcher has observed over a ten-year period that for some adult clients, changing careers is a difficult process. The researcher begins to wonder what distinguishes the people who have difficulty from those who do not. After considerable reflection, more observation, and reading the professional literature, she develops a 100-item questionnaire that assesses barriers associated with changing careers. Such an instrument has not existed before, and little is known about barriers to changing careers. But answering a 100-item questionnaire is time consuming and the questionnaire does not identify or group common barriers together. The researcher can only compute a total score of barriers, or look at individual barrier items. Factor analysis could condense these 100 items by aligning them with factors that characterize the data set. For example, the researcher might conclude through factor analysis that there are three main types of career barriers, reflecting (1) career myths, (2) self-efficacy, and (3) attributional styles. The researcher can now summarize a client's career barriers into these three types and provide scores for each of these factors. A client might score exceptionally high on career myths, which would suggest that interventions are especially needed on this dimension. Moreover, the three factors provide theoretical extensions to the topic of career barriers or the career planning process in general. In sum, factor analysis analyzes a large number of variables and condenses or summarizes them into common or underlying dimensions.

Factor analysis has been used frequently in the counseling literature to identify common dimensions relating to a wide array of topics. For example, this technique has been used to describe dimensions of vocational interest (Fouad, Cudeck, & Hanser, 1984), supervisory styles (Worthington & Stern, 1985), expectancies about counseling (Tinsley, Workman, & Kass, 1980), and perception of counselors (Barak & LaCrosse, 1975). For example, Tinsley et al. (1980) found four factors that account for a large portion of the variance in clients' expectations about counseling: personal commitment, facilitative conditions, counselor expertise, and nurturance. Likewise, Phillips, Friedlander, Pazienza, and Kost (1985) described three dimensions of decision-making styles: rational, intuitive, and dependent.

CONDUCTING A FACTOR ANALYSIS. Factor analysis is a multivariate statistical method that involves a number of choice points, which sometimes entail rather complex procedures with specialized vocabulary. Many of these choice points are beyond the scope of this text; a wide variety of more detailed resources are available for further consultation (for example, Hair et al., 1987; Kerlinger, 1986; Tinsley & Tinsley, 1987).

First and foremost, the researcher must carefully think about the research questions of greatest interest. Is the researcher wanting to summarize or reduce data by identifying underlying dimensions or factors? Would the identification of such factors be helpful to practitioners or researchers in some way? If the answer is yes, then the researcher can proceed with factor analysis in mind. One of the next activities is to decide which variables will serve as the basic data. Often the researcher will develop his or her own questionnaire; those items constitute the variables. A great deal of time, planning, and reflection are needed to develop quality items (see Chapter 10). In factor and cluster analysis there are not independent and dependent variables as we have defined those terms in Chapter 2. Sometimes a researcher might factor-analyze an existing instrument, or factor analyze all of the items from two or three instruments to identify common factors across instruments.

After the variables have been selected or developed, the sample is defined, and then the data are collected and entered into a computer. The researcher then engages in factor-analyzing the data. Computers and statistical software programs have greatly facilitated this process, although several major decision points still exist for the researcher.

The purpose of factor analysis is to identify common dimensions of a set of variables. The researcher also wants to see which items go together to make up a factor. In the example given earlier, the researcher wants to know which factors account for the types of career barriers that people experience, and which of the 100 items make up each factor. While much of the actual factor analysis procedure is technical and beyond the scope of this chapter, you should be aware of two critical choice points that the researcher encounters in performing a factor analysis.

First, the researcher has to decide how many factors exist in a set of data. The actual factor analysis procedure produces a range of possible factor solutions. While specific criteria can be used to suggest how many factors may exist, many times deciding on the number of factors is not a clear-cut process. Two researchers looking at the same data might decide that a different number of factors exist. You should be aware of this situation when you read the report of a factor analysis. One of the major advantages of confirmatory factor analysis is that the number of dimensions is decided on beforehand and the researcher tests whether the data confirm or disconfirm his or her expectations.

Naming the derived factors is a second important decision that the researcher makes. To do this, he or she examines all of the items that make up a factor and attempts to identify a name that captures the conceptual meaning inherent in the items. Obviously, this naming process is subjective and researchers examining the same set of items may derive different names for the same factor. You should also be aware of the subjective nature of the factor-naming process when examining the report of a factor analysis.

AN EXAMPLE OF FACTOR ANALYSIS. Tinsley, Roth, and Lease (1989) used both confirmatory and exploratory factor analysis to examine the dimensions that define group leadership. The main purpose of this study was to attempt to confirm a four-factor model of group leadership originally described by Lieberman, Yalom, and Miles (1973). In a classic study of group leadership, Lieberman et al. found that leader, member, and observer rating of leadership converged on a four-factor structure of leadership. They labeled these factors emotional stimulation, caring, meaning attribution, and executive functioning. Tinsley et al. wanted to determine if group leaders' self-ratings, obtained from a large number of these leaders, would confirm this four-factor structure.

The study by Tinsley et al. used both survey and factor analytic methods. These authors randomly selected 500 members of the Association for Specialists in Group Work and mailed them survey questionnaires. Usable responses were returned by 200 of the 500 identified group leaders. The survey instrument contained 130 items, 5 items measuring each of the 26 leader characteristics studied by Lieberman et al.

Twenty-six scale scores (one score for each of the 26 leader characteristics) were calculated for each subject. These scale scores were used as the data for the factor analysis. First Tinsley et al. used confirmatory factor analysis to ascertain if the 26 scales would result in the four factors described by Lieberman et al. They found that only 8 of the 26 scales loaded on (or scored highest on) the factor that they theoretically should have loaded on. Tinsley et al. concluded that their analysis failed to confirm the factor model proposed by Lieberman et al.

Because of this failure to confirm, Tinsley et al. then used exploratory factor analysis to determine how many and what dimensions accounted for self-rating of leadership. The authors examined eight-, nine-, and ten-factor solutions before adopting an eight-factor solution that they believed best explained the data. Next Tinsley et al. examined the scales that constituted (or loaded on) each factor, and determined a name for the underlying construct that these items represented. For example, the scales managing/limit setting, mirroring command stimulation, cognizing, charismatic leader, and model all loaded on (were a part of) the first factor. Tinsley et al. named the underlying construct "cognitive direction." In a similar manner, they examined the scales that loaded on the other factors and derived names for the underlying constructs. The constructs they named were affective direction, nurturant attractiveness, group functioning, verbal stimulation, charismatic expert, individual functioning, and nonverbal exercises.

Tinsley et al. concluded that the four factors identified by Lieberman et al. could not adequately account for the self-rating of leadership obtained in their sample. In fact, eight factors were used to account for the obtained self-ratings. Tinsley et al. concluded that group leadership is more complicated and multifaceted than the Lieberman et al. model would suggest.

The Tinsley et al. study is an excellent example of the use of factor analysis. It is exemplary because they explicitly delineated for readers the basis for their choice of number of factors and for naming the factors. In this way readers are invited to make their own judgments about the critical choices made by the researchers.

Cluster Analysis

Often in counseling we would like to be able to identify natural groupings or subtypes of clients, counseling responses, or counselors. Cluster analysis is a class of multivariant statistical method the primary purpose of which is to reduce data by identifying and classifying similar entities into subgroups (Hair et al., 1987). This statistical technique classifies objects or variables so that each object is very similar to others in its cluster. Thus, within each cluster, objects are homogeneous, but there is considerable heterogeneity among clusters (Hair et al., 1987).

Frequently, cluster analysis is used to put people into subgroups, which is quite functional for examining individual differences in counseling research. Consider the earlier example about career barriers. Suppose the researcher was interested not in identifying underlying dimensions of career barriers, but rather identifying subgroups of clients, each of whom experienced barriers in changing careers but in different ways. The researcher then might assess 100 clients by administering five or six instruments that she thought would measure some aspect of career barriers (for example, self-esteem, motivation to change, risk-taking propensity). After collecting and entering the data into the computer, she might use cluster analysis procedures to identify, let's say, four subgroups of clients: (1) a low self-esteem group, (2) a low motivation group, (3) a group lacking career information, and (4) a low risk-taking group. These results might suggest that different career planning interventions should be designed for these subgroups of clients. In sum, cluster analysis condenses or summarizes a large number of variables by placing objects (such as people) or variables into categories or subgroups.

Unlike factor analysis, cluster analysis has been used infrequently in the counseling literature until recently. In terms of identifying people, Megargee and Bohn (1979) used cluster analysis to develop a topology of criminal offenders based on MMPI profiles. Hill and O'Grady (1985) used cluster analysis of variables to develop a classification of counselor intentions. Their 19 therapist intentions were collapsed into four categories: assessment, therapeutic work, nonspecific factors, and problems. Using a similar analysis, Hill, Helms, Spiegel, and Tichenor (1988) found five clusters of client reactions. As an example of clustering other objects, Wampold and White (1985) used cluster analysis to analyze research themes in counseling psychology. Examining common citations among 27 articles published during 1982, they concluded that the social influence model was a common underlying theme in the 27 articles.

PERFORMING A CLUSTER ANALYSIS. As with factor analysis, many of the processes involved in cluster analysis are beyond the scope of this text. Interested readers should consult some of the following references for more details: Aldenderfer and Blashfield, 1984; Blashfield, 1984; Borgen and Barnett, 1987; Borgan and Weiss, 1971; Hair et al., 1987; Lorr, 1983.

Similarly to factor analysis, the researcher must determine the appropriateness of the design to the research question. Borgen and Barnett (1987) noted that the purposes of cluster analysis are exploration (to find a certain structure or set of groupings), confirmation (to test an existing classification, perhaps based on theory), and simplification (to reduce a complex data set into a simpler structure). The researcher must also define a sample and select the appropriate instruments. The latter assumes added importance in cluster analysis, because the instruments are the tools for measuring the similarity between objects. To use the flashlight analogy again, the flashlight will only provide light in the direction in which it is pointed. Likewise, the objects will only be determined to be similar in the ways that are measured. After data are collected, the researcher proceeds to the statistical procedures involved in cluster analysis.

The two major decision points in cluster analysis are similar to those involved in factor analysis. Like factor analysis, the cluster analysis procedure produces a number of possible cluster solutions. The researcher must then decide on the best solution for the data set. Fewer guidelines are available in cluster analysis than in factor analysis to help in making this decision, so the number of clusters retained is a subjective decision. Once this decision has been made the researcher attempts to name the clusters. To do this, he or she examines the items or individuals that make up a cluster and tries to identify an underlying commonality or construct. Obviously, this naming process is subjective and there can be disagreement about the meaning of the cluster.

In sum, cluster analysis can be a very powerful data reduction technique, although its application is less well developed than that of factor analysis. Different measures and categorizing techniques often result in different clusters, and thus the researcher must often be cautious and tentative.

AN EXAMPLE OF CLUSTER ANALYSIS. Surprisingly, before 1985 there was no system for classifying helpful and nonhelpful therapeutic events. Such a system can help process researchers describe the counseling process with greater consistency, as well as facilitate training. Elliott (1985) set out to derive a taxonomy of helpful and nonhelpful events in brief counseling. To do this he used a three-step process. First, clients were asked to describe the most and least helpful events in a counseling session. Next, judges sorted the descriptions of events into categories. Finally, these sortings were combined and cluster analyzed.

Twenty-four student clients identified 86 helpful and 70 nonhelpful counselor responses. Their descriptions of these responses were then given to 34 judges who were instructed to create 3 to 12 categories for classifying these descriptions. Similarity was calculated by tabulating the number of judges who put each pair of events into the same category.

Elliott used two clustering methods (average linkage and a maximum linkage) to cluster the data. These methods yielded high levels of agreement. The analysis identified eight kinds of helpful events, which were grouped into two higher-order superclusters (note the hierarchial outcome). One supercluster, the task supercluster, contained the following categories: perspective, problem solution, problem clarification, and focusing awareness. The other supercluster, the interpersonal supercluster, contained the following clusters: understanding, client involvement, reassurance, and personal contact. The six clusters of nonhelpful events were misperception, negative counselor reaction, unwanted responsibility, repetition, misdirection, and unwanted thoughts.

This study is a good example of the process recommended by Borgen and Barnett (1987). Especially noteworthy is the use of two methods of cluster analysis (average and maximum linkage) to examine the stability of the derived clusters. The use of two methods of clustering was a type of within-sample replication in that two different methods resulted in similar solutions. Elliott also validated the derived clusters by examining their relationship to counselor response mode. For example, Elliott found that paraphrases were usually followed by focusing awareness but not by unwanted thoughts. Moreover, he found that particular sets of following responses were nicely described by the derived categories. The major weakness of Elliott's study involves the sampling procedure. He used undergraduates recruited from a psychology class in the research. It is unclear if their responses are generalizable to a client population. This study could have been strengthened by replicating the cluster structure with a more clinical population. Despite this weakness in sample selection, Elliott's study is a good example of carefully designed cluster analytic study. If replicated, the clusters he found could add greatly to research in the counseling process.

Passive Designs

What is the relationship between interest/job congruence and satisfaction with one's job (for example, Gottfredson & Holland, 1990)? Can we predict a student's acquisition of counseling skills by knowing his or her MMPI score? What is the relationship between a person's self-efficacy expectations and his or her choice of career options (Betz & Hackett, 1981, 1987; Lapan, Boggs, & Morrill, 1989)? These are questions that can be addressed by passive designs. Cook and Campbell (1979) refer to these designs as passive because the researcher neither actively forms groups or conditions through random or nonrandom assignment, nor actively manipulates an independent variable.

Passive designs are used to examine the relationship between two or more variables. A simple passive design (sometimes called a correlational design) examines the relationship between two variables (for instance, depression and social skills). More complex designs examine the collective contribution of two or more variables to the variation in a third variable.

In a simple passive study, the investigator collects data on two variables (x and y) and then uses a statistical analysis, typically a Pearson product moment correlation, to describe their relationship. The correlation index, or r, provides an index of the degree of linear relationship. Let's say that as x increases, so do the scores on y; thus, x and y vary together, or covary, and have a "strong positive relationship." If x scores do not vary with y scores, we typically say there is no relationship between x and y. The correlation coefficient, or r, between two scores can range from + 1.00 (a positive relation) to - 1.00 (a negative relation). Thus, the correlation index, r, provides an indication of how much two variables covary. The amount of variance that is accounted for between two variables is the square of the correlation, or r^2. Thus, the correlation between x and y might be + .5, which means that the amount of variance accounted for between these two variables is 25% ($.5^2$).

For example, Hoffman and Weiss (1987) were interested in the relationship between individual psychological separation and healthy adjustment. They developed an inventory of common problems to reflect healthy adjustment, and correlated this measure with scores from another inventory that measured four aspects of psychological separation. Two hundred and sixty-seven white college students completed the two self-report inventories. Hoffman and Weiss found that students with more conflictual dependence on their mothers or fathers reported more problems (r = .43 and .42, respectively). Because the results are correlational, however, the direction of the relationship between conflictual dependence and reported problems cannot be determined. Conflictual dependence may cause more emotional problems, having more problems may lead to more conflictual dependence on parents, or a third variable may cause both conflictual dependence and emotional problems. In short, the correlational design used by Hoffman and Weiss allowed the researchers to describe the degree of relationship between two variables—individual psychological separation and psychological adjustment.

Passive designs have been used throughout the history of counseling research. The use of this design has not been linked to a particular type of question or to a specific content. Rather, studies employing a passive design have been used to describe relationships among a wide variety of variables of interest to counseling researchers.

A study by Nocita and Stiles (1986) is a particularly noteworthy example of the use of a simple passive design. These authors wanted to assess the relationship between a client's level of introversion and his or her perception of counseling sessions. The client's level of introversion was assessed by the Social Introversion scale of the MMPI. Clients also filled out a session evaluation questionnaire at the conclusion of each counseling session. The session evaluation questionnaire assessed the client's perception of session depth and smoothness and his or her feeling of positivity and arousal. Nocita and Stiles correlated the client's social introversion score with each of his or her scores on the four session evaluation questionnaire scales. Introverted clients saw the counseling session as less smooth and felt less positive after the session than the more extraverted clients. The noteworthy and unusual aspect of this study is that the correlational results were replicated with two different client samples. This type of replication is unfortunately uncommon in the counseling literature.

We also want to mention a more recent development in the use of correlational designs. Cole, Lazarick, and Howard (1987) argued that most of the passive, as well as the experimental, research in counseling has underestimated the relationships among the variables examined because researchers tend to examine only manifest variables. A manifest variable is a derived score, usually from an inventory, that is presumed to reflect a person's standing on a construct or latent variable. Manifest variables (for example, the score on the Beck Depression Inventory), however, contain measurement error. Therefore, the relationship between two manifest variables is a function of their relationship and the reliability of the measures. Cole et al. described a method for determining the relationship between the constructs that the manifest variables are presumed to measure.

Cole et al. proposed that confirmatory factor analysis be used to examine the relationship between constructs or latent variables. To use confirmatory factor analysis, the constructs of interest must be assessed by multiple methods. For example, Cole et al. were interested in assessing the relationship between depression and social skills. The authors assessed each of the constructs from four perspectives: self-report (Beck Depression Inventory and Survey of Heterosexual Interactions); behavioral ratings (Nonverbal Cue for Depression and Social Anxiety and Skill Index); interview (Feeling and Concerns Checklist and Interpersonal Adjective Checklist); and significant other (Depression Behavior Rating Scale and a modified version of the Survey of Heterosexual Interactions). Cole et al. (1987) found an average cross-trait correlation of $-.25$ across the four measures of depression and social skills. When confirmatory factor analysis was used to estimate the relationship between the constructs of depression and social skills, a $-.85$ correlation was found. Rather than accounting for only 6% of the variance in depression using a Pearson product moment correlation ($-.25^2$), social skills accounted for approximately 72% ($-.85^2$) of this variance using confirmatory factor analysis.

The procedure described by Cole et al. is an important statistical and conceptual advance in the analysis of passive designs. Counseling researchers are often interested in the relationship between psychological constructs, although we usually only examine the relationship between manifest variables. As with all passive designs, however, this type of analysis does not allow for causal explanation. A causal relationship between social skills and depression can only be established using an experimental design.

In sum, passive designs are extremely important, especially in early stages of investigating phenomena. With these designs, in contrast to experimental designs, a researcher can quickly and relatively easily describe possible relationships among variables. Passive studies can rule out the existence of causal relationships—if no correlation exists between variables, there can be no causal relationship—and can suggest possible causal connections among variables that can be examined later in an experimental design. One of the main weaknesses of most passive studies in counseling is the lack of attention to sample selection. When convenience samples are used, the generalizability or external validity of the results is limited.

Multiple Regression

Whereas a correlation identifies the relationship between two variables, most often researchers are interested in describing the relationships among more than two variables. For example, one might ask: If one knows the correlation between x and y, would it not be more powerful to include variables a, b, and c (along with x) to study y? In many cases, it is, and thus multivariate analysis has become increasingly more popular. We will briefly focus on multiple regression here as a way of increasing our ability to describe the relationships among multiple variables. (For more details, see Cohen & Cohen, 1983; Hair et al., 1987; Pedhazur, 1982; Wampold & Freund, 1987.)

Multiple regression is a statistical method for studying the separate and collective contributions of one or more independent variables to the variation of a dependent variable (Wampold & Freund, 1987). Multiple regression can be used with a passive design to describe how multiple "independent" (predictor) variables are related to a single "dependent" (criterion) variable. Thus, frequently, researchers refer to *predicting* the criterion variable and discuss the extent to which they can accurately predict the criterion. Like simple correlation, multiple regression has been used with a wide variety of variables and research questions. The relationship between a "dependent" variable and a set of multiple "independent" variables is expressed as the multiple correlation coefficient. The multiple correlation coefficient (R) is a measure of how well the predicted scores correspond to the actual scores of dependent variables. The square of the multiple correlation coefficient (R^2) is the proportion of variance in the dependent variable explained by the independent variables. *Explained* here does not necessarily imply a causal relationship, but rather an association of the dependent variable with variability in the independent variables (Wampold & Freund, 1987).

There are three basic methods for entering independent variables in regression equations, and each method serves slightly different purposes and outcomes. It is important for the researcher to be familiar with the strengths and weaknesses of each method (see Wampold & Freund for an overview). In *simultaneous regression,* all of the independent variables are entered (simultaneously) into the regression equation. Simultaneous regression is most often used for the purpose of prediction, and when there is no basis for entering any particular independent variable prior to another. For instance, Parham and Helms (1985) examined the relations between racial identity attitude and self-esteem. Four racial identity attitudes were simultaneously entered in a regression equation predicting self-esteem. Parham and Helms found a multiple R of .36 for the analysis. Thus, racial identity accounted for about 10% of the variance ($.36^2$) in the black subject's self-esteem. Examination of the specific racial identity attitudes revealed that students in the preencounter stage of racial identity formation had lower self-esteem than students in the immersion stage of identity formation.

In *stepwise regression,* independent variables are entered into the regression equation in an order based on a specified criterion. For example, the regression model first enters the variable with the highest correlation with the "dependent" variable. The next variable that is entered is the one that results in the largest increase in R^2. This procedure is repeated until adding variables does not result in a statistically significant increase in R^2. Thus, a stepwise procedure identifies which variables contribute the most unique variance in the equation, and in what order. Cohen and Cohen (1983) recommended that stepwise regression only be used when the research goal is primarily predictive. This is because stepwise methods are subject to biases in the particular sample and thereby are subject to spurious results. Kivlighan and Shapiro (1987) used a stepwise regression as they were interested in predicting who would benefit from a self-help career counseling program. This type of prediction was important because earlier studies had shown that self-help and counselor-directed career interventions had equivalent effects (Krivatsky & Magoon, 1976). Scores for the six Holland types (realistic, investigative, artistic, social, enterprising, conventional) were used as predictor variables. The criterion variable was change in vocational identity (Holland, Daiger, & Power, 1980). The conventional and investigative scores entered the stepwise regression as statistically significant predictors. Participant scores on the two variables accounted for 25% (adjusted R^2) of the variance in outcome. The Kivlighan and Shapiro study is also noteworthy because they used an analysis of covariance to remove the variance in the dependent variable attributable to pretest scores. The pretreatment vocational identity scores were regressed on the posttreatment vocational identity scores. The residuals (the variance in the posttreatment scores that could not be accounted for by the pretreatment scores) from this regression were used as the dependent variable in the stepwise regression. In this manner, the researchers were able to examine how much the Holland scores could accurately predict *change* in vocational identity from a pretest to a posttest period.

In *hierarchical regression,* the researcher specifies the order of entry of the independent variables based on some rationale (for example, research relevance, causal priority, or theoretical grounds). Lent, Brown, and Lankin (1987) were interested in examining the relationships among self-efficacy, interest congruence, consequential thinking, and various career and academic behaviors. One behavior of interest was academic grade point average. In the first step of the regression analysis, a measure of composite ability (high school rank, Preliminary Scholastic Aptitude Test) was entered first to control for the effects of previous academic performance. Next, the three theoretically derived variables (self-efficacy, interest congruence, and consequential thinking) were entered in a stepwise manner. In predicting career indecision, the multiple R for composite ability was .34. When interest congruence was added, the multiple R increased to .44 ($F = 9.62$, $P > .01$). This result indicated that interest congruence added unique predictive variance beyond that accounted for by composite ability. By using a hierarchical model where composite ability was entered first, Lent et al. were able to perform a more stringent test of the relationship between interest congruence and career indecision.

In evaluating the usefulness of multiple regression, it is always important to remember that the results of these types of analyses are based on correlational data. Even though regression research uses terms from experimental designs (*dependent variable, independent variables*), the results obtained are relational, not causal. The choice of a dependent variable and independent variables is always arbitrary. In other words, prediction is not causality. Therefore, causal statements are not appropriate with these designs. Multiple regression is suited to describe and predict the relationship between two or more variables and is especially useful to examine the incremental as well as total explanatory power of many variables (Hair et al., 1987). Perhaps the main caveats for researchers pertain to inadequate sample sizes (see Wampold & Freund, 1987) and spurious results due to methodological procedures.

Ex Post Facto Designs

Many independent variables of interest to counseling researchers cannot be manipulated. For instance, gender, personality type, treatment success (versus failure), and race are important and interesting variables, but they cannot be manipulated. Designs that use these type of variables are also passive designs and are called ex post facto designs. The name literally means "after the fact." In other words, the investigation or research takes place after the groups or conditions have been formed.

In many ways, ex post facto designs resemble the posttest-only quasi-experimental design described in Chapter 6. A simple two-level ex post facto design can be diagrammed as follows:

Selection characteristic (male)　0_1
Selection characteristic (female)　0_2

This diagram shows that the experimenter selects an appropriate independent variable (male versus female) and then observes differences in a dependent variable (counseling skills). For instance, do male and female therapists differ in client-perceived empathy? Ex post facto designs can have multiple levels, or be factorial. For instance, an investigator can simultaneously examine the effect of counselor race and gender on client-perceived empathy. These more complicated designs, however, share the same strengths and limitations as the simpler two-level designs.

The most obvious difference between the ex post facto design and a true experiment involves the manipulation of the independent variable. In addition, the designs also differ in the lack of random assignment in the ex post facto design—for instance, therapy continuers and dropouts are not randomly assigned to the continuer or dropout condition. Kerlinger (1986) warned about a self-selection of subjects into conditions, and this is clearly the case with dropouts. This self-selection implies that there is some basis for the selection. In an ex post facto design, this selection basis—and not the variable of interest—may account for any observed differences across conditions.

Like quasi-experimental designs, ex post facto designs offer a number of problems in interpreting results. One of these problems is the role of chance in the findings. Especially if the researcher examines a large number of variables, it is likely that he or she will find some significant results by chance. For instance, a researcher may want to distinguish between continuing clients and those clients who do not continue in therapy. He or she may give a number of instruments (50 variables in all) to clients as they come to an agency and then at a later point compare the continuers and noncontinuers on these 50 variables. The researcher may find differences between continuing and noncontinuing clients on 5 variables. How important are these findings? Are they a reflection of real differences or chance? Ex post facto designs can capitalize on chance, and the researcher may be misled into erroneous conclusions based on chance findings.

EX POST FACTO DESIGNS: A HISTORICAL PERSPECTIVE. Ex post facto designs have been used extensively in all areas of counseling research. We have consequently chosen only three areas to highlight because of their historical importance. These areas are gender differences, Holland's theory of vocational choice, and therapy dropouts.

The area of gender differences has been one of continuing interest in psychological research in general and counseling research in particular. The variables that have been examined as possible consequences of gender differences are too numerous to list. Some of the more important findings in the counseling realm include consistent gender differences in important career-related variables, including differences in abilities, interests, occupational preferences, vocational schemas, and self-efficacy estimates; and gender differences in terms of client role behavior, including gender differences in use of counseling services, number and type of reported problems, attitudes toward and expectations about counseling, and some counseling process variables. Finally, gender differences have also been reported in a number of counselor role behaviors, including differences in quantity and quality of different counselor skills, attitudes, and values related to therapy, and differences in styles of interaction with clients. In fact, most areas that are central to counseling research have been examined for possible gender differences. As Lee, Heppner, and Gagliardi (1987) have documented, 58% of a sample of recent counseling publications have explicitly examined gender differences as either a primary or a secondary component of the investigation.

Arguably, one of the most heuristic theories in vocational psychology specifically, and counseling research generally, is Holland's (1985) theory of career choice. Because Holland's theory is based on a topology of persons and environments, much of the research conducted within this paradigm has been ex post facto in nature. People of different Holland types have been compared on numerous variables, including such diverse variables as accident proneness, preference for counselor type, reaction to different forms of treatment, styles of vocational decision making, personality characteristics, and preferences for activities. Typically, this research has been conducted by first determining a subject's Holland type (either through inventories or expressed vocational choice) and then comparing people of different Holland types along theoretically important dependent variables. Because the researcher cannot assign subjects to Holland types, this research is passive in nature. The use of theoretically derived variables is critically important. The ex post facto research that has been produced within the Holland paradigm has usually had a strong theoretical base. Dependent variables have been chosen on theoretical grounds. As a result, the research findings have been quite consistent and replicable.

Unfortunately, a reliance on theory has not characterized the research examining therapy dropouts. Like the Holland research, much of the dropout research has been ex post facto in nature. In this research tradition, clients who prematurely leave counseling have been compared on a number of variables to those who complete counseling. This research is ex post facto because the researcher cannot assign a client to a dropout or a continuer condition. This research has usually been undertaken from an empirical perspective (that is, "Let's see which variables differentiate dropouts and continuers"). This area has been plagued by inconsistent and often contradictory findings (for example, in one study, gender is related to dropping out, but not in another study). Also, many studies have failed to replicate the results of previous investigations. The literature on dropouts represents many of the dangers of ex post facto research. Because few studies have had a strong theoretical basis for variable selection, most of the reported findings have capitalized on chance variance. By examining a larger number of variables without strong theoretical links, one runs the risk of obtaining spurious results. Most likely the inconsistencies, contradictions, and failures to replicate with which this literature is replete, are a function of designs that have capitalized on chance.

AN EXAMPLE OF AN EX POST FACTO DESIGN. A study by Gade, Fuqua, and Hurlburt (1988) is an illustration of an ex post facto design because they examined both Holland type and gender. Gade et al. were interested in the relationship between Holland personality type and satisfaction with the educational setting for Native American high school students. They predicted that students of the social and investigative types would be most satisfied with the school environment because school systems tend to be dominated by social and investigative teachers, counselors, principals, and administrators, and this would result in a better person-environment match. In all, 596 Native American students (321 females and 275 males) enrolled in eight high schools served as subjects in the study. The authors specifically selected high schools that represented three different models of education (residential schools, provincially controlled schools that were predominantly Native American, and tribally controlled schools). Students were classified (not assigned) as a particular Holland type by results on the Self-Directed Search (Holland, 1985). Satisfaction with the educational environment was measured by the Teacher Approval and Educational Acceptance scales of the Survey of Study Habits and Attitudes (Brown & Holtzman, 1967).

Two 6 (Holland code) X 2 (Gender) ANOVAS were used to examine differences in teacher approval and educational acceptance. Gade et al. found significant main effects for Holland code on teacher approval and educational acceptance and for gender on educational acceptance. There were no Holland code by gender interactions for either satisfaction variable. In terms of specific Holland codes, investigative and social students had higher school satisfaction than realistic students.

This study is a good example of ex post facto research for a number of reasons. First, the variables examined were theoretically derived. The authors did not ask if students with different Holland types would have different school satisfaction. Rather, they hypothesized (based on Holland's notion of congruence) that there would be a specific difference in school satisfaction for different Holland types, then tested this hypothesis. A second strength was the care the authors took in selecting the sample. Gade et al. deliberately selected students from different types of schools. Because of the sample heterogeneity it is unlikely that the obtained results were caused by some characteristic of students in one particular sample.

This study also illustrates some of the weaknesses of ex post facto research. The examination of gender differences in school satisfaction seemed more empirical than theoretical. The authors never offered a theoretical explanation of why males and females might differ in school satisfaction or why this was an important variable to address. Also, there was no theoretical discussion of possible Holland code by gender interactions. In keeping with this lack of theoretical discussion of gender differences, the authors only noted in passing the significant gender difference found on the Educational Acceptance scale. This lack of discussion seems appropriate given the lack of theoretical attention to gender differences.

RECOMMENDATIONS FOR USING EX POST FACTO DESIGNS. Ex post facto designs have made and will make an important contribution to counseling research, because many of the variables of interest to counseling researchers can only be examined in an ex post facto manner. Ex post facto designs do have some serious limitations. Most important is the possibility of capitalizing on chance when using these designs. The researcher should thoughtfully design ex post facto studies to lessen the role of chance in these designs. We offer three specific recommendations to help in this regard.

First, ex post facto research should be undertaken from a strong theoretical grounding. Researchers would do well to avoid questions such as How do these groups differ? Rather, theory should be used to inform the research, specifically in the determination of the dependent variables examined.

Second, ex post facto designs are strengthened when they contain differential predictions. For example, theory may indicate that a variable (realistic Holland code) might be positively related to one variable (lack of accidents), not related to another (weight), and negatively related to a third (school satisfaction). A study is strengthened when these patterns of relationships are predicted and assessed. Specifically, we recommend that researchers consider examining multiple relationships, especially ones that are predicted to show results in opposite directions.

Our third recommendation is that researchers pay particular attention to sample characteristics. For instance, Gade et al. (1988) purposefully selected a varied sample in an attempt to eliminate any chance results based on sample characteristics. Researchers may want to select samples holding various demographic or psychological characteristics constant. For example, researchers wanting to compare "good" versus "poor" counseling sessions in terms of type of therapist response used may want to only select sessions that are temporally close. This type of selection would lessen the chance that the results were influenced by the stage of therapy.

SUMMARY AND CONCLUSIONS

If, as Greenberg (1986) asserts, the goal of a science is to describe, explain, and predict, the descriptive designs play an important role in describing the existence and establishing characteristics of a particular phenomenon. As we maintained in Chapter 1, the value of a design is not inherent in the design; rather, the value of a design depends on the state of knowledge in a particular area and the particular questions being addressed. Descriptive designs play a unique and important function in the process of scientific exploration.

This chapter has illustrated a number of descriptive designs. All of these designs describe variables by observing systematically, summarizing information, reducing or categorizing information, or providing information about basic relationships among variables. Throughout the chapter, we have emphasized both the reliability and validity in the case of quantitative designs and the replicability in the case of qualitative designs of the observations or instruments, and the representativeness of the sample utilized in the investigation. These are critical issues in descriptive research and directly affect the internal and external validity of the research. In a qualitative study, the researcher becomes intimately and intensely involved with the subjects and data, hopefully without any a priori formulations about what he or she will find. The usefulness of these studies is often dependent on the researcher's ability to put aside biases and preconceptions and to look at her or his data in a naive manner.

Survey designs allow the researcher to describe the occurrence and frequency of variables of interest. In these designs, the researcher is interested in quantitatively describing the occurrence of a variable in a population. The usefulness of the research results depends to a large extent on the measurements used and the adequacy of the sampling techniques. Researchers should make efforts to use or develop psychometrically sound instruments, choose appropriate sampling techniques, maximize return rates, and include both checks between returners and nonreturners as well as between characteristics of the sample and parameters of the population.

Categorization and classification are also important descriptive steps in the scientific endeavor. Factor and cluster analysis are statistical methodologies that can aid in this process. The factors derived from factor analysis, as well as the clusters found in cluster analysis, are dependent on the instruments used and the characteristics of the sample. Therefore, instrument selection and sampling are again important considerations in using these techniques. Factor and cluster solutions should be replicated on disparate samples to assure validity. It is also important to validate clusters and factors by linking them with other variables. Finally, we should remember that both of these procedures involve many decision points, and experts often disagree on criteria for decision making. Thus, the particular methodology or analysis used often affects the results, which suggests the need for further validation.

In correlational designs, the researcher can examine the relationships between two or more variables. The adequacy of these designs is greatly influenced by the reliability of the measures used in operationalizing the variables of interest. Also, the size of the relationship obtained depends to some extent on the sample size; thus, many multiple regression studies include an adjustment for shrinkage to control for sample size. We hope that more researchers will use the strategy advocated by Cole et al. to account for method and error variances when assessing relationships between variables. Like for other descriptive designs, sampling considerations and methodological strategies are extremely important in interpreting the results of correlational and multiple regression studies. We encourage researchers to use random sampling and/or to replicate their results when using correlational designs.

The designs described in this chapter can be important building blocks in the scientific process. Based on a careful analysis of the current state of knowledge in a given area, the researcher can choose a design that will lead to a progressively better understanding of the content area. When chosen wisely, the descriptive designs can serve the important function of describing phenomena of interest in counseling research.

PART THREE
METHODOLOGICAL ISSUES

C H A P T E R   9

DESIGNING AND EVALUATING
THE INDEPENDENT VARIABLE

One of the primary concerns of the research endeavor is to establish a causal relationship between the independent and dependent variables. After a researcher has identified a research question, he or she takes the critical step of selecting or designing appropriate independent and dependent variables. This chapter focuses on issues pertaining to independent variables, while the next chapter focuses on dependent variables.

Selection, design, and evaluation of the independent variable are of critical importance in establishing and interpreting causal relations in a study. If the independent variable is poorly designed, the researcher's effort will be unrewarding—either the expected effect will not be found or the results will be ambiguous or meaningless. Poorly designed independent variables create unwanted bias and extraneous variables, which are clear threats to Kerlinger's "MAXMINCON" principle.

This chapter discusses four issues related to the development and selection of independent variables. The first section discusses operationalizing the independent variable. Even when a researcher has carefully designed an independent variable, there is no assurance that the experimental manipulation will achieve its purpose. Therefore, the second section concerns methods to check or verify the manipulation of the independent variable, often called manipulation checks. The third section focuses on the interpretation of the results of a study, both when the manipulation check indicates the manipulation of the independent variable was successful and when it indicates the manipulation was unsuccessful. Thus, the first section focuses on issues pertaining to the independent variable that are relevant before an experiment begins, the second section on issues during an experiment, and the third section on issues after an experiment has been carried out. Finally, in the last section of the chapter we discuss independent variables that are not amenable to manipulation, which we define as status variables.

OPERATIONALIZING THE INDEPENDENT VARIABLE

Before an experiment begins, four concerns with regard to operationalizing the independent variable are particularly important to the researcher: (1) conditions or levels of the independent variable, (2) adequately reflecting the constructs designated as the cause in the research question, (3) limiting differences between conditions, and (4) establishing salience of differences in conditions.

Determining Conditions

In counseling research, the typical independent variable consists of several conditions. In the between-groups designs discussed in Chapter 5, emphasis was placed on independent variables with two conditions—treatment and no treatment (that is, control group). However, an independent variable can contain any number of conditions. In a treatment study, three treatments as well as a no-treatment condition may be contrasted (that is, four conditions). Or a treatment group may be contrasted with a placebo control group and a no-treatment control group (that is, three conditions). Of course, the independent variable is not restricted to psychological treatments; in a study of preferences for counselors, Anglo-American or Mexican-American counselors (two conditions) would constitute an appropriate independent variable (for example, see Ponce & Atkinson, 1989).

Two notes need to be made about our discussion of conditions. First, we have used the term *conditions* to indicate the groups that constitute the independent variable. However, *levels of the independent variable, groups, categories,* and *treatments* are other terms that are used in the discussion of research design and are interchangeable with *conditions.* In this context, *treatments* refers generically to conditions and not to psychological interventions. Second, we have conceptualized the independent variable as a categorical variable—each discrete category (level, condition, group, or treatment) is different. The independent variable need not be restricted to categories. Classical regression designs involve quantitative independent variables; in this case the conditions reflect differing amounts of something (see Wampold & Drew, 1990). For instance, in a drug study, the independent variable could consist of different dosage levels (for example, no drug, 2 cc, 4 cc, and 6 cc). Because true quantitative independent variables are used infrequently in counseling research, they will not be emphasized here. However, later in this chapter, status variables will be discussed, and these variables are often quantitative.

The most important point is that the nature of the conditions of the independent variable is determined by the researcher. This determination is often referred to as the experimental manipulation. Essentially, the researcher manipulates the independent variable to determine what effect it has on the dependent variable. In this way, the independent variable is related to the cause and the dependent variable is related to the effect.

Adequately Reflecting the Constructs of Interest

It is important that the independent variable be designed to reflect the construct or constructs designated as the cause in the research question. That is to say, the independent variable should be adequately defined or operationalized (see Chapter 2). If the causal construct is inadequately operationalized, alternative explanations for the results can be offered; these alternatives are potential confounds. In this chapter, we will indicate how problems associated with potential confounds can be minimized or eliminated.

To illustrate the importance of adequately reflecting the construct designated as causal, consider a study conducted by Malkiewich and Merluzzi (1980) to test the client-treatment matching model. The research hypothesis stipulated that high conceptual level thinkers would benefit from relatively unstructured counseling, whereas low conceptual level thinkers would benefit from relatively structured counseling. In this study, the structure of the counseling was one of the independent variables. Structure of counseling was operationalized by including three conditions of the independent variable—a desensitization condition, a rational restructuring condition, and a control group. The desensitization group represented high structure and the rational restructuring group, low structure. In this study, the expected interaction effect was not detected and one primary explanation for this null result was that the independent variable did not provide good exemplars of structured and unstructured counseling. It is unclear whether these two groups adequately represented differing structures, as both interventions seem rather structured. To provide a better test of the independent variable (structure of counseling), it might have been useful to provide a type of counseling that is more clearly unstructured. For example, client-centered counseling (which is often characterized as unstructured) could have been used to represent low structure, which would have provided a greater range of structure of counseling.

Limiting Differences between Conditions

The conditions selected for the independent variable should differ only along the dimension of interest. If the conditions are allowed to differ on another dimension, the second dimension becomes a confound. To illustrate this principle, consider a study of perceived credibility of Anglo-American and Mexican-American counselors as a function of counseling style and acculturation (Ponce & Atkinson, 1989). Although several independent variables were considered in a factorial design in this study, we focus on the independent variable related to ethnicity of the counselor. There are many possible ways to operationalize ethnicity of the counselor. In this study, ethnicity was manipulated by showing the subjects photographs of the counselor and by using written introductions. In one condition, subjects saw a photograph of a Mexican-American counselor and the introduction used surnames and birthplaces that reflected the Mexican-American ethnicity (for example, *Chavez* and *Mexico,* respectively). In the other condition, subjects saw a photograph of an Anglo-American counselor and the introduction used surnames and birthplaces that reflected the Anglo-American ethnicity (for example, *Sanders* and *Canada,* respectively). Clearly, this arrangement operationalizes ethnicity of the counselor; the question is whether the two conditions differed on any other dimension. Because Ponce and Atkinson chose to use photographs, there exists the possibility that the Mexican-American and Anglo-American counselors in the photographs also differed in personal attractiveness. Differences in personal attractiveness would provide an alternative explanation for the results pertaining to this independent variable. That is, higher ratings given to Mexican-American counselors by the Mexican-American subjects may be due to either the ethnicity of the counselor or the personal attractiveness of the counselor. Fortunately, Ponce and Atkinson were aware of this potential confound and controlled for it by making sure that the counselors in the photographs were comparable with regard to personal attractiveness (and age, another possible confound).

Before the research is conducted, potential confounds should be considered. It is not always possible to eliminate confounds, but knowing the potential confounds before the study is conducted can enable the researcher to add features to the study that eliminate such confounds (for example, manipulation checks, which are discussed later in this chapter). It is distressing to discover a major confound after the data are collected when some prior thought could have resulted in a modification to the study to rule it out.

Often it is necessary to argue logically that a confound has a low probability of occurring. Personal attractiveness seems to be an important variable in the counselor credibility literature (see Corrigan, Dell, Lewis, & Schmidt, 1980), so taking steps to rule it out was important in the Ponce and Atkinson study. However, Ponce and Atkinson did not rule out the possibility that the results of the study were due to anti-Canadian sentiment due to the then-current difficulty of negotiating a trade agreement with Canada. Although this explanation cannot be ruled out by the design of the experiment, there is no evidence that political relations with the mother country of a counselor affects the credibility of the counselor. On the other hand, neither is there any evidence that these same political relations do not affect credibility. Nevertheless, this confound appears to be trivial. Caution must be used, however, when ruling out confounds based on common sense or logic; after all, the research endeavor is aimed at discovering new knowledge (that is, contradicting what we believe to be true).

There are some troublesome confounds that are unique to treatment studies, one of which is the counselor. Ruling out counselor confounds could be accomplished by holding the counselors constant across treatments. That is, the same counselors would administer all treatments. However, the counselors may be more skilled with one treatment than with another, or the counselors may have allegiance to one treatment or the other, and so forth. Hence, the superiority of a treatment may not be due to the treatment but to the skill or allegiance of the counselor. One alternative is to have experts in a particular treatment administer the treatment. But this strategy introduces possible confounds related to experience, training, and so forth. Another possibility is to select relatively untrained counselors (for example, graduate students in counseling), randomly assign them to treatments, and then give them equal training in their respective treatments. Of course, this reduces the external validity of the study because the results are then generalizable only to treatments administered by inexperienced therapists. Once again, Gelso's (1979) bubble appears—there is no perfect solution to the counselor confound problem. Counselor variables will be considered again in Chapter 11.

Another potential confound in treatment studies is the length of the treatment. If one were comparing the efficacy of behavioral therapy and psychodynamic therapy, limiting the psychodynamic therapy (which is typically a long-term treatment) to the same number of sessions as the behavioral therapy may be unrealistic and may not provide an adequate test of this type of therapy. In this case, the operationalization of psychodynamic therapy would be inadequate.

Credibility of the treatment and client expectations are other potential confounds in treatment studies. Obtained differences between the effectiveness of treatments may be due to client expectations about the efficacy of the treatments and not to actual differences in the treatments. One of the goals of placebo control groups is to control for effects of perceived credibility of the treatments. However, placebo control groups are only valid to the extent that subjects perceive the placebo procedures to be as credible and powerful as the actual treatments (Mahoney, 1978). Although credibility is established to a large extent by the actual activities within a treatment, the way treatments are introduced to the clients is also critical in this regard.

Establishing Salience of Differences in Conditions

The difference between the conditions on the desired dimension should be salient—that is, noticeable—to the subjects. For example, Ponce and Atkinson (1989) could have used only the surname and birthplace of the counselor to operationalize ethnicity. This would have eliminated the personal attractiveness confound and made the research simpler. However, they included the photograph to increase the salience of ethnicity. It would have been easy for the subjects to read the half-page introduction, which focused more on the client, without attending to the surname and birthplace of the counselor.

Sharkin, Mahalik, and Claiborn (1989) conducted a study of motivation of clients to pursue additional counseling that included a manipulation that may not have been salient to the subjects. Subjects were undergraduates who volunteered to participate in a 30-minute counseling session aimed at exploring their communication skills. Depending on whether or not they had completed a list of communication skills, half of the subjects were told near the end of the session either that "by completing the brief list of your communication skills, it shows that you are motivated" or that "by signing up for this study, it shows that you are motivated." No mention of motivation was made to the other half of the subjects. It may well be that given the full range of the 30-minute social interaction, the subjects in the motivation condition did not attend to the one statement about motivation. This conclusion is mitigated to some degree by the fact that differences in one dependent variable were detected for the motivation versus no-motivation independent variable, although interpretation of salience based on the outcome of a study is problematic, as we will see later in this chapter.

Although it appears that salience on the important dimension of the independent variable is vital to the validity of a study, there are dangers when the salience is too great. If the subjects can infer the research hypothesis from the procedure of the study, then there is the possibility that responses will be biased. This is an aspect of hypothesis guessing, a threat to construct validity mentioned in Chapter 3. Often the inference about the hypothesis is based on the stated (to the subject) purpose of the research and various procedures in carrying out the research as well as on the salience of the experimental manipulation. Presumably, subjects who guess the research hypothesis tend to respond in ways that please the researcher and thus confirm the research hypothesis. This phenomenon often is referred to as the Hawthorne effect, after the studies in the Hawthorne industrial plant that found that workers in all experimental conditions attempted to comply with what they perceived the experimenters' expectations to be—in this case, that they would increase productivity.

Hypothesis guessing is a potential threat in the counselor credibility study discussed throughout this chapter (Ponce & Atkinson, 1989). Two Mexican-American researchers asked for Mexican-American volunteers from college classes. Because of these arrangements and because the salience of differences in ethnicity was increased by including photographs, the subjects in the condition where the counselor was Mexican-American may have guessed that the hypothesis involved ethnicity of the counselor and therefore raised (subconsciously) their credibility ratings to please the Mexican-American researchers. Ponce and Atkinson attempted to minimize this by disguising the exact purpose of the research, although generally there are constraints on the degree to which deception can be used in research, as we discussed in Chapter 4.

In sum, the conclusion to be reached about independent variables is that the conditions should vary on the intended dimension and should not vary on other dimensions, and that the intended dimension should reflect the research question of interest. Furthermore, differences between experimental conditions on the intended dimension should be salient but not transparent. Subjects within a condition should be aware of the critical component of the condition but should not be able to infer the research hypothesis. Of course, making decisions between salience and transparency is difficult and is one of the skills that experienced researchers acquire.

MANIPULATION CHECKS

Even when great care has been taken to define and operationalize the independent variable, there is no assurance that the experimental manipulation will achieve its purpose. It is possible for the salience of the independent variable to be misjudged by the researcher. To verify that a manipulation has been adequately designed, it is often advisable to check the characteristics of the manipulation. The goal of manipulation checks is to show one or more of the following: (1) conditions vary on the intended dimension, (2) conditions do not vary on other dimensions, and (3) treatments are implemented in the intended fashion.

To determine whether the conditions vary on the intended dimension, judgments of characteristics related to the dimension should differ across conditions. This determination can be made in a number of ways. First, inquiries can be made of the subjects themselves. For example, Jones and Gelso (1988), in a study of the effects of the style of interpretation, manipulated style by having subjects listen to audiotapes of a counseling session. In one condition, the counselor's interpretations were tentatively phrased and ended with a question, and in the other condition the counselor's interpretations were decisively phrased. The manipulation check was accomplished by having the subjects rate on a seven-point scale whether the counselor's comments were phrased tentatively or decisively, and whether they were in the form of questions or statements. As anticipated, there were significant differences between the conditions on both of the seven-point scales, providing evidence that indeed the manipulation was salient to the subjects.

Another means to assess differences on the intended dimension is to have independent raters (persons other than the subjects or the experimenters) judge the experimental materials. These independent raters could be naive individuals (those untrained in counseling) or experts. In the ethnicity-of-counselor study discussed previously, Ponce and Atkinson (1989) also varied counselor style (directive versus nondirective). Graduate students in counseling psychology rated the dialogue of the sessions and the intended differences in directiveness were found, lending support for the adequacy of the independent variable.

Independent raters and the subjects can also be used to establish that the conditions do not vary on dimensions other than the intended one. Recall that Ponce and Atkinson's use of photographs of the counselors introduced a possible confound related to the personal attractiveness of the counselors. To control for this threat, undergraduates rated the attractiveness of several Anglo-Americans and Mexican-Americans in photographs, and the photographs used in the study were matched on the dimension of personal attractiveness.

As mentioned previously, credibility of treatment is a potential confound in treatment studies. Thus, demonstrating empirically that credibility does not differ across conditions improves the validity of the treatment study. Smith and Nye (1989), in a treatment study of test anxiety, had subjects rate the credibility of their treatment at the end of the first session and at the end of the final session on several dimensions: logic of the program, confidence in it, extent to which they would recommend the program, usefulness, and expected improvement. No differences for the two treatments in this study were found on any of the dimensions at the end of the first session or at the conclusion of the treatments, thus effectively ruling out credibility as a confound. Ratings of credibility can also involve independent raters (for example, Hogg & Deffenbacher, 1988).

In treatment studies it is important that the treatments be delivered to subjects in the intended fashion. This is accomplished, in part, by the training provided to the counselors and by provision of adequate treatment manuals.

Nevertheless, the possibility exists that counselors will deviate from the manual when they are conducting the counseling in the experimental context. Hogg and Deffenbacher (1988) checked on their treatments by having independent judges listen to randomly selected audiotaped segments of sessions and identify the treatment being delivered; they found that the judges reliably were able to identify the treatments correctly.

Manipulation checks can be a very important aspect of a study. When the saliency of a manipulation is in doubt, checks provide a means to verify the researcher's claim that the conditions differ on the intended dimension and do not differ on other dimensions. Whether or not manipulation checks are worth the extra time and effort needed to put them in place is a determination that can only be made in the context of a particular research study.

INTERPRETING RESULTS

The logic of experimental designs is to establish a causal relationship between the independent variable and the dependent variable. To this point, we have presented topics related to design of the independent variable and to checking on the manipulation. Equally important are the results of an experiment, which provide much of the information upon which inferences are based. In this section, various problems in interpreting statistically significant and statistically nonsignificant results with regard to the independent variable are discussed.

Statistically Significant Results

In this instance, the results for each of the conditions are sufficiently different that the null hypothesis of no differences is rejected. That is to say, there appears to be a true difference. For example, in a comparative treatment study, a statistically significant result indicates that some treatments were more effective than others (that is, the null hypothesis of no differences between treatments was rejected).

Although it might appear that statistically significant results are easy to interpret, there is much room for confusion. As discussed earlier, the results may be due to a confound. That is, there may be another explanation for the results other than the intended one; in a treatment study, the experience of the therapist may be a confound. One attempts to design independent variables in such a way that there are few plausible confounds. Nevertheless, no experiment is perfect and several confounds will remain. Manipulation checks can be used to rule out remaining alternatives, but manipulation checks can introduce confusion as well.

One of the most confusing instances is where the manipulation check failed to indicate that the conditions varied on the intended dimension, yet statistically significant differences on the dependent variable were found.

This pattern is ambiguous because there are at least three explanations for the results. First, the results of the check may have been misleading. The failure to find that the conditions varied may be due to Type II error, inadequate measures, poor procedures, and so forth. A second explanation for a failed manipulation check but obtained differences on the dependent variable may be related to the presence of a confound. That is, the manipulation check was accurate (that is, the conditions did not vary on the intended dimension), but the conditions did vary on some other dimension. Although the researcher may have checked other dimensions as well and found no differences, it is not possible to check all confounds. A third possibility is that the statistically significant results were in error (that is, Type I error). Clearly, statistically significant results in the presence of failed manipulation checks are difficult to interpret.

It would seem that the best situation would be that the results were statistically significant and the manipulation check showed that the conditions differed on the desired dimension. But even here, there are some ambiguities. A manipulation check can be reactive and the results may be due to the check and not to the independent variable. When the subjects themselves were queried about the experimental manipulation, there is the possibility that this query sensitized them to many aspects of the study and their responses on the dependent measures were due to this sensitization. For example, asking subjects whether the counselor's comments were phrased tentatively or decisively (for example, Jones & Gelso, 1988) might cause the subjects to review the preceding session critically and retrospectively change their opinion of the counselor. To minimize reactivity, the researcher should consider administering the check after the dependent measure (of course then the check may be influenced by the dependent measure), making the check indirect rather than transparent, embedding the check in filler material, and using unobtrusive measures (see Chapter 10).

It is worth repeating that successfully checking the manipulation to determine that the conditions varied on the intended dimension does not rule out confounds. It is entirely possible that the conditions varied on other dimensions as well. Nevertheless, interpretation is cleanest when the check was successful and the expected differences among conditions were found.

Statistically Nonsignificant Results

From a philosophy of science perspective, null results are very informative. Nevertheless, nonsignificant results can be due to a number of factors other than the lack of a true effect: inadequate statistical power, insensitive instruments, violated assumptions of statistical tests, careless procedures, bias, and so forth. We can now add poorly designed independent variables to this list. As discussed earlier, Malkiewich and Merluzzi's (1980) failure to detect the expected interaction in the client-treatment matching model may have been due to an inadequately designed independent variable. Showing that the experimental manipulation successfully differentiated the conditions helps to fortify the importance of nonsignificant findings. That is, if the conditions indeed were found to be distinct as expected, but the results did not produce the expected pattern, then evidence begins to accumulate that the hypothesized causal relationship is not present. Jones and Gelso's (1988) study of interpretations in counseling did not produce the expected interaction between client type and interpretation style. Without the manipulation check, it would have been easy to attribute the null results to lack of salience of difference in conditions (different interpretation styles). Although Jones and Gelso discussed many possible explanations for their nonsignificant findings, the manipulation check strengthened the possibility that counseling outcomes are not dependent on the interaction of client type and interpretation style, as had been thought.

Nonsignificant findings can also accompany unsuccessful manipulation checks. That is, the check indicates that the conditions did not differ on the intended dimension, and the expected differences on the dependent variable are not found. In this instance, one is left with the distinct possibility that poor design of the independent variable was responsible for the nonsignificant findings; consequently, the importance of the null findings for the field of counseling is mitigated to a large degree.

One of the problems with omitting a check on the manipulation is that the importance of a particular manipulation check is unknown before the data are collected. Consider again the study by Sharkin et al. (1989) that manipulated motivation (half the subjects in a 30-minute interview were told that they were motivated because of an action they had taken). In this study, the results for one dependent variable were significant; this, however, does not indicate whether or not the manipulation was salient because, as we have seen, it is possible that significant results can occur even if the manipulation was not salient. Furthermore, the results for another independent variable were not significant. In this study it is possible that the salience was sufficient to achieve a threshold for one dependent variable and not for the other. Because there was no manipulation check, the degree to which the manipulation was salient is unknown and interpretation of the results of this study is problematic.

STATUS VARIABLES

In this chapter we have emphasized the fact that the nature of the independent variable is determined by the researcher. By designing the independent variable is some particular way, the researcher attempts to examine its effect on the dependent variable. The word *manipulation* was used to characterize this deliberate process. As mentioned previously, a study may contain more than one independent variable; in this case, the effects of the independent variables typically would be examined in a factorial design as discussed in Chapter 5. For example, Ponce and Atkinson (1989) manipulated both counselor ethnicity (Anglo-American or Mexican-American) and counselor style (directive and nondirective) in a 2 × 2 factorial design.

Counseling researchers are often interested in variables that are not amenable to manipulation, either due to ethical constraints or to logical impossibilities. It is not permissible ethically to assign subjects to a spouse-abuse condition, nor is it possible to assign subjects to a gender condition. We define all variables related to subjects that cannot be assigned as status variables. Such variables include personality variables (for example, locus of control), socioeconomic variables (such as education), gender, ethnicity, and so forth. Although many researchers label these variables as independent variables, the distinction between status variables and independent variables is critical to understanding the types of conclusions that can be drawn from these two types of variables.

Independent variables are manipulated and subsequently the effect on the dependent variable is assessed; if everything goes well, a *causal relationship* is established. Status variables cannot be manipulated; therefore, statistical tests involving status variables detect *associations*. For example, Vredenburg, O'Brien, and Krames (1988) classified college students as either depressed or nondepressed; depressed students vis-à-vis nondepressed students were less assertive, had less control over their depressions, had lower degrees of instrumentality and persistence, and had a higher degree of dysfunctional attitudes. Because Vredenburg et al. were not able to randomly assign subjects to levels of depression (for example, manipulate the independent variable), it would not be proper to say depression caused any of the personality variables. The causal relation could be in the opposite direction; for example, dysfunctional attitudes may be the cause of depression for college students. Or a third variable (for example, heredity) could be the cause of both depression and the personality variables.

There is an important point to be made about the statistical analysis of status variables. Although the analysis of status variables often is identical to that of independent variables, because status variables are not manipulated, it is more difficult to make causal inferences (Cook & Campbell, 1979). It is the design and not the analysis that determines the inferential status of the study (Cohen, 1968; Wampold & Freund, 1987). For example, Vredenburg et al. conducted analyses of variance with two groups (depressed and nondepressed); because depression was not manipulated, it cannot be said that depression was the cause of differences in the dependent variables. Parenthetically, note that depression scores in the Vredenburg et al. study were made into a categorical variable (that is, depressed, nondepressed). If the status variable is a continuous variable (for example, depression scores), it should be noted that typically the statistical power of an analysis of a continuous variable is increased by using an analysis that accommodates this continuity (for example, a regression analysis) rather than creating a categorical variable and using an analysis of variance (see Cohen & Cohen, 1983; Wampold & Freund, 1987). Also note that in a regression analysis, the status variable is often referred to as a predictor variable, as we mentioned in Chapter 8.

It is not unusual to include both independent variables and status variables in the same study. Ponce and Atkinson (1989) included acculturation level (a status variable) as well as two independent variables (counseling style and counselor ethnicity). Frequently, research hypotheses are directed toward an interaction of an independent variable with a status variable. Research that addresses the question of which treatments work best with which clients are of this nature. Two studies discussed in this chapter are also of this type. Malkiewich and Merluzzi (1980) examined the interaction of the conceptual level of the client (a status variable) with the structure of the counseling (an independent variable). Jones and Gelso (1988) predicted an interaction between client type (a status variable) and counselor style (an independent variable). When interpreting the results of studies with multiple variables, one needs to keep clearly in mind the distinction between independent and status variables, particularly with reference to causal inferences.

We do not make the distinction between independent variables and status variables so that one type can be considered first class and the other second class. The important point is that independent variables are manipulated so that causal inferences can be made directly. This is not to say that causality can never be attributed to some status variables. However, inferences are made in this case in a much different and more difficult manner. Consider the research on smoking and health. Smoking behavior cannot be ethically manipulated (for example, subjects cannot be assigned to smoking and nonsmoking conditions); nevertheless, there is little ambiguity about the fact that smoking is the cause of a number of diseases (Holland, 1986). However, this causal relationship was established by animal studies, epidemiological surveys, cross-cultural studies, retrospective comparisons, and such. Because smoking cannot be an independent variable, the Tobacco Institute is correct when it states that not *one* study has established scientifically that smoking is the cause of any disease; however, the causal relation has been firmly established over *many* studies. The first step in this process was to establish that there is a relationship between smoking and disease; then alternative explanations were ruled out. Cook and Campbell (1979) provide a good discussion of the problems with attributing causality in field settings.

Finally, it should be noted that there are those who argue that any variable that cannot logically be manipulated cannot be the cause of any effect (Holland, 1986). For example, it is not possible to assign gender to subjects; therefore, gender cannot be a cause. According to this position, differences in rates of depression for men and women are not caused by gender; rather, differences in depression are associated with gender. Cultural or biological factors may be potential causes of this difference because, at least logically, they can be manipulated, although certainly it may not be practical to make such manipulations.

At times, confusing interpretations of studies are made because independent and status variables are not differentiated. A perusal of research articles in counseling will demonstrate that status variables are often called independent variables. Nomenclature is not the issue here; there is little harm when the term *independent variable* is used inclusively. However, attributing causality without justification is an error that should be avoided assiduously. Causality is the strongest claim that can be made about relations between constructs, and one should always carefully examine the basis of causal attributions.

SUMMARY AND CONCLUSIONS

To adequately make causal attributions about the relation between constructs in counseling research, the independent variable must be adequately designed. As we discussed in Chapters 2 and 3, the first step in this process is to clearly state the research question so that the manipulation of the independent variable can adequately operationalize the cause of an effect. Once the critical dimension has been identified, the researcher must design the independent variable such that the conditions vary on the intended dimension but not on other dimensions. When the conditions vary on a dimension other than the intended dimension, it is said that a confound exists. That is, it is not possible to differentiate whether it is the purported construct or the confound that is the cause of an effect. Furthermore, the intended differences among the conditions of the independent variable must be salient so that they have an impact on subjects but not so vivid that they become transparent to subjects. If subjects can guess the hypothesis, then their responses may be affected. If the independent variable does indeed vary on the intended dimension and is salient to the subjects, then between-group variance is *max*imized. Furthermore, avoiding confounds gives the researcher more *con*trol. Clearly, the independent variable is a critical component of Kerlinger's "MAXMINCON" principle.

To demonstrate that the experimental manipulation accomplishes what the researcher had intended, it is often advisable to check on the manipulation. The goal of manipulation checks is to show that the conditions vary on the intended dimension, the conditions do not vary on other dimensions, and/or treatments are implemented in the intended fashion. Manipulation checks typically are made by having the subjects in the experiment or independent raters judge various aspects of the conditions of the independent variable. However, even when manipulation checks are used, the results of an experiment can be confusing. For example, ambiguity results when there are statistically significant differences among groups on the dependent variable but the manipulation check revealed that the conditions did not vary on the intended dimension. When the manipulation check is successful and there are statistically significant differences on the dependent variable, causal attributions are most plausible, although the researcher needs to make sure that the manipulation check was not reactive.

In many counseling studies, status variables are included in the design and analysis. Status variables are variables that have not been manipulated by the researcher, such as personality variables, socioeconomic variables, gender, and ethnicity. Although the analysis of status variables may be identical to the analysis of true independent variables, the inferences that can be made are much different. When status variables are used, statistical tests detect associations rather than causal relations.

Clearly, design of the independent variable is a critical step in designing research. It is not unusual for the researcher to have confidence in his or her manipulations only to discover after the data have been collected that a threatening confound was present. One should always be one's own greatest critic and attempt to think of every possible problem with the independent variable before the study is conducted.

CHAPTER 10

DESIGNING AND CHOOSING THE DEPENDENT VARIABLE

The basic purpose of the dependent variable (sometimes called the dependent measure) is to measure the construct that is hypothesized to be the effect. Thus, selecting or designing dependent variables as well as methods of data collection vis-à-vis the dependent variable are critical activities for the researcher. Poorly designed dependent variables introduce unwanted error variance, which is a serious threat to Kerlinger's "MAXMINCON" principle.

Typically, one subsection of the methods section of a journal article is entitled "Dependent Variables" or "Dependent Measures" and contains a brief description of and some psychometric information about the dependent variables used in the study. Infrequently, however, is a rationale given for the choice of dependent variables: Why were these particular variables included and others excluded? Extreme caution must be exercised in this process because the choice of a dependent variable can be critical to the merits of the research. For example, a mother's report may be used to assess her children's behavior; however, a mother's ratings of her children's behavior may be more affected by her own psychopathology than by the children's actual behavior (Webster-Stratton, 1988). Likewise, the reported outcome of psychotherapy and counseling differs depending on whether the effects are judged by the clients, the therapists, or independent raters (Kazdin, 1980; Orlinsky & Howard, 1986). Investigations with poorly chosen or designed dependent variables at best will be uninformative or uninterpretable and at worst will be erroneous and misleading. Conversely, creatively designing a set of dependent variables might reveal new information that adds greatly to the knowledge base in a particular area.

In the first half of this chapter, we will discuss considerations in choosing or designing the dependent variable. The essential issue is selecting dependent variables that are adequate operationalizations of the effect constructs in the research question. In the last half of the chapter, we will discuss methods of data collection vis-à-vis dependent variables. In that section we will classify and discuss seven nonexclusive methods of data collection that are useful in counseling research. The essential point is that each method of data collection has different advantages and disadvantages. The task of the informed researcher is to collect data with a method that provides the type of information that is most relevant to the research question.

OPERATIONALIZING THE DEPENDENT VARIABLE

Choosing or designing dependent variables that are adequate operationalizations of the effect constructs in the research question is a critical step in research. The dependent variables must be designed or chosen to reflect the constructs embodied in the research question. This section focuses on four issues related to the design and/or selection of dependent variables. The first topic that we examine is the psychometric properties of the variables; we will briefly discuss reliability and validity as considerations in understanding the degree to which a construct is properly operationalized. Second, since no one variable can typically operationalize a construct adequately, we discuss the role of multiple dependent variables to properly reflect the constructs of interest. Third, the researcher must take care to make sure that the dependent variables do not react with the treatment in some way; thus, we briefly discuss the role of reactivity of the dependent variable within the experimental context. Finally, we discuss several procedural issues that can potentially affect subjects' responses to the dependent variable, such as total administration time of dependent variables, order of presentation, and the reading level of the instruments.

A clear research question is critical to the proper choice or design of a dependent variable, as we emphasized in Chapter 2. It is important that the dependent variables be designed to reflect the construct designated as the effect or outcome of the independent variable. For example, in a treatment study of anxiety, it should be mentioned whether the treatment is expected to affect state anxiety, trait anxiety, or both (for example, Smith & Nye, 1989). If the target construct is not easily differentiated from related constructs, the research question (and related discussion) should indicate how it differs. Once the relations among constructs are hypothesized and the constructs differentiated from each other, the researcher's task is to choose or design dependent variables that appropriately operationalize the construct that is expected to change as a function of manipulation of the independent variable.

Psychometric Issues

One important question about the operationalization of a construct involves the psychometric properties of the dependent variable. Researchers need to know to what extent the dependent variables they select to operationalize a construct are reliable and valid. If the estimates of reliability and validity are poor, chances are the operationalization of the construct will be inadequate. Although entire volumes have been devoted to psychometrics, we will review the rudiments nontechnically here because they are critical to understanding the degree to which a construct is properly operationalized. A warning, however, is given: the skilled researcher needs to have a strong background in psychometrics and be knowledgeable about the psychometric properties of the dependent variables used in a study.

Reliability

To be informative, scores on the dependent measure need to vary among the subjects in a study. If everyone obtains the same score on a measure, nothing can be learned about the individuals; however, when one subject scores higher than another, that begins to tell us something about how the two subjects differ. We hope that a difference between two scores is due to true differences in the level of the characteristic of interest (for example, anxiety). Nevertheless, any variance among scores also may be due to error.

The first and most vital factor accounting for variance in scores is related to the central construct being measured. Subjects who possess more of the construct will obtain higher scores on the variable (or lower, depending on how the variable is scaled). Of course, there is no guarantee that the central construct being measured is the construct of interest to the researcher. For example, on a scale designed to measure anxiety, a high score presumably reflects the fact that the subject is truly anxious. However, it is possible that the scale reflects another construct, such as social desirability. That is, the items generally might assess whether the subject responds in the socially desirable manner and not whether the subject is anxious.

In addition to reflecting the true level of functioning on the central construct, scores on the dependent variable may also be related to random errors (that is, error variance). Random error is that component of scores that is not due to systematic factors. As such, random errors do not reflect the central construct and therefore do not measure anything of interest. Obviously, if scores on the dependent variable are composed solely of random error, they will not be informative; in this instance, a statistically significant change in a dependent variable will be due to chance and not to the manipulation of the independent variable.

Random errors can be due to a number of chance factors, such as respondents' carelessness and scoring errors. However, another important source of error to consider is inclusion of items irrelevant to the central construct of the scale. For instance, inclusion on an anxiety scale of an item that measures intelligence will lead to error variance because the intelligence item does not correlate highly with the other items measuring anxiety.

The reliability of a set of scores is the degree to which the scores are due to systematic rather than chance factors. Reliability measures the proportion of variance that is due to true differences. True differences refer to actual differences, not measured differences. For example, when measuring the anxiety of subjects, some of the differences in scores will be due to true differences in anxiety and some will be due to error. If 90% of the variance is due to systematic factors, then the reliability is .90, indicating that 10% of the variance is due to random factors. Clearly, determining reliability is not straightforward because the true scores for any subject are unknown. However, reliability can be estimated in a number of ways; we will briefly discuss two common estimates of reliability: internal consistency and stability.

If the various items of an instrument are measuring the same construct, then scores on the items will tend to covary. That is, someone who has a high level of the construct (for example, is anxious) will tend to answer all the items in one direction (assuming they are all keyed in the same direction), whereas someone who has a low level of the construct (for example, is not anxious) will tend to answer all the items in the other direction. *Internal consistency* is a measure of the homogeneity of the items. When the scores for the various items are highly intercorrelated, the internal consistency will be high. Psychometricians have developed methods to estimate the internal consistency of scores. Cronbach's alpha, the coefficient derived from the Kuder-Richardson 20 formula, and split-half coefficients are estimates of internal consistency and often are seen in discussions of dependent variables in counseling research. It should be noted that the Kuder-Richardson 20 formula is a special case of Cronbach's alpha for dichotomously scored instruments (for example, correct and incorrect) and that estimates using the split-half method are generally inferior to those obtained using either of these other two methods.

A second common estimate of reliability pertains to the *stability* of the scores. Perhaps the most common estimate of stability is the test-retest correlation. If scores on a measure are relatively stable, the correlation between repeated testings is relatively high (r = .8 or .9). Changes in scores from one time to another may be due to error (that is, unreliability of the scale) or to changes in the true level of the construct. For example, if the test-retest index is low for a scale measuring anxiety, it may be due to error or it may be due to changing levels of anxiety over the time period (as would be the case for state anxiety). It should be noted here that a critical element in estimating the stability of the scores on an instrument is the time interval between testings. Typically, shorter time intervals (for example, two weeks) will result in higher estimates of stability than longer time intervals (for example, two years) for the same instrument. Thus, in reporting estimates of stability, it is important to report the time interval as well.

Another method to obtain estimates of stability is to compare alternate forms (or two different measures) of the same instrument. Alternate form indexes also are dependent on two sources—reliability and comparability of forms. That is, low alternate form indexes may be due to the unreliability of the forms, the lack of comparability of the forms, or both. Presumably, high alternate form indexes are due to reliable and comparable forms.

Several points about reliability are important to keep in mind when designing or choosing a dependent variable. First, reliability reflects variance due to true scores, but does not indicate what the true scores are measuring. A set of scores that are internally consistent may be measuring something quite different from what was postulated. For example, a personality measure may be measuring social desirability rather than the targeted construct. Developers of scales often attach names to them that indicate some construct (for example, the ABC Scale of Social Skills); adequate reliability does not establish that the instrument actually measures that construct (for example, social skills). Validity, which will be discussed later in this chapter, is concerned with whether or not the construct being measured is the construct of interest.

A second point is that reliability is based on the scores and not on the instrument from which they were derived. It is the scores themselves that have certain properties. Certainly, the properties of the scores are derived from the characteristics of the instrument, but keeping this distinction in mind will help the researcher avoid some problems. A vital consequence of this distinction is that reliability estimates are restricted to the types of subjects on whom, and conditions under which, the psychometric study was conducted. An instrument may perform adequately for one type of subject but not for another type, or under one set of conditions but not under others. For example, an anxiety measure may yield adequate reliability estimates with undergraduates when administered in a classroom, but be completely useless to measure anxiety of agoraphobics in a laboratory setting. That is, the instrument may be very sensitive to midrange differences in anxiety, but insensitive at the upper range. This is called a *ceiling effect;* all the agoraphobics may score at or near the maximum so that their scores are not reflective of true differences in anxiety. Of course, this problem may also manifest itself at the bottom of the range, creating a *floor effect.* Reliability is also dependent on characteristics of the subjects, such as reading ability and age. An instrument may yield adequate reliability for college students but not for high school dropouts, due to random error created by an inability to read the items. The implication of this discussion is that instruments should be chosen that are sensitive in the range of scores anticipated in the study and with the type of subjects used in the study. One has to read carefully the psychometric studies conducted on various instruments to make this determination. Alternatively, the reliability of the scores actually obtained in a study could be estimated; typically, this is impractical because large numbers of subjects are needed for such studies (typically in excess of 300; Nunnally, 1978) and because reliability estimates are affected by mean differences obtained for the various conditions of the independent variable.

How high should reliability be? Some sources indicate that reliability estimates in excess of .80 are sufficient. Certainly, all things being equal, the instrument that yielded the highest reliability in the desired range would be chosen from among other instruments. However, all things are rarely equal and choices must be made. Other factors need to be considered: validity, time to complete the instrument, costs, and so forth (topics to be discussed later in this chapter). We take the position that the researcher will need to weigh many considerations, such as validity, completion time, properties of alternative measures of the construct, and so forth. Thus, in instances when a construct is elusive, a reliability of .70 may be adequate. Keep in mind, however, that a reliability of .70 means that 30% of the variance of the scores on the dependent variable is due to error. Certainly, reliability indexes below .50 indicate serious psychometric problems that limit the utility of the instrument.

Validity

Psychometric texts list many types of validity. The most important type of validity for research purposes is construct validity. Construct validity refers to the degree to which the scores reflect the desired construct rather than some other construct. Clearly, unreliable scores cannot have construct validity because they are due mostly to random error. Nevertheless, as mentioned previously, reliable scores may reflect one or more constructs other than the one specified. Determining construct validity is complicated and indirect.

One way to establish construct validity is to examine the relationship of scores on the instrument to scores on other instruments intended to measure the same construct and other constructs. Clearly, there should be a high correlation between instruments that measure the same construct. If these expected correlations are found, there is said to be *convergent validity.* Measures of different constructs should not be highly correlated, although a moderate correlation can be tolerated and may even be expected. It is reasonable to expect that certain constructs, although distinct, will be related. For example, anxiety and depression measures are often correlated. Nevertheless, correlation of measures of different constructs should be smaller than correlations of measures of the same construct; if this pattern is found, there is said to be *discriminant validity.*

Convergent and discriminant validity can be examined by constructing a multitrait-multimethod matrix (Campbell & Fiske, 1959). *Multimethod* refers to the use of various means to measure the same trait; for example, behavioral observations, self-report, and report of significant others. *Multitrait* refers to various characteristics of people. Correlations of measures of the same trait but with different methods should be higher than correlations of measures of different traits by the same or different methods. A multitrait-multimethod matrix, with the expected pattern of correlations, is presented in Table 10-1. In this case, Trait A (as well as B and C) is more highly correlated

TABLE 10-1
Multitrait-Multimethod Matrix with Expected Correlations for Convergent and Discriminant Validity

	Method 1			*Method 2*		
	Trait A	*Trait B*	*Trait C*	*Trait A*	*Trait B*	*Trait C*
Method 1						
Trait A		low	low	high	low	low
Trait B			low	low	high	low
Trait C				low	low	high
Method 2						
Trait A					low	low
Trait B						low
Trait C						

across Methods 1 and 2 than with other traits within the same method or between Method 1 and Method 2.

Another means to establish construct validity is through a statistical procedure called factor analysis (Tinsley & Tinsley, 1987), discussed in Chapter 8. Recall that factor analysis is a data reduction procedure that examines the factors that underlie a set of variables. If the variables are the scores on a variety of tests, then factor analysis can be employed to detect a small number of factors that account for the variance in the scores. Variables that measure the same construct will be grouped together in the sense that they will correlate highly (or load on) a single factor. The factors are then interpreted as constructs. For example, examine the results of a factor analysis of a set of six fictitious tests presented in Table 10-2. In this analysis, two factors underlie the six tests. The first factor is a mental abilities factor (or intelligence) because the tests that load on this factor clearly are measures of mental abilities (the ABC Test of Vocabulary, the Peter Test of Problem Solving, and the Amazing Mazes Test). The second factor is a physical abilities factor because the tests that load on this factor clearly are measures of physical abilities (the NBA Test of Eye-Hand Coordination, the Walter Weight-Lifting Test, and the 100-Meter Running Speed). Thus, in this fictitious case, the factor analytic data would indicate construct validity for two factors.

It is not unusual to see subscales of instruments used in counseling research. The presumption is that each of the subscales measures a different, although probably related, construct. A salient example is the Counselor Rating Form (CRF; Barak & LaCrosse, 1975). The CRF is a 36-item scale designed to measure three characteristics of the counselor: trustworthiness, attractiveness, and expertness. Each item contains an adjective and its opposite (for example, logical-illogical) and respondents rate their perceptions of the counselor on a seven-point scale with regard to these adjectives (for example, 1 = logical, 7 = illogical). Typically, subscale scores for trustworthiness, attractiveness, and expertness are determined by summing the scores for the items within each subscale. In the case of the CRF, there are 12 items for trustworthiness, 12 items for attractiveness, and 12 items for expertness.

T A B L E 10-2
Factor Analysis of Six Fictitious Tests

	Factor 1	Factor 2
ABC Test of Vocabulary	.58	.11
Peter Test of Problem Solving	.65	.09
NBA Test of Eye-Hand Coordination	.14	.49
Amazing Mazes Test	.51	.08
Walter Weight-Lifting Test	.02	.62
100-Meter Running Speed	.09	.67

Note. Factor 1 is interpreted as a mental abilities factor because the tests involving mental abilities load on this factor; Factor 2 is interpreted as a physical abilities factor because the tests involving physical abilities load on this factor.

To examine the construct validity of the CRF and the Counselor Effectiveness Rating Scale (CERS; Atkinson & Wampold, 1982), which also measures the same three aspects of the counselor, Atkinson and Wampold (1982) conducted a multitrait-multimethod analysis of these two instruments (traits were the three counselor characteristics and methods were the two instruments). The obtained correlations are presented in Table 10-3. Convergent validity was established by showing that the correlations between corresponding subscales (for example, CRF-Trustworthiness with CERS-Trustworthiness) were high. However, the discriminant validity of these two instruments was suspect because the correlations among all of the subscales were high, casting some doubt on the existence of three separate constructs.

The alternative to using subscales is to use the total score. In the case of the CRF, the total score reflects a global rating of the perception of the counselor and has been labeled generically the "good guy" factor (Ponterotto & Furlong, 1985). One needs to make a decision about whether to use the subscale scores or the total scores as dependent measures in a study. Inclusion of both subscale scores and total scores in the same analysis introduces dependencies that make the results of the analysis uninterpretable (that is, the results will be indeterminate).

Although examining subscale and total scores simultaneously is not advisable, there are ways to study subscale and total scores hierarchically. To illustrate this method as well as demonstrate how factor analysis can be used to establish construct validity, a study of a shortened version of the CRF by Tracey, Glidden, and Kokotovic (1988) is discussed here. The Counselor Rating Form-Short (CRF-S; Corrigan & Schmidt, 1983) is a modification of the CRF containing 12 items, 4 items for each of the three constructs (attractiveness,

TABLE 10-3
Intercorrelations among Three Counselor Dimensions as Measured by Two Instruments

| | Instrument and Dimension | | | | | |
| | CRF | | | CERS | | |
Instrument and Dimension	E	T	A	E	T	A
CRF						
Expertness (E)		.79	.60	.79	.60	.42
Trustworthiness (T)			.76	.63	.73	.59
Attractiveness (A)				.55	.65	.73
CERS						
Expertness (E)					.67	.54
Trustworthiness (T)						.76
Attractiveness (A)						

Note. From "A Comparison of the Counselor Rating Form and the Counselor Effectiveness Rating Scale" by D. R. Atkinson and B. E. Wampold, 1982, *Counselor Education and Supervision, 22,* p. 29. Copyright 1982 by the American Association of Counseling and Development. Reprinted by permission.

expertness, and trustworthiness). Tracey et al. performed various confirmatory factor analyses. Confirmatory factor analyses differ from exploratory factor analyses in that in the confirmatory mode, the researcher posits a factor structure and the analysis indicates the degree to which the posited structure was found (see Fassinger, 1987). Tracey et al. posited several models to explain scores on the CRF-S: one global factor, three independent factors (positing that the three constructs are unrelated), three dependent factors (positing that the constructs are correlated), and a hierarchical model. The hierarchical model involves three constructs and a higher-order factor that accounts for the correlation among the constructs. The higher-order factor represents the global "good guy" factor. It was found that the hierarchical model provided the best fit to the data; the factor loadings for this model (for clients) are presented in Table 10-4. Perusal of these factor loadings shows the existence of three separate constructs (expertness, attractiveness, and trustworthiness), but also the pervasiveness of the global factor (labeled General Evaluation).

The Tracey et al. study demonstrates the complexities involved in understanding the nature of the dependent variable. These complexities can often be critical to detecting psychological phenomena. In a study of premature termination, Kokotovic and Tracey (1987) found that continuers and dropouts were different on the dimensions of trustworthiness and expertness; however, when the effects of general satisfaction (measured on a different instrument) were accounted for, the three CRF scales poorly discriminated continuers from dropouts. Understanding the relationship between general satisfaction and specific dimensions of social influence is critical to interpreting the results of this study.

TABLE 10-4
Standardized Factor Loadings for the Two-Step Hierarchical Model Used to Explain Scores on the CRF-S

Variable	Attractive	Expert	Trustworthy	General Evaluation
Friendly	.63	.00	.00	.56
Likable	.36	.00	.00	.80
Sociable	.59	.00	.00	.68
Warm	.60	.00	.00	.64
Experienced	.00	.44	.00	.77
Expert	.00	.52	.00	.79
Prepared	.00	.19	.00	.81
Skillful	.00	.30	.00	.85
Honest	.00	.00	.35	.74
Reliable	.00	.00	.22	.82
Sincere	.00	.00	.43	.76
Trustworthy	.00	.00	.39	.81

Note. From "Factor Structure of the Counselor Rating Form-Short" by T. J. Tracey, C. E. Glidden, and A. M. Kokotovic, 1988, Journal of Counseling Psychology, 35, p. 333. Copyright 1988 by the American Psychological Association. Reprinted by permission.

Multiple Dependent Variables

Use of more than one dependent variable in a study is often recommended (Cook & Campbell, 1979; Kazdin, 1980). One reason for including multiple dependent variables is that no one variable can adequately operationalize a construct because some of the variance in this variable is due to other constructs and some is due to random error; several variables more adequately represent the construct because one variable will be sensitive to aspects of the construct absent in other variables. To measure mathematical achievement, a researcher may choose to use grade point average (GPA) in math classes as well as the quantitative SAT score. GPA, by itself, is inadequate as a measure because it is also sensitive to motivation, choice of classes, grading practices, and so forth. SAT scores also reflect multiple-choice test taking ability, reading ability, and anxiety. The two measures together, however, more adequately measure achievement than either one alone. The overlap of these variables reflects the essence of the construct, as represented in Figure 10-1.

Another reason for including multiple measures is that the outcomes of experiments are often expected to affect more than one construct. For example, McNamara and Horan (1986) investigated the efficacy of behavioral and cognitive treatments for depression. They were particularly interested in how these treatments affected behavioral and cognitive manifestations of depression. The cognitive battery contained the Automatic Thoughts Questionnaire,

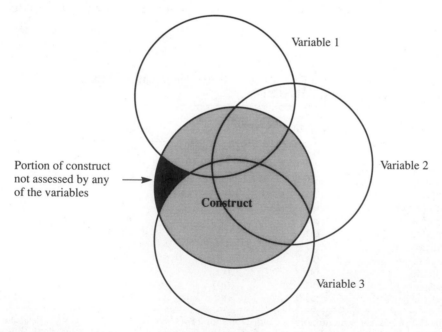

Portion of construct not assessed by any of the variables →

FIGURE 10-1
Use of multiple variables to operationalize a construct.

the Cognitive Scale, and the Recalled Cognitions exercises. The behavioral battery included the Pleasant Events Schedule, the Behavioral Scale, and observer-evaluated social skills ratings. The researchers found that the cognitive treatments strongly attenuated cognitive manifestations of depression with some generalization to behavioral measures, whereas the behavioral treatments appeared to have little effect on either the cognitive or the behavioral measures.

Use of multiple dependent variables raises many concerns for the researcher. The most obvious problem relates to the selection of specific variables. The range of potential dependent variables is vast. For example, in treatment studies, outcomes may be assessed by behavioral observations, self-reports, reports of others, and therapist ratings. In turn, each mode of assessment offers many alternatives. One might ask clients to judge their progress phenomenologically (for example, by asking "How happy are you?") or to report specific cognitions. Moreover, the situation becomes important; a specific behavior may be exhibited in one situation but not in another. Alternatively, variables can be customized for individual subjects, such as is the case with goal attainment scaling (Kiresuk & Sherman, 1968). Further complicating the situation is that time becomes a factor. Is the anticipated effect expected immediately at the end of treatment, a short time thereafter, or at long-term follow-up? Clearly, the researcher must know the area and make informed choices. For example, in a study of anxiety, the researcher needs to know whether anxiety in a particular context would best be measured observationally, physiologically, or by self-report, or some combination of all three. An understanding of the mechanisms of anxiety would be needed to make this determination.

Parenthetically, it is important to note that using multiple dependent measures also complicates the analysis of the data obtained in a study. Treating each variable distinctly (that is, running a univariate analysis for each variable) ignores the interrelationships among the variables and inflates the probability of Type I errors (see Leary & Altmaier, 1980). However, complicated multivariate analyses often obscure different patterns in the data. To select the proper statistical methods, one must be knowledgeable about the interrelationships among the variables and be willing to make predictions about the pattern of results (see Wampold, Davis, & Good, 1990). Statistical analysis is beyond the scope of this text, but the reader is referred to the special 1987 issue of the *Journal of Counseling Psychology* (Wampold, 1987) devoted to the statistical analysis of counseling research.

Reactivity

The dependent variable should be sensitive to some characteristic of the subject, but the assessment process itself should not affect the characteristic directly. That is, the dependent measure should indicate how the subject functions normally. Sometimes, something about obtaining scores on the dependent measure alters the situation so that "false" readings are obtained. Variables that affect the characteristics of the subjects they are intended to measure are said to be *reactive*. For example, a test-anxious subject may report increased anxiety on a self-report instrument because completing the instrument is like taking a test; an aggressive child may display less aggressive behavior when being observed by an adult than at other times; a person may reduce his or her smoking when asked to record the number of cigarettes smoked. Clearly, the reactive nature of dependent variables needs to be considered in designing research; again, knowledge of the substantive area is vital. Later in this chapter, we will discuss unobtrusive measures, which are designed to be nonreactive.

Procedural Considerations

A number of procedural issues need to be considered when selecting or designing the dependent variable. Often, the time involved with the assessment is critical to the success of the study. Subjects will be reluctant to volunteer for studies that demand large amounts of time to complete forms and instruments, or even if they do volunteer they may respond carelessly to items (increasing error variance), especially toward the end of the assessment period. Most psychometric studies assess reliability of scores when only the targeted scale is administered; the researcher must consider that reliability may be considerably less when the scale is administered at the end of a long battery of tests.

As mentioned previously, the readability of instruments is critical to their psychometric performance. Any instrument administered should be checked to insure that the subjects can adequately read the materials. Often the manuals of published tests contain references to the reading level required. Alternatively, the researcher can use one of the relatively easy-to-use methods for determining readability (see Klare, 1974–1975).

The order of the administration of instruments can have an effect on responses. One instrument may sensitize or otherwise influence responses on another instrument. An instrument that draws attention to a subject's own pathology (for example, the Minnesota Multiphasic Personality Inventory) may well affect how the subject rates others (for example, the counselor on the CRF). Order is also important when the same instrument is administered repeatedly. Subsequent performance may be due to previous responding (a testing effect) rather than to the amount of the characteristic. For instance, on an intelligence test, subjects may acquire knowledge about specific questions or tasks (such as picture completion) that improves performance although intelligence remains unchanged.

When repeated measures are used in a study, use of alternative forms is desirable if testing effects are anticipated. Alternative forms enable the researcher to give a pretest and a posttest without having to use the identical instrument.

METHODS OF DATA COLLECTION

The basic purpose of the dependent variable is to measure the effect or outcome of the independent variable. Thus, an essential aspect of any discussion of dependent variables must focus on the collection of data vis-à-vis the dependent variable. To this point, we have emphasized the use of instruments in data collection. Nevertheless, there are a number of other methods to collect data relevant to the dependent variable. For the purposes of this text, we have classified and will discuss several methods of data collection that are relevant in counseling. We have divided these methods into seven nonexclusive categories: (1) self-reports, (2) ratings of other persons and events, (3) behavioral observations, (4) physiological indexes, (5) interviews, (6) projective techniques, and (7) unobtrusive measures. There are other considerations on which to categorize methods; for instance, measures can be dichotomized into objective versus subjective methods. Where relevant these other methods will be discussed. Also note that these seven data collection methods may sometimes overlap; the interview method also is a form of self-report; ratings of other people are sometimes behavioral measures. The main point is that you should become aware of the broad range of data collection methods, as well as their respective advantages and disadvantages. Finally, keep in mind that each method of data collection should be evaluated in terms of its congruence with the research question, psychometric properties, relation to other methods used in the study, reactivity, and so forth.

Self-Reports

For self-report measures, the subject assesses the degree to which some characteristic is present or to which some behavior has taken place. The self-report may be accomplished by responding to items in an inventory, completing a log, or keeping a journal. In any case, the sine qua non of self-reports is that the subject makes the observation or report by himself or herself. Generally, the assumption is made that the report accurately reflects the true state of affairs; that is, that the subject responds honestly and accurately. In this section we will discuss advantages, disadvantages, types of inventories, and scoring formats for self-report inventories.

Advantages

Although there are many forms of self-report, some general advantages make self-reports the most popular assessment device in counseling research. First, they are relatively easy to administer. Most self-report inventories, tests, or questionnaires used in counseling research can be administered to a group of subjects, providing economy of time. Even when administered individually, self-report measures typically do not require special expertise on the part of the administrator; for example, receptionists can give clients inventories to be completed at the end of a session (for example, Kokotovic & Tracey, 1987). Similarly, most self-report inventories are relatively simple to use and require little training of the subject.

Another advantage of self-reports is that they can be used to access areas that otherwise would be impossible or extremely difficult to measure.

Self-reports can assess private cognitions and feelings, behavior in private settings (for example, sexual behavior), and future plans. In addition, subjects can be asked to report about cognitions, feelings, and behaviors in hypothetical situations. For instance, counselors could be asked to report how they would respond to a sexual advance by a client, a situation that would be unethical to arrange experimentally.

Self-reports also are advantageous because they are compatible with phenomenological views of counseling and psychotherapy. According to the phenomenological perspective, the thoughts and feelings of a client are of paramount importance and self-reports of such constructs as happiness, marital satisfaction, and anxiety are more important than other indicants of these constructs, such as therapist ratings of client change, behavioral observations, physiological measures, or other measures that use a locus other than the self. For example, anxiety can be assessed physiologically; nevertheless, the distress caused by anxiety states is the debilitating factor for clients and their self-reports of anxiety are essential to understanding this phenomenon.

Disadvantages

Although self-reports have many advantages, they also have some very conspicuous disadvantages. The most obvious, and the most troublesome, is that self-reports are vulnerable to distortions by the subject. For a variety of reasons, the subject may consciously or unconsciously respond in a way that yields a score that reflects a response bias rather than the construct being measured. For example, subjects may guess the hypothesis of the study and respond (1) in a way that they think will confirm the researcher's conjecture, (2) in a manner that makes them look good, (3) in a way that makes them appear more distressed than is truly the case in order to receive promised services, or (4) in a socially desirable way. Some inventories are constructed to minimize distortions. For example, the Minnesota Multiphasic Personality Inventory-2 (MMPI-2) contains four scales to assess the attitude of the subject. Two scales (*L* and *K*) measure whether the subject is trying to look better than is actually the case; one scale (*F*) measures deviate response sets; and one scale (the "?" scale) indicates the number of questions unanswered, which may indicate the subject's resistance to the test, confusion, or insufficient time to complete the test (Graham, 1990). To avoid subject bias, the Edwards Personality Preference Schedule is constructed so that the two choices for each item are equivalent with regard to social desirability (Sax, 1989).

Another disadvantage of self-report measures is that the subject may not be aware of the characteristic being measured. For example, a test-anxious subject may deny that he or she is anxious and attribute poor performance to inadequate preparation. In such cases, self-report can be used if the characteristic is measured indirectly. For example, the subject may be asked to self-report about the signs of anxiety (such as cold fingers, difficulty concentrating, dizziness). However, the case can be made that subjects do not have access to some mental processes and that self-reports reflect only the products of cognitive processes (for example, Nisbett & Wilson, 1977).

A final disadvantage of self-report measures is the flip side of the advantage related to the congruence between a phenomenological perspective and self-reports. Self-reports are less valued by other theoretical perspectives; for example, self-reports are of minimal importance to behaviorists. In spite of the disadvantages of self-reports, a perusal of the dependent variables used in counseling research clearly indicates that the self-report is the most frequently used dependent measure.

Types of Inventories

There are many different ways to classify self-reports; we will classify self-reports into inventories published by professional publishing companies, those published in the professional literature, and author-generated inventories tailored to a particular study. It is important to note that the different types of inventories present various advantages and disadvantages, which are important in choosing or designing the dependent variable. In addition to briefly discussing these advantages and disadvantages, we will note how to obtain copies of the various inventories.

Many studies in counseling use tests or inventories that are published by professional publishing companies. Many counseling studies use published inventories; well-known examples of published self-report inventories include the Minnesota Multiphasic Personality Inventory (MMPI), the Strong-Campbell Interest Inventory (SCII), and the Wechsler scales of intelligence (for example, WAIS-R). Published inventories can be obtained from the publisher; often there is a discount if the test or inventory is used in a research context.

The advantage of published inventories is that generally a substantial amount of research has been conducted on them. Typically, the manual reports the outcome of reliability and validity studies as well as normative data. Moreover, there are often many other studies published that report psychometric information about the inventory or that have used the inventory in research contexts. For example, there have been thousands of studies using the MMPI, the SCII, and the Wechsler scales. Information obtained from manuals and other studies is invaluable in assessing the appropriateness of the inventory for a particular study. It should be kept in mind, though, that publication does not insure the usefulness of an inventory; that determination needs to be made on an individual basis.

Most published inventories fall into one of the following classes: personality measures, intelligence and aptitude tests, attitude and value scales, achievement tests, and interest inventories. Although many sources provide information about published tests, the most comprehensive is the series of yearbooks published by the Buros Institute. The most recent, *The Ninth Mental Measurements Yearbook* (Mitchell, 1985), contains reviews of tests published since the prior yearbook, an index of test titles, a list of acronyms, a classified-subject index, a publisher directory and index, an index of names of authors and reviewers, and an index of the construct or properties measured. To facilitate locating tests in previous yearbooks, the Buros Institute also publishes *Tests in Print,* the most recent of which is the *Tests in Print III* (Mitchell, 1983).

There are a number of inventories that have been developed by researchers and that appear in various journal articles and books, but that are not published by publishing companies. One of the most widely used inventories in counseling research is the Counselor Rating Form (CRF; Barak & LaCrosse, 1975). As mentioned earlier, the CRF was developed to measure a client's perceptions of a counselor in the areas of attractiveness, expertness, and trustworthiness. Although this inventory has never been professionally published, it has been widely researched, used, and revised (for example, Barak & LaCrosse, 1975; Corrigan & Schmidt, 1983; Epperson & Pecnik, 1985; Heesacker & Heppner, 1983; Tracey, Glidden, & Kokotovic, 1988).

As was the case with professionally published instruments, researchers are advised to consider the psychometric data carefully on instruments that have appeared in the literature. In the case of the CRF and the CRF-S (short form of the CRF), extensive information is available. Other instruments may only have appeared in the literature once or twice and the psychometric properties may be uncertain. It is also advisable to read carefully how these instruments were used or are supposed to be used. Often, the items themselves do not appear in the articles, but can be inferred from tables or other information in the article. For example, the stems of items may be presented with means for the items in tables, and the type of scaling used (for instance, a seven-point bipolar scale) may be described in the text. One must be careful because inventories can perform differently depending on how the items are arranged on the page, the order in which they are presented, and so forth. When inventories from the literature are used, these aspects may vary from one study to another. It is generally advisable to contact the developer of such inventories to obtain permission and a copy of the instrument.

In some instances, researchers cannot find published or previously researched inventories that meet their needs. In such instances, the researcher can develop scales for a particular study. Adequately developing items for a questionnaire can be a long and drawn-out process (often six months or longer) in and of itself, involving writing and rewriting questions, pretesting on a small sample, and additional rewriting. Because subjects often complete these instruments in the absence of the experimenter, the instructions and questions must be crystal clear. The format of the questions must also facilitate the easy identification of all of the items. Even the length of the questionnaire and size of type can influence subjects' response rate, and thus are additional considerations. Again, this process merits very careful planning and thinking; far too many dissertations have produced ambiguous findings because of a hastily developed questionnaire. In short, developing an inventory is a complex process, and well beyond the scope of this chapter; interested readers should consult various test construction sources (for more details, see Babbie, 1979, and Dawis, 1987).

These ad hoc scales can be particularly useful because they can be tailored to measure just what the researcher has in mind. For example, Palmer and Cochran (1988) developed a scale to measure adolescent relations with their parents with regard to career planning and decision making. There is one very difficult problem with using ad hoc inventories; they have unknown psycho-metric properties. Although the reliability of an ad hoc inventory can be assessed by analyzing the scores in the particular study, this option is often unsatisfying. First, it may well be that the reliability of the scores obtained is not sufficiently high to conduct any further analysis using the scores. Second, most studies are not designed to enable the researcher to conduct such inciden-tal psychometric analyses; the most difficult problem here is that typically there are too few subjects for psychometric purposes. Finally, most inventories need to be tested, revised, and retested in a number of contexts before confidence in their performance is obtained. It is not uncommon for a researcher to spend ten years developing an inventory (for example, polishing items, confirming factor structure across sample populations, making multiple estimates of reliability and validity). Although the advantage of tailoring a measure to a particular study is a strong one, the total lack of psychometric information on that measure considerably weakens its utility.

Scoring Formats

Self-report measures can also be described by how they are scored, whether objectively or subjectively. If there is little ambiguity about the score assigned to a subject—if the subject, let's say, circles a number from 1 to 7 for each item and the circled numbers are summed to form a total score—then the inventory is objectively scored. If subjects are asked to record their food intake and scores are determined by estimating the caloric content ingested, then there is ambiguity due to estimation of size of portions, content of food, and so forth, and thus the inventory is subjectively scored. Clearly, objectivity and subjec-tivity are not absolutes. It should be noted that *objective* and *subjective* refer to how the scores are determined and not to the format of the inventory. If the food intake report were scored by counting the number of adjectives used to describe the food, then the report would be scored relatively objectively. Objectively scored self-reports are advantageous because little error variance is introduced by the scoring procedure. Nevertheless, subjectively scored self-reports are often richer in that they sometimes reflect better the con-struct being measured.

Items that can be objectively scored can be classified into several types. One type involves having the subject select one of several choices. The choices may be "agree–disagree," "yes–no," "approve–no opinion–disapprove," or "approve strongly–approve–neutral–disapprove–disapprove strongly." Alter-natively, there may be a point scale with anchors; for example, a seven-point scale with the anchors "agree" and "disagree" might appear as

Agree   1   2   3   4   5   6   7   Disagree

In all these cases, the response to each item is assigned a numeral (for example, yes = 0, no = 1). Typically, the sum of the responses for several items is used as a dependent variable. For example, the CRF-S consists of 12 items, and scores on each of the three subscales are derived by summing the responses for each of 4 items. The use of multiple items to form a scale or subscale score is desirable because it usually enhances the reliability of the scores (assuming that the items relate to the construct being measured). Dependent variables that rely on a single item of this type should be considered cautiously; in fact, the internal consistency of scores of single-item variables cannot be calculated.

Another means to construct objectively scored measures is to have the subjects rank-order a set of stimuli according to some criterion. Rank ordering forces the respondent to make discriminations that he or she might not otherwise make. For example, rather than being asked to rate the effectiveness of a set of possible counselor responses, the subject might be asked to rank-order the counselor responses from least effective to most effective. This could be a good strategy if respondents otherwise tended to rate all the counselor responses as equally effective.

Forced-choice methods require that subjects select one of two alternatives. Often the alternatives appear to be equally favorable or unfavorable. For example, the Edwards Personality Preference Schedule contains alternatives that are matched on the basis of social desirability, and the subject is required to select one of the alternatives that best describes him or her. A variation of the forced-choice method that has great potential for counseling research asks subjects to identify dimensions within a series of ratings. For instance, subjects might be presented descriptions of counselors that vary on certain dimensions (for example, empathy, unconditional positive regard) and asked to indicate which of the pair of counselors they prefer (all possible pairs need to be presented). These data can then be analyzed to indicate the dimensions to which the subjects are attending. Multidimensional scaling is one such method (see Fitzgerald & Hubert, 1987).

Although a few formats for objectively scored scales have been discussed very briefly here, it should be recognized that developing instruments to measure constructs is difficult. In fact, many articles appearing in professional journals in counseling, such as the *Journal of Counseling Psychology,* are related to the development and validation of such instruments. Dawis (1987) provides an introduction to this topic for counseling researchers. Furthermore, various formats will yield data with particular properties, affecting the validity of the statistical tests used. For example, a broader range of statistical analyses are typically available for Likert (1–6) responses than true-false or yes-no responses. Likewise, questions that ask respondents to "*check* all those items below that apply" also restrict the range of statistical analyses possible. Care must be used to select statistical tests that are appropriate for the types of data obtained; refer to measurement and statistical sources for discussion of this complicated issue.

Ratings of Other Persons and Events

Often counseling research relies on ratings made of other persons or of events. The procedures here are similar to those for self-reports except that the respondent rates characteristics of the subject or of the event. Often the respondent is an expert and his or her judgment is assumed to reflect accurately character-istics of the person or event. For example, in treatment studies, the therapist or significant others could rate the degree of dysfunction or improvement of a client. A perusal of the literature in counseling reveals that direct rating of subjects is seldom used. However, many studies derive variables from ratings of events, particularly counseling sessions. For example, the Session Evaluation Questionnaire (SEQ; Stiles, 1980) is designed to measure the depth and smoothness of counseling sessions (for example, Stiles, Shapiro, & Firth-Cozens, 1988).

Ratings of other persons and events share many of the advantages of self-reports, particularly their ease of administration and flexibility. When experts are the raters, their judgments are particularly valuable because they are made with a deep and rich background. Experienced counselors' judgments take into account years of experience with many types of clients. Another advantage is that many rating scales (for example, the SEQ) have proven psychometric properties in various conditions.

The primary problem with ratings of other persons and events is that the ratings may be systematically biased. This is especially a problem when the raters are aware of the hypotheses and cognizant of the condition to which the subjects belong. If counselors are the raters and also are involved in the experimental treatment, they may rate the progress of clients higher because they have an interest in the outcome of the study. If at all possible, raters should be blind to as many factors of the experiment as possible.

When raters are used to make judgments about events, the ratings can reflect characteristics of the rater as well as characteristics of the event. When the participants (counselors and clients) judge the depth and smoothness of interviews on the SEQ, they are actually reporting their perceptions of the interview and in that respect their ratings are self-reports. Thus, when inter-preting ratings of events (or other persons, for that matter), researchers must be careful to separate the variance due to differences in the event from the variance due to the raters themselves. To examine the variance due to raters, the use of neutral or multiple observers is helpful. For example, Hill, Carter, and O'Farrell (1983) compared observers' as well as the counselor's and client's ratings of counseling sessions.

Another problem with ratings is that often they are relatively general, and hence it is not possible to determine what led to the ratings. In the SEQ, raters respond to the stem "The session was" on seven-point scales anchored by adjectives such as "bad–good," "dangerous–safe," and "difficult–easy." However, it is unknown which aspects of a session lead to a rater's respond-ing with "difficult" as opposed to "easy."

An imaginative way to use ratings of events is to have subjects respond to a stimulus and rate these responses in some way. Tracey, Hays, Malone, and Herman (1988) used the Therapist Response Questionnaire to obtain counselors' reactions to various client statements. The counselors indicated how they would normally respond and then these responses were rated on eight dimensions: dominance versus submission, approach versus avoidance, focus on cognition versus affect, immediacy, breadth versus specificity, the extent to which the counselor met the client's demand, verbosity, and confrontation. In this way, Tracey et al. were able to obtain a set of responses to various client statements and then obtain additional dimensional ratings on those counselor responses, which allowed for greater precision and interpretability of the ratings.

Behavioral Measures

Behavioral measures are derived from the observation of overt behavior, most typically by a trained observer. Behavioral psychology has stressed the importance of overt behavior and deemphasized intrapsychic phenomena. Accordingly, observing and recording behavior is the key component of studies in the applied behavior analysis area (see the *Journal of Applied Behavior Analysis* for examples of this type of research). Essentially, behavioral measures are the same as ratings of other persons or events, except that behavioral measures focus on overt, observable behavior and presumably do not rely on inferences by the raters.

As is the case with other modalities of assessment, behavioral assessment encompasses a wide variety of methods (Barlow, 1981; Mash & Terdal, 1981; see also the journal *Behavioral Assessment*). Generally, behavioral assessment requires an operational definition of the behaviors of interest, direct observation of subjects' behavior, recording of occurrences of the targeted behavior, and some presentation or summarization of the data.

The general advantages of behavioral measures are that they are objective and direct measures. Although there can be systematic biases in the observation and recording of overt behavior, they are typically not subject to the personal biases inherent in self-reports. Another advantage of behavioral measures is that subjects can be assessed in various environments. Over and over again, studies have shown that behavior is situation-specific; behavioral measures can be used to assess functioning in several situations. Finally, for many dysfunctions, the behavior itself is problematic (for example, stuttering, social skills deficits, sexual dysfunction, physical avoidance, substance abuse), and thus warrants specific attention.

There are a number of disadvantages of behavioral measures as well. Frequently, problems and concerns of clients do not center around behavior. Marital satisfaction is a construct that is difficult to operationalize behaviorally (although there are many behavioral correlates of marital satisfaction). The central question, as with any operationalization, is whether the behavior chosen reflects the construct of interest.

Another disadvantage of behavioral measures is related to representativeness. A presumption of behavioral assessment is that the behavior sampled is representative of behavior at other times. However, for a number of reasons, the sampled behavior may not be representative. For instance, nonrepresentativeness can occur when behavior is recorded at fixed but unusual times (for example, classroom behavior on Friday afternoons). In addition, the reactivity that results when the subject is aware he or she is being observed leads to observations that may not be representative.

Issues related to reliability are problematic for behavioral assessment. An observer's decision that a particular behavior was emitted may be idiosyncratic to that observer. In the context of behavioral assessment, these reliability issues are judged by calculating indexes of agreement; that is, how well do observers agree about emission of targeted behavior? As was the case for traditional assessment, interobserver agreement is a complex topic (see Suen, 1988).

Even if overt behavior is of paramount importance, it may not be possible or practicable to observe the behavior. Typically, observation of sexual behavior, for instance, is precluded. Other behaviors are difficult to observe and are sometimes assessed in contrived situations. In counseling research, the behavior of a counselor often is assessed with confederate clients who manifest some type of problem. Of course, the representativeness of behavior in contrived situations must be considered.

Behavioral observations have been used successfully in counseling and supervision process research. In the usual paradigm, the interactions between counselor and client (or supervisor and trainee) are recorded and coded as a stream of behaviors. A number of coding systems have been developed or adapted for this use (for example, see Friedlander, Siegel, & Brenock, 1989; Hill et al., 1983; Hill & O'Grady, 1985; Holloway, Freund, Gardner, Nelson, & Walker, 1989; see also Chapter 14). From the sequence of behaviors, measures are derived that can be used to characterize the nature of the counseling or supervision interaction. The simplest measure is the frequency of behaviors. For example, Hill et al. (1983) used the frequency of counselor behaviors to discriminate the best from the worst sessions in a case study of 11 sessions. Simple frequencies, however, are not sensitive to the probabilistic relation between behaviors. More sophisticated methods can be used to detect whether the probability that the behavior of one participant (for example, the client) will be emitted increases in response to the behavior of the other participant (for example, the counselor). Using such methods, Wampold and Kim (1989) showed that the counselor in the Hill et al. study was reinforcing the storytelling behavior of the client. However, methods that look at sequential dependencies are not without their problems or their critics (for example, compare the results of Hill et al., 1983, with Wampold & Kim, 1989; see also Howard, 1983; Lichtenberg & Heck, 1983, 1986; Wampold, 1986).

Physiological Indexes

Often biological responses of subjects can be used to infer psychological states. Many psychological phenomena have physiological correlates that can be used as dependent variables. In fact, physiological responses often can be thought of as direct measures of a construct. For example, whereas self-reports of anxiety can be biased by a number of factors, measures of physiological arousal can be made directly and can be presumed to be free of bias. However, although physiological arousal is a central area in the theoretical conceptualization of anxiety, the relation between physiological states and psychological phenomena has not been found to be as straightforward as was anticipated in the early years of this research. Moreover, physiological measures are expensive, require special expertise, may be reactive, and may be subject to error due to a number of mechanical and electronic factors (such as electrical interference). As a result, physiological measures are infrequently used in counseling research.

Interviews

Interviews are straightforward means to obtain information from subjects. In everyday life, interviewing is the pervasive means; we simply ask people to supply information. The interview typically involves an interpersonal interaction between the interviewer and the interviewee or subject. The interview is usually face-to-face or conducted over the telephone. A third option is to mail questionnaires or surveys. We will briefly discuss face-to-face and telephone interviews.

The personal interview consists of a trained interviewer's asking a subject a set of questions face-to-face, typically in a very structured, prescribed manner, but sometimes in an unstructured manner. In a structured interview, the wording of the questions and their order are fixed. In a semistructured interview, some latitude in follow-up responses is permitted. Unstructured interviews have themes that are pursued, but most questions are developed by the interviewer during the course of the interview. In the more structured interviews, the interviewer follows a list of questions (often called an interview schedule); the schedule of questions is often the result of a laborious process of developing, refining, and piloting. Since the quality of the information obtained in the study is directly dependent on the quality, depth, and scope of the questions, it behooves the researcher to very carefully develop the interview schedule. Developing questions for a detailed interview is often more complex than initially assumed (for details, see Babbie, 1979).

Kerlinger (1986) advocated using personal interviews because of the greater control and depth of information that can be obtained. The depth of information is most often a result of carefully planning and developing the interview schedule. Personal interviews allow flexibility in questionnaire design; the interviewer can provide explanations (and thus reduce subject confusion), make decisions during the interview about the adequacy of a particular response (and probe if necessary), and evaluate the motivation of the subject. The flexibility of the personal interview can be a real advantage if the topic is complex and if subjects are unaware of their answers; interviewer probing can then be extremely beneficial and add considerable depth to the information obtained. Babbie (1979) also observed that personal interviews that are properly executed typically achieve a completion rate of at least 80–85% of the subjects targeted. Interviews rely on the self-report of the subject; however, the human interaction with the interviewer provides another facet to the self-report. In short, the interviewer can also make observations about the subject, which is an additional data source (Babbie, 1979).

Interviews, however, are costly in terms of money and time. If the topics are sensitive (for instance, sexual behavior), then subjects may be more reluctant to divulge information than if they were allowed to respond to an anonymous questionnaire. Interviewers must be recruited and trained. It is also important to standardize procedures across interviews to avoid the introduction of confounding variables due to different interviewer behavior or biases. Often considerable training is needed to standardize procedures (general greeting, introduction of the interview schedule, methods of recording exact responses, manner of asking questions, responses to subjects' questions, handling of unusual subject behavior, and termination of the interview). Thus, interviewer training is another task for the experimenter (see Babbie, 1979, for more details regarding interviewer behavior and training).

The telephone interview consists of a trained interviewer's asking a subject a series of questions over the telephone. This method is usually quick and low cost (financially), unless one is making long-distance calls. Babbie (1979) recommends that the interview be kept short, 10–15 minutes. The shortness, however, often prevents the interviewer from obtaining much depth of information. Moreover, the telephone method reduces the amount of evaluative information that the interviewer can obtain about the subject. As with other personal interviews, an interview schedule needs to be developed, although an added consideration is the generally lower responsiveness of telephone subjects.

Interviews are used infrequently in counseling research. This is unfortunate given the utility of the interview for qualitative designs. McLaughlin, Cormier, and Cormier (1988) used a structured interview to assess the coping strategies used by subjects. The subjects responded as to how often (daily, three times per week, less than three times per week, every other week, infrequently, or never) they employed certain behavioral strategies. The researchers in this study chose an interview format because they wanted the subjects to develop a personal relationship with the research assistants, who were responsible for providing referrals for those subjects who needed assistance after the completion of the study.

Projective Techniques

The rationale behind projective techniques is that subjects' responses to ambiguous stimuli will reveal some facet of their personality. The Thematic Apperception Test (which uses ambiguous drawings) and the Rorschach (which uses inkblots) are probably the two most well-known projective tests. However, a wide variety of possibilities exist: drawing pictures, writing essays, completing sentences, playing with dolls, associating words, and so forth. The assumption is that because the method is indirect, the subjects will not censor their responses. In turn, the responses are indirect measures and need to be inter-preted in some way. Typically, scoring of projective tests is subjective, although there are some very objective systems for scoring them, such as the Exner system for scoring Rorschach responses (Exner, 1974).

One of the advantages as well as disadvantages of projective techniques is that historically they have been associated with psychodynamic approaches to understanding human behavior. As the popularity of psychodynamic approaches has decreased, so has the use of projective techniques. One of the most troublesome aspects of these techniques is that their scoring is subject to systematic biases that tend to confirm preconceived (but incorrect) concep-tions about people (for example, Chapman & Chapman, 1969). Furthermore, the connection between underlying personality characteristics and overt behavior is tenuous.

In spite of the disadvantages, some forms of projective techniques have made a useful contribution to several areas of counseling research. For instance, one of the conspicuous themes in counseling research involves the matching of environmental structure with conceptual level (Holloway & Wampold, 1986). The conceptual level theory states that high-conceptual thinkers will perform best in low-structured environments, whereas low-conceptual thinkers will perform best in high-structured environments. Studies in this area typically have used the Paragraph Completion Method (PCM; Hunt, Butler, Noy, & Rosser, 1978) to measure conceptual level. The PCM asks subjects to respond to six sentence stems; scores are based on the cognitive complexity of the responses.

Unobtrusive Measures

To eliminate reactivity, it is often possible to collect data on subjects without their awareness of this process. Measures that are used in such a way that the subjects are unaware of the assessment procedure are known as unobtrusive measures. These measures have been described in some detail by Webb, Campbell, Schwartz, Sechrest, & Grove (1981). It may be possible to observe subjects without their knowledge in naturalistic settings, to observe subjects in contrived situations (for example, with a confederate), to collect data from archives or other sources (such as school records), or to examine physical traces (like garbage or graffiti). Most psychologists are extremely interested in sources of unobtrusive data. How often do we observe people in public and make interpretations of their behavior?

Of course, the most conspicuous advantage of unobtrusive measures is that they are by definition nonreactive. Because subjects are not aware that the data are being collected, they do not alter their responses. Furthermore, unobtrusive measures are often very accurate. Grade point averages obtained from the registrar will be more accurate than those obtained from subjects' self-reports. Still, there are a number of limitations to unobtrusive measures. Certain types of unobtrusive measures are unethical. For instance, disclosure of personal information by public agencies without the subject's permission is forbidden. Another limitation is that unobtrusive measures are often difficult and/or expensive to obtain. In addition, once the data are obtained, interpretation or classification is often needed. For example, a study of graffiti might involve classifying the graffiti as sexual, drug related, violent, and so forth.

Although use of unobtrusive measures is not widespread in counseling research, a number of studies that have used such measures can be found in the literature. Heesacker, Elliott, and Howe (1988), in a study relating Holland code to job satisfaction and productivity, assessed a number of variables unobtrusively. Productivity was accessed through the payroll office and determined by multiplying the units produced by the value of the unit; absenteeism was obtained from the payroll office; injuries on the job were determined from examining health insurance claims; and demographic information was gleaned from employment applications. Zane (1989) observed subjects in a contrived situation. In a study of placebo procedures, male subjects interacted in the waiting room with a person who they thought was another subject but who actually was a female confederate. The interaction between the subject and the confederate was surreptitiously videotaped and subsequently was rated and coded for indicators of social skills and social anxiety (such as talk time, facial gaze, and smiles).

SUMMARY AND CONCLUSIONS

The basic purpose of the dependent variable is to measure the effect or outcome of the manipulation of the independent variable. We discussed several issues that relate to operationalizing the construct that represents the effect of some cause. Once the construct has been defined, the psychometric properties of the dependent variable vis-à-vis the construct should be established. Reliability and validity are the primary psychometric considerations. *Reliability* refers to the proportion of variance in the dependent variable that is due to true differences among subjects. The remaining variance is error. To be useful, a dependent variable must have adequate reliability. Although there are several types of validity, the one most germane to research design is construct validity. *Construct validity* refers to the degree to which scores reflect the desired construct rather than some other construct. Establishing construct validity is complicated and indirect. Nevertheless, a number of methods can be used to examine construct validity, such as factor analysis and analysis of multitrait-multifactor matrices. Commonly, a single dependent variable will not be able to adequately operationalize a construct; it is often recommended that multiple dependent variables be used. The hope is that each variable reflects some aspect of the construct of interest and together they measure the essence of the construct. However the dependent variables are designed or chosen, they should not react with the treatment. For example, if the dependent variable is derived from behavioral observations, the observations themselves should not have an effect on the subject's behavior. Dependent variables that adequately reflect the effect construct will tend to maximize differences between groups on that construct, an important aspect of Kerlinger's "MAXMINCON" principle.

There are many methods of collecting data related to dependent variables, each of which has its advantages and disadvantages. The most widely used measure in counseling research is the self-report. The sine qua non of the self-report is that the subject makes the observations or report by himself or herself. The advantages of self-reports are that they are relatively easy to administer, can access areas that otherwise would be impossible or difficult to measure (such as sexual behavior), and are compatible with phenomenological views of counseling. The most conspicuous problem with self-reports is that they are vulnerable to distortions by the subject. As well, the subject may not be consciously aware of the construct being measured, and self-reports are incompatible with several theoretical approaches to counseling (for example, behavioral approaches). Self-report instruments may be published, either by professional publishers or in the literature, or tailor-made for a specific study, and can be written in a number of formats.

Less frequently used dependent measures include ratings of other persons and events, behavioral measures, physiological indexes, interviews, projective techniques, and unobtrusive measures. Ratings of other persons and events are useful because experts or possible participants can be used to judge important aspects of counseling, such as the counseling interview itself. Behavioral measures reflect overt behavior and thus are not subject to the distortions that can plague self-reports and ratings of other persons and events; furthermore, they are compatible with behavioral approaches to counseling, although they are, as well, incompatible with other approaches (such as psychodynamic approaches). Physiological responses can be used to infer psychological states because many psychological phenomena (for example, anxiety) have physiological correlates; however, due to lack of reliability, expense, and other problems, physiological indexes are infrequently used in counseling research. Interviews are advantageous because much information can be obtained quickly and because the interviewer can pose follow-up questions, although they are relatively expensive, depend on the skill of the interviewer, and can be biased. Projective techniques use ambiguous stimuli to reveal some facet of personality and can be useful to uncover unconscious aspects of the personality. Unobtrusive measures are designed to eliminate reactivity because the subject is unaware that measurement is being conducted. Given the multitude of data collection methods, the task of the informed researcher is to collect data with a method that provides the type of information that is most relevant to the research question.

Obviously, the selection of the dependent variable and the method of data collection require considerable forethought and examination of the previous research literature. Moreover, these tasks often require creative thinking to tailor measurements to the constructs of interest. Unfortunately, sometimes researchers spend very little time in selecting dependent variables, and weak and disappointing findings result. We firmly believe that careful deliberation and consultation with colleagues can greatly facilitate the selection of dependent variables and enhance the overall quality of research in counseling.

C H A P T E R   11

POPULATION ISSUES

The process of selecting subjects and, subsequently, the generalizability of the results based on the data from those subjects constitute what we call population issues. Although we have not kept a formal count, there is no doubt that the question we are most frequently asked by student researchers is "How many subjects do I need?" Less frequently asked but perhaps more crucial are questions related to how applicable the results of a study are to other contexts. For example, do the results of a treatment study apply to the types of clients seen in mental health agencies? These and many related questions can only be answered when we understand population issues. But population issues are some of the most perplexing issues involved in research design.

The focus of this chapter is on the way in which population issues impinge on the design and interpretation of research in counseling. Key issues for successful research in counseling include (1) what types of subjects to use, (2) how many subjects to study, (3) how to treat different types of subjects in the design and analysis, and (4) to what extent the results are generalizable. To facilitate an understanding of population issues, this chapter focuses on three major topics: sampling theory, the pragmatics of selecting subjects, and generalizability or external validity issues. Selecting subjects for a study typically involves selecting samples from a population of interest. The rationale for using samples from a population is based on sampling theory. Therefore, sampling theory is discussed first. Then, the pragmatics of selecting subjects is addressed, including (1) defining the target population, (2) creating a subject pool, (3) selecting subjects, (4) establishing the validity of research in the absence of random selection, and (5) determining the number of subjects. Finally, the relationship of external validity to population issues is illustrated by considering factorial designs with factors related to person or status variables.

SAMPLING THEORY

Selecting subjects for a study typically involves selecting samples from a population of interest. For example, it would be too cumbersome for an investigator interested in homophobia to interview all Americans about homophobia, so instead the investigator selects a sample of subjects that presumably reflects the larger American population. Sampling theory provides the foundation for understanding the process and the implications of selecting subjects for a particular study. We will briefly discuss sampling theory and elucidate some of the real-life restrictions and subsequent problems that investigators encounter.

The essence of sampling theory revolves around selecting samples that reflect larger or total populations. Typically, we think of a population as a well-defined set of people, such as college students seeking help at a counseling center, depressed adolescents, or counselors-in-training; but technically, a population is a set of observations. That is, it is the observations (or scores) of the people, rather than the people themselves, that constitute the population. The important aspect of populations, whether thought of as people or observations, is that conclusions reached from the research should apply to the population. By necessity, counseling research is conducted with a limited number of subjects; the results for these particular subjects rarely are of primary interest. The object of most research is to generalize from the observations of these subjects in the study to some larger population. That is, an inference is made about the population based on a small number of observations.

The concept of a population, however, is elusive. Some populations are quite real. For example, consider the population that includes the cumulative grade point averages of all college students currently enrolled as of January 3, 1991, and who have completed at least one term of college. The grade point averages (that is, the observations) exist and can be obtained from student records. The size of the population in this instance is fixed and finite, although quite large. Other populations are more ambiguous. For example, examination of depression in college students might involve a population that includes scores on the Beck Depression Inventory (BDI; Beck, Ward, Mendelson, Mock, & Erbaugh, 1961) for all college students currently enrolled as of January 3, 1991. Clearly, not every college student has taken the BDI, so in some sense this is a hypothetical population. Nevertheless, there is little difficulty imagining having each student take the BDI; the population would consist of all these scores. However, it probably would be unwise to limit the population to students enrolled as of January 3, 1991, because to be useful the results of the study should be applicable to students enrolled at different times. A truly hypothetical population might involve college students present (at the time of the research) and future. This hypothetical population is infinite. Clearly, there are some problems with generalizing to infinite hypothetical populations, some of whose scores exist in the future; however, it is just as clear that limiting conclusions to populations in existence only at a given point in time restricts the generalizability of the results.

Inferences about populations are made on the basis of samples selected from populations. Technically, a sample is a subset of the population. That is, the observations in the sample are taken from the set of observations that compose the population. This process is called sampling. Again, inferences about the population of observations are made from the observations in the sample. It should be realized that the validity of the inferences about the population will be dependent on how well the sample represents the population. Representativeness is a complex concept and needs some further explanation.

Certainly, selecting 20 males at an Ivy League college and recording their scores on the BDI would not represent well the population of BDI scores for all college students nationally. Samples that systematically differ from the population in some way are said to be *biased*. More technically, a biased sample is a sample selected in such a way that all observations in the population do not have an equal chance of being selected. In the example of male Ivy Leaguers, the sample is biased because female students do not have the same chance of being selected as males (that is, the probability of selecting a female is zero) and students in non–Ivy League schools do not have the same chance of being selected as students in the Ivy League.

Samples that are not biased are random samples. That is, random samples are samples in which each observation in the population has an equal chance of being selected. Logistically, random samples can be selected by assigning each observation a consecutive number (1, 2, 3 . . .) and then choosing the observations by selecting numbers from a random numbers table or using a computer-assisted random numbers generator. To randomly select a sample of size 20 from all college students, each student would be assigned an eight-digit number; a computer could be used to generate 20 eight-digit random numbers and the BDI scores for the students whose numbers were generated would compose the sample. Clearly, this would be a laborious process (and could never be accomplished), but it illustrates how random selection is undertaken.

Although random selection eliminates systematic bias, there is no guarantee that a random sample will be representative of the population. For example, the random selection process just described could yield a sample of 20 male Ivy League students! Although this would be highly unlikely, it is possible. To understand representativeness and to comprehend how inferences from samples to populations are made, some basic principles of sampling theory are discussed here. Consider a population that has a mean of 100 (that is, the mean of the observations in the population is 100). Typically, this is denoted by writing $\mu = 100$; the Greek symbol μ (mu) indicates a population parameter. A researcher selects a random sample of 25; if the obtained mean M of the 25 observations is close to 100 (say $M = 103.04$), then in one sense the sample is representative. If the mean of the 25 observations is far from 100 (say $M = 91.64$), then it could be said that the sample is not representative. All seems logical here; however, the situation in the real world is such that the population parameter is unknown to the researcher and the researcher selects only one sample. Therefore, it is unclear how representative any given sample is. Fortunately, statistical theory helps us here by allowing calculation of the probability that an obtained mean is an arbitrary distance from a specified population value. More about this later. It should be noted that larger samples will likely be more representative of the population than smaller samples. More about this later as well.

We will now integrate our previous discussion of random assignment from Chapters 3 and 5 with random selection in the context of a particular design (see Wampold & Drew, 1990, for a similar but more technical discussion of these issues). Take the case of a posttest-only control-group design (as discussed in Chapter 5); let's say the researcher is testing the efficacy of an innovative treatment. Two populations are of interest here: the population of individuals who have received the innovative treatment and the population of individuals who have received no treatment. To understand sampling in this example, suppose that 30 subjects are randomly selected from a well-defined population. The researcher does not know how well the sample represents the population, but does know that there are no systematic biases in the sample because the subjects were selected randomly. The next step is to randomly assign the 30 subjects to the two groups (15 in each group). Subjects in the treatment group are administered the treatment and subsequently tested; at the same time, the control subjects are tested. At this point something crucial should be noticed: the 15 observations for the treated group are considered to be randomly selected from a hypothetical population of observations for individuals in the population *who have had the treatment*. Think of it in this way: all people in the well-defined population are eligible to be treated. Hypothetically, all of these people could receive the treatment and subsequently be tested. The 15 observations in the treatment group (that is, the posttest scores) in the study are considered to be randomly selected from the hypothetical population of posttest scores for all persons as if they had been treated. The 15 observations in the control group are considered to be randomly selected from the hypothetical population of posttest scores for persons who have not been treated. These concepts are illustrated in Figure 11-1.

We continue with this example to illustrate a crucial point about experimental design and the tests of statistical hypotheses. The null hypothesis in this case is that the population mean for all individuals who hypothetically could be treated is equal to the population mean for all individuals who are untreated, symbolically stated as $\mu_T - \mu_C = 0$. An appropriate alternative (assuming higher scores indicate a higher level of functioning) is that the population mean for all individuals who hypothetically could be treated is greater than the population mean for all individuals who are untreated: $\mu_T > \mu_C$. If the statistical test (here a two-independent group t test) is statistically significant, the null hypothesis is rejected in favor of the alternative. Statistical hypotheses are written in terms of population parameters. Thus, by deciding to reject the null hypothesis and accept the alternative, the researcher is making an inference about the population of observations based on the sample scores. In this example, if the null hypothesis is rejected in favor of the alternative hypothesis (based on, say, a statistically significant t test), then it is concluded that the mean of scores of treated persons is higher than the mean of scores of untreated persons, in general. However, this conclusion could be incorrect because the samples might not have been representative. For example, it may happen that the 15 subjects assigned to the treatment condition were generally superior initially in some ways to the other persons in the population. Of

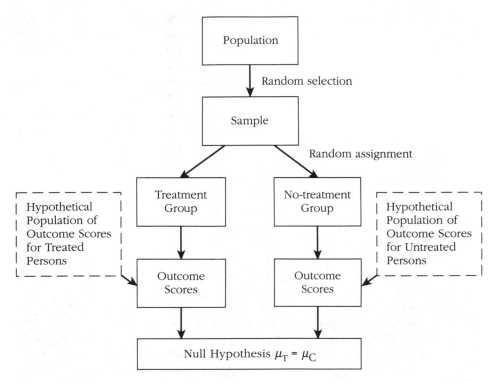

FIGURE 11-1
How sampling is conceptualized for a hypothetical posttest-only control-group design.

course, this cannot be determined from this design. Nevertheless, protection against this possibility is expressed as the alpha level, the probability of falsely rejecting the null hypothesis. When alpha is set at .05, say, the probability that the null hypothesis is rejected when it really is true is less than or equal to .05. Because alpha conventionally is set at low levels (for example, .05 or .01), the probability that significant results will be due to unrepresentative samples will be small. Remember this central point: rejection of a null hypothesis does not mean that the null hypothesis is false. It does mean that the obtained results would be very unusual had the null been true, and thus the decision is made to reject the null. However, there is still the small possibility that the null is true and that sampling error (Type I) was responsible for the obtained results.

Now that we have emphasized random selection from a population, we can also state emphatically that random selection is almost always an impossibility in applied research. A perusal of journals in counseling will convincingly demonstrate that random selection is seldom used. For practical purposes, it is not possible to select subjects for a treatment study from across the country; one is fortunate to be able to afford to select clients locally. Even when random selection is pragmatically feasible (for example, a survey of members of Division 17 of the APA), not all persons selected will choose to participate, creating a bias. In the next section, procedures for conducting research without random selection and the attendant problems are discussed.

THE PRAGMATICS OF SELECTING SUBJECTS

If true random sampling were possible, the researcher would define the target population, identify all people in the population, and randomly select from that group of people. As indicated previously, this process is not pragmatically possible except in the most contrived contexts. In this section we will explore the pragmatics of subject selection by discussing the following topics: (1) defining the target population, (2) creating a subject pool, (3) selecting subjects, (4) establishing validity in the absence of random selection, and (5) determining the number of subjects needed.

Defining the Target Population

The first step in the selection of subjects is to define the target population, or the population to which the investigator wants to generalize. Although technically *population* refers to a set of observations, the population typically is defined in terms of the characteristics of people. Care must be taken to consider carefully many different characteristics in this definition, because ultimately these will be the defining characteristics of the group to which the results of the study will generalize. Defining characteristics may include diagnostic category, gender, ethnicity, age, presenting problem, marital status, and socioeconomic status, among others. For example, Mahalik and Kivlighan (1988) limited subjects in a study of self-help for depression to undergraduates who were mildly depressed (score of 10 or greater on the Beck Depression Inventory), had indicated an interest in participating in a self-help program for mood control, and were not receiving psychotherapy.

One important issue in defining the target population is to decide how heterogeneous the population should be. Heterogeneous populations are desirable because they contain a wide variety of characteristics to which the results of the study may generalize. By limiting the population to undergraduates, Mahalik and Kivlighan restricted the degree to which the results are generalizable. The study does not shed light on the efficacy of self-help procedures with other groups, such as unemployed laborers. Nevertheless, there are problems with heterogeneous populations as well. It is unclear how the results of a study apply to various subgroups of a heterogeneous population (a topic that is revisited in a later section). Furthermore, by their very nature, heterogeneous populations show much variability in responding so that the error variance is greater than it would be for homogeneous populations, creating less-powerful statistical tests. Conversely, homogeneous populations limit the degree to which the results will generalize. Again, as is the case with most decisions in research design, determining the optimal degree of

heterogeneity for a study depends on the nature of the problem being investigated. In terms of Kerlinger's "MAXMINCON" principle, this is a trade-off
between minimizing within-group variance and controlling extraneous variables.

Creating a Subject Pool

After defining the target population, the researcher needs to identify a group
of people who fit this definition, and who are accessible; this group is called
the subject pool. Suppose that the target population is defined as university
counseling center clients. Now clearly it is impossible to identify all such clients.
Often, the subject pool is limited to possible subjects in the vicinity of the
researcher or researchers. Hence, the subject pool may consist of counseling
center clients at the researcher's university, a not uncommon practice (for
example, Tracey, Glidden, & Kokotovic, 1988). Restricting the subject pool
to a subset of all possible subjects introduces a bias. In this case the bias is related
to geography but also includes all factors that are related to geography, such
as socioeconomic factors, ethnicity, and values. In the Tracey et al. (1988)
study, the subjects were clients at a "large midwestern university counseling
center." Are the results of this study applicable to clients at counseling centers
at a small midwestern college, an Ivy League university, or a Southern California
university? Restricting the subject pool restricts the population. Technically,
the results of the study by Tracey et al. are generalizable to clients at that
particular midwestern university counseling center.

There is no empirical means to determine whether restricting a particular
subject pool limits the generalizability of a study other than by investigating
the potential subjects excluded from the subject pool. Clearly, this is not a
feasible solution, because if those subjects were accessible to the researcher,
they would have been included in the study originally. Therefore, a case needs
to be made that restricting the subject pool does not affect the results. Prior
research and knowledge are critical to making this decision. For example,
physiological response to physical stress would not be expected to vary from
one area of the country to another, whereas attitudes toward abortion would.
Of course, restriction of subject pools is not limited to geographical locations;
often subjects are recruited from local mental health agencies, undergraduate
subject pools, school districts, and so forth.

In one sense, all subject pools are restricted. Because it is required that
research subjects participate voluntarily, all subject pools are restricted to
subjects who satisfy the definition of the target population and who volunteer
to participate. A bias is introduced here because volunteer subjects have been
found to be quite different from nonvolunteers; for example, volunteers are
better educated, have a higher need for social approval, are more intelligent,
are less authoritarian, appear to be better adjusted, and seek more stimulation
(Rosenthal & Rosnow, 1969).

Another complicating factor in composing subject pools is that several
of the characteristics contained in the definition of the target population may

not be readily apparent and thus necessitate testing. For example, in the Mahalik and Kivlighan (1988) study of depressed undergraduates, it was necessary to assess the level of depression of every potential subject. Over 800 students were given the Beck Depression Inventory to identify those who were at least mildly depressed.

Selecting Subjects

The final step is to determine those subjects from the subject pool who will participate in the study. Ideally, the subjects would be randomly selected from the subject pool. For example, if the subject pool were students seeking help at a counseling center at a particular university, then the researcher could assign each such student a number and with the aid of a random numbers table or a computer-assisted random numbers generator, randomly select the subjects for the experiment. However, even this process can be pragmatically trouble-some. Often the researcher needs all the subjects to be at the same stage of counseling. At any given time, there may be an insufficient number of such clients. Thus the researcher will likely solicit subjects as they become available. For example, Tracey et al. (1988) had university counseling center clients evaluate their counselor immediately after the intake session. To obtain a sufficient sample, the researchers asked all clients who presented themselves at the center to participate in the study; in all, 192 of 430 clients agreed to participate and completed the study. So in this case there was no random selection from a subject pool because all available subjects were used.

Establishing Validity in the Absence of Random Selection

Although historically, random selection has been identified as a critical element in proper generalization from the results of a study with a particular set of subjects to a larger population (Serlin, 1987), random selection does not typify research in counseling. Nevertheless, available samples may be "good enough for our purpose" (Kruskal & Mosteller, 1979, p. 259). The "good enough" principle stipulates that nonrandom samples can have sufficient characteristics that generalization to a certain population is reasonable. Accordingly, when samples are obtained by a means other than random sampling, "valid inference can be made to a hypothetical population resembling the sample" (Serlin, 1987, p. 300). In this way, generalization is made rationally rather than statistically.

Care must be taken, however, when rationally based generalizations are made. As Serlin (1987) has indicated, generalizations of this type should be theory driven; he cited two areas of counseling research to illustrate this point. The social influence model of change in counseling (Strong, 1968) relies on a credible counselor and an involved client. Thus research with undergraduate psychology majors who are not involved clients is deficient theoretically. However, in other areas of counseling research, undergraduates may be a sufficient sample from which to make valid inferences. The conceptual-level matching model (Holloway & Wampold, 1986) has implications for training beginning counselors. Thus, subjects who are relatively naive with regard to counseling skills are necessary, and psychology undergraduates, because of their interest in behavior and lack of training in counseling, are perfectly appropriate and even desirable subjects. Here undergraduates are "good enough" for studies in this area but not "good enough" for studies of the social influence model.

Thus, in the absence of random sampling, researchers must take great care in determining the characteristics of the subjects used in studies. The burden of proof is on the researcher to establish that the characteristics of the subjects is such that generalizations to a relevant hypothetical population are valid. The vogue in counseling research is to eschew studies with limited generalizability in lieu of field studies with actual clients. Accordingly, for studies investigating anxiety (including treatment studies), clients seeking treatment for anxiety would be favored over mildly anxious undergraduates who had not presented themselves for counseling. Of course, recruiting clients seeking treatment is more difficult than recruiting undergraduates.

Determining the Number of Subjects

The number of subjects used in a study is important because as the number of subjects increases, so does the probability that the sample is representative of the population. The question How many subjects? is intimately involved with the concept of power. Recall that power is the probability of rejecting the null hypothesis when the alternative is true, or the likelihood of detecting an effect when the effect is truly present. For example, suppose that a treatment is effective; that does not mean that a study comparing the treatment group to a control group will necessarily result in a statistically significant finding. It is entirely possible that an effect exists (the alternative hypothesis is true) but that the obtained test statistic is not sufficiently large to reach significance (that is, the null hypothesis is not rejected). Generally, the greater the power, the better the experiment. However, after we discuss factors that lead to increased power, we will present a caveat to this general rule.

Power is dependent on (1) the particular statistical test used, (2) the alpha level, (3) the directionality of statistical test, (4) the effect size, and (5) the number of subjects. Although an in-depth discussion of these factors is more involved with statistics than design, an elementary understanding of them is required before the important question How many subjects? can be answered (see Cohen, 1988; Kraemer & Thiemann, 1987; Wampold & Drew, 1990, for more complete discussions).

Before power can be determined, the researcher has to select a statistical test. For a given situation, there often are several statistical tests that will do the job. For example, for a design with two treatment groups and a control group, the most frequently used test is an analysis of variance. However, non-parametric alternatives exist; in this case, the Kruskall-Wallis test would be appropriate. The relative power of various alternative tests varies depending on the alternative, and a discussion of this is beyond the scope of this book (see, for example, Bradley, 1968). The important point is that power must be calculated for a specific statistical test.

Another factor that affects power is the alpha level set by the researcher. If alpha is set conservatively, say at .01, then it is more difficult to reject the null hypothesis, and power is decreased. So by being careful not to falsely reject the null hypothesis (setting alpha small), the researcher sacrifices power.

The directionality of the test also affects power. If a two-tailed (that is, nondirectional) test is used, the option of rejecting the null hypothesis in either direction is reserved. This is helpful when the researcher is interested in results in both directions and/or is unclear about the direction. For instance, when the researcher is comparing two treatments, knowing whether Treatment A or Treatment B is superior is important. However, keeping options open in both directions costs the researcher because it is more difficult to detect effects in this case than it is when one direction or the other is specified. One-tailed (directional) tests are more powerful when the effect is in the expected direction. For example, when testing the efficacy of a treatment vis-à-vis a control group, it makes sense to test only whether the treatment is more effective than no treatment. Generally, one is not interested in knowing whether the treatment is less effective than no treatment. By specifying the direction (that is, the treatment is superior to no treatment), the researcher increases the power of the statistical test.

The most difficult factor to specify in any determination of power is the size of the true effect. If a treatment is extraordinarily effective, the effect of the treatment is relatively easy to detect and thus power is high. For example, if a treatment of depression reduces self-deprecating statements from an average of 20 per hour to zero, achieving a statistically significant finding will be easy. However, if the reduction is from an average of 20 self-deprecating statements to 18, then it will be difficult to detect this small change. There are many ways to quantify effect size (see Rosenthal, 1984); they all have in common an index of the strength of the relationship between variables.

Specifying the effect size before the study is conducted is problematic. If one knew the effect size for any experiment beforehand, there would be no need to conduct the study. Nevertheless, the effect size must be stipulated before determination of the number of subjects can be made. There are a number of ways in which the effect size can be stipulated. First, prior research in the area or related areas will often give clues about the size of effects. For instance, if the effect of cognitive-behavioral treatments of test anxiety was of a certain size, it would be reasonable to expect that the effect of a cognitive-behavioral treatment of performance anxiety would be about the same size. Haase, Waechter, and Solomon (1982) surveyed the effect sizes obtained in the counseling psychology research in general, although it is unclear how applicable these results are to specific areas within the field. A second means to stipulate effect size is to specify the size of the effect that would have practical or clinical significance. In a treatment study involving a treatment group and a control group, an effect size of 1.00 indicates that at the end of treatment 84% of the treatment group functioned better than the mean of the control group (assuming normality); an effect size of 1.5 indicates that 93% functioned better than the mean of the control group; an effect size of 2.0 indicates that 98% functioned better than the mean of the control group. Translation of effect size into indexes of clinical improvement allows the researcher to gauge how large the effect should be to have an impact clinically. Finally, Cohen (1988) has, based on a number of considerations, classified effects into three categories: small, medium, and large. According to this scheme, one can determine the number of subjects needed to detect each of these three effect sizes. Of course, the researcher still needs to stipulate which of three sizes of effects he or she wishes to detect. Furthermore, Cohen's determination of effect size is arbitrary and cannot apply equally well to all areas of social and behavioral research. Nevertheless, when there are no other guiding lights, stipulation of a "medium"-sized effect has guided many a researcher.

The last determination needed before deciding how many subjects to use in an experiment is the level of power desired. Power of .80 has become the accepted standard (although again this level is arbitrary). Keep in mind that a level of power of .80 refers to a probability level; that is, 80% of the time the stipulated effect size will be detected (that is, the test will be statistically significant). It also means that there is a 20% chance that no statistically significant results will be found when the effect really is present!

Once the researcher has selected the statistical test to be used, chosen whether to use a one-tailed or two-tailed test, set alpha, stipulated a desirable level of power, and determined the effect size to be detected, he or she can determine the number of subjects needed to obtain the stipulated level of power. Typically, this is accomplished by using tables, such as those provided by Cohen (1988) or Kraemer and Thiemann (1987). Cohen provides extensive examples, but his format uses different tables for different tests. Kraemer and Thiemann, by using approximations, have been able to reduce the complexity of the process of determining the number of subjects needed. Perhaps the simplest way to make this important determination is to use computer programs designed for this purpose (for example, Borenstein & Cohen, 1988).

Some caveats are needed about the determination of sample size. First, all of the procedures are based on the fact that the assumptions of the statistical test are met. When assumptions are violated, typically power is decreased, so beware. Second, one often hears rules of thumb about sample sizes: 10 subjects for each variable in a multiple regression, 15 subjects to a cell in a factorial design, and so forth. Be warned that such rules are almost always misleading, as Table 11-1, an abbreviated power table for multiple regression, shows. In some instances less than 10 subjects per variable are needed, and in other instances many more than 10 are needed. Third, the general rule that the more subjects one can obtain for an experiment, the better, also is misleading. Certainly, the researcher wants to have a sufficient number of subjects to have a reasonable opportunity (say 80%) to detect an effect of a size that is interesting to him or her. However, using too many subjects raises the possibility that

TABLE 11-1
Number of Subjects Needed to Achieve Various Levels of Power (α = .05)

| | Number of independent variables | | | | | | | |
| | K = 3 | | | | K = 6 | | | |
R^2	.30	.50	.70	.90	.30	.50	.70	.90
.10	34	56	83	132	47	74	107	164
.30	11	17	25	37	17	24	33	45
.50	7	10	13	18	11	14	18	24

Note. R^2 is the minimum value of R^2 in which the researcher is interested.
*From Wampold & Freund.
SOURCE: "Use of multiple regression in counseling psychology research: A flexible data-analytic strategy" by B. E. Wampold and R. D. Freund, 1987, *Journal of Counseling Psychology, 34,* p. 378. Copyright 1987 by the American Psychological Association.

a very small effect size can be detected (see Meehl, 1978, for an excellent discussion of this issue). Although small effects can be interesting, they often mislead the researcher into believing that something important has occurred when in fact only a trivial finding has been obtained. For example, in a regression problem, a statistically significant finding with a large number of subjects that accounts for only 2% of the variance in the dependent variable most likely will not add to our understanding of psychological processes. Because statistical significance can be obtained for trivial effects, it is often recommended that researchers report effect size and power in addition to significance levels (Cook & Campbell, 1979; Fagley, 1985; Folger, 1989).

EXTERNAL VALIDITY AND POPULATION ISSUES

Recall that external validity refers to the generalizability of findings across persons, settings, or times. The most direct means to increase the external validity of findings is to build into the design variables that represent persons, settings, or times. Because issues related to the generalizability of findings across persons are the most relevant to counseling researchers, we will illustrate these issues and indicate how they might extend to settings or times where important. We will first describe how population issues can be incorporated into factorial designs, and then discuss several general considerations of studying external validity in factorial designs. It is important to note that factorial designs are not the only designs that can examine population issues; factorial designs are used here for illustrative purposes only.

Use of Factorial Designs to Study External Validity

To determine how results apply to various groups of persons, a status variable related to persons can be added to the design to create a factorial design (discussed in Chapter 5). Consider a factorial design with one independent variable (with, say, three levels) and a status variable related to persons (with, say, two levels):

Independent Variable

	I	II	III
Persons I			
II			

To make this strategy more salient, consider the three levels of the independent variable to be three treatments and the two levels of the status variable related to persons to be gender. Now the factorial design can be written as follows:

Treatments

	Treatment A	Treatment B	Treatment C
Gender Males			
Females			

Interpretation of the main effects and the interaction effects of this factorial design will illustrate how it establishes the generality of the results across persons. Suppose that it was found that there was no treatment effect; that is, there was insufficient evidence to establish that one treatment was more effective than any other. External validity seeks to answer the question of whether or not this result applies equally to males and females. It may well be that there was no main effect for gender as well. However, the interaction effect speaks most clearly to external validity. For example, with males, Treatment A may have been most effective, whereas with females, Treatment C may have been most effective, indicating that the results are not generalizable across gender. This prototypic interaction is illustrated in Panel 1 of Figure 11-2. As can be seen in the right side of Panel 1, had the results been analyzed without considering gender, the conclusion that the treatment variable was not important (that is, that there were no differences in treatment) would have been reached. However, were gender included as a factor, a very different conclusion would have been reached. Incidentally, had only males been included in the study, one would have concluded that Treatment A was most effective, the opposite of the conclusion that would have been reached had only females been included. Clearly, considerations of person variables can be vital to the proper understanding of research results. Parenthetically, gender is receiving increased attention in the counseling literature (interested readers could

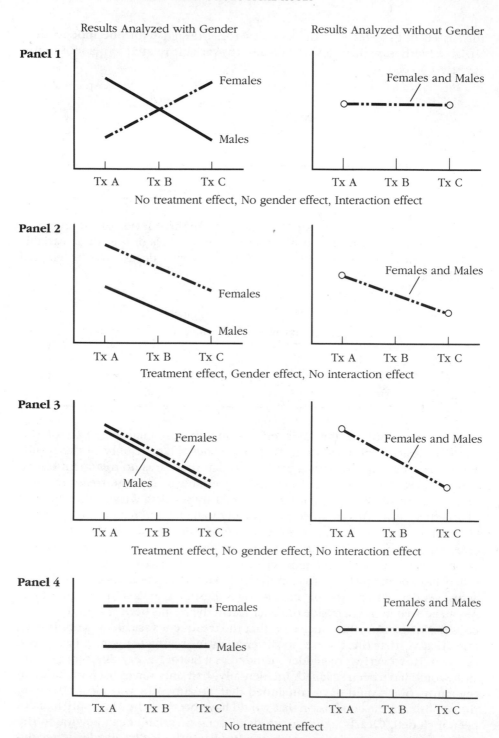

FIGURE 11-2
Comparison of patterns that can result from including a person factor in a factorial design.

examine Cook, 1990; Good, Gilbert, & Scher, 1990; Mintz & O'Neil, 1990; Richardson & Johnson, 1984; Scher & Good, 1990).

Figure 11-2 also illustrates other patterns that can result from including a person factor in a factorial design. In Panel 2, there are main effects for treatment (Treatment A > Treatment B > Treatment C) and for gender (females > males). Clearly, considering gender adds information because females performed better than males. However, the pattern of results is the same for males and females (that is, Treatment A > Treatment B > Treatment C) and therefore the conclusions reached for males, for females, and for persons in general (males and females) are the same. In this case, one would not be misled by ignoring gender in the design. Thus, in this case, external validity is not increased by including gender although information about males and females is gained.

In Panel 3, there is a main effect for treatment but no gender effect nor interaction effect. In this case, the addition of gender does not affect the results in any way. Of course, the absence of gender effect may be interesting, although the usual caveats about interpreting null effects need to be recognized. In Panel 4, there are no main effects for treatment nor interaction effects; however, effects for gender are present because females outperformed males. Here inclusion of gender informs the researcher that females performed better than males; nevertheless, subjects performed equally well in each treatment, a conclusion that would not change by including gender as a factor in the study.

The general principle to be gleaned from this discussion is that when external validity is examined within a design (by including person as a status variable), it is the interaction effect that is most interesting. An interaction effect indicates that the levels of the independent variable interact with the person variable to produce different outcomes. Those with background in educational research will recognize this discussion as essentially that of aptitude-treatment interactions (Cronbach & Snow, 1976); likewise, in career counseling, Fretz (1981) has referred to attribute-treatment interactions.

Some theories in counseling are expressed in terms of interactions between independent variables and person variables. Probably the most conspicuous is the cognitive complexity model (Miller, 1981). According to this model, low conceptual level thinkers benefit from a more structured environment whereas high conceptual level thinkers benefit from a less structured environment. In this model, conceptual level is a person variable and structure of the environment is an independent variable that is manipulated by the researcher. Holloway and Wampold (1986) conducted a meta-analysis of studies investigating this hypothesis and found that the expected interaction effect appears to be operating. The effects found based on 12 studies are represented in Figure 11-3. There is a main effect for environmental structure (generally subjects performed better in structured environments) and a (small) main effect for conceptual level (generally, high conceptual level subjects performed better). However, these conclusions were mitigated by the interaction between environmental structure and conceptual level. According to these results, one should provide more-structured environments to low conceptual level thinkers and less-structured environments to high conceptual level thinkers.

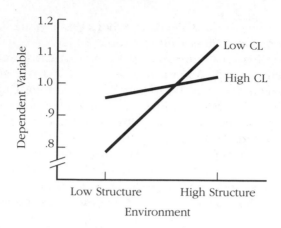

FIGURE 11-3
Means for 12 studies derived from the results of a meta-analysis. Metric of *y*-axis is arbitrary; CL = conceptual level.
SOURCE: "Relation between Conceptual Level and Counseling-Related Tasks: A Meta-analysis" by E. L. Holloway and B. E. Wampold, 1986, *Journal of Counseling Psychology, 33,* p. 316. Copyright 1986 by the American Psychological Association. Reprinted by permission.

So far we have discussed external validity in terms of a factorial design, with an emphasis on the interaction effect. However, examination of interaction effects is not limited to factorial designs (and concomitant analyses of variance). For example, regression analysis accommodates interaction effects nicely as well. Thus, external validity is related to the interaction of independent and person variables, regardless of the analysis.

Considerations in the Use of Factorial Designs

Although the factorial design approach to external validity seems straightforward, there are some issues that need consideration. The most important and most difficult to reconcile is related to choice of the variables related to persons, settings, or times. Panel 1 of Figure 11-2 portrays a case in which including gender is crucial to understanding the phenomenon under investigation. However, the researcher will not know whether this pattern will occur or whether some other pattern (those portrayed in Panels 2 to 4) will occur. Furthermore, the researcher does not know whether an interaction effect crucial to external validity would occur with other person, setting, or time variables. Selecting variables related to external validity is tricky business. The problem is exacerbated by the fact that there are literally hundreds of such variables that might be included in the design, such as gender, ethnicity, age, level of dysfunction, intelligence, personality types, and type of clinic. Even if gender and ethnicity appear to be important variables (as they often are in counseling research), specification of these variables is not straightforward. It might well be that sex-role orientation is more critical than biological gender or that level of acculturation is more critical than ethnicity. At this juncture the usual refrain is invoked: knowledge of the substantive area should drive the choice of variables related to external validity. If prior research or theory, or for that matter common sense, indicates that gender is an important variable, add it to the design. Nevertheless, do not include variables when there is no compelling reason for their inclusion.

There is a subtle issue related to how subjects should be selected and assigned when person variables are included in a factorial design. It is desirable in a factorial design to have equal numbers of subjects in each cell; in this way, main and interaction effects are independent (provided the assumptions of the analysis of variance are met; see Wampold & Drew, 1990). Accordingly, equal numbers of subjects of each type should be selected (recruited). For instance, in the example that examined types of treatment (depicted in Figure 11-2), equal numbers of males and females would be selected and then randomly assigned to the three treatments. For research on gender, this presents no problems; however, when the base rates of various person variables are different, conceptual (as well as statistical) problems occur. For example, selecting equal numbers of Native Americans and Anglo-Americans for a study results in a sample that is not representative of the general population (that is, it is biased toward inclusion of Native Americans). This is problematic because the results are peculiar to the manner in which the sample was obtained. For example, correlations are affected by the proportions of types of subjects included (see Cohen & Cohen, 1983). This is a complex issue and is beyond the scope of this text, but a simple example will illustrate the problem. If one were conducting a study to examine how various types of political commercials affected voting preferences of Anglo-Americans and Native Americans, equal numbers of these persons would be selected. The design of the experiment might involve exposing the subjects to various types of commercials and measuring their attitudes. The results of this study might be theoretically interesting and applicable to political campaigns. However, if one were polling to determine the expected outcome of a political race, one would not want to bias the sample by having equal numbers of Native Americans and Anglo-Americans in the sample. Generally, experimental studies that examine theoretical phenomena or treatment effectiveness should have equal numbers of subjects. However, for studies that examine relations between variables in society, subjects should be selected so that the proportions of the various person variables reflect the proportions in the population.

In all the examples used so far, the person, setting, or time variable has been operationalized such that the results are specific to the groups included in the study. In the case of gender, there are only two types (males and females) and the results are specific to them. In studies that include ethnicity as a variable, the results are typically specific to those ethnicities included (for instance, Anglo-American, Hispanic, and African American). However, there is a strategy called random effects analysis of variance that allows for random sampling of levels of a variable (see Wampold & Drew, 1990). Considering therapists effects will explicate as well as demonstrate the usefulness of this procedure. Selection of therapists is one of the trickiest problems in treatment studies. Clearly, the choice of therapists is an important variable related to external validity. An important question generally is whether individual therapists make a difference. Is Therapist 1 more skilled with Treatment A and Therapist 2 more skilled with Treatment B? One could include a number of therapists in the study and examine these effects. However, by randomly selecting the therapists from a population of therapists, the general question can be answered: Does the therapist make a difference? If therapists are not randomly selected, the results are specific to the particular therapists used in the study. Conversely, if therapists are randomly selected, broader statements can be made about therapists in general. The intricacies of random effects analysis of variance are explained in statistics texts (for example, Hays, 1988; Wampold & Drew, 1990); we encourage counselor researchers to make more use of these methods.

The factorial design approach to external validity also has philosophical implications for various classes of persons. Typically, studies are either conducted on predominantly majority samples (for example, Anglo-Americans) or include person variables that contrast the majority sample with a minority sample (for example, Anglo-Americans versus African Americans). In this way, there is an assumption that Anglo-Americans are somehow the norm and all other groups are contrasted with them (Ponterotto, 1988). As well, there is an assumption that each of these groups is homogeneous. African Americans compose a diverse population, and typically such diversity (in, for example, level of acculturation, racial identity, and generational status; again, see Ponterotto, 1988) must be considered in research designs. Furthermore, there are phenomena that may be culture-specific and for which it is not optimal or even sensible to use a design that contrasts various groups. For instance, the underutilization of mental health clinics by ethnic minorities is a major concern to providers of service. It may well be that the reasons for this phenomenon are best understood by examining intraethnic processes rather than interethnic differences.

It should be realized that external validity is often established in multiple studies. For example, single-subject designs preclude the inclusion of person variables because one or a few subjects are used. Therefore, a strategy called systematic replication is used (Barlow & Hersen, 1984). Systematic replication involves replicating an experiment except for one element. By systematically varying the one element over time, the researcher can identify the effects of this element. For example, a single-subject design that establishes the efficacy of social reinforcement in the attenuation of off-task behavior with students in an urban school with an Anglo-American student body might be replicated in a rural school with an Anglo-American student body, in an urban school with a Hispanic student body, and so forth.

The idea of systematic replication can apply to group studies as well. For example, the interaction effect shown in Panel 1 of Figure 11-2 might have been identified by two studies that differed only in the fact that one had female subjects and the other had male subjects. However, there are some disadvantages of such a strategy. True replication is difficult to accomplish, so that differences between two studies may be due to factors other than the different types of subjects. Furthermore, examination of external validity in one study allows direct estimation of the size of the interaction effect, a procedure that is precluded in the systematic replication strategy.

SUMMARY AND CONCLUSIONS

Population issues impinge on the design and interpretation of research in counseling. A critical issue in the development of a study is the selection of a sample of subjects from a broader target population. Considerable care is needed to (1) define the target population (or the population to which the investigator wishes to generalize), and (2) select subjects that fit the definition of the target population. Theoretically, the generalizability of the results is established by randomly selecting a sample from a population. Because of the practical constraints on most counseling researchers, sampling is rarely conducted through true random selection. Instead, researchers often use nonrandom samples that have similar relevant characteristics to a target population, and rationally argue that the results apply to a population with the same characteristics. Finally, a critical issue in selecting subjects is determining how many subjects are needed to adequately test the relationships among the constructs of interest in the study. The number of subjects needed for any study pertains to statistical power, or the probability of rejecting the null hypothesis when the alternative hypothesis is actually true. With regard to estimating statistical power (and thus the number of subjects needed), we discussed (1) the particular statistical test used, (2) alpha level, (3) directionality of the statistical test, and (4) effect size. Thus, there are a number of decisions that the investigator needs to make in selecting subjects for a study.

Typically, researchers are interested in generalizing the results of a particular study to a larger population of individuals, which is the essence of external validity. External validity also relates to the generalizability of findings across persons, settings, or times. We suggested that the most direct means to increase the external validity of findings is to build into the design factors that represent relevant persons, settings, or times. In this way, external validity can be investigated by examining the interaction of the independent variable and a variable related to persons, settings, or times.

Because counseling is an applied profession designed to help a broad array of individuals in various settings across different times, external validity is very important. Far too often, convenience samples consisting of predominantly white undergraduate subjects are used in counseling research. We strongly encourage efforts to broaden the external validity of research in counseling in order to develop the more extensive data bases that are needed in the counseling profession.

CHAPTER 12

EXPERIMENTER AND SUBJECT BIAS

When a researcher designs a study, he or she seeks to examine the relationships among specified variables. One of the most crucial tasks that confronts the researcher is to control the extraneous variables or reduce the error variance (serious threats to Kerlinger's "MAXMINCON" principle) that may influence the relationships among the experimental variables of interest in a particular study. Most often, when the extraneous variables or sources of measurement error are known, they are relatively easy to control; the problem is that in designing most studies, it is difficult, if not impossible, to identify all of the possible extraneous variables and error variance.

The purpose of this chapter is to identify potential sources of bias in subjects, investigators, and experimenters that are particularly relevant to researchers in counseling. By the term *bias,* we mean systematic introduction of extraneous variables that may distort or disguise the relationships among the experimental variables. Whereas *error variance* (or "noise" or "static") refers to variance due to random events, *bias* refers to creation of differential effects between groups or subgroups of subjects due to some systematic method of errors.

In this chapter, *investigator* will refer to the person who designs the study, and *experimenter* will refer to the person who executes the investigation. The first section of this chapter examines investigator and experimenter bias, particularly with regard to (1) experimenter attributes, (2) investigator and experimenter expectancies, and (3) experimental procedures. The second section of this chapter examines subject bias, particularly with regard to (1) demand characteristics, (2) subject characteristics, and (3) introspective abilities. Throughout both sections we use examples from previous research efforts to clarify different types of bias. Moreover, in discussing the various sources of bias, we will also discuss some strategies for controlling or minimizing these variables.

INVESTIGATOR AND EXPERIMENTER BIAS

In the optimal scenario, we might picture an investigator as an objective, unbiased seeker of truth. This researcher engages in a systematic, scientific enterprise and is able to remain an impartial, passive observer throughout. In this way, the researcher does not contaminate the research in any way, but rather he or she is an unbiased observer of some phenomenon, and subsequently a reporter of the truth. We might even assume that

> All *experimenters* [investigators] are created equal; that they have been endowed by their graduate training with certain interchangeable properties; that among these properties are the anonymity and impersonality which allow them to elicit from the same subject identical data which they then identically observe and record. Just as inches were once supposed to adhere in tables regardless of the identity of the measuring instrument, so needs, motives, traits, IQs, anxieties, and attitudes were supposed to adhere in patients and subjects and to emerge uncontaminated by the identity and attitude of the examiner or experimenter. (Friedman, 1967, pp. 3–4)

We know, however, that investigators do not conduct research in such an unbiased manner. Moreover, we know that experimenters who execute investigations may consciously or unconsciously affect the results of a study. Rather, sometimes the researcher has opinions and beliefs that unconsciously (or even consciously) compromise his or her objectivity, sometimes in very subtle ways. For example, the story of Clever Hans nicely depicts the unintentional effects of the subtle experimental bias. Hans was a horse around the turn of the twentieth century that reliably computed various mathematical problems, identified musical intervals, and had a working knowledge of German. His owner, Herr Wilhelm von Osten, would ask Hans all kinds of questions; Hans would tap numbers out with his hoof or gesture with his head toward objects. Hans passed a number of tests with various local citizens and professionals, much to everyone's amazement. That is, until a young psychologist, Oskar Pfungst, came along. Pfungst discovered that Hans could reliably answer questions (that is, nine times out of ten) only when the interrogator knew the right answers, but his performance dropped to one out of ten if the interrogator was ignorant of the answer. As it turned out, Hans had not learned math, or music, or the German language, but rather he had learned to read subtle cues in the interrogator's posture, breathing, and facial expressions (Pfungst, 1911). More recent research in the 1980s revealed that laboratory animals can learn to read a wide variety of subtle behavioral cues in trainers that give away the intended answer.

In short, investigators and experimenters can be the source of extraneous variables and error variance that may very well bias the results of a study. We will discuss three major types of bias: experimenter attributes, investigator and experimenter expectancies, and experimental procedures. In addition, we will offer some strategies for reducing such biases.

Experimenter Attributes

Experimenter attributes are primarily biological and interpersonal characteristics of the experimenter that may cause differential responses in subjects. Examples include the experimenter's age, gender, race, physical appearance, and interpersonal style. For example, some subjects might respond more honestly to a female (as opposed to a male) researcher investigating sexual harassment. Likewise, an experimenter of age 50 might inhibit younger subjects but facilitate disclosure for older subjects. Likewise, the experimenter's interpersonal style (let's say unfriendly and dominant) might interact with the independent variable (for example, expertness cues) so that some subjects feel uncomfortable or even threatened during the experiment. Another potential biasing characteristic pertains to prior contact between the experimenter and subjects. Some subjects may feel that having some prior knowledge about an experimenter would make it easier for them to respond, while others may feel much less likely to disclose personal information.

In short, a wide range of experimenter characteristics might influence some or all subjects to respond differentially in a particular experiment, thereby confounding the results of the study. In fact, several writers (such as Christensen, 1980; Kazdin, 1980) have reported empirical investigations that document that experimenter characteristics can affect responses given by subjects on various tasks, such as self-report inventories, projective tests, laboratory tasks, and measures of intelligence (for example, Barber, 1976; Johnson, 1976; Masling, 1966; Rumenik, Capasso, & Hendrick, 1977).

In short, experimenter attributes create threats to validity. Consider the following example, which raises questions about construct validity. Imagine an investigator (Professor Kay Tharsis) who has reason to believe that a psychodynamic, insight-oriented therapy group would be more effective in treating bulimic clients than a cognitive-behavioral therapy group. A study is conducted in which two bright, advanced graduate students act as experimenters to conduct the group therapies, each lasting ten weeks. Each student conducts one of the treatment groups. Let's say a broad array of extraneous subject variables are controlled (for example, age, gender, personality dynamics), the treatments are carefully matched, and random assignment of clients is used. Imagine further that the results clearly favor the psychodynamic treatment group on a broad array of dependent variables (such as self-report, behavioral indexes, therapist observations). Nonetheless, in this example the results of the treatment groups cannot be separated from the different experimenter attributes and their potential biases. In reality, it may be that the attributes of the two therapists did not affect clients differentially, but we have no way of determining whether or not this is the case. Thus, if different experimenters are used to administer different treatments, it may be difficult to determine whether the results are due to the different treatments, the different experimenters, or an interaction between the two.

Experimenter attributes can also threaten the external validity or generalizability of a study by interacting in some way with the independent variable. For example, it could be that the results of a study would only generalize to therapists with certain characteristics, such as androgynous men, feminist therapists, or black therapists. Imagine the following modifications to the fictitious example just mentioned. Suppose that Professor Kay Tharsis seeks and uses two female therapists in their thirties with excellent interpersonal skills to co-lead both groups. Within the psychodynamic, insight-oriented treatment, a major therapeutic intervention involves the use of the therapeutic relationship to provide interpersonal feedback and promote awareness of each client's interpersonal style and intrapersonal dynamics (see Yalom, 1985, for such a therapeutic orientation). Again imagine that the insight-oriented therapy clearly results in the more favorable outcomes. Would these obtained results generalize to other female therapists who may not have excellent interpersonal skills, or to male therapists? While this is obviously an empirical question, it is useful to highlight how experimenter attributes might interact with independent variables, and possibly limit the generalizability of specific findings.

There are a number of strategies that investigators can use to reduce the possible effects of experimenter attributes:

1. Avoid using a single experimenter for different levels of the independent variable if at all possible, as this clearly confounds the construct validity of the experiment with experimenter attributes. Whenever possible, use two or more experimenters for each level or all levels of the independent variable.

2. If two or more experimenters are used for each level of the independent variable, statistically analyze the data for differences across experimenters to determine if any differences could be related to experimenter attributes such as gender. Often this is done as a preliminary data analysis to rule out possible confounding variables related to experimenter attributes. For example, McCarthy, Shaw, and Schmeck (1986) were interested in studying whether stylistic differences in client information processing (shallow versus deep processors) would be related to their verbal behaviors during counseling sessions. They used two counselors; each counselor saw half of the subjects across all of the conditions. Before doing their main data analysis, they did a preliminary analysis to determine if there were any main effects or interactions due to the counselors on the dependent variables; no differences were found, suggesting that the counselors did not differentially affect the dependent variables. Thus, the authors were able to rule out differences due to different experimenters and to proceed with their main statistical analyses.

3. Because there are so many unknowns at this time about the effects of experimenter attributes, it would be useful for investigators to specify the characteristics of therapists used in treatment interventions. Perhaps over time patterns pertaining to certain therapist characteristics might emerge. Kazdin (1980) suggested that investigators analyze their data for experimenter characteristics (gender), which might provide a useful knowledge base over time. A recent review of two major counseling journals revealed that on the whole, more authors analyze their results for gender differences than did a decade ago (Lee, Heppner, Gagliardi, & Lee, 1987).

4. Authors need to explicitly discuss the generalizability of their data in terms of experimenter attributes and qualify the conclusions in their discussions accordingly. For example, if researchers used only male therapists, then the discussion of the results should focus on male therapists and not therapists

in general. Gender is a particularly important variable in counseling research. Suffice it for now to note that Lee et al. (1987) found that authors still tended to overgeneralize their results in terms of gender, although less so than a decade ago.

Investigator and Experimenter Expectancies

Investigator and experimenter expectancies are beliefs and desires about either how the subject should perform or the expected results of the study. Kazdin (1980) noted that the effect of these expectancies has been referred to as an "unintentional expectancy effect," because the investigator and experimenter may not intentionally try to influence the subject, but actually do so unconsciously through a range of verbal and nonverbal behaviors (like head nods, smiles, glances, subtle comments). Such bias obviously introduces confounding variables, as illustrated in the Clever Hans story.

Rosenthal was one of the first to investigate this topic in the early 1960s; he found that investigator and experimenter expectancies directly influenced how subjects performed (see Rosenthal, 1966). Later research indicated that investigator and experimenter bias can influence subjects in a wide variety of contexts, such as learning studies, ability studies, psychophysical studies, reaction time studies, inkblot test studies, structured laboratory studies, and person perception studies (see Rosenthal, 1966). While some writers have argued that the effect of experimenter bias has been overstated (Barber, 1976; Barber & Silver, 1968), it is generally concluded that investigators and experimenters can and do influence subject responses (Barber, 1976; Christensen, 1980).

Expectancies can be positive or negative and occur in many different ways. Specifically, investigator and experimenter bias can affect subjects or clients at any time during an investigation, such as during subject recruitment, during data collection, or after treatment interventions. For example, an exuberant experimenter (serving as a therapist) may subtly or not-so-subtly promote the effectiveness of one intervention over others. This form of bias is operative when an investigator is testing a new treatment intervention that perhaps he or she has developed and strongly believes in, and this gets communicated to the experimenter. Thus, a therapist might consciously or unconsciously put forth too much effort in conducting the therapeutic role within a study. Sometimes the desire to be effective even leads experimenters serving as therapists to break protocol and engage in activities outside of the normal therapeutic or experimental procedures. For example, in one study that examined the counseling process, a relatively inexperienced therapist was found engaging in a friendly conversation with the client immediately after the counseling session, during which time the client was completing forms evaluating the counseling session and the counselor.

Investigator and experimenter bias also can influence clients in a negative way. For example, if an experimenter is not very motivated or interested in conducting a study, the lack of enthusiasm can very well affect client recruitment and willingness to participate. Halfhearted attempts by experimenters can result in halfhearted responses by clients. Biases resulting from lack of experimenter motivation can be a particular problem with doctoral dissertations, notably when the author is away from the home institution and asks a friend to assume total responsibility for various aspects of a study (such as recruitment, data collection, monitoring data flow); even most "good friends" will not be as motivated as the researcher, especially as problems arise and frustrations mount. Sometimes inexperienced investigators feel shy or guilty asking clients to participate in a study; telling clients three or four times in an apologetic tone that they do not have to participate is not particularly persuasive. Another probable source of bias arises during the administration of inventories to subjects or clients; a busy counseling center receptionist might get tired at the end of each working day given the added demands of the research, and convey verbally or nonverbally to the last clients, "Hurry up and fill this damn thing out."

In summary, there are many opportunities for investigator and experimenter bias to contaminate the results of a study. Experimenter and investigator expectancies can bias subjects whenever anyone involved in conducting the study interacts with the subject. Experimenter and investigator expectancies can bias the results to favor one treatment over another, or can affect the generalizability of the findings as well. Thus, experimenter and investigator expectancies can affect both construct and external validity in ways similar to the examples discussed with experimenter attributes.

Some strategies to lessen the effects of investigator and experimenter expectancies are as follows:

1. Probably the most common strategy to offset experimenter biases is to keep experimenters "blind" as to the purpose of the study. For example, if an investigator is comparing the effectiveness of two treatment approaches, it may be best if the investigator does not communicate to the experimenters serving as therapists the specific purposes and hypotheses of the study, thereby reducing the probability that the therapists will unintentionally influence subjects in the hypothesized direction. In fact, the investigator may want to keep all the people involved in the study who have contact with subjects (for example, receptionists, therapists, assistants who collect data from subjects) blind as to the specific purpose of the study.

2. Keeping various personnel blind is more difficult in some studies than others. In those studies where it is not possible to keep the personnel involved with the study blind, the investigator may need to resort to a partial-blind strategy. For example, it would be very difficult to keep therapists blind as they administer a cognitive-behavioral group treatment for bulimics versus a placebo nondirective discussion group. In such cases, the investigator might try to keep the therapists as blind as possible, and especially with regard to the specific hypotheses and variables involved in the study. Another strategy is to restrict the amount of contact the partial-blind therapists have with subjects; therapists might only administer the treatments and not be involved

in subject selection, data collection, and debriefing. In short, even when one can only achieve a partial-blind situation, the goal is to keep the experimental personnel as blind as possible to the purpose of the study.

3. Because experimenter expectancies can affect subject responses, another strategy is to assess the accuracy of experimenter expectancies. For instance, an investigator may assess whether the experimenters correctly surmise the purpose of the study, or even the general hypotheses. If the experimenters have accurately pieced together the purpose of the investigation, the potential bias from experimenter expectancies is generally much higher than if the experimenters have not adequately discerned the nature of the study. It is important to note that experimenters might still bias subjects in subtle ways even if they are kept blind about the purpose of a study; there is a lower probability, however, that subjects will be biased in line with the hypotheses. In short, assessing experimenter expectancies allows for an evaluation of the degree to which experimenters have been kept blind as well as assess the accuracy of their expectancies.

4. There are some strategies for decreasing negative experimenter bias due to halfhearted efforts. Investigators should be wary of recruiting "friends" to assume total responsibility for various aspects of a study, especially if the investigator is physically removed from the location of the study. While we do not want to prescribe absolute rules, our experience suggests that no one will do the same quality of work as the researcher most directly affected. Thus, the investigator should try to avoid conducting a study in absentia, or if it is absolutely impossible to avoid such a predicament, the researcher should regularly converse with his or her collaborator and make repeated on-site visits.

Experimental Procedures

After an investigator has carefully developed a study, operationalized constructs, identified variables, and controlled as many extraneous variables as possible, the investigator will usually attempt to conduct the experimental procedure in a constant and consistent manner. A typical study involves a wide range of experimental procedures, such as recruiting subjects, greeting subjects, obtaining informed consent, administering instructions, providing a rationale, administering interventions, recording observations, reminding subjects about returning questionnaires, interviewing subjects, administering questionnaires, and debriefing. Imprecision or inconsistencies in the manner in which the experimental procedures of a study are conducted can be a major source of bias and contamination. Procedural imprecision occurs when the activities, tasks, and instructions of an experiment are vague and not specifically identified. Consequently, an experimenter treats subjects differently because it is unclear exactly how the experimenter is to behave and what he or she is to say or do in specific situations. Thus, the experimenter introduces bias (or error variance if it occurs randomly) into an experiment by the variability in his or her experimental procedures.

For example, an investigator might want to study the effects of training residence hall staff to be career resource specialists. The training given to the staff should be clearly specified, and the specific ways the staff are to interact with students on their hall floors should be clearly delineated as well. Are the staff intended to actually dispense career information? If so, what kind of information? Should they make referrals to the career center? If so, to anyone in particular? Should they administer career assessment inventories? If so, which ones? Should they engage in actual counseling sessions with students? If so, are there any guidelines for topics and number of sessions? Should they promote information-gathering activities? If so, what kind? This example indicates only some of the ways residence hall staff acting as career resource specialists might behave. If the investigator does not specifically delineate what the staff should and should not do, the probability is very high that there will be a wide variability in activities across the different residence hall staff members. Moreover, the lack of delineation of staff responsibilities increases the probability that systematic staff biases might occur, such as preferential treatment for brighter students, same-gender or opposite-gender students, or students who come from higher socio-economic status families.

Even if an investigator has carefully specified the procedures for a particular study, variability across experimenters can occur for a number of reasons. We will briefly discuss three reasons: fatigue, experimenter drift, and noncompliance. An experimenter might become fatigued over time, resulting in a different performance across subjects. This can be a particular problem if experimenters engage in an intensive activity, such as interviewing a lot of subjects or clients in a short period of time. An experimenter may also slowly and unconsciously alter his or her performance over time (experimenter drift); this is of special concern if an experimenter is involved in repetitive tasks over time. Or an experimenter may not comply with the exact experimental procedures over time, perhaps because of a misunderstanding of the importance of some procedures. For example, in one study, toward the end of a data collection process, an experimenter began to estimate a timed task to "about the nearest minute," obviously an imprecise procedure! In another study, designed to compare the effects of two therapists, a researcher was equally chagrined to find one counselor complying within the normal 50-minute sessions, but the other counselor, trying very hard to do well, conducting therapy up to 70 minutes per session! In short, even when procedures are carefully specified, experimenter variability can occur because of fatigue or misunderstandings.

There are at least three problems associated with procedural imprecision. First, as suggested in the preceding example, experimenters will most likely vary among themselves as well as introduce systematic biases over time. Thus, not only would there be a good chance that the residence hall staff each would engage in quite different activities in the name of being a career resource specialist, it also is likely they would act differently from one student to another, and thus add a confounding variable to the study.

Second, if the procedures are unclear, the investigator does not know what actually occurred. It may be uncertain whether the independent variable was administered consistently, or if other variables might have intervened (remember the earlier discussions of construct validity in Chapter 3 and independent variables in Chapter 9). If significant results are found, it is uncertain whether this is to be attributed to the independent variable or other variables. In short, if the investigator does not know what was done in an experiment, not only are his or her conclusions confounded, but it also will be difficult, if not impossible, to discuss the results of the study with much precision.

A third problem of procedural imprecision pertains to a statistical issue of introducing error variance or "noise" into the data. Ideally, variability in the data is due to the independent variable. However, variability in the data due to experimenter variability presents "noise" or unwanted variability. Statistically speaking, the variability due to the experimenter increases the within-group variability. The "noise" attributable to the experimenter variability makes it more difficult to find an effect due to the independent variable (assuming such an effect actually exists). Thus, the independent variable has to be more potent to offset the increased within-group variability due to experimenter differences.

Given the applied nature of much of our research, procedural imprecision is a particular problem in counseling. For many experiments, the procedural details of a study can be specified and followed. For example, Feldman, Strong, and Danser (1982) were interested in comparing the effects of paradoxical and nonparadoxical interpretation and directives on depressed clients. The authors trained master's-level counselors over the course of ten hours to integrate a series of paradoxical and nonparadoxical interpretations and directives into a basic counseling interview. In this case, the interpretations and directives were uniform within different treatment conditions; at the end of training, counselors were able to integrate the interpretative and directive statements verbatim at certain points within the counseling interview. However, other counseling interventions that entail several individuals or therapy sessions are more difficult to control and achieving constancy across experimenters is more difficult. Thus, the amount of control and constancy one can achieve across counselors is a matter of degree and depends a great deal on the type of experimental manipulations involved in the study.

The following strategies can be used to reduce bias due to experimental procedures:

1. Perhaps the most basic strategy is to carefully describe and make explicit the experimental procedures involved in a particular study. Most often it is helpful to put the procedures in writing, both as a way of organizing the investigator's thoughts as well as communicating precise procedures for personnel involved in conducting the study. If experimenters are to make specific statements, it is important that they not only be given verbatim transcripts but also be instructed that smooth verbatim responses are needed. Especially for complex or extended therapeutic interventions, it is often useful to write detailed training manuals that identify and document the specific

interventions of treatment; for example, see O'Neil and Roberts Carroll (1987) for a detailed description of a six-day gender-role conflict workshop (cited in O'Neil & Roberts Carroll, 1988). Such manuals are not only helpful in training experimenters, but also for communicating to other investigators the content of a particular intervention.

2. A common strategy involves attempts to standardize the procedures through some type of structure or even automation. For example, if an investigator were interested in studying the effects of counselor self-disclosure, there may be some difficulties in examining similar types of self-disclosures from different therapists across different clients. However, video or audio recordings depicting counselor self-disclosures can be developed and shown to subjects, which will result in each subject's consistently viewing or hearing a specific counselor self-disclosure (see Dowd & Boroto, 1982, for such an example). Another common example of standardization is to develop a structured interview to guide experimenters to ask the same questions in the same order and using exactly the same words. For example, Josephson and Fong-Beyette (1987) developed a structured interview to identify specific behaviors and characteristics of counselors that were correlated with adult female clients' disclosure of incest during counseling. The structured interview consisted of a list of questions, asked in a particular sequence, within four general areas: demographic questions, questions pertaining to the incest experience and its perceived effects on the participants, questions about counseling experiences during childhood, and questions about all counseling experiences since age 18. Other examples of standardization include formulating verbatim statements for experimenters or receptionists, providing written instructions for subjects to complete tasks or inventories, developing a specific order for subjects to complete instruments, and using structured forms to facilitate the observation and recording of data. The intent of all of these examples is to enhance consistency or constancy throughout various aspects of a study by standardizing or providing structure for some procedure.

3. Given that misunderstandings and different assumptions can lead to important differences in experimenter procedures (for example, 70-minute counseling sessions), sometimes it is also useful to reiterate basic experimental procedures with all personnel before a study begins and at various points throughout the study.

4. Often, training of experimenters is a critical component of achieving standardization. Such training of experimenters involves specific instructions to experimenters about their experimental tasks and interventions, as well as role-playing, feedback, and skill-acquisition exercises. One way to standardize experimenter behavior is to carefully train experimenters to behave exactly in the manner desired. If at all possible, experimenters should be trained simultaneously in one group to ensure they will receive identical information. Typically, training also involves attention to and suggested guidelines for anticipated procedural problems or subject reactions. Ideally, experimenters will have consistent responses to difficult questions (for example, "How did you get my name?") or ways of responding to infrequent but difficult situations

(for instance, strong negative emotional reactions of clients such as crying or pleas for additional help).

5. Another strategy for reducing problems related to experimenter procedures is to maintain close contact with all the personnel involved with the study. Especially as the research is just getting under way, close monitoring of the experimenters' experiences with their assigned tasks often reveals unexpected problems, which sometimes require small changes in the protocol or procedures. In addition, actively encouraging experimenters to report problems, ask questions, and notify the investigator of any errors leads to useful feedback and opens lines of communication. It is particularly important that the investigator be present to closely monitor all stages of a study. For example, it is essential that procedures such as the receptionist's statements and standardized instructions for completing instruments be conducted in the way the investigator intended. Whereas the novice investigator may erroneously believe that he or she can sit back and relax after the experiment actually starts, the veteran researcher spends a considerable amount of time in vigilant monitoring and troubleshooting to ascertain whether the study is proceeding as planned.

6. Investigators have developed different strategies for checking experimenters' performance and combatting experimental fatigue. Most of these strategies are in essence manipulation checks (discussed in Chapter 9). For example, Kazdin (1980) reports that confederate subjects are sometimes used to check on the experimenter. These people are randomly assigned to the various experimental conditions and provide feedback to the experimenter about the adequacy of the experimenter's performance. Sometimes informing experimenters that confederate subjects will be used is enough incentive to maintain performance standards. Likewise, researchers can use audio recordings or direct observations of structured interviews or counseling sessions as a way to evaluate the performance level of the experimenters. For example, Hogg and Deffenbacher (1988) compared cognitive and interpersonal-process group therapy in the treatment of depression. As a check on the adequacy of the experimental manipulation, they trained undergraduates to identify components of cognitive or behavioral treatments. The undergraduates then listened to the sessions of therapy; they were highly accurate (96%) in correctly identifying the type of treatment. Hogg and Deffenbacher concluded that since raters who did not know the details of the experiment were able to discriminate audiotapes of different types of treatment with accuracy and certainty, the therapists were reliably following treatment guidelines. Another strategy is to communicate about the potential problem of experimenter fatigue with the experimenters, and enlist their help in finding solutions to this problem.

SUBJECT BIAS

Similar to our optimal scenario for investigators and experimenters, the prototypical subject could be pictured as an honest, naive person who comes to an experiment without preconceived notions, willingly accepts instructions, and is motivated to respond in as truthful and helpful a way as possible (Christensen, 1980). This type of subject would not be afraid to be seen in a negative light and would be willing to disclose personal information about his or her inner secrets. Likewise, within counseling, such clients would openly discuss their experiences in counseling, the problems they have not been able to solve on their own, the reasons they chose to enter counseling, their perceptions of their counselor, and the ways in which they have changed. Moreover, the ideal subject would be aware of his or her inner subjective experiences as well as the world around him or her, and thus could reliably describe his or her external and internal worlds.

Unfortunately, we know that subjects often come to psychological experiments with preconceived notions, and even sometimes resenting the fact that they need to participate in a research study (Argyris, 1968; Gustav, 1962). As Christensen (1980) observed, subjects entering a psychological experiment are not passive organisms just waiting to respond to the independent variable. Rather, the typical subject brings a host of opinions, preferences, fears, motivations, abilities, and psychological defenses that may or may not affect how he or she responds in different experiments. We will discuss three major sources of subject bias—demand characteristics, subject characteristics, and introspective abilities—and again offer some strategies for guarding against such confounding variables.

Demand Characteristics

One major source of subject bias pertains to what is commonly referred to as demand characteristics. Demand characteristics are cues within an experiment that may influence subjects to respond in a particular way, apart from the independent variable. Demand characteristics may or may not be consistent with an experimenter's expectancies and often include events other than the experimenter's expectancies. Examples of demand characteristics include instructions on a personal problems questionnaire that give the impression that most college students do not have personal problems, nonverbal behaviors from a receptionist that seem to say that the subject should complete a questionnaire, or an experimenter's apologetic nonverbal cues toward subjects in the control group. Demand characteristics are typically subtle influences or pressures, although sometimes they are not so subtle. For example, in a study of client preferences, clients coming to a counseling center were asked very leading questions, such as: "What kind of counselor do you expect to see, expert or inexpert?" Not surprisingly, the results of this study revealed most clients' preferences included counselor expertness, although it is questionable if counselor expertness would have been consistently identified by clients if a more general question were used. Demand characteristics can occur at any point during an experiment, such as in recruiting subjects, during interactions with any personnel involved with the experiment, during the completion of inventories or experimental tasks, and in debriefing.

Demand characteristics operating within a particular study are often difficult to identify. While an investigator's intentions are to be objective and conduct a rigorous study, he or she may be unaware that the specific instructions on an inventory will influence some subjects to withhold personal information. Likewise, very minor comments in recruiting subjects may mask the effects of the independent variable. For example, consider the story of a group of researchers interested in the effects of breaches of confidentiality on the subject's perceptions of counselor trustworthiness. In the pilot study, the researchers were rather shocked to find that blatant breaches of confidentiality within a counseling analogue did not seem to affect how subjects rated the counselor on trustworthiness. For example, the counselor would begin the interview by expressing surprise at the previous subject by saying something like, "Did you see that person who just left? Boy, he has some serious problems!" but after the interview the subject would rate the counselor as quite trustworthy. Close examination of all of the experimental procedures revealed that when subjects were initially contacted, they were asked if they would be willing to participate in a counseling study in which they would talk with a "highly competent professional counselor, a person who is well liked and has a very positive reputation with students on campus." Additional piloting of subjects revealed that omitting this emphasis on prestige in the introduction resulted in more accurate perceptions of the counselor's behaviors. In short, demand characteristics operating on subjects are often subtle and unintentional.

Subject Characteristics

Not all subjects respond in the same way to different experimental tasks and procedures. Some subjects may respond more than others to subtle cues or pressures. A broad range of subject characteristics may affect how subjects respond not only to demand characteristics, but on a larger level to the experimental situation as well. We will briefly discuss the following subject characteristics as they may contribute to biasing subjects' responses: self-presentation style, motivation level, intellectual abilities, and psychological defenses.

Self-presentation Style

Christensen (1980) has suggested that a consistent theme among subject motives in psychological experiments is positive self-presentation, or a desire to present themselves in a positive light. Consequently, some subjects may begin to feel threatened if they believe their performance is inadequate or their responses are "wrong." Other subjects may be reluctant to disclose negative events about themselves or others, especially if they feel that the investigator will be able to connect their responses to their name in some way. For example, a young researcher was shocked while debriefing doctoral trainees in a supervision study when one of the subjects acknowledged that he did not dare report his true perceptions because he "just was not sure" who would see his responses.

Likewise, subjects may feel compelled to respond in socially desirable ways, such as reporting positive outcomes from counseling, or liking their therapist. Social desirability is sometimes a difficult issue when investigating topics that often require socially undesirable responses, such as premature termination from counseling. Former clients may feel reticent to report negative perceptions of the counselor in general, and particularly if they believe that their comments will be disclosed to the counselor or will cause trouble for the counselor.

Subjects with a strong desire to present themselves in a positive manner may be more susceptible to being influenced by demand characteristics. Christensen (1980) has argued that such subjects use available demand characteristics to identify the types of responses that will make them appear most positively. In short, some subjects who want to present themselves well, either consciously or unconsciously, will try to be the "good subject" and respond in a way believed to be consistent with the experimenter's desires or wishes.

Motivation Level

The subject's motivation level can also be a source of bias. Sometimes subjects find themselves in a psychological experiment and at some level really do not want to put forth much energy to be a participant in the study. For some reason, a group of subjects might feel apprehensive about the experimental conditions, apathetic about the experimental tasks, angry about being in a control group, or simply tired. Thus, the subjects may fail to appear for a scheduled appointment, give halfhearted responses, or worse yet, give random responses.

Sometimes in counseling research, some clients may be motivated to "help" their counselor. That is, in studies that evaluate some aspect of the counselor, clients who feel very grateful or even indebted to the therapist may be motivated to give glowing responses to "help" their counselor.

Intellectual Skills

Sometimes bias is introduced into a study because subjects do not have adequate intellectual skills, such as reading or writing skills. For example, one investigator at a midwestern college was interviewing subjects and was surprised to learn that some of the subjects had difficulty reading; this was after she had collected data on three self-report inventories! Another investigator gave four self-report inventories, commonly used with college students, to rural midwestern farmers and learned that such intellectual activities presented quite a demanding task to this group, who required considerably more time to complete the forms. Yet another investigator found that a group of inpatient alcoholics experienced a great deal of difficulty in completing a commonly used instrument; after defining many words in the items, he learned that the average reading level for this group was below the sixth grade. In short, the intellectual skills of the subjects can bias the results of a study and thus should be considered.

Psychological Defenses

Sometimes bias is introduced into a study because of some subjects' psychological defenses. For example, some men feel sexually aroused when viewing even a violent rape film; it is hard for most men to admit such sexual arousal even to themselves, much less to others. Thus, some subjects may feel threatened by their responses to certain material and may deny or repress their true feelings.

There are other times when some subjects may feel defensive or paranoid about revealing their feelings or thoughts about sensitive topics (for example, sexual orientation, race relations, feelings of inadequacy or embarrassment). Likewise, subjects such as inmates from a state or federal prison may be suspicious of any experimenter and withhold or temper responses because of perceived danger. In short, bias may be introduced into a study because subjects perceive some threat, real or imaginary, which consciously or unconsciously tempers their responses.

Subjects' Ability to Report Their Experiences

A topic that has a great deal of relevance for counselors is the ability of clients to accurately report their internal experiences; this discussion extends the previous discussion in Chapter 10 on self-report inventories. Nisbett and Wilson (1977) examined a broad array of data to determine subjects' ability to reliably report their cognitive processes. In general, their analyses suggested that subjects provide more accurate reports when causal stimuli and plausible causes for responses are salient. In addition, subjects more accurately report (1) historical facts, (2) the focus of their attention, (3) current sensations, and (4) knowledge of their plans, evaluations, and emotions. However, a considerable amount of data suggest that subjects have greater difficulty describing their mental processes when the situation is ambiguous, such as when subjects are unaware of the stimuli that trigger cognitive responses.

For example, an experiment conducted by Maier (1931) aptly depicts subjects' inability to connect causal elements in ambiguous situations. Maier used the "string-problem," where two cords were hung about ten feet apart from the ceiling of a laboratory room containing various objects, pliers, poles, lamps, and such. The goal was for subjects to stand between the two cords, holding one in each hand. Some of the subjects, after some trial and error, would find the solution of tying a weight onto one of the cords, swinging it like a pendulum, walking over and grabbing the other cord with one hand, and catching the weighted swinging cord with the other hand. Voilà, the solution. If subjects were unsuccessful in finding a solution, Maier, who had been wandering around the room, would walk by the cords and swing one of the cords in motion. Some of the unsuccessful subjects then would pick some object, tie it to the end of the cord, swing it like a pendulum, and shortly thereafter solve the problem. But when Maier asked the subjects how they had arrived at the solution, he would get answers such as: "It just dawned on me" or "I just realized the cord would swing if I fastened a weight to it." In short, most of Maier's subjects could not accurately report the causal events involved in their cognitive and affective processing. Likewise, more recent research in experimental information processing suggests that subjects have difficulty explaining the causal chain of events in their cognitive processes, particularly with the passage of time (Ericsson & Simon, 1984).

While the work of Nisbett and Wilson (1977) has been the subject of some debate, their observations should be carefully considered when counseling researchers attempt to examine clients' cognitive processes, especially within the often-ambiguous situation we call counseling. For example, the question of why clients changed or what influenced them to change in the course of counseling may be a very difficult one for them to accurately and reliably answer. Likewise, as one researcher learned, asking clients how they decided to seek help at a counseling center resulted in a very broad range of responses, and some incomprehensible ones! In short, counseling researchers in particular need to carefully consider the type of information that can be accurately and reliably obtained about clients' mental processes, particularly on retrospective events. It may very well be that researchers may ask clients to tell us more than they can know, and thus clients may provide misleading self-reports.

Strategies for Reducing Subject Bias

Investigators can use several strategies to reduce subject bias:

1. Perhaps the most commonly used strategy to reduce subject bias due to the "good subject" role is to keep subjects blind or naive to the real purpose of the study. If the subject does not know the purpose of the study, it will be more difficult for the subject to consciously or unconsciously conform in ways similar to the predicted hypotheses. Subjects are kept blind by withholding from them not only information about the hypotheses of the study, but sometimes even about the purpose of the study as well. For example, subjects participating in a study may be asked in an unspecified manner to complete an inventory about their perceptions of the college career center. When both the subject and the experimenter are kept blind, as discussed in the previous section, this is called "double blind." The double-blind procedure tends to reduce both experimenter and subject bias, and is often recommended in counseling research.

2. To reduce bias due to subjects' desire to present themselves in a positive light, a general strategy is to reduce the threat associated with the experiment. Thus, instructions on a questionnaire may explicitly state that "there are no right or wrong answers" and that "this inventory is not a test." The actual title of an inventory might also be altered if it arouses anxiety or introduces demand characteristics. In addition, some researchers attempt to reduce threat by explicitly normalizing typical subject fears. For example, in

a study of the coping process subjects might be told that it is normal to have unresolved personal problems; in fact, "everyone has them."

3. Several procedures can be used to increase subjects' honesty as well as reduce subjects' fears about confidentiality. First and foremost, honest and direct statements from the researcher about his or her desire or need to obtain honest responses to increase the profession's understanding of a phenomenon are often employed. In addition, researchers typically communicate to subjects that their responses will be strictly confidential, and explain the mechanisms for safeguarding confidentiality (for example, coding). Moreover, in research using groups of subjects, it is often helpful for subjects to know that the researcher is interested in how the group of subjects as a whole responds to the items, rather than specific individuals. Sometimes subjects are asked not to include their name on their questionnaires, thereby ensuring anonymity. In some situations, a researcher may need to collect data on several occasions from subjects and match their responses over time. To ensure confidentiality, subjects can be asked to supply a code name in lieu of their actual name; subjects can be asked to generate an alias name or develop an intricate code based on some combination of numbers related to their birthdate, age, social security number, or such (see Kandel, 1973).

4. Often researchers will make appeals to subjects to increase the subjects' motivation level. For example, subjects can be briefly told the importance of the research and possible outcomes of the research (for example, honest responses to the questionnaires will clarify changes or growth within supervision). In exchange, researchers sometimes promise to mail subjects the results of the study, particularly if the study is of a survey nature.

5. Sometimes researchers concerned about demand characteristics and subject bias will conduct a postexperimental inquiry. As per our discussion in Chapter 9, after the experiment is over, the experimenter will assess potential subject bias by asking subjects questions about their understanding of the purpose of the experiment, their beliefs about how the experimenter wanted them to respond, and any problems they encountered. The postexperimental inquiry might consist of a brief questionnaire (with perhaps follow-up inquiries to those subjects who identified the true purpose of a study or those who felt pressured in some way) or be conducted via direct interviewing. Sometimes direct interviewing can introduce demand characteristics in and of itself, and may best be done by someone who has not previously interacted with the subjects. While there is considerable value in postexperimental inquiries, it is important to note a limitation. Subjects may have been biased by some demand characteristic, but may be totally unaware of such influence; postexperimental inquiry will not reveal such subject bias.

6. In addition to withholding information about the purpose of a study, a researcher can reduce subject bias through the more drastic measure of disguise or deception. The purpose of a study can be disguised by providing subjects with information that will lead them to believe that a particular study is investigating another research topic. Such strategies, however, carry important ethical considerations (see Chapter 4). For example, subjects about to

participate in an attitude-change study might be told that they are being asked to evaluate whether the university should institute final oral exams for all undergraduates. Likewise, a study involving client perceptions of counselors might be framed in terms of evaluating the adequacy of the counseling center's service delivery. In short, another strategy to reduce subject bias is to provide information that disguises the true purpose.

7. Given that a considerable amount of research in counseling uses undergraduate students who participate in research to fulfill a class requirement, lack of student motivation or apathy can be a serious source of bias. Sometimes one strategy is to perform "spot checks" on subjects' performance. For example, a question can be inserted in the middle of a questionnaire asking subjects to leave this item blank or mark "strongly agree" (K. Sher, personal communication, September 1989). Subjects who do not follow such simple instructions are then eliminated from the study.

8. With regard to intellectual skills, the researcher can and should evaluate the reading level of all instruments used in a study and match them to the sample. Typically, information about the sample can be obtained from personnel in the corresponding agencies or from colleagues familiar with the subject samples of interest.

9. Researchers in counseling must be attentive to subjects' ability to report their cognitive and affective processes. One strategy is to develop questionnaires based on the cognitive processes that are more readily accessible to subjects. Another strategy is to provide the subject with additional information to facilitate the accurate reporting of the more ambiguous cognitive and affective processes, such as by enabling video or audio replay or by using Interpersonal Process Recall (Kagan, 1975).

SUMMARY AND CONCLUSIONS

The purpose of this chapter was to identify potential sources of bias in subjects, experimenters, and investigators that might disguise or cloud the relationships between the experimental variables of interest; such bias is a major threat to Kerlinger's "MAXMINCON" principle. The more uncontrolled are the conditions of an experiment, the more various biases are likely to operate and create more error variance or extraneous variables. More error variance means that it is more difficult to identify systematic variance due to the independent variables in question. The introduction of extraneous variables means that it is difficult to isolate the variables responsible for change. Thus, subject, experimenter, and investigator biases serve to introduce extraneous variables that may distort or disguise the relationships among the experimental variables.

In this chapter we maintained that investigators and experimenters are subject to biases that may very well affect the results of a study. We discussed three major types of experimenter bias: experimenter attributes, experimenter and investigator expectancies, and experimental procedures. Within subject bias we also discussed three major sources of bias: demand characteristics, subject characteristics, and introspective abilities. For experimenter, investigator, and subject bias we discussed several strategies for controlling or minimizing bias.

Subject, investigator, and experimenter biases represent serious problems for the counseling researcher. These sources of bias can quickly reduce the results of many long hours spent in developing and conducting a study into a pile of meaningless numbers. The veteran researcher becomes vigilant, even hypervigilant, against various sources of bias and constantly monitors the study to detect any biases that might have crept in. Bias is a particularly important issue for counseling researchers because much of our research is conducted in applied settings, where fewer experimental controls are available and thus more sources of bias are potentially operative.

It is important to note that minimizing and eliminating bias is a matter of degree, and often the researcher is uncertain whether various sources of bias were operative. Thus, it is useful to qualify the results of one's research (typically done in the discussion section) based on the possible sources of bias that might have been operative. A general research strategy that is becoming more commonplace is for investigators to statistically test for the existence of various biases and confounds in a series of preliminary analyses. Hogg and Deffenbacher (1988) provide a good example of using such preliminary analyses. Such statistical procedures, as well as frank discussions of other possible sources of bias that were untested, are recommended.

C H A P T E R 13

ANALOGUE RESEARCH

This chapter focuses on analogue research in counseling, which is defined as research that is conducted under conditions that resemble or approximate the therapeutic situation. In an effort to follow Kerlinger's "MAXMINCON" principle, some investigators have sought to reduce bias and extraneous variables by creating tightly controlled conditions that approximate the counseling context. Not surprisingly, analogue research has historically led directly into the heart of the debate on naturalistic versus experimental approaches to research. Bordin aptly depicted the debate in 1965:

> A . . . decision in research strategy is whether to choose the naturalistic or experimental path. This is a familiar controversy with established cliches, e.g., "Only when we bring phenomena under precise control as in the laboratory can true knowledge be gained," versus "Of what use is precision when it is obtained by reduction to the trivial?" A frozen posture is not helpful to psychology or any other scientific discipline. (p. 483)

The first section of this chapter provides a brief historical overview of the use of analogue methodology in counseling. The second and third sections discuss the advantages and limitations of this particular methodology. The fourth section of this chapter proposes that the external validity of analogue research can be evaluated by examining the variables that depict real-life counseling, most notably variables related to the counselor, client, and counseling process. The fifth section maintains that the ultimate utility of analogue methodology must be evaluated within the context of existing knowledge bases and prior research methodologies used in a particular topical area. The use of analogue methodology in social influence research in counseling is analyzed to demonstrate this point.

HISTORICAL OVERVIEW

Real-life counseling is a tremendously complex process. Clients differ, therapists differ, and counseling is such a highly interactive, emotionally charged, and complex communication process that it is difficult to investigate and even succinctly describe. About twenty years ago, such complexity led Heller (1971) to conclude that the counseling interview, "while an excellent source of research hypotheses, is a poor testing group for isolating factors responsible for behavior change. The varied complexity of the therapeutic interaction and the inability to specify and control therapeutic operations make it difficult to obtain reliable information concerning exact agents of change" (p. 127). Heller was a strong believer in the scientific method and experimental control at that time. Part of the solution to investigating and understanding the complexity within counseling was to exercise the experimental control offered in what he called laboratory research. "The purpose of clinical laboratory research is to determine what factors produce change, under what conditions they operate best, and how they should be combined to produce an effective therapeutic package" (Heller, 1971, p. 127).

Basically, a counseling analogue is an experimental simulation of some aspect of the counseling process involving manipulation of some aspects of the counselor, client, and/or counseling process. In the past the analogue has been referred to as "miniature therapy" (Goldstein, Heller, & Sechrest, 1966) or as a "simplification strategy" (Bordin, 1965).

Keet (1948) has been credited with one of the first uses of the analogue methodology in psychotherapy research (for example, Bordin, 1965; Heller, 1971; Kushner, 1978). Keet used volunteer subjects and examined the efficacy of expressive (reflective) versus interpretative therapeutic statements in overcoming previously identified memory blocks on word association tasks. Interpretative statements were found to be more effective. Historically, it is interesting to note that while subsequent research did not replicate Keet's findings (Grummon & Butler, 1953; Merrill, 1952), Bordin (1965) observed that "so great is the attractiveness of control and simplification as a research strategy that this failure [to replicate] only spurred further efforts in this direction" (p. 494). In general, however, the use of analogue research has been late in developing within counseling research. Heller (1971) attributed the tardiness to the fact that analogues are rather foreign to psychotherapy because knowledge in the clinical fields has normally been collected in the more naturalistic tradition (for example, the case studies of Freud). Munley (1974) attributed the slow emergence of the analogue to the reluctance of counselors to accept a contrived and highly controlled methodology that might well be too artificial and unrealistic.

Bordin (1965) wrote one of the earliest theoretical critiques of "simplification," or analogue methodology, in counseling research. He appears to have been keenly aware of the strengths and limitations of this methodology. While the experimental control afforded by the analogue was quickly recognized, there was concern and debate about the generalizability or external validity of the results (for example, Lewin, 1951; Rappaport, 1960). Bordin acknowledged that the criticisms of simplification research focused primarily on its oversimplifying the phenomenon of interest. To counteract such problems, Bordin proposed three rules for achieving "acceptable simplifications," which are as follows:

1. Start from and keep in central focus the natural phenomenon that aroused the researcher's curiosity and about which he or she wished to know more to verify his or her present ideas.
2. The degree to which a researcher can safely depart from the naturalistic setting is proportional to the amount already known about the phenomenon in question.
3. If it is not based on prior knowledge, simplification should be accompanied by empirical investigations of the naturalistic phenomenon to which it is intended to refer.

Researchers initially employed analogue methodology in two general lines of research (Heller, 1971). One line of research involved an analysis of therapies to "find their most potent ingredients and the conditions under which each is optimized" (Heller, 1971, pp. 148–149). This included analogue studies of systematic desensitization, Rogerian facilitative conditions, and free association (pp. 148–149).

The second major approach examined the communication process, particularly in terms of the social influence process. This line of research was sparked by the applications of social psychology to counseling, particularly the work of Goldstein, Heller, and Sechrest (1966) and Strong (1968). The late 1960s and early 1970s saw a flurry of analogue studies, primarily examining the effects of counselors' behavior on client perceptions of the counselors' expertness, attractiveness, and trustworthiness. The social influence research has "continued unabated" (Borgen, 1984a) and has been the focus of most of the analogue research in counseling.

There are several different types of analogue studies. In reviewing the counseling analogue research methods used in the *Journal of Counseling Psychology,* Munley (1974) categorized the analogue studies into five categories: (1) audiovisual counseling studies—counselor behavior as the dependent variable, (2) audiovisual counseling studies—client behavior as the dependent variable, (3) quasi-counseling interview studies—client behavior as the dependent variable, (4) quasi-counseling interview studies—counselor behavior as the dependent variable, and (5) experimental tasks not directly resembling a counseling interview. At this point, the types of analogues that investigators have used are quite broad, ranging from highly artificial nonlive simulations to very realistic live simulations involving multiple sessions.

Despite Bordin's (1965) earlier proposal for "acceptable simplifications," concern and debate over the utility of analogue methodology has persisted. A number of theoretical critiques have now addressed the utility of the analogue methodology (for example, Gelso, 1979; Heller, 1971; Kazdin, 1978, 1980; Strong, 1971). At the center of the controversy is the questionable generalizability of the analogue finding. Goldman (1978) summed up the criticisms best, purporting that the "venerated laboratory experiment has been highly overrated as a way to gain understanding of human behavior as it exists in real life" (p. 8). Furthermore, "the laboratory has become so 'pure' that it has little or nothing to say about how people function in real life" (p. 8).

Before entering into this debate ourselves, we will discuss in greater detail the advantages and limitations of analogue methodology.

ADVANTAGES OF ANALOGUE RESEARCH

The hallmark of analogue research is experimental control. The analogue research methodology enables the experimenter to control the experimental situation, primarily by eliminating extraneous variables, controlling confounding variables, and manipulating specified levels of an independent variable. In a counseling situation, many variables are present pertaining to the client and counselor (for example, personality variables, coping skills, manner of processing information, expectations, demographic variables), the counseling process (for example, counselor interventions; client reactions and disclosures), and the particular situation (for example, room decor and arrangement, cost of therapy, reasons for seeking help). In analogue designs, variables extraneous to the particular research problem can be eliminated or controlled. For example, subjects easily can be randomly assigned to treatment conditions, thereby reducing confounds from subject variability. Subjects also can be selected based on a particular variable (such as locus of control, level of depression), which can be either held constant across treatment conditions or varied to create levels of an independent variable. Therapists' theoretical orientation and interview behaviors can be controlled or even standardized across conditions. In short, analogue research allows for a great deal of situational control by enabling the researcher to manipulate one or more independent variables, eliminate or hold extraneous variables constant, and use random assignment.

Along with providing situational control, analogue methodology has the advantage of enabling the experimenter to achieve a high degree of specificity in the operational definitions of a variable. For example, level of counselor self-disclosure could be manipulated to enable examination of, let's say, three distinct levels of self-disclosure (no self-disclosure, five self-disclosures per session, ten self-disclosures per session). In this sense, the analogue methodology often offers greater precision—not only in terms of the variables under examination but also in terms of experimental procedures.

The increased specificity is a major advantage in isolating specific events or processes in the complex activity called counseling. Thus, within a laboratory analogue it is possible to isolate and examine the effect of rather small events, such as self-involving counselor disclosures, specific counselor introductions, and professional titles, on whatever variables are of interest, such as the client's perceptions of the counselor (see Andersen & Anderson, 1985; Strong & Dixon, 1971).

Another advantage of the analogue methodology is often the reduction of practical and ethical obstacles in experimentally examining some aspect of the counseling process. Many times, real-world constraints such as financial limits and limits on subject availability can be substantially reduced by using client surrogates in an analogue design (for example, Dixon & Claiborn, 1981). Given that real-life counseling involves clients with real-life problems, stresses, and anxieties, experimental procedures such as randomly assigning clients to placebo groups or waiting-list control groups can cause problems. Or certain experimental manipulations, such as varying the type of counselor feedback or type of counselor self-disclosure, may pose serious ethical dilemmas when clients with real problems are used. Creating a situation analogous to counseling or using transcripts, audiotapes, or videotapes of counseling interactions sidesteps ethical problems with manipulations, especially with clients under some kind of duress.

DISADVANTAGES OF ANALOGUE RESEARCH

The major concern about or disadvantage of analogue laboratory research pertains to the generalizability of the research findings, or external validity. External validity is of special importance to those in the counseling profession because the primary focus of our work is on real-life, applied counseling with actual clients.

Sometimes the strength of the analogue methodology (experimental control and internal validity) results in rather artificial circumstances. The investigation may be very high in experimental precision but examine events in such artificial and contrived conditions that they no longer resemble actual counseling conditions. It can even become unclear whether the research is investigating the counseling process, or variables that are so abstract and removed that they are irrelevant to real-life counseling. Thus, the most serious concern pertains to whether the results of a particular study can be generalized to actual counseling practice. The power of the experimental controls may result in the loss of external validity, or as Bordin (1965) stated, "oversimplification."

The limitations of the analogue methodology often leads to discussions about the relative importance of internal versus external validity. The inexperienced student wants to know which is more important, or which one should be the focus of the initial research in an area. Both internal and external validity are important. While reasons have been stated for emphasizing either internal and external validity in undeveloped research areas (for example, Gelso, 1979; Kerlinger, 1986), in our opinion it should be clearly understood that both internal and external validity are needed in all research areas, and that it is most important that the knowledge on any one topic be created by research that represents a balance between internal and external validity. Since knowledge on any one topic will accumulate over time, the issue of which type of validity to examine first is often less important than the larger issue of overall balance.

VARIABLES TO CONSIDER IN EVALUATING THE GENERALIZABILITY OF ANALOGUE STUDIES

The basic question in analogue research is: To what extent does a particular laboratory experiment resemble the actual counseling circumstances? One way to evaluate the external validity of the analogue methodology is to consider some of the variables that depict the situation we typically are trying to generalize to, namely real-life counseling. Several writers have attempted to provide some criteria for evaluating the relevance of analogue methodologies to the practice of counseling (for example, Kazdin, 1980; Strong & Matross, 1973). We propose that the external validity of analogue research also can be evaluated in part by examining the resemblance of some of the variables that depict real-life counseling: (1) the client and his or her presenting problem, (2) the counselor, and (3) the counseling process and setting. Any given study might vary on these variables and resemble the actual counseling situation in varying degrees. Table 13-1 depicts variables pertaining to the client, counselor, and counseling process; each of these variables can be evaluated as having relatively high, moderate, or low degrees of resemblance to real-life counseling. Most likely, not all of the variables will be relevant for each study. One study might be focused primarily on counselor behavior; in terms of evaluating the external validity of the study, the counselor variables we identify would most likely be more important to consider than, let's say, the client variables. For research purposes, it may be useful to increase the specificity of these evaluations by developing Likert-type items to assess each variable. Here we use the three rather general points of low, moderate, and high for each variable primarily to illustrate varying levels of resemblance on each particular dimension. Moreover, variables listed in the table were developed through rational means; empirical research may well add or delete variables in this table that are relevant to determining generalizability.

T A B L E   13-1
Evaluating the Relevance of Analogue Methodologies to Real-Life Counseling

Variables	Relatively high degree of resemblance	Moderate degree of resemblance	Relatively low degree of resemblance
A. Client			
Expectations of change	Client expects treatment and change	Person expects experimental treatment	Subject expects course credit or to learn about psychology
Motivation and distress level	Client is distressed enough to seek help at a treatment center	Person is stressed enough to seek relevant academic experiences and psychological experiments	Subject is not distressed and does not seek help; subject has ulterior motivation (such as course credit) rather than seeking psychological help and change
Selection of treatment	Client often chooses therapists or type of treatment	Subject selects relevant psychological experiments providing treatment	Subject is assigned to treatments and therapists/interviewers

(continued)

TABLE 13-1 (continued)

Variables	Relatively high degree of resemblance	Moderate degree of resemblance	Relatively low degree of resemblance
Presenting problem	Real-life problem typically seen in counseling	Hypothetical problems	Nonproblem or experimental tasks
Knowledge of problem	Relevant and current concern; high level of processing and knowledge	Relevant but not pressing, therefore moderate level of information processing	Irrelevant or new issue; low level of information processing and knowledge
B. Counselor expectations	Client change	Moderate belief of client change	Successful role play or interview
Role credibility	High status, appearance is role congruent	Moderate level of status	Absence of status cues, role incongruent
Knowledge bases	Broad range of knowledge about assessments, personality and counseling theories, and the counseling process	Moderate levels of information about assessment, personality and counseling theories, and the counseling process	Low level of knowledge about assessment, personality and counseling theories, and the counseling process
Counseling skill	High levels of procedural skills within the counseling process	Moderate levels of procedural skills within the counseling process	Low levels of procedural skills within the counseling process
Motivation level	Highly motivated to provide therapeutic relationship and facilitate change	Moderate levels of provided therapy; possibly combined with motivation for experimental change	Not motivated to provide therapy; primary goal is to conduct an interview
Experience level	10 years +	3rd year doctorate	1st year M.A.

C. Counseling process and setting

Assessment	Client is carefully diagnosed and goals established	Client may be assessed to determine congruence with treatment goals	Subject is not assessed; lack of goals for specific individual
Interventions	Specifically targeted to client's presenting problems	Interventions are relevant to client's problem	Interventions are not relevant to subject's concerns or problems
Duration	Extended over several normal-length therapy sessions across time	A few normal-length sessions	One-shot and brief (10 minutes or so)

(continued)

T A B L E 13-1 (continued)

Variables	Relatively high degree of resemblance	Moderate degree of resemblance	Relatively low degree of resemblance
Interpersonal interchange	Counselor and client interact and exchange information	Counselor and client interact on restricted topic or in some defined manner	Subject views counseling scenario, but does not interact with a counselor
Client reactions	Client processes the counseling experience and reacts in some way to the relevant information	Client reacts to restricted topic or semirelevant topic	Subject views counseling scenario and responds hypothetically
Client change or outcome	Client changes or is different in some way because of the counseling interchange	Client may change in some way, providing the treatment is successful	Subject does not change in any way since the counseling scenario was not personally relevant
Environment	Professional treatment center	Facility that may not offer regular treatment services	Laboratory setting or classroom

Client Variables and Presenting Problems

A number of variables pertaining to clients or subjects directly relate to the generalizability of the research findings to actual counseling practice. We will identify several client variables that depict important elements of clients seeking counseling and then relate these variables to evaluating the generalizability of a particular study.

In most actual counseling situations, clients experience personal problems that they have been unable to resolve (Fretz, 1982). These personal problems typically cause anxiety and distress of some sort, as people find themselves "failing" where they want to "succeed" in some way. As people cope with their "current concerns" (Klinger, 1971), they typically engage in a wide range of cognitive, affective, and behavioral trial-and-error processes (Heppner & Krauskopf, 1987). In other words, clients normally have thought about and tried a number of possible solutions and thus have compiled some kind of knowledge base pertaining to this problem (accurate or inaccurate). After unsuccessful problem solving and accompanying levels of distress, a person might seek a wide variety of resources for assistance (see Wills, 1987, for a review of client help-seeking) and perhaps end up at a counseling center or some kind of treatment facility. Most important, people seeking psychological help have expectations about being treated. They often choose a certain therapist based on a recommendation or reputation, and they are motivated to change in some way. In short, typically clients seeking psychological help enter therapy (1) with expectations about change; (2) with expectations about the therapist and treatment; (3) under distress, and thus in a motivated state; (4) with the intent of discussing specific problematic situations; and (5) with a wide range of information or knowledge about their particular problems. Although there may well be other variables that depict other aspects of clients seeking help, we propose to begin evaluating the relevance of the analogue methodology by considering these five client variables.

Table 13-1 depicts these five client variables and suggests what would constitute relatively high, moderate, and low degrees of resemblance of these variables to real-life counseling. For example, a relatively high degree of resemblance for client expectations would entail a client expecting treatment and change, as opposed to a subject simply expecting course credit (low degree of resemblance). Also related to client expectations is the way in which treatment is selected. Often clients choose a type of treatment or therapist based on their presenting problem or a counselor's reputation (high resemblance) rather than being assigned to particular treatments and therapists/interviewers (low resemblance). Distress and motivation levels may also be polarized; a client is distressed enough to seek help at a treatment center (high resemblance) whereas a subject is part of a convenient or captive subject pool and merely seeks course credit (low resemblance) rather than seeking psychological help and change. Perhaps most important, actual clients have both "current concerns" or real problems as well as a high level of information processing and knowledge about that problem (high resemblance); conversely, subjects assigned to a potentially irrelevant task have relatively low knowledge levels about the task and thus represent low resemblance to real-life counseling.

The main point in this discussion is that several client variables need to be considered in evaluating the generalizability of particular analogue methodologies within counseling. In 1978, Strong facetiously referred to subjects typically used in the social influence investigations as "client surrogates." We find this a rather good phrase to underscore the subject substitution and its many implications, all of which commonly occur in most analogue studies. If an experimenter designs a study where the subjects do not closely resemble actual clients, then the generalizability of the findings to actual clients is unclear and probably questionable.

Counselor Variables

A number of variables pertaining to counselors or interviewers also directly relate to the generalizability of research findings to actual counseling practice. Perhaps in the most optimal therapeutic counseling relationship, the counselor is experienced and has a broad range of knowledge about assessment, personality and counseling theories, and about the counseling process in general. In addition, the therapist has high levels of procedural skill; that is, he or she has the interpersonal and counseling skills to actually be therapeutic with a client. The therapist also is highly motivated to provide a therapeutic relationship, perhaps reflected in establishing the Rogerian conditions such as empathy and unconditional positive regard or other ways of establishing a strong working alliance. Thus, the therapist approaches counseling with the expectation that the therapy will be successful and the client will change in desired ways. Finally, the therapist appears to be a credible professional, expert and trustworthy, a person who can provide therapeutic assistance.

Table 13-1 suggests relatively high, moderate, and low degrees of resemblance of six therapist variables to actual counseling. For example, high degrees of resemblance characterize therapists with a broad range of relevant knowledge about counseling as well as high levels of procedural skill. Such counselors have a considerable amount of counseling experience. By contrast, relatively low resemblance to actual therapists characterizes interviewers or inexperienced counselors who lack essential knowledge about counseling as well as the skills to actually do counseling. The other variables can also be polarized, so that people resemble actual therapists when they (1) are highly motivated to provide a therapeutic relationship and facilitate change, (2) expect counseling to be successful and the client to change, and (3) appear credible and congruent within a therapeutic role. Conversely, relatively low resemblance to actual therapists may be characterized as not intending to provide a therapeutic and caring relationship, but rather being motivated solely to conduct an interview. Moreover, often the interviewer reflects an absence of status and credibility cues.

In some of the previous research in counseling, the therapist variables under examination did not closely resemble the role or behaviors of a typical therapist. Several examples can be readily found within what is referred to as the social or interpersonal influence area in counseling (see Corrigan, Dell, Lewis, & Schmidt, 1980; Heppner & Dixon, 1981). In the past, researchers have manipulated a broad range of cues associated with perceived counselor expertness, attractiveness, and trustworthiness. One goal of much of this research has been to identify behaviors and cues that enhance the counselor's credibility and subsequent ability to impact the client. Often a common research strategy has been to examine extreme levels of an independent variable to determine if that particular variable has an effect on client perceptions of the counselor. The important point for this discussion is that sometimes the therapist variables have not closely resembled the role of a typical therapist.

For example, in attempting to lower the perceived expertness of an interviewer, subjects have been told: "We had originally scheduled Dr. _____ to talk with you, but unfortunately he notified us that he wouldn't be able to make it today. In his place we have Mr. _____ , a student, who unfortunately has had no interviewing experience and has been given only a brief explanation of the purpose of this study. I think he should work out all right, though. Now, if you would step this way . . . " (Strong & Schmidt, 1970).

Likewise, the procedural skills of interviewers have been manipulated to produce interviewer behaviors that do not closely resemble those of actual therapists. For example, a counselor portraying an unattractive role "ignored the interviewee when he entered the office, did not smile at him, did not look beyond a few cold glances, leaned away from him, and portrayed disinterest, coldness, and boredom'' (Schmidt & Strong, 1971, p. 349). Gelso (1979) referred to such procedures as "experimental deck stacking," and raised questions about the utility of research on such atypical therapist behaviors. In short, although a considerable amount of information was obtained about events contributing to clients' perceptions of counselor credibility, the generalizability of some of this knowledge to actual counseling practice is questionable because of the relatively low resemblance to actual therapist behaviors.

It is important to note that the focus here is on the extent to which a person in a therapeutic role resembles an experienced therapist in terms of knowledge, skill, and expectations. Thus, it is also quite possible that a trainee—let's say a beginning-level practicum student counseling his or her first actual client—may not closely resemble an actual therapist. At best, the trainee reflects an approximation of a therapist. Thus, it is important not to confuse a trainee with a therapist just because they both counsel an actual client seeking psychological help from a treatment center. In short, to evaluate the generalizability of analogue research to actual counseling practice, it is important that we consider several variables pertaining to the therapist, notably the counselor's knowledge bases, skills, expectations, and role credibility.

Counseling Process and Setting

We must consider another set of variables related to the counseling process when evaluating the external validity of analogue research. In a real-life counseling situation, the counselor and client typically meet for a number of sessions, often once per week, extending over several weeks. Typically, the client and his or her presenting problem are carefully diagnosed, and treatment goals as well as intervention strategies are tailored specifically to this particular client. Most important, the counselor and client freely interact and exchange a wealth of information. The client is not a tabula rasa, but rather assimilates the new information into his or her existing conceptual framework and reacts in some way (see Hill, Helms, Spiegel, & Tichenor, 1988, for a taxonomy of client reactions). In a positive counseling situation, the client changes in some desirable manner, such as learning new behaviors, altering beliefs, attitudes, or feelings, and adapting to environmental demands more effectively. The environmental context for the therapeutic situation is a professional treatment center of some sort, university counseling center, or community mental health center.

Table 13-1 again suggests relatively high, moderate, and low degrees of resemblance of at least seven counseling process variables to actual counseling practice. In terms of assessment and interventions, high resemblance characterizes those situations where the client is carefully diagnosed and interventions are specifically targeted to the client's present problems. Low resemblance involves a lack of assessment, and interventions that are not relevant to a subject's concerns or problems. Analogues that resemble the actual therapy process involve multiple 50-minute sessions, extended over several weeks (versus one-shot, 10-minute counseling scenarios). In addition, analogues that resemble actual counseling include rather extended interactions between the counselor and client where a broad range of information is exchanged, versus analogues that do not include live interactions between the counselor and client. The analogue also can be evaluated in terms of how much and what kind of information the client processes. High resemblance entails the client's processing the counseling experience repeatedly over time whereas low resemblance entails the subject's responding to counseling scenarios in a hypothetical and often irrelevant manner. The analogue might also be evaluated in terms of therapeutic outcomes: Did the client change in some desired manner? High resemblance involves change of personally relevant behaviors, thoughts, or feelings, whereas low resemblance entails a lack of change on the part of the subject, most likely because the counseling scenario was not personally relevant. Finally, the analogue can be evaluated in terms of the environment or context of the counseling situation. Analogues involving a high resemblance to actual practice take place in a professional environment, such as a treatment center or counseling center, whereas an experimental laboratory setting or classroom offers rather low resemblance.

EVALUATING UTILITY WITHIN AN EXISTING KNOWLEDGE BASE

A common goal in counseling is to facilitate change in clients. Such a goal implies that the counselor can favorably affect the client to alter specific thoughts, attitudes, and behaviors. The process of one person influencing the actions, attitudes, or feelings of another has been labeled the interpersonal or social influence process, which has been considered by some the "central core of social psychology" (Zimbardo & Ebbesen, 1970, p. iii). Initially, research in social psychology established the importance of several variables in promoting attitude change: source characteristics (such as perceived expertness, trustworthiness), message variables (like message discrepancy, incongruity), and recipient characteristics (such as locus of control, authoritarianism). Later research has indicated that the attitude change process is more complex, and different persuasion routes have been proposed and empirically substantiated (Petty & Cacioppo, 1981).

Strong (1968) initially conceptualized counseling as an interpersonal or social influence process, as he explicitly integrated social psychological concepts into counseling. Since 1968, considerable research has been conducted on interpersonal influence variables in counseling. Investigators have examined a wide range of variables affecting counselor power, or the counselor's ability to influence a client (see Corrigan, Dell, Lewis, & Schmidt, 1980; Dorn, 1986; Heppner & Claiborn, 1989; Heppner & Dixon, 1981).

The analogue methodology has been used in a very high percentage of the published studies in the interpersonal influence area. Aware of the advantages and disadvantages of the analogue methodology, Strong (1971) proposed five criteria or "boundary conditions" that if met, would increase the external validity or generalizability of analogue methodology. The boundary conditions are as follows: (1) counseling is a conversation between or among persons, (2) status differences between or among interactants constrain the conversation, (3) the duration of contact between interactants in counseling varies and at times is extended, (4) many clients are motivated to change, and (5) many clients are psychologically distressed and are heavily invested in the behaviors they seek to change.

Although other criteria could be used, Heppner and Dixon (1981) used these five conditions to initially assess the external validity of the investigations of the interpersonal influence process in counseling. The third condition (extended duration) was operationally defined as two sessions. Heppner and Dixon reviewed 51 studies that examined events associated with perceived expertness, attractiveness, and trustworthiness; 29 did not meet any of the boundary conditions, 16 met only the first two conditions, 5 studies fulfilled three conditions, and 1 study met four conditions. Over half of the studies reviewed met none of the five boundary conditions.

Heppner and Claiborn (1989) did a similar analysis of the interpersonal influence literature in counseling after 1981. Thirty-seven of the 56 studies reviewed (66%) did not meet any of the boundary conditions. These studies presented the counseling situation to subjects through written, audiotaped, or videotaped materials, which can be considered noninterview analogues. Moreover, these noninterview studies contained an average of only about 12 minutes of stimulus material, which suggests that this research is based on minimal information and initial impressions. Thus, a majority of the interpersonal influence research consists of data collected in situations of questionable generalizability (that is, none of Strong's boundary conditions were met). In addition, these studies are based on only 12 minutes of stimulus material, which is an extremely small sample of counseling. Twenty-nine percent of the studies (n = 16) met three or more boundary conditions, compared to about 12% in the Heppner and Dixon (1981) review. Further analysis of these investigations revealed that seven studies were conducted with counseling center clients during actual counseling. Thus, there appears to be some progress in examining the social influence process under conditions more similar to actual counseling situations; yet relatively little research (n = 7) exists that has examined the influence process in a real-life counseling context over time.

The major methodological point in this analysis of the social influence literature is that the utility of a particular methodology, in this case the analogue methodology, is contingent upon the previous research and the accumulated knowledge bases. There is no doubt that the analogue methodology is powerful and useful. However, when it is by far the most frequently used methodology, the body of knowledge that is created becomes unbalanced and tends to emphasize one methodological strength to the exclusion of other issues. In short, the utility of the knowledge obtained from the analogue methodology diminishes if this methodology is overused relative to other methodologies in a particular research area. Gelso (1979) discussed this issue in terms of paradigm fixation. In addition, when analogues are used that are very dissimilar to the actual counseling experience, additional questions are raised about the generalizability of the results.

The question then becomes: Can additional research using the analogue method significantly increase our knowledge base about the influence process in counseling? While the analogue can still play a powerful role in acquiring knowledge about counseling, it is doubtful whether additional social influence studies using the analogue methodology that do not meet any of Strong's boundary conditions will substantially add to our knowledge base. While it can be argued that new knowledge is created by such research, its value in the area of social influence at this time is doubtful given the generalizability issues.

In sum, the utility of any particular methodology must be evaluated within the context of existing knowledge bases and prior research methodologies used in a particular topical area. Studies that employ the same methodology create a knowledge base that is very weak with regard to the particular disadvantage of that methodology. Moreover, when the overwhelming majority of research in an area employs the same methodology, the strength and utility of the knowledge base is unknown.

SUMMARY AND CONCLUSIONS

As Munley (1974) has pointed out, there are several different types of analogue research, such as audiovisual and quasi-counseling interviews. Without a doubt, the analogue methodology can be and often is a powerful and useful methodology. In short, in terms of Kerlinger's MAXMINCON principle, analogue research typically allows for a great deal of experimental control to manipulate one or more independent variables, eliminate or hold extraneous variables constant, and use random assignment. The major question surrounding the analogue methodology for counselors pertains to the external validity of the results; sometimes analogue methodology examines circumstances so far removed from actual counseling practice that the research becomes oversimplified and artificial. We proposed that the external validity of analogue research can be evaluated in part by examining some of the variables that depict real-life counseling, such as (1) the client and his or her presenting problem, (2) the counselor, and (3) the counseling process and setting.

We suggested that analogues fall on a continuum from low to high resemblance to the counseling situation. For example, an analogue with low resemblance to counseling might involve having students from the psychology subject pool view a videotape of a counseling session and rate some aspect of the counselor's behavior. Given the sparsity of empirical research, at this point it is unclear what the relationship is between analogues with varying degrees of resemblance to actual counseling and real-life counseling. Investigations that have examined the comparability of analogue studies and more applied research have produced mixed results (for example, Elliott, 1979; Helms, 1976, 1978; Kushner, 1978). Clearly, more research is needed.

Nonetheless, as Kerlinger (1986) has indicated, the temptation to incorrectly interpret the results of analogue (laboratory) research as they apply to real-life phenomena is great. When an investigator finds highly statistically significant results in the laboratory, it is easy or tempting to assume that these results would also be similar in actual counseling practice. As a general rule, *it is questionable to generalize beyond the conditions or population that was used in the actual study.* Thus, if an investigator is primarily interested in generalizing about clients, counselors, and/or the counseling process, then the analogue methodology needs to be evaluated with those particular conditions or populations in mind. Depending on the degree of resemblance to actual counseling practice, the investigator may be able to conclude that *maybe* the analogue results would apply to actual counseling. Again, as a general rule, *relationships found in a laboratory need to be tested again in the context we wish to generalize to, typically actual counseling.*

The typical student may well be wondering: Does this mean that *all* analogues should closely resemble the conditions of actual counseling practice? We believe not. In our opinion, a considerable amount of information can be obtained about counseling from tightly controlled analogue studies that do not closely resemble actual counseling. This may well be the case early in a line of research where relatively little is known about certain variables. For example, a substantial amount of knowledge has been collected from tightly controlled analogue studies about events that affect clients' perceptions of counselor expertness, attractiveness, and trustworthiness (see reviews by Corrigan et al., 1980; Heppner & Dixon, 1981).

Another typical question is: To what extent should an investigator emphasize external validity and perhaps sacrifice internal validity when examining events in counseling? It depends on the knowledge base that currently exists in a particular line of research. One argument is that if relatively little is empirically known, the researcher should avoid sacrificing internal validity (see Kerlinger, 1986). This reasoning emphasizes the role of internal validity in making scientific advancement. Another argument is that the powerful analogue methodology can be used to refine knowledge obtained from the less internally valid field situations (see Gelso, 1979). In this way, the strength of the analogue (precision and experimental control) can be taken full advantage of, and the results may be more readily interpreted within the existing base of knowledge collected in the field. Both lines of reasoning have merit. It is important to note that both of these arguments pertain to a central theme of this book, namely that the strengths or weaknesses of any particular methodology for a specific research area are related to the existing knowledge base and prior research methods used in that area. In line with Bordin's 1965 recommendation, we suggest that analogue research be combined with empirical investigations conducted in a field setting to create knowledge bases that emphasize both internal and external validity.

CHAPTER 14

PROCESS RESEARCH

Process research provides an analysis of the counseling interaction that involves the counselor(s), client(s), and the evolving relationship. Often process research is defined in relation to outcome research (Wellman, 1967). Outcome research attempts to address efficacy questions (that is, Does counseling work?). Thus, outcome research is characterized by designs that compare a treatment group or several treatment groups to a control group, or compare several treatments groups. Process research, on the other hand, attempts to characterize what changes occur during counseling. Thus, process researchers may attempt to (1) describe the client, counselor, group, family, or interaction, (2) specify changes in the behavior or actions of the client, counselor, group, or family over time, or (3) link one or more of these process variables to client outcome. Process research does not represent a category of research design per se; rather, it is a specific area of focus within counseling research. Moreover, a number of different research designs are often used to conduct process research, such as intensive single-subject, within-subjects, and between-subjects designs.

One overview of process research in counseling was provided by Hill (1982). Most notably in this article, Hill outlined major choice points in designing process research, such as hypothesis development, the research setting, group versus individual designs, selection of variables, and methodological issues (for example, the training of raters). We recommend this article for researchers as they contemplate the activities involved in designing and conducting process research.

The primary purpose of this chapter is to introduce you to a number of specific methodological issues related to measurement within process research. In doing so, we will discuss much of the current process research in counseling, and thus provide an overview of this research area; it will become clear that counseling researchers have made and do make significant contributions in this area. For more content-oriented reviews, see Garfield and Bergin (1986), Gurman and Razin (1977).

By way of introduction to process research, we will initially discuss some of the early process research in counseling. An examination of the first volume of the *Journal of Counseling Psychology* (*JCP*) attests to the early roots of counseling process research. Not only has process research per se been an important theme within counseling research, but also many of the topics and questions studied today have their roots in research published in 1954 with the first volume of *JCP*. The primary purpose of this section is to compare and contrast the focus of the early researchers with current process researchers as well as identify several methodological and conceptual strategies that began in the early counseling research of the 1950s.

The later sections of this chapter focus on methodological strategies and measurement issues in process research, and in particular on the following questions: What to measure? From whose perspective? How much to measure? and How to analyze it? Moreover, to facilitate examination of the measurement decisions, copies of nine different assessment instruments are provided at the end of this chapter, as Exhibits A–I.

EARLY PROCESS RESEARCH IN COUNSELING

Much of what is currently being examined in process research dates back to at least the early 1950s. Present-day research is, however, more sophisticated methodologically and conceptually because of technical advances in both of these areas.

For example, consider three studies published in the first volume of the *Journal of Counseling Psychology*. Dipboye (1954) was interested in examining differences in counselor style among different content areas of discussion. Nine mutually exclusive categories were used to examine counselor style. These included questions about content, questions about feelings, responses to content, responses to feelings, interpretation of content, interpretation of feelings, suggestions about content, suggestions about feelings, and giving information. These categories bear remarkable similarity to the six categories of response modes (questions, advisements, information, reflection, interpretation, and self-disclosure) that Elliott, Hill, Stiles, Friedlander, Mahrer, and Margison (1987) found to underlie a variety of response mode systems. Content categories included test discussion, interpersonal relations, family relations, educational and vocational problems and planning, self-reference, and study skills. Dipboye (1954) found that four of the six counselors that he examined did change their style of interaction when different content areas were being addressed. Unfortunately, he did not examine specifically which styles were related to which content areas.

The second process study published in Volume 1 of *JCP* involved an examination of counselor directiveness, and the third study explored client nonverbal behavior. Danskin and Robinson (1954) examined counselor directiveness by rating the amount of "lead" in a counselor statement. They defined "lead" as (1) "the extent to which the content of the counselor's remark seems to be ahead of the content of the client's last remark," and (2) "the degree of pressure or definiteness in the counselor's remark that is apparently used to bring about client acceptance of the expressed idea" (pp. 65–67).

Danskin and Robinson's major finding was that the amount of counselor lead was related to the type of problem being discussed. They found that the counselor used more leading statements with clients who had a "skills" problem than with clients who had an "adjustment" problem. This focus on counselor lead bears some similarity to Tracey's research, which had examined control in individual counseling (for example, Tracey & Ray, 1984).

A final study by Berg (1954) examined differences between two groups of clients (those whose presenting problems either were or were not sexually related) in nonverbal behavior displayed during counseling interviews. Based on psychoanalytic theory, the following classes of gestures, which were thought to represent sexual symbolism, were tabulated: rotating and sliding, clasping or wrapping, insertion, pressing, and licking and biting. Although the categories of coding nonverbal behavior seem quite different today, there is still a continuity of this line of research (for example, Hill & Stephany, 1990). Berg found, contrary to his hypothesis, that both groups of clients made a relatively high number of the sexually suggestive gestures. Thus, the content or the presenting concern had little relationship to the type or number of nonverbal gestures exhibited.

There are also important differences between these early studies and more recent process research. Two of the most striking differences involve (1) the emphasis on content in the counseling interview and (2) the link between process and outcome. In two of the studies from Volume 1 of *JCP*, the content of the counseling interview was an important defining variable. As we mentioned earlier, Dipboye (1954) categorized segments of counseling interviews as representing one of six content categories. Likewise, Danskin and Robinson (1954) used four categories to classify the content of their counseling interviews. These categories included special (visiting, making plans, and such), adjustment, skill, or test interpretation. This emphasis on content seen in Volume 1 of *JCP* is representative of the focus that content received in much of the early research. This content focus has been almost completely neglected in more recent process research (see reviews by Highlen & Hill, 1984; Hill, 1982; Parloff, Waskow, & Wolfe, 1978).

A second point of discontinuity concerns the process-outcome link. Early counseling research tended to focus either solely on client outcome or counseling process. None of the early studies reviewed attempted to link the process variables with some measure or outcome. For example, Danskin and Robinson (1954) did not know if for skill problems more-leading interviews were more productive than less-leading interviews. More recently, there has been an emphasis on linking process to outcome within the same study (see Highlen & Hill, 1984; Holloway, Wampold, & Nelson, 1990; Orlinsky & Howard, 1978; Wampold & Kim, 1989). For example, Wampold and Kim (1989) related patterns of client interaction to evaluation of sessions made by counselor, client, and observers.

It is also important to note the continuity of two conceptual systems from the early process research to present-day research. Robinson's book *Principles and Procedures in Student Counseling* (1950) had a seminal influence on early process research. In addition to his emphasis on session content, Robinson also devised a system of classifying counseling behavior based on the concept of counselor roles and subroles. This concept served as the basis for designing past and present category systems used to classify counselor actions. The second conceptual system that influenced early process research was Leary's (1957) system of interpersonal diagnosis. Unlike Robinson's ideas, which lead to the classification of counselor behavior in terms of actions or response modes, Leary's system classified counselor behavior in terms of its interpersonal style. Mueller (1969) used the Leary system to study the manifestation of transference and countertransference in counseling interviews. Researchers continue to apply Leary's system to examine client and counselor interpersonal style (for example, Strong, Hills, Kilmartin, De Vries, Lanier, Nelson, Strickland, & Meyer, 1988).

CURRENT METHODOLOGICAL AND MEASUREMENT ISSUES IN PROCESS RESEARCH

In this section we review current methodological strategies and measurement issues in process research. The emphasis is not on providing exhaustive reviews of the multiple measures for defining counseling process or on summarizing the findings from this literature. Rather, we outline major areas for examining counseling process and discuss methodological and measurement issues in these various areas. This review will be structured around four questions process researchers must address in designing a study of counseling process: What to measure? From whose perspective? How much to measure? and How to analyze these data?

What to Measure?

Assuming that a general research topic has been identified, one of the first methodological issues that a process researcher must address is what aspect of the counseling process he or she wants to examine. At the most basic level, the researcher must decide if he or she wants to examine aspects of the individual participant's behaviors or aspects of the developing relationship or system. Typically, process research focuses on either the participants (counselor, client) or the relationship, or some combination thereof. In group or family counseling, the clients are obviously multiple individuals. Oftentimes in group and family counseling, the counselor dimension also can involve a measurement of the activities of co-counselors. In individual counseling, the relationship involves the measurement of how the client and counselor work together. In group and family process research, this relationship dimension is usually referred to as the group (cohesion, norms) or family (closeness, involvement) process. We will discuss issues pertaining to what to measure specifically with regard to individual participants and the relationship.

The process researcher also must consider two other dimensions in designing his or her study. The first dimension pertains to the particular focus of the process investigation. Elliott et al. (1987) contended that counseling process can be divided into four aspects or focal points: content (what is said), action (what is done), style (how it is said or done), and quality (how well it is said or done). Hill, Helms, Spiegel, and Tichenor (1988) add two other aspects to this list: intention (why it is said or done), and reaction (the internal effect of what is said or done).

Process researchers also must decide at what level they are going to measure these aspects of process. This is an important decision because, as Greenberg (1986) indicated, the lack of standard units or levels of analysis makes it difficult to compare findings across studies. He suggested that three levels of analysis be used in examining counseling process: speech acts, episodes, and the relationship. In counseling process research, *speech acts* refers to the microanalysis of statement-by-statement transactions, *episode* refers to a coherent thematic section of counseling, and *relationship* refers to the ongoing or continuous relationship over multiple sessions. In reality, there are few if any process measures that specifically address the episode level. The measurement of counseling process therefore occurs at either a microscopic (statement-by-statement) or global (more general) level.

To provide some structure and organization for our discussion of measurement issues, we propose the categorization scheme represented in Table 14-1. We arrived at this table by combining the six aspects of the counseling process and the two levels of analysis. The various instruments listed in the table are intended to be representative of measures within each of the cells.

Content—Micro Level

Content refers to the topic or subject of counseling. The Hill Interaction Matrix (HIM; Hill, 1965), which is used in group process research, is an example of a micro-level rating system that focuses on the content of the interaction. The HIM is a statement-by-statement rating system that can be used to rate statements made by either group clients or therapists. The HIM consists of 16 cells formed by combining the dimensions of content (four types) and work style (four types). The content categories in the HIM system are topic, group, personal, and relationship; and the work-style categories are conventional, assentive, speculative, and confrontive. The HIM is used by an outside observer who reviews a transcript and places each client or counselor statement into one of the 16 HIM categories. As an example, a researcher could identify how often a group counselor used statements in each of the 16 cells and compare this counselor rate of use to group members' use of the categories. Research has suggested that the rate of therapist sponsoring is related to the rate of member participation in the different HIM cells (for example, Hill, 1965). Hill therefore concluded that the content (and the style) of the counselor's speech is related to (influences) the content (and style) of the client's speech.

TABLE 14-1
Instruments Representative of Counseling Process Measures, Defined by
Aspect Examined and Level of Measurement

	Level of measurement	
Aspect	Microscopic	Global
Content	Hill Interaction Matrix (Hill, 1965)	Discussion Units (Dipboye, 1954)
Action	Hill Counselor Verbal Response Modes (Hill, 1985)	Supervision Questionnaire (Worthington & Roehlke, 1979)
Style	Interpersonal Communication Rating Scale (Strong et al., 1988)	Checklist of Interpersonal Transactions (Kiesler, 1984)
Intention	Intentions List (Hill & O'Grady, 1985)	Brief Structured Recall (Elliott & Shapiro, 1988)
Quality	Client Experiencing Scales (Klein, Mathieu-Coughlan, & Kiesler, 1986)	Therapist Strategy Rating Form (O'Malley, Foley, Rounsaville, Watkins, Sotsky, Imber, & Elkin, 1988)
Reaction	Client Reactions System (Hill, Helms, Spiegel, & Tichenor, 1988)	Session Evaluation Questionnaire (Stiles & Snow, 1984)

Content—Global Level

Hill's (1965) research suggests that the content of the counselor's response may be a useful focus to examine within the counseling process. The content areas examined, however, have been fairly narrow. Clearly, research in counseling process would be enhanced by the development of a more sophisticated category system to classify the content of the counselor's and client's responses. Moreover, there are few measures that focus on the global level of counselor and client content.

At this global level, several early process studies examined the content of discussion units. Dipboye (1954) defined a discussion unit as the portion of an interview that is devoted to an obvious and clearly recognizable topic of discussion. He defined the following six units of relationship content: (1) test discussion and interpretation, (2) interpersonal relations, (3) family relations, (4) educational and vocational problems and planning, (5) self-reference, and (6) study habits and skills. Dipboye found that the counselors he studied tended to vary their styles (actions) as a function of the topical unit of discussion.

This finding was extended in a recent study by Cummings (1989). She classified problem type or the content of the counseling interaction as either interpersonal or intrapersonal. Like Dipboye (1954), she found that counselors varied their behavior as a function of problem type. Specifically, counselors used more information responses with intrapersonal problems and more reflection responses with interpersonal problems.

The research by Dipboye and Cummings suggests that the content of the material focused on in the relationship affects the counseling process. Relatively few studies, however, focus on this content dimension. This lack of attention to content is quite surprising given that most theories of counseling and therapy specifically advocate the focus on specific content areas, and counselor training focuses a great deal on content.

One major problem is the lack of an agreed-upon classification system for categorizing content material. Dipboye's system of classifying content seems biased toward a counselor's definition of "appropriate" content areas, and thus may be limited. The intrapersonal-interpersonal categorization used by Cummings seems useful but perhaps too simple; future research might explore the utility of developing finer categories rather than the two global categories. For example, Cumming's differentiation between interpersonal and intrapersonal content might be a beginning point for developing a taxonomy. A third major category of impersonal content (weather) could be added. Each of these three main categories could be divided into subcategories. As an example, Horowitz, Rosenberg, Baer, Ureño, and Villaseñor (1988) identified six types of interpersonal problems: hard to be assertive, hard to be sociable, hard to be submissive, hard to be intimate, too responsible, and too controlling. The categories of intrapersonal and nonpersonal content could be subdivided in a similar manner. Another reason for exploring such a differentiated system is that there is strong support in the coping, problem-solving literature that different problem types lead to different problem-solving activities (see Heppner & Krauskopf, 1987, for a review). In short, additional research is needed to further examine the utility of content in the counseling relationship, as well as explore the utility of various classification systems.

Action—Micro Level

Action refers to how the speaking in counseling is done. Some studies have examined linguistic structure (Meara, Shannon, & Pepinsky, 1979; Meara & Patton, 1986); however, most of the studies that examine this action level of counselor or client behavior have relied on measures of response modes. *Response mode* refers to the grammatical structure of the response (for example, closed question, open question, interpretation). Elliott et al. (1987) suggested that 20 to 30 systems for identifying counselor response modes had been developed; the breadth and quality of these systems vary greatly. Accordingly, the researcher wanting to measure this level of counselor action is presented with a plethora of choices but little systematic help in choosing a particular response mode system for his or her study. Elliott et al. (1987) addressed this problem by comparing six of the more widely used response-mode rating systems.

These authors found that a fundamental set of response-mode categories underlay the six systems they examined. These response modes include questions, advisements, information, responses, reflections, interpretations, and self-disclosures. In addition, three other response modes (reassurances, confrontations, acknowledgments) were reliably represented by most of the six systems examined. Unfortunately, Elliott et al. concluded that there was not one best system for rating response modes. Rather, they suggested that researchers examining response modes should use systems that contain results in terms of the six (and probably the three additional) primary response modes. The use of these six to nine categories would promote comparability across studies.

One of the strengths of response-mode systems is conceptual clarity. In addition, most of the systems are atheoretical, which enables them to be used across a variety of treatment modalities. In addition, response-mode systems can reliably differentiate among various therapeutic approaches. Research linking therapist response modes to immediate or long-term outcome, however, has shown only a weak relationship between response-mode use and outcome (Elliott et al., 1987; Hill, Helms, Tichenor, Spiegel, O'Grady, & Perry, 1988). These results suggest that other variables may be more important in accounting for counseling outcomes, and that perhaps the frequency of response mode use in and of itself does not measure a critical ingredient of the change process. After all, the frequency of certain counselor responses tells us little about the myriad of possible client reactions. Given these findings, we recommend that future process researchers not examine response modes in isolation. More useful research could involve examining the interaction between response-mode use and the other aspects (content, style, intention, and quality) of counselor behavior.

An example of this type of research is the study by Hill, et al. (1988). The purpose of their study was to examine the effects of therapist response modes on immediate outcome (client helpfulness ratings, changes in level of client experiencing, client reactions), session outcome (client and therapist ratings of session depth and smoothness), and treatment outcome (changes in anxiety, depression, and self-concept). While certain response modes were significantly correlated with measures of session and treatment outcome, these response modes only accounted for 1% of the variance in immediate outcome. This small relationship between response modes and immediate outcome became more tenuous when other process variables were added to the analysis. In fact, counselor intentions (discussed later) were better predictors of immediate outcome than were response modes. Only when counselor response modes were combined with counselor intentions was an appreciable amount of variance in immediate outcome accounted for in this analysis. The results of this study underscore the need to examine the interaction between therapist response modes and other aspects of counselor behavior in counseling process research.

Unlike the action level of counselor behavior, the action level of client behavior has received little research attention. Thus, fewer systems have been developed to measure client response modes. Client verbal behavior, like that of the counselor, can be categorized in terms of its grammatical structure. This type of category system would result in a measure of client response modes. One such system has been developed by Hill, Greenwald, Reed, Charles, O'Farrell, and Carter (1981). Using this system, client verbal behavior can be classified as simple responses, requests, descriptions, experiencing, insight, discussion of plans, discussion of client-counselor relationship, silence, and other. One problem with this system is that action (that is, requests) is confused or confounded with content (that is, discussion of plans).

We suspect that the area of client action deserves more research attention. Not only are few ways available for comparing or contrasting different approaches to defining client responses, but also few studies have examined the relationship between client response modes and other aspects of client or counselor behavior.

Action—Global Level

The action dimension also has been examined at a more global level. This is particularly true of the literature examining the supervisory process. Almost all of the studies of counselor supervision (with the exception of those done by Holloway and her colleagues—for example, Holloway, Freund, Gardner, Nelson, & Walker, 1989) have relied on supervisor or supervisee ratings of supervision behavior. In this type of research, supervisors and/or supervisees are presented with a list of items describing supervisor behaviors and asked to indicate the frequency with which the behaviors occurred in the supervision session or during the course of supervision.

An example of this type of research is provided by Krause and Allen (1988). Krause and Allen were interested in examining Stoltenberg's (1981) developmental model, which predicted that supervisors would use different behaviors with trainees at different developmental levels. These authors gave a list of 37 items describing supervisor behavior to 87 supervisors and 77 supervisees. The responses of the supervisees and supervisors were factor analyzed separately. Eight factors accounted for the variance in supervisors' ratings. Krause and Allen labeled these factors: teacher, counselor respectful sharing, satisfied colleague, dynamic counselor, perceived impact, laissez-faire, and preparation. A factor analysis of the same items from the supervisees' perspective yielded five factors: supervisor as mentor, supervisor as counselor, directive supervision, supervisor as dynamic counselor, and process supervision.

Krause and Allen used these factors to examine the hypothesis that supervisors would vary their behaviors with supervisees. Using the eight supervisor-derived factors to examine this hypothesis, supervisors rated three of these factors differently depending on the supervisees' training levels. Specifically, structuring and directing behaviors decreased and collegial and consulting relationships increased as supervisees advanced in development. An identical analysis using the five supervisee-derived clusters yielded no differences in supervisee ratings between supervisor behaviors for supervisees at different developmental levels. In sum, the supervisors saw themselves as varying their behaviors with supervisees of different developmental levels but the supervisees did not.

Did the supervisors actually vary their behaviors with the supervisees at different levels? Unfortunately, we cannot provide a complete answer to this question. One reason that this question cannot be answered involves the measures used to examine supervisor actions. Without the benefit of an outside perspective, it is impossible to determine the reliability of either the supervisors' or supervisees' account of the supervisors' behavior.

Style—Global Level

The style of the counselor and the client has been the most widely studied aspect of counseling process. *Style* refers to the verbal manner of the counselor or client, *how* he or she says or does things. Much of the early process literature involved measurement of the necessary and sufficient conditions described by Rogers (1955). The single most widely addressed area has been the assessment of counselor empathy (see review by Parloff, Waskow, & Wolfe, 1978). Usually this assessment has involved trained raters listening to or reading transcripts of segments of counseling sessions and rating the empathy of each counselor response. While having been a focus of much early research, the examination of counselor empathy (at the speech act) has now slowed to a virtual standstill. The exception is research on empathy at the global level.

The Barrett-Lennard Relationship Inventory (Barrett-Lennard, 1962) was designed to measure client perceptions of counselor-offered conditions (style). Generally, clients fill out this inventory after interacting with the counselor over a number of sessions. One of the interesting aspects of the research that has examined counselor empathy is the divergence of findings on the connection between counselor empathy and counseling outcome (see Parloff et al., 1978). Research at the micro or speech act level has generally shown no relationship between counselor-offered empathy and client outcome (Gurman, 1977). At the global level, however, research suggests that there is a moderate relationship between client ratings of counselor empathy and client outcome. These findings suggest that these global ratings of counselor behavior are important to assess. In short, empathy at the global level is an important dimension of counselor behavior. Other aspects of counselor style that can be usefully assessed at this relationship level are unclear at this time.

Another widely used global measure of counselor style has been the Counselor Rating Form (Barak & LaCrosse, 1975). Strong (1968) initially hypothesized that a counselor's power or ability to influence a client (for example, to change an opinion) was related to source characteristics of the counselor—namely, perceived counselor expertness, attractiveness, and trustworthiness. These constructs were operationalized in the Counselor Rating Form as counselor attractiveness, expertness, and trustworthiness. Like the Barrett-Lennard Relationship Inventory, this rating is usually made on a session-to-session basis (although not always).

Scores from the Counselor Rating Form have been used as both dependent (or criterion) and independent (or predictor) variables in research using the social influence paradigm (see reviews by Corrigan, Dell, Lewis, & Schmidt, 1980; Heppner & Claiborn, 1989; Heppner & Dixon, 1981). In short, a large body of research has examined the influence of various independent variables (diplomas, communication style) on client ratings of attractiveness, expertness, and trustworthiness. Another group of studies has examined the relationship of client-rated attractiveness, expertness, and trustworthiness to client outcome.

The client's interpersonal style also has been measured at the global level. At this level, the work of Leary (1957) on interpersonal diagnosis has served as a foundation for most of the examination of client style of interacting. Recently, Elliott and James (1989) reviewed the literature on the client's experience in psychotherapy and proposed three dimensions to account for their findings. These dimensions were positive versus negative affiliation, control versus independence, and interpersonal versus task focus. Two instruments developed by Kiesler (1984, 1987) use the control and affiliation dimension to describe client or counselor interpersonal style. The Impact Message Inventory (IMI; Kiesler, 1987) assesses client style by recording the engagements or pulls that a client has on another interactant or observer (that is, what the person feels, thinks, or wants to do as he or she interacts or observes this client). The Check List of Psychotherapy Transactions (CLOPT) and the Check List of Interpersonal Transactions (CLOIT) define the client's style by describing overt interpersonal actions. The IMI, CLOPT, and CLOIT can characterize clients in terms of 16 interpersonal scores: dominant, competitive, mistrusting, cold, hostile, detached, inhibited, unassured, submissive, deferent, trusting, warm, friendly, sociable, exhibitionistic, and assured. These interpersonal scores can be combined to form octant, quadrant, or axes descriptions of client interpersonal style. We believe research in this area is promising. For example, a positive association between client openness and therapeutic outcome has been noted by Orlinsky and Howard (1986). However, it seems that it may be fruitful to develop more standardized ways of assessing openness.

Style—Micro Level

Counselor and client style also has been assessed at the level of the speech act. This analysis has usually employed some variant of the Leary (1957) system to classify counselor speech along the dimensions of control and affiliation (for example, Penman, 1980). A recent version of this system was developed by Strong et al. (1988). They used the dimensions of control and affiliation to define eight types or styles of counselor or client communication: leading, self-enhancing, critical, distrustful, self-effacing, docile, cooperative, and nurturant.

Compared to the global level, there has been far less research examining counselor style at the level of speech acts. One recent study examined differences in counselor style with successfully versus unsuccessfully treated clients. These authors (Henry, Schacht, & Strupp, 1986) classified counselor speech acts using Benjamin's (1974) system, which like the Strong et al. (1988) system is based on Leary's dimensions of control and affiliation. They found significant differences in counselor style between the successful and unsuccessful cases. Specifically, counselors were less likely to reciprocate client hostility in successful cases.

In short, the vast majority of the research effort with regard to style has focused on the global levels. We suspect that it may be fruitful for more research to address counselor style at the speech act level. It may be especially helpful in this area to have research that examines the relations between counselor style at the speech act level and more global ratings of style.

Intention—Micro Level

Counselor and client intentions are a relatively new and unexplored area of examination in process research. At present, all of the research has examined intentions at the speech act level, and most of the work has focused on counselor as opposed to client intentions. Hill and O'Grady (1985) define a counselor intention as the covert rationale for or the why of counselor behavior. These authors have developed a list of 19 pantheoretical, nominal, nonmutually exclusive intentions: set limits, get information, give information, support, focus, clarify, hope, cathart, cognitions, behaviors, self-control, feelings, insight, chance, reinforce change, resistance, challenge, relationship, and therapist needs. Since intentions are covert, they are only available through counselor introspective reports. To obtain these introspective reports, researchers have counselors review a videotape or audiotape of a recently completed session (Hill and O'Grady recommend that this review take place within 24 hours). For each counselor turn, the counselor lists up to five intentions that described their goals for that intervention.

This intention measure has now been used in several studies examining different aspects of counseling process (for example, Fuller & Hill, 1985; Kivlighan, 1989; Kivlighan & Angelone, 1991). For instance, Hill and O'Grady (1985) found that counselor theoretical orientation was related to differential intention use, and that intention use changed both within and across sessions. More important, Hill, Helms, Tichenor, Spiegel, O'Grady, and Perry (1988) found that counselor intentions were more adequate descriptors of counselor behavior than were response modes. Specifically, intentions either alone or in conjunction with response modes (counselor actions) accounted for significantly more of the variance in immediate outcome ratings than did response mode measures. This finding supports the continued use of intention measures for examining counselor behavior.

There is controversy concerning the measurement of counseling intentions. Hill and her colleagues in their studies have simply asked counselors to record their intentions while reviewing taped sessions. Sometimes this has involved little or no training in using the intentions measure. This method of collecting intentions makes it virtually impossible to obtain estimates of reliability. Martin, Martin, and Slemon (1989) have contended that counselors often use different intention categories to describe nominally identical reasons for behaving. These authors have consequently modified Hill and O'Grady's (1985) procedure for collecting intentions. Martin et al. (1989) asked counselors to review each videotape and for each in turn to describe their intentions or reasons for the intervention. These descriptions were then transcribed and submitted to judges for rating. The judges then placed the descriptions into the categories in the Hill and O'Grady (1985) intentions list. One advantage of this procedure is that the reliability of category placement can be assessed by examining agreement across judges.

Given the concerns of Martin et al. (1989) about counselors using the intentions list in an idiosyncratic manner, we recommend one of two procedures for researchers examining counselor intentions. First, researchers could use a procedure where counselors verbally (Martin et al., 1989) or in writing (Kivlighan, 1990) describe their intentions, and then raters decide on category placement. Second, researchers could develop more extensive training procedures designed to insure that counselors have a common understanding of the intentions list. For example, a researcher could develop a list of counselor-stated reasons for intervening and have potential research participants practice placing these reasons into intention categories until an acceptable level of agreement is reached.

Intention—Global Level

On the global level, there are no measures currently available that operationalize counselor intentions. This is somewhat surprising given the emphasis that these levels receive in counselor training and supervision. One of the most common questions addressed to supervisees involves what he or she was trying to accomplish in a given session or what his or her overall treatment plan involves. Development of this type of measure might be useful in future research and in conceptualizing the counseling process.

Clients also have intentions. In their analysis of the literature, Elliott and James (1989) found eight common themes across the studies that examined client intentions. These eight themes were understanding self and problems, avoiding, getting a personal response from the counselor, feeling relieved or better, changing behavior, getting counselor support, expressing feelings, and following therapeutic directives or procedures. Elliott and Shapiro's (1988) Brief Structured Recall method was designed as a global measure of client intentions. The client completes a structured assessment that identifies his or her intentions during a significant event episode. The intentions include the eight categories described in Elliott and James (1989). Elliott and his colleagues (for example, Elliott, James, Reimschuessel, Cislo, & Sack, 1985) have used free recall to study client intentions at a micro level, but these have not been systematized into a more replicable format. Investigating client intentions is a promising area for future research.

Reactions—Micro Level

Reaction is the internal, subjective response of the client or the counselor to the other's speech act or person. While counseling process research on the client's and counselor's subjective responses to the session has had a long history (for example, Orlinsky & Howard, 1978), examination of the client's or counselor's response to particular speech acts has occurred only recently.

Hill, Helms, Spiegel, and Tichenor (1988) recently developed a system for categorizing client reactions to counselor interventions. This system contains

21 categories of reactions, grouped into 14 positive reactions (understood, supported, hopeful, relief, negative thoughts or behaviors, better self-understanding, clear, feelings, responsibility, unstuck, new perspective, educated, new ways to behave, challenged) and 7 negative reactions (scared, worse, stuck, lack of direction, confused, misunderstood, no reaction).

Clients review a videotape of their counseling session, stopping the tape after each therapist response. The clients then use the Client Reactions List (a list of all 21 reactions) to record their recollected experience. The Client Reactions System has operationalized an important area of counseling process. While most counseling theories advocate attempting to alter both the external behavior of the client and his or her internal processing, until the development of the Client Reactions System there was no way of documenting moment-to-moment changes in the client's internal processes. The other strength of this system is its ability to differentiate among categories of reactions. This enables the researcher to examine specific effects of counselor interventions (for example, what type of counselor intervention precedes client reactions of relief compared to better self-understanding).

The main concern with this rating system pertains to questions of reliability and validity. Previously we mentioned that Martin et al. (1989) reported that counselors seemed to use the Intentions List in an idiosyncratic manner. In other words, they would record different intentions for nominally similar statements of intent. It is likely that the same problem exists with the Client Reactions System. Researchers may want to consider collecting client reactions in a manner similar to that used by Martin et al. (1989) to collect intentions. This would involve having the client review a tape of a session and describe either verbally or in writing his or her response to each counselor intervention. These descriptions could then be given to judges who could categorize the reactions using the Hill, Helms, Spiegel, and Tichenor (1988) rating system. The researcher would then be able to examine the reliability of the categorizations. Moreover, in terms of validity, it is presently unknown to what extent client reactions are influenced by, for instance, self- or other-deception.

Although counselors certainly have reactions to what their clients do, there have been few systematic investigations of this important area. Most researchers seem to view counseling as a one-way interaction, with the counselor influencing the client and the client passively accepting this influence. Heppner and Claiborn (1989) maintained that the client needs to be conceptualized as an active participant in the counseling process who also exerts influence on the counselor. From this perspective, counselors would be expected to have reactions to their clients' influence attempts. Unfortunately, the development of statement-by-statement or micro-level measures of counselor reactions has not kept pace with the theoretical formulations.

Reaction—Global Level

At the global level, one of the most widely used measures of client reactions is the Session Evaluation Questionnaire (SEQ; Stiles & Snow, 1984). The SEQ consists of four scales. The Depth and Smoothness scales measure the client's reactions to characteristics of the session. (These scales are discussed in more detail later when we address process measures of the relationship.) The Positivity and Arousal scales measure postsession mood. Positivity, as the name implies, is a measure of how positive or negative the client feels upon completing the session. The Arousal scale is a measure of how much emotional arousal the client feels after completing the session. These SEQ scales have been used to measure consequences (that is, the relationship between therapist response modes and client postsession mood) and antecedents (that is, the relationship between postsession mood and counseling outcome).

At a global level, counselor reactions have been measured with instruments parallel to those used to measure global client reactions. For instance, the Session Evaluation Questionnaire has been used to record the counselor's reactions at a session-by-session level.

Quality—Micro Level

Quality refers to how well or how completely the counselor carries out a single or a series of interventions, or how well the client enacts his or her role or tasks. Clinically, counselor competence is extremely important, but until recently it has been virtually ignored in the process research. For example, dynamically oriented counselors speak of the timing and correctness of an interpretation. Most research on interpretation, however, has simply examined the presence or amount of interpretation (see the review by Claiborn, 1982).

At the speech act level, one of the most commonly used measures of the quality of the counselor's intervention is the Helpfulness Scale (Elliott, 1985). To use this measure, clients review a recently completed counseling session and rate each of his or her counselor's interventions on a nine-point scale indicating how helpful he or she found each intervention. This method assumes that the client is in fact the best arbitrator of the usefulness of counseling. At present it is unknown whether such a rating of the helpfulness of specific counselor interventions is related to client outcome. For example, when a client rates therapist interventions as more helpful, will he or she have a better outcome than a client who rates his or her therapist's interventions as less helpful?

A second method for examining quality of counselor interventions at the speech act level has been described by Silberschatz, Fretter, and Curtis (1986). These authors maintained that assessing the quality of counselor behaviors involves two processes: (1) identifying the client's problems and needs, and (2) deciding if a given intervention correctly addresses these problems and needs. Specifically, Silberschatz et al. wanted to assess the quality of therapist interpretations. They used two steps in determining the quality of the therapist's interpretation. The first step involved formulating a plan or conceptualization for each client. A prominent part of this plan involved identifying insights that would be helpful to the client. Using assessment instruments and transcripts from an assessment interview, five clinicians independently prepared a plan for each client. The second step involved having a second group of judges rate the extent to which each counselor interpretation fit the plan that had been developed. These judges used a seven-point Likert scale ranging from -3 (strongly antiplan) to $+3$ (strongly proplan) to measure the extent of agreement between the plan and the individual interpretation. Silberschatz et al. found that the compatibility of an interpretation with a plan was a better predictor of immediate outcome (change in client experience) than was type of interpretation (transference versus nontransference).

Silberschatz et al. suggested that their methods or procedures for assessing quality of counselor interventions were transferable to a variety of conceptual frameworks. We agree with this suggestion. To reiterate, this method of assessing quality involves two steps. First, an independent and reliable conceptualization of the client, including a specification of his or her particular learning needs, is needed. Second, an independent and reliable rating of the extent to which particular interventions fit the conceptualization is needed.

Similar to assessing the quality of therapist interventions, there are relatively few agreed-upon measures of client response quality. One obstacle to the development of standardized quality measures is that various theories define the client role differently, and hence the appropriateness or quality of various client responses is viewed in divergent manners. For example, a behavior therapist might construe a client response of questioning or disagreeing with the therapist as a sign of resistance to implementing a treatment protocol, and assign it a low quality rating. A dynamic therapist, on the other hand, may construe the same response as a sign of autonomy, and assign it a high quality rating. Despite these theoretical differences, there is a surprising consistency of use of two particular speech act ratings of client response quality, which we will now discuss.

The most widely used rating of client response quality is the Client Experiencing Scale (Klein, Mathieu-Coughlan, & Kiesler, 1986). The Client Experiencing Scale is a seven-point scale used by trained raters to describe a client's level of involvement. Low levels are characterized by client disclosures that are impersonal or superficial. At high levels of experiencing, feelings and exploration are a basis for problem resolution and/or self-understanding. Klein et al. reported high interrater reliability and validity as evidenced by the relationships between client experiencing and self-exploration, insight, working through, the absence of resistances, and high-quality free association.

The second measure that has been used to operationalize the quality of client responding at the speech act level is the Client Vocal Quality Scale (CVQ; Rice, Koke, Greenberg, & Wagstaff, 1979). Like the Client Experiencing Scale, the CVQ is designed to measure the quality of the client's involvement in the counseling process. Vocal quality is a measure of how the energy of a speech act is expressed. According to this system, voice quality can be characterized as limited, externalizing, emotional, or focused (from low to high voice quality). *Externalizing* vocal quality involves an external or outward movement of energy, designed to produce an effect in a listener. In *limited* vocal quality, there is a lack of energy; the voice has a thinness that seems to suggest a withdrawal of energy. *Emotional* vocal quality contains an overflow of energy, while *focused* vocal quality involves energy that is concentrated and directed inward. Like the Experiencing Scale, the CVQ has good reliability and validity data (Rice et al., 1979).

It is noteworthy that the two most widely used measures of client response quality (at the speech act level) were developed by researchers operating within a client-centered perspective. The client-centered perspective more than any other theoretical formulation places a premium on the client's involvement in the counseling process. Thus, it is probably not surprising that client-centered researchers have concentrated on developing measures of client process. What is surprising is how widely these client response quality measures have been adopted by researchers from other theoretical perspectives. For example, Silberschatz et al. (1986) used the Experiencing Scale to examine the quality of analytic interpretations.

As pointed out earlier, it seems likely that other theoretical perspectives would define client response quality in terms other than quality of client involvement. It may be important to develop process measures that offer complementary views of what constitutes client response quality. A recent example of an alternative perspective for defining client response quality was reported by Martin and Stelmaczonek (1988). These researchers used categories of discourse analysis that were drawn from a theoretical framework of information processing to define the quality of a client's response. Specifically, they rated client speech acts on the following information-processing dimensions: (1) deep-shallow, (2) elaborative-nonelaborative, (3) personal-impersonal, (4) clear-vague, and (5) conclusion oriented-description oriented. Martin and Stelmaczonek found that events that clients recalled as being important when compared to events not recalled were characterized by client speech acts that involved (1) interpretive, critical, and analytic thinking (deep); (2) thinking that involved unique language, images, or metaphors (elaborative); or (3) interpretations or hypotheses (conclusion-oriented). It would be especially interesting to see how these measures of client response quality, derived from information-processing theory, would relate to the more established measures (experiencing and voice quality) derived from client-centered theory. Moreover, other measures of client response quality are clearly needed.

Quality—Global Level

There also has been recent work measuring counselor quality at a global level. O'Malley, Foley, Rounsaville, Watkins, Sotsky, Imber, & Elkin (1988) examined whether counselor competence in conducting interpersonal therapy was related to client outcome. Counselor competence was assessed by both self- and supervisor ratings. Supervisors used two measures to rate counselor competence. The Therapist Strategy Rating Form was designed to evaluate the problem the client presented, the strategies the counselor used to address the specific problem, and the counselor's competence in implementing the strategies. Similarly, the Process Rating Form identified specific techniques (for example, decision analysis, exploration) used in interpersonal therapy. The supervisor determined if a technique was used and then made a rating of the quality of use. Counselor self-ratings of effectiveness were made on a single seven-point scale (not at all effective or detrimental to maximally effective) administered at the completion of the therapy session.

The results of this study confirmed the authors' hypothesis that counselor competence was related to client outcome. For our purposes the most important aspect of the O'Malley et al. (1988) study is the procedures used to operationalize the global level of therapist competence. To do this, the researcher first has to carefully and specifically define the parameters of the treatment. Once the treatment has been specified, then the therapist's behaviors within a session can be rated (by self, supervisor, or observers) on the extent to which they match or represent those specified behaviors. Future researchers may want to use technique-specific scales to obtain therapist self-ratings rather than rely on the rather global self-ratings used by O'Malley et al. (1988).

The assessment of counselor quality is an exciting and virtually untapped area for process researchers. The methods and procedures developed by Silberschatz et al. (1986) and O'Malley et al. (1988) to assess counselor quality can serve as models for researchers wanting to measure the quality of counselor behavior from other theoretical perspectives.

The examination of client response quality at the global level has received even more limited attention. At the global level, one of the most promising dimensions for characterizing client response quality can be formulated in terms of openness versus defensiveness. Orlinsky and Howard (1986) reported that in 88% of the studies examining client openness, there was a positive relationship between this variable and outcome measures. There is, however, little agreement on how this construct at a global level should be measured. Seldom, across the 16 studies that examined client openness, has the same process measure been used to assess this construct. Nor is it known how the different measures that assess client openness relate to one another. Given the positive association between client openness and therapeutic outcome noted by Orlinsky and Howard (1986), it seems important that more standardized ways of assessing this construct at a global level be developed.

Recommendations

Hill (1982) observed that counselor process variables have attracted more theoretical and empirical attention than client process variables. She speculated this was because we as counselors/researchers are more drawn to examining what we do. This difference can be clearly seen by examining the differential attention focused on counselor and client response modes. While 20 to 30 systems have been developed to classify therapist response modes, fewer than 5 systems exist for classifying client response modes. In addition, research has compared several different therapist response mode systems and has identified common elements across these systems. This is not true for client systems. This relative lack of attention to client process is evident both in terms of the types of measures and in the levels of analysis.

We believe this relative lack of attention to client process variables is a critical omission that hampers our understanding of the counseling process. Moreover, we strongly recommend that the client be conceptualized not as a passive agent to whom interventions are administered, but rather as an *active processor* of information in the change process (see Heppner & Claiborn, 1989; Heppner & Krauskopf, 1987; Martin, 1984, 1987; McGuire, 1985; Petty & Cacioppo, 1986). The Martin and Stelmaczonek (1988) investigation is an excellent example of conceptualizing the client as an active processor of information. Since human reasoning is a key activity in how people cope with their problems, a focus on the active process of human reasoning deserves a central place in counseling process research.

Such a perspective might best be examined in both the content and quality aspects of process research. For example, with regard to content, it may be useful to examine how clients represent their presenting problems to themselves (for example, via schemas), and if there are changes in how the client views the problem over time in counseling. Are there changes in the client's knowledge about the problem over time, or in the way the client's knowledge is organized (see Martin, 1985, for an excellent case illustration)? It also may be important to investigate how clients deal with their affective reactions and how they appraise the significance of their problems. In short, we believe it may be very fruitful to examine the internal processes that clients engage in (cognitive, affective, and physiological) as they cope and struggle with their problems before, during, and after counseling. Whereas client satisfaction or perceptions of client expertness provide some information about the client, these variables tell us little about how the client is processing information directly about the most pressing concerns that brought him or her into counseling (Heppner & Claiborn, 1989; Heppner & Frazier, in press).

Relationship Process Measures

The relationship in counseling is more than the sum of the interactants. Just measuring what the client and counselor or the group members do individually does not constitute a measure of this relationship. Process measures also focus on the developing relationship between and among clients and counselors.

The quality of the relationship has recently received a great deal of theoretical and empirical attention. Specifically, in individual counseling the quality of the relationship is usually examined in terms of the therapeutic or working alliance (for example, Horvath & Greenberg, 1989). In group research this quality dimension is usually examined in terms of cohesion (see review by Bednar & Kaul, 1978).

Frank (1974), in summarizing 25 years of research, concluded that "the quality of the therapeutic interaction, to which the patient, therapist, and therapeutic method contribute, is probably the major determinant of short-term therapeutic response" (p. 388). The quality of therapeutic interaction is the focus of the various measures of the therapeutic or working alliance. There are four commonly used measures of the working alliance. Three of these were designed for use by trained observers. These three are the California Psychotherapy Alliance Scales (CALPAS; Marmar, Marziali, Horowitz, & Weiss, 1986), the Penn Helping Alliance Rating Scale (Penn; Morgan, Luborsky, Crits-Christoph, Curtis, & Solomon, 1982), and the Vanderbilt Therapeutic Alliance Scale (VTAS; Hartley & Strupp, 1983). The Working Alliance Inventory (WAI; Horvath & Greenberg, 1989) was designed to capture client and therapist perceptions of the working alliance. It is important to note that all of these measures have been designed to measure the working alliance at a global level.

A recent study by Tichenor and Hill (1989) compared these various measures of the working alliance. These authors also devised an observer form of the WAI (adopted by altering the pronouns to fit an observer perspective). All of the working alliance measures had high internal consistency; coefficient alphas ranged from .90 for the CALPAS to .98 for the WAI-observer form. In addition, the four observer rating forms had high interrater reliability; interclass correlations ranged from .71 for the Penn to .94 for the CALPAS. Three of the four observer measures (CALPAS, VTAS, WAI-observer form) also had high intercorrelations, indicating that they were measuring a single working alliance construct. (The Penn was only significantly correlated with the WAI-observer form.) These findings suggest common elements of working alliance across the four observer measures of the working alliance. In addition, the WAI-observer form was the most economical measure because it did not require any rater training. If the results of the Tichenor and Hill study are replicated, there would be strong support for using the WAI-observer form to operationalize the working alliance.

Tichenor and Hill (1989) also found that there was a lack of relationship between observer, client, and counselor perspectives on working alliance ratings. Thus, it is unclear what the measurements of the working alliance from the different perspectives actually assess; further research is needed to address the lack of agreement across the working alliance perspectives.

Another major issue in assessing the quality of the relationship is the lack of micro-level speech act measures of the working alliance. Bordin's (1979) conceptualizations of the working alliance emphasized the "tear and repair" process. This tear-and-repair process is best conceptualized as occurring at the speech act level. It may be useful to develop speech act measures of the working alliance so an examination of client and therapist behaviors that lead to tearing and repairing the alliance can be examined.

Fuhriman and Burlingame (1990) described cohesion in groups as analogous to the relationship in individual counseling. Kaul and Bednar (1986) declared that the term *cohesion* has such an endemic use in group treatment that descriptions of what happens in "groups would be practically impossible without reference to cohesion". Despite its clinical utility, the concept of cohesion has been a "spectacular embarrassment" for group researchers (Kaul & Bednar, 1986, p. 707). Most researchers have attempted to measure cohesion at a global level. As implied in Kaul and Bednar's comment, there is no agreed-upon definition of or way to operationalize cohesion. Most of the research that examines cohesion has developed idiosyncratic derivatives of the concept, resulting in inconclusive findings and little cumulative knowledge of the construct of cohesion. A useful step for the group counseling field might be to examine the relationship between the different measures of cohesion. A study similar in format to Tichenor and Hill (1989) that examines group cohesion measures might well provide both theoretical and operational clarity for this important but messy area.

We are aware of only one measure of cohesion at the speech act level. Friedlander, Thibodeau, Nichols, Tucker, and Snyder (1985) defined cohesion as the semantic relations within a spoken text that make it cohere or coalesce as a unit. They operationalized a cohesive tie as when the interpretation of one speaker's message depends on information contained in the previous speaker's turn. According to these authors, there are five categories or types of cohesive ties: reference, conjunction, substitution, ellipsis, and lexical. Friedlander et al. argued that semantic cohesion is a measure of conversational involvement, an important component of all definitions of cohesion. The results of the Friedlander et al. study indicated that leader style was related to the number of cohesive ties produced in a group, and that groups with more cohesive ties had better client outcomes. These findings suggest that this speech act measure of cohesion may also be a useful means of studying this elusive group phenomenon.

In summary, the relationship is a key ingredient of the counseling process. Additional research is needed to develop a speech act measure of the working alliance. Only with this type of measure can investigators begin to examine Bordin's notion of the "tear and repair" process in the actual formation of the working alliance. Moreover, additional research is needed to examine how the three perspectives (client, counselor, observer) on working alliance formation interact. Are they complementary, unrelated, or just different? Researchers interested in group cohesion research have a promising speech act measures. It appears that research at the global level could be enhanced by a comparative study of the different measures that purport to measure cohesion.

Whose Perspective?

The second major question that process researchers must address is: From whose perspective does the researcher want to evaluate the counseling process? There is evidence that suggests that client, counselor, and observer perspectives on the counseling process may offer quite diverse views of what happens in counseling. For example, Dill-Standifond, Stiles, and Rorer (1988) found that clients and counselors had very different views of session impact (that is, depth, smoothness, positivity, and arousal). The critical question is no longer: Does it matter from whose perspective we assess counseling process? but rather: "To what extent does it matter?" In this section, we will discuss methodological issues pertaining to the perspective of measurement in process research. Specifically, we will examine (1) differences and similarities across perspectives, as well as (2) the reliability and validity of data obtained from the client, counselor, and observer perspectives.

Differences and Similarities across Perspectives

Gurman (1977) argued that while client ratings of therapist empathy are positively related to therapy outcome, ratings of empathy from outside observers are not. He consequently questioned the value of assessing empathy from the perspective of independent observers. Clearly, Gurman believed that it does matter from whose perspective the process is assessed.

The question of whose perspective to assess from is not so clear when we look at research on the working alliance. The study by Tichenor and Hill (1989) suggested that clients, counselors, and observers have different views of the working relationship (correlations among the three perspectives averaged $r = -.02$). Other research, however, suggests that client and counselor (Horvath & Greenberg, 1989) and observer (for example, Marmar, Marziali, Horowitz, & Weiss, 1986) ratings of the working alliance are all related to client outcome. These results suggest that different perspectives of the working alliance may measure different constructs, but each of them are important.

There is also research that shows little difference between, for example, client and counselor perspectives on the rating of therapist behavior (Carkhuff & Burstein, 1970). Conversely, supervisors and supervisees typically differ when each person is asked to rate the frequency of various supervisor behaviors (for example, Heppner & Roehlke, 1984).

We believe that whether or not there are differences between client, observer, and counselor perspectives depends on what aspect of the process is being measured. Specifically, the more concrete and observable the behavior being assessed, the less discrepancy there will be among the perspectives. For instance, the presence or absence of a specific observable behavior can be reliably assessed from any of three perspectives. Researchers using this type of process variable can choose a perspective based on ease of data collection.

When the process variable assessed is more subjective, however, we suspect that there will be less agreement among client, counselor, and observer perspectives. When a researcher wants to examine these more subjective process variables, he or she should consider obtaining ratings from multiple perspectives. In this way, the researcher can empirically examine the degree of relationship among the perspectives for the particular variable of interest. In addition, the researcher can determine if the different perspectives add useful information. For example, the combination of client, counselor, and observer perspectives on the working alliance may be a better predictor of counseling outcome than any single perspective.

Reliability and Validity of Ratings

Another issue confronting the process researcher is the reliability and validity of the ratings obtained from the counselor, client, and observers. Reliability has been typically addressed when the researcher is using an observer perspective to examine the counseling process. Reliability is examined by obtaining estimates of interrater reliability, and typically addressed by many hours of rater training. We maintain, however, that rater training is important regardless of which process perspective is being examined.

As reported in an earlier section, Martin, Martin, & Slemon (1989) found that counselors used different categories of the Hill and O'Grady (1985) Intentions List to record nominally similar descriptions of intentions. Their solution to this problem was to ask therapists to give verbal descriptions of their intentions and then have raters classify these descriptions. One problem with this solution is that it is very expensive in terms of time and effort. An alternative to this approach might be to train the counselors/raters in the use of the intention system. The training of people who are being asked to introspect has a long history in psychology (Wundt, 1904) but is rarely used in modern process research. For example, counselors could be trained to use the Intentions List by first learning to classify a series of intention statements to a specified criterion level. Only after they reached this level on the practice statements would they start to rate their own intentions. Rater drift could be assessed by administering additional series of intention statements to be rated throughout the study.

Hill (1982) believes that the most important aspect of rater training happens before the actual training starts. Specifically, she believes that the selection of raters is a crucial step in process research. Her three selection criterion are intelligence, motivation for the specific project, and demonstrated ability on a simulated rating task. Once raters are selected, the researcher can begin the actual training. This training usually involves three steps: (1) description of the rating system, (2) rating of sample items, and (3) discussion of the sample ratings.

In the first step, the rater must be introduced to the rating system. This should probably include a discussion of the theory base from which the rating system is derived, as well as a description of the specific system. This introduction to the rating system is enhanced by the use of manuals with examples of expert ratings. Next the rater uses the rating system on a set of sample items. Once these ratings are made, the raters need to discuss the ratings they made and the reasons for making the ratings. This step is enhanced if "expert" ratings of the sample items are available so the trainees can compare their ratings to those of the experts. The last two steps (rating sample items and discussing the ratings) continue until a specified level of agreement exists among the raters.

At this point the raters begin the actual rating task. We believe, however, that rater training should be extended throughout the rating process. For example, periodically during the actual rating process, raters can be given sample items to rate and can then discuss these ratings. This type of procedure helps to assure the researcher that the raters are still using the rating system in a similar manner.

The final aspect of rater training involves the assessment of rater reliability. In some ways this can be considered an assessment of the rater training program. Hill (1982) stated that researchers should calculate both inter- and intrarater reliability. Intrarater reliability assesses whether or not an individual rater is consistent in using the rating system over time. Interrater reliability assesses the amount of agreement between raters. Tinsley and Weiss (1975) should be consulted for methods of calculating inter- and intrarater reliability.

One final issue pertains to the validity of the data obtained from the various rating or coding systems. So far we have discussed the counselor, client, and observer perspectives as representing three separate perspectives. Patton (1989), however, maintained that these three perspectives in reality only represent one perspective, the researcher's. Whenever the researcher chooses a coding scheme, he or she defines a priori and consequently delineates the type of observations that can and will be made, by the structure of the assessment device. In other words, the researcher, in selecting a particular coding scheme, typically defines for the rater, counselor, client, or observer how he or she will describe the process events in question. Patton maintained that the descriptive events produced directly by clients and counselors apart from the structure imposed by researcher-developed questionnaires should be seen as the data for our observation and analysis. Thus, Patton asserted that we have not truly examined counselors' or clients' perspectives concerning the events in counseling because of the predominance of researcher-imposed questionnaires. Patton suggested qualitative methodologies as nonimposing vehicles for examining the process of counseling (see Chapter 8). We believe that Patton raised an important methodological point concerning the conduct of most of counseling process research that merits additional attention and exploration.

In summary, the perspective that the researcher uses to assess the counseling process clearly affects the type of data collected and the type of conclusions drawn. Researchers must not only be aware of the perspective issue, but also explicitly qualify the results of their investigations accordingly. Moreover, the reliability and validity of the data merit careful scrutiny and additional empirical research. The issue of researcher-imposed structure (Patton, 1989) is particularly interesting, and emphasizes the need to assess how both the client and counselor are processing the counseling experience apart from the structure imposed by the researcher.

How Much to Measure?

Process researchers must also decide how much of the session or how many sessions to use in their analyses. In other words, is it sufficient to sample from one session, or does one need to analyze the whole session or even multiple sessions? While there is little empirical evidence pertaining to this issue, we will briefly discuss sampling and underscore its role in counseling process research.

Friedlander, Ellis, Siegel, Raymond, Haase, and Highlen (1988) examined this issue of how much to measure empirically. Specifically, they addressed: (1) What fraction of an interview, if any, best represents the entire interview? and (2) At what starting point in the interview should this "best" sample be drawn? Friedlander et al. found that the answer to the questions depended on the researcher's purpose. If the researcher was interested in group data, such as the process across several different counseling-client dyads, then fairly small segments of sessions were reasonable representations of an entire session. Specifically, in such group designs, as little as 10% of the session was an accurate description of the session as a whole. For a group design, it also did not seem to matter from what point in the interview the researcher drew the sample. Friedlander et al. did recommend, however, that a "mini-generalizability" study be routinely conducted when using a group design. In other words, a subsample of the data could be analyzed to ascertain that the use of small segments is appropriate in a particular case. On the other hand, Friedlander et al. reached a different conclusion concerning process analysis for a single case. They recommended that entire sessions be used when this type of intensive strategy is used. Their data suggested that sampling of single-subject data leads to enormous differences in the conclusions.

Thus, the question of whether to use sample session segments seems to depend on the nature of the design. With group designs, segments of as little as 10% of the session will likely yield acceptable results, while with single-subject designs it is best to use an entire session without sampling. This issue of how much to measure is relatively unexplored and clearly needs more empirical research. Sampling is a critical issue in external validity and merits serious attention in counseling process research.

How to Analyze Process Data?

An important trend in process research has been the move toward studies that explicitly examine the link between counseling process and outcome. With this movement has come important questions about analyzing process data. Traditionally, process has been linked to outcome using a correlational strategy. For instance, the percentage of counselor interpretations could be correlated with session depth. If the researcher found a significant positive relationship between interpretation use and depth, then he or she could infer that interpretation was an important process element. Unfortunately, these correlational designs restrict the researcher from understanding causal relationships (for example, did counselor interpretations cause deeper sessions?).

A second example of a correlational design, this time using an ex post facto design, would involve comparisons across successfully and unsuccessfully treated cases. In this case the researcher would examine if the frequency of occurrence of a response (for example, open-ended questions) differed across the two kinds of cases. Again, if open-ended questions occurred more frequently in the successful cases, does this mean that counselors who use more open-ended questions will be more successful?

In short, correlational designs in counseling process research are often quite limiting. In fact, Gottman and Markman (1978) are quite critical of these types of correlational designs in process research. Rather, they argue for analyses that examine the direct effect of counselor behavior on subsequent client behavior. Stiles (1988) also observed that often counselors use greater frequencies of a behavior not because it is working well, but rather because it is not working well. For instance, a counselor might offer a lot of interpretations because the client is being "resistant" and rejecting the interpretation. This situation would cause a high number of counselor interpretations and probably a low rating for session depth. Thus, the correlation between these two variables alone presents rather misleading information.

An alternative way of examining the relationship between counselor behavior and client response is sequential analysis. Sequential analysis is a set of statistical techniques that examine the mutual influence of counselor and client behaviors. For example, sequential analysis can be used to examine the likelihood of a client response (for example, self-disclosure) given a prior counselor response (for example, interpretation). At a more sophisticated level, these sequential analyses can examine issues like control and power (that is, is the counselor's response made more predictable by knowing the client's preceding response, or vice versa?). An excellent description of these types of analyses can be found in Claiborn and Lichtenberg (1989).

A study by Wampold and Kim (1989) illustrates the power of sequential analysis in examining counseling process. Wampold and Kim reanalyzed data from Hill, Carter, and O'Farrell's (1983) study using an intensive single-subject design across 12 counseling sessions. The process variables used in this study were Hill's counselor and client verbal response category systems. Categories for counselor responses included minimal encourager, silence, approval-reassurance, information, direct guidance, closed question, open question, restatement, reflection, interpretation, confrontation, nonverbal referent, self-disclosure, and other. Client categories included simple response, requests, description, experiencing, insight, discussion of plans, discussion of client-counselor relationship, silence, and other.

The purpose of the study was to examine the reciprocal influence of counselor and client behaviors. We will only highlight a couple findings here to describe the utility of sequential analysis. First, analyses showed what Wampold and Kim called two "circuits" between client and counselor behaviors. One circuit was from client description to counselor minimal encourager back to client description. A second circuit involved client description to counselor confrontation. In addition, Wampold and Kim tested the first circuit for dominance, the dominant member of the dyad being defined as the one with the most influence. For the client description–counselor minimal encourager–client description circuit, the client was dominant. In other words, the counselor's behavior was more predictable from the client's behavior than the other way around. Wampold and Kim concluded that the sequential analysis allowed them to document several important aspects of the client and counselor interactions that had been undetected in the correlational and descriptive analysis used by Hill et al.

We believe that the Wampold and Kim article is an excellent example of how sequential analysis can further our understanding of the counseling process. Accordingly, we recommend that researchers more frequently move beyond the use of correlational designs in their process research.

SUMMARY AND CONCLUSIONS

In this chapter we have addressed some of the measurement issues and methodological decisions that a researcher must confront in designing a process study. Specifically, these included: What to measure? From whose perspective? How much to measure? and How to analyze it? Our recommendations have consistently been to examine the counseling process in a deep rather than broad manner. In other words, we have recommended that process researchers use multiple measures of process, examined from multiple perspectives, and examined in an intensive manner. A logical assumption from this type of recommendation is that we would emphasize single-subject methodologies. To use multiple measures with multiple perspectives in an intensive analysis could be prohibitively expensive in large group-comparison designs. While we do value and recommend single-subject methodologies, we certainly do not think that these should be used to the exclusion of between-groups designs in process research. Moreover, it is important to remember the research of Friedlander et al. (1988) concerning session segment generalizability: for between-groups designs, a segment of as little as 10% of the session can capture the essence of the session process, but 100% of the session is needed in single-subject designs. Thus, using small segments, process researchers can still use multiple process measures from multiple perspectives.

•   •   •   •   •   •   •   •   •   •   •   •   •   •   •   •   •

EXHIBIT A
Hill Interaction Matrix (Hill, 1965)[1]

Work on the Hill first began in 1954 and has been continuing ever since. A comprehensive account of this work appeared in monograph form in 1961 and was revised in 1965. A scoring manual was also published in 1961 and revised in 1965. The present publication has as its purpose updating HIM developments and especially the dissemination of information on the rating scales associated with the HIM. A brief account of the HIM category system is included to provide a context and point of ready reference, especially for those who have not read the HIM Monograph and Scoring Manual.

INTRODUCTION TO HIM CATEGORY SYSTEM

The categories of this interaction rating system were empirically derived by studying intensively a considerable number of therapy groups. This resulted in deriving two basic dimensions which seemed to be paramount in distinguishing groups. Both dimensions are manifested in 'styles' of operation. One dimension deals with the 'content,' that is, what groups talk about. The Content/Style has four categories—Topic, Group, Personal, and Relationship. A group's style can be characterized by talking about the 'here and now' relationships and reactions of members to each other (Relationship, IV), or talking about the problem of a member in a historical manner (Personal, III), or about the group itself (Group, II), or about all the topics external to the group itself, e.g., current events (Topic, I). These categories can be treated as nominal but in the HIM they are put into an ordinal scale of presumed increasing therapeutic potential from I through IV.

The other dimension deals with the level of Work obtaining in a group. Work has five categories, in order of significance, Responsive, Conventional, Assertive, Speculative, and Confrontive. Work, a term borrowed from Bion, is a meaningful concept but elusive of definition. In HIM terms it is characterized by someone in the group playing the helping or therapist role and someone asking for help or playing the patient or client role in an attempt to get self-understanding. Within the Work/Style dimension there are two subdivisions, Work and Pre-Work. In Pre-Work no one is really trying to obtain self-understanding. The lowest level is Responsive (A), which is characterized by the fact that little or nothing is taking place except in response to leader's probes. Next is Conventional (B), which resembles everyday *socio* groups that interact about social amenities, gossip, chit chat, etc. Assertive (C) is the highest ranking of the Pre-Work categories and represents social protest behavior, usually the asserting of independence from group pressure. Superficially, Assertive behavior may look like Work—a member presenting his problem—but he is 'acting-out' his problem, not 'acting-on' it. Work categories are two: Speculative (D) and Confrontive (E): the former being the 'conventional' way of transacting therapy, i.e., playing the therapeutic game. Confrontive style is intended to have real involvement and impact, and is characterized by tension and risk taking. The dimensions are arranged in matrix form with Content/Style on the horizontal axis and Work/Style on the vertical axis. The matrix thereby has twenty cells—each characterizes typical behavior to be found in treatment groups. Figure A-1 presents the cells and determinants of the Hill Interaction Matrix (HIM).

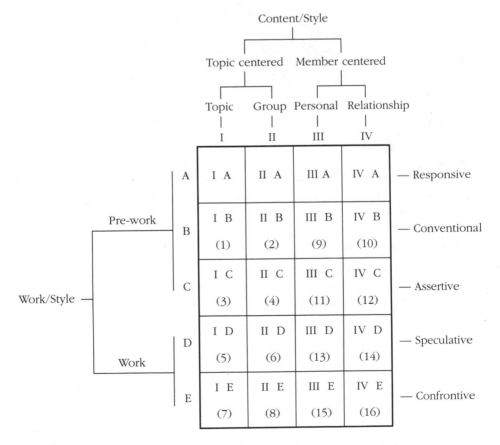

FIGURE A-1
Cells and determinants of the Hill Interaction Matrix.

•   •   •   •   •   •   •   •   •   •   •   •   •   •   •

E X H I B I T   B
Supervision Questionnaire (Worthington and Roehlke, 1979)[2]

SUPERVISION QUESTIONNAIRE

Name: _____   Date of Ph.D. Degree _____

Setting: Counseling Center _____

　　　　　Academic Department _____

Supervisor's approximate number of years since Ph.D. _____

Supervisor's primary placement: Academic _____

　　　　　　　　　　　　　　　　　Counseling Center _____

　　　　　　　　　　　　　　　　　Community Mental Health Center _____

　　　　　　　　　　　　　　　　　Private Practice _____

Is your supervisor a licensed psychologist (Clinical or Counseling)?
　　　　　　　　　　(Circle one)   Yes   No

　　　This questionnaire is designed to evaluate the supervision you received this semester. It has two parts. The first part asks you to rate the effectiveness of the supervision you have received. The second part of the questionnaire is designed to measure more specifically the behaviors of your supervisor. Please consider each item carefully on its own merits. Try to avoid the "halo effect" in which a good supervisor tends to receive "high marks" on everything. Do not mark this second part according to how frequently you think your supervisor "should" have done each behavior; rather, rate the actual frequency of behavior. This form is used at a number of universities and agencies. It is highly likely that your supervisor never did (rating 1) some of the behaviors. Marking a 1 or 2 (or any rating for that matter) is not an indictment of or testimony for your supervisor.

I. <u>Effectiveness of supervision:</u>

　　1. Satisfaction with supervision.

Totally unsatisfied; it could not have been worse.	Mostly unsatisfied; could have been a little worse.	More unsatisfied than not.	So-so; not really satisfied or unsatisfied.	More satisfied than not.	Mostly satisfied; could have been a little better.	Totally satisfied; it could not have been better.

　　2. How competent was your supervisor at giving good supervision?

Totally incompetent	Mostly incompetent	More incompetent than not	So-so	More competent than not	Mostly competent	Totally competent

3. How much did interactions with your supervisor contribute to improvement in your counseling ability?

Had almost no effect	Had a small effect	Had somewhat of an effect	Had a moderate effect	Had a substantial effect	Had a large effect	Had a very large effect

II. Description of your supervisor's behavior:

Please rate each of the following items as to how descriptive it is of your supervisor's behavior. Use the following 5-point scale to make your ratings.

    5—perfectly descriptive of my supervisor's behavior
    4—usually descriptive of my supervisor's behavior
    3—descriptive of my supervisor's behavior
    2—occasionally descriptive of my supervisor's behavior
    1—never (or very infrequently) descriptive of my supervisor's behavior

Behavior (or pseudo behavior) of supervisor — Rating (circle one)

1. Established good rapport with you. 1 2 3 4 5
2. Established clear goals conjointly with you against which progress in supervision was measured. 1 2 3 4 5
3. During the initial sessions the supervisor provided more structure than during later sessions. 1 2 3 4 5
4. Observed you counsel (live observation) at a minimum of one time this semester. 1 2 3 4 5
5. Observed at least three videotapes of your counseling this semester. 1 2 3 4 5
6. Listened to at least three audio tapes of your counseling this semester. 1 2 3 4 5
7. Provided relevant literature or references on specific treatment techniques or assessment techniques. 1 2 3 4 5
8. Gave appropriate feedback to you
    a. About positive counseling behaviors 1 2 3 4 5
    b. About non-facilitative behaviors 1 2 3 4 5
9. Was sensitive to the differences between how you talk about your actions and how you really behave with clients. 1 2 3 4 5
10. Modeled within the supervision session good task-oriented skills. 1 2 3 4 5
11. Gave direct suggestions to you when appropriate. 1 2 3 4 5
12. Supervisor allowed you to observe him or her, do co-counseling with him or her, listen to audio tapes of his or her counseling, or view videotapes of his or her counseling. 1 2 3 4 5
13. Supervisor was available for consulting at times other than regularly scheduled meetings. 1 2 3 4 5
14. Used the relationship between supervisor and supervisee to demonstrate principles of counseling. 1 2 3 4 5

Rating (circle one)

15. Helped you to conceptualize cases. Worked together with you to evolve a joint conceptualization for clients.   1 2 3 4 5

16. Encouraged you to experiment with different assessment and intervention techniques to discover your own unique style.   1 2 3 4 5

17. Suggested specific ways to help you get your client(s) to accept your conceptualization of the client's problems.   1 2 3 4 5

18. Used humor in supervision sessions.   1 2 3 4 5

19. Labeled counselor behavior as effective or ineffective rather than right or wrong.   1 2 3 4 5

20. Helped you develop self-confidence as an emerging counselor.   1 2 3 4 5

21. Helped you realize that trying new skills usually seems awkward at first.   1 2 3 4 5

22. Confronted you when appropriate.   1 2 3 4 5

23. Helped you assess your own:
    a. strengths   1 2 3 4 5
    b. weaknesses   1 2 3 4 5

24. Evaluated you at mid-semester.   1 2 3 4 5

25. Renegotiated goals with you at mid-semester.   1 2 3 4 5

26. Called you by name at least one time per session.   1 2 3 4 5

27. Provided suggestions for alternative ways of conceptualizing clients.   1 2 3 4 5

28. Provided suggestions for alternative ways of intervening with clients.   1 2 3 4 5

29. Discussed with you experiences in the practicus class in addition to clients.   1 2 3 4 5

30. Gave emotional support to you when appropriate.   1 2 3 4 5

31. Supervisor taught you specific counseling behaviors intended to facilitate your style.   1 2 3 4 5

32. Encouraged you to find your own style of counseling.   1 2 3 4 5

33. Helped you with personal problems that may interfere with your counseling.   1 2 3 4 5

34. Supervisor demonstrated, by role playing, techniques of intervention.   1 2 3 4 5

35. Helped you deal with your own defensiveness when it arose in supervision.   1 2 3 4 5

36. Supervisor shared his or her own experiences with clients with you.   1 2 3 4 5

37. Supervisor consulted with you when emergencies arose with your clients.   1 2 3 4 5

Rating (circle one)

38. Supervisor missed no more than one supervisory session   1   2   3   4   5
    per semester. (If a missed session was rescheduled and
    made up, it is not counted as missed.)

39. Supervisory sessions lasted at least 50 minutes.   1   2   3   4   5

40. At least 45 minutes of each supervisory session were   1   2   3   4   5
    spent discussing counseling and/or clients.

41. Focus of most supervision sessions was on the relationship   1   2   3   4   5
    between supervisor and supervisee.

42. Focus of most supervision sessions was on content of   1   2   3   4   5
    counseling sessions.

43. Focus of most supervision sessions was on conceptualizing   1   2   3   4   5
    the dynamics of the client's personality.

44. Supervisor made it easy to give feedback about the   1   2   3   4   5
    supervision process.

45. Helped you develop skills at intake interviews.   1   2   3   4   5

46. Helped prepare you for consultation and case disposition   1   2   3   4   5
    after intake interviews.

●   ●   ●   ●   ●   ●   ●   ●   ●   ●   ●   ●   ●   ●   ●   ●

●   ●   ●   ●   ●   ●   ●   ●   ●   ●   ●   ●   ●   ●   ●   ●

E X H I B I T C
Interpersonal Communication Rating Scale (Strong et al., 1988)[3]

RATING PROCEDURE

The objective of rating is to place each communication unit in an interaction into one of the eight categories of the model and to indicate the extremity of the unit within the category. *A communication unit is defined as a person's communication uninterrupted by another's verbal utterance.* Units are classified in terms of the behaviors they contain. The behaviors are the combination of the content of a communication unit and the person's manner of being during the communication, the linguistic and non-linguistic (kinesic and paralinguistic) aspects of communication. The linguistic aspects of a communication are the words used and their structure. The kinesic and paralinguistic aspects include facial expression, eye gaze, body posture, speech rate, and voice qualities such as tone, volume, and intonation. Rating involves identifying the behaviors the communicator presents in the linguistic *and* non-linguistic aspects of the communication.

    Each communication unit is to be rated as an independent entity. It must be classified on the basis of its own characteristics without regard for the context within which it occurs. The overall tone of the interaction or the nature of the communication units that precede or follow a communication are not to be considered. The Interpersonal Communication Rating Scale was developed to classify communications with the aid of videotapes and transcripts of interactions. Using audiotapes or transcripts alone will alter ratings due to the loss of non-linguistic cues.

Some classification decisions are based primarily on the linguistic characteristics of a communication. Other decisions are based primarily on the non-linguistic characteristics. Still other decisions are based on their combined effects.

The easiest and most reliable way to rate behaviors is to do the judgement task in the following three steps:

1. Concentrate on the linguistic form, structure, and content of the communication unit presented in the transcript. Follow the procedure presented below using the transcript alone and arrive at a preliminary judgement of the best rating for the unit.

2. Concentrate on the non-linguistic aspects of the communication presented in the videotape, noting especially speech rate, voice volume, tone, and intonation, eye gaze, attentiveness to other, body posture, affect, and energy level. Go through the procedure presented below again, this time focusing on the non-linguistic aspects.

3. Base your final judgement of the best rating for the unit on both the linguistic *and* non-linguistic aspects of the communication.

The procedure for classifying each communication unit is as follows:

1. Using both videotape and transcript, determine the communication unit to be rated. A communication unit is defined as a person's communication uninterrupted by another's verbal utterance.

2. Examine the communication unit. Using Figure C-2, identify to which category(s) the behavior(s) may belong.

3. Review the rating conventions and category descriptions. Determine to which category(s) the behavior(s) belongs.

4. If the communication unit contains more than one behavior, determine the predominant behavior in the unit. Assign the unit to the category to which the predominant behavior belongs.

5. Determine the extremity level of the predominant behavior by matching it with the behaviors in the four levels of the chosen category in Figure C-2. Adjust the level assignment as specified in Rating Convention 5, *Softeners.*

6. Finally, record the two-digit rating that identifies the category and level of the unit on the Rating Sheet.

COMMON NON-LINGUISTIC ASPECTS OF BEHAVIORS
Common Leading (1) Non-linguistic Cues

Facial expression is neutral, uplifted, pleasant, and aroused. Holds eyes open, relaxed, and alert; eyes are clear. Maintains direct and personable eye contact with frequent, sustained, and attentive gazes; attention to the other is directive and social. Relaxes eyebrows to a normal (base line) position. Holds mouth in a normal (inexpressive) position, shows a slight smile at the corners, or exposes teeth in an open smile. The face is relaxed, open, and interested. Lips are full and moist.

Paralinguistic cues. Speaks with normal to moderately loud voice, smooth and moderately fast verbal flow, and slightly upward, deep, and full intonation. Air movement is excited but controlled. Laughs rather often, and accompanies laughter with increased eye contact.

Body movements. Holds head straight up and facing the other. Nods with assurance. Sits facing the other in an open, comfortable, and erect position with shoulders

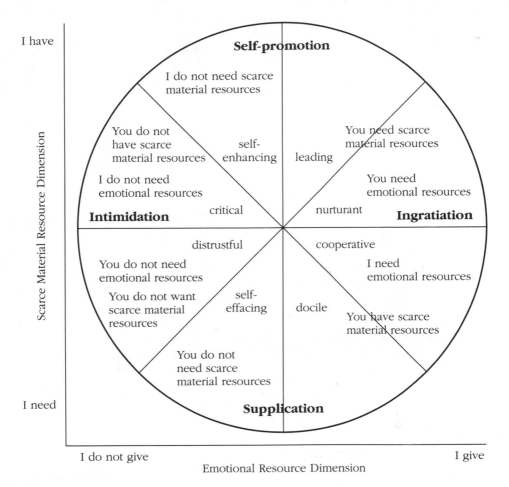

FIGURE C-1
Resource messages of interpersonal behaviors.

back and carried high; may sit on the edge of the seat. Leans slightly forward while listening. Holds arms open. Keeps hands relaxed or actively gesturing. Uses controlled, purposeful, and coordinated gestures and confines them to a small space; holds palms up. May actively point to materials. May preen by throwing head back and brushing hair away to expose face. Orients legs toward the other. Places legs in a casual parallel position with feet flat on the floor, or scissors legs comfortably apart at the knee.

Common Self-enhancing (2) Non-linguistic Cues

Facial expression is animated, aroused, decisive, and excited when speaking, and tense, uplifted, determined, unwavering, firm, and controlled when the other speaks. Opens eyes wide with animation. Does not attend closely when the other speaks, and shows mild irritation through short gazes, eye rolls, and stares into space. Often stares straight ahead when speaking, or may maintain steady and unflinching eye contact with little

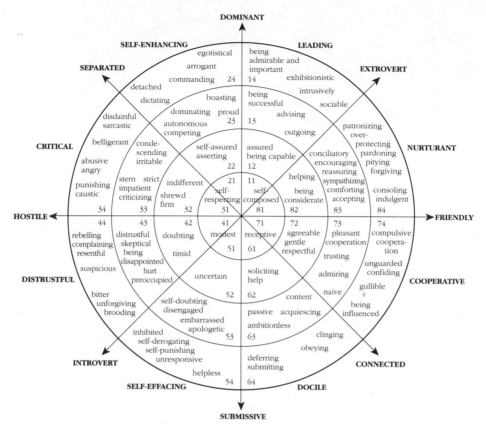

F I G U R E C-2
Classification of interpersonal behavior.

blinking to intimidate the other; dramatic gazes. Raises eyebrows and furrows forehead. Holds mouth in a normal (inexpressive) position and seldom smiles at other. Lips may be tight, set, and dry.

Paralinguistic cues. Speaks with a loud voice, fast and animated verbal flow, and slightly upward, deep, robust, full, and abrupt intonation. Spontaneously clicks tongue, humms, and whistles. Air movement is excited and controlled. May burst into hearty laughter; guffaw.

Body movements. Holds head straight up. May face the other head on during intimidation or short gazes. Nods infrequently; quick, jerky head movements. Body movements are alert, enthusiastic, and energetic. Faces body straight into the room. Sits proudly and erect, with shoulders back and carried high. Sits straight up on the edge of seat without leaning forward even when shown something. May sprawl with an arm or leg thrown over the edge of the chair. Holds arms and hands open and tense. Holds materials in front. May jam hands together and thrust elbows outward to signal authority. Rests elbows on chair arms and laces fingers together placing index fingers up and touching at collarbone level. Uses gestures that are confident, controlled, and open, and generally confines them to a small space. To emphasize a point, may use wide, intrusive, dominant, and animated gestures with palms out. Raises hand slightly

Rating Sheet: Interpersonal Communication Rating Scale (3/25/87)

Person Odd		Person Even		Condition		Part		Rater		Date		Study	
Unit	Rating	Unit	Rating	Unit	Rating	Unit	Rating	Unit	Rating	Unit	Rating	Unit	Rating
1		26		51		76		101				126	
2		27		52		77		102				127	
3		28		53		78		103				128	
4		29		54		79		104				129	
5		30		55		80		105				130	
6		31		56		81		106				131	
7		32		57		82		107				132	
8		33		58		83		108				133	
9		34		59		84		109				134	
10		35		60		85		110				135	
11		36		61		86		111				136	
12		37		62		87		112				137	
13		38		63		88		113				138	
14		39		64		89		114				139	
15		40		65		90		115				140	
16		41		66		91		116				141	
17		42		67		92		117				142	
18		43		68		93		118				143	
19		44		69		94		119				144	
20		45		70		95		120				145	
21		46		71		96		121				146	
22		47		72		97		122				147	
23		48		73		98		123				148	
24		49		74		99		124				149	
25		50		75		100		125				150	

while listening, ready to disagree. Deliberate movements; may drum pencil to communicate disinterest. May hold legs in parallel position with feet flat on the floor.

Common Critical (3) Non-linguistic Cues

Facial expression is scornful, sneering, disdainful, serious, severe, disgusted, rejecting, displeased, disapproving, annoyed, angry, and frustrated. Avoids eye contact. Attends to external stimuli to show irritation or disinterest, but attends to the other during attacks. Glances away from the other into space or looks out a window to show disinterest, or rolls eyes to signal irritation. Darts eyes furtively away, then quickly glares at the other during attack. May glare at the other with a serious and severe look (pin the other down with the eyes). Uses long, frequent blinking. Stares aggressively with eyebrows moved over eye area. Lifts head and lowers eyelids to cut off communication. May lower upper eyelids and raise lower lids into a narrow, tense, and squared pattern; squints. Lowers eyebrows and pulls them together; knits brows; furrows forehead. Dilates and flares nostrils. Smiles infrequently and does not return smiles. May smile cynically when the other has not said anything funny. Draws lips tightly together, turns down corners, raises upper lip and depresses lower lip. The lips are tight, set, and dry. Clenches jaw and displays taunt jaw and facial muscles. Drops jaw.

Paralinguistic cues. Speaks with a normal to loud voice, moderately fast to fast verbal flow, and irregular, up and down, clipped, harsh, icy, cold, and gruff intonation. Spontaneously coughs, sighs, and hisses. Takes short, repressed, and ingressive breaths; snorts. Laughs infrequently; snickers; snide and partially stifled laughs; sardonic laughs that are bitter, scornful, and cynical. Accompanies laughs with nasal aspiration and controlled movements.

Body movements. May hold head straight, tilted, or down; quick, jerky head movements; may throw head back. May face the other head on. Infrequently nods, but occasionally uses forced nods (three or more nods in quick succession). Places chin in palm with index finger on cheek while leaning back to signal negative evaluation. Positions finger between nose and lip while listening to signal displeasure. Pushes up middle of forehead with fingers to signal disinterest. May raise finger and then drop it in coordination with negative head shakes. Posture is tense, tight, and stiff. May sit straight up or slump back and away from the other. Does not lean toward the other even when shown something. Turns body away when the other is speaking; positions body straight at the other when attacking. Occasionally uses quick and forced movements. Blocks the other with shoulder. May cross arms over chest and make fists with hands (a bulwark); may hold self and rock. May push hands into seat while looking away from the other, or lean forward in seat with palms down on thighs (bellicose position). Makes intrusive and attacking gestures that are overly broad, with sharp movements and palms out. Fidgets while the other is speaking to show irritation: taps pencil, drums fingers, looks at watch, picks imaginary lint from clothing, engages in prolonged and agitated self-scratching, rubs eyes, or swings foot. Hold legs tightly together with feet flat on the floor and away from the other, or scissors legs apart at knee away from the other. Shields or masks mouth and face with hands; uses materials and forearms as shields.

Common Distrustful (4) Non-linguistic Cues

Facial expression is miserable, sad, gloomy, droopy, distressed, hesitant, suffering, doubting, resentful, dejected, serious, and frustrated. Avoids eye contact. Does not attend much to the other or to external stimuli; is self-involved. Darts eyes away from the other; long frequent blinks. Emphasizes disbelief and resentment with furtive and guarded sideways glances followed by downward gazes. Looks up suddenly, then down or to the side. Raises inner corners of the upper eyelids and draws eyebrows up at inner corner. May narrow eyelids. Smiles infrequently; fake smiles. May raise upper lip or protrudes lower lip (pouts). May turn corners of the mouth downward. Lips are thin and dry.

Paralinguistic cues. Speaks with a soft to normal voice, slow verbal flow, and up and down, but overall downward, intonation (whiny, breaking, nasal, choking). Spontaneously coughs and sighs. Takes deep, labored, repressed, and ingressive breaths. Laughs infrequently; laughter is incongruous.

Body movements. May hold head down, tilted or bowed slightly, while glancing suspiciously at the other. Shakes head slowly. May hold chin in palm with index finger on cheek while leaning back to show negative evaluation or doubt. May position index finger on the nose or raise finger and drop it to communicate doubt. Slouches, retracts shoulders, and draws body back; body is tense. Moves body cautiously, occasionally shrugs shoulders or blocks the other with shoulder. Faces the other or turns away. Does not lean forward when shown something. May cross arms over chest or hold self and rock. Closes hands almost into fists. May clasp hands or lace fingers tightly in lap. Uses materials and forearms as shields; shields and masks face and mouth with hands. May cover face with hair. May rub eyes or hands; picks; prolonged and agitated self-scratching. Covers forced cough with hand over mouth. Makes tight, uncomfortable, and stiff gestures. Holds legs tightly together in a parallel position. May wrap one foot over the other and tuck feet toward body.

Common Self-effacing (5) Non-linguistic Cues

Facial expression is depressed, suffering, distressed, tense, anxious, sad, droopy, shameful, embarrassed, submissive, and uncertain. Passively attends to the other to look for signs of approval; does not attend to external stimuli. Little gazing; averts eyes to signal submission. Blinks excessively; blank stares. Glances downward to show modesty. Frequently looks down at materials on lap. Raises inner corners of the upper eyelids and draws up inner corners of eyebrows to show sadness. Turns the corners of the lips slightly upwards to show modest smiles. Roles lips inward toward mouth or turns them downward. Bites lips. Lips are dry and thin.

Paralinguistic cues. Speaks with a soft voice that may dwindle to a whisper, slow and hesitant verbal flow with irregular pauses, and downward, shaky, drawling intonation. Spontaneously clears throat, coughs nervously, gasps, and sniffs. Breaths deeply and exhales slowly, or inhales quickly, pauses, then exhales slowly with noise. Laughs infrequently; titters (a restrained nervous giggle accompanied by blushing and head lowering).

Body movements. Holds head down and lower than does the other, looks at the other at an angle to the side and up. Tilts, cocks, or bows head toward the other. Shakes head negatively. May support head with one hand. Sits back in the seat, bows shoulders, sinks chest, and droops as if in surrender; body is tense and defensive; assumes a fetal position. Makes guarded, hesitant, and uncertain body movements. Occasionally squirms nervously. May shrug shoulders. Gathers arms tightly toward the body and holds self. May rock. Hands are tense, almost fists. Clasps hands and laces fingers tightly in the lap. May use materials or forearms as shields or obstacles; may hide or mask mouth and face with hands. May position hair over eyes to close off face. Makes infrequent, hesitant, breaking, awkward, and uncertain gestures. May fondle ring, bracelet, etc., chew on pencil, or play with hair. Places finger on chin or holds finger in mouth to signal uncertainty. May rub eyes. May doodle on materials or pick nails. May position legs in parallel, tuck feet close in toward body, cross legs at the ankle, or keep knees in and touching.

Common Docile (6) Non-linguistic Cues

Facial expression is neutral, a mask, poker-faced, submissive, unresponsive, sleepy, droopy, calm, still, tranquil, tired, serene, placid, even, and steady. Infrequent eye contact; shows lack of involvement with slow, infrequent gazes. Averts eyes to signal submission. Blank stares. Attends to the other passively; unresponsive. Slightly relaxes and lowers upper eyelids. Relaxes eyebrows and mouth to normal (inexpressive) positions. Relaxes jaw. Smiles infrequently.

Paralinguistic cues. Speaks with a soft voice, slow, breaking, and slurred verbal flow with irregular pauses, and flat, monotone, gravelly, dull, and heavy intonation. Breaths deeply and exhales slowly. Occasionally yawns or slowly sighs. Does not laugh.

Body movements. Holds head down, lower than does the other. Looks at the other at an angle; bows head to the side and up. May support head in hands. Nods head slowly and infrequently. Relaxes body into a caved in, slumped, resting, limp, and still position. Moves body passively. Sits back in the chair and positions body slightly toward the other. May stretch out while leaning back. Hangs arms and hands relaxed at sides or in lap with palms up. Places materials in lap. Makes infrequent, faint, and weak gestures. May rub eyes or gently stroke leg with finger. Positions legs in casual parallel with feet on heels or crossed at the ankle; may close legs and tuck feet near body.

Common Cooperative (7) Non-linguistic Cues

Facial expression is relaxed, friendly, pleasant, calm, content, pleased, submissive, respectful, sympathetic, thoughtful, reverent, and loyal. Holds eyes open, relaxed, and clear. Actively attends to the other; shows involvement with the other with frequent, sustained, and intense gazing. Relaxes eyebrows to a normal (base line) position. Holds mouth in a normal (inexpressive) position, shows a slight smile at the corners, or exposes teeth in an open smile. Smiles frequently and in coordination with generous and cooperative responses to the other. Lips are full and moist.

Paralinguistic cues. Speaks with a normal voice, normal and smooth verbal flow, and slightly upward, smooth, and sweet intonation. Breathes normally. Laughs frequently and happily, and accompanies laughter with increased eye contact.

Body movements. Holds head lower than does the other and orients it at an angle (side and up). Shows approval with single and double head nods. May support head with the hands. Centers and keys body position on the other while listening. Relaxes posture with shoulders cupped; sits on the edge of the seat and leans forward to follow the other with interest. Holds arms and hands open and relaxed, positioned at the side or in the lap. Places materials on lap. Makes open, broad and even gestures with the palms up. May preen by slowly patting hair. May tie shoes, take off glasses, or touch hand to chest. Positions legs in casual parallel and places feet flat on the floor, turned in, or crossed at the ankle.

Common Nurturant (8) Non-linguistic Cues

Facial expression is relaxed, warm, pleasant, happy, affectionate, thoughtful, concerned, pitying, empathic, and commiserating. Holds eyes open, relaxed and clear. Actively attends to the other. Emphasizes involvement with frequent, sustained, and intense gazes that communicate concern and empathy. Relaxes eyebrows to a normal (base line) position. Holds mouth in a normal (inexpressive) position, shows a slight smile at the corners, or exposes teeth in an open smile. Holds mouth open and receptive to the other; smiles frequently. Lips are full and moist.

Paralinguistic cues. Speaks with a normal voice, normal verbal flow, and an overall upward, singing, resonant and full intonation (baby talk). Breathes normally. Laughs frequently and happily, and accompanies laughter with increased eye contact.

Body movements. Holds head straight up or tilts it gently; faces the other. Shows approval with single and double head nods. Sits straight up facing the other in a relaxed posture with shoulders comfortably back. Sits on the edge of the seat with a forward lean and follows the other with interest. Sits close to the other. Centers and keys body and face on the other while listening. Places materials in lap. Holds arms open. Uses hands expressively, relaxes them at the side, or places them in lap. Uses broad, open, and even gestures with palms up. May place hand on the chest or touch the other to emphasize a point. Preens by slowly patting hair. May tie shoes, take off glasses. Positions legs in casual parallel and places feet comfortably on the floor, or scissors legs apart at the knee toward the other.

●　●　●　●　●　●　●　●　●　●　●　●　●　●　●　●

●　●　●　●　●　●　●　●　●　●　●　●　●　●　●　●

E X H I B I T D
Check List of Interpersonal Transactions (Transaction Rating Form) (Kiesler, 1984)[4]

DIRECTIONS

The following pages contain lists of actions that can occur in interactions between two persons. Your task is to check each item which accurately describes an action exhibited in your transactions by the person targeted for you.

Make your judgments about occurrence of this person's actions solely on the basis of your personal encounters with that person. Check only those items which describe actions by that person which occurred "live" in your presence.

In order to receive a check, the action described by a particular item must have occurred in your presence *and* must be judged by you as typical of the way that person acts with you. If an item describes an action that does not typically occur in your interactions with this person, leave that item blank.

WHEN IN MY COMPANY, THIS PERSON . . .

_____ 1. suggests topics or issues to discuss, or directions or actions to pursue

_____ 2. is hesitant to express approval or acceptance of me

_____ 3. is careful to speak or act unemotionally or undemonstratively, or with little variation in tone or manner

_____ 4. finds it difficult to take the initative; or looks to me for direction or focus; or shows a desire to do "whatever you want"

_____ 5. is receptive and cooperative to my requests, directions, appeals, or wishes; or is quick to assist or work together with me

_____ 6. expresses pleasure in self; or comments on own accomplishments, awards, or successes

_____ 7. scans carefully to detect any of my reactions, evaluations, or motives that might have a harmful intent

_____ 8. shows little attention, interest, curiosity, or inquisitiveness about my personal life, affairs, feelings, or opinions

_____ 9. waits for or follows my lead regarding topics or issues to discuss, directions or actions to pursue

_____ 10. is quick to express approval or acceptance of me

_____ 11. speaks or acts emotionally or melodramatically, or with much variation in tone or manner

_____ 12. shows an intense task focus or desire to "get down to business"; or suggests directions or objectives

_____ 13. is quick to resist, not cooperate, or refuse to comply with my requests, directions or objectives

_____ 14. makes self-critical statements; or expresses low self-worth; or apologizes frequently

_____ 15. gazes at me in an open, receptive, trusting, or non-searching manner

_____ 16. inquires into or expresses attention, interest, or curiosity about my personal life, affairs, feelings, or opinions

_____ 17. dominates the flow of conversation, or changes topic, or interrupts and "talks down"

_____ 18. avoids at any cost showing affection, warmth, or approval

_____ 19. endlessly prefaces or qualifies statements to the place where points being made get lost, or views or positions are unclear or ambiguous

_____ 20. goes out of way to give me credit for my contributions, or to admire or praise me for my good ideas or suggestions

_____ 21. inconveniences self or sacrifices to contribute, help, assist, or work cooperatively with me

_____ 22. is cocky about own positions or decisions; or makes it abundantly clear s/he can do things by self; or avoids any hint that I can help

_____ 23. in response to my inquiries or probings acts evasively as if hiding important secrets

_____ 24. refrains at all costs from close visual or physical contact or direct body orientation with me

_____ 25. finds it almost impossible to take the lead, or to initiate or change the topic of discussion

_____ 26. constantly expresses approval, affection, or effusive warmth to me

_____ 27. makes startling or "loaded" comments; or takes liberties with facts to embellish stories

_____ 28. works hard to avoid giving me credit for any contribution; or implies or claims that good ideas or suggestions were his/her own

_____ 29. is openly antagonistic, oppositional, or obstructive to my statements, suggestions, or purposes

_____ 30. urgently solicits my advice, help, or counsel even for everyday troubles or difficulties

_____ 31. responds openly, candidly, or revealingly to the point of "telling all"

_____ 32. continually stands, sits, moves or leans toward me to be physically close

_____ 33. expresses firm, strong personal preferences; or stands up for own opinions or positions

_____ 34. acts in a stiff, formal, unfeeling, or evaluative manner

_____ 35. works at being careful or precise in his/her statements; or searches for precise words to express thoughts

_____ 36. is content, unquestioning, or approving about the focus or direction of a given topic of discussion or course of action; or is quick to follow my lead

_____ 37. expresses appreciation, delight, or satisfaction about me, our situation, or our task

_____ 38. is quick to rely on own resources to make decisions or solve problems

_____ 39. claims that I misunderstand, misinterpret, or misjudge his/her intents or actions

_____ 40. remains aloof, distant, remote, or stand-offish from me

_____ 41. expresses own preferences hesitantly or weakly; or yields easily to my viewpoints; or backs down quickly when I question or disagree

_____ 42. acts in a relaxed, informal, warm, or nonjudgmental manner

_____ 43. makes comments or replies that "pop out" quickly and energetically

_____ 44. questions or expresses reservation or disagreement about the focus or direction of the conversation or course of action

_____ 45. grumbles, gripes, nags, or complains about me, our situation, or our task

_____ 46. readily asks me for advice, help, or counsel

_____ 47. communicates that I am sympathetic or fair in interpreting or judging his/her intents or actions

_____ 48. is absorbed in, attentive to, or concentrates intensely on what I say or do

_____ 49. states preferences, opinions, or positions in a dogmatic or unyielding manner

_____ 50. has absolutely no room for sympathy, compromise, or mercy regarding my mistakes, weaknesses, or misconduct

_____ 51. understates or hedges on evaluations of me, events, or objects, or constantly minimizes expressions of emotion

_____ 52. makes statements that are deferentially, softly, or carefully presented as if s/he desperately wants to avoid any implication of disapproval, criticism, or disagreement

_____ 53. seems always to agree with or accommodate me; or seems impossible to rile

_____ 54. brags about achievements, successes, or good-fortune; or "puts on airs" as if in complete control of his/her life

_____ 55. expresses harsh judgment, "never forgetting," or no forgiveness for my mistakes, weaknesses, or injurious actions

_____ 56. seems constantly uncomfortable with me as if s/he wants to leave or be by self

_____ 57. claims s/he doesn't have an opinion, preference, or position, or that "it doesn't matter," "whatever you want," "I don't know," etc.

_____ 58. goes out of way to understand or be sympathetic towards me, or to find something about me to approve of, endorse, or support

_____ 59. constantly overstates evaluations of me, events, or objects; or exaggerates expression of his/her feelings

_____ 60. challenges or disputes my ideas or statements; or attempts to get the better of me or put me down

_____ 61. argumentatively challenges or refutes my statements or suggestions; or "tells me off," "lets me have it" when disagrees

_____ 62. claims s/he is a constant failure, or is helpless, witless, or at the mercy of events and circumstances

_____ 63. expresses unbending sympathy, understanding, or forgiveness for my hurtful or injurious actions

_____ 64. finds it difficult to leave me; or goes out of way to secure more and more of my company

_____ 65. seizes opportunities to instruct or explain things, or to give advice

_____ 66. expresses stringent, exacting, rigorous standards or expectations of me

_____ 67. is slow to make decisions; or deliberates carefully before acting

_____ 68. shares credit with me for good happenings or joint accomplishments; or points out ways I have been helpful; or "plays down" own contributions

_____ 69. is attentive to, considerate or solicitous of my feelings, or sensitive to pressures or stresses in my life

_____ 70. speaks or acts in a composed or graceful manner, confident about what s/he wants, remaining calm and unruffled

_____ 71. expresses doubt, mistrust, or disbelief regarding my intentions or motives

_____ 72. is slow to respond or speak to me; or seems distracted by own thoughts

_____ 73. is quick to ask me for information, instruction, explanations, or opinions

_____ 74. expresses lenient, soft-hearted, or compassionate standards or expectations of me

_____ 75. makes hasty decisions; or jumps into new activities with little premeditation

_____ 76. makes comments that avoid sharing credit with me for good happenings or joint accomplishments; or "plays up" own contributions

_____ 77. ignores, overlooks, or is inconsiderate of my feelings; or disregards pressures or stresses in my life

_____ 78. is unsure or "iffy" about what s/he wants; or acts in an uneasy and inept manner; or is easily embarrassed

_____ 79. expresses belief or trust in, or reliance upon, my claims about good intentions or motives

_____ 80. initiates greetings, chats easily, or shows enjoyment in being with or talking to me

_____ 81. overwhelms or "steamrolls" me by his/her arguments, positions, preferences, or actions

_____ 82. expresses severe, inflexible, or uncompromising expectations for my conduct

_____ 83. endlessly avoids or delays choices, decisions, or actions, or commitment to positions

_____ 84. makes flattering or glowing comments about me, our situation, or our joint task

_____ 85. makes unconditionally supportive, encouraging, endorsing, comforting, or bolstering comments to me

_____ 86. acts as if excessively "full of self," or as feeling special or favored, or as cocksure of his/her future

_____ 87. is bitterly accusatory, suspicious, or disbelieving of me

_____ 88. seems totally unmoved, unaffected, or untouched by my comments or actions

_____ 89. seems unable to assert what s/he wants, or to stand up to me, or to take any opposing position

_____ 90. is unwaveringly tolerant, patient, or lenient in regard to his/her expectations for my conduct

_____ 91. seems compelled to act out feelings with me, or impulsively to jump into new actions or activities

_____ 92. makes critical, demeaning, snide, or derisive statements about me, our situation, or our joint task

_____ 93. swears at me; or makes abusing, disparaging, damaging, or crude comments to me

_____ 94. is constantly dissatisfied with self, guilty or depressed; or feels hopeless about the future

_____ 95. shows blind faith or polyannish trust in me; or believes almost anything I say

_____ 96. seems totally engrossed in me; or is constantly moved, affected, or responsive to my comments or actions

• • • • • • • • • • • • • • • •

• • • • • • • • • • • • • • • •

EXHIBIT E
Client Experiencing Scale (Klein et al., 1986)[5]

SCALE STAGES

These general descriptions of each of the seven scale stages are amplified considerably in the manual (Klein et al., 1969) and also outlined in Table E-1.

STAGE 1   The chief characteristic of this stage is that the content or manner of expression is impersonal. In some cases the content is intrinsically impersonal, being a very abstract, general, superficial, or journalistic account of events or ideas with no personal referent established. In other cases, despite the personal nature of the content, the speaker's involvement is impersonal, so that he or she reveals nothing important about the self and the remarks could as well be about a stranger or an object. As a result feelings are avoided and personal involvement is absent from communication.

STAGE 2   The association between the speaker and the content is explicit. Either the speaker is the central character in the narrative or his or her interest is clear. The speaker's involvement, however, does not go beyond the specific situation or content. All comments, associations, reactions, and remarks serve to get the story or idea across

T A B L E E-1
Short Form of Experiencing Scale (Patient)

Stage	Content	Treatment
1	External events; refusal to participate	Impersonal, detached
2	External events; behavioral or intellectual self-description	Interested, personal, self-participation
3	Personal reactions to external events; limited self-descriptions; behavioral descriptions of feelings	Reactive, emotionally involved
4	Descriptions of feelings and personal experiences	Self-descriptive; associative
5	Problems or propositions about feelings and personal experiences	Exploratory, elaborative, hypo-thetical
6	Felt sense of an inner referent	Focused on there being more about "it"
7	A series of felt senses connecting the content	Evolving, emergent

SOURCE Copyright 1970 by The Regents of the University of Wisconsin. Revised, 1983.

but do not refer to or define the speaker's feelings. Thus the personal perspective emerges somewhat to indicate an intellectual interest or general, but superficial, involvement.

STAGE 3 The content is a narrative or a description of the speaker in external or behavioral terms with added comments on feelings or private experiences. These remarks are limited to the events or situations described, giving the narrative a personal touch without describing the speaker more generally.

Self-descriptions restricted to specific situations or roles are also part of Stage 3. Thus feelings and personal reactions come into clear but limited perspective. They are "owned" but bypassed or rooted in external circumstances.

STAGE 4 At Stage 4 the quality of involvement or "set" shifts to the speaker's attention to the subjective felt flow of experience as referent, rather than to events or abstractions. The content is a clear presentation of the speaker's feelings, giving a personal, internal perspective or account of feelings about the self. Feelings or the experience of events, rather than the events themselves, are the subject of the discourse, requiring the speaker to attempt to hold on to inner referents. By attending to and presenting this experiencing, the speaker communicates what it is like to be him or her. These interior views are presented, listed, or described, but are not the focus for purposeful self-examination or elaboration.

STAGE 5 The content is a purposeful elaboration or exploration of the speaker's feelings and experiencing. There are two necessary components: First, the speaker must pose or define a problem, proposition, or question about the self explicitly in terms of feelings. The problem or proposition may involve the origin, sequence, or implications of feelings or relate feelings to other private processes. Second, the speaker must explore or work with the problem in a personal way. The exploration or elaboration must be clearly related to the initial proposition and must contain inner references that have the potential to expand the speaker's awareness of experiencing. These may also be evidence of and/or references to the process of groping or exploration itself.

TABLE E-2
Additional Stage Criteria

Scale Stage	Grammatical	Expressive	Paralinguistic	Content
1	No first-person pronouns; past or present tense	Remote, impersonal	Fluent	Impersonal, others' activities or events
2	Personal pronouns; past or present tense	Interested, intellectual	Usually fluent	Ideas, events, actions
3	Personal pronouns; past or present tense	Limited reactions	Some affect indicators, e.g., laughs, sighs	Parenthetical or limited references to feelings
4	Present or past tense	Immediate, expressive	Focused voice, expressions of affect	Subjective experiences and associations
5	Present tense, but past can be included; Subjunctive, tense questions	Immediate, groping, tense, tentative	Dysfluency	Questions about unclarity in own awareness
6	Present tense or vivid representation of past	Declarative, fresh, real	Exclamation, alternations of dysfluency and fluency, pauses	Directly sensed and emergent feeling
7	Present tense primarily	Affirmative	More fluency than dysfluency	What one "knows" for oneself

STAGE 6   At Stage 6 the way the person senses the inner referent is different. There is a *felt sense* of the there-and-yet-to-be-fully-discovered, that is, of an unclear inner referent that has a life of its own. It is a sense of potentially more than can be immediately thought or named. This felt sense is more than recognizable feelings such as anger, joy, fear, sadness, or "that feeling of helplessness." If familiar or known feelings are present, there is also a sense of "more" that comes along with the identified feelings.

STAGE 7   The content reveals the speaker's steady and expanding awareness of immediately present feelings and internal processes. He or she clearly demonstrates the ability to move from one inner referent to another, linking and integrating each immediately felt nuance as it occurs in the present experiential moment, so that each new sensing functions as a springboard for further exploration and elaboration.

EXHIBIT F
Intentions List (Hill & O'Grady, 1985)[6]

INSTRUCTIONS

To judge intentions, the therapist should review the tape within 24 hours so that the session is as fresh and vivid in memory as possible. The therapist should stop the tape after each therapist turn (everything the therapist says between two client speech acts, excluding minimal phrases) and indicate as many intentions as applied for that turn. You should strive to remember exactly what was going through your mind right at the time of the intervention *and* be as honest as possible in reporting what you were actually thinking. Remember that there are no right or wrong answers; the purpose is simply to uncover what you planned to do at that moment. Also remember that you should indicate your intentions only for that immediate intervention, rather than report global strategies for the entire session. Note that not every phrase in the definition for each intention needs to fit to judge that the intention applies. In general, the therapist should choose those intentions that best apply, even if all the phrasing is not exactly applicable to the current situations or does not fit the way he or she would say it.

INTENTIONS

1. *Set limits:* To structure, make arrangements, establish goals and objectives of treatment, outline methods to attain goals, correct expectations about treatment, or establish rules or parameters of relationship (e.g., time, fees, cancellation policies, homework).
2. *Get information:* To find out specific facts about history, client functioning, future plans, and so on.
3. *Give information:* To educate, give facts, correct misperceptions or misinformation, give reasons for therapist's behavior or procedures.
4. *Support:* To provide a warm, supportive, empathic environment; increase trust and rapport and build relationship; help client feel accepted, understood, comfortable, reassured, and less anxious; help establish a person-to-person relationship.
5. *Focus:* To help client get back on the track, change subject, channel or structure the discussion if he or she is unable to begin or has been diffuse or rambling.
6. *Clarify:* To provide or solicit more elaboration, emphasis, or specification when client or therapist has been vague, incomplete, confusing, contradictory, or inaudible.
7. *Hope:* To convey the expectation that change is possible and likely to occur, convey that the therapist will be able to help the client, restore morale, build up the client's confidence to make changes.
8. *Cathart:* To promote relief from tension or unhappy feelings, allow the client a chance to let go or talk through feelings and problems.
9. *Cognitions:* To identify maladaptive, illogical, or irrational thoughts or attitudes (e.g., "I must be perfect").
10. *Behaviors:* To identify and give feedback about the client's inappropriate or maladaptive behaviors and/or their consequences, do a behavioral analysis, point out games.
11. *Self-control:* To encourage client to own or gain a sense of mastery or control over his or her own thoughts, feelings, behaviors, or impulses; help client become more appropriately internal rather than inappropriately external in taking responsibility for his or her role.
12. *Feelings:* To identify, intensify, and/or enable acceptance of feelings; encourage or provoke the client to become aware of or deepen underlying or hidden feelings or affect or experience feelings at a deeper level.

13. *Insight:* To encourage understanding of the underlying reasons, dynamics, assumptions, or unconscious motivations for cognitions, behaviors, attitudes, or feelings. May include an understanding of client's reactions to others' behaviors.
14. *Change:* To build and develop new and more adaptive skills, behaviors, or cognitions in dealing with self and others. May be to instill new, more adaptive assumptive models, frameworks, explanations, or conceptualizations. May be to give an assessment or option about client functioning that will help client see self in new way.
15. *Reinforce change:* To give positive reinforcement or feedback about behavioral, cognitive, or affective attempts at change to enhance the probability that the change will be continued or maintained; encourage risk taking and new ways of behaving.
16. *Resistance:* To overcome obstacles to change or progress. May discuss failure to adhere to therapeutic procedures, either in past or to prevent possibility of such failure in future.
17. *Challenge:* To jolt the client out of a present state; shake up current beliefs or feelings; test validity, adequacy, reality, or appropriateness of beliefs, thoughts, feelings, or behaviors; help client question the necessity of maintaining old patterns.
18. *Relationship:* To resolve problems as they arise in the relationship in order to build or maintain a smooth working alliance; heal ruptures in the alliance; deal with dependency issues appropriate to stage in treatment; uncover and resolve distortions in client's thinking about the relationship that are based on past experiences rather than current reality.
19. *Therapist needs:* To protect, relieve, or defend the therapist; alleviate anxiety. May try unduly to persuade, argue, or feel good or superior at the expense of the client.

• • • • • • • • • • • • • • • • •

• • • • • • • • • • • • • • • • •

E X H I B I T   G
Brief Structured Recall (Elliott & Shapiro, 1988)[7]

EVENT RATING FORM—CLIENT

Part D: Client Intentions Ratings

For the following items, please rate what you were doing during the event. Use the following rating scale:

Not at all	Slightly	Somewhat	Pretty much	Very much
1	2	3	4	5

1   2   3   4   5   1. I was wanting or trying to get my therapist to do something for me (e.g., give me information, advice, support, explanation, etc.).

1   2   3   4   5   2. I was agreeing with what my therapist said.

1 2 3 4 5   3. I was disagreeing with what my therapist said.

1 2 3 4 5   4. I was trying to describe something to my therapist; put an experience into words.

1 2 3 4 5   5. I was trying to figure something out about myself; explore an experience or behavior of mine; see if what the therapist said about me fit.

1 2 3 4 5   6. I was trying to figure out what to do about a problem; learn how to do something; see what I thought of a suggestion by my therapist.

1 2 3 4 5   7. I was trying to avoid something I'd rather not deal with or talk about right now.

1 2 3 4 5   8. Other intention(s). (Please describe:)

_____

_____

• • • • • • • • • • • • • • •

• • • • • • • • • • • • • • •

E X H I B I T H
Client Reactions System (Hill, Helms, Spiegel, & Tichenor, 1988)[8]

INSTRUCTIONS

Review the tape immediately after the session. Try to remember what you were experiencing during the session. Stop the tape after each therapist intervention and list the numbers of up to five reactions that you felt when you first heard what the therapist said. Choose those reactions that best describe your experience, even if every part of the definition does not apply or the phrasing is not exactly accurate.

1. *Felt understood:* I felt that my therapist really understood me and knew what I was saying or what was going on with me.
2. *Felt supported:* I felt accepted, reassured, liked, cared for, or safe. I felt like my therapist was on my side or I came to trust, like, respect, or admire my therapist more. This may have involved a change in my relationship with my therapist, such that we resolved a problem between us.
3. *Felt hopeful:* I felt confident, encouraged, optimistic, strong, pleased, or happy, and felt like I could change.
4. *Felt relief:* I felt less depressed, anxious, tense, guilty, angry, or had fewer uncomfortable or painful feelings.
5. *Became aware of negative thoughts or behaviors:* I became aware of specific thoughts or behaviors which cause problems for me or others.
6. *Gained better self-understanding:* I gained new insight about myself, saw new connections, or began to understand *why* I behaved or felt a certain way. This new understanding helped me accept and like myself better.
7. *Became more clear:* I got more focused about what I was really trying to say, what areas I need to change in my life, what my goals are, or what I want to work on in therapy.
8. *Became aware of feelings:* I felt a greater awareness of or deepening of feelings or could express my emotions better.

9. *Took responsibility:* I felt more responsibility for myself, blamed others less, and realized my part in things.

10. *Got unstuck:* I overcame a block and felt freed up and more involved in what I have to do in therapy.

11. *Gained new perspective:* I gained a new understanding of another person, situation, or the world. I found a new framework for understanding *why* people or things are as they are.

12. *Got educated:* I gained greater knowledge or information. I learned something I had not known.

13. *Learned new ways to behave:* I got specific ideas about what I can do differently to cope with particular situations or problems. I solved a problem, made a choice or decision, or decided to take a risk.

14. *Felt challenged:* I felt shook up, forced to question myself, or to look at issues I had been avoiding.

15. *Felt scared:* I felt overwhelmed or afraid. I wanted to avoid or not admit to having some feeling or problem. Perhaps my therapist was too pushy. I may have felt that my therapist would disapprove of me or would not like me.

16. *Felt worse:* I felt less hopeful, sicker, out of control, dumb, incompetent, ashamed, or like giving up. Perhaps my therapist ignored me, criticized me, hurt me, pitied me, or treated me as weak and helpless. I may have felt jealous of or competitive with my therapist.

17. *Felt stuck:* I felt blocked, impatient or bored. I did not know what to do next or how to get out of the situation. I felt dissatisfied with the progress of therapy or having to go over the same things again.

18. *Felt lack of direction:* I felt angry or upset that my therapist didn't give me enough guidance or direction.

19. *Felt confused:* I did not know how I was feeling or felt distracted from what I wanted to say. I was puzzled or could not understand what my therapist was trying to say. I was not sure I agreed with my therapist.

20. *Felt misunderstood:* I felt that my therapist did not really hear what I was trying to say. Perhaps my therapist misjudged me or made assumptions about me that were incorrect.

21. *No reaction:* I did not have a particular reaction to because my therapist was just gathering information, making social conversation, or the statement was too short or unclear.

•   •   •   •   •   •   •   •   •   •   •   •   •   •   •   •   •

•   •   •   •   •   •   •   •   •   •   •   •   •   •   •   •   •

EXHIBIT I
Session Evaluation Questionnaire (Stiles & Snow, 1984)[9]

CLIENT POSTSESSION QUESTIONNAIRE

This session was:

Bad	1	2	3	4	5	6	7	Good
Safe	1	2	3	4	5	6	7	Dangerous

Difficult	1	2	3	4	5	6	7	Easy
Valuable	1	2	3	4	5	6	7	Worthless
Shallow	1	2	3	4	5	6	7	Deep
Relaxed	1	2	3	4	5	6	7	Tense
Unpleasant	1	2	3	4	5	6	7	Pleasant
Full	1	2	3	4	5	6	7	Empty
Weak	1	2	3	4	5	6	7	Powerful
Special	1	2	3	4	5	6	7	Ordinary
Rough	1	2	3	4	5	6	7	Smooth
Comfortable	1	2	3	4	5	6	7	Uncomfortable

Right now I feel:

Happy	1	2	3	4	5	6	7	Sad
Angry	1	2	3	4	5	6	7	Pleased
Moving	1	2	3	4	5	6	7	Still
Uncertain	1	2	3	4	5	6	7	Definite
Calm	1	2	3	4	5	6	7	Excited
Confident	1	2	3	4	5	6	7	Afraid
Wakeful	1	2	3	4	5	6	7	Sleepy
Friendly	1	2	3	4	5	6	7	Unfriendly
Slow	1	2	3	4	5	6	7	Fast
Energetic	1	2	3	4	5	6	7	Peaceful
Involved	1	2	3	4	5	6	7	Detached
Quiet	1	2	3	4	5	6	7	Aroused

•   •   •   •   •   •   •   •   •   •   •   •   •   •   •   •   •

NOTES

1. From *HIM: Hill Interaction Matrix,* by W. F. Hill. Los Angeles: University of Southern California, Youth Study Center. Reprinted by permission of the author.
2. From "Effective supervision as perceived by beginning counselors-in-training," by E. L. Worthington, Jr. and H. J. Roehlke, *Journal of Counseling Psychology,* 1979, *26,* 64–73. Copyright 1979 by the American Psychological Association. Reprinted by permission of the author.
3. From "The dynamic relations among interpersonal behaviors: A test of complementarity and autocomplementarity," by S. R. Strong, et al., *Journal of Personality and Social Psychology,* 1988, *54,* 798–810. Copyright 1988 by the American Psychological Association. Reprinted by permission of the author.
4. From *Check List of Psychotherapy Transactions (CLOPT) and Check List of Interpersonal Transactions (CLOIT).* Richmond: Virginia Commonwealth University. Copyright © 1984 by Donald J. Kiesler. Reprinted by permission.
5. From "The Experiencing Scales," by Kline et al. In L. Greenberg and W. Pinsof (Eds.), *The Psychotherapeutic Process: A Research Handbook,* pp. 21–72. Reprinted by permission of The Guilford Press.
6. From "List of therapist intentions illustrated in a case study and with therapists of varying theoretical orientation," by C. E. Hill and K. E.

O'Grady. In *Journal of Counseling Psychology*, 1985, *32*, 8. Copyright 1985 by the American Psychological Association. Reprinted by permission.

7. From "Brief structured recall: A more efficient method for studying significant therapy events," by R. Elliott and D. A. Shapiro. In *British Journal of Medical Psychology*, 1988, *61*, 141–153. Reprinted by permission of the author.

8. From "Development of a system for categorizing client reactions to therapist interventions," by C. E. Hill, J. E. Helms, S. B. Spiegel, and V. Tichenor. In *Journal of Counseling Psychology*, 1988, *35*, 27–36. Copyright 1988 by the American Psychological Association. Reprinted by permission.

9. From "Counseling session impact as viewed by novice counselors and their clients," by W. B. Stiles and J. S. Snow. In *Journal of Counseling Psychology*, 1984, *31*, 3–12. Reprinted by permission of the author.

PART FOUR
PROFESSIONAL WRITING

CHAPTER 15

THE RESEARCH REPORT

A study is not any better than the written report that discusses it. Although it could be argued that results of studies are disseminated in ways other than written reports (such as conference presentations), the research report is critical. Journal articles, books, dissertations, and to a lesser extent written summaries of conference presentations are the permanent records of counseling research. Unless a study is discussed in one of these sources, it is unlikely that a researcher interested in the topic area will be able to learn about the study. Nevertheless, a poorly written report, even if it is retrieved, will limit the usefulness of the research. It is a shame when the informative results of an elegantly conducted study are obscured by a complex, contorted, and confusing report. The preparation of a clear and informative research report is a critical step in the research process.

No doubt, few readers will begin to conduct research without having had at least some instruction in writing. A critical element in learning to write is practice with feedback. Of all the elements of the research process, writing is the most difficult to communicate didactically. Nevertheless, we would be remiss if we did not discuss important aspects of writing the research report. Others have discussed psychological report writing (for example, APA, 1983; Dorn, 1985; Seeman, 1959; Sternberg, 1988); our emphasis is on the aspects of the report that relate to research design.

Realize that writing style is personal. The opinions of authors, critics, and educators will differ. Furthermore, style varies according to constraints of the publication in which the writing will appear. For example, the American Psychological Association (APA) carefully details required elements of manuscripts submitted to APA journals in the *Publication Manual of the American Psychological Association* (APA, 1983). The APA *Publication Manual* is indispensable for most authors who publish in professional journals. Graduate schools typically have their own requirements for the dissertation.

This chapter will focus on generic components of the research report. First, the major sections of a report are presented and their relation to the principles of research design discussed previously in this book are mentioned.

Although various organizational formats could be discussed, we focus on the title, abstract, introduction, method, results, and discussion. Second, we present some general principles for writing research reports: (1) be informative, (2) be forthright, (3) do not overstate or exaggerate, (4) be logical and organized, (5) have some style, (6) write and rewrite, and (7) if all else fails, just write!

It is also important to underscore at the beginning that everyone has difficulty in writing at one time or another. It may be due to "writer's block," fatigue, a particularly complex writing task, or a myriad of fears and apprehensions about the product (for example, "I will make a mistake, which will be there for everyone to see"; "What I have to say is really not very important"; "If I can't write it perfectly, I won't write anything"). Many of these fears are particularly acute for inexperienced authors, and developmentally normal. Our major point is that writing is just one more skill the researcher needs to acquire; this skill, like any other skill, takes practice, feedback, analyzing successful models of writing (such as published articles), and rewriting. Moreover, even the veteran author experiences fears and apprehensions.

SECTIONS OF A RESEARCH REPORT

The exact organization of a research report varies depending on the publication for which it is intended and the nature of the study. Nevertheless, a perusal of counseling journals reveals a modal organization, roughly as follows:

Title
Abstract
Introduction
Method
     Subjects
     Measures (or Variables or Instruments)
     Materials
     Design (or Design and Analysis)
     Procedure
Results
Discussion (or Conclusions)
References
Tables
Figures

The nature of each of these components depends on the publication and the readership. Nevertheless, there are some aspects of each of these components that are critical to a well-written research report. In this discussion we will focus on those aspects of the components that relate to research design (see APA, 1983; Dorn, 1985; Sternberg, 1988, for other discussions related to these components). We will not discuss reference lists, tables, and figures, as these are clearly described in the APA *Publication Manual*. As we discuss these components sequentially, keep in mind that the components are held together by a common focus, the research hypotheses. This common focus helps the reader comprehend the study as a whole. For example, presentation of the results should mirror presentation of the design used to test the research hypothesis that was discussed in the method section.

Title

The title of a research report does much more than just name the report. Titles are used in a variety of ways to call attention to the research report. Many services depend on titles to index and abstract publications; users of these services often see only the title. Furthermore, readers perusing journals or other sources (such as *Current Contents* or *PsychScan*) often will decide to read the report solely on the basis of the title. Therefore, choose the title carefully.

A title should accurately summarize the research. Attempt to describe the topic, the independent and dependent variables, the design, and the outcome succinctly (in 12 to 15 words, according to most sources). Given the limitations on the length of titles, redundancies and irrelevancies need to be avoided. Omit such phrases as "A Study of" or "The Relation between." However, even within these constraints, interesting and stylistic titles can be developed.

Alloy and Abramson (1979) provide an example of a seminal article that has a title that is both descriptive and attention-getting: "Judgment of Contingency in Depressed and Nondepressed Students: Sadder but Wiser?" The title describes the independent variable (depressed versus nondepressed), the dependent variable (judgment of contingency), the subjects (students), and the results (sadder but wiser). The phrase "Sadder but Wiser?" adds interest because the results become a mnemonic; this phrase is often used to refer to this article.

Abstract

The abstract is a summary of the research report. As with the title, the abstract is used for indexing and retrieving articles. After the title, the abstract is the most often read portion of a research report. Therefore, the abstract should be succinct, accurate, and comprehensive. It should summarize the content of each of the major sections of the report, including the hypotheses, method (subjects, measures, materials, design, and procedure), results, and conclusions. Remember that nonsignificant results are informative; typically, it is useful to report and discuss all results, not just those that were expected. The length of abstracts is dependent on the publication; APA journals require abstracts of empirical studies to be between 100 and 150 words. Writing accurate as well as interesting abstracts is a difficult task.

The abstract should be self-contained. The reader should not need to depend on any other section of the report to make sense of the abstract. Therefore, avoid abbreviations and acronyms to the extent possible, or at the very least make sure that they are defined in the abstract. Explain unique and technical terms. Because readers of abstracts often do not have access to the entire research report, do not reference other articles in an abstract. Exceptions to this rule include abstracts of reaction articles (for instance, an article written in response to a previous article or a reanalysis of data from a published article).

Introduction

The introduction to the research report sets the stage for the study. It should orient the reader to the problem, develop the logic for the study, and indicate as specifically as possible the hypotheses being tested. Several questions should be answered in the introduction: Why is this an important topic to study? What previous work (empirical and theoretical) bears on the topic? How does this previous work logically lead to the authors' research question and hypotheses? How will this question be researched? What predictions can be made? To answer these questions, the introduction of a research report typically contains three elements: (1) introduction to the problem, (2) development of the framework for the study, and (3) statement of the research hypotheses. In journal articles, these three elements often blend together; theses and dissertations may require formal separation of these elements in different chapters.

The introduction to the problem should begin by orienting the reader to the topic and indicating why this is an important area to investigate. This discussion should be achieved with broad strokes. A study of child abuse might begin with some general statistics about the prevalence of child abuse and its implications for society; a study of supervision may begin by discussing difficulties with understanding the supervisory process (for example, see Friedlander, Siegel, & Brenock, 1989); a study of social support vis-à-vis the effectiveness of group therapy might begin with a statement about the widespread finding that social support mediates stressful life changes (see Mallinckrodt, 1989). The introduction to the problem should begin to narrow the topic by identifying important developments in the topic area. In the child abuse area, the identification of stress as a precursor of abuse could be identified (if that is the direction the researcher will pursue). The introduction to the problem can be concluded with a statement of the problem in general terms.

The second element in an introduction is the development of a rationale for the study. The framework for the rationale is built through the logical interconnectedness of empirical results and theory that leads to a critical, unanswered research question. Quite deliberately, we avoid the use of the more traditional term *literature review*. *Literature review* implies (at least to some) a synopsis of one study after another along with considerable integration and synthesis of the findings; in contrast, a framework depends on a logical case. In some ways, the development of a framework is similar to a legal brief. When the case is solid, there should be one inescapable conclusion; by the time the reader has completed reading this section, he or she should be saying "I know exactly what research question should be asked" and then find that the author goes on to ask that research question.

CHAPTER 15 / THE RESEARCH REPORT   379

Literature cited in the development of the framework should be pertinent to this particular research study. If reviews of the literature exist, cite the reviews rather than the original studies if this is sufficient to build the case. In any discussion of a previous study, discuss only the pertinent aspects of that study; typically, the pertinent aspects of a study are related to the findings of that study, but might also include methodological issues, such as type of subjects, design, statistical tests, and so forth. For example, reference to a study would not mention the number of subjects used in that study unless that was pertinent, which would be the case if the point being made was related to inadequate power to detect an effect. Discussion of previous findings and theory need to be intertwined logically. When you discuss a particular study or theory, the purpose of the discussion vis-à-vis the framework should be clear to the reader. Don't hesitate to inform the reader directly: "Left and Write's (1980) application of the Direct Counseling Approach (DCA) is important because it extends previous studies using DCA to children." Furthermore, you should integrate the material reviewed. Often studies result in contradictory findings; you need to speculate about the reasons for the discrepancy and to indicate how these discrepancies (and the reasons behind them) relate to the present study.

A word about completeness is needed. Certainly, the scope of the framework and the literature reviewed in it is determined by the publication for which it is intended. More completeness is needed for a dissertation than for a journal article. Nevertheless, the principle is the same. The goal is to develop a logical argument that will lead to a research question and/or hypothesis, not to review all studies ever written on a topic. Generally, this element of the introduction should be complete enough that it mentions issues raised elsewhere in the research report; it should not be necessary to review literature when hypotheses are stated or when dependent variables are operationalized. One exception to this rule is that it is common to report psychometric information under the measures subsection of the method section.

If the framework has been developed properly, the purpose of the present research should be readily apparent. The purpose might be to reconcile discrepancies in previous research; that is, the study will explain why contradictory findings have been obtained. Another purpose might be to apply results from a noncounseling area to problems in counseling (see, for example, the social influence model, Strong, 1968). Or the purpose of the study might be to extend previous results to a different population.

The final element of the introduction is the statement of the research hypotheses. Occasionally, some writers will also include their research questions at this time, or earlier as they are building their rationale. To repeat what should be clear by now: the research hypotheses should be logically derived from the framework built previously. The hypotheses stated at this point should be a critical test of some important theoretical or practical question (Cook & Campbell, 1979; Wampold, Davis, & Good, 1990). A good theory will allow several implications to be drawn from it. A hypothesis is critical to the extent that it tests an implication from a theory and that the implication is unique to that theory (see Wampold, Davis, & Good, 1990). In that way, knowledge progresses because theories are winnowed.

Research hypotheses are written in terms of theoretical constructs; operationalization of the constructs comes later. For example, the research hypothesis might state that a cognitive-behavioral treatment will lower state but not trait anxiety. Unless there is some particular issue with operationalization that this study addresses directly, operationalization of state and trait anxiety would typically be discussed under the measures subsection of the method section. Thus, discussion of particular measures used to operationalize a construct should not be included in the introduction, unless a particular operationalization is related to the research hypothesis (for example, the study differs from previous studies in the manner in which a construct is operationalized).

Research hypotheses should be stated unambiguously. Of course, the degree to which a hypothesis can be specific is dependent on the specificity of the theory. However, statements such as "the purpose of the present study is to explore the relation between . . ." or "the purpose is to determine the relation between . . ." are insufficient because some relation will always be discovered (even if the relation is null—that is, no relation). It is not clear how the discovered relation relates to theoretical predictions, and the researcher must create post-hoc explanations. An example of an unambiguous research hypothesis is provided by Ponce and Atkinson (1989):

> The purpose of this study was to examine the effects of counselor ethnicity, subject acculturation, and counseling style on the perceptions of counselor credibility and influence that Mexican-American subjects hold. It was hypothesized that subject acculturation would interact with both counselor ethnicity and counseling style in such a way that unacculturated subjects would prefer a Mexican-American counselor who used a directive style, whereas acculturated clients would have no preference for either counselor ethnicity or counseling style. (p. 204)

Method

The method section describes how the research hypotheses were tested. That is, this section details all aspects of how the study was conducted. Enough detail is needed so that a reader can (1) determine the validity of the study and (2) replicate the study. It is interesting to note that of all the sections of a manuscript, the method section has the highest correlation with editorial decisions to reject or accept a manuscript for publication in the *Journal of Counseling Psychology* (Munley, Sharkin, & Gelso, 1988); therefore it is imperative that the method section be well written.

Typically, the method section is divided into subsections. These subsections are not prescribed, but research in counseling usually contains subsections on subjects, measures (or variables or instruments), Materials, Design, and Procedures. Each of these subsections is briefly described here. Organization of the method section depends, to a great extent, on the nature of the study.

The order of the subsections may be altered (for instance, design often appears as either the first or the last subsection). However, the subsections of the method section should fit together like a puzzle, providing at the end a very clear picture of what was done and how it was done. Furthermore, it should be clear to the reader how the researcher will analyze the data so that the reader is primed for the presentation of the results.

Subjects

The subsection on subjects should indicate, at a minimum, (1) the total number of subjects, (2) how the subjects were selected, and (3) characteristics of the subjects relevant to the outcome of the study (for example, age, educational level, gender, ethnicity, geographical area of residence, pretest level of functioning, and/or others, depending on the study). Other aspects that may be mentioned in this section include assignment of subjects to conditions of the independent variable (including number of subjects in each condition), attrition, statistical power, and circumstances under which the subjects participated (for instance, financial remuneration, course credit).

The issue of power needs further comment. Previously, we mentioned the importance of designing studies with adequate power. If a power analysis was conducted to determine the number of subjects needed, mention of this analysis should be included either here or in the design subsection.

Measures (or Variables or Instruments)

The purpose of the measures subsection is to operationalize the constructs to which the research hypotheses referred. Recall that Ponce and Atkinson (1989) mentioned counselor ethnicity, subject acculturation, counseling style, and perceptions of counselor credibility in their statement of the research hypothesis. Counselor ethnicity was a subject characteristic and counseling style was a manipulated independent variable; subject acculturation and perceptions of counselor credibility were operationalized by using the Acculturation Rating Scale for Mexican-Americans (ARSMA) and the Counselor Effectiveness Rating Scale (CERS), respectively. Therefore, Ponce and Atkinson discussed the ARSMA and the CERS under a subsection called "Instruments."

The measures subsection discusses the operationalization of constructs. The rationale for choosing particular instruments should be presented here. Why was a particular instrument chosen? Why were three measures of a construct used rather than one (or two, or four)? Why were commonly used measures omitted? Furthermore, the measures subsection should include a discussion of each instrument chosen, including the title of the instrument, citation (manual, article, or other source that is primary), description of instrument (for example, number and type of items, direction of scoring), factors or subscales, and psychometric properties (such as reliability and validity). With regard to psychometric properties, statements about reliability and validity estimates should refer to the context in which these estimates were calculated (for example, the population).

Because of the need to justify choice of operationalizations, the measures subsection is one conspicuous place in the method section where it is not unusual to cite a number of studies (for instance, studies of psychometric properties). However, if the operationalization of a construct is controversial and therefore critical to the experiment, then discussion of these issues probably fits best in the introduction (that is it is part of the development of the framework). This would be the case should the researcher claim that previous attempts to corroborate a theory were unsuccessful because of improper operationalization of the dependent variable and the present study used different instruments to measure the same construct.

In a treatment study, operationalization of the independent variable is vital. This operationalization usually takes the form of describing the treatments for each condition. Sometimes the amount of detail needed to adequately describe a particular treatment intervention becomes prohibitive; in such cases it often is helpful to develop a detailed treatment manual that can be footnoted for interested readers (for example, see O'Neil & Roberts Carroll, 1988).

Materials

The materials subsection describes any materials used in the study. Pilot testing of the materials would also be described in this section. Sufficient information should be given that an independent researcher could reproduce the materials and replicate the study. If this is impossible to do given space restrictions, it is customary to indicate in a footnote that additional information or the materials themselves are available from the author.

Design (or Design and Analysis)

This subsection describes the design of the study. After reading this section, one should have a clear understanding of the independent, status, and dependent variables and the manner in which subjects were assigned to levels of the independent variables. For example, if a factorial design is used, the factors should be labeled, the number of conditions within a factor should be indicated, and the nature of the factors (such as between versus within or random versus fixed) should be stated. If the analyses are mentioned (for example, a two-way analysis of variance applied to a factorial design), change the name of the subsection to include "Analysis." If a power analysis was conducted, it can be included in this subsection.

One point about the design subsection needs emphasis. The connection between the design and the research hypotheses should be clear. That is to say, after reading this subsection, the reader should realize how the hypotheses were tested (see Wampold, Davis, & Good, 1990). Often (especially in the dissertation), the research hypotheses are restated in operationalized form. For example, at this stage in a report, the following statement might be included:

"To test the research hypothesis that [statement of hypothesis], a two-way analysis of variance was conducted. [Explain factors and indicate dependent variable.] It was predicted that a statistically significant F test for the interaction would be obtained."

Procedure

The procedure subsection describes how the research was conducted with the subjects. Discuss everything that the researchers did with the subjects, from beginning to end, including instructions to the subjects, formation of groups, and experimental manipulations. Typically, the procedure subsection is organized chronologically. Enough detail should be given so that the study can be replicated. If a separate design subsection is not included, details related to randomization and other features of the design can be included in this subsection.

Results

The purpose of the results section is to summarize the data and the results of the statistical analysis. Generally, two types of results should be reported: (1) summary statistics and results of preliminary analyses and (2) results related to research hypotheses. The summary statistics typically include the means and standard deviations of the dependent variables for each level of the independent variable (or combination of levels, as in a factorial design). Results of preliminary analyses may be related to manipulation checks, dropouts, verification of stimulus materials, and so forth.

Results related to research hypotheses should be organized so that the reader can tie the results of specific statistical tests to research hypotheses stated earlier in the report. There should be a one-to-one correspondence between the hypotheses and the statistical tests (see Wampold, Davis, & Good, 1990). This organization is facilitated by subsections titled appropriately. Subsections titled "Preliminary Analyses," "Summary Statistics," "Test of Hypothesis 1," "Test of Hypothesis 2," and so forth would clearly organize the results for the reader.

The results section should report the findings, but discussion of the results is saved for the discussion section. Nevertheless, introduce each result so that its purpose is clear. For example, indicate why a preliminary analysis was conducted and what various outcomes mean: "A preliminary analysis on the observers' ratings of the therapy sessions was conducted to determine whether or not the treatments were perceived as different. The [name of statistical test] was statistically significant [give information about test statistic], indicating that the observers did indeed rate the treatments differently."

Often there is confusion about what information to include with regard to statistical tests. The APA *Publication Manual* (1983) gives specifics about reporting statistical tests in the text and in tables. However, these specifications are inadequate because they indicate, for the most part, *how* to report rather than *what* to report. There has been a trend to report less; for example, one rarely sees analysis of variance source tables anymore. More disturbing is the tendency not to report important information (like size of test statistic and probability levels) when results are nonsignificant. This minimalist point of view puts the emphasis on statistical significance and ignores concepts such as effect size, estimation, and power. Failure to report information other than significance levels makes it difficult or impossible for readers to verify results, calculate other indexes (such as effect size or power), and conduct meta-analyses. Although not adopted by many, a persuasive argument can be made for reporting size of test statistics, exact probability levels (rather than, say, $p < .05$) for significant and nonsignificant findings, some measure of effect size, power, and other indexes as appropriate (Rosnow & Rosenthal, 1988). An article by Ellis, Robbins, Shult, Ladany, & Banker (1990) provides a good example of reporting a variety of indexes other than level of significance.

Often results are presented in tables or figures. Tables and figures are useful because results can be presented in a minimal amount of space and because the information presented can be easily understood. Locating important results in text is much more difficult than finding them in a well-organized table. Figures are particularly useful for illustrating a pattern of results, such as an interaction in an analysis of variance. When tables or figures are used, total recapitulation of the results in the text should be avoided, although sometimes it is useful to summarize key findings in the tables. The writer must, however, tell the reader what to look for in the tables. For example, one might say, "The main effects of the 3 (treatment) by 2 (gender) analysis of variance were statistically significant, as shown in Table 1"; it is unnecessary then to note, for example, the degrees of freedom, the F statistics, and so forth, because that information is in the table.

Discussion

The discussion should include (1) an explanation of whether or not the data support the research hypotheses, (2) a statement of the conclusions, (3) an indication of the limitations, and (4) a discussion of the implications. This section provides an opportunity for the author to expand on the findings and to place them in the context of previous research and theorizing on this topic.

Typically, the discussion begins with a statement of whether or not the research hypotheses were supported. Although the study reported is primary, you may choose at this point to integrate your findings with previous research.

After indicating whether or not the hypotheses were supported, you will probably feel the need to discuss these results. What conclusions can be reached from the results? If you believe that new knowledge has been generated by support of the hypotheses, state this. If the data lead to reformulated hypotheses, state the new hypotheses, but indicate that they have been formulated post hoc (that is, have not been tested directly). If future research is needed, indicate what types of hypotheses should be tested and how future studies should be designed.

Every discussion of results should include a statement of the limitations. Typically, limitations are related to low power, analogue nature of the study, violated assumptions of statistical tests, confounds, and so forth. Remember that no study is perfect. It is best to be forthright about the limitations and discuss how the results are interpretable in spite of the limitations.

Finally, given the support (or nonsupport) for the hypotheses and the limitations, you are free to indicate the implications of the study for theory and for practice. Be cautioned, however, that the results of one study are rarely important enough by themselves to revise theory or to change practice. So avoid statements such as "Practitioners should refrain from Treatment X and only use Treatment Y."

GENERAL PRINCIPLES FOR WRITING RESEARCH REPORTS

Although it is difficult to identify general principles in writing, we would like to highlight a few ideas. We will briefly discuss seven general considerations: (1) be informative, (2) be forthright, (3) do not overstate or exaggerate, (4) be logical and organized, (5) have some style, (6) write and rewrite, and (7) if all else fails, just write!

Principle 1: Be Informative

The goal of the research report is to inform the reader about the study. Provide enough detail for the reader to understand what you are explaining, but do not provide so much detail that the reader becomes bogged down. Of course, level of detail is determined by the publication for which the writing is intended. Dissertations require the most detail. Some journals are more technical than others and thus require more detail. Are the readers of a particular journal primarily practitioners, other researchers, or statisticians? The best way to ascertain how much detail to include is to select the journal for which the manuscript is intended and then emulate those articles that you like the best in the journal. Most journals also publish from time to time editorials or other information about the materials to be contained in articles that they publish (see the inside covers of most journals for descriptions of appropriate articles).

In any report, discuss the central points and minimize digressions. Obviously, you should not report everything that you did. Include only information that will be needed to understand the study. For example, preparation of stimulus materials often involves many successive stages of development. It is not necessary to explain each iteration; rather, describe the final product and summarize the development process in a sentence or two. However, do not omit important details, either. Frequently, authors refer to a decision that was made but do not discuss the decision rule; for example, "three outliers were omitted from the analysis." On what basis was it determined that the three data were outliers? Was this decision rule formulated before the data were analyzed?

Principle 2: Be Forthright

Every study has flaws (Gelso, 1979). It is rare that a researcher would not alter a study, had he or she the chance of doing it over again. Authors should be forthright about limitations of the study and discuss ramifications of the limitations rather than attempt to hide the flaw in some way. Signs of hidden flaws include obtuse language, esoteric statistical tests (with improper justification), omitted information, overstated justifications, and so forth. Reviewers of manuscripts submitted for publication are especially annoyed when they uncover hidden flaws or when they have a vague (intuitive) sense that the author has not been forthright with regard to some limitation.

The author has a fundamental decision to make. If a flaw is fatal to the study (for example, a confound that cannot be minimized), then it is best to consider the study as a time-consuming learning experience. If the flaw is problematic but the results of the study are informative nevertheless, then the author should indicate how the flaw affects the interpretation and why the study remains important. But keep in mind that judgments in this regard typically are made by others: dissertation committees, editors, and reviewers. Although the author may think that a flaw is not fatal, a journal editor may decide otherwise.

Principle 3: Do Not Overstate

There is a widely shared tendency to believe that every study that we conduct will change the course of the field. When this tendency is expressed in written reports, it appears as unjustified claims about the importance of the results for the field of counseling. To take the proper perspective, it is important to understand that it is highly unusual that any one research study in counseling is sufficient to stand alone. It is only the accumulation of the results from many studies that adds to our knowledge. For example, the conclusion that smoking is detrimental to health was established from years of research; alternative explanations in one study were ruled out in other studies. Progress toward the conclusion that a link exists between smoking and health was made inch by inch (Holland, 1986). Interestingly, it is not unusual for the results of seminal studies to be contradicted by future research. For example, Rosenthal and Jacobson's (1968) conclusion that teacher expectations influence student achievement has often been unsupported by subsequent research (Brophy & Good, 1974).

Unsupported statements usually appear in the discussion and conclusions sections of a report. Refrain from stating that, based on the results of your study, practitioners should change their practice or that researchers should abandon some theoretical position. If you feel strongly about a position, state that "the results of this study as well as previous studies [cite those studies] suggest that Theory X should be reconsidered." Let the scientific community decide whether, based on this suggestion, Theory X should be abandoned.

An issue related to overstatement centers around the appraisal of other authors' work. Generally, it is not advisable to be overly critical of others, especially at the beginning of one's career. Again, let the scientific community make judgments about the worth of various schools of thought or of the contributions of a researcher. It is acceptable to point out differences of opinion, but do it tactfully. Wampold and Kim (1989) reanalyzed a case study presented by Hill, Carter, & O'Farrell (1983) and came to different conclusions from those reached in the original study. Rather than argue that their conclusions were justified, Wampold and Kim provided several possible explanations for the differences and made the following conclusion: "Whether Hill et al.'s observations or the patterns revealed by the sequential analysis [conducted by Wampold & Kim] are reflective of the essential nature of the counseling process in this study remains an unanswered epistemological question" (p. 362). Readers are left to draw their own conclusions.

Principle 4: Be Logical and Organized

The written report is not simply a report; it is the presentation of a position. The author must persuade the reader that claims made are justified. For example, the research question should be justified given the literature reviewed. As we indicated previously, the logic and organization of the introduction should make the case for the research question. Don't force the reader to guess how the research question followed logically from the studies reviewed; explain it!

A few general considerations will aid in organization and logic. First, work from an outline. The outline should not just list various parts of the report, but should neatly summarize the logical organization. Often, authors are at a loss to provide an outline of the introduction of a report. Second, provide advance organizers and summaries of complex materials. That is, tell the reader what is to follow and how it is organized, and, if necessary, summarize at the end of the explanation. If the material is lengthy, use headings. Transition statements are particularly helpful when the logic shifts gears.

Writing can be an aid to logic. What may seem perfectly logical in one's own mind may indeed be illogical when explained fully in writing. Writing the method section of a report before the study is conducted often reveals faulty logic. Of course, this is the utility of research proposals.

Principle 5: Have Some Style

Although technical writing is constrained by various parameters, style remains important. Make the research report interesting. Would a reader mildly interested in this topic want to read the entire report? Often, style is the determining factor. Of course, the style should be congruent with the publication in which the article will appear (for example, more informal style for *Psychology Today* than for a dissertation). However, even the most technical writing should be made readable to the fullest extent possible.

Several considerations will aid in preparing readable reports. Interest the reader at the outset; this can be accomplished by good titles, quotations from important sources (ancient Greek sources seem to be the most prestigious), and so forth. A second suggestion is that abbreviations should be avoided. Keep in mind that many readers will attend to one or two sections of the report; if they have to flip around to understand abbreviations, they will tend to quit reading entirely. Particularly annoying are idiosyncratic abbreviations of variables used in statistical analysis programs that make sense only to the author (for example, NCOCLIN—number of counselor/client interactions). A third suggestion (and one probably made by all sources on style) is that simpler words and sentence structures are preferable to more complex ones. The corollary of this suggestion is that precision of expression is desirable.

Principle 6: Write and Rewrite

One fact is clear: except for the extraordinary few, authors need to do some rewriting to prepare a quality research report. Writers use different methods. Some write as fast as possible and rely heavily on the revision process to create a polished product; others write the first draft carefully and minimize time with revisions. Some like to let the original "age" before revising, while others progress as quickly as possible to the final product.

Often authors are so absorbed with their project that they lose objectivity. Having discussed and thought about a procedure, they are convinced that their explanation of it is clear and concise. However, an outside person may have a very different view. We recommend strongly that all authors have a colleague or advisor read and critique research reports as part of the revision process. Unjustified compliments are not helpful, so choose someone who will be critical. (Similarly, if asked to review someone else's report, provide direct and helpful comments.) Different types of comments will be provided by different types of readers. Consider readers who are unfamiliar with the area as well as those who are knowledgeable. Often someone who disagrees with the author's point of view can identify problems with the logic. Remember that these critiques are not binding and the author may choose to ignore them. As a courtesy, authors should ask those who provide critiques whether they wish to be credited in the author footnote (for example, "I express my appreciation to Ima Kritiq for her helpful comments").

Principle 7: Just Write!

We would be remiss if we did not mention problems related to procrastination. Many of us who enjoy conducting research avoid settling down to write the research report. At one time or another, we venture to say, all researchers have agonized about the actual writing of the research report. Rather than stating that "misery loves company," let us give a suggestion: write! Even if you think what you are writing is terrible, write anyway. Drafts can be changed or discarded. In fact, it is usually much easier to revise a draft than it is to create a first draft. Write a few pages and then later determine if it is any good. Once started, writing becomes increasingly easy.

SUMMARY AND CONCLUSIONS

The research report is critical to the research endeavor because it is the typical vehicle by which the results of studies are disseminated. The entire research process is summarized in the research report, from the statement of the problem to the discussion of the results. A coherently organized and well written report will increase the likelihood that the research study will influence the scientific community.

Although organization of the research report varies, most reports contain a title, an abstract, an introduction, a description of the method (subjects, measures, materials, design, and procedure), a presentation of the results, and a discussion or conclusion. The content of these sections is determined, to a great extent, by the design of the research.

The style of the written report varies, certainly; each of us has our own style, which we in turn vary depending on the publication for which our writing is intended. Nevertheless, as general principles, authors should (1) be informative, (2) be forthright, (3) not overstate or exaggerate, (4) be logical and organized, (5) write in an interesting way, and (6) revise their reports to obtain a polished product.

Professional writing is a complex skill that takes years of practice and feedback. Moreover, it is a skill that involves one's personal style of communicating. Procrastination and other avoidance patterns are common reactions of both inexperienced and experienced authors. One of the most effective strategies to improve one's professional writing is to work closely with a successful author, writing drafts, receiving feedback, rewriting, and polishing. It is not atypical for graduate students to spend two to three years co-writing with a faculty member to enhance their professional writing skills as well as to enhance their research skills in general. Thus, we strongly urge students to actively solicit feedback on their writing and seek co-writing experiences with established authors.

APPENDIX A

ETHICAL STANDARDS

of the American Association

for Counseling and Development

PREAMBLE

The Association is an educational, scientific, and professional organization whose members are dedicated to the enhancement of the worth, dignity, potential, and uniqueness of each individual and thus to the service of society.

The Association recognizes that the role of definitions and work settings of its members include a wide variety of academic disciplines, levels of academic preparation, and agency services. This diversity reflects the breadth of the Association's interest and influence. It also poses challenging complexities in efforts to set standards for the performance of members, desired requisite preparation or practice, and supporting social, legal, and ethical controls.

The specification of ethical standards enables the Association to clarify to present and future members and to those served by members the nature of ethical responsibilities held in common by its members.

The existence of such standards serves to stimulate greater concern by members for their own professional functioning and for the conduct of fellow professionals such as counselors, guidance and student personnel workers, and others in the helping professions. As the ethical code of the Association, this document establishes principles that define the ethical behavior of Association members. Additional ethical guidelines developed by the Association's Divisions for their specialty areas may further define a member's ethical behavior.

SECTION A: GENERAL

1. The member influences the development of the profession by continuous efforts to improve professional practices, teaching, services, and research. Professional growth is continuous throughout the member's career and is exemplified by the development of a philosophy that explains why and how a member functions in the helping relationship. Members must gather data on their effectiveness and be guided by the findings. Members recognize the need for continuing education to ensure competent service.

2. The member has a responsibility both to the individual who is served and to the institution within which the service is performed to maintain high standards of professional conduct. The member strives to maintain the highest levels of professional services offered to the individuals to be served. The member also strives to assist the agency, organization, or institution in providing the highest caliber of professional

services. The acceptance of employment in an institution implies that the member is in agreement with the general policies and principles of the institution. Therefore the professional activities of the member are also in accord with the objectives of the institution. If, despite concerted efforts, the member cannot reach agreement with the employer as to acceptable standards of conduct that allow for changes in institutional policy conducive to the positive growth and development of clients, then terminating the affiliation should be seriously considered.

3. Ethical behavior among professional associates, both members and nonmembers, must be expected at all times. When information is possessed that raises doubt as to the ethical behavior of professional colleagues, whether Association members or not, the member must take action to attempt to rectify such a condition. Such action shall use the institution's channels first and then use procedures established by the Association.

4. The member neither claims nor implies professional qualifications exceeding those possessed and is responsible for correcting any misrepresentations of these qualifications by others.

5. In establishing fees for professional counseling services, members must consider the financial status of clients and locality. In the event that the established fee structure is inappropriate for a client, assistance must be provided in finding comparable services of acceptable cost.

6. When members provide information to the public or to subordinates, peers, or supervisors, they have a responsibility to ensure that the content is general, unidentified client information that is accurate, unbiased, and consists of objective, factual data.

7. Members recognize their boundaries of competence and provide only those services and use only those techniques for which they are qualified by training or experience. Members should only accept those positions for which they are professionally qualified.

8. In the counseling relationship, the counselor is aware of the intimacy of the relationship and maintains respect for the client and avoids engaging in activities that seek to meet the counselor's personal needs at the expense of that client.

9. Members do not condone or engage in sexual harassment which is defined as deliberate or repeated comments, gestures, or physical contacts of a sexual nature.

10. The member avoids bringing personal issues into the counseling relationship, especially if the potential for harm is present. Through awareness of the negative impact of both racial and sexual stereotyping and discrimination, the counselor guards the individual rights and personal dignity of the client in the counseling relationship.

11. Products or services provided by the member by means of classroom instruction, public lectures, demonstrations, written articles, radio or television programs, or other types of media must meet the criteria cited in these standards.

SECTION B: COUNSELING RELATIONSHIP

This section refers to practices and procedures of individual and/or group counseling relationships.

The member must recognize the need for client freedom of choice. Under those circumstances where this is not possible, the member must apprise clients of restrictions that may limit their freedom of choice.

1. The member's primary obligation is to respect the integrity and promote the welfare of the client(s), whether the client(s) is (are) assisted individually or in a group relationship. In a group setting, the member is also responsible for taking reasonable

precautions to protect individuals from physical and/or psychological trauma resulting from interaction within the group.

2. Members make provisions for maintaining confidentiality in the storage and disposal of records and follow an established record retention and disposition policy. The counseling relationship and information resulting therefrom must be kept confidential, consistent with the obligations of the member as a professional person. In a group counseling setting, the counselor must set a norm of confidentiality regarding all group participants' disclosures.

3. If an individual is already in a counseling relationship with another professional person, the member does not enter into a counseling relationship without first contacting and receiving the approval of that other professional. If the member discovers that the client is in another counseling relationship after the counseling relationship begins, the member must gain the consent of the other professional or terminate the relationship, unless the client elects to terminate the other relationship.

4. When the client's condition indicates that there is clear and imminent danger to the client or others, the member must take reasonable personal action or inform responsible authorities. Consultation with other professionals must be used where possible. The assumption of responsibility for the client's(s') behavior must be taken only after careful deliberation. The client must be involved in the resumption of responsibility as quickly as possible.

5. Records of the counseling relationship, including interview notes, test data, correspondence, tape recordings, electronic data storage, and other documents are to be considered professional information for use in counseling, and they should not be considered a part of the records of the institution or agency in which the counselor is employed unless specified by state statute or regulation. Revelation to others of counseling material must occur only upon the expressed consent of the client.

6. In view of the extensive data storage and processing capacities of the computer, the member must ensure that data maintained on a computer is: (a) limited to information that is appropriate and necessary for the services being provided; (b) destroyed after it is determined that the information is no longer of any value in providing services; and (c) restricted in terms of access to appropriate staff members involved in the provision of services by using the best computer security methods available.

7. Use of data derived from a counseling relationship for purposes of counselor training or research shall be confined to content that can be disguised to ensure full protection of the identity of the subject client.

8. The member must inform the client of the purposes, goals, techniques, rules of procedure, and limitations that may affect the relationship at or before the time that the counseling relationship is entered. When working with minors or persons who are unable to give consent, the member protects these clients' best interests.

9. In view of common misconceptions related to the perceived inherent validity of computer-generated data and narrative reports, the member must ensure that the client is provided with information as part of the counseling relationship that adequately explains the limitations of computer technology.

10. The member must screen prospective group participants, especially when the emphasis is on self-understanding and growth through self-disclosure. The member must maintain an awareness of the group participants' compatibility throughout the life of the group.

11. The member may choose to consult with any other professionally competent person about a client. In choosing a consultant, the member must avoid placing the consultant in a conflict of interest situation that would preclude the consultant's being a proper party to the member's efforts to help the client.

12. If the member determines an inability to be of professional assistance to the client, the member must either avoid initiating the counseling relationship or immediately terminate that relationship. In either event, the member must suggest appropriate alternatives. (The member must be knowledgeable about referral resources so that a satisfactory referral can be initiated.) In the event the client declines the suggested referral, the member is not obligated to continue the relationship.

13. When the member has other relationships, particularly of an administrative, supervisory, and/or evaluative nature with an individual seeking counseling services, the member must not serve as the counselor but should refer the individual to another professional. Only in instances where such an alternative is unavailable and where the individual's situation warrants counseling intervention should the member enter into and/or maintain a counseling relationship. Dual relationships with clients that might impair the member's objectivity and professional judgement (e.g., as with close friends or relatives) must be avoided and/or the counseling relationship terminated through referral to another competent professional.

14. The member will avoid any type of sexual intimacies with clients. Sexual relationships with clients are unethical.

15. All experimental methods of treatment must be clearly indicated to prospective recipients, and safety precautions are to be adhered to by the member.

16. When computer applications are used as a component of counseling services, the member must ensure that: (a) the client is intellectually, emotionally, and physically capable of using the computer application; (b) the computer application is appropriate for the needs of the client; (c) the client understands the purpose and operation of the computer application; and (d) a follow-up of client use of a computer application is provided to both correct possible problems (misconceptions or inappropriate use) and assess subsequent needs.

17. When the member is engaged in short-term group treatment/training programs (e.g., marathons and other encounter-type or growth groups), the member ensures that there is professional assistance available during and following the group experience.

18. Should the member be engaged in a work setting that calls for any variation from the above statements, the member is obligated to consult with other professionals whenever possible to consider justifiable alternatives.

19. The member must ensure that members of various ethnic, racial, religious, disability, and socioeconomic groups have equal access to computer applications used to support counseling services and that the content of available computer applications does not discriminate against the groups described above.

20. When computer applications are developed by the member for use by the general public as self-help/stand-alone computer software, the member must ensure that: (a) self-help computer applications are designed from the beginning to function in a stand-alone manner, as opposed to modifying software that was originally designed to require support from a counselor; (b) self-help computer applications will include within the program statements regarding intended user outcomes, suggestions for using the software, a description of the conditions under which self-help computer applications might not be appropriate, and a description of when and how counseling services might be beneficial; and (c) the manual for such applications will include the qualifications of the developer, the development process, validation data, and operating procedures.

SECTION C: MEASUREMENT & EVALUATION

The primary purpose of educational and psychological testing is to provide descriptive measures that are objective and interpretable in either comparative or absolute terms.

The member must recognize the need to interpret the statements that follow as applying to the whole range of appraisal techniques including test and nontest data. Test results constitute only one of a variety of pertinent sources of information for personnel, guidance, and counseling decisions.

1. The member must provide specific orientation or information to the examinee(s) prior to and following the test administration so that the results of testing may be placed in proper perspective with other relevant factors. In so doing, the member must recognize the effects of socioeconomic, ethnic, and cultural factors on test scores. It is the member's professional responsibility to use additional unvalidated information carefully in modifying interpretation of the test results.

2. In selecting tests for use in a given situation or with a particular client, the member must consider carefully the specific validity, reliability, and appropriateness of the test(s). General validity, reliability, and related issues may be questioned legally as well as ethically when tests are used for vocational and educational selection, placement, or counseling.

3. When making any statements to the public about tests and testing, the member must give accurate information and avoid false claims or misconceptions. Special efforts are often required to avoid unwarranted connotations of such terms as IQ and grade equivalent scores.

4. Different tests demand different levels of competence for administration, scoring, and interpretation. Members must recognize the limits of their competence and perform only those functions for which they are prepared. In particular, members using computer-based test interpretations must be trained in the construct being measured and the specific instrument being used prior to using this type of computer application.

5. In situations where a computer is used for test administration and scoring, the member is responsible for ensuring that administration and scoring programs function properly to provide clients with accurate test results.

6. Tests must be administered under the same conditions that were established in their standardization. When tests are not administered under standard conditions or when unusual behavior or irregularities occur during the testing session, those conditions must be noted and the results designated as invalid or of questionable validity. Unsupervised or inadequately supervised test-taking, such as the use of tests through the mails, is considered unethical. On the other hand, the use of instruments that are so designed or standardized to be self-administered and self-scored, such as interest inventories, is to be encouraged.

7. The meaningfulness of test results used in personnel, guidance, and counseling functions generally depends on the examinee's unfamiliarity with the specific items on the test. Any prior coaching or dissemination of the test materials can invalidate test results. Therefore, test security is one of the professional obligations of the member. Conditions that produce most favorable test results must be made known to the examinee.

8. The purpose of testing and the explicit use of the results must be made known to the examinee prior to testing. The counselor must ensure that instrument limitations are not exceeded and that periodic review and/or retesting are made to prevent client stereotyping.

9. The examinee's welfare and explicit prior understanding must be the criteria for determining the recipients of the test results. The member must see that specific interpretation accompanies any release of individual or group test data. The interpretation of test data must be related to the examinee's particular concerns.

10. Members responsible for making decisions based on test results have an understanding of educational and psychological measurement, validation criteria, and test research.

11. The member must be cautious when interpreting the results of research instruments possessing insufficient technical data. The specific purposes for the use of such instruments must be stated explicitly to examinees.

12. The member must proceed with caution when attempting to evaluate and interpret the performance of minority group members or other persons who are not represented in the norm group on which the instrument was standardized.

13. When computer-based test interpretations are developed by the member to support the assessment process, the member must ensure that the validity of such interpretation is established prior to the commercial distribution of such a computer application.

14. The member recognizes that test results may become obsolete. The member will avoid and prevent the misuse of obsolete test results.

15. The member must guard against the appropriation, reproduction, or modification of published tests or parts thereof without acknowledgement and permission from the previous publisher.

16. Regarding the preparation, publication, and distribution of tests, reference should be made to:
   a. "Standards for Educational and Psychological Testing," revised edition, 1985, published by the American Psychological Association on behalf of itself, the American Educational Research Association and the National Council of Measurement in Education.
   b. "The Responsible Use of Tests: A Position Paper of AMEG, APGA, and NCME," *Measurement and Evaluation in Guidance*, 1972, 5, 385–388.
   c. "Responsibilities of Users of Standardized Tests," APGA, *Guidepost*, October 5, 1978, pp. 5–8.

SECTION D: RESEARCH AND PUBLICATION

   1. Guidelines on research with human subjects shall be adhered to, such as:
   a. *Ethical Principles in the Conduct of Research with Human Participants*, Washington, D.C.: American Psychological Association, Inc., 1982.
   b. Code of Federal Regulation, Title 45, Subtitle A, Part 46, as currently issued.
   c. *Ethical Principles of Psychologists*, American Psychological Association, Principle #9: Research with Human Participants.
   d. Family Educational Rights and Privacy Act (the Buckley Amendment).
   e. Current federal regulations and various state rights privacy acts.

2. In planning any research activity dealing with human subjects, the member must be aware of and responsive to all pertinent ethical principles and ensure that the research problem, design, and execution are in full compliance with them.

3. Responsibility for ethical research practice lies with the principal researcher, while others involved in the research activities share ethical obligation and full responsibility for their own actions.

4. In research with human subjects, researchers are responsible for the subjects' welfare throughout the experiment, and they must take all reasonable precautions to avoid causing injurious psychological, physical, or social effects on their subjects.

5. All research subjects must be informed of the purpose of the study except when withholding information or providing misinformation to them is essential to the

investigation. In such research the member must be responsible for corrective action as soon as possible following completion of the research.

6. Participation in research must be voluntary. Involuntary participation is appropriate only when it can be demonstrated that participation will have no harmful effects on subjects and is essential to the investigation.

7. When reporting research results, explicit mention must be made of all variables and conditions known to the investigator that might affect the outcome of the investigation or the interpretation of the data.

8. The member must be responsible for conducting and reporting investigations in a manner that minimizes the possibility that results will be misleading.

9. The member has an obligation to make available sufficient original research data to qualified others who may wish to replicate the study.

10. When supplying data, aiding in the research of another person, reporting research results, or making original data available, due care must be taken to disguise the identity of the subjects in the absence of specific authorization from such subjects to do otherwise.

11. When conducting and reporting research, the member must be familiar with and give recognition to previous work on the topic, as well as to observe all copyright laws and follow the principles of giving full credit to all to whom credit is due.

12. The member must give due credit through joint authorship, acknowledgement, footnote statements, or other appropriate means to those who have contributed significantly to the research and/or publication, in accordance with such contributions.

13. The member must communicate to other members the results of any research judged to be of professional or scientific value. Results reflecting unfavorably on institutions, programs, services, or vested interests must not be withheld for such reasons.

14. If members agree to cooperate with another individual in research and/or publication, they incur an obligation to cooperate as promised in terms of punctuality of performance and with full regard to the completeness and accuracy of the information required.

15. Ethical practice requires that authors not submit the same manuscript or one essentially similar in content for simultaneous publication consideration by two or more journals. In addition, manuscripts published in whole or in substantial part in another journal or published work should not be submitted for publication without acknowledgement and permission from the previous publication.

SECTION E: CONSULTING

Consultation refers to a voluntary relationship between a professional helper and help-needing individual, group, or social unit in which the consultant is providing help to the client(s) in defining and solving a work-related problem or potential problem with a client or client system.

1. The member acting as consultant must have a high degree of self-awareness of his/her own values, knowledge, skills, limitations, and needs in entering a helping relationship that involves human and/or organizational change and that the focus of the relationship be on the issues to be resolved and not on the person(s) presenting the problem.

2. There must be understanding and agreement between member and client for the problem definition, change of goals, and prediction of consequences of interventions selected.

3. The member must be reasonably certain that she/he or the organization represented has the necessary competencies and resources for giving the kind of help

that is needed now or may be needed later and that appropriate referral resources are available to the consultant.

   4. The consulting relationship must be one in which client adaptability and growth toward self-direction are encouraged and cultivated. The member must maintain this role consistently and not become a decision maker for the client or create a future dependency on the consultant.

   5. When announcing consultant availability for services, the member conscientiously adheres to the Association's Ethical Standards.

   6. The member must refuse a private fee or other remuneration for consultation with persons who are entitled to these services through the member's employing institution or agency. The policies of a particular agency may make explicit provisions for private practice with agency clients by members of its staff. In such instances, the clients must be apprised of other options open to them should they seek private counseling services.

SECTION F: PRIVATE PRACTICE

   1. The member should assist the profession by facilitating the availability of counseling services in private as well as public settings.

   2. In advertising services as a private practitioner, the member must advertise the services in a manner that accurately informs the public of professional services, expertise, and techniques of counseling available. A member who assumes an executive leadership role in the organization shall not permit his/her name to be used in professional notices during periods when he/she is not actively engaged in the private practice of counseling.

   3. The member may list the following: highest relevant degree, type and level of certification and/or license, address, telephone number, office hours, type and/or description of services, and other relevant information. Such information must not contain false, inaccurate, misleading, partial, out-of-context, or deceptive material or statements.

   4. Members do not present their affiliation with any organization in such a way that would imply inaccurate sponsorship or certification by that organization.

   5. Members may join in partnership/corporation with other members and/or other professionals provided that each member of the partnership or corporation makes clear the separate specialties by name in compliance with the regulations of the locality.

   6. A member has an obligation to withdraw from a counseling relationship if it is believed that employment will result in violation of the Ethical Standards. If the mental or physical condition of the member renders it difficult to carry out an effective professional relationship or if the member is discharged by the client because the counseling relationship is no longer productive for the client, then the member is obligated to terminate the counseling relationship.

   7. A member must adhere to the regulations for private practice of the locality where the services are offered.

   8. It is unethical to use one's institutional affiliation to recruit clients for one's private practice.

SECTION G: PERSONNEL ADMINISTRATION

It is recognized that most members are employed in public or quasi-public institutions. The functioning of a member within an institution must contribute to the goals of the institution and vice versa if either is to accomplish their respective goals or objectives.

It is therefore essential that the member and the institution function in ways to: (a) make the institutional goals specific; and public; (b) make the member's contribution to institutional goals specific; and (c) foster mutual accountability for goal achievement.

To accomplish these objectives, it is recognized that the member and the employer must share responsibilities in the formulation and implementation of personnel policies.

1. Members must define and describe the parameters and levels of their professional competency.

2. Members must establish interpersonal relations and working agreements with supervisors and subordinates regarding counseling or clinical relationships, confidentiality, distinction between public and private material, maintenance and dissemination of recorded information, work load, and accountability. Working agreements in each instance must be specified and made known to those concerned.

3. Members must alert their employers to conditions that may be potentially disruptive or damaging.

4. Members must inform employers of conditions that may limit their effectiveness.

5. Members must submit regularly to professional review and evaluation.

6. Members must be responsible for in-service development of self and/or staff.

7. Members must inform their staff of goals and programs.

8. Members must provide personnel practices that guarantee and enhance the rights and welfare of each recipient of their service.

9. Members must select competent persons and assign responsibilities compatible with their skills and experiences.

10. The member, at the onset of a counseling relationship, will inform the client of the member's intended use of supervisors regarding the disclosure of information concerning this case. The member will clearly inform the client of the limits of confidentiality in the relationship.

11. Members, as either employers or employees, do not engage in or condone practices that are inhumane, illegal, or unjustifiable (such as considerations based on sex, handicap, age, race) in hiring, promotion, or training.

SECTION H: PREPARATION STANDARDS

Members who are responsible for training others must be guided by the preparation standards of the Association and relevant Division(s). The member who functions in the capacity of trainer assumes unique ethical responsibilities that frequently go beyond that of the member who does not function in a training capacity. These ethical responsibilities are outlined as follows:

1. Members must orient students to program expectations, basic skills development, and employment prospects prior to admission to the program.

2. Members in charge of learning experiences must establish programs that integrate academic study and supervised practice.

3. Members must establish a program directed toward developing students' skills, knowledge, and self-understanding, stated whenever possible in competency or performance terms.

4. Members must identify the levels of competencies of their students in compliance with relevant Division standards. These competencies must accommodate the paraprofessional as well as the professional.

5. Members, through continual student evaluation and appraisal, must be aware of the personal limitations of the learner that might impede future performance. The

instructor must not only assist the learner in securing remedial assistance but also screen from the program those individuals who are unable to provide competent services.

6. Members must provide a program that includes training in research commensurate with levels of role functioning. Paraprofessional and technician-level personnel must be trained as consumers of research. In addition, personnel must learn how to evaluate their own and their program's effectiveness. Graduate training, especially at the doctoral level, would include preparation for original research by the member.

7. Members must make students aware of the ethical responsibilities and standards of the profession.

8. Preparatory programs must encourage students to value the ideals of service to individuals and to society. In this regard, direct financial remuneration or lack thereof must not be allowed to overshadow professional and humanitarian needs.

9. Members responsible for educational programs must be skilled as teachers and practitioners.

10. Members must present thoroughly varied theoretical positions so that students may make comparisons and have the opportunity to select a position.

11. Members must develop clear policies within their educational institutions regarding field placement and the roles of the student and the instructor in such placement.

12. Members must ensure that forms of learning focusing on self-understanding or growth are voluntary, or if required as part of the educational program, are made known to prospective students prior to entering the program. When the educational program offers a growth experience with an emphasis on self-disclosure or other relatively intimate or personal involvement, the member must have no administrative, supervisory, or evaluating authority regarding the participant.

13. The member will at all times provide students with clear and equally acceptable alternatives for self-understanding or growth experiences. The member will assure students that they have a right to accept these alternatives without prejudice or penalty.

14. Members must conduct an educational program in keeping with the current relevant guidelines of the Association.

APPENDIX B

THE AMERICAN PSYCHOLOGICAL ASSOCIATION'S ETHICAL PRINCIPLES OF PSYCHOLOGISTS

Author's note: At the time of printing, these Ethical Principles were under review by the APA membership. Readers should consult the approved Ethical Principles for possible modifications. *

INTRODUCTION

The *Ethical Principles of Psychologists* consists of the General Preamble followed by six general ethical principles. The general principles state ethical ideals that guide psychologists to the highest standards of the profession. Each general principle is followed by ethical standards that set forth minimal behavioral expectations for upholding the principle. Both the general principles and the ethical standards should be considered in arriving at an ethical decision. Whenever possible, the standards are written broadly so as to apply to all psychologists regardless of the professional role they occupy.

Membership in the American Psychological Association commits members to adhere to the Association's *Ethical Principles of Psychologists,* also called the Ethical Code. The Code is also intended to educate and guide students of psychology and others who do work of a psychological nature.

GENERAL PREAMBLE

Psychologists promote the welfare and respect the dignity and worth of the individual, and strive to preserve and protect fundamental human rights. To do so requires that psychologists understand and consider such variables as age, disability, ethnicity, gender, national origin, race, religion, sexual orientation, and social class. In whatever their roles, psychologists strive for honesty, integrity, and respect for others.

Psychologists are committed to increasing knowledge of behavior and to using this knowledge to promote human welfare. Psychologists are sensitive to how their behavior affects individuals, groups, and society. They make every effort to prevent harmful consequences to others.

Because psychologists require for themselves freedom of inquiry and communication, they accept the responsibilities that freedom requires: competence, objectivity, and concern for the best interests of those with whom they work. In their areas of competence, psychologists have adequate education and training. They stay current with and informed about relevant literature and ethical issues. They examine their personal values as these may influence their professional conduct. They recognize limitations and changes in their personal competence that might adversely affect others, and take appropriate measures. When uncertain about an ethical choice, they consult with others; they serve as resources to their colleagues and peers facing similar dilemmas.

Psychologists aspire to the highest ideals of ethical behavior, described in these *Ethical Principles:* Respect for Rights and Dignity of Persons, Promoting Welfare of Others, Social Responsibility, Integrity, Competence, and Professional Responsibility.

PRINCIPLE I: RESPECT FOR RIGHTS AND DIGNITY OF PERSONS
General Principle:

Psychologists respect the fundamental rights, dignity, and worth of people and respect human differences, including those due to age, disability, ethnicity, gender, national origin, race, religion, sexual orientation, and social class. Psychologists promote the rights of individuals to privacy, self-determination, and autonomy.

A. Rights and Responsibilities

1. Psychologists do not engage in or condone practices that are inhumane or that result in illegal or unjustifiable actions. — *Avoiding illegal or unjustifiable actions*

2. Psychologists establish, maintain, and use fair procedures in addressing situations in which rights are at risk. — *Procedural fairness*

3. Psychologists use fair measures for evaluating performance and take appropriate actions when performance is inadequate. — *Fair evaluations*

4. After making their expectations clear, and using remedial strategies when applicable, psychologists withhold degrees, credentials, and promotions, or impose other appropriate consequences for those whose performance does not meet established criteria. — *Assessing inadequate performance*

5. Psychologists respect the rights of others to hold diverse values, attitudes, and opinions. — *Respecting diversity*

B. Confidentiality

1. Psychologists have an obligation to maintain the confidentiality of information obtained in the course of their work. — *Maintaining confidentiality*

2. Information or data obtained in the course of professional relationships are disclosed to peers only for professional purposes and only to professionals clearly concerned with the case. — *Professional consultations with peers*

3. When consulting, psychologists share with others information that could lead to the identification of a client only to the extent necessary to achieve the purposes of that consultation. — *Minimizing identifying data*

4. In order to avoid invasions of privacy, written and oral reports present only data germane to the purposes of the psychological service being rendered. — *Minimizing invasion of privacy*

5. When possible and appropriate, psychologists inform people at the outset of a professional relationship of those constraints on confidentiality that can be reasonably anticipated. — *Informing others of legal limits of confidentiality*

6. When working with individuals from cultures in which rules of confidentiality are more strictly applied, psychologists respect those restrictions to the extent possible.

Confidentiality and differing cultural standards

7. Psychologists reveal confidential information only with the formal consent of the person or person's legal representative, except in those unusual circumstances in which a psychologist reasonably determines that releasing the information is necessary to prevent a clear danger to the person or other persons or if warranted and appropriate to comply with a legal requirement.

Release of information and formal consent

8. Psychologists maintain confidentiality in storing and disposing of written and electronic records, and in providing for such records in the event of their death or incapacitation.

Maintenance of records and procedures for therapist's death

9. Psychologists who present personal information obtained during the course of professional work in their writings, lectures, or other public forums, either obtain prior consent to do so or take reasonable steps to assure that personal identities are not revealed.

Use of confidential information for didactic purposes

C. Informing Consumers and Research Participants

1. Psychologists inform consumers as to the purpose and nature of an evaluation, research, treatment, or educational procedure in language commensurate with the individual's level of comprehension.

Clarifying expectations

2. Whenever possible, psychologists obtain informed consent from children and from individuals with diminished mental capacity regarding their participation in psychological services or research. If they object to participation, the psychologist considers the individual's basic rights in light of such factors as age, psychological maturity, and the judgment of the individual's parents or legal guardians. The psychologist's decision is based upon the best interests of the individual.

Minors and those with diminished capacity

3. Psychologists inform recipients as to the voluntary or mandatory nature of the assessment, treatment, research, educational, or training procedure. When a procedure is voluntary, psychologists inform the clients, students, or research participants of their freedom of choice and any alternatives to participation.

Voluntary and mandatory procedures

4. Psychologists obtain permission from clients, students, and research participants prior to the use of observation or electronic taping, recording, or filming procedures.

Electronic recording and filming

5. When the possibility exists that others may obtain access to confidential information, psychologists explain this possibility, together with plans for protecting confidentiality, to clients, students, or participants as part of the procedure for obtaining informed consent.

Access to confidential information by others

6. In offering clinical or other professional services as an inducement for obtaining research participants, psychologists make clear the nature of the services as well as the risks and obligations.

Inducements for research participants

7. When conducting research, psychologists clearly communicate to participants the experiences they are likely to have, especially those that they might find negative, such as physical risk or discomfort, negative emotional reactions, etcetera.

Research involving risk or discomfort

8. Individuals are ordinarily free to decline to participate in research or to withdraw from research without adverse consequences. When research participation is mandated by a third party, psychologists describe the probable consequences of consenting, declining to participate, or subsequently withdrawing from the research.

Freedom to avoid or withdraw from research

9. When psychologists conduct research with individuals whose real or ascribed power is different than that of the psychologist, special care is taken to protect their rights to decline participation or withdraw from research.

Protecting right of individual to avoid or withdraw from research

10. Before deciding to waive informed consent, psychologists planning research that may not require informed consent, such as certain types of archival research or anonymous naturalistic observations, consult with APA, federal and state guidelines, or human subject review committees.

Waiving informed consent

11. Prior to conducting research, psychologists establish a clear and fair agreement with participants that clarifies the obligations and responsibilities of each party.

Research obligations and responsibilities

12. Psychologists inform research participants of procedures for contacting them within a reasonable time period following participation should stress, harm, or related questions or concerns arise.

Post research consultation with participants

13. When conducting research, psychologists provide participants, regardless of age or diminished mental capacity, with the opportunity to receive information about the general results and conclusions of that research.

Providing participants research results and conclusions

14. Psychologists clarify in advance their plans for sharing and utilizing research data with participants and any other persons.

Sharing and utilizing data

15. When psychologists have access to data collected by others, they obtain permission from research participants, whenever possible, to utilize the data. In any case, psychologists have a special obligation to ensure that information is obtained and stored in such a way as to preserve the anonymity of participants.

Permission: Access to another's data

16. Psychologists explain clearly their financial arrangements, including fees and billing procedures, as early as feasible in their contacts with consumers, and as appropriate throughout the time that services are rendered. They explain the possibility of initiating collection procedures prior to using such procedures. Records regarding services already rendered may not be withheld because payment has not been received.

Financial arrangements

17. When psychologists agree to provide services to a client at the request of a third party, psychologists assume the

Third-party referrals

responsibility for informing each party about the nature of their relationships. Such information includes defining the role of the psychologist (for example, therapist, diagnostician, expert witness), as well as the probable uses of the information gathered and conclusions reached. If there is a risk of conflicting alliances in the provision of services, due to the involvement of a third party, psychologists clarify the nature and direction of their responsibilities and keep all parties appropriately informed.

18. When psychologists agree to provide assessment, evaluation, treatment, or other psychological services to an individual or group, regardless of the origin of the request and regardless of the age or competence of the person making the request, psychologists provide the individual or group with information about the results, conclusions, and rationale. If a psychologist is prohibited by law or by professional role within an organization from doing so, then the psychologist must so inform the individual or group at the outset of psychological service.

Providing results of psychological services

PRINCIPLE II: WELFARE OF OTHERS
General Principle:

Psychologists contribute to and promote the welfare of those with whom they work. Promoting the welfare of others requires that psychologists function without causing foreseeable harm or injury. When conflicts do occur among their obligations, they attempt to do the least amount of harm. They are sensitive to real and ascribed differences in power between themselves and others and are careful to avoid exploiting or misleading other people.

A. General Psychological Services

1. Psychologists take reasonable steps to protect the welfare of consumers, research participants, students, and others with whom they work, and to avoid actions that could be of foreseeable harm to them.

Avoiding harm to consumers

2. Psychologists use their skills in a manner consistent with these principles. They do not participate in activities that might lead to a misuse of their skills.

Misuse of skills

3. Psychologists make referrals in light of all relevant considerations, including applicable law and contractual limitations, keeping paramount the best interests of the consumer. They neither give nor receive remuneration for making or accepting referrals for professional services, without full disclosure in advance to the consumer of the terms of such an agreement.

Referrals based on consumer welfare

4. In deciding whether to offer services to someone already receiving similar services elsewhere, psychologists carefully consider the treatment issues and the potential client's welfare. The psychologist discusses these issues with the client to minimize the probable risks of confusion and conflict, and proceeds with caution and sensitivity to the therapeutic issues.

Offering services to clients of others

5. Psychologists avoid relationships that may impair their objectivity or create a conflict of interest. They avoid dual relationships that could impair their professional judgment or increase

Avoiding dual relationships

the risk of exploitation, such as sexual relationships with their current students, supervisees, or trainees. Engaging in either therapy or assessment of clients generally precludes social or business relationships with those clients.

6. Psychologists do not engage in sexual intimacies with current or former psychotherapy clients.

Prohibiting sex with clients

7. Psychologists do not exploit, sexually or otherwise, their professional relationships with clients, supervisees, students, employees, research participants, or others.

Prohibiting exploitation in professional relationships

8. Psychologists terminate a professional relationship when it becomes reasonably clear that the consumer is not benefiting or is being harmed by continued contact. They offer options for alternative sources of assistance.

Unproductive professional relationships

9. Psychologists provide for the transfer of records and referral of clients, in the event of the psychologist's departure or death, in a manner that promotes the client's welfare. They also attempt to provide for continuity of care when psychological services are interrupted by such factors as the client's departure or financial limitations.

Interruptions to treatment

10. Psychologists do not condone or engage in harassment based on either age, disability, ethnicity, gender, national origin, race, religion, sexual orientation, or social class.

Avoiding harassment

11. Psychologists know and take into account the function and role of other professionals and cooperate with them when to do so is in the best interest of the consumer.

Cooperating with other professionals

B. Assessment

1. Psychologists avoid misuse of assessment results and interpretations, and strive to prevent others from engaging in such misuse.

Misuse of assessment results

2. Psychologists apply the same ethical standards concerning confidentiality, competence, and consumer welfare whether using automated or nonautomated procedures for testing, assessment, or other psychological services.

Automated psychological services

C. Research

1. In planning a study, psychologists carefully evaluate its ethical acceptability. If the weighing of scientific and human values suggests the possibility of a violation of any principle, psychologists seek ethical advice through peer consultation and institutional review boards, and observe stringent safeguards to protect the rights of human participants and the welfare of animal subjects.

Planning research

2. When working with animal subjects, psychologists ensure that the animals will be treated humanely. They only inflict discomfort, illness, or pain when the objectives of the research cannot be achieved by other methods. Any procedures that do inflict pain, stress, or privation must be strongly justified by their prospective scientific, educational, or applied value.

Animal subjects' welfare

3. Assessing the degree of risk to research participants, according to recognized standards, is of primary ethical concern to psychologists. They protect human participants from physical and mental harm as well as any danger that may arise from research procedures.

Assessing level of risk and protecting human participants

4. In planning, implementing, or interpreting socially sensitive research, or in situations where investigator bias may be a factor, psychologists have a duty to consult with those knowledgeable about the individuals or groups most likely to be affected, in order to preserve the integrity of the research methodology and to prevent harm.

Socially sensitive research and duty to consult

5. Research procedures likely to cause serious or lasting harm to a human participant are not used unless the failure to use these procedures might expose the participant to greater harm, or unless the research has significant potential benefit. In either case, psychologists obtain fully informed, voluntary consent from each participant.

Justification for risks of serious harm

6. Psychologists do not deceive human participants about the experience of participating in a study, especially those aspects that subjects might find negative, such as physical risk, discomfort, or unpleasant emotional experiences. Any deceptive aspects of a study must be explained at its conclusion or earlier. Before conducting such a study, psychologists have a special responsibility to (a) determine whether the use of deceptive techniques is justified by the study's prospective scientific, educational, or applied value; and (b) determine whether alternative procedures are available that do not use concealment or deception.

Deception and debriefing

7. Interference with the milieu in which data are collected is kept to a minimum.

Minimizing invasiveness of data gathering

8. After data are collected, psychologists provide an opportunity to human participants to obtain information about the nature of the research, and they attempt to correct any misconceptions that may have arisen. If scientific or human values justify delaying or withholding this information, the psychologist incurs a special responsibility to monitor the research and to ensure that there are no damaging consequences for the participant.

Providing participants with information about the study

PRINCIPLE III: SOCIAL RESPONSIBILITY
General Principle:

Psychologists have a responsibility to the societies in which they work and live. They apply and make public their knowledge of psychology to contribute to human justice and welfare. When undertaking research, they consider how to contribute to human welfare as well as to the science of psychology. Psychologists are cognizant of cultural and individual differences and work to eliminate biases based on age, disability, ethnicity, gender, national origin, race, religion, sexual orientation, or social class. Psychologists are concerned with the development of such legal and quasi-legal regulations as best serve the public interest, and they work toward changing existing regulations that are not beneficial to the public interest. Social responsibility implies that professional contributions should not be guided solely by monetary remuneration, but by concern for societal and individual welfare. Therefore, psychologists contribute a portion of their professional time for little or no remuneration.

A. General Responsibility

1. Psychologists adhere to relevant governmental laws and institutional regulations. When these laws are in conflict with sections of this code, they make known their commitment to the APA *Ethical Principles* and, whenever possible, work toward a resolution of the conflict.

Conflict between laws or institutional regulations and *Ethical Principles*

2. As practitioners, psychologists know that they bear a heavy social responsibility because their recommendations and professional actions may alter the lives of others. They are alert to personal, social, organizational, financial, or political situations and pressures that might lead to misuse of their influence.

Social responsibility and misuse of influence

B. Research

1. Psychologists plan and carry out investigations in a manner consistent with federal and state regulations as well as professional standards governing the conduct of research with human participants and animal subjects.

Federal and state regulations and professional standards

2. Psychologists provide a discussion of the limitations of their studies, especially where their work touches on social policy or might be construed to the detriment of persons in groups of specific age, disability, ethnicity, gender, national origin, race, religion, sexual orientation, social class, or other vulnerable groups.

Reporting limitations of study

3. Psychologists do not engage in fraudulent research or distort, fabricate, misrepresent, or bias their results. They never suppress disconfirming data, and they acknowledge the existence of alternative hypotheses and explanations of their findings.

Fraudulent research

4. Psychologists attempt to prevent distortion or misuse of psychological findings by their employing institution or agency.

Preventing misuse of research results

5. After research results are in the public domain, psychologists do not withhold the data on which their conclusions are based from other competent professionals, assuming the confidentiality of the participants can be protected.

Sharing data

C. Public Statements and Accountability

1. Psychologists are responsible for substantiating their professional recommendations and actions, particularly as these affect the lives of others. They take special care to substantiate claims that may affect such groups as those identified by age, disability, ethnicity, gender, national origin, religion, sexual orientation, race, or social class.

Substantiating professional recommendations and actions

2. In presenting their services, products, and publications in public statements, psychologists are guided by the primary obligation to aid the public in developing informed judgments, opinions,

Advertising and public statements

and choices. Public statements include but are not limited to: communication by means of print, electronic media, lectures, expert witness testimony, or other public presentation.

PRINCIPLE IV: INTEGRITY
General Principle:

Psychologists are honest, fair, and respectful of others during the course of their professional work. They avoid deceit in describing their qualifications, services, research, or products. Psychologists strive to be aware of their own belief systems, values, needs, and limitations.

A. Advertising, Announcements, and Public Statements

    1. Psychologists do not make false, fraudulent, misleading, or deceptive statements in: (a) announcements or advertisements of psychological products, publications, or services; (b) public statements about individuals, groups, or organizations; (c) announcements, descriptions, or advertisements of educational offerings such as programs, seminars, or courses, and; (d) statements about their qualifications, education, experience, competence, and affiliations.

Fraud in public statements

    2. Psychologists do not claim organizational memberships (for example, APA) in a manner that suggests specialized competence or qualifications that the psychologist does not have.

Accurate claims of organizational membership

    3. Psychologists do not solicit testimonial endorsements from current psychotherapy clients or other persons who, because of their particular circumstances, are also vulnerable to undue influence. Psychologists do not solicit consent from such persons to use statements or testimonial endorsements previously made by them.

Avoiding client testimonials

    4. Psychologists make reasonable efforts to ensure that announcements or advertisements about them or their services which are developed by non-psychologists are consistent with these ethical principles.

Responsibility for advertising done by others

    5. Psychologists do not engage in uninvited, in-person solicitation of business from actual or potential clients or others who, because of their particular circumstances, are vulnerable to undue influence.

Prohibiting overbearing solicitation

B. Research

    1. Psychologists secure appropriate approval from host institutions or organizations prior to conducting research. They provide accurate information about their research proposal, carry out the research as agreed, and give the host proper acknowledgment.

Approval from host institutions

    2. Psychologists generally disclose funding sources and sponsors in reporting research results.

Acknowledging funding source

    3. When conducting research, psychologists honor all commitments to participants.

Honoring commitments to participants

C. Publications

　　1. Psychologists take credit only for work they have actually done, including publication credit.

Accurate claims

　　2. Publication credit accurately reflects the relative contribution of the individuals involved, regardless of professional status. A student generally is listed as the principal author of any multiply authored article based primarily on the student's thesis or dissertation. Minor contributions to publications are acknowledged in footnotes or in an introductory statement.

Publication credit

　　3. Plagiarism in either written or oral form is unethical. Acknowledgment through specific citations is made for unpublished as well as published material that has directly influenced the research or writing.

Acknowledging all sources

PRINCIPLE V: COMPETENCE
General Principle:

The maintenance of high standards of competence is a responsibility shared by all psychologists in the interest of the public and the professional as a whole. Psychologists recognize the boundaries of their competence and the limitations of their techniques. They only provide services and only use techniques for which they are qualified by training and experience. In those areas in which recognized standards do not yet exist, psychologists take whatever precautions are necessary to protect the welfare of their clients. They maintain knowledge of current scientific and professional information related to the services they render, and recognize the need for ongoing education.

　　Psychologists make full use of all professional, technical, and administrative resources that serve the best interests of consumers, research participants, students, and others with whom they work.

A. General Competence

　　1. Diagnostic and therapeutic services are provided only in the context of a professional psychological relationship.

Context for diagnostic or therapeutic services

　　2. Psychologists do not practice or conduct research outside the boundaries of their demonstrated competence or the limitations of their techniques, training, and supervised experience.

Boundaries of competence

　　3. In those areas for which performance standards do not yet exist, psychologists take all reasonable steps to ensure the competence of their work.

Caution when standards are lacking

　　4. Psychologists recognize that personal problems and conflicts may interfere with professional effectiveness. Accordingly, they refrain from undertaking any activity in which their personal problems are likely to lead to inadequate performance or harm to a client, colleague, student, or research participant. If engaged in such activity when they become aware of their personal problems, they seek competent professional assistance to determine whether they should suspend, terminate, or limit the scope of their professional and/or scientific activities.

Personal problems and conflicts

5. Psychologists who become aware that personal impairment has compromised their competence are obligated to seek competent consultation and/or supervision and treatment.

Responsibilities of impaired psychologists

B. Public Statements

1. Psychologists claim as evidence of educational qualifications only those degrees obtained from institutions acceptable under the Bylaws and Rules of Council of the American Psychological Association.

Academic degrees

2. Psychologists maintain appropriate standards of scholarship by presenting psychological information fully and accurately.

Presentation of psychological information

3. When providing psychological information, professional opinions, or information about the availability of psychological products, publications, and services, psychologists make public statements consistent with scientifically acceptable psychological findings and techniques, which appropriately recognize the inherent limits and uncertainties of such evidence.

Public statements about products and services

4. When personal advice is given by means of public lectures or demonstrations, newspaper or magazine articles, radio or television programs, mail, or similar media, psychologists utilize the most current relevant data and exercises the highest level of professional judgment.

Exercising competent judgment when providing advice

C. Ongoing Professional Education

1. Psychologists perform their duties consistent with current scientific and professional information related to their work.

Remaining knowledgeable about current scientific research

2. Psychologists recognize differences among people such as those that may be associated with age, disability, ethnicity, gender, national origin, race, religion, sexual orientation, or social class. They obtain training, experience, or supervision to ensure competent service or research relating to such persons.

Remaining knowledgeable about clients with special needs

D. Research

1. Psychologists accept responsibility for the methods used in scientific investigation, analyses, and reports.

Ultimate responsibility for research study

2. Responsibilities and activities of psychologists participating in research are consistent with their respective competencies.

Competence of assistants with human subjects

3. Psychologists who conduct research with animal subjects are trained in appropriate research methods, as well as in the humane care and maintenance of animals.

Competence with animal subjects

E. Assessment

1. Psychologists use, administer, score, and interpret psychological assessment techniques competently.

Competence in assessment

2. Psychologists who use assessment techniques maintain current knowledge about research developments and revisions concerning the techniques that they use.

Remaining knowledgeable about current research and assessment

3. When conducting assessments, psychologists are familiar with their reliability and validity and related standardization studies. Psychologists recognize the limits to the certainty with which predictions can be made about individuals, including those to whom the norms may not apply due to factors such as their age, disability, ethnicity, gender, national origin, race, religion, sexual orientation, social class, or language.

Reliability, validity, and special populations

4. When interpreting assessment results, including automated interpretations, psychologists take into account the various factors that should temper their judgments and may reduce an interpretation's accuracy. They indicate reservations about their conclusions, assessment circumstances, and/or the degree to which norms may not be applicable.

Reporting assessment results

5. Psychologists make diagnostic or evaluative statements only about those whom they have assessed in the context of a professional relationship.

Diagnosis and evaluation in professional context

6. Psychologists promote the appropriate use of psychological assessment techniques. When assessment results are provided by other qualified professionals, whether under the psychologist's supervision or by automated interpretation services, procedures are established for ensuring the adequacy of these explanations.

Appropriate use of tests and automated psychological services

7. Psychologists select scoring and interpretation services based on evidence of the validity of the programs and procedures used in arriving at interpretations.

Test scoring and interpretation services

8. Psychologists make decisions based on test results in a manner consistent with principles of psychological or educational measurement.

Use of tests in decisions

9. Psychologists do not base recommendations or decisions on obsolete tests results.

Rejecting obsolete test results

10. Psychologists who develop and standardize psychological tests and other assessment techniques use established scientific procedures and observe the relevant APA standards and guidelines.

Scientific procedures in test construction

11. Psychologists maintain the security of tests and other assessment techniques within the limits of legal mandates.

Maintaining test security

PRINCIPLE VI: PROFESSIONAL RESPONSIBILITY
General Principle:

Psychologists uphold high professional standards, accept full responsibility for their behavior, clarify their obligations to and expectations of others, and adapt their methods to the needs of different populations. They are sensitive to the ethical conduct of their peers. Psychologists' moral and ethical standards of behavior are a personal matter to the same degree for any other citizen, except as such standards may compromise the fulfillment of their professional responsibilities or reduce the public trust in psychology and psychologists. Psychologists are also aware of the possible impact of their public behavior upon the ability of colleagues to perform their professional duties.

A. Accountability

1. Psychologists accept responsibility for the consequences of their acts and make every effort to ensure that their services are used appropriately.

Accountability for provision of services

2. Psychologists take reasonable precautions to ensure that their employees act responsibly, competently, and ethically.

Ensuring competency in employees

3. Psychologists always retain responsibility for ethical practices in human or animal research conducted by those under their direction.

Research responsibilities

4. Psychologists responsible for training conduct periodic evaluations of their programs to ensure that established goals are met.

Periodic evaluation of training programs

5. Within the limitations of the institutional setting, psychologists who employ or supervise other professionals provide appropriate working conditions, timely performance evaluations, constructive consultation, appropriate supervision, and access to relevant training experiences.

Supervisory and employer relationships

6. Psychologists appropriately document their professional work to ensure accountability.

Documentation of professional work

B. Ethical Conflicts

1. When the demands of an organization conflict with the *Ethical Principles,* psychologists clarify the nature of the conflict between the demands and the principles. Psychologists affirm their responsibility to uphold the *Ethical Principles.*

Conflict between ethics and organizational demands

2. When psychologists are uncertain whether a situation constitutes a violation of the *Ethical Principles,* they consult with other psychologists or state, national, or other ethics committees.

Uncertainty regarding ethical choice

3. When psychologists know of an ethical violation by another psychologist, and it seems appropriate, they attempt to resolve the issue by informally bringing the behavior to the attention of the psychologist. If the misconduct is of a minor nature or appears to be due to lack of sensitivity, knowledge, or experience, an informal solution is usually appropriate. Informal corrective efforts are made with sensitivity to any rights to confidentiality involved.

Minor ethical violations

4. If an ethical violation does not seem amenable to an informal solution, or is of a more serious nature, psychologists take appropriate action such as referral to state or national committees on professional ethics, or state licensing boards, unless such reporting would conflict with rights of privilege or confidentiality.

Major ethical violations

5. Psychologists cooperate with the Ethics Committee of the American Psychological Association by responding personally to inquiries. Failure to do so is, in itself, an ethics violation.

Cooperating with ethics committees

Psychologists also respond to inquiries from duly constituted state psychological association ethics committees and professional standards review committees.

GLOSSARY

Note: The Glossary is still in developmental stages and will be expanded at a later date.

Conflict of interest: A conflict between the private interests and needs of a psychologist and his or her official responsibilities toward a client, student, research participant, or other consumer.

Client: A person or group of persons receiving benefits or services from a psychologist.

Cultural diversity: The inevitable variety that exists among groups from different ethnic, racial, or national backgrounds who come into contact.

Culture: The unique set of elements—knowledge, beliefs, values, assumptions, and practices or art—found in every society.

Dual relationships: Relationships in which one individual is simultaneously participating in two or more role categories with another. Such relationships may be benign or exploitative.

Electronic recordings: The use of equipment for recording sound or images, such as audio or videotape recording, motion picture film, or any other mechanical or electronic means.

Ethnic minority groups: Asian-American/Pacific Islanders, African-Americans, Hispanics, Native Americans.

Exploitative dual relationships: Relationships in which the psychologist is simultaneously or sequentially participating in two or more role categories that conflict or compete in such a way that the other person is at risk of being harmed. Either the relationship creates a conflict of interest for the psychologist, or in some other way the conflict leads the psychologist to use the other person for the psychologist's advantage or benefit.

Fundamental human rights: Basic human rights which may or may not be fully protected by existing laws and statutes. Of particular significance to psychologists are rights to equal justice, privacy, self-determination, and autonomy. Protection of some aspects of these rights may involve encouraging practices not contained or controlled within current laws and statutes. Fundamental rights are not limited to those mentioned in this definition.

Informed consent: When an individual voluntarily agrees to participate in research, education, or treatment based on adequate knowledge and comprehension of the anticipated experience, its possible risks, and benefits.

Public statements: Public statements include but are not limited to communication by means of print, electronic media, lecturing, or direct conversation.

Sexual harassment: Sexual harassment is defined as deliberate or repeated comments, gestures, or physical contacts of a sexual nature that are unwanted by the recipient or expressed in a relationship wherein power differential is a factor. A power differential may imply that the recipient does not have equal choice in the relationship.

Vulnerable groups: Those who are members of groups that, relative to society, have less opportunity, power, or freedom to determine outcomes in their lives or to make decisions that affect their situation because of their age, disability, ethnicity, gender, national origin, race, religion, sexual orientation, or social class.

*American Psychological Association (in press.) Ethical principles for psychologists. Draft printed in *The APA Monitor,* 1990, *21*(6), 28–32. Copyright 1990. Reprinted by permission.

REFERENCES

Abramson, L. Y. (Ed.). (1988). *Social cognition and clinical psychology: A synthesis.* New York: Guilford Press.

Albee, G. W. (1970). The uncertain future of clinical psychology. *American Psychologist, 25,* 1071–1080.

Aldenderfer, M. S., & Blashfield, R. K. (1984). *Cluster analysis.* Beverly Hills, CA: Sage.

Alloy, L. B., & Abramson, L. Y. (1979). Judgment of contingency in depressed and nondepressed students: Sadder but wiser? *Journal of Experimental Psychology, 108,* 441–485.

American Association for Counseling and Development. (1977). Standards for the preparation of counselors and other personnel services specialists. *Personnel and Guidance Journal, 55,* 596–601.

American Association for Counseling and Development. (1988). *Ethical standards.* Alexandria, VA: Author. (Originally published by American Personnel and Guidance Association)

American Psychological Association. (1983). *Publication manual of the American Psychological Association* (3rd ed.). Washington, DC: American Psychological Association.

American Psychological Association. (1990). Ethical principles of psychologists (amended June 1989). *American Psychologist, 45,* 390–395.

American Psychological Association. (in press). Ethical principles for psychologists. Draft printed in *The APA Monitor,* 1990, *21*(6), 28–32.

American Psychological Association Ethics Committee. (1983, February 19). *Authorship guidelines for dissertation supervision.*

Andersen, B., & Anderson, W. (1985). Client perceptions of counselors using positive and negative self-involving statements. *Journal of Counseling Psychology, 32,* 462–465.

Anderson, J. R. (1983). *The architecture of cognition.* Cambridge, MA: Harvard University Press.

Anderson, T. R., Hogg, J. A., & Magoon, T. M. (1987). Length of time on a waiting list and attrition after intake. *Journal of Counseling Psychology, 34,* 93–95.

Anderson, W. P., & Heppner, P. P. (1986). Counselor applications of research findings to practice: Learning to stay current. *Journal of Counseling and Development, 65,* 152–155.

Argyris, C. (1968). Some unintended consequences of rigorous research. *Psychological Bulletin, 70,* 185–197.

Atkinson, D. R. (1983). Ethnic similarity in counseling psychology: A review of the research. *The Counseling Psychologist, 11,* 79–92.

Atkinson, D. R., & Wampold, B. E. (1982). A comparison of the Counselor Rating Form and the Counselor Effectiveness Rating Scale. *Counselor Education and Supervision, 22,* 25–36.

Babbie, E. R. (1979). *The practice of social research* (2nd ed.). Belmont, CA: Wadsworth.

Baer, D. M., Wolf, M. M., & Risley, T. R. (1968). Some current dimensions of applied behavioral analysis. *Journal of Applied Behavior Analysis, 1,* 91–97.

Barak, A., & LaCrosse, M. B. (1975). Multidimensional perception of counselor behavior. *Journal of Counseling Psychology, 22,* 471–476.

Barber, T. X. (1976). *Pitfalls in human research: Ten pivotal points.* New York: Pergamon Press.

Barber, T. X., & Silver, M. J. (1968). Fact, fiction, and the experimenter bias effect. *Psychological Bulletin Monograph, 70,* 1–29.

Barlow, D. H. (Ed.). (1981). *Behavioral assessment of adult disorders.* New York: Guilford Press.

Barlow, D. H., & Hersen, M. (1984). *Single case experimental designs: Strategies for studying behavior change* (2nd ed.). New York: Pergamon Press.

Barrett-Lennard, G. T. (1962). Dimensions of therapist response as causal factors in therapeutic change. *Psychological Monographs, 76* (43, Whole No. 562).

Baumrind, D. (1976). *Nature and definition of informed consent in research involving deception.* Background paper prepared for the National Commission for the Protection of Human Subjects of Biomedical and Behavioral Research. Washington, DC: Department of Health, Education, and Welfare.

Beauchamp, T. L., & Childress, J. F. (1979). *Principles of biomedical ethics.* Oxford, England: Oxford University Press.

Beck, A. T., Rush, A. J., Shaw, B. F., & Emery, G. (1979). *Cognitive therapy of depression.* New York: Guilford Press.

Beck, A. T., Ward, C. H., Mendelson, M., Mock, J., & Erbaugh, J. (1961). An inventory for measuring depression. *Archives of General Psychiatry, 4,* 561–571.

Bednar, R. L., & Kaul, T. J. (1978). Experiential group research: Current perspectives. In S. L. Garfield & A. E. Bergin (Eds.), *Handbook of psychotherapy and behavior change* (2nd ed., pp. 769–816). New York: Wiley.

Benn, S. I. (1967). Justice. In P. Edwards (Ed.), *The encyclopedia of philosophy* (Vol. 4, pp. 298–302). New York: Macmillan.

Berdie, R. F. (1972). The 1980 counselor: Applied behavioral scientist. *Personnel and Guidance Journal, 50,* 451–456.

Berg, I. A. (1954). Ideomotor response set: Symbolic sexual gesture in the counseling interview. *Journal of Counseling Psychology, 1,* 180–183.

Bergin, A. E., & Garfield, S. L. (1971). *Handbook of psychotherapy and behavior change.* New York: Wiley.

Bergin, A. E., & Lambert, M. J. (1978). The evaluation of therapeutic outcomes. In S. L. Garfield & A. E. Bergin (Eds.), *Handbook of psychotherapy and behavior change,* 2nd ed. (pp. 139–190). New York: Wiley.

Bergin, A. E., & Strupp, H. H. (1970). New directions in psychotherapy research. *Journal of Abnormal Psychology, 76,* 13–26.

Betz, N. E. (1986). Research training in counseling psychology: Have we addressed the real issues? *The Counseling Psychologist, 14,* 107–113.

Betz, N. E., & Hackett, G. (1981). The relationship of career-related self-efficacy expectations to perceived career options in college women and men. *Journal of Counseling Psychology, 28,* 399–410.

Betz, N. E., & Hackett, G. (1987). The concept of agency in educational and career development. *Journal of Counseling Psychology, 34,* 299–308.

Bhaskar, R. (1975). *A realist theory of science.* Leeds, England: Leeds Books.

Blashfield, R. K. (1984). *The classification of psychopathology: Neo-Kraepelinian and quantitative approaches.* New York: Plenum.

Blos, P. (1946). Psychological counseling of college students. *American Journal of Orthopsychiatry, 16,* 571–580.

Bordin, E. S. (1965). Simplification as a research strategy in psychotherapy. *Journal of Consulting Psychology, 29,* 493–503.

Bordin, E. S. (1979). The generalizability of the psychoanalytic concept of working alliance. *Psychotherapy: Theory, Research and Practice, 16,* 252–260.

Borenstein, M., & Cohen, J. (1988). *Statistical power analysis: A computer program.* Hillsdale, NJ: Erlbaum.

Borgen, F. H. (1984a). Counseling psychology. *Annual Review of Psychology, 35,* 579–604.

Borgen, F. H. (1984b). Are there necessary linkages between research practices and the philosophy of science? *Journal of Counseling Psychology, 31,* 457–460.

Borgen, F. H., & Barnett, D. C. (1987). Applying cluster analysis in counseling psychology research. *Journal of Counseling Psychology, 34,* 456–468.

Borgen, F. H., & Weiss, D. J. (1971). Cluster analysis and counseling research. *Journal of Counseling Psychology, 18,* 583–591.

Bracht, G. H., & Glass, V. V. (1968). The external validity of experiments. *American Educational Research Journal, 5,* 437–474.

Bradley, J. V. (1968). *Distribution-free statistical tests.* Englewood Cliffs, NJ: Prentice-Hall.

Breuer, J., & Freud, S. (1955). Studies on hysteria. In J. Strachey (Ed. and Trans.), *The standard edition of the complete psychological works of Sigmund Freud* (Vol. 2). London: Hogarth Press. (Original work published 1893–1895)

Bridgewater, C. A., Bornstein, P. H., & Walkenbach, J. (1981). Ethical issues and the assignment of publication credit. *American Psychologist, 36,* 524–525.

Broad, W., & Wade, N. (1982). *Betrayers of the truth.* New York: Simon & Schuster.

Brophy, J. E., & Good, T. L. (1974). *Teacher-student relationships: Causes and consequences.* New York: Holt, Rinehart & Winston.

Brotemarkle, R. A. (1927). College student personnel problems. *Journal of Applied Psychology, 11,* 415–436.

Brown, F. (1982). The ethics of psychodiagnostic assessment. In M. Rosenbaum (Ed.), *Ethics and values in psychotherapy.* New York: Free Press.

Brown, S. D., & Lent, R. W. (Eds.). (1984). *Handbook of counseling psychology.* New York: Wiley.

Brown, W., & Holtzman, W. (1967). *Manual, Survey of Study Habits and Attitudes.* New York: The Psychological Corporation.

Buchler, J. (Ed.). (1955). *Philosophical writings of Peirce.* New York: Dover.

Burt, M. R. (1980). Cultural myths and supports for rape. *Journal of Personality and Social Psychology, 38,* 217–230.

Campbell, D. T., & Fiske, D. W. (1959). Convergent and discriminant validation by the multitrait-multimethod matrix. *Psychological Bulletin, 56,* 81–105.

Campbell, D. T., & Stanley, J. C. (1963). *Experimental and quasi-experimental designs for research.* Chicago: Rand McNally.

Campbell, L. M., III. (1973). A variation of thought stopping in a twelve-year-old boy: A case report. *Journal of Behavior Therapy and Experimental Psychiatry, 4,* 69–70.

Caple, R. B. (1985). Counseling and the self-organization paradigm. *Journal of Counseling and Development, 64,* 173–178.

Caple, R. B. (in press.) Editorial. *Journal of College Student Development.*

Carkhuff, R. R. (1968). A "non-traditional" assessment of graduate education in the helping professions. *Counselor Education and Supervision, 8,* 252–261.

Carkhuff, R. R., & Burstein, J. W. (1970). Objective therapist and client ratings of therapist-offered facilitative conditions of moderate to low functioning therapist. *Journal of Clinical Psychology, 26,* 394–395.

Carney, C. G., & Barak, A. (1976). A survey of student needs and student personnel services. *Journal of College Student Personnel, 17,* 280–284.

Chapman, L. J., & Chapman, J. P. (1969). Illusory correlations as an obstacle to the use of valid psychodiagnostic tests. *Journal of Abnormal Psychology, 74,* 271–280.

Chickering, A. W. (1969). *Education and identity.* San Francisco: Jossey Bass.

Christensen, L. B. (1980). *Experimental methodology* (2nd ed.). Boston: Allyn & Bacon.

Claiborn, C. D. (1982). Interpretation and change in counseling. *Journal of Counseling Psychology, 29,* 439–453.

Claiborn, C. D. (1984). Training students in research. In R. B. Pipes (Chair), *Basic issues faced by counseling psychology training programs.* Symposium conducted at the annual meeting of the American Psychological Association, Toronto, Canada.

Claiborn, C. D. (1985). Harold B. Pepinsky: A life of science and practice. *Journal of Counseling and Development, 64,* 5–13.

Claiborn, C. D. (1987). Science and practice: Reconsidering the Pepinskys. *Journal of Counseling and Development, 65,* 286–288.

Claiborn, C. D., & Lichtenberg, J. W. (1989). Interactional counseling. *The Counseling Psychologist, 17,* 355–453.

Cohen, J. (1968). Multiple regression as a general data-analytic strategy. *Psychological Bulletin, 70,* 426–443.

Cohen, J. (1988). *Statistical power analysis for the behavioral sciences* (2nd ed.). Hillsdale, NJ: Erlbaum.

Cohen, J., & Cohen, P. (1983). *Applied multiple regression/correlation analysis for the behavioral sciences* (2nd ed.). Hillsdale, NJ: Erlbaum.

Cohen, M. R., & Nagel, E. (1934). *An introduction to logic and scientific method.* New York: Harcourt, Brace & Company.

Cole, D. A., Lazarick, D. L., & Howard, G. S. (1987). Construct validity and the relation between depression and social skill. *Journal of Counseling Psychology, 34,* 315–321.

Cook, E. P. (1990). Gender and psychological distress. *Journal of Counseling and Development, 68,* 371–375.

Cook, T. D., & Campbell, D. T. (1979). *Quasi-experimentation: Design and analysis issues for field settings.* Boston: Houghton Mifflin.

Cooke, R. A. (1982). The ethics and regulation of research involving children. In B. B. Wolman (Ed.), *Handbook of developmental psychology.* Englewood Cliffs, NJ: Prentice-Hall.

Coopersmith, S. (1981). *SEI, self-esteem inventories.* Palo Alto, CA: Consulting Psychologists Press.

Corazzini, J. (1980). The theory and practice of loss therapy. In B. Mark Schoenberg (Ed.), *Bereavement counseling: A multi-disciplinary handbook* (pp. 71–85). Westport, CT: Greenwood Press.

Corrigan, J. D., Dell, D. M., Lewis, K. N., & Schmidt, L. D. (1980). Counseling as a social influence process: A review [Monograph]. *Journal of Counseling Psychology, 27,* 395–441.

Corrigan, J. D., & Schmidt, L. D. (1983). Development and validation of revisions in the Counselor Rating Form. *Journal of Counseling Psychology, 30,* 64–75.

Crites, J. O. (1978). *Career Maturity Inventory.* Monterey, California: McGraw-Hill.

Cronbach, L. J., & Snow, R. E. (1976). *Aptitudes and instructional methods: A handbook for research on interactions.* New York: Irvington.

Cummings, A. L. (1989). Relationship of client problem type to novice counselor response modes. *Journal of Counseling Psychology, 36,* 331–335.

Daniels, L. K. (1976). An extension of thought stopping in the treatment of obsessional thinking. *Behavior Therapy, 7,* 131.

Danskin, D. G., & Robinson, F. P. (1954). Differences in "degree of lead" among experienced counselors. *Journal of Counseling Psychology, 1,* 78–83.

Dar, R. (1987). Another look at Meehl, Lakatos, and the scientific practices of psychologists. *American Psychologist, 42,* 145–151.

Davis, H. T. (1941). *The analysis of economic time series.* Bloomington, IN: Principia Press.

Dawis, R. V. (1984). Of old philosophies and new kids on the block. *Journal of Counseling Psychology, 31,* 467–469.

Dawis, R. V. (1987). Scale construction. *Journal of Counseling Psychology, 34,* 481–489.

Denton, D. E. (1980). Understanding the life world of the counselor. *Personnel and Guidance Journal, 59,* 596–599.

Department of Health and Human Services. (1989). Responsibilities of awardee and applicant institutions for dealing with and reporting possible misconduct in science. *Federal Register, 54*(151), 32446–32451.

DeProspero, A., & Cohen, S. (1979). Inconsistent visual analysis of intrasubject data. *Journal of Applied Behavior Analysis, 12,* 573–579.

DeSena, P. A. (1966). Problems of consistent over-, under-, and normal-achieving college students as identified by the Mooney Problem Checklist. *Journal of Educational Research, 59,* 351–355.

Diener, E., & Crandall, R. (1978). *Ethics in social and behavioral research.* Chicago: University of Chicago Press.

Dill-Standifond, T. J., Stiles, W. B., & Rorer, L. G. (1988). Counselor-client agreement on session impact. *Journal of Counseling Psychology, 35,* 47–55.

Dipboye, W. J. (1954). Analysis of counselor style by discussion units. *Journal of Counseling Psychology, 1,* 21–26.

Dixon, D. N., & Claiborn, C. D. (1981). Effects of need and commitment on career exploration behaviors. *Journal of Counseling Psychology, 28,* 411–415.

Dixon, D. N., & Glover, J. A. (1984). *Counseling: A problem-solving approach.* New York: Wiley.

Dixon, D. N., Heppner, P. P., Petersen, C. H., & Ronning, R. R. (1979). Problem-solving workshop training. *Journal of Counseling Psychology, 26,* 133–139.

Dixon, W. A. (1989). *Self-appraised problem solving ability, stress, and suicide ideation in a college population.* Unpublished master's thesis, University of Missouri-Columbia.

Dolliver, R. H. (1969). Strong Vocational Blank versus expressed vocational interests: A review. *Psychological Bulletin, 72,* 95–107.

Dorn, F. J. (1985). *Publishing for professional development.* Muncie, IN: Accelerated Development.

Dorn, F. J. (Ed.). (1986). *Social influence processes in counseling and psychotherapy.* Springfield, IL: Charles C Thomas.

Dowd, E. T., & Boroto, D. R. (1982). Differential effects of counselor self-disclosure, self-involving statements, and interpretation. *Journal of Counseling Psychology, 29,* 8–13.

Drane, J. F. (1982). Ethics and psychotherapy: A philosophical perspective. In M. Rosenbaum (Ed.), *Ethics and values in psychotherapy: A guidebook.* New York: Free Press.

Drew, C. F. (1980). *Introduction to designing and conducting research* (2nd ed.). St. Louis: C. V. Mosby.

D'Zurilla, T. J. (1986). *Problem-solving therapy: A social competence approach to clinical intervention.* New York: Springer.

Edgington, E. S. (1980). *Randomization tests.* New York: Marcel Dekker.

Edgington, E. (1982). Nonparametric tests for single-subject multiple schedule experiments. *Behavioral Assessment, 4,* 83–91.

Edgington, E. S. (1987). Randomized single-subject experiments and statistical tests. *Journal of Counseling Psychology, 34,* 437–442.

Elliott, R. (1979). How clients perceive helper behaviors. *Journal of Counseling Psychology, 26,* 285–294.

Elliott, R. (1985). Helpful and nonhelpful events in brief counseling interviews: An empirical taxonomy. *Journal of Counseling Psychology, 32,* 307–322.

Elliott, R., Hill, C. E., Stiles, W. B., Friedlander, M. L., Mahrer, A. R., & Margison, F. R. (1987). Primary therapist response modes: Comparison of six rating systems. *Journal of Consulting and Clinical Psychology, 55,* 218–223.

Elliott, R., & James, E. (1989). Varieties of client experience in psychotherapy: An analysis of the literature. *Clinical Psychology Review, 9,* 443–467.

Elliott, R., James, E., Reimschuessel, C., Cislo, D., & Sack, N. (1985). Significant events and the analysis of immediate therapeutic impacts. *Psychotherapy, 22,* 620–630.

Elliott, R., & Shapiro, D. A. (1988). Brief structured recall: A more efficient method for studying significant therapy events. *British Journal of Medical Psychology, 61,* 141–153.

Ellis, J. V., Robbins, E. S., Shult, D., Ladany, N., & Banker, J. (1990). Anchoring errors in clinical judgments: Type I error, adjustment, or mitigation. *Journal of Counseling Psychology, 37,* 343–351.

Epperson, D. L., & Pecnik, J. A. (1985). Counselor Rating Form-Short version: Further validation and comparison to the long form. *Journal of Counseling Psychology, 32,* 143–146.

Ericsson, K. A., & Simon, H. A. (1984). *Protocol analysis: Verbal reports as data.* Cambridge, MA: MIT Press.

Exner, J. E., Jr. (1974). *The Rorschach: A comprehensive system* (Vol. 1). New York: Wiley.

Eysenck, H. J. (1952). The effects of psychotherapy: An evaluation. *Journal of Consulting Psychology, 16,* 319–324.

Eysenck, H. J. (1961). The effects of psychotherapy. In H. J. Eysenck (Ed.), *Handbook of abnormal psychology* (pp. 697–725). New York: Basic Books.

Eysenck, H. J. (1965). The effects of psychotherapy. *International Journal of Psychology, 1,* 97–178.

Fagley, N. S. (1985). Applied statistical power analysis and the interpretation of non-significant results by research consumers. *Journal of Counseling Psychology, 32,* 391–396.

Fassinger, R. E. (1987). Use of structural equation modeling in counseling psychology research. *Journal of Counseling Psychology, 34,* 425–436.

Feldman, D. A., Strong, S. R., & Danser, D. B. (1982). A comparison of paradoxical and nonparadoxical interpretations and directives. *Journal of Counseling Psychology, 29,* 572–579.

Fiske, S. T., & Taylor, S. E. (1984). *Social cognition.* Reading, MA: Addison-Wesley.

Fitzgerald, L. F., & Hubert, L. J. (1987). Multidimensional scaling: Some possibilities for counseling psychology. *Journal of Counseling Psychology, 34,* 469–480.

Folger, R. (1989). Significance tests and the duplicity of binary decisions. *Psychological Bulletin, 106,* 155–160.

Folkman, S., & Lazarus, R. S. (1980). An analysis of coping in a middle-aged community sample. *Journal of Health and Social Behavior, 21,* 219–239.

Ford, D. H. (1984). Reexamining guiding assumptions: Theoretical and methodological implications. *Journal of Counseling Psychology, 31,* 461–466.

Fouad, N. A., Cudeck, R., & Hansen, J. (1984). Convergent validity of Spanish and English forms of the Strong-Campbell Interest Inventory for bilingual Hispanic high school students. *Journal of Counseling Psychology, 31,* 339–348.

Frank, G. (1984). The Boulder model: History, rationale, and critique. *Professional Psychology: Research and Practice, 15,* 417–435.

Frank, J. D. (1961). *Persuasion and healing: A comparative study of psychotherapy.* Baltimore: Johns Hopkins University Press.

Frank, J. D. (1974). Therapeutic components of psychotherapy. *Journal of Nervous and Mental Disease, 159,* 325–342.

Frankena, W. K. (1963). *Ethics.* Englewood Cliffs, NJ: Prentice-Hall.

Freidman, N. (1967). *The social nature of psychological research.* New York: Basic Books.

Fremont, S., & Anderson, W. P. (1986). What client behaviors make counselors angry? An exploratory study. *Journal of Counseling and Development, 65,* 67–70.

Fretz, B. R. (1981). Evaluating the effectiveness of career interventions. *Journal of Counseling Psychology, 28,* 77–90.

Fretz, B. R. (1982). Perspective and definitions. *The Counseling Psychologist, 10*(2), 15–19.

Friedlander, M. L., Ellis, M. V., Siegel, S. M., Raymond, L., Haase, R. F., & Highlen, P. S. (1988). Generalizing from segments to sessions: Should it be done? *Journal of Counseling Psychology, 35,* 243–250.

Friedlander, M. L., Siegel, S. M., & Brenock, K. (1989). Parallel processes in counseling and supervision: A case study. *Journal of Counseling Psychology, 36,* 149–157.

Friedlander, M. L., Thibodeau, J. R., Nichols, M. P., Tucker, C., & Snyder, J. (1985). Introducing semantic cohesion analysis: A study of group talk. *Small Group Behavior, 16,* 285–302.

Friedlander, M. L., Thibodeau, J. R., & Ward, L. G. (1985). Discriminating the "good" from the "bad" therapy hour: A study of dyadic interaction. *Psychotherapy, 22,* 631–642.

Fuchs, C. Z., & Rehm, L. P. (1977). A self-control behavior therapy program for depression. *Journal of Consulting and Clinical Psychology, 45,* 206–215.

Fuhriman, A., & Burlingame, G. M. (1990). Consistency of matter: A comparative analysis of individual and group process variables. *The Counseling Psychologist, 1(18),* 6–63.

Fuller, F., & Hill, C. E. (1985). Counselor and helpee perceptions of counselor intentions in relation to outcome in a single counseling session. *Journal of Counseling Psychology, 32,* 329–338.

Furlong, M. J., & Wampold, B. E. (1982). Intervention effects and relative variation as dimensions in experts' use of visual inference. *Journal of Applied Behavior Analysis, 15,* 415–421.

Furst, J. B., & Cooper, A. (1970). Combined use of imaginal and interoceptive stimuli in desensitizing fear of heart attacks. *Journal of Behavior Therapy and Experimental Psychiatry, 1,* 87–89.

Gade, E., Fuqua, D., & Hurlburt, G. (1988). The relationship of Holland's personality types to educational satisfaction with a native American high school population. *Journal of Counseling Psychology, 35,* 183–186.

Gadlin, H., & Ingle, G. (1975). Through the one-way mirror, the limits of experimental self-reflection. *American Psychologist, 30,* 1003–1009.

Garfield, S. L., & Bergin, A. E. (Eds.). (1978). *Handbook of psychotherapy and behavior change* (2nd ed.). New York: Wiley.

Garfield, S. L., & Bergin, A. E. (Eds.). (1986). *Handbook of psychotherapy and behavior change* (3rd ed.). New York: Wiley.

Gelatt, H. B. (1989). Positive uncertainty: A new decision-making framework for counseling. *Journal of Counseling Psychology, 36,* 252–256.

Gelso, C. J. (1979). Research in counseling: Methodological and professional issues. *The Counseling Psychologist, 8*(3), 7–35.

Gelso, C. J. (1982). Editorial. *Journal of Counseling Psychology, 29,* 3–7.

Gelso, C. J. (1985). Rigor, relevance, and counseling research: On the need to maintain our course between Scylla and Charybdis. *Journal of Counseling and Development, 63,* 551–553.

Gelso, C. J., Betz, N. E., Friedlander, M. L., Helms, J. E., Hill, C. E., Patton, M. J., Super, D. E., & Wampold, B. E. (1988). Research in counseling psychology: Prospects and recommendations. *The Counseling Psychologist, 16,* 385–406.

Gelso, C. J., & Fassinger, R. E. (1990). Counseling psychology: Theory and research on interventions. *Annual Review of Psychology, 41,* 355–386.

Gelso, C. J., Raphael, R., Black, S. M., Rardin, D., & Skalkos, O. (1983). Research training in counseling psychology: Some preliminary data. *Journal of Counseling Psychology, 30,* 611–614.

Glaser, B., & Strauss, A. (1967). *The discovery of grounded theory: Strategies for qualitative research.* Chicago: Aldine.

Glass, G. V, Willson, V. L., & Gottman, J. M. (1974). *Design and analysis of time-series experiments.* Boulder, CO: Colorado Associated University Press.

Gleitman, H. (1986). *Psychology* (2nd ed.). New York: Norton.

Glock, C. Y. (Ed.). (1967). *Survey research in the social sciences.* New York: Russell Sage Foundation.

Goldman, L. (1976). A revolution in counseling research. *Journal of Counseling Psychology, 23,* 543–552.

Goldman, L. (1977). Toward more meaningful research. *Personnel and Guidance Journal, 55,* 363–368.

Goldman, L. (Ed.). (1978). *Research methods for counselors: Practical approaches in field settings.* New York: Wiley.

Goldman, L. (1982). Defining non-traditional research. *The Counseling Psychologist, 10*(4), 87–89.

Goldstein, A. P., Heller, K., & Sechrest, L. B. (1966). *Psychotherapy and the psychology of behavior change.* New York: Wiley.

Good, G. E., Gilbert, L. A., & Scher, M. (1990). Gender aware therapy: A synthesis of feminist therapy and knowledge about gender. *Journal of Counseling and Development, 68,* 376–380.

Goodyear, R. K., & Benton, S. (1986). The roles of science and research in the counselor's work. In A. J. Palmo & W. J. Weikel (Eds.), *Foundations of mental health counseling* (pp. 287–308). Springfield, IL: Charles C Thomas.

Gottfredson, G. D., & Holland, J. L. (1990). A longitudinal test of the influence of congruence: Job satisfaction, competency utilization, and counterproductive behavior. *Journal of Counseling Psychology, 37,* 389–398.

Gottman, J. M. (1973). N-of-one and N-of-two research in psychotherapy. *Psychological Bulletin, 80,* 93–105.

Gottman, J. M. (1979). Detecting cyclicity in social interaction. *Psychological Bulletin, 86,* 338–348.

Gottman, J. M., & Markman, H. J. (1978). Experimental designs in psychotherapy research. In S. L. Garfield & A. E. Bergin (Eds.), *Handbook of psychotherapy and behavior change* (2nd ed., pp. 23–62). New York: Wiley.

Gottman, J. M., McFall, R. M., & Barnett, J. T. (1969). Design and analysis of research using time series. *Psychological Bulletin, 72,* 299–306.

Graham, J. R. (1990). *MMPI-2: Assessing personality and psychopathology.* New York: Oxford University Press.

Greenberg, L. S. (1986). Change process research. *Journal of Consulting and Clinical Psychology, 54,* 4–9.

Grummon, D. L., & Butler, J. M. (1953). Another failure to replicate Keet's study, two verbal techniques in a miniature counseling situation. *Journal of Abnormal and Social Psychology, 48,* 597.

Gurin, G., Veroff, J., & Feld, S. (1960). *Americans view their mental health.* New York: Basic Books.

Gurman, A. S. (1977). The patient's perception of the therapeutic relationship. In A. S. Gurman & A. M. Razin (Eds.), *Effective psychotherapy: A handbook of research* (pp. 503–543). New York: Pergamon Press.

Gurman, A. S., & Razin, A. M. (Eds.). (1977). *Effective psychotherapy: A handbook of research.* New York: Pergamon Press.

Gustav, A. (1962). Students' attitudes toward compulsory participation in experiments. *Journal of Psychology, 53,* 119–125.

Gysbers, N. C., & Associates. (1984). *Designing careers: Counseling to enhance the quality of education, work, and leisure.* San Francisco, CA: Jossey-Bass.

Gysbers, N. C., & Henderson, P. (1988). *Developing and managing your school guidance program.* Washington, DC: American Association for Counseling and Development.

Haase, R. F., Waechter, D. M., & Solomon, G. S. (1982). How significant is a significant difference? Average effect size of research in counseling psychology. *Journal of Counseling Psychology, 29,* 58–65.

Hackett, G. (1981). Survey research methods. *Personnel and Guidance Journal, 59,* 599–604.

Hair, J. F., Jr., Anderson, R. E., & Tatham, R. L. (1987). *Multivariate data analysis: With readings* (2nd ed.). New York: Macmillan.

Hanfling, O. (1981). *Logical positivism.* Oxford: Blackwell.

Hardin, S. I., Subich, L. M., & Holvey, J. M. (1988). Expectancies for counseling in relation to premature termination. *Journal of Counseling Psychology, 35*, 37–40.

Harmon, L. W. (1981). The life and career plans of young adult college women: A follow-up study. *Journal of Counseling Psychology, 28*, 416–427.

Harmon, L. (1982). Scientific affairs: The next decade. *The Counseling Psychologist, 10*(2), 31–38.

Harmon, L. W. (1989). Changes in women's career aspirations over time: Developmental or historical. *Journal of Vocational Behavior, 33*, 46–65.

Harré, R. (1950). *Social being: A theory for social psychology.* Totowa, NJ: Littlefield Adams.

Harré, R. (1970). *The principles of scientific thinking.* Chicago: University of Chicago Press.

Harré, R. (1972). *Philosophies of science: An introductory survey.* Oxford, England: Oxford University Press.

Harré, R. (1974). Blueprint for a new science. In A. Nigel (Ed.), *Reconstructing social psychology.* Baltimore: Penguin Books.

Harré, R. (1980). *Social being: A theory of social psychology.* Totowa, NJ: Rowman & Littlefield.

Hartley, D. E., & Strupp, H. H. (1983). The therapeutic alliance: Its relationship to outcome in brief psychotherapy. In J. Masling (Ed.), *Empirical studies of psychoanalytic theories* (Vol. 1; pp. 1–37). Hillsdale, NJ: The Analytic Press.

Harvey, O. J., Hunt, D. E., & Schroder, H. M. (1961). *Conceptual systems and personality organization.* New York: Wiley.

Hathaway, S. R., & McKinley, J. C. (1942). A multiphasic personality schedule (Minnesota): III. The measurement of symptomatic depression. *The Journal of Psychology, 14*, 73–84.

Hathaway, S. R., & McKinley, J. C. (1967). *MMPI manual* (Rev. ed.). New York: Psychological Corporation.

Haupt, S. G. (1990). *Client Christian belief issues in psychotherapy.* Unpublished doctoral dissertation, University of Missouri, Columbia.

Hays, W. L. (1988). *Statistics* (4th ed.). New York: Holt, Rinehart & Winston.

Heesacker, M., Elliott, T. R., & Howe, L. A. (1988). Does the Holland code predict job satisfaction and productivity in clothing factory workers? *Journal of Counseling Psychology, 35*, 144–148.

Heesacker, M., & Heppner, P. P. (1983). Using real-client perceptions to examine psychometric properties of the Counselor Rating Form. *Journal of Counseling Psychology, 30*, 180–187.

Heller, K. (1971). Laboratory interview research as an analogue to treatment. In A. E. Bergin & S. L. Garfield (Eds.), *Handbook of psychotherapy and behavior change* (pp. 126–153). New York: Wiley.

Helms, J. E. (1976). Comparison of two types of counseling analogue. *Journal of Counseling Psychology, 23*, 422–427.

Helms, J. E. (1978). Counselor reactions to female clients: Generalizing from analogue research to a counseling setting. *Journal of Counseling Psychology, 25*, 193–199.

Henry, W. P., Schacht, T. E., & Strupp, H. H. (1986). Structural analysis of social behavior: Application to a study of interpersonal processes in differential psychotherapeutic outcome. *Journal of Consulting and Clinical Psychology, 54*, 27–31.

Heppner, P. P. (1978a). A review of the problem-solving literature and its relationship to the counseling process. *Journal of Counseling Psychology, 25*, 366–375.

Heppner, P. P. (1978b). The clinical alteration of covert thoughts: A critical review. *Behavior Therapy, 9,* 717–734.

Heppner, P. P. (1979). The effects of client perceived need and counselor role on clients' behaviors (doctoral dissertation, University of Nebraska, 1979). *Dissertation Abstracts International, 39,* 5950A–5951A. (University Microfilms No. 79–07,542)

Heppner, P. P. (1989). Identifying the complexities within clients' thinking and decision making. *Journal of Counseling Psychology, 36,* 257–259.

Heppner, P. P., & Anderson, W. P. (1985). On the perceived non-utility of research in counseling. *Journal of Counseling and Development, 63,* 545–547.

Heppner, P. P., Baumgardner, A. H., Larson, L. M., & Petty, R. E. (1988). The utility of problem-solving training that emphasizes self-management principles. *Counselling Psychology Quarterly, 1,* 129–143.

Heppner, P. P., & Claiborn, C. D. (1989). Social influence research in counseling: A review and critique [Monograph]. *Journal of Counseling Psychology, 36,* 365–387.

Heppner, P. P., & Dixon, D. N. (1981). A review of the interpersonal influence process in counseling. *Personnel and Guidance Journal, 59,* 542–550.

Heppner, P. P., & Frazier, P. A. (in press). Social psychological processes in psychotherapy: Extrapolating basic research to counseling psychology. In S. D. Brown & R. W. Lent (Eds.), *Handbook of counseling psychology* (2nd ed.). New York: Wiley.

Heppner, P. P., Gelso, C. J., & Dolliver, R. H. (1987). Three approaches to research training in counseling. *Journal of Counseling and Development, 66,* 45–49.

Heppner, P. P., & Krauskopf, C. J. (1987). An information-processing approach to personal problem solving. *The Counseling Psychologist, 15*(3), 371–447.

Heppner, P. P., & Neal, G. W. (1983). Holding up the mirror: Research on the roles and functions of counseling centers in higher education. *The Counseling Psychologist, 11*(1), 81–89.

Heppner, P. P., & Petersen, C. H. (1982). The development and implications of a personal problem-solving inventory. *Journal of Counseling Psychology, 29,* 66–75.

Heppner, P. P., & Roehlke, H. J. (1984). Differences among supervisees at different levels of training: Implications for a developmental model of supervision. *Journal of Counseling Psychology, 31,* 76–90.

Heppner, P. P., Rogers, M. E., & Lee, L. A. (1984). Carl Rogers: Reflections on his life. *Journal of Counseling and Development, 63,* 14–20.

Hermansson, G. L., Webster, A. C., & McFarland, K. (1988). Counselor deliberate postural lean and communication of facilitative conditions. *Journal of Counseling Psychology, 35,* 149–153.

Hersen, M., & Barlow, D. H. (1976). *Single case experimental designs: Strategies for studying behavior change.* New York: Pergamon Press.

Highlen, P. S., & Hill, C. E. (1984). Factors affecting client change in counseling: Current status and theoretical speculations. In S. D. Brown & R. W. Lent (Eds.), *Handbook of counseling psychology* (pp. 334–396). New York: Wiley.

Hill, C. E. (1982). Counseling process researcher: Philosophical and methodological dilemmas. *The Counseling Psychologist, 10*(4), 7–20.

Hill, C. E. (1984). A personal account of the process of becoming a counseling process researcher. *The Counseling Psychologist, 12*(3), 99–109.

Hill, C. E. (1985). *Manual for the Hill Counselor Verbal Response Modes Category System* (rev. ed.). Unpublished manuscript, University of Maryland.

Hill, C. E., Carter, J. A., & O'Farrell, M. K. (1983). A case study of the process and outcome of time-limited counseling. *Journal of Counseling Psychology, 30,* 3–18.

Hill, C. E., Greenwald, C., Reed, K. A., Charles, D., O'Farrell, M. K., & Carter, J. A. (1981). *Manual for the counselor and client verbal response category systems.* Columbus, OH: Marathon Consulting and Press.

Hill, C. E., & Gronsky, B. R. (1984). Researcher: Why and how? In J. M. Whiteley, N. Kagan, L. W. Harmon, B. R. Fretz, & F. Tanney (Eds.), *The coming decade in counseling psychology* (pp. 149–159). Schenectady, NY: Character Researcher Press.

Hill, C. E., Helms, J. E., Spiegel, S. B., & Tichenor, V. (1988). Development of a system for categorizing client reactions to therapist interventions. *Journal of Counseling Psychology, 35,* 27–36.

Hill, C. E., Helms, J. E., Tichenor, V., Spiegel, S. B., O'Grady, K. E., & Perry, E. S. (1988). Effects of therapist response modes in brief psychotherapy. *Journal of Counseling Psychology, 35,* 222–233.

Hill, C. E., & O'Grady, K. E. (1985). List of therapist intentions illustrated in a case study and with therapists of varying theoretical orientations. *Journal of Counseling Psychology, 32,* 3–22.

Hill, C. E., & Stephany, A. (1990). Relation of nonverbal behavior to client reactions. *Journal of Counseling Psychology, 37,* 22–26.

Hill, W. F. (1965). *HIM: Hill Interaction Matrix.* Los Angeles: University of Southern California, Youth Study Center.

Hoch, P. H., & Zubin, J. (Eds.). (1964). *The evaluation of psychiatric treatment.* New York: Grune & Stratton.

Hoffman, J., & Weiss, B. (1987). Family dynamics and presenting problems in college students. *Journal of Counseling Psychology, 34,* 157–163.

Hogg, J. A., & Deffenbacher, J. L. (1988). A comparison of cognitive and interpersonal-process group therapies in the treatment of depression among college students. *Journal of Counseling Psychology, 35,* 304–310.

Holland, J. L. (1985). *Making vocational choices: A theory of vocational personalities and work environments.* Englewood Cliffs, NJ: Prentice-Hall.

Holland, J. L. (1986). Student selection, training, and research performance. *The Counseling Psychologist, 14*(1), 121–125.

Holland, J. L. (1987). *Manual supplement for the Self-Directed Search.* Odessa, FL: Psychological Assessment Resources.

Holland, J. L., Daiger, D. C., & Power, P. G. (1980). Some diagnostic scales for research in decision-making and personality: Identity, information, and barriers. *Journal of Personality and Social Psychology, 39,* 1191–1200.

Holland, P. W. (1986). Statistics and causal inference. *Journal of the American Statistical Association, 81,* 945–960.

Hollon, S. D., & Kendall, D. C. (1980). Cognitive self-statements in depression: Development of an Automatic Thoughts Questionnaire. *Cognitive Therapy and Research, 4,* 383–395.

Holloway, E. L. (1987). Developmental models of supervision: Is it development? *Professional Psychology; Research and Practice, 18,* 209–216.

Holloway, E. L., Freund, R. D., Gardner, S. L., Nelson, M. L., & Walker, B. R. (1989). Relation of power and involvement to theoretical orientation in supervision: An analysis of discourse. *Journal of Counseling Psychology, 36,* 88–102.

Holloway, E. L., & Wampold, B. E. (1986). Relation between conceptual level and counseling-related tasks: A meta-analysis. *Journal of Counseling Psychology, 33,* 310–319.

Holloway, E. L., Wampold, B. E., & Nelson, M. L. (1990). Use of a paradoxical intervention with a couple: An interactional analysis. *Journal of Family Psychology, 3,* 385–402.

Horan, J. J. (1979). *Counseling for effective decision making: A cognitive-behavioral perspective.* North Scituate, MA: Duxbury Press.

Horowitz, L. M., Rosenberg, S. E., Baer, B. A., Ureño, G., & Villaseñor, V. S. (1988). Inventory of Interpersonal Problems: Psychometric properties and clinical applications. *Journal of Consulting and Clinical Psychology, 56,* 885–892.

Horvath, A. O., & Greenberg, L. S. (1989). Development and validation of the Working Alliance Inventory. *Journal of Counseling Psychology, 36,* 223–233.

Hoshmand, L. L. S. T. (1989). Alternate research paradigms: A review and teaching proposal. *The Counseling Psychologist, 17,* 3–79.

Howard, G. S. (1982). Improving methodology via research on research methods. *Journal of Counseling Psychology, 29,* 318–326.

Howard, G. S. (1983). Toward methodological pluralism. *Journal of Counseling Psychology, 30,* 19–21.

Howard, G. S. (1984). A modest proposal for a revision of strategies in counseling research. *Journal of Counseling Psychology, 31,* 430–441.

Howard, G. S. (1985). Can research in the human sciences become more relevant to practice? *Journal of Counseling and Development, 63,* 539–544.

Huck, S. W., & McLean, R. A. (1975). Using a repeated measures ANOVA to analyze the data from a pretest-posttest design: A potentially confusing task. *Psychological Bulletin, 82,* 511–518.

Hughes, E. C. (1952). Psychology: Science and/or profession. *American Psychologist, 7,* 441–443.

Hunt, D. W., Butler, L. F., Noy, J. E., & Rosser, M. E. (1978). *Assessing conceptual level by the paragraph completion method.* Toronto, Canada: The Ontario Institute for Studies in Education.

Ingram, R. (Ed.). (1986). *Information processing approaches to clinical psychology.* Orlando, FL: Academic Press.

Jauquet, C. A. (1987). The effects of an agenda setting exercise on process involvement in a counseling training group. Unpublished master's thesis, University of Missouri, Columbia, MO.

Jayaratne, S., & Levy, R. L. (1979). *Empirical clinical practice.* New York: Columbia University Press.

Jensen, A. R. (1969). How much can we boost IQ and scholastic achievement? *Harvard Educational Review, 39,* 1–123.

Jensen, A. R. (1985). The nature of the black-white difference on various psychometric tests: Spearman's hypothesis. *The Behavioral and Brain Sciences, 8,* 193–263.

Johnson, R.F.Q. (1976). The experimenter attributes effect: A methodological analysis. *Psychological Record, 26,* 67–78.

Johnston, J. A., Buescher, K. L., & Heppner, M. J. (1988). Computerized career information and guidance systems: Caveat emptor. *Journal of Counseling and Development, 67,* 39–41.

Jones, H. G. (1956). The application of conditioning and learning techniques to the treatment of a psychiatric patient. *Journal of Abnormal and Social Psychology, 52,* 414–419.

Jones, A. S., & Gelso, C. J. (1988). Differential effects of style of interpretation: Another look. *Journal of Counseling Psychology, 35,* 363–369.

Josephson, G. S., & Fong-Beyette, M. L. (1987). Factors assisting female clients' disclosure of incest during counseling. *Journal of Counseling and Development, 65,* 475–478.

Kagan, N. (1975). Influencing human interaction: Eleven years with IPR. *Canadian Counselor, 9,* 44–51.

Kandel, D. K. (1973). Adolescent marijuana use: Role of parents and peers. *Science, 181,* 1067–1070.

Kanfer, F. H., & Busemeyer, J. R. (1982). The use of problem solving and decision making in behavior therapy. *Clinical Psychological Review, 2,* 239–266.

Kaul, T., & Bednar, R. L. (1986). Experiential group research. In S. L. Garfield & A. E. Bergin (Eds.), *Handbook of psychotherapy and behavior change* (3rd ed., pp. 671–714). New York: Wiley.

Kazdin, A. E. (1976). Statistical analyses for single-case experimental designs. In M. Hersen & D. H. Barlow (Eds.), *Single-case experimental designs: Strategies for studying behavioral change* (pp. 265–316). New York: Academic Press.

Kazdin, A. E. (1978). Methodology of applied behavior analysis. In A. C. Catania & T. A. Brigham (Eds.), *Handbook of applied behavior analysis: Social and instructional processes* (pp. 61–104). New York: Irvington Press/Halstead Press.

Kazdin, A. E. (1980). *Research design in clinical psychology.* New York: Harper & Row.

Kazdin, A. E. (1982). *Single-case research designs: Methods for clinical and applied settings.* New York: Oxford University Press.

Kazdin, A. D., & Kopel, S. A. (1975). On resolving ambiguities of the multiple-baseline design: Problems and recommendations. *Behavior Therapy, 6,* 601–608.

Keet, C. D. (1948). Two verbal techniques in a miniature counseling situation. *Psychological Monographs, 62* (7, Whole No. 294).

Keith-Spiegel, P., & Koocher, G. P. (1985). *Ethics in psychology: Professional standards and cases.* New York: Random House.

Kerlinger, F. N. (1986). *Foundations of behavioral research* (3rd ed.). New York: Holt, Rinehart & Winston.

Kiesler, D. J. (1966). Some myths of psychotherapy research and the search for a paradigm. *Psychological Bulletin, 65,* 110–136.

Kiesler, D. J. (1971). Experimental designs in psychotherapy research. In A. E. Bergin & S. L Garfield (Eds.), *Handbook of psychotherapy and behavior change* (pp. 36–74). New York: Wiley.

Kiesler, D. J. (1984). *Check List of Psychotherapy Transactions (CLOPT) and Check List of Interpersonal Transactions (CLOIT).* Richmond: Virginia Commonwealth University.

Kiesler, D. J. (1987). *Research manual for the Impact Message Inventory.* Palo Alto, CA: Consulting Psychologists Press.

Kiresuk, T. J., & Sherman, R. E. (1968). Goal attainment scaling: A general method for evaluating comprehensive community mental health programs. *Community Mental Health Journal, 4,* 443–453.

Kitchener, K. S. (1984). Intuition, critical evaluation and ethical principles: The foundation for ethical decision in counseling psychology. *The Counseling Psychologist, 12*(3), 43–55.

Kivlighan, D. M., Jr. (1989). Changes in counselor intentions and response modes and client reactions and session evaluation following training. *Journal of Counseling Psychology, 36,* 471–476.

Kivlighan, D. M., Jr. (1990). Relation between counselors' use of intentions and clients' perception of working alliance. *Journal of Counseling Psychology, 37,* 27–32.

Kivlighan, D. M., Sr., & Angelone, E. O. (1991). Helpee introversion, novice counselor intention use, and counseling session impact. *Journal of Counseling Psychology, 38,* 25–29.

Kivlighan, D. M., Jr., Hageseth, J., Tipton, R., & McGovern, T. M. (1981). The effects of matching treatment approaches and personality types in group vocational counseling. *Journal of Counseling Psychology, 28,* 315–320.

Kivlighan, D. M., Jr., & Jauquet, C. A. (1990). Quality of group member agendas and group session climate. *Small Group Research, 21,* 205–219.

Kivlighan, D. M., Jr., & Shapiro, R. M. (1987). Holland type as a predictor of benefit from self-help career counseling. *Journal of Counseling Psychology, 34,* 326–329.

Klare, G. R. (1974–1975). Assessing readability. *Reading Research Quarterly, 10,* 62–102.

Klein, M. H., Mathieu-Coughlan, P., & Kiesler, D. J. (1986). The Experiencing Scales. In L. Greenberg & W. Pinsof (Eds.), *The psychotherapeutic process* (pp. 21–77). New York: Guilford Press.

Klingelhofer, E. L. (1954). The relationship of academic advisement to the scholastic performance of failing college students. *Journal of Counseling Psychology, 1,* 125–131.

Klinger, E. (1971). *Structure and functions of fantasy.* New York: Wiley.

Koile, E. A., & Bird, D. J. (1956). Preferences for counselor help on freshman problems. *Journal of Counseling Psychology, 3,* 97–106.

Kokotovic, A. M., & Tracey, T. J. (1987). Premature termination at a university counseling center. *Journal of Counseling Psychology, 34,* 80–82.

Koplik, E. K., & DeVito, A. J. (1986). Problems of freshmen: Comparison of classes of 1976 and 1986. *Journal of College Student Personnel, 27,* 124–131.

Kraemer, H. C., & Thiemann, S. (1987). *How many subjects?: Statistical power analysis in research.* Newbury Park, CA: Sage.

Kratochwill, T. R. (Ed.). (1978). *Single subject research: Strategies for evaluating change.* New York: Academic Press.

Krause, A. A., & Allen, G. J. (1988). Perceptions of counselor supervision: An examination of Stoltenberg's model from the perspectives of supervisor and supervisee. *Journal of Counseling Psychology, 35,* 77–80.

Krivatsky, S. E., & Magoon, T. M. (1976). Differential effects of three vocational counseling treatments. *Journal of Counseling Psychology, 23,* 112–117.

Krop, H., & Krause, S. (1976). The elimination of shark phobia by self-administered systematic desensitization: A case study. *Journal of Behavior Therapy and Experimental Psychiatry, 7,* 293–294.

Krumboltz, J. D., & Mitchell, L. K. (1979). Relevant rigorous research. *The Counseling Psychologist, 8*(3), 50–52.

Kruskal, W., & Mosteller, F. (1979). Representative sampling III: The current statistical literature. *International Statistical Review, 47,* 245–265.

Kuhn, T. S. (1970). *The structure of scientific revolutions* (2nd ed.). Chicago: University of Chicago Press.

Kushner, K. (1978). On the external validity of two psychotherapy analogues. *Journal of Consulting and Clinical Psychology, 46,* 1394–1402.

Lakatos, I. (1970). Falsification and the methodology of scientific research programmes. In I. Lakatos & A. Musgrave (Eds.), *Criticism and the growth of knowledge* (pp. 91–196). Cambridge, England: Cambridge University Press.

Lambert, M. J., Bergin, A. E., & Collins, J. L. (1977). Therapist-induced deterioration in psychotherapy. In A. S. Gurman & A. M. Razin (Eds.), *Effective psychotherapy: A handbook of research* (pp. 452–481). New York: Pergamon Press.

Lapan, R. T., Boggs, K. R., & Morrill, W. H. (1989). Self-efficacy as a mediation of investigative and realistic general occupational themes of the Strong-Campbell Interest Inventory. *Journal of Counseling Psychology, 36,* 176–182.

Larson, L. M., Heppner, P. P., Ham, T., & Dugan, K. (1988). Investigating multiple subtypes of career indecision through cluster analysis. *Journal of Counseling Psychology, 35,* 439–446.

Leary, M. R., & Altmaier, E. M. (1980). Type I error in counseling research: A plea for multivariate analyses. *Journal of Counseling Psychology, 27,* 611–615.

Leary, T. (1957). *Interpersonal diagnosis of personality.* New York: Ronald Press.

Lee, L. A., Heppner, P. P., & Gagliardi, J. (1987). Gender bias in subject samples in counseling psychology. *Journal of Counseling Psychology, 34,* 73–76.

Lent, R. W., Brown, S. D., & Lankin, K. C. (1987). Comparison of three theoretically derived variables in predicting career and academic behavior: Self-efficacy, interest consequence, and consequence thinking. *Journal of Counseling Psychology, 34,* 293–298.

Lent, R. W., Russell, R. K., & Zamostny, K. P. (1981). Comparison of cue-controlled desensitization, rational restructuring, and a credible placebo in the treatment of speech anxiety. *Journal of Consulting and Clinical Psychology, 49,* 608–610.

Levine, M. (1974). Scientific method and the adversary model, some preliminary thoughts. *American Psychologist, 29,* 661–677.

Lewin, K. (1951). Formalization and progress in psychology. In D. Cartwright (Ed.), *Field theory in social science* (pp. 1–41). New York: Harper.

Lewinsohn, P. M., Mischel, W., Chapel, W., & Barton, R. (1980). Social competence and depression: The role of illusory self-perceptions. *Journal of Abnormal Psychology, 89,* 203–212.

Lichtenberg, J. W. (1984). Believing when the facts don't fit. *Journal of Counseling and Development, 63,* 10–11.

Lichtenberg, J. W., & Heck, E. J. (1983). Use of sequential analysis in counseling process research: A reply to Hill, Carter, and O'Farrell and to Howard. *Journal of Counseling Psychology, 30,* 615–618.

Lichtenberg, J. W., & Heck, E. J. (1986). Analysis of sequence and pattern in process research. *Journal of Counseling Psychology, 33,* 170–181.

Lichtenberg, J. W., & Hummel, T. J. (1976). Counseling as a stochastic process: Fitting a Markov chain model to initial counseling interviews. *Journal of Counseling Psychology, 23,* 310–315.

Lieberman, M. A., Yalom, I., & Miles, M. (1973). *Encounter groups: First facts.* New York: Basic Books.

Lindsey, R. T. (1984). Informed consent and deception in psychotherapy research: An ethical analysis. *The Counseling Psychologist, 12,* 79–86.

Lorr, M. (1983). *Cluster analysis for social scientists.* San Francisco: Jossey-Bass.

MacKenzie, K. R. (1983). The clinical application of a group climate measure. In R. R. Dies & K. R. MacKenzie (Eds.), *Advances in group psychotherapy: Integrating research and practice* (pp. 159–170). New York: International Universities Press.

Magoon, T. M., & Holland, J. L. (1984). Research training and supervision. In S. D. Brown & R. W. Lent (Eds.), *Handbook of counseling psychology* (pp. 682–715). New York: Wiley.

Mahalik, J. R., & Kivlighan, D. M., Jr. (1988). Self-help treatment for depression: Who succeeds? *Journal of Counseling Psychology, 35,* 237–242.

Mahoney, M. J. (1978). Experimental methods and outcome evaluation. *Journal of Consulting and Clinical Psychology, 46,* 660–672.

Maier, N.R.F. (1931). Reasoning in humans: II. The solution of a problem and its appearance in consciousness. *Journal of Comparative Psychology, 12,* 181–194.

Malkiewich, L. E., & Merluzzi, T. V. (1980). Rational restructuring versus desensitization with clients of diverse conceptual levels: A test of client-treatment matching model. *Journal of Counseling Psychology, 27,* 453–461.

Mallinckrodt, B. (1989). Social support and the effectiveness of group therapy. *Journal of Counseling Psychology, 36,* 170–175.

Mallinckrodt, B., & Helms, J. E. (1986). Effect of disabled counselor's self-disclosures on client perceptions of the counselor. *Journal of Counseling Psychology, 33,* 343–348.

Manicas, P. T., & Secord, P. F. (1983). Implications for psychology of the new philosophy of science. *American Psychologist, 38,* 399–413.

Marmar, C. R., Marziali, E., Horowitz, M. J., & Weiss, D. S. (1986). The development of the therapeutic alliance rating system. In L. S. Greenberg & W. M. Pinsof (Eds.), *The psychotherapeutic process: A research handbook* (pp. 367–390). New York: Guilford Press.

Martin, J. (1984). The cognitive mediational paradigm for research on counseling. *Journal of Counseling Psychology, 31,* 558–571.

Martin, J. (1985). Measuring clients' cognitive competence in research on counseling. *Journal of Counseling and Development, 63,* 556–560.

Martin, J. (1987). *Cognitive-instructional counseling.* London, Ontario, Canada: Althouse Press.

Martin, J. S., Goodyear, R. K., & Newton, F. B. (1987). Clinical supervision: An intensive case study. *Professional Psychology: Research and Practice, 18,* 225–235.

Martin, J., Martin, W., & Slemon, A. G. (1989). Cognitive-mediational models of action-act sequences in counseling. *Journal of Counseling Psychology, 36,* 8–16.

Martin, J., & Stelmaczonek, K. (1988). Participants' identification and recall of important events in counseling. *Journal of Counseling Psychology, 35,* 385–390.

Maruyama, M. (1963). The second cybernetics: Deviation-amplifying mutual causal processes. *American Scientist, 51,* 169–179.

Marx, J. A., & Gelso, C. J. (1987). Termination of individual counseling in a university counseling center. *Journal of Counseling Psychology, 34,* 3–9.

Mash, E. J., & Terdal, L. G. (Eds.). (1981). *Behavioral assessment of childhood disorders.* New York: Guilford Press.

Masling, J. (1966). Role-related behavior of the subject and psychologist and its effect upon psychological data. In D. Levine (Ed.), *Nebraska Symposium on Motivation, 14,* 67–103.

Max, L. W. (1935). Breaking up a homosexual fixation by the conditioned reaction technique: A case study. *Psychological Bulletin, 32,* 734.

McCarthy, P. R., Shaw, T., & Schmeck, R. R. (1986). Behavioral analysis of client learning style during counseling. *Journal of Counseling Psychology, 33,* 249–254.

McCullough, L., & Farrel, A. D. (1983). The Computerized Assessment for Psychotherapy Evaluation and Research [Computer program]. New York: Beth Israel Medical Center, Department of Psychiatry.

McCullough, L., Farrell, A. D., & Longabaugh, R. (1986). The development of a microcomputer-based mental health information system: A potential tool for bridging the scientist-practitioner gap. *American Psychologist, 41,* 207–214.

McGuire, W. J. (1985). Attitudes and attitude change. In G. Lindzey & E. Aronson (Eds.), *Handbook of social psychology* (3rd ed., Vol. 2, pp. 233–346). New York: Random House.

McKinney, F. (1945). Four years of a college adjustment clinic: I. Organization of clinic and problems of counselors. *Journal of Consulting Psychology, 9,* 203–212.

McLaughlin, M., Cormier, L. S., & Cormier, W. H. (1988). Relation between coping strategies and distress, stress, and marital adjustment of multiple-role women. *Journal of Counseling Psychology, 35,* 187–193.

McNamara, K., & Horan, J. J. (1986). Experimental construct validity in the evaluation of cognitive and behavioral treatments for depression. *Journal of Counseling Psychology, 33,* 23–30.

Meara, N. M., & Patton, M. J. (1986). Language use and social influence in counseling. In F. J. Dorn (Ed.), *The social influence process in counseling and psychotherapy* (pp. 85–93). Springfield, IL: Charles C Thomas.

Meara, N. M., Schmidt, L. D., Carrington, C. H., Davis, K. L., Dixon, D. N., Fretz, B. R., Myers, R. A., Ridley, C. R. & Suinn, R. M. (1988). Training and accreditation in counseling psychology. *The Counseling Psychologist, 16,* 366–384.

Meara, N. M., Shannon, J. W., & Pepinsky, H. B. (1979). Comparison of the stylistic complexity of the language of counselor and client across three theoretical orientations. *Journal of Counseling Psychology, 28,* 110–118.

Meehl, P. E. (1971). A scientific, scholarly nonresearch doctorate for clinical practitioners. In R. R. Holt (Ed.), *New horizon for psychotherapy: Autonomy as a profession* (pp. 37–81). New York: International Universities Press.

Meehl, P. E. (1978). Theoretical risks and tabular asterisks: Sir Karl, Sir Ronald, and the slow progress of soft psychology. *Journal of Consulting and Clinical Psychology, 46,* 806–834.

Meehl, P. E. (1987). Why summaries of research on a psychological theory are often uninterpretable. In R. Snow & D. E. Wiley (Eds.), *Strategic thinking: A volume in honor of Lee J. Cronbach.* San Francisco: Jossey-Bass.

Megargee, E. I., & Bohn, M. J. (1979). *Classifying criminal offenders: A new system based on the MMPI.* Beverly Hills, CA: Sage.

Merrill, R. M. (1952). On Keet's study, "two verbal techniques in a miniature counseling situation." *Journal of Abnormal and Social Psychology, 47,* 722.

Meyer, V. (1957). The treatment of two phobic patients on the basis of learning principles. *Journal of Abnormal and Social Psychology, 55,* 261–266.

Mill, J. S. (1953). A system of logic, Book VI, On the logic of the moral sciences. In P. P. Weiner (Ed.), *Readings in philosophy of science* (pp. 255–281). New York: Scribner's. (Original work published 1843)

Miller, A. (1981). Conceptual matching models and interactional research in education. *Review of Educational Research, 51,* 33–84.

Mills, E. A. (1924). *Rocky Mountain National Park.* Garden City, NY: Doubleday, Page, & Co.

Mintz, L. B., & O'Neil, J. M. (1990). Gender roles, sex, and the process of psychotherapy: Many questions and few answers. *Journal of Counseling and Development, 68,* 381–387.

Mitchell, J. V., Jr. (Ed.). (1983). *Tests in print III.* Lincoln: University of Nebraska Press.

Mitchell, J. V., Jr. (Ed.). (1985). *The ninth mental measurements yearbook.* Lincoln: The Buros Institute of Mental Measurements of the University of Nebraska-Lincoln.

Mitchell, K. M., Bozarth, J. D., & Kraft, C. C. (1977). A reappraisal of the therapeutic effectiveness of accurate empathy, nonpossessive warmth and genuineness. In A. S. Gurman & A. M. Razin (Eds.), *Effective psychotherapy: A handbook of research* (pp. 482–502). New York: Pergamon Press.

Monte, C. F. (1980). *Beneath the mask: An introduction to theories of personality* (2nd ed.). New York: Holt, Rinehart & Winston.

Mooney, R. L., & Gordon, L. V. (1950). *Manual: The Mooney problem checklists.* New York: Psychological Corporation.

Morgan, R., Luborsky, L., Crits-Christoph, P., Curtis, H., & Solomon, J. (1982). Predicting the outcomes of psychotherapy by the Penn Helping Alliance Rating Method. *Archives of General Psychiatry, 39,* 397–402.

Morrison, L. A., & Shapiro, D. A. (1987). Expectancy and outcome in prescription vs. exploratory psychotherapy. *British Journal of Clinical Psychology, 29,* 54–60.

Muehlenhard, C. L., & Linton, M. A. (1987). Date rape and sexual aggression in dating situations: Incidence and risk factors. *Journal of Counseling Psychology, 34,* 186–196.

Mueller, W. J. (1969). Patterns of behavior and their reciprocal impact in the family and in psychotherapy [Monograph]. *Journal of Counseling Psychology, 16,* 1–25.

Munley, P. H. (1974). A review of counseling analogue research methods. *Journal of Counseling Psychology, 21,* 320–330.

Munley, P. H., Sharkin, B., & Gelso, C. J. (1988). Reviewer ratings and agreement on manuscripts reviewed for the *Journal of Counseling Psychology. Journal of Counseling Psychology, 35,* 198–202.

Nagelberg, D. B., Pillsbury, E. C., & Balzor, D. M. (1983). The prevalence of depression as a function of gender and facility usage in college students. *Journal of College Student Personnel, 24,* 525–529.

Neimeyer, G., & Resnikoff, A. (1982). Major contribution: Qualitative strategies in counseling research. *The Counseling Psychologist, 10*(4), 75–85.

Neisser, U. (1976). *Cognition and reality: Principles and implications of cognitive psychology.* San Francisco: Freeman.

Nezu, A. M. (1986). Efficacy of a social problem-solving therapy approach for unipolar depression. *Journal of Consulting and Clinical Psychology, 54,* 196–202.

Nezu, A. M., Nezu, C. M., & Perri, M. G. (1989). *Problem-solving therapy for depression: Theory, research, and clinical guidelines.* New York: Wiley.

Nisbett, R. E., & Ross, L. (1980). *Human inference: Strategies and shortcomings of social judgment.* Englewood Cliffs, NJ: Prentice-Hall.

Nisbett, R. E., & Wilson, T. D. (1977). Telling more than we can know: Verbal reports on mental processes. *Psychological Review, 84,* 231–259.

Nocita, A., & Stiles, W. B. (1986). Client introversion and counseling session impact. *Journal of Counseling Psychology, 33,* 235–241.

Nunnally, J. C. (1978). *Psychometric theory.* New York: McGraw-Hill.

O'Farrell, M. K., Hill, C. E., & Patton, S. M. (1986). A comparison of two cases of counseling with the same counselor. *Journal of Counseling and Development, 65,* 141–145.

O'Malley, S. S., Foley, S. H., Rounsaville, B. J., Watkins, J. T., Sotsky, S. M., Imber, S. D., & Elkin, I. (1988). Therapist competence and patient outcome in interpersonal psychotherapy of depression. *Journal of Consulting and Clinical Psychology, 56,* 496–501.

O'Neil, J. M., & Roberts Carroll, M. (1987). *A six-day workshop on gender role conflict and strain: Helping adult men and women take the gender role journey.* Storrs, CT: University of Connecticut, Department of Educational Psychology, Counseling Psychology Program. (ERIC Document Reproduction Service No. ED 275963)

O'Neil, J. M., & Roberts Carroll, M. (1988). A gender role workshop focused on sexism, gender role conflict, and the gender role journey. *Journal of Counseling and Development, 67,* 193–197.

Orlinsky, D. E., & Howard, K. I. (1978). The relation of process to outcome in psychotherapy. In S. L. Garfield & A. E. Bergin (Eds.), *Handbook of psychotherapy and behavior change* (2nd ed., pp. 283–330). New York: Wiley.

Orlinsky, D. E., & Howard, K. I. (1986). The relation of process to outcome in psychotherapy. In S. L. Garfield & A. E. Bergin (Eds.), *Handbook of psychotherapy and behavior change* (3rd ed., pp. 311–381). New York: Wiley.

Palmer, S., & Cochran, L. (1988). Parents as agents of career development. *Journal of Counseling Psychology, 35,* 71–76.

Parham, T. A., & Helms, J. E. (1985). Attitudes of racial identity and self-esteem of black students: An exploratory investigation. *Journal of College Student Personnel, 26,* 143–147.

Parloff, M. B., Waskow, I. E., & Wolfe, B. E. (1978). Research on therapist variables in relation to process and outcome. In S. L. Garfield & A. E. Bergin (Eds.), *Handbook of psychotherapy and behavior change* (2nd ed., pp. 233–282). New York: Wiley.

Patterson, G. R., & Forgatch, M. S. (1985). Therapist behavior as a determinant for client noncompliance: A paradox for the behavior modifier. *Journal of Consulting and Clinical Psychology, 53,* 846–851.

Patton, M. J. (1984). Managing social interaction in counseling: A contribution from the philosophy of science. *Journal of Counseling Psychology, 31,* 442–456.

Patton, M. J. (1989). Problems with and alternatives to the use of coding schemes in research or counseling. *The Counseling Psychologist, 17,* 490–506.

Patton, M. J. (in press). The qualitative approach to research on college students: Some methodological considerations. *Journal of College Student Development.*

Paul, G. L. (1967). Strategy of outcome research in psychotherapy. *Journal of Consulting Psychology, 31,* 109–118.

Pedhazur, E. (1982). *Multiple regression in behavioral research: Explanation and prediction* (2nd ed.). New York: Holt, Rinehart & Winston.

Penman, R. (1980). *Communication processes and relationships.* London: Academic Press.

Pepinsky, H. B. (1984). Language and the production and interpretation of social interactions. In H. F. Fisher (Ed.), *Language and logic in personality and society* (pp. 93–129). New York: Columbia University Press.

Pepinsky, H. B., & Pepinsky, P. N. (1954). *Counseling theory and practice.* New York: Ronald Press.

Petty, R. E., & Cacioppo, J. T. (1981). *Attitudes and persuasion: Classic and contemporary approaches.* Dubuque, IA: William C. Brown.

Petty, R. E., & Cacioppo, J. T. (1986). *Communication and persuasion: Central and peripheral routes to attitude change.* New York: Springer-Verlag.

Pfungst, O. (1911). *A contribution to experimental, animal, and human psychology.* New York: Holt, Rinehart & Winston.

Phillips, S. D., Friedlander, M. L., Pazienza, N. J., & Kost, P. P. (1985). A factor analytic investigation of career decision-making styles. *Journal of Vocational Behavior, 26,* 106–115.

Polkinghorne, D. (1983). *Methodology for the human sciences: Systems of inquiry.* Albany, NY: State University of New York.

Polkinghorne, D. E. (1984). Further extensions of methodological diversity for counseling psychology. *Journal of Counseling Psychology, 31,* 416–429.

Ponce, F. Q., & Atkinson, D. R. (1989). Mexican-American acculturation, counselor ethnicity, counseling style, and perceived credibility. *Journal of Counseling Psychology, 36,* 203–208.

Ponterotto, J. G. (1988). Racial/ethnic minority research in the *Journal of Counseling Psychology*: A content analysis and methodological critique. *Journal of Counseling Psychology, 35,* 410–418.

Ponterotto, J. G., & Furlong, M. J. (1985). Evaluating counselor effectiveness: A critical review of rating scale instruments. *Journal of Counseling Psychology, 32,* 597–616.

Porter, A. C., & Raudenbush, S. W. (1987). Analysis of covariance: Its model and use in psychological research. *Journal of Counseling Psychology, 34,* 383–392.

Powell, C. J. (1984). Ethical principles and issues of competence in counseling adolescents. *The Counseling Psychologist, 12*(3), 57–68.

Putman, H. (1962). What theories are not. In E. P. Nagel, P. Suppes, & A. Tarski (Eds.), *Logic, methodology, and philosophy of science: Proceedings of the 1960 international congress* (pp. 240–251). Stanford, CA: Stanford University Press.

Rabinowitz, F. E., Heppner, P. P., & Roehlke, H. J. (1986). Descriptive study of process and outcome variables of supervision over time. *Journal of Counseling Psychology, 33,* 292–300.

Raimy, V. (Ed.). (1950). *Training in clinical psychology.* New York: Prentice-Hall.

Ramsey, P. (1970). *The patient as person.* New Haven: Yale University.

Rappaport, D. (1960). The structure of psychoanalytic theory. *Psychological Issues,* Monograph 6. New York: International Universities Press.

Raush, H. L. (1974). Research, practice, and accountability. *American Psychologist, 29,* 678–681.

Reising, G. N., & Daniels, M. H. (1983). A study of Hogan's model of counselor development and supervision. *Journal of Counseling Psychology, 30,* 235–244.

Rennie, D. L., & Brewer, L. (1987). A grounded theory of thesis blocking. *Teaching of Psychology, 14,* 10–16.

Rennie, D. L., Phillips, J. R., & Quartaro, G. K. (1988). Grounded theory: A promising approach to conceptualization in psychology? *Canadian Psychology/Psychologie Canadienne, 29,* 139–150.

Resnikoff, A. (1978). Scientific affairs committee report, 1975–1977: A discussion of methodology. *The Counseling Psychologist, 7*(4), 67–71.

Rice, L. N., Koke, L. J., Greenberg, L. S., & Wagstaff (1979). *Manual for client vocal quality, Volume 1: Information for the investigation.* Toronto: Counseling and Development Center, York University.

Richardson, M. S., & Johnson, M. (1984). Counseling women. In S. R. Brown & R. W. Lent (Eds.), *Handbook of counseling psychology* (pp. 832–877). New York: Wiley.

Robinson, F. P. (1950). *Principles and procedures in student counseling.* New York: Harper & Brothers.

Rogers, C. R. (1955). Persons or science? A philosophical question. *American Psychologist, 10,* 267–278.

Rogers, C. R. (1961). *On becoming a person.* Boston: Houghton Mifflin.

Rokeach, M. (1973). *The nature of human values.* New York: Free Press.

Rosenbaum, M. (1982). Ethical problems of group psychotherapy. In M. Rosenbaum (Ed.), *Ethics and values in psychotherapy.* New York: Free Press.

Rosenthal, R. (1966). *Experimenter effects in behavioral research.* New York: Meredith.

Rosenthal, R. (1984). *Meta-analytic procedures for social research.* Beverly Hills, CA: Sage.

Rosenthal, R., & Jacobson, L. (1968). *Pygmalion in the classroom: Teacher expectations of the disadvantaged.* New York: Holt, Rinehart & Winston.

Rosenthal, R., & Rosnow, R. L. (1969). The volunteer subject. In R. Rosenthal & R. L. Rosnow (Eds.), *Artifact in behavioral research* (pp. 61–118). New York: Academic Press.

Ross, A. O. (1981). Of rigor and relevance. *Professional Psychology, 12,* 318–327.

Ross, R. R., & Altmaier, E. M. (1990). Job analysis of psychology internships in counseling center settings. *Journal of Counseling Psychology, 37,* 459–464.

Ross, W. D. (1930). *The right and the good.* Oxford, England: Clarendon.

Rotter, J. B. (1966). Generalized expectancies for internal versus external control of reinforcement. *Psychological Monographs: General and Applied, 80*(1, Whole No. 609).

Royalty, G. M., Gelso, C. J., Mallinckrodt, B., & Garrett, K. D. (1986). The environment and the student in counseling psychology: Does the research training environment influence graduate students' attitude toward research? *The Counseling Psychologist, 14,* 9–30.

Royalty, G. M., & Magoon, T. M. (1985). Correlates of scholarly productivity among counseling psychologists. *Journal of Counseling Psychology, 32,* 458–461.

Rubinton, N. (1980). Instruction in career decision making and decision-making styles. *Journal of Counseling Psychology, 27,* 581–588.

Ruch, F. L., & Zimbardo, P. G. (1970). *Psychology and life* (8th ed.). Glenview, IL: Scott, Foresman.

Rumenik, D. K., Capasso, D. R., & Hendrick, C. (1977). Experimenter sex effects in behavioral research. *Psychological Bulletin, 84,* 852–877.

Russell, R. K., & Lent, R. W. (1982). Cue-controlled relaxation and systematic desensitization versus nonspecific factors in treating test anxiety. *Journal of Counseling Psychology, 29,* 100–103.

Russell, R. K., & Sipich, J. F. (1973). Cue-controlled relaxation in the treatment of test anxiety. *Journal of Behavior Therapy and Experimental Psychiatry, 4,* 47–50.

Rust, R. E., & Davie, J. S. (1961). The personal problems of college students. *Mental Hygiene, 45,* 247–257.

Sax, G. (1989). *Principles of educational and psychological measurement and evaluation* (3rd ed.). Belmont, CA: Wadsworth.

Scheidler, G. G., & Berdie, R. F. (1942). Representativeness of college students who receive counseling services. *Journal of Educational Psychology, 33,* 545–551.

Scher, M., & Good, G. E. (1990). Gender and counseling in the twenty-first century: What does the future hold? *Journal of Counseling and Development, 68,* 388–391.

Schmidt, L. D., & Meara, N. M. (1984). Ethical, professional, and legal issues in counseling psychology. In S. D. Brown & R. W. Lent (Eds.), *Handbook of Counseling Psychology* (pp. 56–96). New York: Wiley.

Schmidt, L. D., & Strong, S. R. (1971). Attractiveness and influence in counseling. *Journal of Counseling Psychology, 18,* 348–351.

Schotte, D., & Clum, G. (1982). Suicide ideation in a college population: A test of a model. *Journal of Consulting and Clinical Psychology, 50,* 690–696.

Schutz, A. (1964). *Collected papers II: Studies in social theory* (A. Broderson, Ed.). The Hague, The Netherlands: Martinus-Nijhoff.

Seeman, J. (1959). Organizing a thesis proposal. *American Psychologist, 9,* 794–797.

Seeman, J. (1969). Deception in psychological research. *American Psychologist, 24,* 1025–1028.

Seeman, J. (1973). On supervising student research. *American Psychologist, 28,* 900–906.

Serlin, R. C. (1987). Hypothesis testing, theory building, and the philosophy of science. *Journal of Counseling Psychology, 34,* 365–371.

Serlin, R. C., & Lapsley, D. K. (1985). Rationality in psychological research: The good-enough principle. *American Psychologist, 40,* 73–83.

Sharkin, B. S., Mahalik, J. R., & Claiborn, C. D. (1989). Application of the foot-in-the-door effect in counseling. *Journal of Counseling Psychology, 36,* 248–251.

Shaw, B. F. (1977). Comparison of cognitive therapy and behavior therapy in the treatment of depression. *Journal of Consulting and Clinical Psychology, 45,* 543–551.

Shlien, J. M., Mosak, H. H., Dreikurs, R. (1962). Effects of time limits: A comparison of two psychotherapies. *Journal of Counseling Psychology, 9,* 31–34.

Silberschatz, G., Fretter, P. B., & Curtis, J. T. (1986). How do interpretations influence the process of therapy? *Journal of Consulting and Clinical Psychology, 54,* 646–652.

Sime, W. E., Ansorge, C. J., Olson, J., Parker, C., & Lukin, M. (1987). Coping with mathematics anxiety: Stress management and academic performance. *Journal of College Student Personnel, 28*(5), 431–437.

Sipich, J. F., Russell, R. K., & Tobias, L. L. (1974). A comparison of covert sensitization and "nonspecific" treatment in the modification of smoking behavior. *Journal of Behavior, Therapy, and Experimental Psychiatry, 5,* 201–203.

Slate, J. R., & Jones, C. H. (1989). Can teaching of the WISC-R be improved? Quasi-experimental exploration. *Professional Psychology Research and Practice, 20,* 408–410.

Slusher, M. P., & Anderson, C. A. (1989). Belief perseverance and self-defeating behavior. In R. Curtis (Ed.), *Self-defeating behaviors: Experimental research, clinical impressions, and practical implications* (pp. 11–40). New York: Plenum.

Smith, M. L. (1981). Naturalistic research. *Personnel and Guidance Journal, 59,* 585–589.

Smith, R. E., & Nye, S. L. (1989). Comparison of induced effect and covert rehearsal in the acquisition of stress management coping skills. *Journal of Counseling Psychology, 36,* 17–23.

Spence, J. T., & Helmreich, R. (1972). The Attitudes Toward Women Scale: An objective instrument to measure attitudes toward the rights and roles of women in contemporary society. *JSAS Catalog of Selected Documents in Psychology, 2,* 1–48.

Spiegel, D., & Keith-Spiegel, P. (1970). Assignment of publication credits: Ethics and practices of psychologists. *American Psychologist, 25,* 738–747.

Stein, M. L., & Stone, G. L. (1978). Effects of conceptual level and structure on initial interview behavior. *Journal of Counseling Psychology, 25,* 96–102.

Sternberg, R. J. (1988). *The psychologist's companion: A guide to scientific writing for students and researchers* (2nd. ed.). New York: Cambridge University Press.

Stiles, W. B. (1980). Measurement of the impact of psychotherapy sessions. *Journal of Consulting and Clinical Psychology, 48,* 176–185.

Stiles, W. B. (1988). Psychotherapy process-outcome correlations may be misleading. *Psychotherapy, 25,* 27–35.

Stiles, W. B., Shapiro, D. A., & Firth-Cozens, J. A. (1988). Do sessions of different treatments have different impacts? *Journal of Counseling Psychology, 35,* 391–396.

Stiles, W. B., & Snow, J. S. (1984). Counseling session impact as viewed by novice counselors and their clients. *Journal of Counseling Psychology, 31,* 3–12.

Stoltenberg, C. (1981). Approaching supervision from a developmental perspective: The counselor complexity model. *Journal of Counseling Psychology, 28,* 59–65.

Stone, G. L. (1984). Reaction: In defense of the "artificial." *Journal of Counseling Psychology, 31,* 108–110.

Stricker, G. (1982). Ethical issues in psychotherapy research. In M. Rosenbaum (Ed.), *Ethics and values in psychotherapy: A guidebook* (pp. 403–424). New York: Free Press.

Strohmer, D. C., & Blustein, D. L. (1990). The adult problem solver as personal scientist. *Journal of Cognitive Psychotherapy: An International Quarterly, 4,* 281–292.

Strohmer, D. C., & Newman, L. J. (1983). Counselor hypothesis-testing strategies. *Journal of Counseling Psychology, 30,* 557–565.

Strong, S. R. (1968). Counseling: An interpersonal influence process. *Journal of Counseling Psychology, 15,* 215–224.

Strong, S. R. (1971). Experimental laboratory research in counseling. *Journal of Counseling Psychology, 18,* 106–110.

Strong, S. R. (1978). Social psychological approach to psychotherapy research. In J. Garfield & A. Bergin (Eds.), *Handbook of psychotherapy and behavior change* (2nd ed., pp. 101–136). New York: Wiley.

Strong, S. R. (1984). Reflections on human nature, science, and progress in counseling psychology. *Journal of Counseling Psychology, 31,* 470–473.

Strong, S. R., & Dixon, D. N. (1971). Expertness, attractiveness, and influence in counseling. *Journal of Counseling Psychology, 18,* 562–570.

Strong, S. R., Hills, H. I., Kilmartin, C. T., De Vries, H., Lanier, K., Nelson, B., Strickland, D., & Meyer, C. W. (1988). The dynamic relations among interpersonal behaviors: A test of complementarity and autocomplementarity. *Journal of Personality and Social Psychology, 54,* 798–810.

Strong, S. R., & Matross, R. P. (1973). Change processes in counseling and psychotherapy. *Journal of Counseling Psychology, 20,* 25–37.

Strong, S. R., & Schmidt, L. D. (1970). Expertness and influence in counseling. *Journal of Counseling Psychology, 17,* 81–87.

Strupp, H. H. (1980a). Success and failure in time-limited psychotherapy: A systematic comparison of two cases—Comparison 1. *Archives of General Psychiatry, 37,* 595–603.

Strupp, H. H. (1980b). Success and failure in time-limited psychotherapy: A systematic comparison of two cases—Comparison 2. *Archives of General Psychiatry, 37,* 708–716.

Strupp, H. H. (1980c). Success and failure in time-limited psychotherapy: Further evidence—Comparison 4. *Archives of General Psychiatry, 37,* 947–954.

Strupp, H. H. (1981). Clinical research, practice, and the crisis of confidence. *Journal of Consulting and Clinical Psychology, 49,* 216–219.

Suen, H. K. (1988). Agreement, reliability, accuracy, and validity: Toward a clarification. *Behavioral Assessment, 10,* 343–366.

Super, D. (1957). *The psychology of careers.* New York: McGraw-Hill.

Suppe, F. (1977). *The structure of scientific theories* (2nd ed.). Urbana, IL: University of Illinois Press.

Taussig, I. M. (1987). Comparative responses of Mexican Americans and Anglo-Americans to early goal setting in a public mental health clinic. *Journal of Counseling Psychology, 34,* 214–217.

Thigpen, C. H., & Cleckley, H. M. (1954). A case of multiple personality. *Journal of Abnormal and Social Psychology, 49,* 135–151.

Thigpen, C. H., & Cleckley, H. M. (1957). *Three faces of Eve.* New York: McGraw-Hill.

Thoreson, R. W., Budd, F. C., & Krauskopf, C. J. (1986). Alcoholism among psychologists: Factors in relapse and recovery. *Professional Psychology: Research and Practice, 17,* 497–503.

Thoreson, R. W., Kardash, K. A., Leuthold, D. A., Morrow, K. A. (1990). Gender differences in the academic career. *Research in Higher Education, 3*(2), 193–209.

Thoreson, R. W., Miller, M., & Krauskopf, C. J. (1989). The distressed psychologist: Prevalence and treatment considerations. *Professional Psychology: Research and Practice, 20,* 153–158.

Tichenor, V., & Hill, C. E. (1989). A comparison of six measures of working alliance. *Psychotherapy, 26,* 195–199.

Tinsley, H.E.A., Bowman, S. L., & Ray, S. B. (1988). Manipulation of expectancies about counseling and psychotherapy: Review and analysis of expectancy manipulation strategies and results. *Journal of Counseling Psychology, 35,* 99–108.

Tinsley, H.E.A., Roth, J. A., & Lease, S. H. (1989). Dimensions of leadership and leadership style among group intervention specialists. *Journal of Counseling Psychology, 36,* 48–53.

Tinsley, H.E.A., & Tinsley, D. J. (1987). Use of factor analysis in counseling psychology research. *Journal of Counseling Psychology, 34,* 414–424.

Tinsley, H.E.A., & Weiss, D. J. (1975). Interrater reliability and agreement of subjective judgments. *Journal of Counseling Psychology, 22,* 358–376.

Tinsley, H.E.A., Workman, K. R., & Kass, R. A. (1980). Factor analysis of the domain of client expectancies about counseling. *Journal of Counseling Psychology, 27,* 561–570.

Toulmin, S. (1972). *Human understanding: The collecting use and evolution of concepts.* Princeton: Princeton University Press.

Tracey, T. J. (1983). Single case research: An added tool for counselors and supervisors. *Counselor Education and Supervision, 22,* 185–196.

Tracey, T. J. (1985). The N of 1 Markov chain design as a means of studying the stages of psychotherapy. *Psychiatry, 48,* 196–204.

Tracey, T. J. (1986). Interactional correlates of premature termination. *Journal of Consulting and Clinical Psychology, 54,* 784–788.

Tracey, T. J., Glidden, C. E., & Kokotovic, A. M. (1988). Factor structure of the Counselor Rating Form-Short. *Journal of Counseling Psychology, 35,* 330–335.

Tracey, T. J., Hays, K. A., Malone, J., & Herman, B. (1988). Changes in counselor response as a function of experience. *Journal of Counseling Psychology, 35,* 119–126.

Tracey, T. J., Leong, F.T.L., & Glidden, C. (1986). Help seeking and problem perception among Asian Americans. *Journal of Counseling Psychology, 33,* 331–336.

Tracey, T. J., & Ray, P. B. (1984). Stages of successful time-limited counseling: An interactional examination. *Journal of Counseling Psychology, 31,* 13–27.

Truax, C. B., & Carkhuff, R. R. (1967). *Toward effective counseling and psychotherapy: Training and practice.* Chicago: Aldine.

Truax, C. B., & Wargo, D. G. (1966). Psychotherapeutic encounters that change behavior: For better or for worse. *American Journal of Psychotherapy, 20,* 499–520.

Turk, D. C., & Salovey, P. (Ed.). (1988). *Reasoning, inference, and judgment in clinical psychology.* New York: Free Press.

Turnbull, H. R., III (Ed.). (1977). *Consent handbook.* Washington, DC: American Association on Mental Deficiency.

Tversky, A., & Kahneman, D. (1974). Judgment under uncertainty: Heuristics and biases. *Science, 185,* 1124–1131.

Tversky, A., & Kahneman, D. (1981). The framing of decisions and the psychology of choice. *Science, 211,* 453–458.

Tyler, L. E. (1984). Further implications for counseling research. *Journal of Counseling Psychology, 31,* 474–476.

Underwood, B. J. (1966). *Experimental psychology.* New York: Appleton-Century-Crofts.

Vredenburg, K., O'Brien, E., & Krames, L. (1988). Depression in college students: Personality and experiential factors. *Journal of Counseling Psychology, 35,* 419–425.

Wallenstein, R. S. (1971). The role of researcher training. How much, what kind, how? In R. R. Holt (Ed.), *New horizon for psychotherapy.* New York: International Universities Press.

Wallenstein, R. S. (1989). The psychotherapy research project of the Menninger Foundation: An overview. *Journal of Consulting and Clinical Psychology, 57,* 195–205.

Wampold, B. E. (1986). State of the art in sequential analysis: Comment on Lichtenberg and Heck. *Journal of Counseling Psychology, 33,* 182–185.

Wampold, B. E., Davis, B., Good, R. H. III (1990). Hypothesis validity of clinical research. *Journal of Consulting and Clinical Psychology, 58,* 360–367.

Wampold, B. E., & Drew, C. J. (1990). *Theory and application of statistics.* New York: McGraw-Hill.

Wampold, B. E., & Freund, R. D. (1987). Use of multiple regression in counseling psychology research: A flexible data-analytic strategy. *Journal of Counseling Psychology, 34,* 372–382.

Wampold, B. E., & Freund, R. D. (in press). Statistical issues in clinical research. In M. Hersen, A. E. Kazdin, & A. S. Bellack (Eds.), *The clinical psychology handbook* (2nd ed.). Elmsford, NY: Pergamon Press.

Wampold, B. E., & Furlong, M. J. (1981a). The heuristics of visual inference. *Behavioral Assessment, 3,* 79–82.

Wampold, B. E., & Furlong, M. J. (1981b). Randomization tests in single-subject designs: Illustrative examples. *Journal of Behavioral Assessment, 3,* 329–341.

Wampold, B. E., & Kim, K. H. (1989). Sequential analysis applied to counseling process and outcomes: A case study revisited. *Journal of Counseling Psychology, 36,* 357–364.

Wampold, B. E., & White, T. B. (1985). Research themes in counseling psychology: A cluster analysis of citations in the process and outcomes section of the *Journal of Counseling Psychology. Journal of Counseling Psychology, 32,* 123–126.

Wampold, B. E., & Worsham, N. L. (1986). Randomization tests for multiple-baseline designs. *Behavioral Assessment, 8,* 135–143.

Warchal, P., & Southern, S. (1986). Perceived importance of counseling needs among adult students. *Journal of College Student Personnel, 27,* 43–48.

Webb, E. J., Campbell, D. T., Schwartz, R. C., & Sechrest, L. (1966). *Unobtrusive measures: Nonreactive research in the social sciences.* Chicago: Rand McNally.

Webster-Stratton, C. (1988). Mothers' and fathers' perceptions of child deviance: Roles of parent and child behaviors and parent adjustment. *Journal of Consulting and Clinical Psychology, 56,* 909–915.

Wellman, F. (1967). A conceptual framework for the derivation of guidance objectives and outcome criteria: Preliminary statement. In J. M. Whiteley (Ed.), *Research in counseling: Evaluation and refocus* (pp. 153–174). Columbus, OH: Merrill.

White, M. D., & White, C. A. (1981). Involuntarily committed patients' constituted right to refuse treatment. *American Psychologist, 36,* 953–962.

White, O. R. (1974). The "split middle": A "quickie" method for trend estimation. Seattle: University of Washington, Experimental Education Unit, Child Development and Mental Retardation Center.

Whiteley, J. M. (1984). A historical perspective on the development of counseling psychology as a profession. In S. D. Brown & R. W. Lent (Eds.), *Handbook of counseling psychology* (pp. 3–55). New York: Wiley.

Wiley, M. O., & Ray, P. B. (1986). Counseling supervision by developmental level. *Journal of Counseling Psychology, 33,* 439–445.

Williams, J. E. (1962). Changes in self and other perceptions following brief educational-vocational counseling. *Journal of Counseling Psychology, 9,* 18–30.

Wills, T. A. (1987). Help seeking as a coping mechanism. In C. R. Snyder & C. E. Ford (Eds.), *Coping with negative life events: Clinical and psychological perspectives* (pp. 19–50). New York: Plenum.

Winston, Roger B., Jr. (1985). A suggested procedure for determining order of authorship in research publications. *Journal of Counseling and Development, 63,* 515–519.

Wolpe, J. (1969). *The practice of behavior therapy.* New York: Pergamon Press.

Worthington, E. L., Jr. (1984). Empirical investigation of supervision of counselors as they gain experience. *Journal of Counseling Psychology, 31,* 63–75.

Worthington, E. L., & Stern, A. (1985). Effects of supervision and supervisor degree level and gender on supervisory relationship. *Journal of Counseling Psychology, 32,* 252–262.

Worthington, E. L., Jr., & Roehlke, H. J. (1979). Effective supervision as perceived by beginning counselors-in-training. *Journal of Counseling Psychology, 26,* 64–73.

Wrenn, R. L. (1985). The evolution of Anne Roe. *Journal of Counseling and Development, 63,* 267–275.

Wundt, W. (1904). *Principles of physiological psychology.* New York: Macmillan.

Wundt, W. (1916). *Elements of folk psychology.* London: Allen & Unwin. (Original work published 1900)

Yalom, I. D. (1985). *The theory and practice of group psychotherapy* (3rd ed.). New York: Basic Books.

Yates, A. J. (1958). The application of learning theory to the treatment of tics. *Journal of Abnormal and Social Psychology, 56,* 175–182.

Zane, N.W.S. (1989). Change mechanisms in placebo procedures: Effects of suggestion, social demand, and contingent success on improvement in treatment. *Journal of Counseling Psychology, 36,* 234–243.

Zimbardo, P. G., & Ebbesen, E. B. (1970). *Influencing attitudes and changing behavior.* Reading, MA: Addison-Wesley.

AUTHOR INDEX

SUBJECT INDEX

TO THE OWNER OF THIS BOOK:

We hope that you have found *Research Design in Counseling*, useful. So that this book can be improved in a future edition, would you take the time to complete this sheet and return it? Thank you.

School and address: _____

Department: _____

Instructor's name: _____

1. What I like most about this book is: _____

_____

2. What I like least about this book is: _____

_____

3. My general reaction to this book is: _____

_____

4. The name of the course in which I used this book is: _____

_____

5. Were all of the chapters of the book assigned for you to read? _____

   If not, which ones weren't? _____

_____

6. In the space below, or on a separate sheet of paper, please write specific suggestions for improving this book and anything else you'd care to share about your experience in using this book.

_____

_____

_____

_____

_____

_____

Optional:

Your name: _____ Date: _____

May Brooks/Cole quote you, either in promotion for *Research Design in Counseling*, or in future publishing ventures?

Yes: _____ No: _____

Sincerely,

P. Paul Heppner
Dennis Kivlighan
Bruce Wampold

- -

FOLD HERE

NO POSTAGE
NECESSARY
IF MAILED
IN THE
UNITED STATES

BUSINESS REPLY MAIL

FIRST CLASS   PERMIT NO. 358   PACIFIC GROVE, CA

POSTAGE WILL BE PAID BY ADDRESSEE

ATT: *Heppner, Kivlighan & Wampold*

**Brooks/Cole Publishing Company
511 Forest Lodge Road
Pacific Grove, California 93950-9968**

FOLD HERE